The Church of Scotland: An Economic Survey

J.N. Wolfe
and
M. Pickford

Geoffrey Chapman
London

A Geoffrey Chapman book published by
Cassell Ltd.,
35 Red Lion Square, London WC1R 4SG
and at Sydney, Auckland, Toronto, Johannesburg
an affiliate of
Macmillan Publishing Co. Inc.
New York

© J. N. Wolfe and M. Pickford, 1980

All rights reserved. No part of this publication may be reproduced, stored in a retrieval system, or transmitted, in any form or by any means, mechanical, photocopying, recording or otherwise, without the prior permission in writing of the publishers.

Wolfe, James Nathaniel
  The Church of Scotland.
  1. Church of Scotland – Finance
  I. Title II. Pickford, M
    262   BX 9072

ISBN 0 225 66250 7

Typeset by Colset Private Limited, Singapore

Printed and bound in Great Britain at
The Camelot Press Ltd, Southampton

Contents

List of Tables.. v
List of Figures... xii
Preface... xv
Introduction.. xvii

I General Background to the Study

1 A Brief History of the Church....................................... 3
2 Constitution and Government...................................... 31
3 The Property and Funds of the Church............................ 55

II Economic Analysis and Forecasts

4 Membership.. 69
5 Income.. 98
6 Expenditure... 116
7 Ministers and Lay Workers.. 154
8 Charges and Congregations....................................... 180
9 Forecasts of the Financial Position in 1981 and 2001......... 202

III The Ministry

10 Funding the Ministry... 219
11 Stipend.. 243
12 Congregational Finance.. 268
13 Union and Readjustment of Congregations................... 307
14 Education and Training for the Ministry...................... 326
15 New Forms of Ministry.. 337

IV Mission and Stewardship

16 Mission and Service.. 349
17 Fund-raising and Stewardship.................................. 369

V Further Proposals to Improve Finances

18 Deeds of Covenant.. 397
19 Investment and Property... 409
20 Church Government and Administration...................... 431

Conclusions... 442
Summary of Main Recommendations................................. 447
Appendix... 452
Selected Bibliography.. 459

List of Tables

1 The proportion of members, elders, and office-bearers aged under 35 in a sample of 30 congregations, 1970	71
2 Statistics of the population of Scotland, 1970	71
3 A comparison of the age-distribution of the Church of Scotland membership with that of the Scottish population, 1970	72
4 A chi-square test of significance on the relationship between age and Church membership	72
5 Statistics of membership for 1946, 1956 and 1975	75
6 Ranking of a selection of Presbyteries by membership decline, 1960-73	77
7 The age distribution of the Scottish population for the years 1946, 1956 and 1972	79
8 The decline of admissions on Profession of Faith compared with the decline in total membership, 1957-75	83
9 The decline in infant baptisms, Sunday School pupils and Bible Class pupils, 1956-1974	85
10 Net loss of membership through removals by certificate, 1947-74	85
11 Forecasts of the membership for the period 1976-2001	90
12 Forecasts of the membership for 1981 and 2001, compared with the predicted figure for 1976	90
13 The total income of the Church of Scotland and its main components, 1975	99
14 The main components of Church income expressed as percentages of total income, 1966-75	102
15 Changes in the income of the Church (in real terms at 1975 prices) between 1948, 1953, 1967 and 1975	105
16 Calculations of real personal income *per capita* in the United Kingdom for selected years, 1950-75	109
17 Alternative forecasts of the membership of the Church for 1981 and 2001	110

18 Forecasts of the four independent variables of the income equation and of real total Church income, 1976-2001	111
19 Forecasts of real total Church income for 1981 and 2001	113
20 Percentage distribution of congregational income (or liberality) between the three major spending agencies of the Church, 1961-75	120
21 The proportion of 'special' liberality to total liberality, 1970-5	121
22 Distribution of congregational income (or liberality) 1961-75 (in money terms)	124
23 Distribution of congregational income (or liberality) 1961-75 (in real terms at 1975 prices)	125
24 The liberality income devoted to congregational expenses in money terms and in real terms at 1975 prices, 1961-75	127
25 The income and expenditure of the Church and Ministry Department, 1961-75 (in money terms)	129
26 The income and expenditure of the Church and Ministry Department, 1961-75 (in real terms at 1975 prices)	130
27 The payment of stipend in the Church, 1961-75	132
28 The income and expenditure of the committees within the Mission and Service Fund (excluding National Church Extension), 1961-75 (in money terms)	135
29 The income and expenditure of the committees within the Mission and Service Fund (excluding National Church Extension), 1961-75 (in real terms at 1975 prices)	136
30 The income and expenditure of National Church Extension, 1961-75 (in money terms)	139
31 The income and expenditure of National Church Extension, 1961-75 (in real terms at 1975 prices)	140
32 Summary of the income of the Church of Scotland, broken down by major areas of expenditure, 1961-75 (in money terms)	142-143
33 Summary of the income of the Church of Scotland, broken down by major areas of expenditure, 1961-75 (in real terms at 1975 prices)	142-143
34 Summary of the expenditures of the Church, 1961-75 (in money terms)	144-145
35 Summary of the expenditures of the Church, 1961-75 (in real terms at 1975 prices)	144-145
36 The total income and expenditure of the Church in money terms and in real terms at 1975 prices, 1961-75	146
37 The proportion of total Church income received by the committees within the Mission and Service Fund in 1962 and 1975	148

38 The apportionment of the total income of the Church for 1975, and the forecasts for 1981 and 2001, between the ministry, and mission and service	148
39 Age-distribution of active parish ministers in the Church of Scotland as at July 1974	156
40 Number of ministers employed by the Church as at July 1974	157
41 Inflow of ministers into the ministry of the Church of Scotland by age, 1969-73	159
42 Outflow of ministers from the ministry of the Church of Scotland, 1969-73	161
43 Breakdown of the outflow of ministers from the ministry, 1969-73	162
44 Changes in the numbers of parish ministers in the Church, 1953-73	164
45 Inflows and outflows of parish ministers to the ministry, 1969-73	164
46 The scaling up of the inflow and outflow figures of parish ministers	165
47 The ministerial manpower forecast for the ministry: basic data and the results for selected years	166-167
48 A forecast of the parish ministerial manpower of the Church of Scotland, 1975-2001	170
49 The ministerial manpower forecast under alternative assumptions	171
50 Comparisons of the numbers of members, ministers and lay workers for 1949, 1957 and 1973	175
51 Forecasts of members and lay workers for 1981 and 2001	177
52 The numbers of congregations, charges, ministers and vacancies as at 31 December 1945-75	188
53 A summary of the work of the Committee on Unions and Readjustments for the period 1945-75	190-191
54 Analysis of the financial position in 1971 of those charges considered for union or readjustment in 1972	195
55 The numbers of charges, congregations, parish ministers and 'net vacancies', 1945-75	197
56 A forecast of the number of charges in the Church of Scotland, 1974-2001	199
57 Projections of members per charge in 1981	203
58 Projections of members per charge in 2001	203
59 Projections of real income per charge (at 1975 prices) in 1981	205
60 Projections of real income per charge (at 1975 prices) in 2001	205
61 Projections of real liberality per member (at 1975 prices) in 1981	205
62 Projections of real liberality per member (at 1975 prices) in 2001	206

63 Estimates of the expenditure of the average charge in real terms (at 1975 prices) for 1975, 1981 and 2001 under different assumptions	206
64 Forecasts of the income and expenditure of the ministry in real terms (at 1975 prices), 1975-2001	209
65 Projections of the financial position of the ministry in real terms (at 1975 prices) in 1981	211
66 Projections of the financial position of the ministry in real terms (at 1975 prices) in 2001	211
67 Forecasts of the income and expenditure of mission and service in real terms (at 1975 prices), 1975-2001	213
68 Projections of the financial position of mission and service in 1981	214
69 Projections of the financial position of mission and service in 2001	214
70 The reallocation of standardized stipend in the period 1930-9	225
71 Details of some of the grants and other expenses met by the Maintenance of the Ministry Fund, 1968-74	238
72 A representative sample of 34 charges drawn from the Church total in 1974	244
73 The distribution of the stipends of the sample of 34 charges in 1976	244
74 The number and estimated value of manses in 1975	246
75 A comparison of the incomes of ministers with the salary scales of university academic staff, 1976	250
76 A comparison of the minimum stipends paid in several United Kingdom churches, 1975 and 1976	251
77 Changes in the minimum stipend in money and real terms, and compared to average earnings, 1961-76	252
78 Estimating the impact of the proposal to re-allocate endowment stipend, based on a sample of 157 congregations, 1973	261
79 The frequency distribution of the number of congregations per Presbytery, 1973	269
80 The frequency distribution of Presbytery memberships, 1973	271
81 The frequency distribution of the average membership per congregation by Presbytery, 1973	271
82 The frequency distribution of the normal liberality per congregation by Presbytery, 1973	273
83 The frequency distribution of the 'normal liberality' per member by Presbytery, 1973	273
84 The numbers of congregations giving aid to, or receiving aid from, the Fund for the Maintenance of the Ministry in 1973	275

85 The average net aid per congregation given to (+) or received from (−) the fund by Presbytery in 1973	275
86 The Synods where the numbers of aid-receiving congregations exceeded aid-giving congregations in 1973	275
87 The Synods which were net receivers of aid from the fund in 1973	277
88 Aid-giving and aid-receiving congregations in the four Synods in 1973	278
89 The Mission and Service Fund allocations and contributions of the four 'city' Presbyteries, 1973	278
90 The Mission and Service Fund allocations and contributions of the four 'city' Synods, 1973	279
91 The significance in Church finance of certain urban and rural Presbyteries and Synods in 1973	280
92 A weighted sample of 40 congregations (sample 1)	282
93 Estimates of the income of congregations in 1973 with different levels of membership, based on equation (19)	284
94 Estimates of the expenditure of a non-linked congregation in 1973 with increasing levels of membership, based on equation (27)	288
95 Estimates of the expenditure of a linked congregation in 1973 with increasing levels of membership, based on equation (28)	288
96 Estimates of the average expenditure per member of a congregation in 1973 with different levels of membership, based on equation (26)	289
97 Estimates of the income of congregations in 1973 with different levels of membership, based on equation (34)	294
98 Information on the subsidiary accounts which appeared in the annual accounts of the sample of 33 congregations in 1973	297
99 Information on the total income of the sample of 33 congregations as recorded in their annual accounts for 1973	298
100 Estimates of Church total congregational income in 1973	300
101 Estimates of the actual total income of the Church in 1973	301
102 Information on the capital balances held in the accounts of the sample of 33 congregations in 1973	302
103 Estimate of the total capital balances held by congregations in 1973	302
104 Comparisons of annual changes in membership of united charges with the Church as a whole, 1960-74	308
105 Comparisons of annual changes of income (normal liberality) of united charges with the Church as a whole, 1960-74	309
106 Alternative calculations of the savings arising from the uniting of pairs of congregations with different aggregate levels of membership	314-315

107 Alternative calculations of the savings arising from the linking of pairs of congregations with different aggregate levels of membership   320-321

108 Estimates of the savings to the Church (at 1973 prices) of union and readjustment, 1975-86   322

109 The selection of candidates for the ministry, 1967-75   329

110 Distribution by university of students in training for the ministry, 1966/7-1975/6   329

111 Number of students in training for the ministry by course and university, 1975-6   331

112 Breakdown of the average working week of a parish minister from a survey in 1966-7   333

113 Relative costs of ministers and assistants in the Church of Scotland, 1975   342

114 Liberality received by committees within the Mission and Service Fund, 1961-75   354-355

115 Allocation of Mission and Service Fund budget to groups of congregations, 1973-6   360-361

116 Minimum (group B) and maximum (group Q) rates of Mission and Service Fund levy on groups of congregations, 1973-6   362

117 A breakdown of the numbers of congregations which met, exceeded, and failed to meet, their Mission and Service Fund allocations in the years 1971-3   364

118 A calculation of the increase in income to the Mission and Service Fund in 1973 assuming that (A) all Presbyteries, and (B) all congregations, had at least achieved their allocations   365

119 The number of charges participating in each of the four types of fund-raising campaign, 1963-72   379

120 The geographical distribution by Presbytery of charges participating in fund-raising campaigns, 1963-72   380

121 A comparison of the 'average' characteristics of charges in each of the four fund-raising campaign categories with those of the control group between 1964 and 1972   382

122 Mean annual percentage changes in the membership and income of charges participating in the Wells Three-Year Plan, 1963-9   383

123 Mean annual percentage changes in the membership and income of charges participating in the Parish Development Programme, 1967-8   384

124 Mean annual percentage changes in membership and income of charges in control sample I for comparison with the charges participating in the Wells Three-Year Plan   384

125 Mean annual percentage changes in membership and income of

charges in control sample II, for comparison with the charges participating in the Parish Development Programme	385
126 Estimating the effectiveness of the Wells Three-Year Plan in raising the income of charges	387
127 The cost of a Wells Three-Year Plan campaign, 1965-7	388
128 Details of Deeds of Covenant held by the Church of Scotland	398
129 Details of the stratified sample of parishes in the Church	399
130 A disaggregation of congregational income showing the proportion raised by Deed of Covenant for the five groups of charges in 1973	401
131 Proportions of charges not using Deeds of Covenant	402
132 A calculation of the potential increase in income per charge from income tax recovered on covenants in 1973	405
133 A calculation of the potential increase in income of the Church from income tax recovered on covenants in 1973	406
134 The potential increase in the income of the Church from income tax recovered on covenants compared to total income in 1973	406
135 A summary of the changes in the income of the Church between 1946, 1960 and 1975 (in money terms)	410
136 A summary of the changes in the income of the Church between 1946, 1960 and 1975 (in real terms at 1975 prices)	412
137 Sales and purchases of manses, as reported in the minutes of the General Trustees, 1972/3-1976/7	418
138 Sales and purchases of church properties other than manses, as reported in the minutes of the General Trustees, 1972/3-1976/7	420
139 Estimates of the cost of the ministerial contribution to Church government and administration, 1966 and 1975	432
140 The cost of the General Assembly and the central departments, 1975	435
141 The estimated real total savings (at 1975 prices) of the main quantifiable proposals, 1976-85	443

List of Figures

1 A simplified diagram of the 'family tree' of Christian Churches	4
2 Divisions and Reunions of the Scottish Church, 1960-1929	19
3 Communicant membership, annual communicants, and Supplementary Roll numbers, 1921-75	74
4 Comparisons of membership with membership/population ratios, 1921-75	79
5 Removals and admissions of members, and the membership turnover, 1921-75	80
6 A breakdown of the removals from membership, 1921-75	81
7 A breakdown of the admissions to membership, 1921-75	82
8 Linear regression trend lines fitted to the membership data, 1956-75	88
9 The total income (TI), liberality (L), and other income (OI) of the Church shown at current prices and in real terms at 1975 prices, 1950-75	103
10 Forecasts of the real total income of the Church (at 1975 prices) for 1976-2001, compared to the actual figures for 1967-75	113
11 The total income and expenditure of the Church in money terms and in real terms at 1975 prices, 1961-75	147
12 Age-distribution of active parish ministers in the Church of Scotland as at July 1974	155
13 A flow diagram showing the main flows of ministers into and out of the ministry	158
14 The number of ministers entering and leaving the ministry each year over the period 1969-73, averaged by age for each age group	163
15 A forecast of the age distribution of parish ministers for selected years, based on the manpower forecast	172
16 Forecasts of the number of ministers in the parish ministry, 1974-2001	174
17 The numbers of congregations, charges, ministers, and net vacancies in the Church, 1950-75	187

18 The numbers of unions and readjustments in the Church, 1950-75	192
19 Forecasts of the income and expenditure of the ministry in real terms (at 1975 prices), 1975-2001	210
20 Forecasts of the income and expenditure of mission and service in real terms (at 1975 prices), 1975-2001	213
21 Linear regressions of stipend against congregational income, expenditure, membership and aid for a sample of charges, 1973	255
22 A map of Scotland showing the four 'city' Synods	270
23 A map of Scotland showing the four net aid-receiving synods in 1973	272
24 Frequency polygon of endowment and investment income	285
25 Congregational income and expenditure equations	289
26 The financial 'break even' membership of congregations	291
27 The simultaneous equation model of congregational income and expenditure	295
28 Income ($I4_1$) and expenditure (E_2) as functions of membership for a sample of non-linked congregations, 1973	313
29 Income ($I4_1$) and expenditure (E_3) as functions of membership for a sample of linked congregations, 1973	318

Preface

This book is the product of the research work conducted by the Church of Scotland Economic Survey, which was established in the Department of Economics at the University of Edinburgh in November 1972 under the direction of Professor J.N. Wolfe. The work was financed by a generous grant from the Church of Scotland. The first full-time research staff were appointed in September 1973, and the research was completed four years later, in September 1977. The remit of the Economic Survey was notified to the General Assembly of the Church of Scotland in 1973, and was further considered at the General Assembly of 1974. A steering committee, composed of eminent people in the Church, was appointed to help in the formulation of research aims, and to receive and comment upon reports of the research at regular intervals.

We have been very aware throughout our work that the Economic Survey has been breaking new ground. To the best of our knowledge, no previous attempt has been made to undertake an economic analysis of an institutional Church. Although originally there may have been doubts as to how far economic analysis would be applicable to the Church, these were soon dispelled once the research got under way. It gradually became clear that the scope for economic analysis is as great in the Church as in other institutions, once the special features of the history, organization and traditions are fully understood.

The book concentrates, firstly, on understanding the organization and procedures of the Church, particularly with regard to financial affairs, and, secondly, with examining proposals which, if implemented, might improve the financial position and prospects of the Church. Our research has proceeded through the framing of hypotheses about different aspects of the Church's work, and then testing the hypotheses by subjecting the appropriate data to statistical tests. As far as possible, therefore, given the necessarily limited time and resources at our disposal, we have attempted to make this book an expression of fact, rather than of opinion.

On many questions, however, it is not possible to devise clear-cut tests, either because the nature of the problem does not lend it to statistical testing, or because of the lack of the appropriate data. Even where tests can be made the results may not be conclusive, or they may be subject to varying interpretations. In many of our proposals, therefore, the statistical tests have had to be supplemented by our judgement as to what is the best policy to follow. It should be clear in the text when that is the case.

The analysis is confined largely to the economic and financial issues involved.

While we have tried to ensure that the proposals conflict as little as possible with present Church practice and procedure, it is inevitable that some of the proposals will raise theological questions, and others challenge Church traditions. Such questions are beyond our competence to resolve, however, and must be left to the Church to consider.

A number of people have assisted our research work, including M.E. Corboy, D.E. Pitfield, and C. Wilkinson, who spent periods as research associates on the Economic Survey. In addition, several researchers in the Department of Economics carried out short projects for the survey, and we have benefited from discussions with a number of other members of staff within the University of Edinburgh. Among these are included Mrs S.L. Bowen, C.R. Brand, S.N. Brissimis, R.C. Cressy, J.P. Dunne, V. Droucopoulos, L. Gill, R.M. Gill, M.J. Prentice, N.W. Shrock, and Miss G. Watson.

We owe a debt of gratitude to the many people in the Church — parish ministers, lay officials, and secretaries at the Church offices — who have readily co-operated in our frequent requests for information and advice. Amongst those we should especially like to thank are Rev. H.C.M. Eggo, Rev. G.L. Lugton, and Rev. T. Balfour of the Church and Ministry Department. We should also like to record our gratitude to the late Rev. K.S.G. Greenlaw, who first conceived the idea of an economic survey, and was responsible for setting the survey in motion.

Finally, to acknowledge the use of certain copyright material in chapter 1 taken from: J.H.S. Burleigh, *A Church History of Scotland*, (1960), reprinted by permission of Oxford University Press; J.D. Mackie, *A History of Scotland*, (Pelican Original, 1964), reprinted by permission of Penguin Books Ltd.; from the *Oxford Junior Encyclopaedia*, (Volume I, 1960), the use of a diagram modified as our figure 1, by permission of Oxford University Press; and in chapters 2 and 3 from: J.T. Cox, *Practice and Procedure in the Church of Scotland*, (6th ed., edited by Rev. D.F.M. Macdonald, 1976), by permission of the editor.

University of EdinburghM. Pickford
July 1977J.N. Wolfe

Introduction

The Church of Scotland is a Presbyterian church, and is the established Church in Scotland. With just over one million communicant members, together with a large number of baptized children and adults, out of a Scottish population of 5.2 million, it is easily the largest Church in Scotland. The Church is organized territorially, covering the whole of Scotland with about 1,700 parishes, each with its own resident minister. Every parish has one, and sometimes two or more, congregations, each having its own church building, governing body (the Kirk Session), method of congregational management, and separate identity.

The Church is governed by a hierarchical system of courts. The first is the congregational Kirk Session, which is composed of minister and elders, and is responsible for managing the affairs of the congregation. The parishes are grouped by district into Presbyteries, which are composed of the minister and Presbytery elder from each parish, and the Presbyteries are grouped by region into Synods. There are forty-seven Presbyteries and twelve Synods of the Church in Scotland. The supreme governing body is the General Assembly, which meets annually, and is composed of one-quarter of the ministers by rotation in each Presbytery, together with an equal number of elders.

In 1975 the published total income of the Church was £17,644,424, of which 73.5 per cent was raised by the congregations, largely from the giving of individual members. The remainder is collected in the form of bequests, grants, donations, investment income, and feu-duties by the Church central authorities.

While each congregation is a semi-independent unit which manages its own financial affairs, all participate in a central fund called the Maintenance of the Ministry Fund, which is managed by the Maintenance of the Ministry Committee. The main purpose of this fund is to 'support' the ministry by maintaining stipends in all charges at least at the minimum level declared in advance for the year. Annual grants are made from the Fund to support the stipend in those charges which are not financially self-supporting, these grants being financed by an annual contribution from those charges which are self-sufficient. In 1976 the minimum stipend was £2,560, together with a manse. Parishes which are self-supporting are permitted to pay their minister a stipend above the minimum.

The second major activity of the Church is the mission and service work. This covers a variety of activities, usually of an evangelistic nature, which overlaps with, and complements, the work of the ministry. These activities include religious education and publications, work overseas, social work in homes and hostels, and the employment of ministers as chaplains to hospitals, industry, and the Forces. The income for this work is derived partly from a system of levies imposed upon the income of congregations through the Mission and Service Fund, and partly from a proportion of the income collected centrally.

In this book the analysis of the Church of Scotland is divided into five parts. Part I provides the background to the study, without which much in the present position of the Church cannot be fully understood. In chapter 1 we present a brief history of the Church from the Middle Ages up to the present day. This is followed in chapter 2 by an outline of the present constitution and method of government of the Church. Chapter 3 deals with the ownership of the property and funds of the Church.

In part II we turn to the analysis and forecasting of some of the main economic variables in the Church. Chapter 4 examines the composition of the membership of the Church, analyses where members are being gained and lost, and suggests policies for halting the decline in numbers which started two decades ago. In chapter 5 we turn to the question of Church income, analyse its main components, and develop a statistical model for making income forecasts. Chapter 6 examines the breakdown in the expenditures of the Church between the main spending agencies, and shows how it is closely related to income. In chapter 7 we develop forecasts of the number of parish ministers, based on the age distribution of the present population of ministers, and on the recent trends in the intake of new ministers and losses of existing ministers. In the following chapter the distinction between parish 'charges' and 'congregations' is made clear, and the policy of union and readjustment by which the number is being reduced is described. Forecasts are made on the basis of the forecast number of ministers. Part II is concluded with chapter 9 which draws together the forecasts of the main Church economic variables in order to make forecasts of the financial position of the Church in 1981 and 2001.

In part III we turn our attention to the parish ministry, the first main area of the Church's work. Chapter 10 is a largely factual account of the way in which the ministry is financed. This is followed in chapter 11 by an analysis of stipend, which leads to the formulation of proposals for stipend policy. Chapter 12 is devoted to an examination of the finances of congregations. This includes a statistical analysis to determine the main factors which influence the income and expenditure of congregations, and thus whether a congregation is likely to be self-supporting or in receipt of aid from the fund. Then in chapter 13 we investigate the economic implications of the rationalization of the parish structure through the policy of union and readjustment. By the uniting and 'linking' of congregations, the policy serves to reduce their number, and therefore the cost of the ministry. Chapter 14 examines the important question of the education and training received by candidates for the Ministry. The training is compared with the requirements of the job. Finally, chapter 15 examines the economic implications of forms of Ministry other than the traditional 'one man – one parish' form of organization.

Part IV is concerned with mission and stewardship. In chapter 16 we examine the work of the Stewardship and Budget Committee in organizing the financing of the mission and service work through the fund of that name. This is followed in chapter 17 by an analysis of the Committee's work in promoting stewardship and fund-raising amongst the congregations. We describe a comparative statistical analysis of the effectiveness of different forms of Stewardship campaign.

In part V further proposals are made to improve the overall financial position of the Church. Chapter 18 examines the importance to the income of the Church of members channelling their contributions through Deeds of Covenant. Chapter 19 deals with the complex question of the investments of the Church. We outline the principles of an investment strategy which, if implemented, should extend the Church's investments, and increase the amount of investment income accordingly. Finally, in chapter 20 we put forward a number of proposals to streamline the government and administration of the Church, which should reduce costs and lead to increased efficiency in the organization.

The conclusion draws together the main themes of the book, and assesses the possible impact of our main proposals on the financial position of the Church over the next ten years.

I
General Background To The Study

Chapter 1

A brief history of the Church of Scotland

1 Introduction
In this chapter is presented a brief outline of the history of the Churches in Scotland, with particular emphasis on the Church of Scotland. This should provide a backcloth against which the present position of the Church can be better understood, and should put our study in an historical perspective.

No claim is made to originality in any of the material presented here. It is simply a summary of what, to the authors, seemed interesting and important points, and is drawn from certain secondary sources, mainly Burleigh, Gibson and Mackie.[1] In keeping with the economic nature of our study, the emphasis is on the structure and organization of the Church, particularly financial organization, rather than on matters of theology and doctrine.

In section 2 a brief sketch is given of the history of the western Christian Church from the Middle Ages to the present day, in order to understand better the changes and developments in the Church history of Scotland. Then in section 3 the historical development of the Churches in Scotland is dealt with in greater detail, again over the period from the Middle Ages to the present day.

2 The western Christian Church
During the Middle Ages the Church, with its centre at Rome, had become the single religious authority throughout western Christendom. About the year 1200, Pope Innocent III declared that the Pope was head of a feudal world and that kings held their kingdoms as fiefs from the Pope. Later, there were attempts to reform the Church by such men as Wycliffe and Huss, but their influence was relatively restricted and local.

By the sixteenth century conditions had changed. The supremacy of the Pope over temporal affairs was increasingly brought into question by the development of new nation states which looked for a Church managed on a constitutional basis where national interests could also be represented. Apart from these political considerations, the inquiring spirit of the age (the Renaissance) led people to question things which they had merely accepted before, and to condemn abuses in the Church. Humanist scholars, such as Erasmus (?1469-1536), studied the Bible in its original texts, and pointed out where the practice of the Church differed from the original teachings of Jesus and St Paul. Also, many were shocked by the abuses which had grown up in the Church – for example, by the sale of indulgences and benefices, and by the worldliness of the Popes.

At first those who protested against the abuses sought only to reform the

FIGURE 1. A simplified diagram of the 'family tree' of Christian Churches
SOURCE: adapted from *Oxford Junior Encyclopedia,* (Oxford University Press, 1960), Volume I, p. 119.

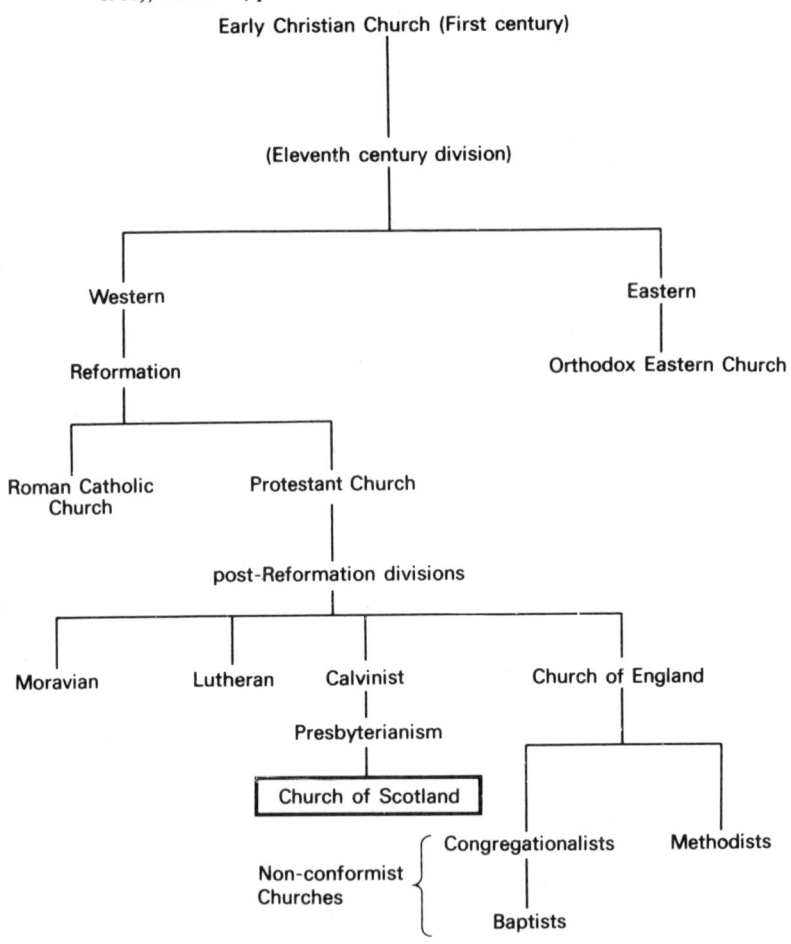

```
              Early Christian Church (First century)
                              |
                   (Eleventh century division)
                              |
              ┌───────────────┴───────────────┐
           Western                         Eastern
              |                               |
         Reformation                 Orthodox Eastern Church
              |
      ┌───────┴───────┐
  Roman Catholic   Protestant Church
     Church             |
                post-Reformation divisions
                        |
      ┌────────┬────────┼──────────────┐
  Moravian  Lutheran  Calvinist    Church of England
                        |               |
                 Presbyterianism  ┌─────┴──────┐
                        |
                 Church of Scotland
                                Congregationalists   Methodists
                Non-conformist  {        |
                  Churches              Baptists
```

Church; they had no wish to break from it. But attempts at reform were resisted by those who benefited from the abuses, and the reformers were forced to choose between the Bible and the Pope. They chose the Bible, and soon built up large followings. In 1517 Martin Luther started the break from Rome in Germany. This led to the formation of the Lutheran Church, to which most people in north Germany, Denmark, Norway and Sweden now belong (*see figure 1*). In 1536 Calvin started in Geneva the movement which resulted in the establishment of the Calvinist Church, which spread over western Germany, France, the Netherlands, and Scotland.

The custom in the Roman Church was to set apart as a priest, by the solemn act of ordination, the man who was to make the Communion-offering. However, with many of the Protestant Churches established during the Reformation the ancient line of bishops, priests and deacons was brought to an end, and in its place a new order of ministers was established. Their chief work lay in preaching the Gospel, acting as shepherds of their flocks, and ministering to a congregation, rather than in acting as attendants at the altar during worship.

The English Reformation left the medieval church order less disturbed, except for the dissolution of the monasteries, and many of the old forms of service were kept in the Church of England. In Scotland, the papacy was overthrown in 1560, but the Presbyterian Church of Scotland was not finally established until 1690.

In the sixteenth and eighteenth centuries groups of English people, dissatisfied with the reformation of the Anglican Church, broke away and formed separate denominations. Among these are included the Congregationalists and Baptists in the earlier period, and the Methodists in the later period. These denominations are called 'nonconformist' because they would not accept the one-style religion which the State laid down. They had little impact in Scotland, where the main stream of evangelism was retained within the Church of Scotland.

The Roman Church met the Reformation with a counter-Reformation, in which it stiffened its own discipline, removed many abuses, and attempted to win back members by the use of propaganda and persecution through the instrument of the Inquisition. The Church also launched, largely through the Jesuits, a great Christian expansion which carried Christianity to the New World, Africa, and the East Indies. Although the Roman Church retained its power in south Europe, France and Belgium, the Protestant Churches remained entrenched in northern Europe.

Today there is more concern about the unity between the Churches than at any time since the Reformation, although the ecumenical movement has not made rapid progress. Like most established institutions the Churches have generally been conservative and slow to accept new ideas. Such conservatism leads to security against the risk of falling victim to false doctrines, although the immediate effect may be unprogressive.

3 A Church history of Scotland

1 The Church during the Middle Ages
By the eleventh century Christianity in Scotland had survived the troublesome period of the Norse invasions and the unification of the different racial groups in northern Britain, and had increased its hold on the people. The Church had outgrown the missionary conditions with which it had begun, and was identified with the nation. *Ecclesia Scoticana* emerged from the period of the Dark Ages with a bishop (of St Andrews) at its head, with its properties, rights and privileges recognized by the crown, and ministering to the people from many centres.

Local churches were founded chiefly by local lairds and endowed with glebe lands. Out of these emerged the parish churches to administer the sacraments to the parishioners. Moreover, the Church claimed on the grounds of Scripture the tithe or tenth part (or 'teind' in Scotland) of the annual produce of the parish, and this claim was enforced by royal commands. The teinds became the main subsidy in Scotland of ministers' stipends for the next seven centuries to around 1850. In addition, offerings were expected on certain occasions, such as baptisms, marriages, funerals and the celebration of the Mass, especially on Easter Day.

These were supposed to be voluntary, but they became customary, and custom came to have the force of law. The income from all these sources together formed the parochial benefice which might be held by a parson or rector appointed by the founder, or his heirs or patron.

The teinds became known as 'Spiritualities' because of their Biblical origin and history. They were distinguished from other revenues, known as 'Temporalities', which the Church held under no particular privilege, but in the same way as other owners. The principle temporalities were the vast landed estates which had come into the possession of the Church. For the most part they were gifted before 1300 by private persons, encouraged by the example of David I (1124-53). Most of the larger Scottish monasteries were founded in his reign, and it was largely by him that the lavish endowments were given. Apart from land, they included to some the privilege of administering baronial justice to their tenants or of erecting a burgh with the customary trading rights. Just before the Reformation, according to Gibson, the lands held by the Church amounted to one-third of the area of the country, and produced about one half of the wealth. At this time Cardinal Sermoneta was able to report to Rome that 'the clergy of Scotland far surpassed the laity in the wealth and abundance of their resources.'

However, this wealth was unevenly distributed among the clergy. In the twelfth century it became usual for the founder of a parish church to hand over his church to some favoured monastery, which thereby became the permanent 'rector', appropriated the fruits to its own uses, and appointed a priest ('Vicar') to perform the parochial duties on a salary which was only a fraction of the parish revenue. By the middle of the thirteenth century each of the larger abbeys is found in possession of a considerable number of these 'appropriated' churches, not all of them in its vicinity. Thus Kelso had 37, Holyrood 27, Paisley 29, and Arbroath 33.

The weakness of the system was that cathedrals and monasteries tended to draw to themselves too large a share of ecclesiastical endowments, leaving the parochial ministry poor and ineffective. Vicars were commonly badly paid and poorly educated. It seems clear that the 'cure of souls', the task of the parochial ministry, was seriously undervalued and became a dead-end occupation, not to be accepted by anyone in search of higher preferment. This situation was not peculiar to Scotland, but obtained everywhere throughout the western Church, and it proved to be its fatal weakness.

While the monasteries were the prevailing form of religious devotion in the reign of David I, there seems to have been a deterioration of standards from the fourteenth century. From 1488, abbots, the heads of monasteries, were nominated by the Crown for the first time, and appointed by the Pope. Such appointments were bestowed on royal favourites, whether clerical or not, so that it was not surprising that the monastic ideal fell into discredit. The obvious abuses attracted criticism of the Church, and attention was drawn to the difference between the Church at the time of the Apostles and the Church which now had become wealthy. Church councils which met from 1549 to 1559 in order to stem the Reformation by reform were out-spoken in their criticism of monastic abuses, but the same abuses were criticised in 1559 as had been first raised in 1549, so that little reform seems to have been achieved.

2 The Reformation in Scotland, 1560

The Reformation in Scotland was not only a great religious issue; political and economic factors were also involved. The first cause of the Reformation was the laxity and corruption of the higher clergy, which led men to wonder whether the services rendered by the Church were commensurate with the great privileges it enjoyed. Among the abuses condemned were clerical 'concubinage', the granting of feus with the expropriation of old tenants, non-residence, pluralities, the dilapidation of hospitals, and the lack of good preaching. The real work of the Church was neglected, as the ordinary parish priest was starved while the bulk of the income went to the bishops, to the maintenance of large, unproductive monasteries and other religious houses, and to meet Papal exactions from Rome.

Then there was the economic background. On the eve of the Reformation the revenue of the Church is estimated to have been at least £300,000 a year. This compares with the Crown's patrimony of about £17,500, which, together with other sources, produced a total income which was far less than that of the Church at a time when its obligations were increasing. The enemies of the Church suggested spoliation. Also, many teinds had been appropriated to sees or religious houses, while the parochial work was done by poorly paid curates who tended to collect the 'small teinds' with vigour and thus became unpopular. 'Pillaged by the crown, envied by the nobles, distrusted by the poor, the Church was very open to the attacks of those who hoped to cure their economic grievances by enbracing the cause of the Reformation.'[2]

The third cause of the Reformation was political. Scotland, enfeebled since her defeat against the English at Flodden (1513), and later reduced by ineffectual rule, could not stand alone. She had to have the support of one of her two powerful, and rival, neighbours – England and France. This struggle took a religious complexion, since France stood for the old religion while England, from 1534 with her break from Rome under Henry VIII, was at least anti-papal. Under James V (1513-42) Scotland inclined towards France, and the ties between the two countries were strengthened when Mary Queen of Scots married the Dauphin in 1558. She secretly signed three documents which would have the effect of conveying Scotland to the King of France if she should die without heir. Thus in 1558 Scotland was in danger of being absorbed by France, a danger which spurred on the reformers.

Matters were well advanced by the time John Knox, the greatest agent of the Reformation in Scotland, returned there in 1559. Protestantism had grown apace over the previous decade, and had been reinforced by the Marian exiles from England. Even in 1555-6, on a previous visit, Knox had found sporadic congregations springing up here and there, and was astonished at the progress Protestantism had made in Edinburgh. In December 1557 there was signed by some great nobles and others the first formal 'covenant', whereby they undertook 'to apply their whole power, substance and very lives to maintain and forward and establish the most blessed work of God and His Congregation.' So came into being the instrument which, revived four times, served to unite the Protestants during the crisis of 1559-60, and expanded and altered, was to play a great part in the history of the Scottish Kirk until 1689 and after.

In August 1560 the Scottish Parliament met. On the 17th it passed Knox's Confession of Faith, and on the 24th it passed three Acts which destroyed the

Roman Church in Scotland, viz., (a) all legislation in favour of the Roman Church was repealed; (b) the jurisdiction of the Pope within Scotland was abolished; and (c) the number of sacraments were reduced to two, and celebration of the Mass was made punishable by a series of penalties, culminating in death for the third offence. 'Such was the Protestant Revolution, carried out by the Estates in defiance of the "pleasure" of the absentee sovereign, but its stability had still to be tested . . . the Reformers had gained nothing from Parliament except the legalizing of their creed. A long struggle confronted them before their ideal of a Reformed Church could be realized.'[3]

The foundation of the Reformed Church was the Confession of Faith, the drawing-up of which was appropriate, since the Reformation claimed above all else to be a return to the pure Gospel and scriptural truth. The Confession asserted that truth and righteousness could be established from the Bible, but gave to the Sprit of God the sole right of intrepretation. By implication, ministers would be the most likely interpreters, and so special emphasis was placed on the education and personal qualities of ministers. Ordination became a solemn admission to the pastoral office in a particular charge, thereby laying new emphasis on the pastoral obligations in ordination which had been scandalously neglected.

It was also a fundamental principle of the Calvinist Reformation that the Church 'shows its face' where the Christian people gather for instruction and worship. A wider organization, whether national or ecumenical, may be helpful to refute heresies or declare the faith, but the life of the Church is in the local congregation. Moreover, the interpretation of the Scriptures pertains to the Spirit of God, and not to any individual or body. Since there could be nothing higher than the ministry of Word and sacraments, ministers and bishops were regarded as identical. This explains the absence of bishops in the Church of Scotland, and the fact that all ministers are regarded as equals.

The Confession accepts two sacraments as dominical – Baptism and the Supper – and criticizes the 'adulterated' sacraments of the Roman Church, and especially the Mass, as superstitious and idolatrous. If the efficacy of the sacraments depends on true faith, then it is necessary for ministers and participants to know their meaning and purpose, and to fulfil the moral conditions of worthy participation. For this reason, and since the parochial minister was to be elected by congregations, an educated congregation was a necessity. Hence in the *Book of Discipline* the reformers aimed at organizing, not only the Kirk, but the whole nation, in accordance with the will of God. Proceeding on the assumption that the revenues of the old Kirk would be available, they envisaged the establishment of ministers throughout Scotland, a national system of education, and some arrangement for poor relief. Realizing that some time would elapse before a sufficient number of good ministers could be trained, the authors provided for the appointment of 'readers', who might do some parochial work under supervision.

A further characteristic feature of the Reformed Church of Scotland was the elders who were to be elected by the congregation to assist with the minister in the government of the congregation. Their duties, among others, were to watch over the manners and conversation of all – including the minister and his family! In this way the reformers sought to prevent in the new Church the clerical indiscipline that had been a notorious feature of the old.

From the beginning it was recognised by all parties that the Roman Church no longer had any right to Spiritualities (i.e. the teinds), but the leaders of the Reformed Church were remarkably moderate in their demands. They agreed to an arrangement, passed by Act of Council in 1562, whereby Roman priests, deprived of their livelihood, received for their lifetime two-thirds of the parochial teinds, the remaining one-third passing to the Protestant Church for the new ministers. This was intended to be a temporary arrangement until life interests had died out.

As for the temporalities, the reformers, according to Gibson, 'put forward no claim at all to them for reasons that to this day are not fully understood.' This alone approximately halved the income of the Church, and, together with the fall in the teinds, reduced the annual income of the Protestant Church to one-sixth of that of the pre-Reformation Church. The Crown repossessed itself of much of the land given by past monarchs, and often neighbouring proprietors simply took possession without having any real claim.

The poverty of the Reformed Church made it impossible for it to undertake the ambitious programme of providing for every parish a church and school together with a minister and schoolmaster, as well as income for sustaining the poor. The clergy were poorly paid; even by 1567 there were only 257 ministers for 1080 churches, with some 600 readers and 'exhorters'.

The institutions of the new Church took shape only in a haphazard way. The congregational Kirk Session was there from the start, and the General Assembly appeared in 1560, although at first it was predominantly a lay body. The Synod, or provincial assembly, was introduced in 1562. But the Presbytery, or district assembly, came into being only about 1580, and then partly in imitation of English practice.

A general explanation of the divergence between the Churches in Scotland and English is that Scotland accepted Calvinism wholeheartedly while England did not. But Mackie points out that the official religion of England after the Civil War was, for a time, Presbyterian, and that it was from England that Scotland was to receive the 1647 Westminister Confession of Faith, which to this day remains the principal subordinate standard of the Church of Scotland. Mackie argues that while it may be true that Scotland as a whole accepted the logical system of Calvin, whereas England found the means of tempering its austerities, the fundamental cause of the differences lay, not in doctorine, but in discipline. In England the Crown arrogated to itself the power of the Pope; the monarch became head of the Church, and the government of the Church was authoritarian. The monarch, as head of the Church, was thus able to persecute religious dissidents on the grounds that they were enemies of the State. The Reformation in England was therefore more political than doctrinal.

The Scottish Church, however, was born in revolution against an absentee Queen who was a Papist. The Church generally received only half-hearted support from the Crown, and could not rely on it to suppress opponents. There were also fears of papist invasion. Hence the new Church had always to stand to its defence, and not unnaturally it developed the Calvinist doctrine that civil government, though regarded as a necessity, was to be recognized only when it was conducted according to the Word of God.

This had two consequences. Firstly, the Church came to claim a spiritual authority outside the authority of the State in what became known as the doctrine of the 'two kingdoms'. Secondly, because the authority of the Church rested on moral conviction, ministers must display in their own lives, and demand from their people, an exact obedience to the Word of God. It has been suggested that the emphasis on discipline has bred in the Scottish people the idea of God as arbitrary and severe; but at the same time it has encouraged high standards of moral and self-responsibility which helped safeguard the Church against the storms which threatened it in the years after its foundation.

Mary Queen of Scots, although a convinced Catholic and connected by the closest ties with France, at first made no effort to suppress the infant Kirk, although neither did she encourage it. After her marriage in July 1565 to Lord Darnley, however, her policy turned sharply and disastrously towards Catholicism, and in 1567 she was compelled to abdicate.

The period 1567-78 saw four regencies, all supported by England, by which the Protestant cause was maintained in Scotland. However, the position of the infant Church was not secure. In 1567 practically all abbacies were in the hands of lay commendators, usually members of noble families, and all but four bishoprics were still held by prelates of the old Church.

The first bishopric to fall vacant was that of St Andrews in 1571. The appointment of Douglas by the lawful patron, the Regent acting on behalf of the Crown, aroused protests. Although a prominent Protestant, Douglas was an infirm old man, unfit for the arduous duties of the office. Also, the Superintendent of Angus protested to the Regent on the grounds that Douglas had not been examined or admitted by any ecclessiastical authority. As a result of the protest a Commission, or extraordinary General Assembly, met in Leith in 1572. It appointed a strong committee with full powers to confer with a committee of the Privy Council.

The result is known as the Concordat of Leith. It was agreed that archbishoprics and bishoprics were to remain, at least until the King attained his majority. After consecretion, the new bishops were required to take an oath of allegiance to the King. Ecclesiastically, they were to have no more power than the superintendents had, and were also, like the latter, to be subject to the General Assembly. In these and other questions the Concordat evinced a sympathy towards vested interests and traditional institutions. This reflected the fact that the country was engaged in civil war, and that all the bishops in possession were on the Queen's side.

The Regent, the Earl of Morton, also had a hand in formulating the Articles, and they mirrored his ideas. The acquiescence of the General Assembly in August 1572 to the Articles indicates that the Reformed Church could not afford to quarrel with Morton, who was the destroyer of the Queen's party and the champion of Protestantism. But it soon became evident that Morton was aiming at the enhancement of royal authority over the Church. Some of his nominees to bishoprics did not inspire confidence, which led the Assembly to claim the right to examine them before their admission. The opposition found a leader in Andrew Melville.

The Assembly appointed a committee of six, including Melville, to examine the question of the bishops. They concluded that a bishop is essentially the pastor of one congregation, and that any supervision he may excercise beyond his own congregation is a duty entrusted to him by the Church authority. This position emphasised in the *Second Book of Discipline*, which the General Assembly approved in 1578. The book sought to preserve the liberty of the Church in relation to the State by asserting that the Kirk derived its power directly from God, and thereby attempted to erect a spiritual authority outside that of the State. The Christian magistrate may purge the Church when it is corrupt, but when the ministry is lawfully constituted and does its duty faithfully, the magistrate ought to assist in its maintenance. In 1580 the Assembly took power into its own hands by declaring the office of bishop as understood within the realm to be unlawful, and those who held the office were ordered to demit it. In the following year it was agreed to group the 600 parishes in the country into fifty Presbyteries, of which thirteen were to be established immediately. Hence a cleavage developed between the Crown, which favoured the authoritarian bishops, and the Presbyteries, who held that the reappearance of bishops might presage a return to Rome.

In 1578 James VI came to the throne at the age of eleven. Although in 1589 he was to marry a Protestant bride — Anne of Denmark — he followed a middle course between Catholics and Protestants, his policy being conditioned by the desire to succeed Elizabeth to the English throne. Thus he mildly favoured Protestantism for the sake of England, but did not go so far as to discourage Catholic candidates or oppose the Pope. Judging it politic to come to terms with the Kirk, he invited an Assembly to meet in 1586, the first time for three years.

A scheme for the organizing of Presbyteries covering practically the whole country was drawn up, with bishops to be the moderators of the presbyteries within whose bounds they resided. However, the scheme broke down as the result of opposition to bishops within the Assembly. In 1587, the king probably having decided that bishops of this kind could not serve his purpose, Parliament passed on Act of Annexation appropriating to the Crown the temporalities (*i.e.* the landed properties) of bishoprics, abbeys and other prelacies. This Act had the effect of destroying the episcopate.

Following his marriage in 1589, James warmed to the Kirk. In 1592 an Act was passed which has been regarded as the charter of Presbyterianism. The Act in the main affirmed the *Second Book of Discipline*, which set forth the principles of what has come to be known as Presbyterianism. Episcopal jurisdictions were abolished, and the government of the Church by assemblies in which ministers and elders take equal part was approved. These Courts are arranged in a hierarchy — Kirk Session, Presbytery, Synod and General Assembly — in which the acts of the lower courts are subject to review in a higher. The General Assembly overrules the lower courts and takes responsibility for all important matters concerning the welfare and good order of the national Church. Authority was given for an annual meeting of the General Assembly, providing that the King, or his commissioner, is present, and that he should appoint the time and place of the next meeting during the sitting.

All seemed set fair for relations between King and Kirk in 1592, but thereafter the wind was to change.

3 The struggle between Presbyterianism and Episcopacy in the seventeenth century

Anti-Romanist sentiments in the Kirk had always been strong, so that the moderation shown by James towards the Catholic earls aroused suspicion as to his Protestantism, and led to many furious attacks from the pulpit. Matters were not helped by the Kirk's assertion of the doctrine of the 'two Kingdoms', and by the vehemence of Andrew Melville. There is the famous scene in Falkland Palace in 1596 in which Melville called James 'God's silly vassal', and forcibly reminded him that, while he was the King of Scotland, he was but a member of the Kirk, which was the Kingdom of Jesus Christ. It is not surprising that James developed a lasting antipathy to Presbyterianism.

James sought to counter these attacks by undermining both the General Assembly, which was the main expression of the political power of the Kirk, and the doctrine of ministerial parity, which was used to claim for every minister the right to speak as he would from the pulpit as an instrument of divine truth. Ignoring the Act of 1592, he arrogated to himself by degrees the power of appointing the time and place for meetings of the General Assembly. By choosing such places as Dundee and Montrose, he was able to secure the attendance of north country ministers, who tended to be more conservative than the ministers from Fife and the Lothians who dominated the Assemblies held in Edinburgh. In 1598 he succeeded in persuading the Assembly to vote for fifty-one ministers – the number of clerics in the medieval Parliament – to have a place in Parliament, thereby weakening the doctrine of ministerial parity.

Once seated on the English throne, James fell under the influence of Laud and became even more 'high' in outlook. He initiated a series of measures which led to the struggle between Presbyterianism and Episcopacy in the Kirk during the seventeenth century. He overthrew the General Assembly by not holding it from 1603-5. In 1606 by Act of Parliament 'the Estate of the Bishops' was restored. An Act of 1609 restored to prelates the jurisdictions they had lost at the time of the Reformation. Finally, in 1610, the General Assembly accepted these innovations without undue influence.

The extremists were outraged, but many moderate Presbyterians were prepared to receive the bishops, though not to welcome them. Local church courts and ordinary services were little altered, and Popery was condemned.

But James did not stop there; he prejudiced his victory in two ways. By using bishops in political affairs and increasing their power, he showed them to be agents for royal absolutism, since they were nominated by the Crown. He also began to interfere with the ordinary services of the Church by encouraging ritual, as in the Five Articles of Perth of 1618, which were passed under duress by the Assembly. These changes aroused much opposition, and ended any chance of a united Episcopal Kirk in Scotland, although the consequences did not immediately appear.

Worse was to come when Charles I ascended the throne in 1625. He felt that the monarchy should be absolute, and was strengthened in this view by the support of Archbishop Laud and other Arminian divines who, liking the trappings of Rome but refusing papal supremacy, magnified the King as head of the Church. Charles gave bishops a still greater part in the government of the Scottish Church, and in 1635, without reference to the General Assembly or to

Parliament, authorized a *Book of Canons* which gave the King the title of Head of the Church, ordained an unpopular ritual, and commanded exclusive use of a new liturgy which had not yet been published. When it appeared, the new Service Book was found to be more 'Papistical' than the English *Book of common prayer* and a riot ensued when the Dean of Edinburgh attempted to read from it in St Giles' Kirk.

The inheritors of the Reformed Kirk were now determined that their legacy should not be stolen from them by an enforced system from England. After further public riots, the more sober and senior Presbyterians signed the National Covenant in 1638 at Greyfriars Church, Edinburgh, pledging themselves to defend the King, but utterly to reject his Church enforcements unless approved by a free Assembly and Parliament. The Covenant was then signed publicly throughout most of Scotland, except Aberdeen and the Highlands. In the same year the General Assembly held in Glasgow abolished Episcopacy and re-established the pure Presbyterian system.

Charles tried to temporize, but war became inevitable. The Bishop's Wars of 1639-40 which followed generated considerable enthusiasm in Scottish, and Charles suffered a humiliating defeat when the Scottish army occupied Newcastle. His position in England was also weakening as the result of clashes with Parliament, and in 1642 the Civil War began.

At first the Scots remained aloof from the Civil War, but before the end both King and Parliament were to appeal to the Scots for support. The Scots chose Parliament, and the resulting treaty took the form of the Solemn League and Covenant of 1643. The contracting parties agreed to preserve the reformed religion in England and Ireland; to try to extirpate papacy and prelacy; to maintain the rights of Parliament and the King's personal authority in preservation of the true religion and liberties of the kingdom; to suppress all opponents of the League; and to preserve peace between England and Scotland.

In the same year the Westminster Assembly held its first meeting. The Assembly was not an ecclesiastical body, but a sort of Parliamentary advisory commission, composed mainly of ministers, and set up by Parliament to reform the doctrine, worship and government of the Church of England. The Scottish Church sent representatives who took a prominent part in the debates, since they could speak from experience about the working of the Presbyterian system. As a result of the Assembly's deliberations, the English *Book of common prayer* was replaced by a *Directory for the Public Worship of God,* and a confession of faith and two catechisms were introduced. The Westminister documents 'set forth . . . a Calvinism more rigid than Calvin's', and have remained the official standards of the Church of Scotland ever since.

However, there were differences between the two parties to the Covenant. England was for a civil league, while Scotland was for a religious covenant. Moreover, although both Capital and Commons were at this time Presbyterian in sentiment, a great part of Puritan England was not. Misgivings between the allies soon became evident. When the English Parliament abolished Episcopacy in 1646 it kept the new Presbyterian establishment under its own control, and to the Scots this was Erastianism. These misgivings increased as the English army, Puritan in outlook with Cromwell, an Independent, at its head, gained ascendancy in English politics.

When Cromwell executed Charles I in 1649 he cared little that he was also executing the King of Scots. The Scots were horrified, but saw an opportunity of resolving the conflict between their faith and their loyalty to the King by inviting Charle's exiled son and heir, later to be Charles II, to Scotland and crowning him, on condition that he supported both Covenants. To proclaim Charles as king was as good as a declaration of war on the English Commonwealth, and Cromwell hastened north. He defeated the Scots army at Dunbar in 1650, and finally at Worcester in 1651, thereby ending the Civil War. Charles fled abroad, and until the restoration of the monarchy in 1660 Cromwell ruled over Scotland as part of a single Commonwealth. The form of religion practised in England was very like that of the Scottish Kirk, but it declined to accept Presbyterianism as the one true form, and established its own more tolerant system. By the terms of the Humble Petition, toleration was not extended to Papists and Prelatists, but even they were left alone if they did not call attention to themselves. The Presbyterian Kirk was no longer able to make civil penalties follow upon its censures, but the Kirk Sessions, Presbyteries and Synods continued to function as before.

The return of Charles to London was at first welcomed by the Scots for, as they were rid of the Cromwellian occupation, they anticipated relief from heavy taxation, and hoped for the continued support by the King of the Covenant, which he had given as a youth and almost under duress. But Charles soon resolved three things: not to be ousted again; to rule as far as possible as an absolute king; and, if possible, to make Britain Roman Catholic again. His general policy was the same in both countries. He developed arbitrary government with the aid of the bishops; he introduced a profession of tolerance which might appease the Dissenters and would help the Roman Catholics; and he promoted the interests of the Roman Catholics.

In Scotland the Episcopal System was restored by an Act which rescinded all Acts in favour of Presbyterial church government, and especially that of 1592 (the so-called Charter of Presbyterianism). The Parliament of 1662 also declared all livings filled since 1649 to be vacant, and that every such minister must apply to the patron for a presentation and to the bishop for collation. There was no question of ordination, but to seek collation from a bishop was to give recognition to the hierarchy. At least 270 ministers refused to comply, and they were excluded from their charges and replaced by licentiates drawn from other parts of the country. Although these licentiates were not all as scandalous and ignorant as has been said, they failed to satisfy the people, many of whom sought the services of their former ministers. These worshipped in what were known as 'conventicles' sometimes on remote hillsides, especially in the south-west.

An Act of Council was passed designed to keep the deprived clergy away from their flocks by forbidding them to reside within twenty miles of their former parish. The licentiates were used as informers, and the method of having troops to collect fines for non-churchgoing produced a revolt which was defeated in 1666.

The government regarded the conventicles as seedbeds of sedition, and greater severity was used against the nonconformists. As Act of 1670 made preaching at a field conventicle punishable by death; the harbouring or in any way helping an ousted minister was to incur severe penalties; and absence from church on three successive Sundays involved a fine. In 1674 heritors (i.e. land-owners) and masters were made responsible for their tenants and servants. So began the persecution of the Convenanters, who worshipped at conventicles. When the Convenanters reacted in 1679 by killing Archbishop Sharp, they were defeated at Bothwell Brig.

The south-west still remained to be pacified. Here the strong supporters of the Covenants and the true Church found a leader in Richard Cameron, and hence became known as the Cameronians. They were mainly humble folk who were regarded as extremists by nearly all of their Presbyterian brethren at the time. They supported Presbyterian Church government *jure divino,* loyalty to the Convenants, and were opposed to Erastianism. The Cameronians were savagely repressed in the years between 1680 and 1688.

In 1685 Charles II died. He had kept the throne secure, made himself well-nigh absolute, and had secured the succession of his brother – James VII and II – who was openly Romanist.

James seriously underestimated the people's Protestant convictions. He dismissed Protestants from offices of State, Privy Council, the judiciary, the military councils, and even town councils, and replaced them with Romanists, thereby alienating many powerful people. In 1687 he issued two Proclamations of Indulgence, which permitted people of both faiths freedom of expression as long as they did not teach disloyalty. Many suspected that this was a subtle attempt to reintroduce Catholicism by means of a 'free for all', but it enabled the ousted Presbyterian ministers to return to their parishes where the influence they exercised was to play a great part in the Revolution of 1688. People were also worried by events in France, where the revocation of the Edict of Nantes of 1685 marked the culmination of an almost successful campaign by Louis XIV to exterminate the Protestant Hugenots.

The attack by James on the privileges of the Church of England proved to be his final undoing; by the end of 1688 he had fled to France, and William and Mary ruled in his place. Episcopalians had no wish for a Dutch Calvinist as King; they had sworn allegiance to James, the Lord's annointed. Their cause was lost when he landed in England in November. In the west of Scotland men rose against their 'curates', and on Christmas Day began a visitation which ejected some 200 households of episcopalian ministers.

Presbyterianism had played an important part in the Revolution. The Crown was absolutist, and therefore had the support of the Episcopalians who revered the principle of authority; and in resisting despotism, the Covenanters were champions of liberality, the more heroic because the struggle in which they were engaged was so unequal.

4 The Revolution Settlement, 1690

The Settlement of the Church of Scotland was of great importance. In 1690 the Act of Supremacy was repealed and Presbyterianism established. The Westminster Confession of Faith was approved as the public confession of the Church. The government of the Church by Kirk Sessions, Presbyteries, Synods and General Assembly, as established in 1592, was confirmed. Ministers ejected in 1662 were restored to their parishes whether vacant or not. Finally, patronage was abolished, except in the case of town councils. When a rural parish fell vacant the heritors and elders were to nominate a minister to the congregation for approval or disapproval, and reasons for disapproval were to be given to the Presbytery of the bounds, which should have the final decision. 'Such was the Revolution Settlement which brought to an end the long, bitter and complicated struggle between Church and Crown begun with Knox at the Reformation in 1560, and continued by Andrew Melville and the Covenanters . . . the government of the Church of Scotland was recognized by law to be Presbyterian and so it has remained.'[4]

In 1707 the Scots Parliament agreed to the Treaty of Union by which it would merge with the English Parliament. It was agreed that the two nations should become one in the United Kingdom of Great Britain under one sovereign, Queen Anne, whose successors must not be Papists nor married to Papists. As part of this process, the Scots Parliament passed an Act securing the Protestant religion and Presbyterian Church government, which was to be regarded as part of the Treaty; a corresponding Act securing the Church of England in England was passed by the English Parliament. The Act of Union was a remarkable achievement. It made the two countries one, yet it deliberately preserved the Church, law, judicial system, and some of the characteristics of the smaller Kingdom, thereby ensuring that Scotland should preserve the distinctive nationality which she had won for herself.

After the Settlement there were still many Jacobites (i.e. supporters of James II who had fled to the continent) in the north and the Highlands. In 1708, 1715, 1719 and 1745, attempts were made to reinstate the Stuarts, all unsuccessful. During the Jacobite Rebellion of 1745-46 in particular the Presbyterian ministers of Scotland were distinguished by their faithfulness to the government. Subsequently, it was thought that an effort to raise stipends might be supported by the government, so that the General Assembly asked Parliament to facilitate processes in the Court of Teinds to raise by one-quarter the stipends fixed in 1633. However, this move was opposed by the heritors, who would have to meet the increase, and so it was unsuccessful.

The Revolution Settlement had established a Kirk based on the Act of 1592 in structure and on the Westminster Confession of 1647 in doctrine, but this Kirk did not embrace all Scots. The Roman Catholics, Episcopalians, and some Presbyterians did not accept it.

The Roman Catholics, who had thrived under James VII, decreased in numbers during the eighteenth century. Popery was still esteemed a danger, and the aftermath of the '45 took its toll. By 1755 it is reckoned that there were only some 16,500 communicant members in Scotland, distributed over the shires of Banff, Aberdeen, Inverness, and Argyll.

The Episcopalians had a similar, though less extreme, experience to the Catholics because the majority remained constant in their Jacobitism. They prospered under Queen Anne (1702-14), whose partiality for the Episcopal clergy was well known, but vigorous adherence to the 1715 Rebellion cost them dear in membership support. They also had internal troubles, both administrative and liturgical, but by 1766 these had been overcome and they had organized themselves territorially as the Scottish Episcopal Church.

The Cameronians refused to accept an uncovenanted Church; but their numbers were few and they abstained from political action. In 1743 they established themselves as the Reformed Presbyterian Church. Their strength at first lay in the west, especially in rural areas, but they came to establish themselves in the towns. The Church still has a few congregations, though in 1876 most of the members joined the Free Church.

5 Schisms in the Church in the eighteenth century

The national Church had to reckon not only with those Churches which remained outside it, but also with dissensions within, which before long produced the First Secession.

In 1710 a general election gave the Tories a large majority in the new Parliament, with a Scottish contingent hostile to the Revolution and to the establishment of the Church. In 1712 they passed an Act which restored lay patronage (i.e. the right of an individual or body to nominate a minister to a vacant charge) without consulting the Church in any way, and in open breach of the Act for the Security of the Scottish Church. This Act deprived Presbyterian congregations of what they felt to be a fundamental right – the choice of their own minister. Instead, they had to accept the choice of the patron – a local landowner – regardless of whether or not he had any concern for the Church.

Although the immediate cause of the secessions was the controversy about patronage, Mackie argues that the root cause was the development during the eighteenth century of two parties, or two conflicting approaches to religion, in the Church. On the one side was the Evangelical or Popular Party (from their opposition to patronage), whose view of religion was austere and traditional, and who insisted upon strict moral rectitude. They were supported by devout people in many parishes, who formed praying societies where the services of the Church were supplemented by communal devotions; for the most part they belonged to the humbler classes of society. On the other side were the Moderates. These appeared in the Church in the early eighteenth century with a new generation of ministers who had had no experience of the Covenanting struggles, and 'in the enjoyment of Hanoverian security and growing prosperity was coming to dislike "enthusiasm", that deadly sin of the eighteenth century.' The Moderates believed that the law of patronage must be obeyed, regardless of the opposition in the parishes, and that it would lead to a better ministry, as patrons were thought to be better judges of quality of ministers than congregations. The Evangelical party probably embraced the bulk of the ministers until about 1750, even after the secession had drawn off many 'hotheads', after which the Moderates gained the ascendancy in the Church.

Under the ancient patronage system the right to nominate a minister for a vacant parish was vested in the heritors and the elders. The congregation might then approve or disapprove the choice, and the Presbytery had the final say. In the event of no nomination being made within six months, the Presbytery itself might make the appointment; in the years following the passing of the 1712 Act the shortage of ministers often resulted in presbyterical appointments. Also, the General Assembly began to uphold the action of patrons, who had started to exercise their powers; and, when grievances about such 'intrusions' multiplied, the General Assembly overruled the recalcitrant Presbyteries. A notorious case occurred at Kinross when the parish fell vacant in 1726 and remained unoccupied for six years. The people desired to call Ebenezer Erskine, minister of Stirling, while the patron presented a certain Robert Stark. The Presbytery of Dunfermline refuse to recognise Stark, even by order of Assembly in 1732 and 1733. This confrontation threatened schism in the Church and endangered its unity, at a time when the Church was coming into its own. In 1732 Erskine defied the General Assembly in a sermon, and in the following year he and three supporters constituted themselves a separate presbytery; in 1737 they were joined by four other ministers. Many, perhaps most, ministers agreed with them, and the General Assembly tried to make amends. It was only in 1740 that the Assembly finally decided to expel them, when all efforts at reconciliation had failed. In 1744 the 'Dissidents' formed a new Secession Church, which grew quickly around the nucleus of the praying societies. As early as 1740 there were forty congregations widely scattered, mainly in the rural areas and county towns of the lowlands. The members were mainly peasants and artisans who, if not prosperous, could afford to build new churches and pay the ministers.

Although the Secession Church was narrowly exclusive, it soon quarrelled over the admissibility of a seceder to take the Burgess Oath, which required the burgesses of certain cities to acknowledge the true religion, publicly preached within the realm and authorized by law. The oath was aimed against Jacobitism in 1745, and was applicable only to a few cities; but its wording seemed to assert that the only true religion in Scotland was that of the Established Church. In 1747 the Secession Church split between the Burghers, including Erskine, who considered that the taking of the Oath was admissible, and the Anti-Burghers, who did not. Both communions grew slowly and steadily at the expense of the national church, attracting to themselves ministers on the evangelical side who were dissatisfied with patronage, or with the laxity in matters of doctrine and discipline under the Moderates.

Around the turn of the century new dissensions appeared in both communions over the section of the Confession of Faith which dealt with the duties of the civil magistrate in ecclesiastical affairs. Both set about revising their testimonies in order publicly to disavow 'compulsory and persecuting principles', and in both there were conservatives rendering this difficult. When the New Light prevailed (in 1799 among the Burghers; in 1806 among the Anti-Burghers), the 'Auld Licht' remnants hived off from both to maintain the traditional positions. In 1820 the 'New Lichts' of both communions joined to form the United Secession Church, composed of 280 congregations, which in 1847 joined with the Relief Church (see below) to form the United Presbyterian Church. Most of the 'Auld Licht' Burghers joined the Established Church in 1839. The 'Auld Licht' Anti-Burghers continued until 1852, when the majority joined the new Free Church (see below); the minority went on as the Original Secession Church until 1956, when it joined the Church of Scotland. These and other divisions and reunions in the Church of Scotland are shown in the diagram in figure 2.

In the face of these disputes amongst their enemies, the Moderates took control of the General Assembly, and asserted the importance of discipline in Church government. In 1752 the General Assembly censured the Presbytery of Dunfermline for refusing to induct a presentee at Inverkeithing, one Andrew Richardson, who was opposed by the town council, the Kirk Session, and the mass of the people, and deposed one of the offending ministers, Thomas Gillespie of Carnock. Gillespie surrendered his church and manse, and preached in the open air at Dunfermline until his followers built him a 'meeting house'. In 1761

FIGURE 2. Divisions and Reunions of the Scottish Church, 1690-1929
Note: The original Secession Church joined the Church of Scotland in 1956.
SOURCE: J.H.S. Burleigh, *A Church History of Scotland,* (Oxford University Press) 1960.

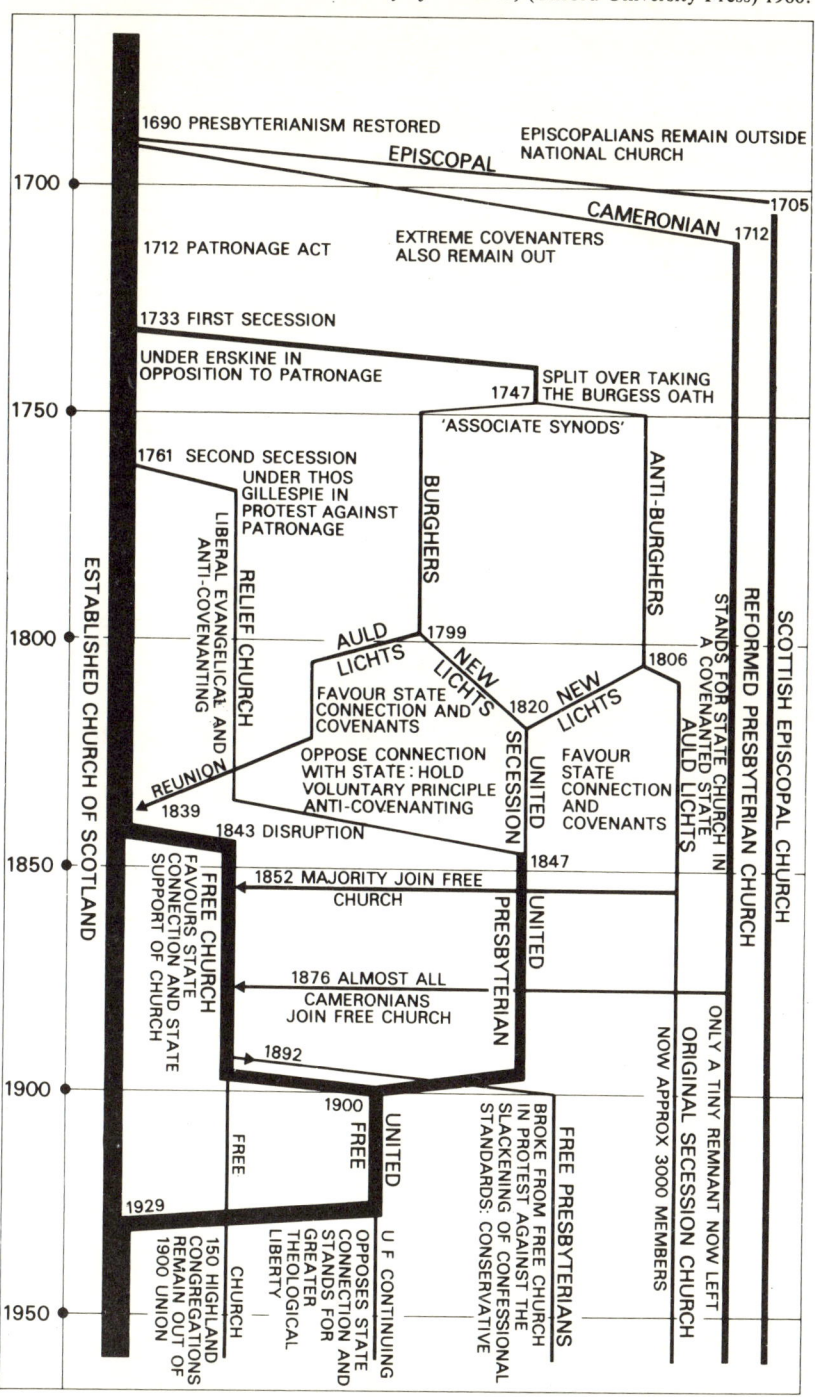

he and two others founded the Relief Church. As with the Secession Church, the congregations of the Relief Church were the important unit, since the obligation was laid on the congregation to provide a reasonable stipend for the minister and to pay for the building of the church and manse. Hence care was taken in deciding where new congregations were to be established, since they were mindful of the need for self-finance. It was said that by 1766 the two dissenting bodies had as many as 120 places for worship attended by 100,000 persons.

Meanwhile, after the disposition of Gillespie, the Presbytery of Dunfermline carried through the induction of Richardson. Henceforth, Presbyteries did not attempt to resist the rulings of the General Assembly, and found means to settle presentees even if they were unpopular with parishioners.

6 Church extension in the eighteenth and early nineteenth centuries

During the eighteenth century there was established a number of Burgh churches in the growing cities and towns of Scotland. They were built by the municipal authorities to meet the needs of the growing population, and the stipend was paid generally out of the city's, or burgh's, fund for the common good.

Church extension also began at this time. As today, the new churches were built in areas where large increases in population put a strain on the existing parishes. Unlike today, however, church extension was carried out locally by individual congregations, rather than by a central committee. The usual practice was for the congregation of the parish to build a chapel-of-ease from its own resources for the people in an outlying part of the parish. These eventually became parishes *quoad sacra* under the New Parishes Act, 1844, by the disjunction of a portion of the parish of the original congregation. Their stipends derived partly from an endowment and partly from the offerings of members of the congregation. The new parishes were given the name *quoad sacra* (i.e. in so far as regards sacred matters) because the parish area was only of significance for Church organization, whereas the old parishes, which were *quoad omnia* (i.e. as regards all matters, civil and sacred), were the unit of organization for both civil and Church affairs.

Church extension had proved satisfactory in centres of increasing population, but in the second half of the eighteenth century emerged another type of case where a new church was badly needed, but where existing procedures could not be employed because the districts were remote and the population was small and poor. In 1824 the government provided a sum of £50,000 for the building of a church and manse in such areas, together with a stipend for the minister and a salary for a precentor (i.e. organist) and beadle (i.e. church officer). The outcome was the establishment in the Highlands and Islands of forty-two new churches and parishes. They are still called 'Parliamentary parishes', and their endowed stipend is still called an 'Exchequer Living'.

While the provisions of the 1824 Act were being implemented in outlying areas, church extension in cities, which began towards the end of the eighteenth century, was taken up strongly, and became in the 1830s a popular movement under the leadership of Dr Thomas Chalmers, one-time minister of one of the Glasgow burgh churches. He believed that the parochial system must be made really effective in the cities, where more churches with more manageable parishes attached to them were needed. In 1834 a Committee on Church Accommodation, convened by Chalmers, was set up by the General Assembly. Appeals were sent out to individuals and congregations, and in four years over £200,000 was raised, largely due to Chalmers' enormous energy and organizing ability. By the time of the Disruption in 1843, 200 new churches had been erected. Parishioners would be expected to pay seat rents to support the new churches, but it was felt that such rents had to be kept low, so that even the poorest could afford them. An endowment was therefore required to pay the ministers' stipends, and an approach was made to the government. Members of the government expressed sympathy, but opposition was aroused, especially from the Scottish Dissenters, who saw in church extension an endeavour on the part of the Established Church to counteract their influence. In the end, the government only provided a little help to rural parishes.

During the eighteenth century ministers were poor, and became poorer with the gradual rise in the cost of living. The strain on the teinds, which had been increased by the secessions, was temporarily relieved towards the end of the eighteenth century when the responsibility for Poor Relief and education was partially taken over from the Church by the secular authorities. The rise in prices would not have mattered much if all teind stipends had continued to be paid in grain or in accordance with fiars prices,[5] the legal method of securing from year to year that payments made in lieu of actual sheaves were fair and in accordance with market prices. But a provision had been included in an Act of Teinds whereby a heritor could substitute a fixed money payment in place of the sum that varied from year to year. According to Gibson, many heritors had taken advantage of this provision.

In 1788 an attempt was made again to induce the government to augment stipends, but again failed because of the determined resistance of the heritors. The inflation of the Napoleonic Wars brought the situation to a crisis. In 1810 an Act was passed setting aside from public revenues a sum of £10,000 a year to augment the smaller stipends of ministers of the Church of Scotland. This Act fixed the first minimum stipend at £150 p.a. with manse and glebe; £180 p.a. with manse or glebe; and £200 without either. Careful provision was made so that actual stipends from all sources might be ascertained, and where these were found to be less than the minimum, an annual sum was allocated to bring the actual stipend up to the minimum. Allocations made in 1810, or soon after, were to be reviewed every five years but, according to Gibson, this important provision scarcely ever operated and fell into disuse. Consequently, parishes came to regard the grants as private endowments of their own. Some managed to greatly increase their incomes over the years, but none felt that they should relinquish their grant in favour of other poorer parishes. It was not until 1927, when the administration of these Exchequer monies was handed over to the Church of Scotland, that the grant in such cases was restored to its original and proper use.

The end of the eighteenth century saw an evangelical revival in England with the growth of Methodism and the beginning of the modern missionary movement. Wesley visited Scotland twenty-two times between 1751 and 1790, but was less successful than in England because of the effectiveness of the Scottish ministry. Also, the missionary movement in the 1790s in Scotland was far behind that of England, and in 1796 the General Assembly refused to countenance support for missionary activity. But a new generation of Evangelical ministers were coming into the Church of Scotland, and they increased in numbers and influence as the new century wore on. By them the main stream of Evangelism was retained within the Church of Scotland, and the 'rival' Baptist and Congregationalist denominations remained small. The dominant figure in this movement was Chalmers, who occupied the Chair of Divinity in Edinburgh over the period 1828-43.

7 The Disruption of 1843 and its consequences

In 1832 the Reform Bill was passed. The established Churches of England and Scotland felt themselves threatened by the extension of the franchise, since it increased the political influence of the Dissenters and of rationalists hostile to all religion. Disestablishment seemed a possibility, unless something could be done to popularize the Church itself. The Evangelicals had been the 'popular' party, because they had championed the rights of congregations in connexion with the appointment of their ministers when the nominees of the patron gave dissatisfaction. But not all of them objected to patronage as such; Chalmers realized the danger of unbridled popular choice. On the other hand, patrons generally belonged to the opponents of reform, and their unpopularity reflected on the Church.

Through the eighteenth century it was customary for a presentee to preach before the congregation, and then members of the congregation to be given an opportunity to sign a call in his favour. However, under the Moderate regime less and less importance had been attached to the call. In 1834 the General Assembly, in which the Evangelical Party was predominant for the first time, carried a motion that enabled a majority of male heads of households, as members of the Church, to veto an appointment in regard to the spiritual interests of the appointee or the congregation. This procedure was put into force by an Interim Act, which by-passed the Barrier Act[6] and deprived Presbyteries of the judicial function that was legally theirs. It gave some recognition to popular rights by curbing patronage, rather than abolishing it.

The operation of the Veto Act in Auchterarder in 1835 led to conflict. The rejected presentee took his case to court which judged, in 1838, in favour of the pursuer. By this decision the Supreme Court had virtually declared 'that in passing the Veto Act the Church had acted *ultra vires*, and that, in operating it, it infringed the statutory civil rights of patrons and presentees.' Moreover, as a national establishment, the Church was judicially declared to be a creation of the State, deriving all its powers from specific Acts of Parliament. When it was urged that the Church had always claimed an independent spiritual power, and had exercised it, the answer was given that that was in a time of rebellion and confusion now happily long past.

Such an interpretation of 'establishment' might have been acceptable to most churchmen in the Moderate ascendancy, but in 1838 it could hardly be agreeable to any party within the Church. The Church appealed to the House of Lords, but in 1839 the appeal was rejected. It declared that patron's rights were absolute, and that no objections on the part of parishioners were relevant.

Relations between Church and State steadily worsened. The Assembly of 1842 protested against patronage, declaring that 'patronage is a grievance, has been attended with much injury to the cause of true religion in this Church and kingdom, is the main cause of the difficulties in which the Church is at present involved, and that it ought to be abolished.' The Assembly also adopted a lengthy resolution which was to become famous as the Claim of Right. It took its stand on the Westminster Confession regarding the independent jurisdiction in spiritual matters of the Church, and went on to quote Parliamentary Acts recognizing and ratifying that jurisdiction, especially the Act of 1690 which abolished in Scotland the royal supremacy in spiritual and ecclesiastical causes.

The resolution against patronage and the Claim of Right brought an uncompromising response from the Government. In November 1842 a Convocation of 'Non-Intrusionist' ministers was held in Edinburgh. The possibility of secession was openly discussed, and Chalmers put forward a plan for financing it based on his experience in church extension. A resolution was adopted which deplored the encroachments of the civil courts on the spiritual powers of the Church. Thereafter country-wide propaganda was organized with public meetings. Rural parishes were visited by enthusiastic deputations, and when the minister was unsympathetic, attempts were made to detach his people from him.

At the General Assembly of 1843 it was speculated that, if the Non-Intrusionists had the majority, they might seek to end the Church's connexion with the State. However, the Non-Intrusionists were in the minority for the first time in ten years. The retiring Moderator, instead of formally opening the Assembly, announced that he and others could not regard it as a free assembly, and were resolved to leave it. He read a protest setting out the reasons, and then left the chamber with about 190 ministers and elders. They were joined by ministers and elders from all parts of the country, and constituted themselves as the first General Assembly of the Free Church of Scotland, with Chalmers as Moderator. A total of 451 ministers signed the deed of demission whereby they relinquished all emoluments and privileges which they had enjoyed within the Established Church; 752 ministers remained in the Established Church.

It is estimated that the Church as a whole lost about a third of its members, in large part its more active membership, and all classes were represented. In parishes where the minister 'went out', he was commonly followed by the bulk of his congregation, and in the northern counties of Ross, Sutherland and Caithness, practically all ministers went out, followed by their congregations.

The task set the new Church was an enormous one — nothing less than that of producing a complete and exact replica of the Established Church they had left, relying on the resources which the members could supply. Moreover, since 1834 successive General Assemblies had commended to the liberality of their people certain specific enterprises or schemes of the Church, such as education, foreign missions, church extension, and aid to colonial churches. In 1843 the missionaries and other agents adhered almost unanimously to the Free Church, which without hesitation accepted responsibility for carrying on their work.

The main problem was that they had plenty of ministers and a great many probationers, but, apart from some fifty or so recently constituted *quoad sacra* churches which they were able to retain, they had no churches, manses or stipends. However, Chalmers had already proposed at the Convocation of Ministers and Elders in 1842 that if they followed the example of the Parliamentary parishes, with their stipend of £120 a year, they would require an annual income of about £50,000. Every congregation was instructed to contribute at least £100, or as much as they could, to a central Sustentation Fund, from which their ministers would receive what was called an 'equal dividend'. The larger and wealthier congregations, in addition to their contributions to the central fund, would be expected to supplement their own minister's stipend, while in this system the ministers of the poorer congregations would not be wholly at the mercy of their own people.

The idea caught on, and, before the actual Disruption took place, informal associations of sympathizers were formed in congregations and began to make regular collections. A distinctive method of collecting by regular visits, usually monthly, at the home of every member and adherent, was developed and put under the responsibility of the deacon.

The income of the fund in the first year was £68,704, which exceeded all expectations, and in the second year was £77,630. The 'equal dividend' was set at £105 (instead of £100) in the first year, and £122 in the second year. In 1867 a Surplus Fund was introduced for the purpose of increasing the stipend paid. From this fund was given a small grant, in addition to the equal dividend, to the ministers of a number of both aid-receiving and aid-giving congregations in recognition of the high rate per member that the congregation had contributed.

Church building also proceeded apace. A total of 470 churches were completed in the first year, usually on sites in close proximity to the old parish church. By 1847 the Free Church had over 700 churches. Also, when it seemed probable that the school-teachers who adhered to them would be expelled from their posts, it created schools of its own. In 1869, shortly before an Act was passed which took over denominational schools in Scotland into a national system, it was reported in Parliament that the Free Church had 598 schools, and had raised for educational purposes since the Disruption not less than £600,000. The New College at Edinburgh, for the training of ministers, was completed in 1850, and within the next five years others were added at Aberdeen and Glasgow.

The Free Church grew in strength through the rest of the nineteenth century, although in 1892 two ministers and 4,000 members, mainly in the Highlands, seceded from the Free Church in protest against a slackening of confessional standards. They formed the Free Presbyterian Church, which exists to this day as a conservative communion with about fifty congregations in the Highlands (see figure 2).

The Free Church stood on the two principles recognized by the Revolution Settlement, which had not been seriously questioned until 1838 when the civil courts, it was held, gave a new interpretation of the law and encroached upon the rights and privileges of the Church. These were the independent spiritual jurisdiction of the Church, and the right and duty of the civil magistrate to protect and further religion by supporting the national church (i.e. the Establishment principle). The Free Church claimed that it maintained the historic position and testimony of the Church of Scotland, necessarily outside the Establishment, unless and until Parliament should put matters right.

In 1847 the union of the United Secession Church with the Relief Church to form the United Presbyterian Church was effected with some difficulty because they differed considerably in ethos. The new Church opposed Establishment and repudiated the religious and ecclesiastical rights and duties of the civil magistrate. In having 518 congregations it was almost as strong as the Free Church; but, owing to the method of finance, it was confined chiefly to cities and towns, whereas in the Highlands almost the entire population adhered to the Free Church.

Although the United Presbyterian Church had the example of the success of the Sustentation Fund before it, it decided not to follow that example, because the position of the United Presbyterian Church in 1847 was very different from that of the Free Church in 1843. Whereas the latter was free to build from scratch, the United Presbyterian Church was constituted from existing congregations, some one hundred years old, and was thus bound by existing practice in individual congregations. In fact, that practice had to be very efficient if the congregation was to survive. The United Secession Church had for some years prior to 1847 helped smaller congregations with grants from central funds. After 1847 the Home Mission Board of the United Presbyterian Church assumed this responsibility. This was a sign that despite the care in siting new congregations, changes over the years made some support necessary. In 1868 an Augmentation Fund was established, and developed along similar lines to the Sustentation Fund of the Free Church, but the aid given was much smaller, although the level of stipend in the two denominations was similar. Gibson makes the following comment: 'The strength of the United Presbyterian method of payment of stipend direct from the congregation to the ministers "lay in impressing upon congregations with limited resources the claim which their own minister had upon them for adequate support." '

The most pressing problem facing the Established Church after the Disruption of 1843 was in filling the 451 vacancies resulting. The Church was able to call upon a large number of probationers, mostly employed as school-masters, but not all proved satisfactory. Patronage also remained a problem, for in the period 1843-69 there were 61 cases of disputed settlements.

Another problem that faced the Church in 1843 was that of church extension. Chalmers's campaign had resulted in the erection of some 200 churches, but the attempt of the Church to give to their ministers the powers and status of parish ministers through the Chapels Act of 1834 had been declared *ultra vires* by the Court of Session. Owing to the steady deterioration of relations between Church and State in the years before 1843, there was no likelihood of the government taking action that would extricate the Church out of its difficulties. However, the shock of the Disruption prompted Parliament to examine the problem of the church extension charges, and in 1844 the New Parishes Act was passed which removed the procedural difficulties of previous legislation. The hope that the government would deal with the charges in the same way as with the Parliamentary parishes by providing an endowment for stipend was not realised. Instead, the government insisted that before any of these charges could be erected into a parish church and so get the benefit of the Act, an endowment for stipend of at least £100 a year, or £120 without a manse, would have to be provided.

In 1843 the Assembly had set up a Committee to consider the plight of the new congregations, and in 1847 this Committee became the Endowment Committee. It had just been decided in the law courts that the 200 churches remained the property of the Church of Scotland, but it was found that the outstanding debt on the buildings was over £30,000. In addition, there was the need to raise £600,000 in order to provide sums of £20,000 – £24,000 a year for endowment. The great champion of endowment was James Robertson, professor of ecclesiastical history in the University of Edinburgh from 1844. With his enthusiastic support a sum of £400,000 was raised in twelve years.

The aim from the start was to encourage congregations to help provide their own endowment, and the normal arrangement at first was that when the congregation raised half of the endowment – £50 or £60 – the Committee provided the other half. These arrangements were modified after the foundation of the Baird Trust in 1873, which has given considerable help to new congregations trying to raise their share of the capital required for the statutory endowment of the *quoad sacra* parishes. The size of the endowment has also been increased; before the First World War it was decided that the desirable endowment was not less than £160 a year, and then it was increased to £200.

In 1866 a public meeting was held in Glasgow under the aegis of the General Assembly and attended by many leading laymen of the Church, who held that the work of improving small stipends was a duty incumbent on the lay membership. The meeting formed a new association called the Church of Scotland Association for Augmenting the Smaller Livings of the Clergy. The Association aimed to raise a capital fund of £100,000 to supply interest income to raise livings under £200 per year to that amount. For the first time an appeal was made to the ordinary membership of the Church to give financial support for an annual fund for the maintenance of the ministry. This proved to be the first step along a very important road. It was found quickly that the Association, as a body only ancillary to the Church, was handicapped in appealing to Church members for annual subscription. Consequently in 1877 the General Assembly set up a new standing committee called the Small Livings Committee, which encouraged all parishes to make an annual collection for it. By this means the minimum stipend was gradually increased to £180 and a manse in 1914, and £300 and a manse by 1928.

In 1920 the two committees on Endowments and Small Livings were brought together under the name of the Committee on the Maintenance of the Ministry. This Committee had an Endowment Branch and an Annual Branch corresponding with former separate committees, and the name was perpetuated after the 1929 Union.[7]

8 Unification and organization of the Church in the twentieth century
From the last quarter of the nineteenth century onwards the ecclesiastical history of Scotland is marked by unification and organization. The existence from 1847 of two major Presbyterian Churches outside the Established Church led men to consider whether reunion was possible. At first it was thought that patronage was the stumbling block to union of the Free Church with the Established Church, and with the passing of the Patronage Act in 1874 many thought that the way was clear for a return of the Free Church to the establishment. This Act declared that the right of electing and appointing ministers is vested in congregations, and that the power to regulate the procedures, and the final and conclusive right to decide all questions as to the appointment of ministers, belongs to the Church courts. The rights of patrons were extinguished, and an agreed sum by way of compensation was to be paid to private patrons who claimed it.

However, the Free Church took alarm at these moves, and, finding evangelism a safer ground for union than the common acceptance of the idea of Establishment, moved closer to the 'voluntaries' of the United Presbyterian Church. Discussions for union had begun as early as 1863, and eventually in 1900 the two Churches united under the name of the United Free Church of Scotland. The Free Church brought 1,100 parishes to the Union, and the United Presbyterians 600, which together was greater than the 1,457 parishes of the Auld Kirk. About twenty or thirty ministers of the Free Church and a considerable body of its people, chiefly in the Highlands, refused to enter the Union, and claimed to inherit all the wealth of that Church. This claim was rejected in Scotland, but upheld by the House of Lords – a decision which aroused intense anger. However, by a subsequent Act of 1905 the United Free Church gained possession of the churches and manses which the minority (the 'wee Frees') were in no position to use, but the Sustentation Fund lost to the Free Church £100,000 of its capital. Today the Free Church has about 150 congregations, and is the dominant Church in parts of the north-west of Scotland and on some of the islands.

After these problems had been settled, a Central Fund of the United Free Church was set up in 1908. For the period 1900-8 interim arrangements had been introduced whereby the two funds – Sustentation and Augmentation – co-existed as before. This system continued with little change after 1908, except that the Surplus Grant Fund of the Augmentation Fund and the Supplementary Fund of the Sustentation Fund were added together, and called the Surplus Fund of the Central Fund. The income of the Surplus Fund was divided amongst all ministers whose stipend from every other source was less than £200; hence it was not yet a true minimum stipend fund, since the £200 per minister was not necessarily achieved. In 1925, prior to the Union, the regulations of the Central Fund were revised, under which a true minimum stipend was established, with no minister who received aid from the fund having a higher total than any other.

It became evident that the United Free Church did not differ much from the Auld Kirk in doctrine, discipline, government or worship, and there was even an interchange of pulpits between the ministers of the various denominations. The successful accomplishment of one union in 1900 turned men's minds to the possibility of another. In 1908 the General Assembly issued an invitation to the United Free Church 'to confer in a friendly and generous spirit on the present ecclesiastical situation in Scotland, and to consider how a larger measure of Christian fellowship and co-operation could be brought about so as to prepare the way for union for which so many were hoping and praying.' The reply of the United Free Church was cordial, but, as on the occassion in 1886, it asked that the conference should be without restriction, implying the inclusion of the Establishment question. The Auld Kirk accepted in an historic decision which meant that Establishment was no longer regarded as sacrosanct.

In 1911 a report was presented to the Assembly, giving suggestions as to the action the Church might take in order to meet the complaint that its existing constitution was inconsistent with the principle of spiritual freedom. It proposed that the Church might approach Parliament with a request to rescind certain clauses in ancient statutes on which the legal judgements that forced on the Disruption had been based, and to pass a Declaratory Act recognizing that the powers the Church claimed in matters spiritual were inherent in the Church as the Church of Christ. It was believed that these measures would avoid the danger alleged to lurk in the old statutory connexion of the Church with the State, and the no less serious danger into which the Free Church had fallen in 1904 of being, in the eyes of the law, simply a voluntary association based on contract.

In 1913 the Church of Scotland committee dealing with the question of union was instructed to produce draft Articles of a constitution embodying the spiritual powers claimed to be inherent in the Church. There was opposition from those who feared that, in abandoning the time-honoured expression 'The Church by law established', they were throwing away the advantages implied in establishment for a vague recognition of the Church by the State. Then the war supervened, and discussions were not resumed until the spring of 1918. In the following year the Articles were completed and almost unanimously approved by the Presbyteries. The United Free Church also approved them, though not without a considerable number of dissensions, and in July 1921 Parliament without a division passed an Enabling Act, which recognized the right of the Church of Scotland to adopt the Articles as a statement of its basic constitution. 'In so doing the 'civil magistrate' for the first time since the Reformation acknowledged in the fullest sense the freedom of a Church in matters affecting its own spiritual life and work.'

There remained the difficult problem of the Church's ancient patrimony — the churches, manses, glebes, teinds, and other statutory revenues and claims, which had been formerly the subject of much dispute. Burleigh points out that in the United Free Church it had come to be widely accepted that the ecclesiastical endowments should not be secularized, but should be conserved for religious purposes: it was insisted that these properties should be vested in the Church in such a way that it had full control over them. To transfer them to a central body of Church trustees proved to be a complex problem, since agreement as to their valuation and conveyance had to be reached with interested parties, particularly the landowners of Scotland who paid the teinds and had certain statutory responsibilities for the unkeep of churches and manses. In 1924 the Church of Scotland Properties and Endowments Bill was introduced to Parliament and, despite vigorous opposition, was passed in May 1925. In the following year the Church ratified the articles and enacted them as its constitution.

Finally, a Basis and Plan of Union was prepared, which set out the substantial agreement between the Churches as regards doctrine, discipline, government and worship, as vouched for in their historic documents from the Reformation down to the articles of 1926, and outlined a scheme for combining the various agencies through which they had carried on their work. The Basis and Plan was approved in May 1929, and in October of that year the two Assemblies became one, and the Church of Scotland was reunited. A few dissidents remained outside, and formed a continuing United Free Church.

The Reunited Church brought together more than four-fifths of the church-going Protestant population of Scotland. At the union it was hoped 'to revitalize the parochial system, which in the large towns at all events had been little regarded.' To each church was now assigned a manageable area as its parish, for the spiritual supervision of which it was responsible. Ministers, elders, and church workers were encouraged to undertake the systematic visitation of all homes in the parish.

Further changes in the parish ministry were also required, since the successive unions had saddled the Church of Scotland with an excess of church buildings and manses. During the period 1843-1929 the Free and United Presbyterian Churches had built many churches in direct rivalry with the Auld Kirk, and many were built where changes in population rendered them unnecessary. A policy of amalgamations and linkings followed, which has succeeded in reducing the number of parishes from about 3,000 at the Union to about 1,700 today. At the same time a scheme of church extension to new towns and housing areas has been followed. Since the financial strain of establishing new churches had become too great for individual congregations, church extension became from 1933 a national movement under the Rev. Dr John White. The building of new churches was financed by a national fund rather than by individual local congregations. Two methods were used. One was the establishing of an entirely new congregation. The second was the 'transportation' of an old congregation from a city centre or other declining area to form the nucleus of a new congregation in a new housing area. In Edinburgh since 1930 there have been as many congregations transported as new congregations founded.

Although the Church of Scotland is the largest denomination in Scotland, with 2,000 congregations and a million members out of a Scottish population of over five million, Mackie argues that even to a casual inspection, the secular spirit has advanced. 'Sixty years ago the streets of a provincial town on a Sunday forenoon would have been black with people thronging to church. Scotland seems to be less "Kirk-hungry" now.'[8]

The second largest denomination in Scotland is the Roman Church, with perhaps 700,000 adherents. The Church survived the Reformation and was able to maintain and expound the faith in the Highlands and Islands even under the penal laws. Indigenous Catholicism was preserved in certain mainland areas, such as Banffshire, and in some islands, such as the southern Outer Isles, where the Mass is now in Gaelic. The faith was kept alive by the people, rather than as in England by the power of recusant families. Only in 1878, and then with considerable hesitation, was the hierarchy restored and organized into territorial dioceses comprising two archbishoprics and six bishoprics. By then the Church had been reinforced by the massive immigration of Irish labour into the industrial towns, especially Glasgow, where its strength still lies.

The Scottish Episcopal Church originated with those who refused to accept the Revolution Settlement of 1689, and suffered subsequently for its loyalty to the Stuart dynasty. The Church made its peace with the government of George III in 1792. Although its membership has remained numerically small – currently around 80,000 – it wields a proportionately greater influence because of the many well-to-do people found among its members. The Church prizes its roots in Scottish history, but to many it appears rather a Scottish province of the Church of England, with which it is in full communion. It is organized into seven dioceses with a Primus at its head.

4 Conclusions

The main purpose of this chapter has been to outline the history of the Church of Scotland from the Middle Ages to the present day, in the hope that it will shed light on the present position and problems of the Church.

We saw the struggle of the infant Church to establish itself after the Reformation in 1560 to the Presbyterian settlement in 1592. Then followed the struggle between Presbyterianism and Episcopacy through the seventeenth century, until the Revolution settlement of 1690 finally established the Church of Scotland as a Presbyterian Church. During the eighteenth century the Church was shaken by schisms over the question of patronage, and relations between Church and State worsened in the early nineteenth century over the State's enforcement of the rights of patrons. This led to the Disruption of 1843, when about a third of the ministers and members went out to form the evangelical Free Church. However, patronage was ended by an Act of 1874, and a more liberal attitude in the Auld Kirk made reunion a possibility. This was finally accomplished in 1929.

Notes

1 J.H.S. Burleigh, *A Church History of Scotland*: (Oxford University Press, 1960); A.J.H. Gibson, *Stipend in the Church of Scotland* (Blackwood, 1961); and J.D. Mackie, *A History of Scotland* (Penguin Books, 1973).

2 Mackie, p. 147.

3 Burleigh, p. 150.

4 ibid., p. 255.

5 Fiars prices were the average prices of the different kinds of grain of one year's crop, judicially determined by the Fiars Court.

6 The Barrier Act, passed by the General Assembly of 1697, decreed that all legislation which effects the constitution of the Church in its doctrine, government, worship or discipline, and which has been proposed to, and approved by the Assembly, must be ratified by a majority of Presbyteries before being enacted as law by a later Assembly. The Act is described in greater detail in chapter 2, section *2.6*.

7 The work of this committee is described in chapter 10.

8 Mackie, p. 363.

Chapter 2

Constitution and government

1 Introduction
The purpose of this chapter is to outline the present constitution and government of the Church of Scotland. Like the first chapter, it should form a useful background against which our proposals for the strengthening of the financial position of the Church can be examined. The chapter is based largely on Cox, and on certain other secondary sources.[1]

Section 2 deals with the constitution of the Church. After a brief look at certain important documents which lay down the constitution, we then describe the principles of the constitution which they expound. These principles concern doctrine, worship, discipline and government, together with relations between Church and State, and the operation of the Barrier Act, 1697. The complexities arising over the question of Church property and endowments are left until chapter 3.

In the following section we examine the government of the Church through the hierarchical system of courts, namely Kirk Session, Presbytery, Synod, and General Assembly. Attention is first paid to those features which the courts share, before the organization and functions of each court are examined in some detail. The section ends with a brief outline of the functions of the Assembly standing committees.

2 The constitution
The constitution of the Church of Scotland is set forth in certain important documents which have been framed comparatively recently. They are briefly as follows:

Articles Declaratory of the Constitution of the Church of Scotland in Matters Spiritual (1921). These are a series of Articles prepared by the Church of Scotland in anticipation of the Union with the United Free Church in 1929. The Articles lay down the substance of the Church's doctrine, assert that the Church is in historical continuity with the Church of Scotland which was reformed in 1560, and deal with the mutual obligations of Church and State. They were approved by Presbyteries and ratified by the Commission of Assembly of the Church in 1919, and approved by the United Free Church in the same year. The Articles were then ratified by Parliament and given the Royal Assent in 1921, which declared that the Articles were lawful for the Church of Scotland to hold. They became effective in 1926, and are appended to the Uniting Act (see below).

Act anent Spiritual Independence of the Church (1906). The Act passed by the United Free Church corresponding to the above Articles of the Church of Scotland, and likewise appended to the Uniting Act.

Basis of Union (1929). Unlike the first two documents, the Basis of Union is the product of the two Churches at a joint conference. After long consideration by the Presbyteries, it was finally approved by them, and ratified by the General Assembly of each Church in 1929. It forms part of the Act of Union (1929).

The Basis of Union affirms certain historical documents, called 'leading documents', which set forth the doctrine, government, worship and discipline of the Church, together with the principles of spirituality and freedom of the Church and the national recognition of religion. By the Act, these documents are declared to be the 'standards' of the Church.

Preamble, Questions, and Formula (1929) : these are to be used on the ordination or induction of a minister. They are important because they summarize the main elements of the constitution and apply them to the particular occasion of the entrance of each of the office-bearers of the Church. The document is also included in the Act of Union.

Standing laws. The body of standing laws (apart from merely administrative regulations) which were brought into the common stock of legislation of the Church by each uniting Church, and not repealed or amended in accordance with the law of the Church as stated in the Basis of Union, or with any law constitutionally enacted since the Union.

The above documents set out the main principles of the Constitution of the Church; these concern doctrine, government, worship and discipline, together with relations between Church and State. There is also the operation of the Barrier Act (1697). We shall deal with each in turn.

1 Doctrine

The Church of Scotland 'is, and must remain, a Christian Church, Trinitarian in its creed, evangelical in its character, maintaining, teaching, and promulgating the great facts of the faith once delivered unto the saints, in full accord with the Scriptures of the Old and New Testaments, as interpreted from time to time by the ever-living and quickening Spirit, whose office is to guide into truth.'

These principles are secured and reaffirmed in the Basis of Union, and declared in the first of the *Articles Declaratory of the Constitution of the Church of Scotland in Matters Spiritual.* The supreme standard is declared to be the Scriptures of the Old and New Testaments. The second Article states that the principal subordinate standard of the Church is the Westminster Confession, approved by the General Assembly of 1647.

The Church of Scotland adheres to the Scottish Reformation and is Protestant in its testimony.

2 Government

The government of the Church of Scotland is Presbyterian, which sets it apart from the hierarchical system of Episcopacy on the one hand and the independent system of Congregationalism on the other. During the Reformation in Europe the aim of reformers was to re-establish the simplicity and equality which they discerned in the early Church, and which they felt had been overridden by the development of a hierarchical organisation in the form of the Papacy. When the Papacy was overthrown in Scotland, the leaders of the Scottish Reformation set up a Presbyterian polity in its place. Since 1690 this has been recognized by the Crown, and its maintenance was ratified in the Treaty of Union, 1707, by an Act of Security. Among the leading documents referring to the government of the Church and mentioned in the Basis of Union is *The Form of Presbyterial Church Government and of Ordination of Ministers,* 1645.

Three main features of Presbyterianism in the government of the Church of Scotland may be mentioned. The first is the parity of ministers. No minister is set in a superior position to others in the ministry. At meetings of ministers where one member is called to preside, that person is termed the 'Moderator', but he is regarded only as *primus inter pares* (first amongst equals). Presbyterianism differs in this respect from the hierarchical system of Episcopacy.

The share of the laity in the government of the Church of Scotland is a second significant feature of Presbyterianism. The government of the Church of Scotland is based on the co-ordinate authority of ministers (ordained by the Presbytery) and elders (laymen set apart for office by the minister). In all courts of the Church the two sit and vote as one body; there is no 'vote by orders', as in the Church of England. In the Kirk Session there is necessarily a predominance of laymen, but in all higher courts the numbers of ministers and elders are the same.

The laity also share in the appointment of parish ministers. The system of patronage, or the appointment of parish ministers by private or other patrons, was abolished by an Act of Parliament of 1874. Ministers are now appointed to parish charges through a system of election by the members of the particular charge concerned. Members include all communicants, together with 'adherents', who are those admitted by the Kirk Session for their personal interest or share in the work and worship of the congregation.

The third feature of Presbyterianism within the government of the Church of Scotland is that it is conciliar in polity. There is a system of courts of the Church, inferior and superior in ascending scale. This feature distinguishes the Church from the independent system of Congregationalism.

The system of courts is briefly as follows. The lowest court is the Kirk Session, which concerns itself with the affairs of the Church in a single parish area, to which only one minister (or presbyter) is appointed. The Kirk Session is composed of the minister, who is the Moderator, together with a number of ruling (or lay) elders. In all congregations of the Church the Kirk Session deals with ecclesiastical matters (i.e. all matters other than those concerning the ordinary finances of the congregation and the care and maintenance of property). The Kirk Session is not answerable to the congregation, but only to superior courts. Practice varies with regard to the temporal (i.e. financial) affairs of the charge. In former *quoad omnia* charges all financial matters are in the hands of the Kirk Session. In *quoad sacra* parishes (i.e. which includes all charges formed since 1844 and nearly all charges formed from the union of two or more congregations) and those of the former Free Church persuasion, financial matters are in the hands of a Congregational Board, or Deacon's Court, or Board of Management.

The next court is the Presbytery, which consists of a group of ministers who have been inducted to charges within a larger area, together with one elder as representative of each charge. The Presbytery also includes theological teachers in the Scottish universities if they have been ordained to the ministry, and in most cases those who have retired from charges (who are declared eligible for the retention of a seat in the Presbytery in which they last ministered). A certain number of additional elders are elected by the Presbytery itself from charges within its bounds to equalize the numbers of ministers and elders. The Presbytery is the characteristic court of the Church. It directly superintends not only the Kirk Sessions but the whole of the ecclesiastical activity within its bounds, as well as electing annually those ministers and elders who are to constitute the General Assembly.

The next court in order of superiority is the Synod. It includes all members of Presbyteries within a wider area, together with such corresponding members (a minister and an elder) as may be appointed from each of the adjacent Synods. Each Synod contains at least two Presbyteries, with the exception of the three Presbyteries of Shetland, Orkney and England, where each Presbytery is vested with synodical powers. The prime functions of the Synod are to exercise a general superintendence of Presbyteries within its area of jurisdiction, and to act as a court of appeal between Presbyteries and General Assembly. By an Act of 1933 (amended in 1947 and 1962) the General Assembly has enacted that finality of judgement should belong to the Synod in all cases of dissent and complaint, or of appeal, other than those involving doctrine, worship, censure of ministers or other office-bearers, cases of licensing of students, and cases of union and readjustment. The General Assembly remains the court of appeal in these cases.

The supreme court of the Church is the General Assembly. The membership is elected annually by each Presbytery in proportion to its size. One minister (including theological teachers) in four, or part of four, is elected, together with an equal number of elders. The General Assembly is not convened by the Crown, but may meet on its own initiative, this right being explicitly recognized by the Scottish Parliament of 1592. The annual meeting is held in May. It is usual for each Assembly to fix the time and place of the meeting for its successor. The Lord High Commissioner, who attends the Assembly as representative of the Sovereign, presents a royal letter, addresses the Assembly, and dissolves it after the Moderator has dismissed it in the name of Christ. The Lord High Commissioner is not a member of the Assembly, and exercises no control over its business.

The Assembly possesses full powers of legislation and administration. It can, within prescribed limits, alter its constitution. It can also alter the constitution of the Church within prescribed limits through the operation of the Barrier Act (see below). The Assembly deals finally with appeals from lower courts, and of petitions from individuals or external bodies. It also deals with overtures (i.e. proposals for change in the law or practice of the Church) from Presbyteries or Synods. The Assembly receives and considers reports of the work of the Church at home and abroad from its various standing and *ad hoc* committees. It generally attends to all matters which affect the efficiency of the Church and the religious and spiritual condition of the nation.

Some of the business of the General Assembly is dealt with by a Commission of Assembly, which holds two meetings between Assemblies, and may meet at other times if specially convened. The membership consists of all commissioners of the appointing Assembly, plus one minister nominated by the Moderator of that Assembly. The Moderator of the Commission is chosen by the Commission, and is usually, but not necessarily, the Moderator of the preceding Assembly. The Commission is appointed by the General Assembly and is not a court of the Church. It cannot deal with business which has not been expressly devolved by the Assembly or not implied in its terms of appointment, nor can it legislate.

3 Worship

The standard of the Church is nominally the Directory of Public Worship of 1645. It is included among the leading documents mentioned in the Basis of Union, but is subject to modification by the General Assembly on the grounds that a document framed so many years ago cannot have an exclusive validity today. The Church is constitutionally entitled to modify its manner of worship as it feels guided by the Spirit of God, without restraint of any form which is the product of a single age. The purity of worship is maintained in the words of the Formula, which every minister and elder is required to sign, and in which he undertakes to observe the order of worship and administration of all public ordinances as allowed by the Church.

4 Discipline

Discipline in the government of the Church derives from scriptural authority, and refers to the correction of misdemeanour and the avoidance or removal of scandal in the Church. Various social and other changes have resulted in the Form of Process of 1707 becoming largely out of date, although it remains the disciplinary instrument of the Church. The document is mentioned in the Basis of Union, but like the Directory is subject to amendment by the General Assembly.

Discipline consists of the administration of the appropriate censures of the Church to those whose conduct requires it. The scale of censures, arranged in ascending order of severity, are admonition, rebuke, suspension from communion, deposition from office, and excommunication. They are administered only on confession, or on proof of sin or of offence. Cases are tried by Church courts in much the same way as civil courts. Such courts have the power to summon any person within their bounds as a party, witness, or otherwise, and to examine them. The Kirk Session is the court of first instance in cases of elders, deacons, communicants, and baptized persons who are adherents; the Presbytery is the court of first instance in cases against ministers or probationers. The proceedings or judgement of a civil court in cases involving immoral conduct can be no substitute for due process in a Church court, but may occasionally aid in determining whether to enter on a process. In discipline, Church courts form their own judgements independently of proceedings in other courts.

5 Church and state

The part of the constitution of the Church which deals with relations between Church and State is very important. The whole concept of religious and civil government has changed since the Reformation, when there was no clearly defined boundary between the two provinces. Today there is a clearer distinction between the magistrate and the minister, and a greater desire that neither should have authority in the province of the other.

The position is laid out in the *Articles Declaratory of the Constitution of the Church of Scotland in Matters Spiritual:*[2]

IV This church ... wherein the Lord Jesus Christ has appointed a government in the hands of Church office bearers, receives from Him ... the right and power, subject to no civil authority, to legislate, and to adjudicate finally, in all matters of doctrine, worship, government, and discipline in the Church ... Recognition by civil authority of the separate and independent government and jurisdiction of this Church in matters spiritual ... does not in any way affect the character of this government and jurisdiction as derived from the Divine Head of the Church alone, or give to the civil authority any right of interference with the proceedings or judgements of the Church within the sphere of its spiritual government and jurisdiction.

VI This Church acknowledges the divine appointment and authority of the civil magistrate within his own sphere, and maintains its historic testimony to the duty of the nation acting in its corporate capacity to render homage to God, to acknowledge the Lord Jesus Christ to be King over the nations ... to honour His Church, and to promote in all appropriate ways the Kingdom of God. The Church and the State owe mutual duties to each other, and acting within their respective spheres may signally promote each other's welfare ...

These *Articles* were accepted alike by the Church and by the Crown through Parliament.

The civil courts cannot interfere with anything done within the sphere of jurisdiction of the ecclesiastical courts, which are recognized judicatures of the realm. In no cases will the civil court entertain an appeal from a judgement of an ecclesiastical court on a question of doctrine, or enter into an examination of the soundness of such judgement before enforcing its civil consequences. However, it is conceivable – although extremely improbable – that a case could arise in which a flagrant departure from the form and purity of worship established by the Act of 1707, if uncorrected by the ecclesiastical courts, would justify an appeal to the civil courts. No appeal lies to a civil court in matters of discipline, or on the ground of excess of punishment, unless there is excess of jurisdiction (e.g. unless punishment is inflicted for obeying the law of the land). On the other hand, the civil power is bound to give all due assistance for making the sentences and censures of the Church and her judicatures to be obeyed. Also, the civil courts hear and determine appeals on matters connected with church property, glebe, repair of churches, and the like.

The *Articles* quoted above not only safeguard the present position of the Church of Scotland, but give it full liberty of determination in future action within the limits of the constitution, which are widely drawn. The Church is not, as in former days, bound to formularies devised at any particular time, so long as it rests on the Word of God as the supreme rule of faith and life. On the other hand, the Presbyterian form of Church government, and the Confession of Faith, are part of the constitution which is approved by the State, and the State would therefore have the right to be consulted on any proposal for changing them.

6 Barrier Act, 1697

Before any change can be made which affects the constitution of the Church in its doctrine, government, worship or discipline, a certain procedure must be followed which involves consulting the whole Church through the Presbyteries; the General Assembly alone cannot effect the change. The procedure is known as the operation of the Barrier Act. The intention is to prevent the passing of hasty and ill-considered legislation. The procedure is as follows. Before any Acts are passed which are 'to be binding rules and constitutions to the Church', these should first be proposed in the form of an overture to the Assembly. If the overture is approved, it must be remitted to the Presbyteries for consideration, and for report to the following Assembly. If the majority of Presbyteries approve, the General Assembly may either pass the overture into an Act, or resolve that it not be passed, or send it down to Presbyteries in amended form for further consideration. If half or more Presbyteries disapprove of the overture, it is regarded as disapproved by the Assembly, though it may be sent down again in amended form

The Barrier Act is not part of the constitution of the Church, but it plays an important role in the framing of the constitution. It exercises a restraining influence on changes to the constitution by the weight given to rural congregations, which probably tend to be more conservative than congregations in urban areas. Whereas the General Assembly is broadly representative of all congregations in the Church, the Presbyteries, because of their disparate sizes with urban charges mainly grouped in a few large Presbyteries, tend to be weighted in favour of rural congregations.

In matters other than those concerned with doctrine, government, worship and discipline, the Assembly may pass Declaratory Acts stating what *is* the law. Providing that these do not contravene anything which has already been enacted with regard to the categories concerned, and do not contain anything inconsistent with the law as formerly existing, the Assembly are entitled to pass legislation and bring it immediately into effect.

The Assembly may also pass interim Acts to effect an immediate change in the law if urgently necessary, even when the operation of the Barrier Act is obligatory, as long as the Barrier Act is operated in the usual way. Such an interim Act may have force only until the following Assembly, when it may be made a permanent law if the Presbyteries approve.

3 The government of the Church
We have seen that the Church is governed by a system of courts, inferior and superior in ascending scale, viz, Kirk Session, Presbytery, Synod and General Assembly. These courts have many features in common. The purpose of this section is to describe some of the points of similarity and contrast before examining each court in some detail. The section ends with a brief description of the functions of the major central committees of the Church.

1 Courts of the Church
The courts of the Church are established by law. They comprise ministers and lay members in equal numbers, except in the Kirk Session, where lay members predominate. Each court votes as a single body; there is no voting 'by orders', as in the Church of England. In courts other than the General Assembly the practice has been for the quorum to be three; in the Kirk Session the quorum has been definitely fixed at three, comprising the minister and two elders. In the General Assembly and Commission of Assembly the quorum has been fixed at thirty-one, of whom not less than sixteen must be ministers.

The Kirk Session is presumed to be a closed court, unless it resolves to be open, which it never has any necessity to do. The other courts are presumed to be open, unless they resolve to be closed. These courts normally sit alone when dealing, amongst other things, with matters of conscience. Each court must meet within its own bounds, unless permission to do otherwise is obtained from a superior court. Similarly, a court cannot sit when a superior court is sitting, unless it obtains permission to do so from that court.

In every court one of the members acts as Moderator. The Moderator of the Kirk Session is the minister of the congregation. In higher courts it is now the invariable practice to appoint a minister as Moderator, and he is chosen by election. The Moderator is responsible for calling a meeting; he acts as chairman, but has a casting vote only. His signature as Moderator is understood to mean he signs for the court and by its authority.

Every court must have a clerk. His appointment is not for life, unless so specified. The office may be held by a person who is not a member of the court. The clerk is the custodian of the court records, and is the only legal extractor of the records.

Each of the four courts of the Church has authority over those below it and, with the exception of a very few cases, may review and reverse their proceedings. One example is that the Kirk Session's decision is final on claims for enrolment as adherents. Another example is that the judgement of the Synod is final in all cases of appeal, except those involving doctrine, worship, the censure of a minister or other office-bearer, the licensing of students, and the question of union and readjustment. The General Assembly is the court of appeal in all other cases. A superior court has the right to satisfy itself that a trust, regulation or Act is being properly administered by a lower court. The orders of a superior court must be obeyed by an inferior court, and the minister and elders come under obligations to such obedience. Any book kept by any court is ordered to be revised and attested annually by the next superior court, where it is examined by a committee of ministers.

A part of the business of Church courts, especially the General Assembly, involves dealing with petitions and overtures. The ordinary use of petitions is to initiate business in the court of first instance. The business generally concerns only the affairs of the petitioners. The General Assembly is in many matters the court of first instance, as when a minister of another Church seeks admission to the Church of Scotland. A petition is not received by the court unless a person appears at the bar in support of it; the General Assembly frequently receives a petition from an association external to the Church.

'Overture' is the name given to the formal proposal submitted to a court by an inferior court, or by one or more members of the court itself, to initiate legislation or executive action of a general kind not limited to the business of the overturers. Overtures are submitted most frequently to the General Assembly, especially from Presbyteries, these having to be forwarded through Synods. Kirk Sessions may overture the Presbytery, but not the General Assembly. Overtures to the General Assembly are often sent down for consideration of the Presbyteries, or for examination by an Assembly committee. Under the Barrier Act, overtures to modify the doctrine, worship, discipline or government of the Church must be passed down to Presbyteries for their consideration.

Committees are appointed, in general, to deal with a part of the official business assigned to a court. By law, these must be composed of members of the court. In committees whose work has been supported by the weight of the authority of a court, members other than members of the court may be included. In such cases the number and composition of members of the committee is determined by standing orders of the General Assembly. But every member of a committee is under the jurisdiction of an appointing court, so that such members may be called to account by it. The chairman of a committee has only a casting vote. It is out of order for a committee member to dissent from, or complain about, a decision of the Committee, or to write a minority report; he may approach the court which appointed the committee with a petition, or, if he is a member of the court, he may make an appropriate motion when the report of the committee is submitted.

It is a principle of Common Law that a court cannot review its own decrees, which therefore must stand until set aside by a competent court. The principle applies to Church courts in all matters, to the extent of including all decrees of the nature of a judicial deliverance. The principle is not strictly applied to non-judicial resolutions.

The General Assembly, as a supreme court, has the power called *nobile officium*, which enables it to rule upon matters necessary in a pending case, and for which there is no legal provision. The Assembly cannot overrule the law, but only supply the want of it where necessary.

2. The Kirk Session

The basic unit of organization of the Church is the congregation. A congregation is defined as a company of persons — communicant members, adherents and their children — associated together in a particular locality for Christian worship, instruction, fellowship and work.

The Kirk Session is the court which governs the affairs of the congregation.

A slightly different term is the 'charge', which means a sphere of pastoral duty — usually a geographically defined area, or parish — to which a minister or ministers are appointed. The great majority of parish charges have one congregation which is ministered to by one minister. However, there are variations from this standard unit of parish organization. Many charges, especially in sparsely populated rural areas, have two or even three congregations under the care of one minister. The congregations in these 'linked' charges each have their own Kirk Session. Also, in some linked charges, and in certain large, urban parishes with single congregations, the minister is supported by an assistant minister or lay missionary.[3]

The Kirk Session is responsible for the overseeing of church members. The members of the congregation in full communion (i.e. those permitted to attend the Communion service) are those who have been admitted as such by the Kirk Session of the congregation. Communicants may be admitted on the Profession of Faith of new members, by Certificate of Transference from another congregation, and by resolution of the Kirk Session in special cases. The Kirk Session is required to keep a Communion Roll containing the names and addresses of communicants. The Roll is supposed to be revised annually, as at 31st December, but this duty is sometimes neglected. The Roll is also revised when a vacancy occurs in the charge. The Kirk Session may remove the names of persons giving no evidence of real interest or participation in the Church's work and worship. Normally, their names are entered on to a Supplementary Roll in the hope that they can be brought back into full membership at some later date. They may take part in communion, but they are not eligible for election as office-bearers or to take part in congregational meetings.

Baptized persons connected with the congregation, but not admitted to full communion, are members and are under the care of the Kirk Session. A list of their names should be entered on a roll kept by the Kirk Session. Among these are included adherents, who are persons of mature age who desire to be permanently connected with the congregation, or are associated with it in its interests and work, and where no reason exists for refusing to admit them to Communion if they were to apply.

It is the duty of the Kirk Session to see that parents instruct their children in the faith, and to aid them by establishing Sunday Schools. The minister is in charge of the instruction of the young, although another person often acts as superintendent.

Only members in full communion have the right to take part in the business of congregational meetings, with the exception that adherents of twenty-one years of age and over may have their names added to the Electoral Roll, and take part in meetings concerned with a vacancy and the election of a minister.

When a vacancy occurs in a charge, the Presbytery of the bounds appoints one of its ministers to be the Interim Moderator of the Kirk Session. His function is to undertake as far as possible the duties of minister, and to preside at all congregational meetings held in connection with the vacancy. The Kirk Session makes up the Electoral Register of the congregation. A vacancy committee is appointed by a meeting of the congregation, and made up from its members, for the purpose of putting forward a candidate or candidates to preach before the congregation. The committee may resolve to nominate only one candidate, or more than one candidate, for election. Election is open or by ballot, the method to be chosen by the congregation. All present at the election are invited to sign the call to the person elected. The Presbytery of the bounds sustains the call by inducting the minister (or by ordaining and inducting a probationer) to the vacant charge at a service of public worship. A minister is inducted to a charge *ad vitam aut culpam* ('for life or until fault'), with the provision that all ministers inducted from 1972 shall have their ministry terminated at age 70.

A parish minister is employed by, and is subjected to the control and direction of, the Presbytery.[4] His duties fall into three main categories. Firstly, the minister is responsible for the spiritual welfare of the members of his congregation and parish. His duties include the ministry of the Word, the conduct of public worship, the administration of the sacraments, the introduction of the young to the Church, and the preparation of first communicants. Secondly, the minister has duties concerning the Proclamation of Banns of marriage. Thirdly, a minister may also undertake certain civil duties. Since 1959 there has been no Church impediment to a minister becoming a member of any civil or criminal judiciary, or sitting in Parliament, although there is a civil prohibition against ministers becoming members of the House of Commons. All ministers are exempt from serving on juries. The General Assembly has enacted that no minister in a regular charge shall undertake any paid employment either within or outside the Church without previously having obtained the approval of the Presbytery of the bounds, or of a higher Court. A minister may act as a notary.

A minister's field of ministerial work and responsibility lies within, and does not extend beyond, his own parish. Parish boundaries are determined by the Presbytery of the bounds. He may enter another parish in order to minister to members of his own congregation, or to officiate at a marriage or funeral by private invitation, but not to recruit new members.

Congregational meetings are of two kinds — those held for ecclesiastical, and those for temporal, purposes. Meetings for ecclesiastical purposes are called by the Kirk Session, and deal with all matters other than those concerning the ordinary finances of the congregation and the care and maintenance of Church property.[5] Practice varies with regard to the temporal, or financial, affairs of the congregation. In former *quoad omnia* charges all financial matters are in the hands of the Kirk Session. In *quoad sacra* congregations, and those of the former Free Church persuasion, financial affairs are in the hands of a Congregational Board, or Deacons' court, or Board of Management.

The Kirk Session in any congregation consists of the minister along with the elders. All members of the Session are elders; the minister is both a teaching and ruling elder, while the lay members are only ruling elders. The minister and elders have an equal voice on every subject as members of the church court, and all have the same responsibility. The Kirk Session is not answerable to the congregation, but only to superior courts. A quorum is formed by three, including the minister.

Elders are elected for life, either by resolution of the Kirk Session or by vote of the congregation. In the latter case, a vote is taken only if the number nominated exceeds the number required, although the result is subject to the judgement of the Kirk Session concerning the qualifications of those elected. Elders must be of good and worthy character, at least twenty-one years of age, and in full communion with the Church. It belongs to the Kirk Session to determine how many should be appointed. Elders are ordained and admitted to office by the Kirk Session. As with other members on the Communion Roll, they are under the jurisdiction of the Kirk Session.

The Kirk Session should arrange for the division of the parish into convenient districts, and appoint one or more elders to have a special spiritual oversight of each district. It is the duty of such elders to visit families in their districts.

The minister is *ex officio* the Moderator of the Kirk Session. He has a casting vote. His duties are to convene the meeting, and to preside over it; to constitute and close each meeting with prayer; to ensure that the business is properly ordered and recorded; to take the vote and announce the decisions of the Kirk Session; and to act for the Kirk Session in carrying out its decisions. The minister is not responsible to the Kirk Session for the discharge of his office, but if he seems to neglect his duties, the Presbytery may be approached by petition. He is bound by decisions of the Kirk Session in all matters in which it is entitled to decide.

The Kirk Session appoints a clerk, whose duty is to take regular minutes of the Session's procedure which are included in a permanent record, to take charge of all sessional documents, and to prepare and issue all extracts of minutes and papers authorized by Session. The Kirk Session appoints a treasurer and a precentor, or organist, and defines their duties. It may also appoint an officer or beadle, who waits upon its meetings and executes its orders. He should be a communicant. The same person may be a church officer in charge of the place of worship. The salaries (if any) of these office-bearers are determined by the body responsible for financial affairs.

The duty of the Kirk Session is to 'maintain good order, to cause Acts of the Assembly to be put into execution, to administer discipline, to judge and determine cases, and to superintend the religious and moral condition of the parish.' The Kirk Session, with the minister, regulates the hours of public worship and fixes the number of services. For the proper conduct of services, the minister is responsible to the Presbytery. The Kirk Session also provides for the administration of Baptism and the observance of the Lord's Supper. The Kirk Session has the constitutional right in all congregations to watch over all the interests of the congregation, and to intervene when it believes that the welfare of the congregation demands it.

The proceedings of the Kirk Session are subject to the review and direction of the Presbytery and superior courts of the Church. It is charged with carrying out the decisions of superior courts in matters within its province, and of furnishing such information as they may require. Congregations are visited quinquennially by a Visiting Committee of Presbytery, when the general state of the congregation is discussed.

Congregational finances are administered by the Kirk Session in former *quoad omnia* congregations, and by the Congregational Board and other bodies in former *quoad sacra* and Free Church congregations. The income of congregations is derived mainly from collections and fund-raising drives amongst members. Congregational expenses include the following items : maintenance of an adequate fabric fund; the insurance premiums and local rates and taxes on property; the stipend and 'Listed Expenses' (e.g. travelling expenses) of the minister, and the appropriate aid (if any) given to the Maintenance of the Ministry Fund; the heating, lighting and cleaning of the church, and other expenses connected with public worship; the salaries of the church officer (if any), organist, and other officials; payment of premium to the Aged and Infirm Ministers' Fund; contributions to the Mission and Service Fund of the Church; assessments levied by the Presbytery, Synod and General Assembly to meet their expenses; and any other fixed charge falling upon the Kirk Session or congregation.

The financial affairs of former United Free congregations are managed by Deacons' Courts. These consist of the minister (who is Moderator), the elders, and deacons.

Deacons are elected, and ordained, or admitted, in the same way as elders for the purpose of assisting in the management of the temporal affairs of the congregation. They must be at least eighteen years of age. Members of the congregation in full communion form the electorate. The Kirk Session determines when there shall be an election of deacons, and the numbers required. Deacons may hold office in one of two ways. The old way is election for life, and ordination to the office by the Kirk Session; the new way is election to office for three years only, with no ordination.

The Deacons' Court has the management and charge of all the temporal affairs of the congregation. It is required to apply spiritual principles to the management of temporal affairs. It has no power of discipline. The court is bound to call a meeting of the congregation as soon as possible after the auditing of the annual accounts. At the meeting the court presents a report of its proceedings for the previous year, and answers any questions asked by members of the congregation.

The financial affairs of former United Presbyterian congregations are managed by committees of management. These differ between congregations, because each had its own constitution derived from the power, under the authority of the Presbytery, to amend the terms of its constitution. The following is the usual pattern. The membership of the committee consists of communicant members of the congregation elected by the congregation, and usually between six and fifteen in number. The minister and elders are eligible for election. One third of managers retire annually by rotation, and these and other vacant places are filled at the annual meeting of the congregation. Retiring managers are usually eligible for re-election. The congregation either elects itself, or empowers the managers to appoint from their own number, a chairman of committee, a clerk, and a treasurer. The managers present their report at the annual meeting of the congregation. They are not allowed to spend in one year on repairs and alterations to buildings more than a sum fixed by the congregation without the express authority of the congregation; nor have they the power to contract debt on the security of property belonging to the congregation without the special authority of the congregation.

A large number of congregations have adopted the Congregational Board, as constituted under the Model Deed of Constitution, 1965, and approved by the General Assembly. The Model Deed of Constitution was devised to overcome the misunderstanding and confusion amongst ministers and office-bearers caused by the diversity in the forms of constitution of congregations. The constitution is based on the Congregational Board of former United Free Church congregations. The Congregational Board consists of the minister with all or a certain number of elders, and a certain number of communicants elected at the annual meeting of the congregation. The elected members must be over eighteen years of age, and their numbers, to be decided by the congregation, must not exceed the number of elders at the time of the election. One third of the elected members retire annually, but are eligible for re-election. At its first meeting, the Board appoints a clerk and treasurer, who need not be of their own number. It also appoints annually an auditor or auditors, who need not be of their own number. If, at the year end, there is a credit balance in the Ordinary Account after the usual payments have been made, the money is to be applied for congregational and/or general church purposes, including the following: a supplement to the minister to the extent necessary to provide for the Appropriate Stipend and Listed Expenses, if not already provided for; additions to the Fabric Fund account; further contributions to the Mission and Service Fund, to a Reserve Fund to meet extraordinary expenditures in connection with church property, and to a Reserve Fund for stipend or further endowment.

3 The Presbytery
The Presbytery is perhaps the characteristic and fundamental court of the Church. It directly superintends the Kirk Sessions and the whole ecclesiastical

activity within the bounds, and elects annually those ministers and elders who are to constitute the General Assembly. Yet the earliest form of Church government after the Scottish Reformation comprised only congregational, provincial and national assemblies. It is said that Presbyteries arose partly out of the weekly meetings of ministers and church members in local districts to discuss the Scriptures, and partly from the need of Synods to delegate some of their duties. The General Assembly of 1581 set out a regular pattern of Presbyteries to replace the bishops which it had deposed, and which formed the prototype of the existing organization. Since then, Presbyteries have gradually taken over many of the duties of Synods. The General Assembly has the power to change the numbers and boundaries of Presbyteries.

The membership of the Presbytery consists of those ministers who have been inducted to charges within the bounds of the Presbytery, together with one ruling elder as a representative of each charge. Also included are most ministers who have left the ministry for retirement or for another church or job, along with the academic staff of the Faculties of Divinity of the Scottish universities who have been ordained to the ministry. The latter may sit in the Presbytery within whose bounds the university is situated. Most Presbyteries, including all the larger ones, meet monthly for nine to eleven months of the year. Some smaller Presbyteries meet between four and eight times a year.

The Moderator is elected by the court from its ministerial members on the recommendation of the Business, or other committee of Presbytery. He holds office for a year at least, and is eligible for re-election. He has a casting vote. The Presbytery appoints one or more clerks who hold office during the pleasure of the court. It has the right to assess congregations under its jurisdiction to obtain funds necessary for carrying on its business. A treasurer may be appointed to take care of the funds.

The Presbytery meets when required, but two meetings are required at the end of the year to elect commissioners to the General Assembly. The court cannot meet when the General Assembly or the Synod of the district are meeting. The quorum is three, at least two of whom are ministers. The Presbytery is an open court, but it may sit in private when it judges necessary, or is required to do so by the law of the Church.

Functions. The functions of the Presbytery may be summarized as follows:

(i) to maintain and enforce the existing laws and usages of the Church in matters connected with the performance of public worship and the administration of ordinances; to ensure that the Word of God is purely preached within its bounds, the sacraments rightly administered, and the discipline maintained;

(ii) to make rules for good order in the churches, with power of visitation and sanction to make good defects; to give counsel and advice in cases where congregations are declared to be in an unsatisfactory state; to review decisions of congregational meetings;

(iii) to exercise special oversight of a congregation in which the pastoral office is vacant; to ensure that ordinances are duly administered and discipline maintained, including the appointment of an Interim Moderator from among the ministers to perform as far as possible the duties of the minister, and to carry out the laws of the Church regarding the filling of the vacancy;

(iv) to supervise, examine, and license students of divinity; to judge appointments and calls, and reject or admit those appointed; to oversee the conduct of ministers and the discharge of their professional duties, with power to indict, try, and sentence them;

(v) to cause ordinances made by the Synod and General Assembly to be kept and put in execution; to participate in the legislation of the Church by approving or disapproving overtures transmitted by the General Assembly under the Barrier Act; and by commenting on draft regulations sent down by the Assembly;

(vi) to consider the question of union and readjustment of charges in a vacancy, in conjunction with the General Assembly's Committee on Union and Readjustments; to delimit ecclesiastical parishes, and alter their bounds as required;

(vii) to vindicate the Church's claim to funds or property, and to guard them from injury or improper use;

(viii) to deal with matters brought before it by Kirk Sessions;

(ix) to determine, in conjuction with the Maintenance of the Ministry Committee, appropriate figures for stipend and aid and, in conjunction with the Stewardship and Budget Committee, the Mission and Service Fund allocations, for all charges within the bounds.

The Presbytery may appoint committees from its members for the consideration of the more detailed aspects of its business. All Presbyteries have committees which parallel in name and business some of the standing committees of the General Assembly, such as the Maintenance of the Ministry Committee, the Union and Readjustments Committee, and the Stewardship and Budget Committee. These committees report to Presbytery.

Presbyteries have the general duty of supervision in all matters affecting the spiritual welfare of the Church and of its members within their respective bounds. They may give counsel and admonition, and public declarations of opinion, on such matters.

4 The Synod

The General Assembly determines the numbers and constituent Presbyteries of each Synod. The Synod consists of all members of the Presbyteries within the province, together with such corresponding members (a minister and an elder) as may be appointed from each of the adjacent Synods. There are currently twelve Synods in the Church, and each contains at least two Presbyteries. In addition, there are three Presbyteries – those of Shetland, Orkney and England – which are not part of any Synod, but are each vested with synodical powers.

The Moderator of the Synod is elected from amongst the ministerial members of the court. He holds office for at least one year, and is eligible for re-election. The Synod appoints one or more clerks, as well as an officer who attends meetings and executes its orders. It is entitled to assess congregations under its jurisdiction for funds required for its business; this is done by an annual assessment on Presbyteries, which then reclaim the amount from each congregation.

The Synod is an open court, but it may meet in private when it judges that to be necessary. It meets at least once a year. The quorum is three, two of whom must be ministers. The usual custom is to have a standing Business Committee which meets beforehand to suggest the order of business, and to act as a Committee on Bills and Overtures. The Synod cannot legislate, but it can give orders to redress things omitted or wrongly done. Its prime functions are to exercise a general superintendence of Presbyteries within its area of jurisdiction, and to act as a court of appeal between Presbyteries and General Assembly.

By an Act of 1933 (amended in 1947 and 1962), the General Assembly has enacted that finality of judgement should belong to the Synod in all cases of dissent or appeal, other than those involving doctrine, worship, censure of ministers or other office-bearers, cases of licensing of students, and cases of union and readjustment. The General Assembly remains the Court of Appeal in these cases. In the three Presbyteries vested with synodical powers, the General Assembly is the final Court of Appeal.

Functions. The detailed business of Synods covers the following matters:

(i) the examination of Presbytery records, which is done annually;

(ii) the receiving and judging of the reports of the quinquennial visitation of congregations by Presbyteries; the Synod acts with the Presbytery to remedy congregations found to be in an unsatisfactory state; it has the power, in consultation with the Presbytery in which it falls, to visit any congregation when it is thought to be necessary;

(iii) the supervision of the delimitation of ecclesiastical boundaries; in any such matter the judgement of the Synod is final, unless the matter affects the bounds of the Synod itself; the Synod deals with the transportation, reduction and dissolution of charges, and has the power to transfer charges from one Presbytery to another;

(iv) the supervision over Presbyteries of the schemes of the Church, i.e. the Maintenance of the Ministry and Mission and Service Funds;

(v) the judgement of appeals and complaints from Presbyteries, but with right of appeal to the General Assembly in cases of doctrine, worship, censure of a minister or other office-bearer, licensing of students, and in cases of union and readjustment;

(vi) the participation in the legislation of the Church through the transmission to the General Assembly of overtures originating in the Synod itself or from Presbyteries; in the latter case, the overture may be transmitted with or without the approval of the Synod;

(vii) when the General Assembly sends down to Presbyteries draft regulations (not under the Barrier Act) for suggestions, the regulations are also sent to Synods, which may send in suggestions;

(viii) the receiving and disposing of petitions by ministers who have demitted their charges on the grounds of age or infirmity, for transference from one Presbytery to another;

(ix) each Synod appoints members to certain of the standing committees of the General Assembly (e.g. each Synod appoints one member to the Committee on Education for the Ministry, holding office for four years);

(x) reports on the activities of the General Assembly's Home Board, etc., carried on within the bounds, are made periodically to Synod.

The Synod is entrusted with the general supervision of the interests of the Church within its bounds, and with the promotion of the life of the Church.

5 The General Assembly

The General Assembly is the supreme court of the Church. In spiritual matters its decisions are final, and are not subject to review by any civil court. The Assembly also determines the number and boundaries of Presbyteries and Synods. The membership (commissioners) is elected annually by each Presbytery in proportion to its size. One minister in four, or part of four, is elected, together with an equal number of elders. In 1976 there were 1,312 commissioners eligible to attend the Assembly. The Assembly clerks, procurator and law agent are *ex officiis* members, and have all the rights of commissioners. Missionaries at home on furlough and secretaries of standing committees are corresponding members, but have no vote. The Assembly also receives delegates from other Churches and visitors. The quorum is thirty-one of whom sixteen must be ministers.

The Moderator is nominated by a committee, but elected by the Assembly immediately after it is constituted by the Moderator of the previous Assembly. His duties are to preside over the Assembly; to visit Presbyteries under the scheme of visitation sanctioned by the Assembly; to perform such duties as may be directed by the Assembly; to represent the Church of Scotland on national occasions; and other duties as he may choose during his term of office.

The General Assembly is not convened by the Crown, but may meet on its own initiative, this right being explicitly recognized by the Scottish Parliament of 1592. The annual meeting is held in May. It is usual for each Assembly to fix the time and place of the meeting for its successor.

Once the Assembly is constituted and the Moderator appointed, the Lord High Commissioner, who attends the Assembly as representative of the Sovereign, presents a royal letter and addresses the Assembly. Later he dissolves the Assembly after the Moderator has dismissed it in the name of Christ. The Lord High Commissioner is not a member of the Assembly, and exercises no control over its business.

Functions. The main functions of the General Assembly are as follows:

(i) The Assembly possesses full powers of legislation and administration. It can deliberate on matters concerning the whole Church in doctrine, worship, discipline and government, and declare the mind of the Church. It may do so by a Declaratory Act, which declares for the guidance of the Church what the Assembly holds to be the law of the Church on any particular point. Such an Act may be sent down to Presbyteries for comment before being passed by the Assembly if difficulties arise. The Assembly can alter the constitution of the Church within prescribed limits through the operation of the Barrier Act. Urgent Acts can be passed as Interim Acts, which are valid until the next Assembly, while approval is being sought from Presbyteries through the operation of the Barrier Act.

(ii) The Assembly deals finally with appeals from lower courts, and of petitions from individuals or external bodies. Being the Supreme Court of the Church, the Assembly has the power of *nobile officium*, where it may deal finally with any matter which may arise and is not otherwise provided for. It may also review *mero motu* the decisions of lower courts.

(iii) The Assembly deals with overtures (i.e. proposals for change in the law or practice of the Church) from Presbyteries and Synods.

(iv) The Assembly may set up a special commission of members by an Act to examine any special case, the powers of the commission being defined in the Act. The Assembly also receives and considers reports of the work of the Church at home and abroad from its various standing committees.

(v) The Assembly determines the numbers and boundaries of Synods and Presbyteries within the Church. In an Act of 1975 the General Assembly effected a major reorganization of the structure of Synods and Presbyteries. From 1 January 1976 the number of Presbyteries in Scotland was reduced from fifty-seven to forty-seven; in addition, there are Presbyteries of England, Europe, and Jerusalem. The numbers and boundaries of parishes are determined by Presbyteries.

(vi) The Assembly generally attends to all matters which affect the efficiency of the Church and the religious and spiritual condition of the nation.

The Commission of Assembly

Some of the judicial and administrative (but not legislative) business of the General Assembly is delegated to a Commission of Assembly. The commission is appointed each year by an Act of Assembly, and is not a court of the Church. It holds two meetings in October and February between Assemblies, and may meet at other times if specially convened. It cannot deal with business which has not been expressly devolved by the Assembly, or not implied in its terms of appointment. Past decisions of the commission suggest that, as long as it keeps within the powers conferred by the Act and the procedure is regular, the judgements are treated as final by succeeding Assemblies. The membership of the commission consists of all commissioners of the appointing Assembly, plus one minister nominated by the Moderator of that Assembly. The Moderator is chosen by the commission, and is usually, but not necessarily, the Moderator of the preceeding Assembly. The quorum is as for the General Assembly.

Functions. The duties of the commission are as follows:

(i) to determine finally in every matter referred to it by the General Assembly;

(ii) to receive any references and appeals from Synods in matters of doctrine;

(iii) to make appointments on behalf of the Assembly to any governing body set up before the following Assembly;

(iv) to give all needed advice and assistance to Synods, Presbyteries, and committees of Assembly;

(v) to receive information on the progress of missionary schemes of the Church. The commission is empowered to do the following:

(i) to dispose of all references from Synods in matters connected with Calls, translations, retiral or settlement of ministers, and the status of congregations and readjustment of agencies; it also disposes of cases of union and readjustment brought up by the Committee on Union and Readjustment;

(ii) to fill any vacancy in the membership of a special commission appointed to deal with a case of readjustment;

(iii) to dispose of cases urgently requiring settlement in the spiritual interests of the parish concerned, where a minister is demitting a charge;

(iv) on the Report from the Law, Property Cases, and Discipline Committee, to dispose of all petitions for sale of property;

(v) to dispose of any matter brought before the General Administration Committee affecting the general interests of the Church at home or abroad requiring immediate action, given the limitation of its powers prescribed in the appointing Act.

The officials of the General Assembly — clerks, procurator and solicitor — are appointed subject to a retirement age of seventy, and are *ex officiis* members of the Assembly. They form a standing committee to report on the commissions to the Assembly and on the returns of Presbyteries to overtures.

The General Assembly has appointed a number of committees to deal with the general work of the Church at home and abroad. These we examine next.

6 The central committees
The general work of the Church at home and abroad, which is directly maintained and regulated by the General Assembly, requires constant administration through the year. The need was recognized in the Basis and Plan of Union of 1929, which established a number of standing committees to deal with it. These are grouped into seven departments as follows: Administration and Special Interests Department; Church and Ministry Department; Home Department; Social Responsibility Department; the Overseas Council; Education Department; and Department of Publicity and Publication. Each department is staffed with permanent officials or secretaries appointed by the General Assembly. The Church offices are at 121, George Street, Edinburgh. The committees discharge their functions under Acts passed, or regulations approved, by the General Assembly. They report annually to the Assembly.

An outline of the committees which make up each department, together with a brief summary of their functions, now follows:

A Administration and Special Interests Department
The committees grouped in the Administration and Special Interests Department have no common bond, apart from the service of one secretariat, and the fact that their concern is either administration in the wide sense or some special interest not covered by the work of any other department.

They are divided into two groups. The first group (administrative) comprises the General Administration Committee; Committee to Nominate the Moderator; Judicial Committee; Committee on Law, Property Cases and Discipline; General Trustees; Nomination Committee; Church of Scotland Trust; General Finance Committee; and Stewardship and Budget Committee. The second group (Special Interests) includes the Church and Nation Committee; Panel on Doctrine; and the Committee on Public Worship and Aids to Devotion.

Among the more important of these committees is the General Administration Committee. It is charged with making arrangements for the meetings of the General Assembly and of the Commission, including the printing and circulation of reports; it is responsible for the care of Assembly buildings; it deals with questions of Church law and procedure brought before it, and advises in the preparation of all legislative measures coming before the Assembly; and it compiles statistics of the Church (except youth and finance).

The General Finance Committee is charged with the care of the buildings and furnishings of the offices of the Church. It exercises control of the General Treasurer's Department, the preparation and issue of schedules for local financial returns, and the preparation and publication of the accounts of the Church. It is responsible for the general supervision of the conduct, duties, salaries, and work of the clerks and subordinate officials employed in the Church offices. The committee also receives annually in February from the General Administration Committee, and from the committees having no funds, an estimate of their expenditure for the current year, and submits in its report to the Assembly proposals for raising from Presbyteries the amount to meet such expenditure (the General Purposes Fund).

The General Trustees are the body in which a large part of the congregational property of the Church is vested.[6] They are responsible for the supervision and care of this property, fire insurances, rating and valuation, the glebe lands, investment funds for fabric and other purposes held on behalf of congregations, and the administration and collection of the standardized stipend.

The Church of Scotland Trust, incorporated by Act of Parliament, is empowered to hold properties and investments on behalf of any court, committee or congregation of the Church.[7] Its main function is the operation of three different funds for the investment of committees and congregations.

The Stewardship and Budget Committee was appointed by Act of Assembly in 1959 to promote the wider work of the Church.[8] It brought into one fund — the Mission and Service Fund — all the contributions made by the congregations of the Church to the Home Board (including Church Extension), the Overseas Council, the Social Responsibility Department and the Department of Education. The wider work of the Church means broadly all those activities of Christian mission and service which stretch beyond the pastoral task in the parishes. The Stewardship and Budget Committee is therefore complementary to the Maintenance of the Ministry Committee, and along with that committee it takes in the whole task of evangelism, service and education for which the Church exists in the world.

The promotion task of the committee has two main aspects. Firstly, the committee has the administrative task of determining the total annual budget required, on the basis of budgets put forward by the benefiting Committees, and of determining the proportion of that budget required from each Presbytery and group of congregations. Secondly, the committee is charged with education in Christian stewardship, i.e. with 'the education of the membership of the Church in the spiritual basis of Christian giving, and in the adoption of the best methods of ingathering and systematic giving.' That educational task is done through Stewardship Campaigns in congregations; by publicity about the work of the committees in the Mission and Service Fund; by guiding financial authorities in congregations on the best fund-raising methods; and by the appointment of a Stewardship promoter in each congregation.

The general purpose of the Church and Nation Committee is 'to watch over developments of the nation's life in which moral and spiritual considerations specially arise, and to consider what action the Church from time to time may be advised to take to further the highest interests of the people.'

The Panel on Doctrine deals, as its name implies, with doctrinal matters.

B Church and Ministry Department

The Church and Ministry Department was created by the Basis and Plan of Union in 1929, was enlarged in 1965, and is responsible for the work of the committees on the Maintenance of the Ministry; Aged and Infirm Ministers' Fund and

Pension Fund; Unions and Readjustments; Probationers and Transference of Ministers; Admission of Ministers of Other Churches; as well as Chaplains to H.M. forces, and the Oxford Chaplaincy Consultative Committee.

The first responsibility of the Church of Scotland is 'to maintain religious ordinances throughout the land, and to provide ministry of Word and sacraments to all our people by means of a territorial ministry.' This responsibility is discharged by means of a settled parochial ministry supported by the fund called 'the Fund for the Maintenance of the Ministry.' The fund consists of the income from nearly all endowments held by the Church for stipend, and all sums received from congregations, individuals, legacies, trusts, and other sources for stipend purposes. The fund is administered by the Committee on the Maintenance of the Ministry.[9] The committee also provides, in certain cases, new endowments for parishes and various grants and expenses to parish ministers.

The function of the Committee on Unions and Readjustments is to eliminate the wasteful use of men, money and material arising from the duplication of churches brought about by the Union of 1929, and subsequent movements in population and other factors. This work is done by uniting adjacent congregations and various other forms of readjustment.[10]

The purpose of the Aged and Infirm Ministers' Fund is to make provision for ministers in their retirement. All congregations are required to contribute annually to the fund a sum fixed in relation to the stipend of the previous year.

The Committee on Probationers and Transference of Ministers deals with the allocation of probationers as candidates in parish vacancies, and it administers a scheme for the transference of ministers under regulations approved by the General Assembly. The committee also controls pulpit supply, i.e. the provision of ministers and others to take services in vacant congregations.

C *Home Department*

The Home Board was established as a standing committee in 1936 to co-ordinate the work of five committees previously independent, namely the Home Mission, Women's Home Mission, National Church Extension, Highlands and Islands, and Church and Manse Building. In 1967 the General Assembly approved a reorganization of the board's structure by which all its work is administered by three sub-committees, namely Home Mission, Church Extension, and Property.

The function of the Home Mission Committee is to promote the spread of the Gospel in Scotland. This is done by reinforcing in a variety of ways the life and witness of congregations, most notably through the employment of over 100 lay field staff. The committee also initiates enterprises in mission which can only effectively be organized on a national basis, such as summer missions, the training of Church members for the work of evangelism (at St Ninian's, Creiff, an ecumenical mission to industry employing four full-time chaplains, and the appointment of full-time and part-time chaplains to all the hospitals in Scotland.

The National Church Extension Committee is charged with the responsibility of deciding, in consultation with Presbyteries, where new church buildings are required to serve the needs of new housing areas, and of then arranging and financing such projects as are agreed. In most cases a new charge with a complete suite of new buildings has been necessary. In some cases, an existing parish church has been able to cope, provided that additional hall accommodation is erected in the new area. Out of about 240 projects completed since the Second

World War, about half represent the creation of new parishes.

The function of the Property Committee is, firstly, to maintain the property owned by the Home Board, and, secondly, to help congregations to maintain their properties in a good state of repair. The committee has at its disposal a loan fund of £275,000, from which it makes loans to congregations for the construction or purchase of new premises, or for repairs to existing premises. The committee also makes grants to poor congregations for building repairs, from a grants fund of about £20,000 derived from the givings of congregations through the Mission and Service Fund.

D Social Responsibility

The Department of Social Responsibility came into being on 1st January 1976 to unify the work of three committees, namely Social Service, Moral Welfare, and the Women's Committee on Social and Moral Welfare.

The broad purpose of the department is (a) to secure in the Church informed opinion on contemporary social and ethical issues; (b) to encourage balanced judgements on these issues in the light of Christian faith and practice, and to press these judgements at all levels of influence; and (c) to offer service through the varied establishments it operates, and to encourage and enable increasing caring work at parish level. The committees in the department run a large number of homes for children, hostels for young people, rehabilitation centres, and homes for the elderly.

E The Overseas Council

The Overseas Council was created in 1964 to bring together four constituent committees, namely Foreign Mission, Colonial and Continental, Church and Israel, and Christian Aid. The overseas work of the Church is now administered by three Area Committees dealing respectively with (a) Asia and Australasia, (b) Africa, and (c) Europe, Israel and the Americas. There are, in addition, Home Organisation, Staffing and Finance Committees concerned with the entire scope of the Council's responsibility, and there is a Christian Aid Committee. The Overseas Council is itself the final authority as well as the body which co-ordinates the work of its area and other committees. The chief function of the Overseas Council is to provide missionaries to serve within the indigenous Churches overseas. There are Church of Scotland missionaries and chaplains serving in seven areas of Africa, eight areas in India, in Pakistan, in Yemen, in Taiwan, in different islands or areas of the West Indies, in ten countries of Europe, in three countries of South America, in Israel, and in Mauritius and Sri Lanka.

F Education Department

The Department of Education comprises the committees on Education, Education for the Ministry, and Parish Education, together with the Board of St Colm's College and the Board of Nomination to Church Chairs.

The Committee on Education acts for the General Assembly on all matters of education in schools, colleges or universities, and fosters co-operation between church and school. It co-operates with the Educational Institute for Scotland and other Churches on the Scottish Joint Committee on Religious Education; provides in-service training for school chaplains; confers with teachers interested in religious instruction in school; and appoints representatives of the General Assembly to the governing bodies of eight colleges of education, and one representative interested in the promotion of religious education to each of the education committees of the regional and island councils.

The Committee on Education for the Ministry is charged with the recruitment, selection and education of candidates for the ministry. It provides bursaries for candidates who are not eligible for Scottish Education Department awards, and arranges and supervises the probationary period which students serve after their academic course has been completed. It provides in-service training courses for ministers who have been some years in a parish.[11]

The Committee on Parish Education is responsible for the work done previously by the Committee on the Religious Instruction of Youth and the Committee on Adult Christian Education. It operates through three divisions: – children, youth and adults. Its executive co-ordinates the work of the divisions in providing for the voluntary education of the Church's people.

St Colm's College is concerned with training for the home and overseas mission of the Church.

G Department of Publicity and Publication

The Department of Publicity and Publication was set up by the General Assembly in 1964, and replaced the Publications Committee which had been a standing committee for over 100 years. The new department was charged with the responsibility for public relations and publicity, both internal and external; for the production of periodicals, such as the Church's monthly magazine *Life and Work;* the publishing of Christian literature through the St Andrew's Press; and the provision of bookshops (six now exist). There are two committees: the committee on Publicity and the Committee on Publication.

Apart from these standing committees, the General Assembly may also appoint temporary and occasional (or *ad hoc*) committees as required, to examine particular issues. Their functions and powers depend upon the minute of appointment.

Conclusions

The purpose of this chapter has been to describe the constitution and government of the Church of Scotland. We have seen that the constitution of the Church has been ratified and confirmed, rather than conferred, by the State.

Adhering to the substance of the faith of the Reformed Churches and the Presbyterian form of Church government, the Church has a right to (a) frame its subordinate standards; (b) constitute its own courts; (c) legislate and judge in all matters of doctrine, government, worship and discipline, membership and office; (d) appoint its agents and their spheres of service; and (e) alter its own constitution within proscribed limits and in accordance with proscribed procedure. The authority of the civil courts is fully recognized in matters of property and civil right.

We saw that the Church is governed by a hierarchy of courts, inferior and superior, in ascending scale, viz. the Kirk Session (for the congregation), the Presbytery (for the congregations in the district), the Synod (for the Presbyteries in the province), and the General Assembly (the national court). Each court has, with very few exceptions, authority over those below it, and may review and reverse their proceedings. The General Assembly is the Supreme Court of the Church. In spiritual matters its decisions are final, and are not subject to review by any civil court. It alone may legislate. The membership of the Church courts is made up of equal numbers of ministers and elders, with the exception of the Kirk Session, where elders predominate. In every court one of the ministers acts as Moderator. In the Kirk Session the Moderator is the minister of the congregation.

All courts have committees of their members to deal with detailed items of business and to report. Many of the committees in the inferior courts parallel the standing committees of the General Assembly, which deal with the day-to-day administration of the Church's work at home and abroad. These standing committees are grouped into seven departments, each staffed by a full-time secretariat.

Notes

1 J.T. Cox, *Practice and Procedure in the Church of Scotland,* 6th ed., edited by Rev. D.F.M. Macdonald (Blackwood, 1976); Church of England, *Church and State: Report of the Archbishop's Commission* appendix E (Church Information Office, 1970); A.J.H. Gibson, *Stipend in the Church of Scotland* (Blackwood, 1960); and Andrew Herron (ed.), *The Church of Scotland Yearbook, 1976,* (Saint Andrew Press, 1976).

2 The *Articles* are printed in Cox, pp. 390-2.

3 A further note on nomenclature is required. The word 'church' has a variety of meanings, and is sometimes confused with congregation, charge or parish. In this book the word is used in the following ways, although this usage does not have official sanction. The term 'church', with a lower-case first letter, denotes the building in which the congregation meets for worship. Written with an upper-case first letter, the term means the Church of Scotland, or some other named denomination. The plural of Church denotes more than one denomination, usually in a particular region or country (e.g. the British Churches), or of a particular theological persuasion (e.g. the Protestant Churches). We do not use the term 'the Church' to mean 'the Christian Church', which by implication includes all Churches in a single body.

4 Some ministers are employed full-time in non-parochial work under the supervision of the standing committees of the General Assembly.

5 The erection or substantial alteration of a church, hall or manse buildings, or the installation of an organ, are matters of ecclesiastical business.

6 The work of the General Trustees is dealt with in greater detail in chapter 3.

7 The work of the Church of Scotland Trust is described briefly in the following chapter, and in greater detail in chapter 19.

8 The organization and working of the Stewardship and Budget Committee is analysed in detail in chapters 16 and 17.

9 The work of the Maintenance of the Ministry Committee is described and analysed in detail in chapter 10.

10 The economic implications of the policy of union and readjustment are analysed in chapter 13.

11 The education and training of ministers is examined in chapter 14.

Chapter 3

The property and funds of the Church

1 Introduction

During the course of its history, the Church of Scotland has accumulated a great deal of property and funds from a variety of different sources. An important part of the constitution of the Church deals with the Church's tenure of these endowments. The purpose of this chapter is to examine the constitutional question of Church property and funds in some detail, and to outline the responsibilities of the various bodies concerned.

The historical background to the question is examined briefly in section 2. Then in the following section we describe the impact of the passing of the Church of Scotland (Property and Endowments) Act of 1925 on the property and funds of the pre-Union Church of Scotland and United Free Church. The Act revolutionized parochial ecclesiastical law in Scotland. The developments arising from the Union of 1929 are also briefly described. Finally, in section 4 we look at the position today regarding the ownership of Church endowments and the maintenance of fabric.

2 Historical background

Since the property and funds of the Church of Scotland have been accumulated over a long period of time, and from many different sources, the present position of these endowments can only be properly understood when seen against the historical background. The purpose of this short section is to sketch in briefly some of this background and, in particular, to draw the distinction between *quoad omnia* and *quoad sacra* parishes.

At the time of the Reformation in Scotland in 1560, the whole of the country was divided into over 800 parishes. These were parishes *quoad omnia* (i.e. parishes for civil and ecclesiastical purposes), so-called because they were the geographical unit of organization for local government, education and other civil affairs, as well as for the Church.[1] The church and the manse (the minister's house) of these parishes were erected and maintained by the heritors, who were the landowners of the parish. This responsibility, which had started as a custom during the early Middle Ages, became a statutory obligation from the sixteenth century onwards. The responsibility was only brought to an end with the passing of the Church of Scotland (Property and Endowments) Act, 1925, when the Church assumed full control of these properties. The stipends (the clerical equivalent of salaries) of *quoad omnia* parishes were derived largely from the teinds, or tithes, also paid by the heritors from the produce of the land.

Church extension, or the building of new churches to cater for new areas of population, occurred from the seventeenth century onwards. The need arose from the growth of the population, and its movement towards the towns and cities where the existing churches were unable to cope. The normal procedure was for *quoad omnia* charges to build chapels-of-ease to minister to outlying centres of population within the parish. As these populations grew and the chapels-of-ease became stronger, they were eventually erected into parishes *quoad sacra* on application to the Court of Teinds under the New Parishes Act, 1844. These new parishes were formed by the disjunction of a portion of the territory of the existing *quoad omnia* parish; they were called parishes *quoad sacra* because they were parishes for ecclesiastical purposes only; the area of the *quoad omnia* parish remained the parish for civil purposes.[2] The normal conditions for erection to *quoad sacra* status under the Act were that a church should be built and inalienably secured as the church of the new parish in connection with the Church of Scotland; that provision should be made for future maintenance of fabric; and that an endowment for stipend of a specified minimum amount should be provided with a suitable manse inalienably secured (or, if no manse, a correspondingly larger minimum stipend). The minimum endowment was £100 per annum with a manse provided, or £120 without a manse. At first the normal arrangement was for the congregation to raise half the endowment – £50 or £60 according to whether there was a manse – with the remaining half being supplied by the central Endowment Committee. This arrangement was modified with the foundation of the Baird Trust in 1873, which today gives an endowment for stipend to congregations trying to raise their share of the capital required for the statutory endowment of a *quoad sacra* parish.

With the growth of cities and towns during the eighteenth century, a number of burgh councils built churches and endowed them for stipend. These churches and endowments are still known as burgh churches and stipends.

The government also contributed to the building of new churches through an Act of 1824, which made funds available for the establishment of forty-two new parishes in the remoter areas of the Highlands and Islands. Each parish was provided with a church, a manse, and an endowment for stipend of £120 per annum. These parishes became known as Parliamentary parishes, and the endowed stipend as an Exchequer living.

The Free Church, and after 1900 the United Free Church, was not organized on a parish basis, although the geographical distribution of church buildings was similar to that of the Established Church. At the Disruption in 1843 the newly-constituted Free Church had only about fifty churches, but a large number of new churches were built within a few years with funds raised by national campaigns. This procedure differed from that in the Established Church, where new churches were built locally with local funds.

Much of the practical significance of the distinction between *quoad omnia* and *quoad sacra* parishes was brought to an end in 1929 by two measures. Firstly, the united Church of Scotland was given the power to redraw its parish boundaries in order to incorporate the churches of the United Free Church into the parish system. Secondly, 1929 also saw the Act which reorganized local government in Scotland. The Act had the effect of divorcing local government organization from the parish system. The churches of the United Free Church became parishes *quoad sacra* at the Union, as do most 'church extension' parishes today on their erection to full status.

The terms *quoad omnia* and *quoad sacra* are still in use, though parishes tend to be referred to as 'former *quoad omnia*' (or 'former old parish') and 'former *quoad sacra*' parishes. No practical consequence now follows from the distinction, except in the fact that *quoad sacra* parishes have a separate financial court.

3 Property and funds before and after 1925[3]

In this section we examine the position of Church property and funds before the passing of the Church of Scotland (Property and Endowment) Act of 1925, and the position after 1925 as changed by the Act. The property and funds of the pre-Union Church of Scotland and the United Free Church are examined in turn. We then briefly describe the impact of the 1929 Union.

1 The Church of Scotland

The position regarding the property and funds in the pre-Union Church of Scotland prior to the Act of 1925 was as follows. Parishes *quoad onmia* held the following property and funds: churches and manses erected and maintained by heritors or the town councils of burghs; stipends payable out of the teinds; stipends of burgh churches; Exchequer grants; the glebe lands.

There were also parishes *quoad sacra*. The statutory requirements were that such parishes should normally have a church and a manse, together with an endowment for stipend of a specified minimum amount. In addition to these statutory endowments, there were frequently other endowments held in trust by individual or *ex officiis* trustees.

A third category of church was found in the small number of Parliamentary churches in the Highlands and Islands, so-called because their ministers were supported by the income of funds voted by Parliament under statute. Some of these were later erected as parishes *quoad sacra*.

In addition, large amounts of property and funds were held by the central committees of the Church. These consisted of heritable properties and securities, and investments in moveable property. They were frequently held in the names of individuals as trustees, whose death or resignation required transfers or other legal proceedings involving considerable expense and inconvenience. With a view to obviating this, the Church in 1921 obtained a Provisional Order, confirmed by Act of Parliament, known as The Church of Scotland (General Trustees) Order Confirmation Act, 1921, which incorporated the General Trustees. The order provided for the transfer to the General Trustees of various specified properties, securities and investments, and for its accepting from, and holding on behalf of, any funds, property or investments from any committee or association making a report to the General Assembly. (The properties and investments so transferred and vested in the General Trustees are now vested in the Church of Scotland Trust, incorporated by The Church of Scotland Trust Order Confirmation Act, 1932.)

This, briefly, was the state of affairs prior to the Church of Scotland (Property and Endowments) Act, 1925, which was passed with a view to the 1929 Union. The position following that Act, and the Amendment Act of 1933, was as follows.

In parishes *quoad omnia* the following changes took place. The teind stipend was standardized, and made payable to the General Trustees;[4] this had the effect of changing it from a personal debt of heritors to a 'standard charge' on the lands. Burgh stipends and Exchequer grants were redeemed by capital payments to the General Trustees. The Act of 1925 ended the obligation of heritors to maintain and repair the property specified, and all rights of property were fully vested in the General Trustees. Burgh churches and manses, and other endowments held for the benefit of ministers by way of stipend, were vested in the General Trustees. Under the 1925 Act, glebe lands became vested in the General Trustees. Glebe feu-duties and investments resulting from the sale of glebe lands were also vested in the General Trustees, who have the right to sell or feu a glebe, subject to the direction of the General Assembly and to the right of adjoining heritors.

Parishes *quoad sacra* were affected in the following way by the 1925 and 1933 Acts. Under the Act of 1925 the statutory properties and endowments of those parishes erected before the passing of the Act were transferred to the General Trustees. Under the 1933 Act the General Trustees can require that non-statutory properties of parishes *quoad sacra* be vested in the General Trustees, or in a permanent body of local trustees – usually the minister, session clerk and treasurer of the congregation. The statutory properties and endowments vested in the General Trustees or other trustees may be sold, if the General Assembly agrees through an Act. Non-statutory property and endowments may also be sold, subject to any trust under which they are held and to the approval of Presbytery.

All the churches and manses of the Parliamentary parishes were transferred to the General Trustees. Such property can be sold, subject to the consent of the General Assembly through an Act of Assembly and to the provisions of a trust (if any).

With regard to endowments, the 1925 Act specifies that '. . . all monies received by the General Trustees with respect to any parish . . . shall be appropriated in the first place to meeting the proper requirements of that parish or its neighbourhood . . .' This applies to standardized stipend and Exchequer monies in charges which fall vacant, and to the proceeds of sales of property.[5] The 'proper requirements' are determined by the General Assembly, which by an Act of 1953 delegated this authority to the Committee on the Maintenance of the Ministry.

2 The United Free Church of Scotland
The property which before the 1929 Union belonged to the United Free Church of Scotland comprised: (i) the property which before the 1900 Union belonged to the Free Church of Scotland; (ii) the property which before the 1900 Union belonged to the United Presbyterian Church; (iii) the property acquired by the United Free Church after the 1900 Union.

The properties belonging to Free Church congregations prior to 1900 were held largely by local trustees – usually the minister and office-bearers – for their respective congregations. In a few instances, the title was in favour of the General Trustees of the Free Church. In nearly all cases, titles took the form of the Model Trust Deed of the Free Church. This declared that the trustees holding property had no power to burden them with debt, or to sell them, except for the purpose of providing another place of worship or manse, and then only with the consent of the General Assembly. A few congregations held property on titles not under the Model Trust Deed, which gave them the power to dispose of their property without the consent of the General Assembly.

After the Union of 1900, and the decision in 1905 of the House of Lords which allocated a very large majority of the properties of the former Free Church to the united Church, it was further effected that properties held in the name of the General Trustees of the Free Church were transferred to the General Trustees of the United Free Church, and, in cases where titles were in favour of local trustees, properties were transferred to the ministers and office-bearers of the respective congregations. Subject to the regulation and direction of the General Assembly, the Trustees have the power to sell property and to burden it with debt, except in cases where the titles prior to Union did not give to the General Assembly of the Free Church any power of regulation, where the same situation prevailed.

The congregational properties belonging to United Presbyterian Church congregations prior to 1900 were vested in trustees for the congregation. The trustees comprised either various office-bearers of the congregation with, in a few cases, the Moderator and Clerk of Presbytery, or individuals in full communion elected by members of the congregation. In many cases the trustees held property on terms specified in the Model Trust Deed of 1892.

Finally, there are the properties acquired by congregations of the United Free Church after the 1900 Union. In former United Presbyterian Church congregations the titles of those properties were usually taken in the same terms as the titles of the existing properties of congregations. In other cases they were taken in the names of the Minister, session clerk and Deacons' Court of the congregation, as trustees for the congregation. Normally, the trustees, subject to the regulation and direction of the General Assembly of the Church, have the power to sell property or burden it with debt.

In addition to churches, manses and other congregational buildings, the United Free Church at the 1929 Union possessed other properties and investments belonging to various committees, associations and bodies. The titles to these were vested in the General Trustees of the Church, the United Free Church of Scotland Trust, trustees acting under a variety of trusts, or individuals holding on behalf of the Church. The properties and investments formerly vested in the General Trustees and Trust, and in certain cases in other trusts and individuals, are now all vested in the Church of Scotland Trust.

3 The 1929 Union and after

By virtue of the Union between the Free Church and the United Presbyterian Church in 1900 to form the United Free Church, and the Union of the United Free Church with the Church of Scotland in 1929, the properties belonging to the United Free Church and its branches now belong to the Church of Scotland.

Since 1929 some of the properties of the former United Free Church have been transferred by congregational trustees to the General Trustees on behalf of the congregations concerned. By early 1977 some 427 properties – churches, halls and manses – had been transferred; this figure includes about 200 churches. Only a small proportion of these transfers have been voluntary on the part of local trustees, since voluntary transfers are discouraged by the legal expenses involved. Most transfers have occurred as a result of a union,[6] where it is proposed to use some of the proceeds of the sale of a building vested in the General Trustees to be held as a fabric fund for the congregation concerned to repair a former Free Church property, where that property is not vested in the General Trustees. In these circumstances the trustees insist that the property is vested in themselves. Such transfers are therefore by no means automatic on the occurrence of a union involving a former Free Church congregation, since their church may already be vested in the General Trustees; or it may be the building which is to be made redundant as a result of the union.

Other cases of transfer occur where grants are received by a congregation from the Home Mission Committee or Property Committee of the Home Board, or any other committee making grants out of general Church funds for the maintenance and repair of congregational property. The General Assembly have directed that in all such cases the grants are made on the condition that the title to the ecclesiastical property concerned is either (a) transferred to the General Trustees, subject to the direction and control of the General Assembly, or (b) vested in a body of local trustees *ex officiis*, under the express condition that the property concerned should not be sold or burdened with debt except with the consent of the General Assembly.

4 The position today
In this section we attempt to summarize the present position regarding the general disposition of the ownership of Church property, and the responsibilities of the various bodies concerned with the repair and maintenance of that property. We also briefly examine the role of the Church of Scotland Trust.

1 The General Trustees
The General Trustees are the largest property-owning body in the Church. As we have seen, they were created and incorporated under the Church of Scotland (General Trustees) Order Confirmation Act, 1921, to hold properties and investments for the Assembly committees of the pre-Union Church of Scotland.

Their duties and powers were greatly extended by the Church of Scotland (Property and Endowments) Act, 1925, as amended in 1933. Under this Act the trustees became an administrative as well as a holding body, subject always to the directions of the General Assembly. The principal duty of the General Trustees under the Act was to ensure that the whole properties and endowments of the pre-Union Church of Scotland were legally transferred to, and vested in them on behalf of the whole Church, thus placing the Church in a position of absolute ownership of those properties and endowments which it had not held since the Reformation.

The properties and investments vested in the Trustees under the 1921 Act were transferred to the Church of Scotland Trust on its incorporation under the Church of Scotland Trust Order Confirmation Act, 1932. The intention of this Act was that there should be two bodies of central trustees, one – the Church of Scotland Trust – holding the properties and funds of central committees, and the other – the General Trustees – holding congregational properties and funds with statutory powers of administration and disposal. Today the properties vested in the trust include the Church's social service homes and its headquarters at 121, George Street, Edinburgh. However, the trust is essentially an investment body; it merely holds these properties, and exercises almost no administrative functions over them.

2 Ownership of property

In examining the ownership of congregational property, the basic distinction is whether the property is vested or is not vested in the General Trustees. We examine each possibility in turn.

A Property vested in the General Trustees.

Although no exact figures are available, it is estimated that at least three-fifths of congregational property (in terms of the numbers of congregations involved) is vested in the General Trustees. The great bulk of this property comprises pre-1929 Church of Scotland congregational property transferred to the trustees following the 1925 Act. Some pre-1929 Church of Scotland property is vested in the congregations concerned. The bulk of former Free Church congregational property is not vested in the trustees, although 427 such properties have been transferred to the trustees since 1929.

All properties vested in the General Trustees must be insured through them. They effect insurance through the Church of Scotland Insurance Trust, which ensures that the risk is shared by a number of leading insurance companies. The amount of insurance cover should be reviewed from time to time to meet increasing building costs. Fire insurance effected by the General Trustees totalled £144 millions in 1975.[7]

B Property not vested in the General Trustees.

The remaining two-fifths or less of Church property is not vested in the General Trustees. This groups falls largely into two categories, as follows.

The first category, which forms as much as 80 per cent of the group (or over 30 per cent of the total), comprises those properties whose sale is subject to the consent of the General Assembly. Two different forms of consent are required in different cases. The consent of the General Assembly by Act of Assembly is required in cases of statutory and certain non-statutory *quoad sacra* properties, burgh churches, Parliamentary properties, certain *quoad omnia* properties and certain mission properties. The consent of the General Assembly by a deliverance is required in cases of most former United Free properties and properties acquired since 1929 and put under Assembly control.

The Custodier of Titles is the official who submits proposals for the sale of property in this category for the approval of the General Assembly and Commission of Assembly. However, these bodies have only a loose control of such property, and some properties are sold without their approval being sought by the congregations concerned.

The second category of property not vested in the General Trustees, forming about 20 per cent of the group (or less than 10 per cent of the total), comprises those properties whose sale is not subject to the approval of the General Assembly. These properties include former United Presbyterian, Free Church, and some *quoad omnia* church congregational property. Such property is normally sold subject to the consent of the Presbytery of the bounds.

It is a curious paradox that while, broadly speaking, the properties now vested centrally in the General Trustees were mainly built locally — the pre-1929 Church of Scotland congregational property was built largely by the heritors of the parish

— the Free Church congregational properties, which are owned locally, were built mainly using funds raised centrally for church extension.

3 Repair and maintenance of property
Under the 1925 Act the General Trustees have a continuing obligation to see that the properties vested in them are carefully preserved and maintained for the Church. Since no funds are provided by the General Assembly for this purpose, the actual cost of upkeep is borne by congregations. It is the duty of the Kirk Session or financial court to maintain in proper order and repair all congregational property, whether vested in the General Trustees or otherwise. Under an Act of Assembly of 1961, fabric committees must be appointed in every congregation to inspect all ecclesiastical properties each year, although this duty is sometimes neglected. A property register must be kept and submitted annually to Presbytery for attestation. The Presbytery reports annually to Synod, and the Synod to the General Assembly through the General Administration Committee. No building operations or repairs to Church buildings may start without the consent of Presbytery and, in the case of property vested in the General Trustees, without the further consent of the Trustees.[8] To finance such repair and maintenance work, it has been recommended by the General Assembly that the maintenance of an adequate local fabric fund should be a first charge on the income of the congregation. The Assembly has further recommended that the fabric fund should be such as to produce an annual income of not less than ½ of 1 per cent of the insurable value of the ecclesiastical property in the parish.[9]

The fabric requirements of the parish are normally the first charge on the proceeds of sale of property. Many of the fabric funds of individual congregations are derived from the proceeds of sale of property, and these funds form the bulk of the total. They are held on behalf of the congregation by the General Trustees or the General Treasurer, or by the congregation itself.

The General Trustees hold the bulk of the congregational fabric funds derived from sales of property. In 1976 the capital and revenue combined amounted to over £4 millions. These funds are derived from sales of property vested in the trustees. When a property has been sold and the proceeds of sale are to be applied in this way, the secretary of the trustees asks the views of the local financial court as to whether the fund should be invested in the General (Unit) Investment Fund or the Deposit Fund of the Church of Scotland Trust, or partly in one and partly in the other. The trend in recent years has been more towards retaining such funds with the Deposit Fund.[10]

For the congregational property of the Church not vested in the General Trustees, but where sales have to be approved by the General Assembly, the Assembly normally directs the proceeds to the General Treasurer of the Church, and specifies the use to which the funds are to be put. Usually the General Treasurer holds such funds for fabric purposes.

In those congregations whose property is not vested in the General Trustees, and where sales have to be approved by Presbytery but not by the General Assembly, the proceeds are retained by the congregations, normally for fabric purposes. In one famous case several years ago a Glasgow congregation sold its church, which was situated in the centre of the city, for £750,000. The proceeds were retained by the congregation.

The Church and Ministry Department holds a small amount of fabric funds for church extension charges.

The Property Committee of the Home Board also has funds available for fabric repairs and building works, for which any congregation is entitled to apply.

4 The Church of Scotland Trust

In 1929 both the Church of Scotland and the United Free Church had a body of trustees. Also, various persons or sets of persons, either as trustees or as individuals, had the titles to Church properties and investments in their names. With a view to all these properties and investments being held by a single body of trustees for the Church of Scotland, the Church of Scotland Trust was incorporated in 1932 by the Church of Scotland Trust Order, 1932. The order vested in the trust all the properties and investments detailed in a schedule, to be held by the trust for the same ends, uses and purposes for which they were held by the trustees in whom they were formerly vested. The trust may also accept from, and hold on behalf of, any committee, congregation, association, trustees, or body connected with the Church, any properties and investments which they may desire to transfer to the trust. They may receive on behalf of the Church, General Assembly, or any committee, etc., any gift, legacy or bequest to which it has become entitled. The trust has the power on behalf of the Church, General Assembly, etc., to sue for and recover all property and funds to which it may be entitled.

The funds held by the trust on behalf of committees, congregations, etc., are held in the General Investment Fund, Special Investment Account, and Deposit Fund. The funds in the General Investment Fund are held in a common pool in the form of a 'unit trust' for permanent and long-term investment. The investment policy is determined by a Committee of Trustees comprising mainly elders of the Church who have a wide professional investment experience; there is no limit to the amount which can be invested. The Special Investment Account is used for the investments of committees, congregations, etc., and under their direction (i.e. for the investment in a particular security). The Deposit Fund is for the short-term investments of committees and congregations. The investments are held in a common pool. Units may be purchased at £5 each up to a maximum of £50,000. The minimum period of investment is three months, and withdrawals may be made at seven days' notice.

The trust has taken advantage of the 1961 Trustee Investments Act. Formerly, trust funds were restricted to a very limited range of investments in fixed interest securities under the Trusts (Scotland) Act, 1921. The real value of such investments tends to decline with inflation. Under the 1961 Act, however, a trustee may divide trust funds into two equal parts. The first half, called the 'narrower range', is limited to investments authorized by the 1921 Act, together with some other types of fixed interest securities. The second half, called the 'wider range', may consist of ordinary and preference shares and stocks of companies incorporated in the United Kingdom, having issued paid up capital of at least £1 million, and having paid a dividend on all ordinary shares for the preceding five years; shares in designated building societies; and unit trusts. Once the initial investment has been separated into two parts of equal value, the parts must remain separate with no net transfers between the two. Under the Act, the trustees may invest funds in the following investments without obtaining advice: Defence Bonds, National

Savings Certificates, deposits in the Post Office Savings Bank, ordinary deposits in Trustee Savings Banks, and deposits in banks. In all other investments, the trustees are required to obtain written advice before making any investment from a person whom they reasonably believe to be qualified by ability and practical experience.

5 The Baird Trust
The Baird Trust was established in 1873 as a private trust. It makes grants for the erection of churches and church halls; the enlargement, renovation and improvement of churches and halls; and the endowment and further endowment of churches. It is customary to insert in the titles the condition that the subjects are inalieniably secured in the Church of Scotland.

5 Conclusions
In this chapter we conclude our background survey of the history and constitution of the Church of Scotland by dealing with the Church's tenure of its property and funds, and with the responsibilities of the various bodies concerned.

Section 2 briefly outlined how the Church accumulated over the years the property and funds which it now holds, and drew the distinction between *quoad omnia* and *quoad sacra* parishes.

In the following section we described how the property and funds held centrally in the pre-Union Church of Scotland were transferred to the General Trustees, which were established under the Church of Scotland (General Trustees) Order Confirmation Act, 1921. These endowments were later transferred to the Church of Scotland Trust when it was incorporated by the Church of Scotland Trust Order Confirmation Act, 1932. In the case of congregational property, the great bulk of the pre-Union Church of Scotland property was transferred to the General Trustees under the Church of Scotland (Property and Endowments) Act, 1925 which also made the trustees an administrative as well as a holding body. The congregational properties of the United Free Church and its branches became the property of the Church of Scotland at the Union of 1929. Subsequent to the Union, a small proportion of these properties have been transferred to the General Trustees, although the bulk remains vested locally.

Finally, in section 4 we saw that today at least three-fifths of congregational property is vested in the General Trustees, and that the remainder is vested locally, although in the latter case most of the property can only be sold with the approval of the General Assembly.

Under the 1925 Act the Trustees have the obligation to keep in good repair all properties vested in them. Since the General Assembly votes no funds for this purpose, the actual cost of upkeep is borne by congregations. It is the duty of Kirk Sessions and financial courts to keep in good repair all property, whether vested in the General Trustees or not. To this end, the General Assembly have recommended that the maintenance of an adequate fabric fund should be the first charge on the income of the congregation. The bulk of such funds are derived from the proceeds of sale of property, most of which are held centrally by the General Trustees and General Treasurer.

A large part of the investments of the Church, including much of the centrally held fabric funds, are held in the Church of Scotland Trust. The Trust has taken advantage of the Trustee Investments Act, 1961 to invest in non-fixed interest bearing securities.

Notes

1 Some new *quoad omnia* parishes were established subsequent to 1560 by application to the Court of Sessions.

2 Certain parish churches, such as St Giles' and St Cuthbert's in Edinburgh, had a great tradition of building new churches.

3 Much of the material in this section is taken from J.T. Cox, op.cit.

4 The various endowments for stipend, including the standardized stipend, are described in detail in chapter 10.

5 The present procedure regarding the reallocation of endowments is described in chapter 10, and an alternative procedure, formulated in connection with policy towards stipend, is proposed in chapter 11.

6 A 'union' is the merging of two or more congregations into one under one minister and Kirk Session. This normally results in the buildings of one or more congregations being made redundant. A fuller explanation is given in chapter 13.

7 The General Trustees also deal with the rating and valuation of property, the administration of glebes, the collection of standardized stipend, and the sale, feuing and let of property held. A commission of eight per cent is currently charged on all funds collected for stipend and other purposes.

8 Cox, p.43.

9 ibid., p. 28.

10 The Church of Scotland Trust is described briefly in this chapter, and analysed in greater detail in chapter 19.

II
Economic analysis and forecasts

Chapter 4

Membership

1 Introduction
In our view, the question of membership is one of the most important the Church has to face. The life of the Church centres around the congregations, and if many of these are weakened through a steady erosion of membership numbers and active support, then the strength of the Church as a whole will be sapped. This view is supported by many in the Church. 'The root issue for the Church of Scotland today . . . is the issue of membership . . . The Church cannot put off dealing with a situation in which half of its so-called members are unrecognisable as such. We have to identify and marshall our real task force.'[1]

Various statistical studies have revealed the importance of the membership in the financial position of the Church. In our Church income forecasting equation, which is described in the following chapter, the membership of the Church is one of the two most important determining variables, and the only one of the four independent variables over which the Church has some direct influence. Similarly, the analysis of congregational finance in chapter 12 reveals that a large part of the variation in income between congregations is accounted for by the membership numbers. In both cases, an increase in membership is associated with an increase in income.

The purpose of this chapter is to describe the membership of the Church, to analyse the trends in numbers during this century, to make forecasts of numbers up to the end of the century, and to suggest measures to counter the present membership decline.

We start in section 2 by defining membership, and within the membership draw the distinctions between communicants, baptized persons, and adherents. The demographic characteristics of the membership population is described with the help of several different surveys.

This is followed in section 3 by the analysis of membership trends over the period 1891-1975. The numbers of communicant members, annual communicants, and members on the Supplementary Roll are examined in turn. Variations in the trends of communicant members, disaggregated by Presbytery, are examined. Various membership/population ratios are calculated to test the secularization hypothesis that there is a long-run decline both in religious activity and in the Churches.

The reasons for the fluctuations in membership numbers from year to year are examined in section 4, particularly the reversal in 1956 of the upward trend in members following the war. Then in the following section an attempt is made to forecast membership numbers up to the year 2001; attempts to build an econometric model of membership prove unsuccessful, so that recourse is had to linear regression.

Finally, in section 6 we turn to the question of membership policy. Various policy measures are suggested which should help to reduce, if not reverse, the twenty year decline in membership numbers.

2 The membership

The membership of the Church comprises members in full-communion and baptized persons. Members in full communion (otherwise known as 'communicants' or 'communicant members') are those who are permitted to attend Communion service, and who have been admitted as such by the Kirk Session of the congregation. The names and addresses of communicant members appear on the Communion Roll of the congregation to which they belong. The total number on the Rolls in 1975 (at 31 December) was 1,041,772.[2]

Baptized persons connected with the congregation, but not admitted to full communion, are members and are under the care of the Kirk Session. A list of their names is normally kept on a roll by the Kirk Session. Many of the baptized persons will be the children of communicant members. Also included in this group are 'adherents'. Adherents are persons of mature age who may attend services regularly, be active in the life of the congregation, and contribute to the life of the Church, but who usually do not feel themselves *ready* to make a formal Profession of Faith and to take part in Communion. While their numbers are not large in relation to the total communicant membership, they may outnumber such members by as much as 2:1 or more in some of the small congregations in the Highlands. Adherents are a feature of the Free Church tradition, and their geographical distribution reflects the strength of the former Free Church in those areas.

The duties of members are defined as follows: 'It is the duty of members to give faithful attendance on Gospel ordinances; to give their minister all due honour and respect in the Lord; to submit to the Kirk Session as over them in the Lord; to cherish a brotherly spirit among themselves; to promote the peace and prosperity of the congregation; and to share with their minister the responsibility for Christian witness and Christian service. It is also their duty to take a lively interest in all that concerns the welfare of the whole Church and to give of their means, as the Lord shall prosper them, for the maintenance of the Christian ministry and the furtherance of the Gospel at home and abroad; and to manifest a Christian spirit in all relationships of life.'[3]

Only members in full communion have the right to take part in the business of congregational meetings, with the exception that adherents of twenty-one years of age and over may have their names added to the Electoral Roll, and may take part in meetings concerned with a vacancy and the election of a minister.

As a rule people do not become communicant members of the Church of Scotland until at least the age of seventeen, so that the communicant membership comprises people over that age. Evidence suggests that the age distribution of members is weighted towards the middle-aged and old, in common with the memberships of many other western denominations. In 1970 the Advisory Board obtained information on the role of young people in the Church by means of a survey of forty congregations: 'These were selected on a basis of population, fifteen being city charges, eleven urban and fourteen rural. A letter was sent to the session clerks and replies to a simple questionnaire were asked of the session clerks themselves, an older elder, a committee member of the Woman's Guild. and an office-bearer or member under the age of thirty-five. Of the congregations approached there were replies from thirty-four, and of 160 possible individual replies 123 were received. A summary was made of the results, account being taken of material from the National Council of Youth Fellowships and from others whose work has been in the same field . . .'[4]

The analysis of the percentage of membership and of office-bearers under thirty-five years of age is shown in table 1. Assuming that the thirty congregations are reasonably representative of the Church as a whole, the figures indicate that in 1970 just over one-fifth (21.67 per cent) of the membership of the Church of Scotland was under thirty-five years of age. This figure varied slightly between congregations, urban congregations having the highest average proportion of members under thirty-five (25.29 per cent) and rural congregations the lowest proportion (19.42 per cent). The numbers of elders and of all office-bearers under thirty-five was found to be 6.3 per cent and 9.8 per cent respectively, indicating that the young age-group is very much under-represented amongst lay church officials.

TABLE 1
The proportion of members, elders, and office-bearers aged under 35 in a sample of 30 congregations, 1970.

	All	City	Urban	Rural
Number of congregations	30	11	8	11
Members under 35 (%)	21.67	20.30	25.29	19.42
Elders under 35 (%)	6.3	3.4	8.5	9.5
All office-bearers under 35 (%)	9.8	8.9	10.5	12.3

These figures only become significant when they are compared with the proportion of the Scottish population in the relevant age-groups, which means taking those people aged under thirty-five but excluding those who are too young to be considered as potential church members. If we take seventeen as the age when young people join the Church in numbers, then the breakdown of the Scottish population for 1970 into the relevant age groups is shown in table 2.

TABLE 2
Statistics of the population of Scotland, 1970

Total population of Scotland	5,199,000
Population aged 17 and over	3,679,000
Population aged 17-34	1,248,900
Population aged 35 and over	2,430,100

SOURCE: Central Statistic Office, *Annual Abstract of Statistics* No. 108, (H.M.S.O. 1971), Table 10, p. 11.

Since we have assumed that all members of the Church are aged seventeen and over, it is necessary, in order to avoid distorting the percentage figures, to exclude the 'under 17' age group from the population figures by setting the '17 and over' group equal to 100 per cent. On this basis, the percentage comparison of the age distribution of the Church membership with the age distribution of the Scottish population at large is as shown in table 3. The percentage figures reveal a considerable under-representation of younger people in the Church membership, and a corresponding over-representation of older people, compared with the age distribution of the Scottish population. Whereas in the Scottish population aged 17 and over almost 34 in every hundred people are aged 17 – 34, in the Church of Scotland less than 22 in every hundred members are in that age group. Similarly, in the Scottish population aged 17 and over, just over 66 in every 100 people are aged 35 and over, whereas in the Church of Scotland over 78 in every hundred members are in that age group.

TABLE 3

A comparison of the age-distribution of the Church of Scotland membership with that of the Scottish population, 1970.

	Church of Scotland membership		Scottish population	
	%	numbers*	%	numbers
17 – 34	21.67	250,118	33.95	1,248,900
35 and over	78.33	904,093	66.05	2,430,100
TOTAL	100.00	1,154,211	100.00	3,679,000

*Estimated figures, based on percentage results in table 1.

A chi-square (X^2) test was carried out on the data to test its statistical significance, using the percentages of the Scottish population and Church membership age under 35 and 35 and over. The null hypothesis is that the age split in the Church population should be the same as that for the Scottish population as a whole, implying that there is no relation between age and Church membership. The observed data is shown in table 4. With one degree of freedom, the chi-square statistic is significant at the 1 per cent level. This means that there is only a one-in-a-hundred chance that the observed data arose at random, thus strongly implying that there is a positive relation between age and Church membership.

TABLE 4

A chi-square test of significance on the relationship between age and Church membership.

	Percentage of ages	
	17 – 35	35 and over
Scottish population	33.95	66.05
Church membership	21.67	78.33

$$x^2 = 6.724$$
$$(n = 1; x^2_{.01} = 6.635, x^2_{.001} = 10.827)$$

Table 3 also indicates that the 1,154,211 members of the Church of Scotland in 1970 formed almost a third (31.4 per cent) of the Scottish population aged 17 and over.

We have concentrated on the age distribution of the membership of the Church of Scotland because of its significance in what follows. Further evidence shows that the composition of the membership of that Church is also biased in other directions, i.e. in relation to the male/female breakdown, social class and the like. This evidence is provided by Sissons' study of Falkirk,[5] and by the work of Robertson[6] and Watson[7] in Edinburgh. Their findings may be very briefly summarised as follows:

Male/female breakdown. One feature which strongly emerged from the studies was the predominance of women in the samples of those attending church. Sissons produced a figure of 67 per cent for his sample of five churches in Falkirk; Watson calculated a figure of 63 per cent for her sample of three churches in Edinburgh. Sissons points out that while 'all the churches in Falkirk have a larger percentage of women than men in their congregations, the Church of Scotland stands out in a statistically significant manner as having an unusually high percentage of women amongst the church members.'[8]

Social class: Sissons found that the membership of the Churches in Falkirk was predominantly middle-class; there was a relative absence of partly-skilled and unskilled manual workers and their families. This imbalance was felt most acutely by the congregations of the Church of Scotland, and closely associated with it was the absence, particularly from Church of Scotland congregations, of those members of the population with little or no further education. In the study conducted by Robertson in 1965 of the relationship to the church of middle-class and working-class men in a district of Edinburgh, a 'relative working-class abstention from the church' was found.

Marital status: A disproportionate percentage of church members consists of single people, although this is at least partly related to age, since a high proportion is found in the older age-groups. Both Sissons and Watson found that 21 per cent of their samples were composed of single people. In Falkirk the proportion of non-Church members who were single was 17 per cent.

From the limited information available from these various studies, none of which are based on a fully representative sample of Church of Scotland members, it seems that the membership is disproportionately weighted in favour of the middle-aged and old, women, single people, the middle-class, and the well educated. Surveys of other Protestant churches have produced similar findings.

3 Membership trends 1891-1975

In the previous section we saw that the membership of the Church of Scotland comprises two groups: members in full communion, and baptised persons. Only statistics of the former group are collected centrally and published, and it is this group which is normally referred to as the membership of the Church. For the rest of this book we take members in full communion as forming the membership of the Church.

Figure 3 shows the membership figures for the Church of Scotland for the years 1921 and 1926, and for the period 1928-73. Figures are also available for 1891, 1901 and 1911. All the pre-1929 figures show the pre-union joint membership of the Church of Scotland and United Free Church.

FIGURE 3 Communicant membership, annual communicants, and Supplementary Roll numbers, 1921-75.

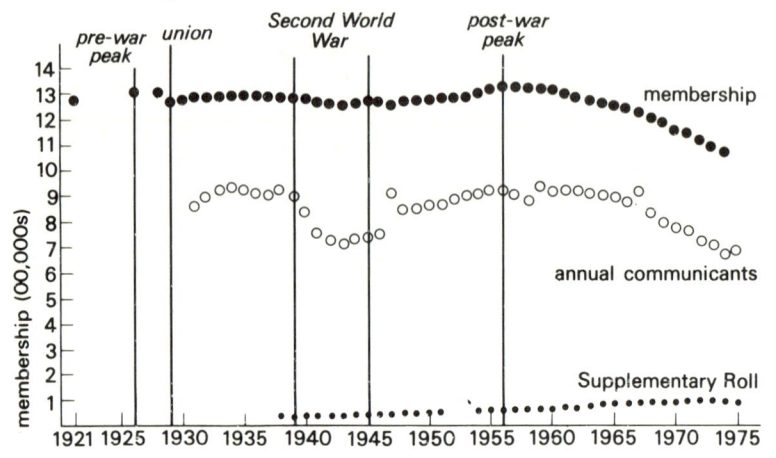

Some key statistics for 1946, 1956 and 1975 given in Table 5 indicate that membership reached a pre-war (and an all-time) peak of almost 1.3 million in 1926. In 1929 the membership figure shows a sharp drop of over 25,000 as a result of the establishment of a continuing United Free Church following the Union. Numbers recovered a little in subsequent years before falling during the Second World War, reaching a low point of 1,256,000 in 1947. Following the war, the membership numbers slowly recovered again, reaching a post-war (and all-time) peak of 1,319,000 in 1956. This peaking of the figures may have been helped by a Billy Graham crusade in Britain in 1955. Since 1956 membership has fallen in every year without exception to the present, fairly slowly at first, but at a faster rate from 1967 onwards. By 1975 membership totalled 1,041,772, giving a fall of 21.1 per cent since 1956, as shown in table 5. Thus, contrary to some views which seem to imply that declining membership in the Church of Scotland is a long-run phenomenon, the membership figures in figure 3 show no very marked trends between 1926 and 1956, but indicate that the sharp decline has occurred only in the last twenty years.

We have seen that the membership of the Church is made up of the total number of people on the parish Communion Rolls at any one time. However, the limitations of these statistics should be borne in mind. While Kirk Sessions are required to revise the Rolls annually as at 31 December, this duty is often neglected, so that in many cases they are out-of-date. Even where revisions are periodically carried out, it appears that there is a reluctance to strike 'lapsed' members from the Rolls. This may reflect a desire to hold on to members, however tenuously, at a time when the total Church membership is in decline.

TABLE 5
Statistics of membership for 1946, 1956 and 1975

		1946	1956	Percentage change between 1 and 2	1975	Percentage change between 2 and 4
		1	2	3	4	5
1	TOTAL MEMBERSHIP	1,261,646	1,319,574	+4.6%	1,041,772	−21.1%
2	Removals,					
	by death	20,041	20,671	+3.1%	20,445	−1.1%
	by certificate	36,580	42,846	+17.1%	27,819	−35.1%
	without certificate	21,660	18,591	−14.2%	16,842	−9.4%
	TOTAL	78,281	82,108	+4.9%	65,106	−20.7%
3	Admissions					
	on Profession of Faith	38,731	41,804	+7.9%	13,797	−67.0%
	by certificate	34,795	43,493	+25.0%	24,495	−43.7%
	by resolution	6,474	9,329	+44.1%	5,880	−37.0%
	TOTAL	80,000	94,626	+18.3%	44,172	−53.3%
4	Turnover of the membership per year (i.e. 2 and 3)	158,281	176,734	+11.7%	109,278	−38.2%
5	Proportion of turnover 4 to membership 1	12.55%	13.39%	+6.7%	10.49%	−21.7%
6	Average annual change in membership	—	+579	—	−14,621	—
7	Annual communicants	747,862	914,031	+22.2%	669,773	−26.7%
8	Proportion of annual communicants 7 to membership 1	59.28%	69.27%	+16.9%	64.29%	−7.2%
9	Average annual change in Annual communicants	—	+1,662	—	−12,856	—
10	Supplementary roll	39,605	55,944	+41.3%	89,357	+59.7%
11	Membership 1: Population ratio	1:3.91	1:3.90	−0.3%	1:5.00	−28.2%
12	Membership 1: adult population (i.e. 20 years +) ratio	1:2.65	1:2.65	0.0%	1:3.36	−26.8%
13	Membership (1): older population (i.e. 35 years +) ratio	1:1.86	1:1.84	−1.1%	1:2.21*	−20.1%*

*Figures for 1972.

A better measure of the *active* membership, who engage in the activities of the Church on a regular basis, would be provided by data giving the frequency with which members attend services. Unfortunately, the Church does not collect such information centrally, and it is doubtful whether many congregations collect the information even on an irregular basis locally. In surveys of church attenders by Sissons in Falkirk[9] and Watson in Edinburgh,[10] both found high frequencies of church attendance; 54 per cent and 58 per cent respectively attended church every Sunday. However, these results hardly reflect the rates of attendance of all the members in the congregations concerned, since the samples of church attenders were certain to be biased in favour of the frequent attenders. Sissons attempted to make an approximate estimate of church attendance patterns amongst the members of the five churches in his sample on the basis of data obtained from the Church of Scotland population and the returns submitted by all congregations to Presbytery. He estimated that 8 per cent of the members attended every Sunday, 15 per cent attended two or three times a month, 3 per cent attended monthly, 34 per cent attended infrequently, and 39 per cent never attended worship. However, these figures for Falkirk almost certainly under-estimate frequencies of attendance for the church as a whole. While Sissons estimates that only 60 per cent of the membership of his five Falkirk churches attend church at all, in the Church as a whole about 65 per cent of the membership attends Communion at least once every year.

An alternative measure of the active membership is provided by the number of members who attend the Communion service at least once a year during any particular year (henceforth called 'annual communicants'). In congregations of the Church of Scotland, Communion is held only two, three or four times a year, depending upon which of the pre-Union traditions the congregation adheres to.[11] It was formerly a requirement of communicants that they should attend Communion at least once every three years, but this measure was revoked a few years ago by the General Assembly.

The numbers of annual communicants for the period 1931-73 are shown in figure 3. The figures should be treated with some caution, however. In most years some congregations fail to make a return of the numbers of their annual communicants, so that the actual figure is under-stated to some extent. Figure 3 shows that, with the exception of the period of the Second World War, the trend in annual communicants parallels quite closely the trend in membership as a whole. Over the whole period between 1931 and 1975 the proportion of annual communicants to members varied only between 64 and 72 per cent, except during the period 1941-6, when annual communicants fell much more sharply than the membership to give percentages of between 56 and 59 per cent; this was probably due to the number of people away from home on war service. Following the war the numbers of annual communicants increased rather more quickly than the membership, and then maintained a plateau level during the late 1950s and early 1960s, when the membership started to fall, so that throughout this period the proportion of annual communicants to members tended to improve, reaching a peak of 71.59 per cent in 1964. Since then, however, the numbers of annual communicants has tended to fall rather more quickly than the membership, so that after 1964 the proportion has fallen quite sharply, reaching a new post-1947 low of 64.29 per cent in 1975.

Also shown in figure 3 is the number of people on the Supplementary Rolls of congregations. These are individuals who through lack of interest or other cause have lapsed from membership, and who have been placed on the Supplementary Roll in the hope that they will eventually return to membership. The numbers on the rolls increased steadily from 1938, when the rolls were introduced, and reached over 89,000 in 1975 — this, no doubt, reflecting the accumulation in the numbers of lapsed members as the membership has declined. Members on the Supplementary Roll are allowed to attend Communion, and may be restored to the Communion Roll by special resolution of the Kirk Session, but they are not eligible to be elected as office-bearers or to take part in congregational meetings.

So far we have been concerned with total Church membership. The overall decline in Church membership should not be allowed to conceal the fact, however, that while the membership in some congregations will be falling quickly, in others it will be rising. A casual examination of the membership trends in a variety of congregations suggested that membership might be tending to fall more rapidly in urban congregations than in rural congregations. In order to test this possibility, membership trends over the period 1960-73 were examined for all Presbyteries. Presbyteries were chosen as the unit of measurement partly because they would cancel out the local variations in the memberships of individual congregations arising from local conditions, and partly because they could be used as rough proxy measures for 'urban' and 'rural' districts.

TABLE 6
Ranking of a selection of Presbyteries by membership decline, 1960-73

Presbytery (reference number in brackets)		Membership 1960	1973	percentage change
(53)	Lochcarron	277	309	+ 11.6
(28)	Lochaber	2,053	2,169	+ 5.7
(3)	Linlithgow & Falkirk	40,796	41,481	+ 1.7
(48)	Inverness	8,521	8,486	− 0.4
(54)	Skye	533	524	− 1.7
(6)	Haddington & Dunbar	17,437	16,800	− 3.7
(5)	Dalkeith	21,581	20,641	− 4.4
(32)	Stirling & Dunblane	31,650	29,491	− 6.8
(4)	Peebles	5,801	5,324	− 8.2
(13)	Wigtown & Stranraer	12,560	11,451	− 8.8
(50)	Tain	1,246	1,126	− 9.6
(25)	Kintyre	3,461	3,116	− 10.0
(36)	St Andrews	11,795	10,536	− 10.7
(37)	Dundee	56,704	50,079	− 11.7
(11)	Dumfries	21,254	18,720	− 11.9
(21)	Lanark	17,529	15,384	− 12.2
(17)	Paisley	47,534	41,185	− 13.4
(14)	Ayr	45,409	39,088	− 13.9
(30)	Perth	24,993	21,346	− 14.6
(20)	Hamilton	78,092	66,611	− 14.7
(7)	Duns	7,306	6,210	− 15.0
(8)	Jedburgh	18,193	15,182	− 16.6
(29)	Dunkeld	4,748	3,943	− 17.0
(46)	Abernethy	2,568	2,130	− 17.1
(39)	Angus & Mearns	41,564	34,171	− 17.8
(40)	Aberdeen	81,386	66,403	− 18.4
(56)	Lewis	1,305	1,055	− 19.2
(58)	Shetland	4,162	3,326	− 20.1
(1)	Edinburgh	129,510	96,676	− 25.4
(19)	Glasgow	201,166	140,543	− 30.1
ALL PRESBYTERY TOTALS		1,308,816	1,093,459	− 16.5

SOURCE OF MEMBERSHIP FIGURES: Church of Scotland, *Reports to the General Assembly*, 1961 and 1974, table A.

The results for a representative sample of about half the Presbyteries are shown in table 6. The average change in membership over the period 1960-73 was − 16.5 per cent, but individual Presbyteries ranged from +11.6 per cent for the Presbytery of Lochcarron to − 30.1 per cent for the Presbytery of Glasgow. The variation in membership changes between Presbyteries is larger than expected, considering the degree of aggregation of the data involved, and is not easy to explain. While the Scottish population has remained virtually stationary over the period, there can be little doubt that population movements have been a factor causing membership changes in at least some Presbyteries. The exceptionally large fall in Church membership in the Presbytery of Glasgow (− 30.1 per cent) must be partly explained by the steady decline in the population of the city over the period. Similarly, the increases in membership in the Presbytery of Linlithgow and Falkirk (+ 1.7 per cent) and the Presbytery of Livingston and Bathgate (+ 6.1 per cent), both very much against the overall trend, have almost certainly been helped by the influx of Glasgow overspill into those towns.

Overall, however, there appears to be few clear-cut trends. The Presbyteries of Glasgow and Edinburgh, which cover the two largest cities in Scotland, have the largest membership declines of all the Presbyteries in Scotland (− 30.1 and − 25.4 per cent respectively). With those exceptions, and possibly also that of Aberdeen (− 18.4 per cent), there appears to be no grouping of urban Presbyteries at the fast declining end of the spectrum, nor of rural Presbyteries at the slow declining end. For example, the three Presbyteries of Uist (− 21.6 per cent), Shetland (− 20.1 per cent) and Lewis (− 19.2 per cent), which can all be classified as rural, join those of Glasgow and Edinburgh to make the five Scottish Presbyteries with the fastest declining memberships. On the other hand, such urban Presbyteries as those of Dundee (− 11.7 per cent) and of Irving and Kilmarnock (− 10.8 per cent) have membership declines well below the average.

Until now we have been dealing with membership of the Church of Scotland in terms of absolute numbers. Figure 4 provides a means of comparing the number of members with the size of the Scottish population for the period 1921-75. The three ratios illustrated relate membership to total population, adult population (aged 20 years and over), and older population (aged 35 years and over). Table 5 indicates that the value of these ratios in 1975 were 1:5.00, 1:3.36 and 1:2.21 (1972 figure) respectively. In the short run, which in this case may be a period of several years, the size of the Scottish population and its age structure will not change greatly, so that the ratio of membership to population tends to vary directly with variations in membership, i.e. an increasing membership leads to an increasing membership/population ratio, and vice versa. Thus, for example, all three ratios rose after the war, reaching high points in 1955 or 1956 which coincided with the 1956 peak in membership, and thereafter began to fall as membership fell.

In the longer run, however, the population of Scotland has tended to increase very slowly, and from the Second World War at least there has been a change in its age composition. These changes are shown in table 7 for the years 1946, 1956 and 1972. The relatively high birth-rate has led to an increase in the proportion of children and young people, while migration has resulted in a fall in the proportion of the population in the 20-34 age group. The proportion of the population over the age of 60 has increased sharply, largely in the latter part of the period. These changes have probably effected the ratios shown in figure 4. For example, the

FIGURE 4. Comparison of membership with membership/population ratios, 1921-75.

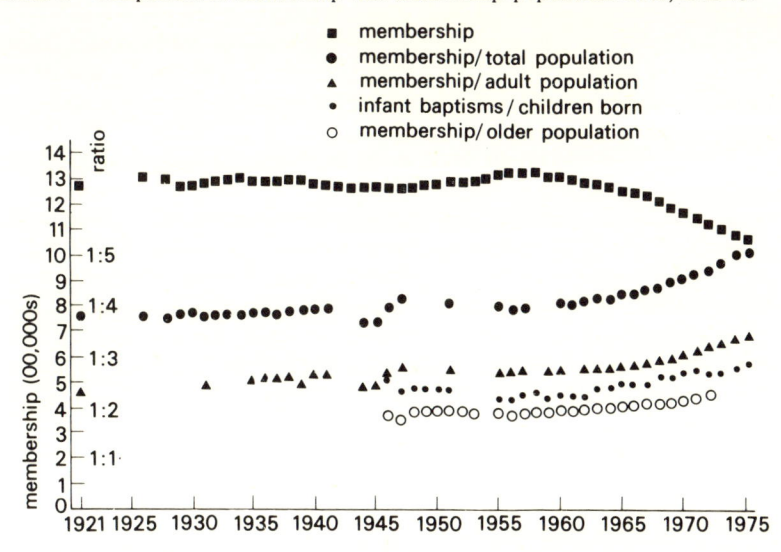

- ■ membership
- ● membership/total population
- ▲ membership/adult population
- • infant baptisms/children born
- ○ membership/older population

growing proportion of the population in the 0-19 age group, who are mostly too young to become Church members, probably accounts for the fact that since 1956 the membership/total population ratio has fallen more quickly than the membership/adult population ratio. Also, in the long-run, where short-term variations such as those caused by the Second World War are ignored, the trend seems to be for a gradual fall in the membership/adult population ratio dating back to 1921 and before. This gives some support to the 'secularization hypothesis', which states that there is a long-run decline in religious participation and in the social role of the Churches; but the fact that the trend has accelerated since 1967 with the sharper rate of fall in membership suggests that changes in the short-run cannot be ignored.

TABLE 7
The age distribution of the Scottish population for the years 1946, 1956 and 1972

	0-19	20-34	35-59	60 and over	Total (000s)
1946	1,533,000	1,154,000	1,623,000	725,000	
	(30.45)	(22.92)	(32.23)	(14.40)	5,035.0
1956	1,649,500	1,061,900	1,670,100	763,100	
	(32.06)	(20.64)	(32.46)	(14.83)	5,144.6
1972	1,739,700	1,011,200	1,514,400	940,100	
	(33.39)	(19.41)	(29.06)	(18.04)	5,205.4

Note: The lower figures are percentages.
SOURCE: *Annual Abstracts of Statistics.*

4 Changes in Membership

The change in membership from year to year results from the difference between the numbers of 'removals' (i.e. those people who are removed from membership each year) and 'admissions' (i.e. those people who are admitted to membership each year). The sum of removals and admissions measures the annual turnover of members. All four elements are shown for the years 1946, 1956 and 1975 in table 5 and are plotted for the period 1921-75 in figure 5. Apart from some small discrepancies between the change in membership from one year to the next and the difference between removals and admissions for the second year in certain years of the period, a deficit of admissions under removals in paralleled by a fall in membership and vice versa. The difference in the membership figures were used where the discrepancies occurred. Until recently the gap between the two has been quite small, indicating the relative constancy of membership. In 1958, however, admissions fell below removals, and the gap has tended to widen ever since, as shown in figure 5, thereby resulting in the sharp fall in membership which has already been noted.

FIGURE 5. Removals and admissions of members, and the membership turnover, 1921-75.

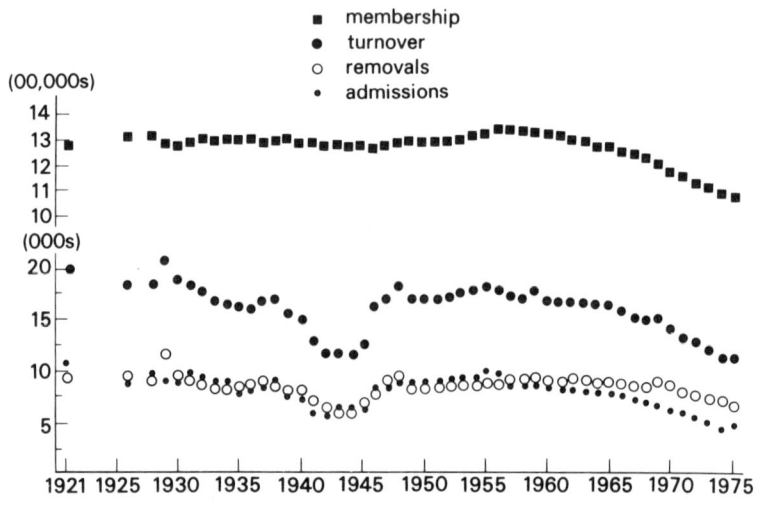

The figures for membership turnover in figure 5 are exaggerated, because they include those people moving between congregations. Since 1949 the trend in turnover has paralleled quite closely the trend in membership, reaching a peak in 1955 when membership was at its height, and declining thereafter. However, the decline in turnover has been proportionately greater than the decline in membership, the proportion of turnover to membership falling from 13.87 per cent in 1955 to 10.49 per cent in 1975. This reflects, at least partly, the growing inability of the Church to attract new members, and perhaps also a reluctance to strike lapsed members off the roll in order to maintain the level of membership in numerical terms.

There are three categories of removals — by death, by certificate, and without certificate — and three categories of admission — on Profession of Faith, by certificate and by resolution. The trends of these different categories are plotted for removals in figure 6, and for admissions in figure 7. The statistics for 1946, 1956 and 1975 are given in table 5. We deal with removals first.

The category 'removals by death' is self-evident. The figures have remained remarkably constant throughout the period under survey, although the fact that membership has declined sharply in recent years means that the proportion of deaths to members has increased. In the ten years 1966-75, removals by death averaged 20,634, with annual figures varying by no more than +2.5 per cent and −3.9 per cent.

'Removal by certificate' involves the transfer of a member from one congregation to another, usually as a result of his moving house. He is given a Transferance Certificate, which indicates that he is in full communion with the Church, and this he is required to lodge with the minister or the session clerk of his new parish. Consequently the 'removal by certificate' category on the removals side is paralleled by an 'admissions by certificate' on the admissions side. The two should be numerically equal, though in practice this is rarely the case, partly because some transferring members take time to choose their new congregation, and partly because others fail to register at all.

The third and final category of removals is 'without certificate'. This category covers those members who are removed for disciplinary reasons or through a lack of interest in the Church, those who emigrate and are unlikely to return, and those who leave the local community and cannot be traced. In recent years the numbers of 'removals without certificate' have fluctuated around 20,000.

Figure 6 shows that because of the relative constancy of removals by death and without certificate and the relatively large numbers of removals by Certificate, the last is responsible for a large part of the variation in total removals. Like most of the figures relating to membership, removals by certificate dropped sharply during the war years, but recovered quickly thereafter. The numbers reached a vaguely defined maximum in the mid-1950s, after which they declined slowly. Since 1969 the decline has been particularly sharp, falling by 26.4 per cent from 40,251 to 27,819 in 1975. This fall may reflect a decline in the geographical mobility

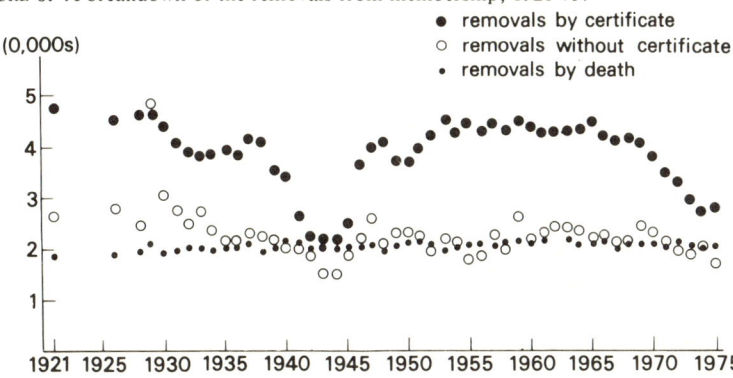

FIGURE 6. A breakdown of the removals from membership, 1921-75.

● removals by certificate
○ removals without certificate
· removals by death

of people in recent years, as the result of job uncertainty caused by the country's recurring economic problems.

As in the case of removals, there are three categories of admissions: on Profession of Faith, by certificate, and by resolution. Figure 7 plots the trends in each of these categories for the period 1921-75, though the figures for admissions by certificate and by resolution are only available separately from 1935.

FIGURE 7. A breakdown of the admissions to membership, 1921-75.

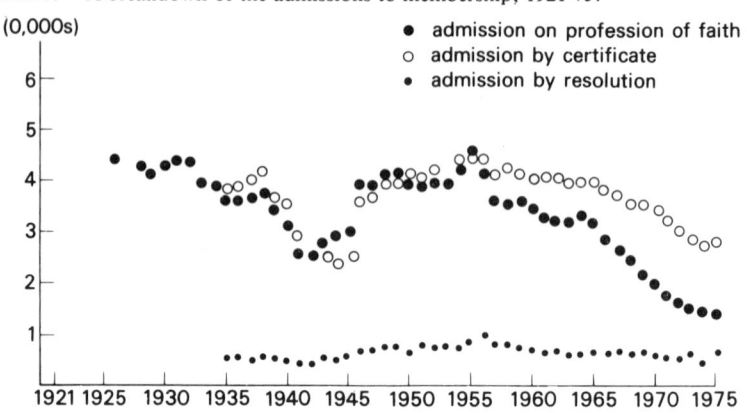

- admission on profession of faith
- ○ admission by certificate
- · admission by resolution

Those entering the Church on Profession of Faith constitute new members of the Church. The Profession of Faith is usually preceded by a process of religious nurture, a process which is formally expressed in the Sunday School and Bible Class, and less formally in the family and school. There is no fixed minimum age of eligibility for membership of the Church, but few join before the age of seventeen. Mostly they come from church-going families. Figure 7 shows that their numbers follow the familiar trend, with a sharp decline during the war followed by a rise in their numbers thereafter. A very pronounced peak was reached in 1955, coinciding with the year of the Billy Graham crusade, followed by a sharp decline, especially from 1964 onwards. In the twelve years between 1964 and 1975 admissions on Profession of Faith declined from 32,385 to 13,797 per year, a fall of 57.4 per cent.

The second category of admissions, by certificate follows a similar trend to removals by certificate, except that it declines less sharply after 1969, as shown in Figure 7.

The third and final category is 'admission by resolution'. This category involves the admission of members of another Church which is similar in doctrine and worship to that of the Church of Scotland. While such members may be in full communion with their own Church, they have no certificate of membership of the Church of Scotland. In these cases, the Kirk Session of the congregation concerned 'resolves' to admit them. Also included in this category are former members who have been removed for disciplinary reasons, and who may be readmitted by resolution of the Kirk Session if they are considered to come up to membership standard. Figure 7 indicates that this category of admissions has remained fairly constant at around 5,000 a year in recent years, although their numbers were somewhat larger after the war, and reached a peak in 1956.

An examination of the post-war trends in removals and admissions suggests that two factors largely account for the sudden reversal in 1956 of the rising trend in membership numbers, both of them potentially avoidable by the Church. By far the most important of these factors is the decline in admissions on Profession of Faith. Their numbers follow the now familiar trend, rising after the war to reach a very pronounced peak in 1955, followed by a sharp decline, particularly from 1964 onwards. In the twelve years between 1964 and 1975 admissions on Profession of Faith declined from 32,385 to 13,797, a fall of 57.4 per cent. The significance of this decline in terms of the overall decline in membership is shown in table 8. Column 1 gives the difference between the actual annual intake of admissions on Profession of Faith for each of the years in 1957-75 and the average annual intake of 39,636 for the years 1948-54. The minus figures in this column illustrate the magnitude of the decline in these admissions. These figures can be compared with the annual fall in total membership shown in column 2. Most of the figures in column 1 are only a little smaller than the corresponding ones in column 2, indicating that the bulk of the decline in membership can be attributed to the decline in admissions on Profession of Faith.

TABLE 8
The decline of admissions on Profession of Faith compared with the decline in total membership, 1957-75

Year	Difference between the actual annual intake of admissions on Profession of Faith and the average of 39,636 for the period 1948-54 1	Annual change in total membership 2
1957	− 4,321	− 3,994
1958	− 4,761	− 164
1959	− 4,145	− 8,805
1960	− 5,994	− 5,381
1961	− 7,366	− 8,663
1962	− 8,292	− 11,058
1963	− 8,669	− 12,672
1964	− 7,251	− 9,725
1965	− 8,875	− 11,190
1966	− 12,011	− 14,164
1967	− 14,309	− 13,785
1968	− 15,835	− 18,190
1969	− 18,501	− 23,499
1970	− 20,432	− 24,123
1971	− 21,915	− 20,696
1972	− 23,889	− 23,328
1973	− 25,189	− 21,314
1974	− 25,526	− 27,167
1975	− 25,839	− 19,934
TOTAL	− 263,120	− 277,795

Over the period of 1957-75, table 8 indicates that the decline in admissions on Profession of Faith below the annual average level for 1948-54 resulted in a total loss of 263,120 members, compared to a decline in total membership of 277,795 over the same period. This suggests that the decline of admissions on Profession of Faith accounted for over ninety per cent of the decline in total membership between 1957 and 1975. The significance of these admissions on the membership decline is somewhat exaggerated, however, to the extent that some of the new members calculated on the basis of a constant intake of admissions on Profession of Faith would have ceased membership at some later date in the period as a result of death, lapsing, emigration and the like. Consequently, the overall decline in membership would have been greater than actually occurred, so reducing the impact of admissions on Profession of Faith rather below ninety per cent. Nonetheless, it seems clear that the single overriding cause of the membership decline since 1956 has been in the rapid decline in the recruitment of new members, which largely means young people.

No conclusive evidence has been provided to explain this apparent disenchantment of the young with the Church. Sissons, in his study of church life in Falkirk,[12] suggested that the high attendance at Sunday School by Church of Scotland children indicates the strong influence of the family during early childhood, but that this influence declines with adolescence. He describes how many parents interviewed were able to encourage their children to attend church when they were young, and their reluctance to be persistent with their children about church attendance and involvement once they reached adolescence. He found that 65 per cent of the church members' children who were of church membership age had not become members of any church, despite the enormous expenditure of money and effort in Christian education and the youth organizations of various kinds. The reasons given for the defection of adolescents from the Church varied, but they mostly indicated disenchantment with the Church in some way. Loss of interest, boredom, 'couldn't see the point' were amongst the reasons given by the informants themselves. Only 6 per cent of those ceasing to attend church cited loss of belief as the cause of their non-attendance. Sissons gives the following explanation of the phenomenon: 'There is a lack of continuity between primary and secondary religious socialization within the church and within the family. Where the Bible Class and Youth organizations function well they are not reinforced by the family to the extent that the Sunday Schools are. The social world of the churches is so closely associated with the family . . . that the adolescent who is beginning to move out of the family also begins to move out of the church, finding both to be inhibiting and repressive.'[13]

The argument that the decline in the number of new members is caused by the failure of religious socialization in the family and Church is broadly supported by the figures in table 9. These show the declining trends in the ratio of infant baptisms in the Church of Scotland to children born in Scotland, and in the numbers of Sunday School pupils and Bible Class pupils. These are the channels which traditionally have supplied a large proportion of new members for the Church.

The second cause of the post-1956 decline in membership, although much less important that the decline in the number of new members, involves the net loss of members through removals by certificate. This loss arises through members moving house. When the distance moved is not great, it seems that members often remain associated with the same congregation, even though they reside outside the parish area.

TABLE 9
The decline in infant baptisms, Sunday School pupils and Bible Class pupils between 1956 and 1974

	1956	1974	Percentage change between 1956 and 1974
Infant baptisms in Church of Scotland children born in Scotland ratio	1:2.15	1:2.92	−35.8%
Sunday School pupils	316,769*	156,205	−50.7%
Bible Class pupils	64,564*	48,069	−25.5%

*Figure for 1955.

TABLE 10
Net loss of membership through removals by certificate, 1947-74.

	Removals by certificate	Admission by certificate	Net gain (+)/ loss (−) of members	Average annual net gain (+)/ loss (−) of members
1947	39,400	37,022	− 2,378	
1948	40,514	39,717	− 797	
1949	37,278	39,242	+ 1,832	
1950	37,278	29,318	− 7,960	
1951	39,692	39,455	− 237	− 786
1952	41,929	41,785	− 144	
1953	42,812	42,391	− 421	
1954	42,369	43,676	+ 1,307	
1955	44,331	44,623	+ 292	
1956	42,846	43,493	+ 647	
1957	44,291	40,476	− 3,815	
1958	43,378	41,936	− 1,442	
1959	44,270	40,652	− 3,618	
1960	43,325	39,703	− 3,622	
1961	42,665	39,626	− 3,039	− 3,797
1962	42,713	39,776	− 2,937	
1963	42,655	38,606	− 4,049	
1964	42,756	38,649	− 4,107	
1965	44,628	38,174	− 6,454	
1966	41,776	36,892	− 4,884	
1967	40,968	36,465	− 4,503	
1968	40,951	34,756	− 6,195	
1969	40,251	34,817	− 5,434	
1970	37,508	32,575	− 4,933	− 3,905
1971	34,380	31,382	− 2,998	
1972	32,058	29,494	− 2,564	
1973	29,624	27,779	− 1,845	
1974	27,034	23,683	− 3,351	
1975	27,819	24,495	− 3,324	
TOTAL	1,151,631	1,070,658	−80,973	−2,792

The phenomenon of members attending a church further afield than their parish church is a common features in urban areas. The congregations which tend to gain members from these movements are those of certain prestigious central city churches, and to a lesser extent those of old parish churches in towns. It is sometimes argued, however, that the comparatively lengthy journey to church involved, especially in the cities, eventually leads in some cases to members lapsing.

When a member moves a greater distance, making it impractical for him to attend his present church, he is given a Transference Certificate which he is required to lodge with the minister or session clerk of the new congregation. In a proportion of cases, however, these members fail to join a new congregation, and effectively 'lapse' from membership. The impact of this factor on the decline in church membership since 1956 is shown in table 10. In the ten year period 1947-56, when church membership was increasing, the average annual net loss of members was only 786. In four of those years admissions by certificate actually exceeded removals by certificate, which illustrates the fact that members do carry the certificate for some time before lodging it with their new congregation.

For the period after 1956, the removals by certificate exceed the admissions by certificate in every year, so leading to a net loss of members in every year. Over the ten year period 1957-66 the average annual loss was 3,797, and over the nine year period 1967-75 the average annual loss was 3,905. In recent years the trend seems to be reducing one, since the average annual net loss in the triennium 1973-5 was only 2,840, as compared to 5,521 in the triennium 1968-70. It is unlikely that this loss arises from emigration, since members intending to emigrate and not return would not normally be given a Transference Certificate. They would be classified in the removals without certificate category.

It is important to note that in this section we have only been concerned to explain the reversal in 1956 of the post-war upward trend in membership. In the following section we turn to the question of forecasting membership numbers in the last quarter of the twentieth century.

5 Membership forecasts

So far we have seen that membership of the church increased after the Second World War to reach a peak in 1956, and then entered into a downward trend which was accentuated from 1967. Efforts have been made by us to explain these trends in terms of demographic and other factors, but so far with limited success. If an explanatory equation could be developed, then future projections of the variables involved would enable projections of the membership to be made.

A wide range of variables were tested for their possible significance. The total Scottish population was included on the hypothesis that it might be positively related to membership.[14] The population was also broken down into four age cohorts, viz. 0-20, 21-34, 35-59 and 60 and over, which were tested individually as percentages of the total population. Since the membership of the Church is strongly biased towards the middle and older age groups, it was thought that the two younger age cohorts might have a negative impact on membership, while the two older age cohorts might have a positive effect. Further demographic factors tested included migration outflows and inflows; both may have a negative effect on church membership. Outward migrants are likely to be predominantly of

Scottish origin, many of whom will be Church of Scotland members who may be lost to the Church. Inward migrants will include some returning Scots who are potential Church of Scotland members, but the bulk may not come from a Presbyterian background, and are therefore unlikely to join the Church of Scotland; for example, English migrants to Scotland are more likely to join the Scottish Episcopal Church than the Church of Scotland, since the former resembles the Church of England, with which it is in full communion.

Other variables tested included the levels of car and house ownership, and the amount of building society mortgage advances. These were included as proxy measures of economic or social class, on the grounds that many studies have shown that Church membership is much stronger among middle-income or middle-class people than lower-income or working-class people. These variables were therefore expected to vary positively with membership.

The number of car licences was also used, along with the number of television licences, as a proxy measure for the growth of the entertainments industry, which may act as a competitor to involvement in the Church. It was hypothesized that these variables might have a negative impact on membership.

A linear regression model was used to test the significance of all these variables in different combinations and with different model forms. Some of the variables, particularly the demographic factors, proved to be significant, although they did not always have the expected relationship (i.e. positive or negative) with membership. However, all the equations suffered from auto-correlation, which rendered them unreliable for forecasting purposes.

An alternative course is to fit a line by statistical means to the annual membership figures for past years. A membership forecast can then be made by extending this line, or trend, into the future. Such a line was fitted to the membership figures for the twenty-one years 1956-75 by means of least squares regression. The following equation resulted, where M denotes membership and YR the year (starting at $YR = 0 = 1956$):

$$M = 1,373,190 - 14,908.6 \, YR \qquad \ldots \qquad (1)$$
$$(9,894.91) \quad (826.01)$$

$N = 20$, *1956-75*
$R^2 = 0.9476$
Durbin-Watson statistic $= 0.1295$

The R^2 is very high (almost one), and the standard error of the coefficient term (in brackets) is low in relation to the value of the term. These indicate that the equation provides a close fit for the data. On the other hand, the value of the Durbin-Watson statistic is low, which indicates serial correlation. This reflects the slight break in the trend in 1967, when the rate of membership decline was accentuated. The equation is plotted in figure 8, where the break in the trend can be seen. The equation indicates that the membership of the Church can be calculated by starting with a figure of 1,373,190 for 1956, and subtracting 14,908.6 to calculate the figure for each succeeding year. In other words, over the period 1956-75 the membership has fallen at an average rate of 14,908.6 per year.

Segmented linear regressions were then carried out on the data for the periods 1956-67 and 1967-75, in recognition of the apparent break in the trend in 1967.

88   The Church of Scotland: An Economic Survey

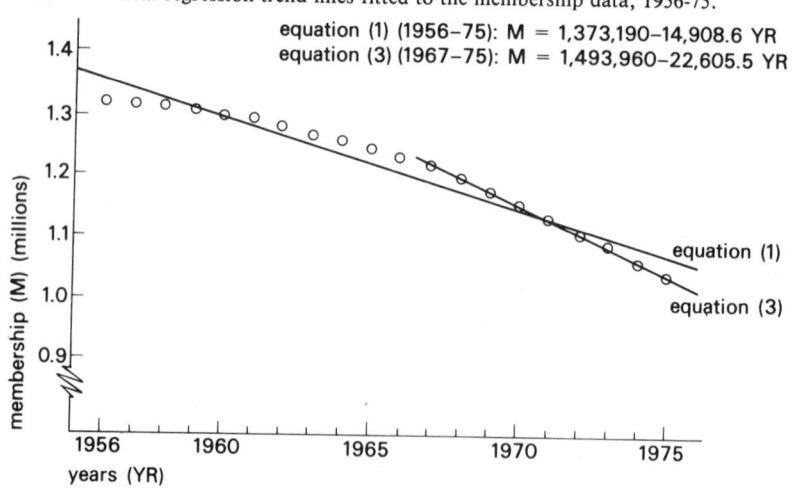

FIGURE 8. Linear regression trend lines fitted to the membership data, 1956-75.

equation (1) (1956–75): M = 1,373,190–14,908.6 YR
equation (3) (1967–75): M = 1,493,960–22,605.5 YR

[Graph: membership (M) (millions) vs years (YR), 1956–1975, showing data points declining from ~1.32 to ~1.0 with equation (1) and equation (3) trend lines]

The following two equations were estimated:

$$M = 1{,}340{,}440 - 9{,}264.55\ YR \qquad \ldots \qquad (2)$$
$$= (4{,}168{,}50)\quad (566.39)$$

N = 12, *1956-67*
R^2 = 0.9640

Durbin-Watson statistic = 0.4141

$$M = 1{,}493{,}960 - 22{,}605.5\ YR \qquad \ldots \qquad (3)$$
$$= (3{,}875.21)\quad (239.11)$$

N = 9, *1967-75*
R^2 = 0.9972

Durbin-Watson statistic = 2.3481

The statistical indicators imply an even better fit than in equation (1). This is to be expected whenever data is analysed is a more refined, segmented fashion, but such a gain is not always worth while if it does not indicate a structurally significant change in the pattern of the data. However, a comparison of the annual decline in membership for 1956-67 of 9,265 with that of 22,606 for the period 1967-75 indicates that some sort of structural change in membership occurred in 1967. Equation (3) is plotted in figure 8, where the closeness of the fit to the data can be observed.

Equations (1), (2), and (3) were recalculated experimentally using logarithmic transformations for membership, but the resulting equations were no improvement on the linear equations. Also, we attempted to account for the non-linearity of the data over the period 1956-75 by fitting a cosine model. This model assumes that the membership decline over the period does not reflect a continuing downward trend, but is part of a cyclical downswing which may be followed by an upswing at some time in the future. While the estimated equation provides as good a fit for the data as the linear equations, its use for predictive purposes was discounted as the forecasts produced were thought to be unrealistic. The linear equations were used, therefore, for making membership forecasts.

It is possible to make predictions of the future levels of membership by extending forward into the future the linear trends calculated by means of the regression analysis. However, this simple procedure makes two important assumptions which may not be borne out in practice. The first is that the trends which are discernible in the data sample will continue throughout the period of the prediction; and the second is that no unforeseen changes, or changes of policy by the Church, will effect the issue in the future. Since the observed trends are more likely to change, and unforeseen or deliberate changes more likely to intrude, the further the forecast is made into the future, the error of any prediction made for future periods in excess of five or ten years is likely to be large. It should also be noted that the linear trend, by giving rise to a constant absolute decline in numbers each year, implies an increasing annual percentage fall as the total membership falls.

The predictions for membership numbers for the period 1977-2001 are shown in table 11. On the basis of equation (1), which is based on the trend for 1956-75, membership is predicted to fall from 1,060,109 in 1976 to 985,566 in 1981, and to 687,394 by 2001. Table 12 shows that these figures constitute falls of 7.0 and 35.2 per cent respectively on the predicted 1976 figure. By comparison, equation (3), which is based on the period 1967-75 when the membership decline accelerated, leads to a rather larger predicted decline in membership. Between 1976 and 1981 the membership falls by 11.1 per cent from 1,019,245 to 906,217, and by 2001 it has fallen by 55.4 per cent to 454,107.

If the present trend continues, therefore, the Church is likely to suffer a decline of between a third and a half in its membership over the remaining years of the century. However, much depends upon two important factors, viz.:
(i) whether the rapid decline over the past twenty years in the number of young people admitted on Profession of Faith continues into the future; and
(ii) whether the large number of young people who failed to become church members over the past twenty years will join when they are older.

The first factor is serious because it eats away at the supply of the new generation of church members, and the second is important because a large proportion of the existing members will cease membership over the next twenty-five years for reasons of old age and death. If admissions on Profession of Faith continue to decline, and the young people who failed to join the Church over the past twenty years do not return to the Church in later life, then the prospects for membership in the future appear to be gloomy, and the predictions based on equation (3) in tables 11 and 12 could be borne out. On the other hand, if the young people who have not been joining the Church in recent years do become members in later life, then even if admissions on Profession of Faith do not increase, but reach a plateau level, the prospects for membership are much better. The proportion of young people in church membership would become even smaller, and the average age of members would rise; but the total membership might be expected to stabilize at a level rather lower than at present, but higher than the levels predicted in equation (3) above. In this case, the forecast based on equation (1) might prove to be reasonably accurate.

At present it is not possible to say which of these outcomes is the most likely to occur. The decline of admissions on Profession of Faith started in the late 1950s, so that some of the young people involved would now be in their early or mid 30s, and possibly nearing the age when they might be expected to join the Church.

TABLE 11
Forecasts of the membership for the period 1976-2001

	Membership forecast based on equation (1) 1	Membership forecast based on equation (3) 2
1976	1,060,109	1,019,245
1977	1,045,201	996,639
1978	1,030,292	974,034
1979	1,015,384	951,428
1980	1,000,475	928,823
1981	985,566	906,217
1986	911,023	793,190
1991	836,480	680,162
1996	761,937	567,135
2001	687,394	454,107

TABLE 12
Forecasts of the membership for 1981 and 2001 compared with the predicted figure for 1976

	Predicted figure for 1976 1	Predicted figure for 1981 2	Percentage change between 1 and 2 3	Predicted figure for 2001 4	Percentage change between 4 and 1 5
Equation (1)	1,060,109	985,566	7.0%	687,394	35.2%
Equation (3)	1,019,245	906,217	11.1%	454,107	55.4%

Evidence in future years will reveal whether this resurgence in membership is to occur, but the Church would be well advised as a matter of urgency to seek ways of encouraging greater participation by young people in its activities.

6 Policies for membership

Since 1956 we have seen that the number of members of the Church has fallen every year without exception, and at a steeper rate from 1967 onwards. Our forecasts suggest that, on the basis of past trends, the current membership of just over one million might fall by between one-third and one-half by the year 2001. The decline in membership has a serious depressing effect on the growth in Church income, and therefore on the financial position of the Church. It seems clear that one of the best ways for the Church to improve its financial position is by attempting at least to slow down, if not halt or even reverse, the downward trend in membership. There is little doubt that the financial position of the Church would be greatly improved if the membership could be held constant at the present level. This does not mean relaxing the qualifications for membership in order to retain more nominal members on the rolls, but holding or increasing the members who are active in the Church and contribute to its income.

A rough example of the extent to which the Church may benefit from the lifetime contributions of the average member is as follows. In 1973 the average member contributed £8.72 to the Church. The average member may be a member of the Church for, say, 40 years. This assumes that he joins in his late teens, allows for periods of little interest in the Church, and assumes that his membership is terminated by death. If our average member joined the Church in 1973, then according to our forecasts of individual contributions, which allow for an increase in personal disposable income in line with economic growth and inflation, he might be contributing over £100 a year by the termination of his membership.[15] Thus his total contribution to the Church over the forty year period of his membership might be of the order of £2,000. In addition, he may encourage his family, relatives and friends to become church-goers, he may contribute his time and energy in the social and other affairs of the congregation, and he may leave a bequest to the Church at death. Thus in purely financial terms (leaving aside the spiritual and social benefits of Church membership) it is worth while for the Church to make considerable efforts to conserve the existing membership and to encourage new members to enrol.

We now examine each of these broad policy options in turn, and make various policy proposals.

1 Encouraging new members to enrol

Here we examine various measures aimed at increasing the number of new members joining the Church.

A Young people

We have seen that the main reason for the reversal in 1956 of the upward trend in membership numbers was the sharp decline in the annual number of admissions on Profession of Faith. These are people admitted to membership of the Church for the first time. Many are young people. No complete explanation has been provided for the apparent disenchantment of the young with the Church, but it seems to arise in part from a lack of parental and school encouragement of church-going in adolescence.

We suggest that the Church should attack this problem on a broad front, as follows:

(i) The Church should concentrate on encouraging young people initially to join organizations affiliated to congregations, such as youth clubs, sports clubs, and the like, rather than on joining the Church, in the hope that Church membership may come at a later stage. The emphasis should be placed on the social, rather than the spiritual, aspects of congregational life. The Church might also attempt to bring younger people into positions of responsibility within its organization, for example as elders and other office-bearers.

(ii) The Church should encourage its parent members to attend services more frequently, since this apparently has an important bearing on the frequency of attendance of their children. These members should also be encouraged to make efforts to ensure that their children attend church.

(ii) The Church should press more strongly for a return to more formal religious education in the schools.

B Older people

While it may not be easy to attract young people to church, there is plenty of scope for congregations to recruit more older members. These efforts are likely to be more successful if concentrated, at least initially, on 'fringe' people, *i.e.* on people who already have some connection with the church, rather than on people who have no connection at all. Potential new members might be found in the following groups: the non-member parents of children attending Sunday School and other church organizations (e.g. Bible Class, Boys' Brigade, etc.); families where only one spouse is in membership; former members on the Supplementary Roll; all old people, since they have a much higher than average propensity to attend church.

In many parishes it is probable that the potential membership, even when limited to these groups, is large. We propose that every Kirk Session should establish a Membership Committee, with the minister as convenor, whose function would be to keep a list of these potential members. The members of the committee, together with the elders of the districts concerned, would have the responsibility of tackling each person on the list every year about joining the church.

A further point is that stewards in attendance at services should be instructed to watch for the arrival of newcomers, and to make them especially welcome.

2 Conserving the existing members
We now turn to measures designed to retain existing members within the membership of the Church.

A Loss of members through geographical mobility
We saw above that members who move house and are issued with a Certificate of Transference appear to be especially vulnerable to lapsing from membership. The danger is that after they have moved they are outside the reach of their former parish minister, and will be unknown to the minister of their new parish.

In order to curb this loss of members we recommend that the following procedure be employed. In all cases where Certificates of Transference are issued, the minister or session clerk should write to the minister of the parish to which the member is moving. The letter, which might be of a standard form, would give the name and new address of the member, and his expected date of arrival in the new parish. These members would then be placed high on the list of people to be visited by their new minister.

B Loss of members by removals without certificate
The greatest loss of members suffered by the Church which lies within its power to correct is through removals without certificate. These are members who are removed from the Communion Roll for disciplinary reasons or for a long-term lack of interest in the Church, who emigrate, or who leave the local community and cannot be traced. In recent years their numbers have been around 20,000 a year on a declining trend. The elimination of this loss of members would alone almost halt the current rate of decline in the membership. Although a proportion of the loss through emigration cannot be avoided, the remaining areas of loss seem to reflect a failure of pastoral care. Sissons found that those who had formerly been members of the Church had ceased to be members for a large variety of reasons. In some cases 'the non-church members had unfortunate experiences of particular congregations and ministers which had resulted in disillusionment, and in others church membership had just lapsed as the outcome of growing disinterest.'[16]

We see this as reflecting a need for a strengthening in the pastoral care work of congregations. Our proposed Membership Committee should have a role to play here.

C Inactive members

A substantial proportion of the members of the Church are inactive. Sissons has estimated in Falkirk that about 39 per cent of members never attend services.[17] The Stewardship and Budget Committee has suggested that half of the membership is inactive.[18] The danger is that these members may eventually be removed from membership without certificate. Again, we feel that this reflects shortcomings in the organization and effectiveness of pastoral care.

3 Parish geography

We consider it essential that the parish system should operate effectively. One important aspect of the effective operation lies in the training and retraining of ministers in pastoral care; this question is examined in chapter 14. A further aspect concerns the geographical boundaries of parishes, which we examine now. We believe that members should be encouraged (but not obliged) to attend the church of the parish in which they reside. This would reduce the time consumed by ministers in travelling outside the parish to visit members in their own homes. The ministry would also be made more effective, in that the minister would be able to concentrate his efforts within the parish, where his responsibilities lie. The minister may visit members of his congregation residing outside the parish, but he cannot recruit new members there.[19]

The effective operation of the parish system also requires that the parish boundaries are drawn up in a logical fashion. These boundaries are adjusted from time to time to take account of changing circumstances. We suggest that it would help congregations concerned in raising their memberships if, in modifying parish boundaries, the following two considerations were to be borne in mind:

(i) Where obstacles exist which impede communications, they should be adopted as parish boundaries. Such obstacles may be of a minor nature, but are nonetheless significant. For example, in Edinburgh there is a parish, one corner of which is cut off from the parish church by the presence of a railway line, over which there is no bridge. People living in that corner of the parish who walk to church may either be discouraged from frequent attendance, or they may attend the church of an adjacent parish which is more accessible.

(ii) As far as possible parishes should cover districts which are socially homogeneous, in recognition of the principle that 'birds of a feather flock together'. People would then not be discouraged from attending the parish church because they felt that they did not fit in, nor would there be the risk of lapsing associated with travelling outside the parish to church. An example of the problems which can arise when this principle is violated is found in Edinburgh. In the suburbs of the city there are two adjacent parishes centred on very different areas; one covers a working-class district, and the other a middle-class district. However, the line of the boundary between the two parishes is such that a part of the middle-class district forms an enclave within the parish of the working-class church. That church only draws a handful of members from the enclave, the rest preferring to attend the church of the middle-class district. Although efforts have been made to transfer the enclave to the parish of the middle-class church in recognition of the residents' preferences, this has been successfully resisted by the working-class church on the ground that an affluent district would be lost from what is otherwise a poor parish.

(iii) Congregations should give careful consideration to the introduction of house groups in congregations. These are formed from the members living in one street or district of the parish, who meet weekly or fortnightly in the home of one of the group. The small size of such groups facilitates a greater degree of fellowship than is possible in the larger meetings of the congregation. They might also form the unit of organization at the grass-roots for fund-raising.

7 Conclusions

In this chapter we have gone to some lengths to describe the membership of the Church of Scotland, to analyse the trends in numbers and the factors underlying the trends, to make forecasts for the future, and to propose ways in which the Church should seek to reverse the twenty-year decline in members. All this reflects the central position which the membership occupies in relation to the life and the financial position of the Church, and to our strategy for improving that financial position.

In section 2 we saw that the membership of the Church is made up of members in full communion and baptized persons, the latter group including adherents. Baptized persons do not normally become communicants on Profession of Faith until at least the age of seventeen. The names and addresses of all communicants are entered on the Communion Roll of the congregation to which they belong, and the total of all the names on the rolls constitutes the communicant membership of the Church. In 1975 the communicant membership numbered 1,041,772 out of a Scottish population of 5.2 millions.

An examination of the demographic features of the membership population, based on limited information from several studies, found that it is disproportionately weighted in favour of the middle-aged and old, women, single people, the middle class, and the well educated.

In section 3 we went on to examine how the number of members (henceforth taken as communicant members) had fluctuated over the period 1891-75. We saw that membership numbers reached a high point of 1.3 million in 1926, before declining a little during the 1930s and '40s. Following the war the membership increased to reach an all-time peak of 1,319,000 in 1956, after which it fell every year without exception up to the present, and at a greater rate from 1967 onwards. Between 1956 and 1975 membership fell by 21.1 per cent.

The Communion Rolls are not always kept up-to-date, and may include many inactive members. One measure of the active membership might be based on attendance frequencies, but the Church collects no such information. Sissons has estimated in his study in Falkirk that 8 per cent of members attend church every Sunday, while 39 per cent did not attend at all.

An alternative measure of the active membership is the number of annual communicants (i.e. those who attend Communion at least once during the year). The annual communicant: membership ratio broadly follows the fluctuations in membership. The ratio reached a peak value in 1964, when 71.59 per cent of the membership attended Communion, after which it declined as annual communicants fell faster than the membership, reaching a post-1947 low of 64.7 per cent in 1973.

An examination of the membership trends in Presbyteries did not confirm the hypothesis that membership is falling faster in urban than in rural areas, notwithstanding the fact that the greatest falls in membership over the period 1960-73 occurred in the Presbyteries of Glasgow (30.1 per cent) and Edinburgh (25.4 per cent). In the former case the decline in membership was at least partly caused by the sharp decline in the population of the city over the period. These falls compare to a membership decline for the whole Church of 16.5 per cent. In a few Presbyteries membership has actually increased slightly over the period.

The membership figures assume greater significance when compared to the population figures of the whole country. This revealed that just over a fifth of the entire population (20.9 per cent) were members of the Church in 1973. An examination of membership/population ratios suggested that the long-run trend is for a fall in the ratios, caused by the long-term slow increase in population, and the decline in membership, particularly over the last 20 years.

Section 4 was concerned with the analysis of the changes in membership arising from the difference between the admission of new members and the removal of existing members. We saw that removals arose by deaths; by certificate, through members moving from the parish; and without certificate as the result of expulsion, lack of interest, emigration, and the like. Admissions arise from the Profession of Faith of new members; the joining of members by certificate from other congregations; and by resolution in special cases. An analysis of these elements revealed that the sudden reversal of the upward trend in members in 1956 was caused largely by changes in two factors: firstly, the numbers admitted on Profession of Faith dropped sharply from 1956; secondly, the number of members lapsing through a failure to register with their new congregation on moving house sharply increased after 1956.

After having analysed the trends in membership numbers up to the present, we turned in section 5 to the problem of making forecasts of membership. Attempts to build an econometric model of membership related to demographic and other factors were largely unsuccessful, because all the equations produced were subject to auto-correlation, which rendered them unreliable for forecasting. The fitting of linear trend lines to the time-series of membership data by least squares regression proved much more successful.

Trend lines were fitted for the period 1956-75, thus covering the period since the membership decline started, and for the periods 1956-67 and 1967-75 in recognition of the acceleration of the trend in 1967. All of the resulting equations fitted the data well, although the two segmented equations were slightly better, revealing the structural change in 1967 which produced a sharply accelerated decline in membership from that date. The equation for the period 1956-75 suggested that membership was falling at a rate of about 14,909 a year, and the second equation for the period 1967-75 that it was falling at about 22,606 a year. Extending these trends into the future produced membership totals of 985,566 and 906,217 respectively in 1981, and 687,394 and 454,107 respectively in 2001. The predictions for 2001 represent falls of 35.2 per cent and 55.4 per cent respectively on the 1976 predicted figure. We argued that if admissions on Profession of Faith continue their present downward trend, and the young people who failed to join the Church in the past twenty years do not join in later life, than the prospects for Church membership appear gloomy, and the lower membership forecast looks the more likely. In contast, if the young people who have not been joining the Church in recent years do become members in later life, then even if the admissions of young people on Profession of Faith do not increase, the prospects for membership are much better, and the high forecast should be vindicated.

In section 6 the seriousness of the depressing effect of the declining membership on the financial position of the Church was emphasized. Measures were proposed to encourage new members to join the Church, and to strengthen the existing membership. New members might be found especially among young people who in former years would have joined the Church, particularly the children of Church members, and amongst older people who have some connection with the Church. We suggested that each Kirk Session should establish a Membership Committee to compile a list of potential Church members in the parish, and to tackle them annually about joining the Church.

We also pinpointed areas where the Church should seek to stem losses of existing members. The loss of members through removals by certificate could be avoided if the ministers of the parishes to which the members move are informed of their coming. A larger loss occurs through members being removed from the rolls through a lack of interest in the Church. This suggests that the organization and effectiveness of pastoral care in congregations is inadequate, as does the substantial proportion of inactive members. The effectiveness of the parish system can be improved by relatively minor adjustments in parish boundaries. The introduction of small groups might prove beneficial. The important question of the training of ministers in pastoral care is the subject of a later chapter.

Notes

1 Church of Scotland, 'Report of the Stewardship and Budget Committee', *Reports to the General Assembly, 1970*, pp. 87-8.
2 'Report of the Committee on General Administration', *Reports to the General Assembly, 1976*, appendix B, p. 23.
3 Cox, p. 19.
4 'Report of the Advisory Board' *Reports to the General Assembly, 1971*, pp. 117-18.
5 P.L. Sissons, *The Social Significance of Church Membership in the Burgh of Falkirk* (Blackwood, 1973).
6 D.R. Robertson, 'The Relationship of Church and Class in Scotland', in D. Martin (ed.), *A Sociological Yearbook of Religion in Britain*, Vol. I: (SCM Press Ltd., 1968), pp. 11-31.
7 Gillian Watson, 'To Examine the Perception of the Church of Scotland as seen by its Members' (unpublished dissertation, University of Edinburgh, 1975).
8 Sissons, p. 288.
9 ibid. table 15, p. 68.
10 Watson, p. 32.
11 The relative infrequency in the holding of Communion in the Church of Scotland compared to the Church of England and the Roman Catholic Church is said to have arisen from Knox's insistence that the service should resemble the Last Supper as closely as possible, e.g. to the extent that members should sit around a large table covered with a white tablecloth. As a result, it was only possible for a limited number of members of the congregation to attend each service, so that each member came to attend Communion only a few times each year.
12 Sissons, pp. 207–8.

13 ibid., p.293.

14 A positive relationship between the numerical values of two variables is said to exist when the dependent variable increases as the independent variable increases, and vice versa. In the example quoted above, it is hypothesized that, when the Scottish population increases, the membership of the Church increases, and vice versa. The membership is thought to *depend* upon the population, and is therefore called the 'dependent' variable. A negative relationship means that the dependent variable increases when the independent variable decreases, and vice versa. Readers who are puzzled by these terms in what follows are directed to such non-technical introductory works on statistics as: Daniel B. Suits, *Statistics: an Introduction to Quantitative Economic Research* (Murray, 1965).

15 This simple calculation does not allow for variations in an individual's annual contribution according to his age and income.

16 Sissons, p. 252.

17 ibid., p. 69.

18 'Report of the Stewardship and Budget Committee' op. cit.

19 Cox, p. 53.

Chapter 5

Income

1 Introduction

The purpose of this chapter is to examine the income of the Church, and to make forecasts of how income might change over the last decades of this century.

In section 2 we describe the main components of Church income, paying particular attention to the distinction between the income raised by individual congregations, and that income received by the central authorities from various sources. Section 3 is then devoted to an examination of the trends in total income and its main components over the post-war period. Comparisons are made between 'money' income and income expressed in 'real' terms. Finally, in section 4 the statistical work involved in developing a Church income forecasting equation is outlined. The main factors which appear to influence income are analysed, and forecasts of income are made from the present up to the turn of the century.

2 Description of income

The income of the Church of Scotland derives from two main sources, as follows:[1]

(i) the income received by congregations from members, interest on invested funds, proceeds of sales of work, etc., all as recorded by congregations in the Schedule of Financial Statistics compiled by them each year and lodged with the General Finance Committee;

(ii) the income received directly by the General Treasurer of the Church for the work of committees, and consisting of donations and grants, bequests, interest on investments and other miscellaneous receipts.

Together these items comprise the total income of the Church. The figures for 1975 are shown in table 13. The total income amounts to £17,644,424, of which £12,976,298, or 73.5 per cent, comprises 'congregational income' ((i) above), and the remaining £4,668,126, or 26.5 per cent, comprises 'other income' ((ii) above). We now examine each of these main components of income in turn.

1 Congregational income

The figure for congregational income is regarded as the best measure of Christian liberality, which is the giving of individual Church members. The full definition given by the *Yearbook* is as follows: 'The total amount of Christian liberality received by parishes and charges . . . includes all ordinary and special collections, contributions, donations, proceeds from sales of work and seat rents, from congregations and their Sunday Schools, Bible Classes, young men's guilds, women's guilds, girls' associations and all other agencies for all purposes, but it excludes capital of invested funds, trusts, mortifications, grants from Baird Trust, Ferguson Bequests, or other similar sources, and grants from Maintenance of the Ministry, Home Mission, Home Mission Property, or other committees of the Church.'[2]

It can be seen that, although congregational income is made up largely of the contributions of individual members in the current year through various types of collections, donations, and the income tax recovered on Deeds of Covenant, also included is the income from such items as sales of work, the income from endowments given to the congregation by past members, and the interest on bank deposits from congregational savings. Every year each congregation completes a Financial Schedule of its income for the previous year and returns it to the central General Finance Committee. These returns are used to calculate the congregational income of the Church.

On the schedule congregations are required to distinguish between 'normal' and 'extraordinary and special' income. 'Normal income' is defined as: '. . . all *regularly recurring* receipts which are available for meeting normal congregational payments, i.e. for meeting the cost of the ministry, Mission and Service Fund and wider work, and payments for local congregational purposes.'[3] On the other hand, 'extraordinary and special income' covers those receipts which do not recur from year to year, and therefore cannot be regarded as a source of income for meeting regular expenses. Items which may fall in this category include net proceeds of sales of work (where such income is non-recurring), legacies, grants, income from investments, donations, and collections for special appeals. Table 13 shows that normal income forms the bulk of congregational income, comprising 59.4 per cent of Church total income compared to 14.1 per cent for Special Income.

TABLE 13
The total income of the Church of Scotland and its main components, 1975.

	£	%
1 Congregational income		
normal	10,484,603	59.4
special	2,491,695	14.1
sub-total	12,976,298	73.5
2 Other income		
donations, grants, income from trusts and miscellaneous	1,852,470	10.5
bequests	853,840	4.9
income from investments	1,446,003	8.2
standardized stipend, etc., collected by and received from the General Trustees	515,813	2.9
sub-total	4,668,126	26.5
3 Total income of Church (i.e. 1 and 2)	17,644,424	100.0

SOURCE: Church of Scotland, 'Reports of the General Finance Committee', *Reports to the General Assembly, 1976*, Appendix I, p. 49.

Congregations are able to exercise some discretion over what items of income are included in the schedule, and in the breakdown of those items between the 'normal' and 'special' categories of income. This discretion is important in that the normal income is used as the base for allocating over Presbyteries and congregations the annual sum to be raised for the Mission and Service Fund, which finances the wider work of the Church. We have found that certain direct donations and payments by members to fabric and other accounts of their congregations are not recorded by the congregations in their financial schedules, although some, at least, of these omissions are permissible; the question is discussed below in chapter 12. It is also clear that there is a certain flexibility in the congregations' interpretation of the distinction between normal and special income, which is examined in chapter 16.

2 Other income

The second source of Church income is the income from various sources accruing to the central authorities and collected by the General Treasurer. The various items are grouped into four components, which together amounted to £4,668,126, or just over a quarter (26.5 per cent), of total income in 1975. We examine each component in turn.

A Donations, grants, income from trusts and miscellaneous

Income from donations, grants, trusts and other sources amounted to £1,852,470, or 10.5 per cent of total income, in 1975. These are sums donated directly to central funds, and usually designated by the donors to support the work of one or other committee.

The departments whose general funds chiefly benefited from this source in 1973 were as follows:

	%
Church and Ministry Department	37
Home Board	27
Overseas Council	29
Total	93

This component of income includes the income of a number of trusts, by far the largest of which is the F.G. Salvesen Trust. The approximate annual income of this trust is £350,000, and it is divided between five committees of the Church. The capital consists of ordinary and preference shares in Christian Salvesen Limited (the Church is the major equity holder), together with holdings of gilts, debentures, and equities of other companies. There are no other trusts administered by the Church of Scotland which produce an annual income in excess of £10,000.

B Bequests

The income received during 1975 from bequests amounted to £853,840, or 4.9 per cent of total income. Bequests are usually tied to a specific purpose. Care is now taken in such cases where a trust is being established to ensure that the purpose is fairly widely defined, in order to avoid the problems associated with bequests given to the Church in the 1880s. Many of these have become frustrated because of the difficulty in finding a suitable outlet for the income within their narrowly defined purpose. These purposes can be broadened by application to the Court of Session for a *cy près* scheme, but the procedure is involved and expensive.

C Income from investments
The income from investments amounted to £1,446,003, or 8.2 per cent of total Church income, in 1975. All of this income derives from the investments in the Church of Scotland Trust. These investments are held in three separate funds, which together had a market value of £20,371,889 in 1975, as follows:[4]

	Market Value £
General Investment Fund	11,734,800
Special Investment Account	3,117,089
Deposit Fund	5,520,000
Total	20,371,889

In the following year the funds held in the trust were distributed approximately as follows:

	%
Central committees	56.1
General Trustees	29.9
Congregations	11.0
Free Church property cases	3.0
Total	100.0

The central committees account for 56.1 per cent of the investment in the trust. Most of the money from which these investments originate has been given either to a committee for their general use, or for a specific objective in the committee's field. In many cases the donor has specified that only the interest on the money can be used for the stated objective, and that the original capital sum cannot be realised.

Since the investments attributed to the General Trustees and Free Church property cases are almost entirely fabric funds held on behalf of congregations, the investments in the trust made by or on behalf of congregations form the bulk of the remainder. The income accruing to congregations from these investments is in addition to the congregational income described above.

D Standardized stipend, etc.
This category of income may be looked upon as an investment income derived from various endowments for stipend. In 1975 these items amounted to £515,813, or 2.9 per cent of total Church income. About £400,000 of this constitutes the feuduties of the standardized stipend,[5] which are comparable to a tax on land. The standardized stipend is the modern form of the teinds of Scotland, and is collected by the General Trustees. Under the Land Tenure Reform (Scotland) Act, 1974, these feuduties may now be redeemed at the discretion of the feuars, the opportunity arising twice each year in May and November. The basis of redemption is a consolidated stock equivalent, i.e. a sum of money which would, if invested in 2½ per cent consolidated stock, produce an annual income equal to the feuduty. The current redemption rate (July 1977) would be 7.65. In the case of a feuduty being redeemed now, the Church would thus exchange an annual income in perpetuity for a single sum of 7.65 times that annual sum. The first

opportunity to redeem feuduties under the Act occurred in November 1974 when about a third of the feus, having a quarter of the total value, were redeemed. Thus the smaller fues tended to be redeemed first. It is estimated that about 40 per cent of the feus had been redeemed after the November 1976 redemption. However, when a property is sold the redemption of the feu is compulsory, so that in the long run the feuing system will disappear. Because the feuduties have been redeemed at values less than their original book values, it has been calculated that the income of the Church from this source will fall from £400,000 to £350,000. The funds realized by the redemptions have been invested largely in long-term government stock and local authority bonds.

The remainder of this category of income, amounting to roughly £100,000 in 1975, is made up of other types of endowment for stipend. The bulk – about £70,000 – comprises glebe rents and monies. Glebe monies is the income arising from the invested proceeds of sales of glebe land. Much of the rest is made up of interest on invested funds realised from previous *ad hoc* redemptions of individual feus, when the rate set depended very much on an arrangement agreed between the buyer and the individual seller.

Conclusion This completes our description of the main components of the income of the Church. We now turn in the following section to examining the trends in income since the Second World War.

3 Trends in Church income, 1945-75

The purpose of this section is to examine the trends in Church total income, and its main components, over the period since the Second World War.

Table 14 gives the main components of Church income expressed as percentages of total income for the decade 1966-75. The proportion of congregational income to total income has remained fairly constant over the period, varying only between 69.5 and 73.5 per cent. Because the proportion is so large, a change in the size of congregational income causes a similar change in total income, leaving the proportion roughly constant. However, the constancy of the proportion conceals large annual variations in the special income component of congrega-

TABLE 14
The main components of Church income expressed as rounded percentages of total income, 1966-75.

	1966	1967	1968	1969	1970	1971	1972	1973	1974	1975
1 Congregational income										
normal	62.4	61.6	60.4	60.5	61.7	62.2	60.1	59.0	58.3	59.4
special	9.3	9.1	9.5	11.6	7.8	7.2	10.8	12.7	13.2	14.1
sub-total	71.7	70.7	69.9	72.1	69.5	69.4	70.9	71.7	71.5	73.5
2 Other income										
donations, etc.	12.8	13.8	14.7	12.1	14.0	13.8	12.4	12.2	11.2	10.5
bequests	3.4	3.5	3.1	3.6	3.9	4.4	4.2	3.4	4.8	4.9
investments	6.7	6.8	7.3	7.5	7.9	7.9	8.2	8.7	8.8	8.2
stipend, etc.	5.4	5.2	5.0	4.7	4.7	4.5	4.3	4.0	3.7	2.9
sub-total	28.3	29.3	30.1	27.9	30.5	30.6	29.1	28.3	28.5	26.5
3 Total income (i.e. 1 and 2)	100.0	100.0	100.0	100.0	100.0	100.0	100.0	100.0	100.0	100.0

tional income, which has varied between 7.2 and 14.1 per cent of total income. Special liberality increased particularly sharply after 1971.[6]

The General Finance Committee has reported that the sums received within 'other income' 'tend by their nature to fluctuate from year to year.'[7] Table 14 shows that this is particularly true of two of the four categories, namely bequests, which has varied over the period 1966-75 between 3.1 and 4.9 per cent of total income, and donations, etc., which has a range of 10.5 to 14.7 per cent. The variability of these items is not surprising, since all of the first item and a substantial part of the second are composed of gifts by private individuals, the total of which may be expected to vary from year to year. The remaining two components exhibit more stable trends. Income from investments shows a fairly even rising trend from 6.7 per cent of total income in 1966 to 8.2 per cent in 1975, caused partly by a steady growth in the volume of funds invested, and partly by the effect of higher interest rates. In contrast, the income from the standardized stipend, etc., has declined steadily from 5.4 to 2.9 per cent over the period 1966-75. The income from this source, and particularly the standardized stipend, has increased only very slowly compared to total income.

FIGURE 9. The total income (TI), liberality (L), and other income (OI) of the Church shown at current prices and in 'real' terms at 1975 prices, 1950-75

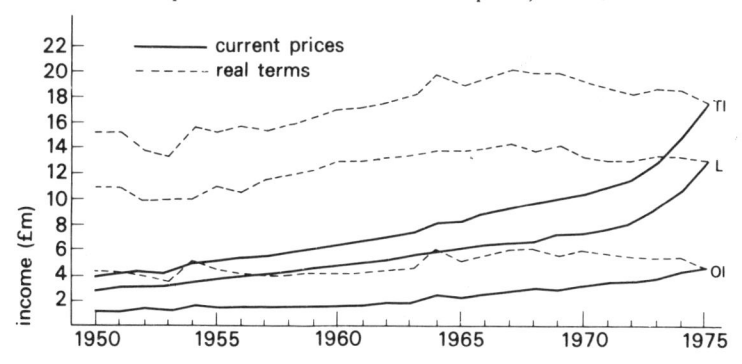

The changes in Church income over the period 1950-75 in both 'money' terms and in 'real' terms at 1975 prices is plotted in figure 9. The calculation of the 'real' values involved scaling up the money figures for each year prior to 1975 by the proportionate increase in the Retail Index between the year concerned and 1975. Thus, for example, the Retail Price Index (1947 = 100) increased from 359 in 1974 to 446 in 1975, so that all the 'money' figures in 1974 had to be multiplied by the fraction 446/359 in order to raise them to their equivalent in 1975 prices. However, this procedure raised the problem that, while the Retail Price Index is based on the prices of a representative sample of consumer goods and services purchased by the community as a whole, the Church uses its income to purchase a 'basket' of goods and services which probably differs very much from that on which the index is based. For example, the Church spends over a quarter of its income on the stipends of ministers, the services of which are not purchased by the ordinary consumer. Thus the problem arises that, if the average price level of the goods on which the Church spends its income diverges significantly from that measured by the Retail Price Index, the index would not be a suitable scale with which to convert the Church's income into real terms. Unfortunately, there is no index of Church costs, and so we have to assume that changes in such costs are measured reasonably accurately by the Retail Price Index.[8]

Figure 9 shows the plots of total income, congregational income, and other income of the Church of Scotland for the period 1950-75 in both 'money' terms and in 'real' terms at 1975 prices. When presented in money terms, all three items show a fairly steady increase year by year, even accelerating in recent years. However, when these sums are expressed in real terms (i.e. in terms of money with a constant purchasing power), a somewhat different picture emerges, with periods of both rising and falling real income. The main turning points – 1948, 1953, 1967 and 1975 – are given in table 15 where the figures are expressed in real terms. The table shows that between 1948 and 1953 the total income of the Church fell in real terms by 15.3 per cent (row 3), with other income (row 2) declining more quickly (−20.8 per cent) than congregational income (row 1) (−13.2 per cent). Between 1953 and 1967 the trend was reversed, with total income increasing in 'real' terms by 50.3 per cent. This was the time of the Church's relative prosperity in the post-war period, when liberality increased by 47.3 per cent and other income by 69.7 per cent. Since 1967, however, the real income of the Church has fallen steadily, apart from a decided upturn in 1973 as the result of a real increase in congregational income. Between 1967 and 1975, total real income fell by 12.9 per cent, which is composed of a fall of 9.3 per cent in liberality and 21.5 per cent in other income.

Taking the period 1948-75 as a whole, the table shows that the total real income of the Church increased by 10.9 per cent. This is composed of a 12.9 per cent increase in liberality, and a 5.6 per cent increase in other income.

The main conclusion which emerges from table 15 is that the Church today has an income which has done little more than keep pace with the rise in the cost of living since the end of the War. The implications of this for expenditure are examined in the following chapter. Meanwhile, in the next section we turn to the question of forecasting Church income.

4 Forecasting Church income

In order to make forecasts of Church income, it is necessary to develop an equation by statistical means which can explain changes in income in the recent past and predict changes in income in the near future. The sample period 1949-75 was taken for the purposes of the study, and regression analysis was used to test the possible correspondence from year to year between total income, Liberality, and the other main components of income on the one hand, and a number of independent or 'explanatory' variables on the other.[9] The independent variables tested included the following: Church membership; United Kingdom (U.K.) personal income *per capita*; the number of television licences; the number of car licences; the number of private house completions; the number of building society mortgage advances; the Retail Price Index; and the base rate of income tax. Since liberality forms such a large proportion of total Church income, and other income tends to vary with liberality, the best approach was found to be to treat other income as dependent on total income, rather than to attempt to deal

TABLE 15

Changes in the income of the Church (in real terms at 1975 prices) between 1948, 1953, 1967 and 1975.

	1948 £	1953 £	Percentage change between 1948 and 1953 %	1967 £	Percentage change between 1953 and 1967 %	1975 £	Percentage change between 1967 and 1975 %	Percentage change between 1948 and 1975 %
1 Congregational income	11,483,457	9,966,026	−13.2	14,305,887	+47.3	12,976,298	−9.3	+12.9
2 Other income								
donations, grants, income from trusts, and miscellaneous bequests	865,077	658,093	−23.9	2,802,137	+325.8	1,852,470	−33.9	+114.1
income from investments	827,284	653,254	−21.0	715,079	+9.5	853,840	+19.4	+3.2
	1,023,962	915,674	−10.6	1,365,080	+49.1	1,446,003	+5.9	+41.2
standardized stipend	1,706,092	1,275,888	−25.2	1,060,638	−16.9	515,813	−51.4	−69.8
sub-total	4,422,415	3,502,909	−20.8	5,942,934	+69.7	4,668,126	−21.5	+5.6
3 TOTAL INCOME OF THE CHURCH (1 and 2 above)	15,905,872	13,468,935	−15.3	20,248,821	+50.3	17,644,424	−12.9	+10.9

separately with each of its four components. This enabled total income to be treated as the single dependent variable. The independent variables which were closely correlated with liberality were found also to be correlated with total income.

The values of the variables were expressed in logarithmic form, since it was thought that their effect was multiplicative. Natural logarithms were used, since the coefficients of the variables could be interpreted as their elasticity with respect to total income. It was also found convenient to express money variables in real terms (at 1975 prices), which avoided the problem of having to forecast separately movements in the price level.

The equation which finally emerged as the best predictor of total income took the following form:

$$\begin{aligned}
\text{Log } TI = \quad &-24.7444 \quad + \quad 1.41205 \text{ Log } Y + \quad 2.30584 \text{ Log } M \\
&(3.90115) \qquad (0.1087) \qquad\qquad (0.2388) \\
&(-6.3429) \qquad (12.9858) \qquad\qquad (9.6574) \\
&+ 0.943553 \text{ Log } T - 0.0764422 \text{ Log } TV \qquad \ldots \qquad (4) \\
&\quad (0.3312) \qquad\qquad (0.0123) \\
&\quad (2.8489) \qquad\qquad (-6.1938)
\end{aligned}$$

$N = 27, 1949 - 75$
$R^2 = 0.9461$
Durbin-Watson statistic $= 2.1464$

where:
$TI =$ total Church income at 1975 prices.
$Y =$ U.K. personal income (before tax) *per capita* at 1975 prices.
$M =$ Church communicant membership
$T =$ standard rate of income tax plus 1
$TV =$ number of U.K. television licences

The equation provides a good fit for the data. The R^2 is high, and the Durbin-Watson statistic is close to the value two, indicating the near absence of auto-correlation. All the independent variables are significant at the 5 per cent level or better, as indicated by the relatively low values of the standard errors (in the first set of brackets), and the relatively high values of the T-statistic (in the second set of brackets).

The equation suggests that the real total income of the Church is related to four explanatory variables viz. real personal income *per capita*, the number of Church members, the standard rate of income tax, and the number of television licences. The first three variables all exert a positive influence on real income (e.g. an increase in membership serves to increase real income, and vice versa), while the fourth variable — the number of television licences — has a negative effect (i.e. an increase in the number serves to reduce real income, and vice versa). Since the variables are expressed in natural logarithms, their coefficients may be interpreted as their elasticities with respect to real Church income. Thus a 1 per cent increase in real personal income per capita leads to a 1.41 per cent increase in real Church income; a 1 per cent increase in membership leads to a 2.31 per cent increase in real Church income; a 1 per cent increase in the standard rate of income tax leads to a 0.94 per cent increase in real income; and a 1 per cent increase in the stock of television licences leads to a 0.08 per cent fall in real Church income.

Of these variables, personal income and membership appear to have the greatest impact. Their influence appears to be the obvious one, that an increase in the number of members, or in the average real personal incomes of members, leads to an increase in real Church income, and vice versa. If this is correct, then the decline in the real income of the Church since 1967 is explained largely by the acceleration in the decline in membership from that year, and by the slow and unsteady growth in real personal income following the pound sterling crises in the British economy, which started in the mid-1960s. The financial position of the Church thus appears to be related to its ability to maintain its membership numbers, and to the performance of the British economy.

The tax variable probably exerts an influence on Church income through the recovery of income tax on Deeds of Covenant, so that the higher the standard rate of tax, the greater the amount of tax recovered on a given amount of covenants.[10]

The significance of the television licences variable is an interesting result, since it offers support to the views of many clergymen that the spread of television over the last two decades has been a factor encouraging reduced church attendance. Indeed, the variable may be a proxy measure for the mushrooming growth of the entertainments and leisure industry in general, which may form a competing activity to involvement in the Church. Since there appears to be a close correspondence between a member's frequency of attendance at services and the amount he contributes to the Church, the link between the spread of television and Church income is clear. However, the fact that television is now received over virtually the whole of Scotland suggests that the adverse influence on Church income of this factor may have abated.

A further significant point about the equation is that inflation does not appear to have an important influence on the real income of the Church, since the equation is statistically significant when the money variables are expressed in real terms. This is a striking result which runs contrary to the fears of many people that the Church would be hit badly by the recent high levels of inflation. The income of the Church is insulated against the worst impact of high rates of inflation by the fact that during inflationary periods, personal incomes also tend to rise, albeit not as fast as prices. Any fall in real Church total income is likely to reflect only the resulting decline in real personal income *per capita*, rather than the much larger depreciation in the value of the pound sterling. It is possible, however, that the decline relative to other groups in the last few years of the income of middle-class families, who form the mainstay of Church membership, has meant that total Church income has declined further in real terms than might have been expected.

The income equation can be used to make forecasts of the real total income of the Church. While our remit requires us to make forecasts of income as far ahead as 2001, it should be obvious that such long-term forecasts will be much less reliable than forecasts extending only two or three years into the future. Indeed, the accuracy of the forecast can be expected to decline in direct proportion to the length of the forecast period. This arises because forecasts from regression equations are dependent on a number of conditions being met, but the likelihood of these conditions actually being realized diminishes, the further the forecast is extended beyond the sample period.

The first of these conditions is that the relationship between the dependent variable and explanatory variables will continue to be the same in the forecast period as it was during the sample period; that is, one must assume that the parameters do not change in the period of the forecast. The second condition is that factors assumed constant when the equation was estimated, such as broad social and political background factors, do not change in the forecast period. The final condition is that the independent variables take the values assumed in the forecast period. The values of the four explanatory variables in the income equation themselves have to be forecast, and the values for a particular year inserted into the equation in order to calculate the predicted value of total income for that year.

We now describe briefly the methods used to make forecasts for each of the four explanatory variables in the regression equation, and then go on to make forecasts of real total Church income.

1 *Real personal income* per capita

There are no reliable forecasts of the path that real personal income *per capita* may take over the long term. Perhaps the simplest method of obtaining long-term forecasts of this variable is to take its value at a base period and project it forward, on the assumption that its previous average annual rate of growth will be maintained. Thus if we assume that real *per capita* income is growing at a constant rate, we can establish its value in any year after the base year from the following formula:

$$Y_t = Y_o (1 + r)^t$$

where Y_t is real per capita income at time t, Y_o is real *per capita* income at any selected base period, r is the constant rate of growth, and t is the number of time periods (years, in this case).

Over the period 1949-75, real personal income *per capita* in the U.K. increased from £857.05 to £1,710.09, giving an average annual rate of growth of 2.7 per cent. The figures for selected years are shown in table 16. Column 1 of table 16 gives the total personal income of the U.K. These figures are then converted into real terms at 1975 prices by means of the Retail Price Index given in column 2. Total personal income at 1975 prices is given in column 3. These figures can be converted into *per capita* terms by dividing them by the total home population, which is shown in column 4. The resulting U.K. real personal income *per capita* figures are presented in column 5. The percentage changes in these figures over the previous year are given in column 6. They indicate the considerable fluctuations from year to year in the growth of real personal income *per capita*.

There are no published forecasts of U.K. personal income. We have calculated that real personal income *per capita* in 1976 was £1,711.10, which represents an increase over the 1975 figure of only 0.06 per cent. The slow growth in personal income in recent years reflects the problems caused by the rise in the price of oil in 1973, and its consequences. In making our forecasts of real personal income *per capita*, we assume that after 1976 improvements in the U.K. economy will allow the post-war growth rate of 2.7 per cent a year to be continued. These forecasts are shown in column 1 of table 18, where they are expressed in real terms at 1975 prices. Real personal income *per capita* is expected to rise from the actual figure of £1,711.10 in 1976 to £3,330.70 in 2001, an increase of 94.7 per cent. It is important to remember, however, that even if the forecast growth rate is attained, the growth will fluctuate from year to year about the forecast trend. These fluctuations would influence our forecasts of Church income.

TABLE 16.
Calculations of real personal income per capita in the United Kingdom for selected years, 1950-75.

	Total personal income+	Retail Price Index* (1947 = 100)	Total personal income at 1975 prices	Total home population (mid year estimates)× (000s)	Real personal income per capita (i.e 3/4)	Percentage change in 5 on previous year
	1	2	3	4	5	6
	£m		£m		£	%
1950	110,370	114	431,798	50,616	853.05	− 0.47
1955	156,000	148	470,108	50,946	922.78	+ 1.32
1960	212,370	166	570,584	52,372	1,089.48	+ 5.51
1965	300,830	193	695,182	54,218	1,282.20	+ 3.92
1970	433,230	241	801,745	55,421	1,446.64	+ 4.49
1971	477,440	264	806,584	55,610	1,450.43	+ 0.26
1972	542,280	283	854,618	55,793	1,531.77	+ 5.61
1973	627,750	309	906,073	55,933	1,619.92	+ 5.75
1974	758,500	359	942,315	55,965	1,683.76	+ 3.94
1975	957,000	446	957,000	55,962	1,710.09	+ 1.56

+ SOURCE: Central Statistical Office, *Annual Abstract of Statistics* (HMSO).
* SOURCE: Adapted to 1947 base from the index published in *Department of Employment Gazette* (HMSO).
× SOURCE: *Annual Abstract of Statistics.*

2 Membership

The trend in the total membership over the next twenty-five years will be crucial to the organization and the financial position of the Church. Of the four independent variables in the income forecasting equation, membership is the only one over which the Church is in a position to exert some direct influence.

Forecasting future trends in membership has already been dealt with in chapter 4, but, because of its importance and the uncertainty over forecasts made several years and more ahead, a range of membership forecasts have been calculated, as shown in table 17. Forecast 1 is based on equation (1), which gives the least pessimistic forecast fall in membership from the actual figure of 1,041,772 in 1975 to 687,395 in 2001. Forecast 1 for 1981 is made on the basis that membership declines on a straight line between the above figures for 1975 and 2001. Forecast 3 is based on equation (3), which is statistically the best of the membership equations. This equation produces a decline of 56.4 per cent, from the actual figure of 1,041,772 in 1975 to 454,108 in 2001. However, the equation is based on the limited number of observations for the period 1967-75, when the post-1956 membership decline accelerated; this fast rate of decline may not continue indefinitely into the future. The third forecast – forecast 2 – is the mid-way between the first and third forecasts. This gives a fall in membership to 570,751, or 45.2 per cent of the 1975 actual figure.

There is no wholly scientific way in which to choose which is the 'best' of these forecasts, and much will depend upon the efforts of the Church to improve the membership situation. However, if we were compelled to make such a choice, then it would be for forecast 2. All three membership forecasts are given in columns 2, 3, and 4 of table 18.

TABLE 17
Alternative forecasts of the membership of the Church for 1981 and 2001.

		Annual rate of fall	1981	2001	Percentage change between 1975* and 2001
1	Equation (1)+	13,630	959,993	687,395	34.0%
2	—	18,116	933,075	570,751	45.2%
3	Equation (3)	22,603	906,157	454,108	56.4%

* In 1975 the membership was 1,041,772.
+ For 2001 only (see text).

3 The tax rate
The standard rate of income tax under the unified system is assumed to remain at 35 per cent throughout the forecast period. The value of this variable is shown in column 5 of table 18.

4 U.K. television licences
In order to determine how the number of U.K. television licences (monochrome and colour) might grow in future years, a variety of mathematical trend curves were fitted to the number of television licences held over the period 1949-75.[11] The series was approximated most closely by a second degree polynomial, a curve which exhibits increasing amounts of increase or decrease. While satisfactory for short-term forecasting, such curves are often inappropriate for forecasting in the long term. This is so in the case of television licences, where the curve fitted leads to the prediction that the number of licences held would reach a maximum in 1982 and decrease thereafter. The most appropriate trend curves for the long-term forecasting of television licences would appear to be curves which possess the characteristic of increasing by a decreasing amount (or proportion) throughout their length. Curves of this type approach a ceiling or asymptote, which in the case of television licences might be interpreted as the saturation point when everyone who wants a television has one. The best fit was provided by a simple modified exponential curve, which describes a trend in which the amount of growth increases (or declines) by a constant percentage and approaches an asymptote k:

$$Y_t = k + ab^{X_t}$$

TABLE 18
Forecasts of the four independent variables of the income equation and of real total Church income, 1976-2001.

	Real personal income per capita	\multicolumn{3}{c	}{Membership}	Basic min. rate of income tax + 1	Number of television licences	\multicolumn{3}{c	}{Forecasts of real church income}
		Forecast 1	Forecast 2	Forecast 3			Forecast 1	Forecast 2	Forecast 3
	1	2	3	4	5	6	7	8	9
	£						£	£	£
1976	1,711.10*	1,028,142	1,023,656	1,019,170	1.35	17,892,443	17,806,900	17,628,200	17,450,800
1977	1,757.30	1,014,512	1,005,540	996,567	1.35	18,100,262	17,913,500	17,550,400	17,191,300
1978	1,804.75	1,000,882	987,423	973,965	1.35	18,293,083	18,014,400	17,460,900	16,917,000
1979	1,853.47	987,252	969,307	951,362	1.35	18,470,908	18,109,500	17,359,400	16,627,300
1980	1,903.52	973,623	951,191	928,760	1.35	18,633,735	18,198,400	17,246,200	16,322,600
1981	1,954.91	959,993	933,075	906,157	1.35	18,785,850	18,280,200	17,119,800	16,002,300
1982	2,007.70	946,363	914,959	883,555	1.35	18,925,110	18,355,100	16,980,900	15,666,900
1983	2,061.90	932,733	896,842	860,952	1.35	19,055,800	18,421,900	16,828,200	15,315,900
1984	2,117.57	919,103	878,726	838,350	1.35	19,173,636	18,481,000	16,662,300	14,949,700
1985	2,174.75	905,473	860,610	815,747	1.35	19,285,044	18,531,600	16,482,600	14,568,200
1986	2,233.47	891,843	842,494	793,145	1.35	19,385,735	18,573,200	16,288,500	14,172,300
1987	2,293.77	878,213	824,378	770,542	1.35	19,480,000	18,605,500	16,080,100	13,761,400
1988	2,355.70	864,583	806,261	747,940	1.35	19,567,849	18,627,900	15,857,200	13,336,200
1989	2,419.31	850,953	788,145	725,337	1.35	19,647,120	18,640,400	15,619,700	12,897,700
1990	2,484.63	837,324	770,029	702,735	1.35	19,722,106	18,642,400	15,367,200	12,445,700
1991	2,551.71	823,694	751,913	680,132	1.35	19,790,665	18,633,100	15,100,100	11,981,300
1992	2,620.61	810,064	733,797	657,530	1.35	19,854,935	18,612,600	14,817,800	11,505,100
1993	2,691.36	796,434	715,680	634,927	1.35	19,912,785	18,580,300	14,520,700	11,017,800
1994	2,764.03	782,804	697,564	612,325	1.35	19,966,347	18,536,100	14,209,100	10,520,800
1995	2,838.66	769,174	679,448	589,722	1.35	20,017,766	18,479,000	13,882,500	10,014,700
1996	2,915.30	755,544	661,332	567,120	1.35	20,062,758	18,409,200	13,541,400	9,500,880
1997	2,994.02	741,914	643,216	544,517	1.35	20,105,607	18,326,300	13,186,200	8,980,570
1998	3,074.86	728,284	625,099	521,915	1.35	20,144,171	18,229,800	12,816,900	8,455,140
1999	3,157.88	714,654	606,983	499,312	1.35	20,180,593	18,119,400	12,433,900	7,926,150
2000	3,243.14	701,025	588,867	476,710	1.35	20,214,873	17,994,600	12,037,800	7,395,280
2001	3,330.70	687,395	570,751	454,108	1.35	20,244,867	17,855,100	11,629,000	6,864,360

* Actual figure

where Y is the dependent variable and X_t is time. The equation estimated was as follows:

$$TV_t = 20621.94 - (21424.63)(0.9238^{X_t}) \qquad \ldots \qquad (5)$$

The equation suggests that the stock of television licences will reach a maximum of 20.622 millions, although growth will be extremely slow after the mid-1990s when the total number reaches 20.0 millions. The forecasts for 1981 and 2001 are 18,785,850 and 20,244,867 respectively, compared with an actual figure of 17,675,000 in 1975. The forecasts of the number of television licences for every year over the period 1976-2001 is given in column 6 of table 18.

5 Forecasts of Church income

Once the forecasts of the values of the independent variables have been made for each year over the period 1976-2001, the forecast for the real total income of the Church for those years can be calculated. The three forecasts based on the three membership forecasts, are shown in columns 7, 8, and 9 of table 18, and are plotted in figure 10. An examination of figure 10 reveals that all three lines are concave to the origin. This feature results from the relative impacts of the personal income and membership variables. While real personal income *per capita* is assumed to grow at a constant rate, the constant absolute falls in membership each year implied by the linear trends result in increasing percentage falls as each year passes. Although the growth of personal income has a continuing buoying impact on real Church income throughout the period of the forecast, the depressing effect of the gradual acceleration in the membership decline comes to wield an increasing impact on Church income. This causes the forecast income trends to bend downwards.

In the most optimistic forecast 1 the real income of the Church rises gradually to reach a high point of £18,648,000 in 1990, or 5.69 per cent above the actual figure for 1975 of £17,644,424. Thereafter, real income declines gradually to reach £17,860,000 by 2001, which is 4.23 per cent below the high point but 1.22 per cent above the 1975 figure, as shown in table 19. However, the forecast is based on the assumption that membership falls at the rate of 13,630 a year, which is considerably less than the annual fall of 22,603 established over the period 1967-75. The latter rate of membership decline forms the basis for forecast 3, which gives rise to the most pessimistic income forecast. Under this forecast, real Church income would fall from £17,644,424 in 1975 to £16,005,100 in 1981, and to £6,865,000 by 2001, giving falls on the 1975 figure of 9.29 and 61.09 per cent respectively. These forecasts are shown in table 19. Such falls would give rise to very serious financial problems for the Church. Weight is given to this forecast when figure 10 is examined, which suggests that the trend in real Church income is a continuation of the downward trend in income established from 1967, the actual points of which are also plotted.

Alternatively, forecast 2 is derived from a rate of fall in membership which is intermediate between those on which forecasts 1 and 3 are based. This forecast suggests that real Church income may fall by 2.97 per cent to £17,121,000 in 1981, and by 34.06 per cent to £11,635,000 in 2001. However, even this forecast is based on a rate of membership decline which is a substantial improvement on the rate obtaining in recent years.

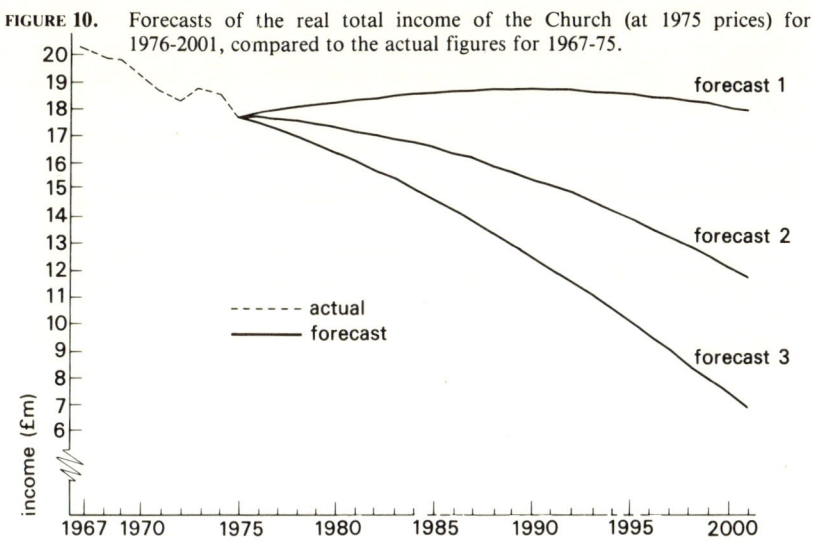

FIGURE 10. Forecasts of the real total income of the Church (at 1975 prices) for 1976-2001, compared to the actual figures for 1967-75.

These results lend weight to our contention that the future trends in membership are crucial to the financial well-being of the Church. Further evidence of the importance of membership to the income of the Church is supplied by using the income equation to predict real income, on the assumption that the membership is held constant at about the present level, i.e. at one million members. The calculations suggest that the Church's real income would rise very sharply from the actual figure of £17,644,424 in 1975 to £20,090,000 in 1981, and to £42,390,000 in 2001, as shown in table 19. These represent increases of 13.86 and 75.98 per cent over the 1975 level. While the Church should redouble its efforts to raise the level of giving per member, it seems clear that a more effective way of consolidating and increasing Church income would be through a policy of membership recruitment and conservation.

TABLE 19
Forecasts of real total Church income for 1981 and 2001.

Forecast	Actual income in 1975	Forecast for 1981	Percentage change between 1975 and 1981	Forecast for 2001	Percentage change between 1975 and 2001
	1	2	3	4	5
	£	£	%	£	%
1	17,644,424	18,285,000*	+3.63	17,860,000	+1.22
2	17,644,424	17,121,000	−2.97	11,635,000	−34.06
3	17,644,424	16,005,100	−9.29	6,865,000	−61.09
Constant membership forecast	17,644,424	20,090,000	+13.86	42,390,000	+75.98

* A high point of £18,648,000 is reached in 1990.

5 Conclusions

The purpose of this chapter has been to examine the sources of the Church's income, and to forecast how that income is likely to grow over the remaining years of this century.

In section 2 we saw that about 70 per cent of the income of the Church comprises Christian liberality, collected by the congregations largely from the giving of individual members on the plate, by envelope, and through covenants. Liberality is divided between 'normal' and 'special' income, the former being the normal, recurring, income for congregational purposes, and the latter being the income raised by special efforts for special purposes. The remaining 30 per cent or so of total income is 'other income', which comprises donations, grants, etc.; bequests; income from investments; the standardized stipend, etc. This income is received centrally by the General Treasurer, and the bulk is used by the central departments.

In section 3 we went on to examine how the Church's income had changed since the war. The proportionate division between liberality and other income has remained fairly constant over the period, although the components of each have fluctuated. This is particularly true of the division between normal and special liberality, and of the donations, grants, etc., and bequests components of 'other income.' The proportion of income from investments to total income has gradually increased, while the proportion of standardized stipend, etc. has diminished.

We saw also that, while the income of the Church has increased steadily since the war, the income when expressed in real terms has fluctuated significantly over the period. Real total income declined sharply between 1948 and 1953; it then enjoyed a sustained growth until 1967, which was followed by another decline to 1975. Over the period as a whole real income increased by 11.1 per cent, showing that the Church has just managed to keep ahead of inflation.

Finally, in section 4 we turned to the question of forecasting Church income. Statistical analysis suggested that the real total income of the Church is determined largely by four variables, of which the first two are the most important, viz. real personal disposable income per head; the communicant membership of the Church; the basic rate of income tax; and the number of television licences. It was suggested that the reason for the decline in the real income of the Church since 1967 is explained partly by the acceleration in the membership decline from that date, and partly by the unsteady growth in real personal disposable income.

Three income forecasts were made, based on three different rates of membership fall. On the most optimistic assumptions about membership, real Church income is forecast to rise slowly by 5.69 per cent from an actual figure of £17,644,424 in 1975 to £18,648,000 in 1990, and then to fall by 4.23 per cent to £17,860,000 by 2001. Under the most pessimistic assumptions about the membership decline, real income is forecast to fall quickly, reaching £16,005,100 in 1981 and £6,865,000 in 2001. Alternatively, in the intermediate forecast, which we tend to favour, real income might fall by 2.97 per cent from £17,644,424 in 1975 to £17,121,000 in 1981, and by 34.06 per cent to reach £11,635,000 in 2001. It is important to remember, however, that we do not claim to foresee the future, but simply project forward current trends. If the British economy should grow faster than anticipated, or the membership decline slow down or reverse, then the financial position of the Church could be better than forecast.

The importance of the number of members to the income position of the Church is further emphasised by the sharp increase in real income that would occur if membership could be held constant at the current level.

Notes

1 Church of Scotland, 'Report of the General Finance Committee', *Reports to the General Assembly, 1974*, p. 61.

2 Andrew Herron (ed.), *The Church of Scotland Yearbook, 1976* (St Andrew Press, 1976), p. 28.

3 Church of Scotland, *Schedule of Financial Statistics* (General Treasurer's Office), p. 5.

4 The investments of the Church of Scotland Trust are examined in more detail in chapter 19.

5 The standardized stipend is discussed in much greater detail in chapter 10.

6 An explanation of this increase is given in the following chapter.

7 'Report of the General Finance Committee, op.cit.

8 A further point is that, since the minimum stipend is an 'administered' price, the Church would be able to influence the rate of change of an index of Church costs, and thereby the rate of change in its real income. However, since the Church has sought in recent years to at least maintain the real value of the minimum stipend as measured by the Retail Price Index, the Church must aim, as a rough approximation, at least to maintain its total income in real terms by the same measure. This question is discussed in more detail in chapters 6 and 9.

9 For a brief definition of these terms, see chapter 4 footnote 14.

10 The significance of Deeds of Covenant for the income of the Church is examined in chapter 18.

11 Central Statistical Office, *Monthly Digest of Statistics* (HMSO).

Chapter 6

Expenditure

1 Introduction
The purpose of this chapter is to present a general overview of the expenditure of the Church, with special reference to the division of expenditure between the three main spending agencies, viz. the Church and Ministry Department, the congregations, and the committees in the Mission and Service Fund. These three agencies are responsible, respectively, for the stipend and expenses of ministers, the expenditure of congregations, and the wider work of the Church beyond the parish ministry. The analysis is carried further in respect of each of those topics in chapter 10 on funding the ministry, chapter 12 on congregational finance, and chapter 16 on mission and service.

In this chapter our central theme is that expenditure cannot be understood properly except in relation to income, since the Church spends each year more or less what it receives in income. An analysis of expenditure, therefore, must also include more than a passing reference to income.

Two important implications follow from this perception. Firstly, although the three major spending agencies in the Church plan ahead their finances over three year periods, their budgeting is essentially a year-to-year process.[1] The budget for next year is largely determined by the *expected* income for next year, the word 'expected' being emphasized, because the income figure can only be a forecast based on past trends and the performance in the current year. The uncertainty involved is likely to encourage budgeting for a small surplus, so that a small shortfall in expected income is less likely to be serious and, in the event of a surplus, funds can be added to the reserves to meet the possibility of future deficits.

Secondly, the methods used in distributing income between spending units are important, for when virtually all income is spent each year the expenditures of each spending unit will be determined by the allocation procedures used. Thus the analysis of the allocation procedures becomes almost as important as the analysis of the expenditures themselves, and this is a topic to which we turn below.

Nonetheless, an examination of expenditures is important in at least two respects. Firstly, given that the income of the Church is limited relative to the many activities in which it could engage, the expenditures should indicate the relative priorities which the Church assigns to the different activities at any point in time. Secondly, the analysis of expenditures over time is important. If real income rises over time, then no spending unit need suffer a cut in its income and expenditure, and there will be a surplus which can be used to meet new priorities. On the other hand, if real income falls, or even remains static in the face of urgent new demands, then important questions of priority and problems of readjustment are raised. Over the period since the war the Church of Scotland has experienced both of these situations.

We start in section 2 by conducting a preliminary survey of the method by which the congregational income, or liberality, of the Church is divided between the main spending agencies; the formal procedure, and the various forces at play, are described and analysed. Then in section 3 we go on to examine the results of the allocation procedures by looking at the income and expenditures of the main spending agencies in turn over the period 1961-75. The Church's income from other sources is included in the discussion. This process leads to the calculation of the total expenditure figures of the Church, which are then compared with the published total income figures. Finally, in section 4 we devise a procedure for apportioning the total income of the Church between the ministry (i.e. the congregations and the Church and Ministry Department) and mission and service. This procedure is then used to apportion the forecast total income figures of the Church made in the previous chapter between those two major areas of the Church's work.

2 A preliminary survey

A formal method has been developed by the Stewardship and Budget Committee for apportioning congregational income (or liberality), which forms about 70 per cent of the Church's income, between the Church and Ministry Department, the congregations, and the committees within the Mission and Service Fund. The method is called the 'available balance' method. It was employed for the first time in 1974, though it does not differ greatly from the less formal methods used previously.

The available balance method is described in some detail in chapter 16, but the essence of the process is as follows. The total 'normal' recurring income of each congregation is calculated and averaged over a recent three-year period. The 'normal' congregational income, or liberality, is distinct from the 'special' income, as described in the previous chapter. From this sum is subtracted the net cost of the maintenance of the ministry, i.e. the congregation's contribution to the stipend, pension and travelling expenses of the minister together with the contribution to the salary of the assistant minister, deaconess or lay missionary (if any). The remainder is the available balance of the congregation, on which the Mission and Service Fund contribution is calculated by the Stewardship and Budget Committee. After the Mission and Service Fund 'levy' has been made, the remaining normal recurring income accrues to the congregation, along with all of the special or non-recurring income.

The 'available balance' formula provides a method of apportioning congregational income, or liberality, between the three major spending agencies. Thus, the larger the slice of liberality taken by any one of the spending agencies, the smaller will be the amounts received by the other two. For example, a large increase in stipend may lead to a squeeze on the liberality accruing to the congregations and to mission and service. However, it is not the formula itself which determines the apportionment, but the way in which it is used.

We now examine some of the forces at play, concentrating first on relations between the two central spending agencies – the Church and Ministry Department and the committees within the Mission and Service Fund – and the congregations.

The allocation process is influenced partly by the implicit priority given to stipend, and partly by the supposed sanctions which the maintenance of the Ministry Committee can impose on congregations which fail to meet their contributions to stipend and aid (if any) to the Maintenance of the Ministry Fund. The level of these contributions for each congregation is determined for a three-year period ahead by the committee in consultation with the Presybteries, and is based on the known resources of the congregation and the expected increase in income over the period. Congregations often have the belief, more imagined than real, that if they have a poor record of meeting their contributions to stipend and aid, the Maintenance of the Ministry Committee may raise difficulties over the call of a new minister when they fall vacant.

The Stewardship and Budget Committee has no such sanction to support its allocations. The committee allocates the Mission and Service Fund budget each year to Presbyteries on the basis of an assessment of the congregations in the bounds, and it is left to the Presbyteries to make the allocation to the congregations concerned within certain prescribed limits. The allocation is intended to represent the minimum contributions they are expected to make. However, the allocation is not legally binding, and congregations are able to exercise a 'veto', in the sense that they do not pay the full allocation. In 1973, for example, 977 congregations (47.9 per cent) met their allocation in full, 307 (15.0 per cent) exceeded it, and 757 (37.1 per cent) failed to meet it. Congregations are also able to complain through their Presbyteries that the Mission and Service Fund allocations are reaching the limit of their ability to pay. For example, in 1971 the Stewardship and Budget Committee deferred any increase in the budget for the year, largely because it was advised in the previous year by a large number of Presbyteries that another substantial increase in the budget would make their task of allocation to congregations seriously difficult.

On the other hand, concern has been expressed jointly by the Maintenance of the Ministry and the Stewardship and Budget Committees about the financial performance of congregations. They have criticized the 'low standard of Christian giving' in many congregations, and the high proportion of funds which tend to be used for local fabric purposes.[2]

In 1972 the two committees attempted to draw some of the apparently surplus funds of congregations to the centre by putting forward the following proposal to the General Assembly: 'The Maintenance of the Ministry Committee is asking for authority to ensure that congregations having attained to their appropriate stipends and appropriate contributions to the fund for 1977 and to the Mission and Service Fund, and wishing to increase their minister's stipend above the appropriate figure agreed upon for 1977, will make a corresponding increase pound for pound, to be divided equally between the Mission and Service and Minimum Stipend Funds.'[3]

However, the General Assembly of 1972 ruled that, instead of a 'pound for pound' increase equally divided between the two funds, there should instead be given 'further contribution to the Minimum Stipend Fund and to the Mission and Service Fund deemed by the Presbytery to be appropriate.' This amounts to a serious weakening of the original proposal.

The operation of the available balance formula for allocating liberality between the three major spending agencies can also be examined in terms of the relationship between the two central agencies. The establishment of a joint Consultative Committee of the Maintenance of the Ministry Committee and the Stewardship and Budget Committee may be seen as a measure to institutionalize the potential conflicts between the two. The joint Consultative Committee developed from meetings between the two constituent committees and the General Finance Committee at the behest of the General Assembly of 1965. The General Finance Committee made the following point in its Supplementary Report: 'These two groups constitute the principal spending agencies of the Church and it is therefore desirable that their methods and financial situations should be considered. The conference was anxious to avoid any suggestion that it looked on the two bodies as competitors for the available funds, but equally it considered that a proper survey of their respective positions was essential to the fulfilment of its remit.'[4]

Secondly, the conference recognized that priority is given to the requirements of the maintenance of the ministry in the statement that 'the minimum stipend, as it may be declared from time to time, has first call on congregations' resources.'[5] Nonetheless, the interdependence of the requirements of the Maintenance of the Ministry Fund and of the Mission and Service Fund was recognized. If one increases its demands for funds faster than the growth in congregational income, then the other will suffer. During the early 1960s, for example, the Maintenance of the Ministry Committee deliberately limited increases in the minimum stipend below the level which its income would have permitted. This was done partly so that congregations on the margin of self-support would not have too great difficulty in meeting their respective stipend commitment, and would not therefore be tempted to reduce their contributions to the Mission and Service Fund, and partly in order to build up the reserves in the Maintenance of the Ministry Fund.[6]

Another example of the interdependence of the two funds is shown in the case of the large number of congregations which receive aid from the Maintenance of the Ministry Fund. If the Mission and Service Fund were to make increasing allocations to those congregations, such allocations might be met only at the expense of the maintenance of the ministry, either through an increase in the amount of aid given by the fund to congregations, or through a cutback in congregational expenditure in charges where the expenditure may be already very low. Consequently, it was reported in 1972 that a common policy with regard to the requirements of the aid-receiving congregations had been agreed, as follows:

(a) All congregations, whatever their financial position, will give their members an opportunity to contribute to the Mission and Service Fund.
(b) In the new proposals for allocation put forward . . . by the Stewardship and Budget Committee, aid-receiving congregations will form a special group.
(c) In the present quinquennium no allocation to an aid receiving congregations may be increased above its present level, without prior consultation with the Maintenance of the Ministry Committee.
(d) Before the end of this quinquennium, to take effect after 1977, allocations to all aid-receiving congregations both for maintenance of the ministry and for mission and service requirements will be renegotiated between the two Committees, in consultation with Presbyteries and congregations.[7]

Finally, it is interesting to note that the task of stewardship and fund-raising is assigned to the Stewardship and Budget Committee, yet the degree of success achieved affects the ministry as well as the Mission and Service Fund. Thus, if the rate of growth of congregational income is increased by successful stewardship campaigns, the Maintenance of the Ministry Committee will be able to increase the minimum stipend faster than would otherwise be the case. On the other hand, since the maintenance of the ministry is acknowledged to have first priority, the income of the Mission and Service Fund is determined by the anticipated surplus funds likely to be available once the necessary requirements of the maintenance of the ministry and of the congregations have been met. There is a certain logic, therefore, in making responsible for stewardship that committee which stands to gain most from any increase in the income surplus to the requirements of the ministry.[8]

The outcome of the allocation of congregational income between the three major spending agencies in the Church is shown in table 20. While the table covers the period 1961-75, the available balance formula was in operation for only the last two years of the period. Nonetheless, the forces at play behind the allocation have remained the same throughout the period. The three spending agencies involved can be aggregated into two groups in two different ways in order to show the changes over time. Firstly, the congregations can be distinguished from the two central spending agencies – the Church and Ministry Department and the Mission and Service Fund. An examination of the table shows that over the period 1961-71 an increasing proportion of congregational income accrued to the centre, and a diminishing proportion to the congregations. Thus, while the congregations' share of liberality declined from 58 per cent in 1961 to 49 per cent in 1971, the share of the two central spending units increased over the same period from 42 per cent to 51 per cent. Over the period 1972-5 this trend has been reversed, with the congregations' share of liberality rising from 48 to 55 per cent, and the share of the central spending agencies falling to 45 per cent.

Further light is shed on this question when we consider the second way of aggregating the liberality income of the three spending agencies. Since the bulk of

TABLE 20.
Percentage distribution of congregational income (or liberality) between the three major spending agencies of the Church, 1961-75.

	1961	1962	1963	1964	1965	1966	1967	1968	1969	1970	1971	1972	1973	1974	1975
	%	%	%	%	%	%	%	%	%	%	%	%	%	%	%
Congregations	58	57	55	55	54	54	54	53	54	50	49	51	52	55	55
Church and ministry	28	29	31	31	32	32	32	33	32	35	35	34	34	32	33
Mission and service	14	14	14	14	14	14	14	14	14	15	16	15	14	13	12
TOTAL	100	100	100	100	100	100	100	100	100	100	100	100	100	100	100

SOURCE: 'Report of the General Finance Committee', *Reports to the General Assembly*, 1969 and 1973, appendix II, schedule A. Later figures were supplied by the general treasurer.
Percentages are rounded.

the expenditure of the Church and Ministry Department is devoted to supplementing stipend and the income of the congregations, the expenditures of these two spending agencies together amount to the cost of the upkeep of the ministry. Since the congregations are the source of the income in the first place, the Mission and Service Fund may be seen as using the surplus income generated when the needs of the ministry have been met. This grouping implicitly recognizes the priority given to the ministry, which must be the case when the bulk of the Church's income is derived from that source. The new grouping is interesting in that the relative shares of the two groups have changed remarkable little over the period. Indeed, in the period of 1961-9 the proportion was constant, with the Mission and Service Fund taking 14 per cent of the total. Only in the early 1970s did the proportion increase to 15 and then 16 per cent, before slipping back to 12 per cent. The decline in the proportion of liberality accruing to the Mission and Service Fund over the period 1971-5 from 16 to 12 per cent largely accounts for the financial problems of the fund. The relative constancy of the share of congregational income accruing to the ministry conceals a significant shift in its distribution from congregations to the Church and Ministry Department. While the share of congregations has fallen from 58 to 51 per cent over the period 1961-72, this was matched almost exactly by an increase in the share going to Church and Ministry from 28 per cent to 34 per cent. Here lies the principal shift in the distribution of liberality in recent years. The shift probably reflects the increasing amounts of aid given by affluent congregations to the Maintenance of the Ministry Fund in order to support the stipend in poor congregations.

Of the increase in the share of liberality accruing to the congregations from 49 per cent in 1971 to 55 per cent in 1975, two-thirds was taken from the Mission and Service Fund and one-third from the Church and Ministry Department. This, in part, may reflect the difficulty of the central authorities in budgeting during a period of unprecedently high inflation. The actual increase in congregational income may have been greater than anticipated, so that the Maintenance of the Ministry Committee and the Mission and Service Fund allocations made in advance may have been set too low. However, the fact that the Mission and Service Fund suffered more than the Church and Ministry Department suggests that another factor was involved. A possible explanation may be found in the fact that the proportion of total liberality collected in the form of 'special' (i.e. non-recurring) liberality has increased sharply in recent years, as shown in table 21.

TABLE 21.
The proportion of 'special' liberality to total liberality, 1970-5

	'Special' liberality 1	Total liberality 2	Proportion of 'special' to total liberality 3
	£	£	%
1970	805,128	7,205,220	11.2
1971	794,600	7,659,815	10.4
1972	1,252,218	8,234,737	15.2
1973	1,635,608	9,258,343	17.7
1974	1,973,203	10,681,947	18.5
1975	2,491,695	12,976,298	19.2

The proportion increased from 10.4 per cent in 1971, to 15.2 per cent in 1972, 17.7 per cent in 1973, and 19.2 per cent in 1975. Since it is the individual congregations which decide the disposition of the liberality they raise between the 'normal' and 'special' categories, albeit on the basis of a definition laid down by the General Finance Committee, it seems likely that the explanation of the phenomenon should be sought in the actions of congregations.

One explanation lies in the recent introduction of the available balance formula to calculate the contribution each congregation is asked to make to the Mission and Service Fund. As we noted above, this allocation is based on the normal recurring income of the congregations, the special element being specifically excluded. If the policy of individual congregations was to reduce their allocations from the Mission and Service Fund, they could do that by increasing the proportion of their income in the 'special' category. This would reduce the amount of their normal income, and therefore the size of their available balances, which in turn would lead to a lower allocation.

This seems precisely to have been what has happened, for the scheme was first proposed in 1971,[9] and the shift in the disposition of income occurred in the following two years. It should be remembered that the available balance calculations for each year are based necessarily on the income of previous years, so that there was an incentive for congregations to make the changes in income prior to the start of the scheme in 1974. Total liberality also declined in real terms in 1970 and 1971 from a post-war peak in 1969, so encouraging congregations to reduce payments to the centre in order to conserve income for congregational expenses. It seems clear that the distinction between 'normal' and 'special' liberality needs to be more rigorously defined in order to avoid a recurrence of this problem.

The discussion of the apportionment of Church income between the three main spending agencies has so far concentrated on congregational income, or liberality. The difficulty of undertaking a similar analysis of other income arises partly because a large proportion of that income is tied by the donors to particular purposes, so that the question of apportionment does not arise, and partly that there is little detailed information available on how those tied funds are distributed.

However, in very broad terms the Church's 'other income' is distributed as follows. The income from donations, grants and trusts, and from bequests, is received centrally, and is usually designated for a particular purpose in the Church and Ministry Department or in one or other of the committees in the Mission and Service Fund. The investment income, derived from the Church of Scotland Trust, is made over to the investors, which are to be found in all of the three main spending agencies. The standardized stipend and other endowments for stipend, although collected centrally, are made over to the ministers of the congregations concerned.

3 The disaggregation of total income and expenditure
In this section an attempt is made to break down the total income and expenditure of the Church between the main spending agencies. We deal in turn with the congregations, Church and Ministry Department, the committees within the Mission and Service Fund (excluding National Church Extension), and National Church Extension. The last-named is one of the committees which receives funds

through the Mission and Service Fund, but it is dealt with separately because of its special features. In all cases, the income of the spending agencies is composed of congregational income, or liberality, and elements of 'other income', as described in the previous chapter. We shall find that that proportion of 'other income' committed by the donors to particular purposes is *excluded* from the published summaries of the income figures of the spending agencies concerned. To that extent the income and expenditure figures of the agencies are understated. We estimate the size of these 'tied' funds at the end of this section.

1 Congregations
The income of congregations for congregational expenses – i.e. for those expenses remaining after stipend and ministerial expenses and Mission and Service Fund contributions have been met – is derived almost entirely from the congregations' share of liberality. Some congregations also receive income from their investments in the Church of Scotland Trust (classified in the 'income from investments' component of 'other income').

The distribution of liberality, together with the share accruing to the congregations, is shown in table 22 for the period 1961-75. In table 23 the same figures have been converted into real terms at 1975 prices. Starting at the top of table 22, the first three lines show total liberality each year and its breakdown between 'normal' and 'extraordinary' (or 'special') liberality. On the next line, the total liberality is broken down between that retained by the congregations, which in most years has accounted for just over half of all liberality, and that which passes on for other uses. Just over a quarter of the remainder goes towards the 'payment of stipend', which is the contribution that the congregations make towards the stipend of their minister. Formerly, much of this money was paid direct to the minister without passing through the centre, especially in self-supporting congregations which paid all of their minister's stipend, but from April 1974 all stipend monies pass through the Maintenance of the Ministry Fund. The 'payment for stipend' item is usually included as part of the expenditure of the Church and Ministry Department, which itself augments stipend funds from its own income (see below).

The remaining sum, amounting to between a fifth and a quarter of liberality, accrues to central funds. The Church and Ministry Department receives about 6 or 7 per cent of total liberality, this being the payment of aid to the Maintenance of the Ministry Fund by aid-giving congregations, together with congregational contributions to the Aged and Infirm Ministers' Fund for ministers' pensions. The Mission and Service Fund (including National Church Extension) receives the remaining 12 to 15 per cent of liberality through the contributions of congregations. The National Church Extension Committee receives about 2 per cent of the total.

A summary of the liberality income devoted to congregational expenses in money terms and in real terms at 1975 prices is shown in table 24 for the period 1961-75. In money terms this income has increased unsteadily, unlike total liberality, except in the last few years, when both have increased sharply under the influence of inflation. When expressed in real terms, the liberality income devoted to congregational expenses has fluctuated from year to year, but on a generally declining trend. The sharp fall in 1963 is probably explained by the

TABLE 22.
Distribution of congregational income (or liberality), 1961-75 (in money terms)

	1961	%	1962	%	1963	%	1964	%	1965	%	1966	%	1967	%	1968	%	1969	%	1970	%	1971	%	1972	%	1973	%	1974	%	1975	%
Christian Liberality																														
normal	4344	84	4584	84	4781	86	4987	88	5232	87	5532	87	5730	87	5821	87	6118	86	6400	84	6865	89	6983	90	7623	85	8709	82	10485	81
extraordinary	689	16	660	16	664	14	745	12	768	13	826	13	846	13	912	13	1170	14	805	16	795	11	1252	10	1635	15	1973	18	2492	19
TOTAL	5033	100	5244	100	5445	100	5732	100	6000	100	6358	100	6576	100	6733	100	7288	100	7205	100	7660	100	8235	100	9258	100	10682	100	12977	100
less retained by																														
congregations	2921	58	3007	58	2981	57	3125	55	3253	55	3463	54	3579	54	3565	54	3919	53	3632	54	3789	50	4195	49	4819	51	5877	52	7115	55
	2112	42	2237	42	2464	43	2607	45	2747	45	2895	46	2997	46	3168	46	3369	47	3573	46	3871	50	4040	51	4439	49	4805	48	5862	45
less payment of stipend	1140	23	1206	23	1384	23	1459	25	1550	25	1630	26	1678	26	1808	26	1924	27	2001	26	2143	28	2259	28	2553	27	2798	28	3365	26
Contributions to central funds divided:																														
	972	19	1031	19	1080	20	1148	20	1197	20	1265	20	1319	20	1360	20	1445	20	1572	20	1728	22	1781	23	1886	22	2007	20	2497	19
Church and ministry	269	5	285	6	298	6	329	6	358	6	384	6	399	6	419	6	462	6	492	6	524	7	568	7	593	7	636	6	988	8
Mission and Service Fund																														
National Church Extension	108	2	124	2	135	2	130	2	131	2	152	2	159	2	164	2	167	2	193	2	204	3	218	3	232	3	248	2	285	2
other committees	595	12	622	12	647	12	689	12	708	12	729	12	761	12	777	12	816	12	887	12	1000	12	995	13	1061	12	1123	11	1224	9
	703	14	746	14	782	14	819	14	839	14	881	14	920	14	941	14	983	14	1080	14	1024	15	1213	16	1293	15	1371	14	1509	11

SOURCE: 'Report of the General Finance Committee', *Reports to the General Assembly*, 1969 and 1973, appendix II, schedule A. Information for later years supplied by the general treasurer.
Figures to nearest £000; percentages are rounded.
'Church and Ministry' also usually includes 'payment of stipend', which is given separately above.

TABLE 23.
Distribution of congregational income (or liberality), 1961-75 (in real terms at 1975 prices)

	1961	%	1962	%	1963	%	1964	%	1965	%	1966	%	1967	%	1968	%	1969	%	1970	%	1971	%	1972	%	1973	%	1974	%	1975	%
Christian liberality																														
normal	11330	84	11616	86	11913	88	12023	87	12091	87	12214	87	12466	87	12019	87	11968	86	11844	84	11598	89	11005	90	11003	85	10820	82	10485	81
extraordinary	1797	16	1673	14	1654	12	1796	13	1775	13	1824	13	1841	13	1883	13	2288	14	1490	16	1343	11	1973	10	2360	15	2451	18	2492	19
	13127	100	13289	100	13567	100	13819	100	13866	100	14038	100	14307	100	13902	100	14256	100	13334	100	12941	100	12978	100	13363	100	13271	100	12977	100
less retained by congregations	7619	58	7620	57	7428	55	7534	55	7518	55	7646	54	7787	54	7361	54	7666	53	6721	54	6401	50	6611	49	6956	51	7301	52	7115	55
less payment of stipend	5508	42	5669	43	6139	45	6285	45	6348	45	6392	46	6520	46	6541	46	6590	47	6613	46	6540	50	6367	51	6407	49	5970	48	5862	45
Contributions to central funds divided:	2973	23	3056	23	3448	23	3517	25	3582	25	3599	26	3651	26	3733	26	3764	27	3704	26	3620	28	3560	28	3685	27	3476	28	3365	26
	2535	19	2613	20	2691	20	2768	20	2766	20	2793	20	2869	20	2808	20	2826	20	2909	20	2919	22	2807	22	2722	20	2494	19	2497	19
Church and ministry	702	5	722	6	743	6	793	6	827	6	846	6	868	6	865	6	904	6	911	6	885	7	895	6	856	6	790	6	988	8
Mission and Service Fund																														
(a) National Church extension	281	2	314	2	336	2	313	2	303	2	336	2	345	2	339	2	327	2	357	2	345	3	344	3	335	3	308	3	285	2
(b) other committees	1552	12	1577	12	1612	12	1662	12	1636	12	1611	12	1656	12	1604	12	1595	12	1641	12	1689	12	1568	13	1531	12	1395	11	1224	9
	1833	14	1891	14	1948	14	1975	14	1939	14	1947	14	2001	14	1943	14	1922	14	1998	14	2034	15	1912	16	1866	14	1703	14	1509	11

SOURCE. Figures converted to real terms from those in table 22.
Figures to nearest £000; percentages are rounded.
'Church and ministry' also usually includes 'payment of stipend', which is given separately above.

introduction of the payment of ministerial travelling expenses for all congregations, which took that element of income over to ministerial expenses under the Church and Ministry Department. Over the period 1961-75 the real income of congregations fell by 6.6 per cent from £7,619,000 to £7,115,000.

Throughout the period, however, the policy of union and readjustment was continuing to reduce the number of congregations by mergers and other forms of adjustment.[10] Between 1961 and 1975 the number of congregations fell from 2,212 to 1,964, a decline of 11.2 per cent. This has had the effect of cushioning congregations against the downward trend in real income. Indeed, in 1975 the liberality income for congregational expenses of the average congregation was £3,623, or 5.2 per cent above the 1961 figure of £3,444 in real terms.

So far the discussion has centred on congregational income. Unfortunately, no information is collected centrally on the expenditures of congregations. The nearest it is possible to get to a figure for the expenditure of congregations is to assume that all income is spent, in which case total expenditure equals total income. From the viewpoint of the central authorities this assumption may be realistic in that income once allocated to the congregations cannot easily be tapped, but from the standpoint of the congregations the assumption is less realistic, because congregations can and do make savings from their income. We do know, however, that congregational expenditures include the following items: the maintenance of an adequate fabric fund; the insurance premiums and local rates and taxes on property; the heating, lighting and cleaning of the church, and other expenses connected with public worship; the salaries (if any) of the church officer, organist and other officials; the assessments levied by the Presbytery, Synod and General Assembly to meet their expenses; and any other fixed charge falling upon the Kirk Session or congregation.

A report of the General Finance Committee in 1967[11] stressed that, because the expenditure of congregations on local expenses absorbed more than 40 per cent of the total income of the Church, such expenditure 'should be kept under constant review to ensure that due economy is observed'. The report went on to draw attention to certain possible economies in congregational finance. Firstly, the report stated that 'more might be done to discourage expenditure on activities outside the Church and on amenities which are not justified at a time when the wider work of the Church is curtailed by lack of funds.' Secondly, the report stated that an examination of congregational accounts shows that there is a tendency for some of the larger and wealthier congregations to transfer their surplus income to reserve against unforeseen contingencies. The comment was not intended to be critical of 'the practice of transferring a reasonable sum each year to a fabric fund', but was aimed at 'unreasonably large transfers, especially when there is no specific object in view.' These are some of the questions we examine in our survey of congregational finance in chapter 12.

2 Church and Ministry Department
The second major spending agency in the Church is the Church and Ministry Department. With the congregations, it accounts for the total income and expenditure of the ministry. The main component of the Church and Ministry Department is the Maintenance of the Ministry Committee. The purpose of this committee is described as follows: 'The first responsibility of the Church of Scotland is to

TABLE 24.

The liberality income devoted to congregational expenses in money terms and in real terms at 1975 prices, 1961-75

	1961	1962	1963	1964	1965	1966	1967	1968	1969	1970	1971	1972	1973	1974	1975
1 Liberality in money terms retained by congregations (£000s)	2,921	3,007	2,981	3,125	3,253	3,463	3,579	3,565	3,919	3,632	3,789	4,195	4,819	5,877	7,117
2 Liberality in real terms retained by congregations (£000s)	7,619	7,843	7,428	7,534	7,518	7,646	7,787	7,361	7,666	6,721	6,401	6,611	6,055	7,301	7,115
3 Number of congregations	2,212	2,200	2,199	2,192	2,179	2,166	2,150	2,115	2,124	2,097	2,088	2,067	2,009	1,993	1,964
4 Average money liberality per congregation, (i.e. 1/3) (£)	1,321	1,367	1,356	1,426	1,493	1,599	1,665	1,686	1,845	1,732	1,815	2,030	2,399	2,949	3,624
5 Average real liberality per congregation, (i.e. 2/3) (£)	3,444	3,565	3,378	3,437	3,450	3,530	3,622	3,480	3,609	3,205	3,066	3,198	3,014	3,663	3,623

maintain religious ordinances throughout the land, and to provide ministry of Word and Sacraments to all our people by means of a settled parochial ministry supported by the fund called the Fund for the Maintenance of the Ministry. This fund is administered by . . . The Committee on the Maintenance of the Ministry.'[12]

The purpose of the fund is partly to act as a vehicle through which congregations pay the stipend of their minister. More importantly, the fund also draws additional sums, called 'aid', from the relatively affluent congregations which can afford to pay in full the stipend of their minister. This it uses to subsidize the stipends of ministers in poor congregations which cannot afford to pay their ministers the minimum stipend. The minimum stipend is the stipend below which no minister is allowed to fall; in 1975 it was declared at £2,258. Thus, if a small necessary congregation is able to give, say, only £1,500 towards the stipend of its minister, the committee then has to find the difference, i.e. £758, to bring the minister's stipend up to the minimum.

The other important expenditure-generating body within the Church and Ministry Department is the Aged and Infirm Ministers' Fund and Pension Fund. This fund gives pensions to retired ministers from income derived largely from congregational contributions of 15 per cent of the stipend paid in the previous year.

The income and expenditure of the Church and Ministry Department are shown in broad outline for the period 1961-75 in table 25. The corresponding figures expressed in terms of constant prices set at the 1975 level are given in table 26. The tables indicate that the income of the department derives from two sources. The first source is the contribution of liberality from congregations through aid given to the fund, and through contributions to the Aged and Infirm Ministers' Fund, as described above in the distribution of liberality, and shown in tables 22 and 23. The second source of income is the department's share of the Church's other income. As we have already pointed out, these figures exclude that proportion of the department's other income designated by the donors for particular purposes, so that the income (and expenditure) of the department is significantly understated in tables 25 and 26.

Table 25 shows that congregational contributions have increased in money terms every year between 1961 and 1975, whereas 'other income' has fluctuated significantly, although on an upward trend. As a result, the proportion of congregational contributions to total income has increased substantially from 29.6 per cent in 1961 to 48.1 per cent in 1975. When expressed in real terms as in table 26, congregational contributions rose every year over the period 1961-70 but fluctuated thereafter, giving an increase of 40.7 per cent over the period 1961-75. The particularly large increase in 1975 is probably accounted for by the large increase in congregational contributions to the Aged and Infirm Ministers' Fund in that year. This was caused by the increase in the annual contribution from 5 to 15 per cent of the stipend of the previous year. On the other hand, income from other sources fluctuated on a downward trend, falling by 36.2 per cent between 1961 and 1975. This is probably largely accounted for by the decline in the real value of the standardized stipend. Taking both components together, total real income increased sharply from 1961, reaching a peak of £2,700,000 in 1964. Thereafter, real income declined on a fluctuating trend, so that by 1975 it stood

TABLE 25.
The income and expenditure of the Church and Ministry Department, 1961-75 (in money terms)

	1961	1962	1963	1964	1965	1966	1967	1968	1969	1970	1971	1972	1973	1974	1975
INCOME															
congregational contributions	269	285	298	329	358	384	399	419	462	492	524	568	593	636	988
income from other sources	639	680	685	791	772	750	817	776	769	836	802	883	848	922	1064
TOTAL	908	965	983	1120	1130	1134	1216	1195	1231	1328	1326	1451	1441	1558	2052
EXPENDITURE															
stipends, etc.	1830	1874	2139	2202	2317	2467	2545	2701	2786	2864	3036	3148	3501	3810	4474
less: paid by congregations	1140	1206	1384	1459	1550	1630	1678	1808	1924	2001	2143	2259	2553	2798	3365
retiring allowances, etc.	690	668	755	743	767	837	867	893	862	863	893	889	948	1012	1109
grants for endowments of stipend	142	164	174	185	189	194	202	237	258	264	267	302	329	354	365
	20	12	13	8	2	19	64	66	30	17	68	2	—	30	60
administration	19	21	22	25	34	37	37	35	37	41	44	47	57	68	77
TOTAL	871	865	964	961	992	1087	1170	1231	1187	1185	1272	1240	1334	1464	1611
surplus(+)/deficit(−)	+37	+100	+19	+159	+138	+47	+46	−36	+44	+143	+53	+211	+108	+94	+441
add: Special distribution from F.G. Salvesen bequest				+197							+321				
Profit(+)/loss(−) on investment transactions		+141	−2						−77		−28		+2		−8
funds at beginning of year	417	454	695	712	1068	1206	1253	1299	1263	1230	1373	1719	1930	2040	2134
FUNDS AT END OF YEAR	454	695	712	1068	1206	1253	1299	1263	1230	1373	1719	1930	2040	2134	2567

SOURCE: 'Report of the General Finance Committee', *Reports to the General Assembly*, 1969 and 1973, appendix II, schedule B (1969) and schedule D (1973). Information for later years supplied by the general treasurer.
Figures to nearest £000.

TABLE 26.
The income and expenditure of the Church and Ministry Department, 1961-75 (in real terms at 1975 prices)

	1961	1962	1963	1964	1965	1966	1967	1968	1969	1970	1971	1972	1973	1974	1975
INCOME															
congregational contributions	702	722	743	793	827	848	868	865	904	911	885	895	856	790	988
income from other sources	1667	1723	1707	1907	1784	1656	1777	1602	1504	1547	1355	1392	1224	1145	1064
TOTAL	2369	2445	2450	2700	2611	2504	2645	2467	2408	2458	2240	2287	2080	1935	2052
EXPENDITURE															
stipends, etc.	4773	4749	5330	5309	5354	5447	5537	5577	5450	5300	5129	4961	5053	4733	4474
less: paid by congregations	2973	3056	3448	3517	3582	3599	3651	3733	3764	3703	3620	3560	3685	3476	3365
retiring allowances, etc.	1800	1693	1882	1792	1772	1848	1886	1844	1686	1597	1509	1401	1368	1257	1109
	370	416	434	446	437	428	439	489	505	489	451	476	475	440	365
grants for endowments of stipends	52	30	32	19	5	42	139	136	59	31	115	3	—	37	60
administration	50	53	55	60	79	82	81	72	72	76	74	74	82	84	70
TOTAL	2272	2192	2403	2317	2293	2400	2545	2541	2322	2193	2149	1954	1925	1818	1611
Surplus(+)/deficit(−)	+97	+253	+47	+383	+319	+103	+100	−74	+86	+265	+90	+333	+156	+117	+441
add: Special distribution of F.G. Salvesen Bequest				+475							+542				
Profit(+)/loss(−) on investment transactions		+357	−5						−151		−47		+3		−8
funds at beginning of year	1088	1150	1732	1716	2468	2663	2726	2682	2471	2276	2320	2709	2786	2534	2134
FUNDS AT END OF YEAR	1185	1760	1774	2574	2787	2766	2826	2608	2406	2541	2905	3042	2945	2651	2567

SOURCE: figures converted to real terms from those in table 25.
Figures to nearest £000.

13.4 per cent below that of fifteen years previously. What seems to have happened over the period is that the department has attempted to increase congregational contributions as quickly as possible in order to offset the real decline in other income.

The first item under the expenditure heading in table 25 is labelled 'stipends, etc.' This item covers the total stipend payments of the Church, together with the payments of various expenses relating to ministers, such as car grants, driving grants, widows' and next-of-kin grants, vacancy expenses, removal expenses, and expenses involving retirements in the interest of union.[13] It is thought that stipend payments formed about 90 per cent of this category of expenditure in 1975.

The bulk of stipend payments and the expenses of ministers are paid by the congregations, through the Maintenance of the Ministry Fund in the case of stipends, and direct to the minister in the case of expenses. The proportion of these expenditures paid by congregations has shown a tendency to increase over the period under review, from 62.3 per cent in 1961 to 75.2 per cent in 1975. The remaining proportion is paid from the income of the Maintenance of the Ministry Committee. Table 25 shows that congregational contributions are not sufficient to cover the committee's contributions to stipend and ministerial expenses.

The total payment of stipend and ministerial expenses is sometimes included within the income and expenditure accounts of the Church and Ministry Department, partly because the stipend to be contributed by each congregation for a three-year period ahead is determined by the Maintenance of the Ministry Committee in conjunction with the Presbytery, and partly because all stipend payments to ministers are now made through the department. However, even if only that proportion of the expenditure made from the fund is considered, it still forms the bulk of total departmental expenditure. In 1975 expenditures on stipend and ministerial expenses amounted to 68.8 per cent of total departmental expenditure, this proportion having declined over the preceding fifteen years from 79.2 per cent in 1961.

The bulk of the remaining expenditure is taken up with retiring allowances and the like paid by the Aged and Infirm Ministers' Fund. These have tended to form an increasing proportion of total departmental expenditure, rising from 16.3 per cent in 1961 to 22.7 per cent in 1975. Also, sizeable sums are devoted to grants to individual congregations in certain cases for endowments of stipend, such as on the occasion when a Church Extension charge reaches full status.[14] Expenditure on administration accounted for between about four and four-and-a-half per cent of total expenditure in the last few years of the period.

Table 25 shows that the Church and Ministry Department had surpluses of income over expenditure every year over the period 1961-75 with the single exception of 1969, even before including the net flow of funds from certain special sources, such as the F.G. Salvesen bequest. The reserves of the department have therefore increased steadily over the period from £454,000 in 1961 to £2,567,000 in 1975. The 1975 figure compares to a total expenditure in that year of £1,611,000. In real terms at 1975 prices the reserves have increased over the period by 116.6 per cent from £1,185,000 to £2,567,000.

We have seen that the bulk of the expenditure of the Church and Ministry Department is devoted to stipend and ministerial expenses, and that the congregations contribute an even larger sum to those items. All told, the expenditure of the

TABLE 27
The payment of stipend in the Church, 1961-75

Year	Minimum Stipend 1	Retail Price Index 2	Minimum Stipend at 1975 prices 3	Number of parish ministers 4	Total Minimum Stipend 'bill' at 1975 prices (i.e. 3 × 4) 5	Expenditure on 'Stipends, etc.' at 1975 prices 6	Difference between 5 and 6 7	($\frac{7}{6} \times 100\%$) 8
1961	800	171	2,087	1,928	4,023,736	4,773,000	749,264	15.7
1962	870	176	2,205	1,927	4,249,035	4,749,000	499,965	10.5
1963	900	179	2,242	1,890	4,237,380	5,330,000	1,092,620	20.5
1964	925	185	2,230	1,888	4,210,240	5,309,000	1,098,760	20.7
1965	950	193	2,195	1,885	4,137,575	5,354,000	1,216,425	22.7
1966	1,000	202	2,208	1,859	4,104,672	5,447,000	1,342,328	24.6
1967	1,100+	205	2,393	1,814	4,340,902	5,537,000	1,196,098	21.6
1968	1,150	216	2,375	1,827	4,339,125	5,577,000	1,237,875	22.2
1969	1,200	228	2,347	1,789	4,198,783	5,450,000	1,251,217	23.0
1970	1,250	241	2,313	1,754	4,057,002	5,300,000	1,242,998	23.5
1971	1,392	264	2,352	1,745	4,104,240	5,129,000	1,024,760	20.0
1972	1,500	283	2,364	1,687	3,988,068	4,961,000	972,932	19.6
1973	1,674	309	2,416	1,660	4,010,560	5,053,000	1,042,440	20.6
1974	1,872	359	2,326	1,631	3,793,706	4,733,000	939,294	19.8
1975	2,258	446	2,258	1,588	3,585,704	4,474,000	888,296	19.9

+ Increase deferred for six months until 1.7.67 because of prices and incomes standstill. The figure in column 5 has been adjusted accordingly.

Church devoted to stipend and related expenses as a proportion of total income varied only between 25.4 and 29.5 per cent for the period 1961-75. The annual average for the whole period was 27.1 per cent. The connection between stipend and Church income is explored more closely in table 27. Column 1 of the table shows the value of the minimum stipend each year over the period 1961-75. In that period it has increased 2.8 times, from £800 to £2,258. Column 3 gives the minimum stipend in real terms at 1975 prices, having been converted using the Retail Price Index (column 2). Although fluctuating from year to year, the real minimum stipend stood 14.7 per cent higher in 1967 than in 1961, but then only managed to roughly maintain its real value between 1967 and 1973, when it increased overall by just under 1 per cent. In 1974 and 1975 the real minimum stipend declined sharply. This pattern roughly reflects the trend in the real total income of the Church and Ministry Department, which reached a high point in the mid-1960s; but it does not explain the constancy of the real minimum stipend in the period 1967-73, when the real income of the department was declining. The answer seems to lie in the gradual decline over the whole period 1961-75 in the numbers of ministers, together with charges. Column 4 of table 27 indicates that the number of parish ministers was 1,588 in 1975, or 17.6 per cent fewer than the total of 1,928 in 1961. If the number of ministers in each year is multiplied by the ruling minimum stipend in each year, the total minimum stipend 'bill' for each year can be calculated, and these are shown in column 5. The total annual minimum stipend payments increased, if somewhat unevenly, up to 1968, and then declined, thereby giving a closer fit with the total income of the department than the minimum stipend alone, and indicating as a result the role played by the numbers of ministers in determining total expenditures.

Thus the decline in the number of ministers over the period 1961-75 served to accentuate the increase in real minimum stipend up to 1967, and to maintain its real value between 1967 and 1973, when the real total income devoted to stipend was falling. The significance of this factor can be illustrated by calculating what would have happened had the number of ministers stayed constant in the face of the total real minimum stipend payments actually made. If the 1,928 ministers in 1961 had remained in 1967, with the 1967 total real minimum stipend bill staying the same, the real minimum stipend would have been £2,251. This figure is only 7.9 per cent above the figure for 1961 of £2,087 and 6.3 per cent below the actual real figure of £2,393. Similarly, if the 1,814 ministers in service in 1967 had survived until 1975, then the minimum stipend would probably have been about £1,977, or 14.2 per cent below the 1975 minimum of £2,258. It seems clear, therefore, that the maintenance of the real value of the minimum stipend in the present financial circumstances of the Church depends very much on a continued decline in the number of ministers and charges.

Finally, column 7 in table 27 shows the difference between the total annual expenditure on minimum stipends and the annual expenditure on total stipends and related expenses of ministers, both expressed in real terms at 1975 prices. The sums given in column 7 thus comprise partly the various ministerial expenses enumerated above, and partly that element of stipend above the minimum which ministers in a large proportion of charges receive. Some of these charges are affluent, and so can afford to pay their minister more than the minimum; in other special cases, such as in Church Extension and linked charges, the minister is automatically given a supplementary allowance over and above the minimum, even though the charge remains technically a minimum stipend charge. Column 8 of table 27 gives the figures of column 7 as a percentage of total stipend and related expenses. The percentage averages about 20 per cent in recent years. The large increase in the percentage in 1963 probably arose from the making of ministerial travelling expenses obligatory upon all congregations in February 1963.[15]

3 Mission and service
In this section we turn to examine briefly the income and expenditures of the committees receiving income from the Mission and Service Fund. These Committees are concerned with the work of the Church which extends beyond the ministry. Table 28 presents the aggregate income and expenditures of the committees for the period 1961-75. Although the National Church Extension Committee receives income from the fund, it is dealt with separately in the next section because of its special situation. Table 29 gives the same income and expenditure figures expressed in real terms at 1975 prices.

Like the income of the Church as a whole, the income of the committees within the Mission and Service Fund derives from congregational contributions and income from other sources. The congregational contributions are received entirely through the Mission and Service Fund. The income from other sources includes donations, bequests, grants and the like given directly to the committees concerned. Again it must be recalled that elements of 'other income' designated by their donors for particular purposes are not included in the figures in tables 28 and 29, and to that extent the income of the committees within the fund is understated.

Although the income of the committees has been roughly the same as that of the Church and Ministry Department, hovering around £2.5 millions in real terms at 1975 prices, the proportions received from the two sources are very different. Whereas the Church and Ministry Department has, at least until the last year or two, received roughly two-thirds of its income as income from other sources, the position of the committees in the Mission and Service Fund is the reverse, with roughly two-thirds of the income derived from congregational contributions. The Fund is thus very dependent on the annual contributions of congregations. This dependency helps to explain the emphasis in the work of the Stewardship and Budget Committee on developing and refining methods of allocating the Mission and Service Fund budget to the congregations.

The congregational contributions to the committees within the Mission and Service Fund (excluding National Church Extension) increased every year over the period 1961-75, with the single exception of 1972. Income from other sources also increased, but on a less steady upward path. Taking the period as a whole, the total income of mission and service increased about two-and-a-quarter times from £895,000 in 1961 to £2,036,000 in 1975. The picture changes, however, when these figures are converted into real terms. Real total income of mission and service increased sharply in the early years following the inception of the fund (formerly the Co-ordinated Appeal) in 1961, but in 1965 it levelled off, and then fell sharply in 1966 as a result of an unexpected decline in income from other sources. In the years 1968-72 total real income stabilized at just under £2.5 millions, but in the last three years has tended to decline, falling to nearly

TABLE 28.

The income and expenditure of the committees within the Mission and Service Fund (excluding National Church Extension), 1961-75, (in money terms)

	1961	1962	1963	1964	1965	1966	1967	1968	1969	1970	1971	1972	1973	1974	1975
INCOME															
congregational contributions	595	622	647	689	708	729	761	777	816	887	1000	995	1061	1123	1224
income from other sources	300	339	377	428	456	375	484	422	439	484	439	557	526	741	812
TOTAL	895	961	1024	1117	1164	1104	1245	1199	1255	1371	1439	1552	1587	1864	2036
EXPENDITURE															
work of committees	745	798	865	930	943	1039	1034	1024	1122	1147	1204	1155	1338	1605	1549
administration	132	149	164	173	194	191	202	204	209	223	249	258	274	326	388
TOTAL	877	947	1029	1103	1137	1230	1236	1228	1331	1370	1453	1413	1612	1931	1937
surplus(+)/deficit(−)	+18	+14	−5	+14	+27	−126	+9	−29	−76	+1	−14	+139	−25	−67	+99
add: Special distribution from F.G. Salvesen bequest				+148							+242				
Profit(+)/loss(−) on investment transactions		−19					+47				−1			−19	−10
funds at beginning of year	591	609	604	599	761	788	682	738	709	633	634	793*	932	907	821
FUNDS AT END OF YEAR	609	604	599	761	788	662	738	709	633	634	861	932	907	821	910

* Made up as follows: funds at beginning of year £861
  less: residual funds of huts and canteens   68
                                              _____
                                              £793

SOURCE: 'Report of the General Finance Committee', *Reports to the General Assembly*, 1969, 1973 appendix II, schedule D (1969) and schedule C (1973). Information for later years supplied by the general treasurer. Figures to nearest £000.

TABLE 29.

The income and expenditure of the committees within the Mission and Service Fund (excluding National Church Extension) 1961-75
(in real terms at 1975 prices)

	1961	1962	1963	1964	1965	1966	1967	1968	1969	1970	1971	1972	1973	1974	1975
INCOME															
congregational contributions	1552	1576	1612	1661	1636	1610	1656	1604	1596	1642	1689	1568	1531	1395	1224
income from other sources	782	859	939	1032	1054	828	1053	871	859	896	742	878	759	921	812
TOTAL	2334	2435	2551	2693	2690	2438	2709	2475	2455	2538	2431	2446	2290	2316	2036
EXPENDITURE —															
work of committees	1943	2022	2155	2242	2179	2294	2250	2114	2195	2123	2034	1820	1931	1994	1549
administration	344	378	409	417	448	422	439	421	409	413	421	407	395	405	388
TOTAL	2287	2400	2564	2659	2627	2716	2689	2535	2604	2536	2455	2227	2326	2399	1937
Surplus(+)/deficit(−)	+47	+35	−12	+34	+62	−278	+20	−60	−149	+2	−24	+219	−36	−83	+99
add: special distribution from F.G. Salvesen bequest				357							409				
Profit(+)/loss(−) on investment transactions		−48					+102				−2			−24	−10
funds at beginning of year	1541	1543	1504	1444	1759	1740	1484	1524	1387	1171	1071	1250*	1345	1127	821
FUNDS AT END OF YEAR	1588	1530	1492	1835	1821	1462	1606	1464	1238	1173	1454	1469	1309	1020	910

* Made up as follows: funds at beginning of year — £1357
  less: residual funds of huts and canteens — 107
                              1250

SOURCE: Figures converted to real terms from those in table 28. Figures to nearest £000.

£2 millions by 1975. In that year total real income stood 12.8 per cent below the 1961 level.

In tables 28 and 29 the expenditures of the committees within the Mission and Service Fund are broken down only between 'administration' and 'work of committees', but this is sufficient to reveal an apparently high proportion of expenditure devoted to administration. Over the period 1961-75 the proportion of total expenditure devoted to administration varied between 15.0 and 20.0 per cent.

As expected, expenditure has closely followed income, although a sizeable deficit was incurred in 1966 as the result of an unexpected drop in income. If the special distributions from the F.G. Salvesen bequest in 1964 and 1971 are taken into account, the reserves funds of the committees increased by 54.0 per cent from £591,000 at the beginning of 1961 to £910,000 at the end of 1975. However, if the effect of the rise in prices is also included, the size of the reserve funds fell by 40.9 per cent between the two dates from £1,541,000 to £910,000. This is a further indication of the financial weakness of the committees within the Mission and Service Fund. A further point is that a large proportion of the reserve funds were tied up in the loan to the National Church Extension Committee from the mid-1960s (see below).

The operation of the Mission and Service Fund illustrates in a very clear way how the desired expenditure of the committees, as expressed in their budgets submitted each year to the Stewardship and Budget Committee, has to be reduced to match expected income. In its 1965 report, the Stewardship and Budget Committee pointed out that from its inception it had worked 'on a tight budget'.[16] Once again the committee had 'to encourage committees to prune their budgets, so that the total could be fitted in to what the Church is ready to provide.' The budgeting procedure illustrates the weak position of the Stewardship and Budget Committee, which by its terms of reference is instructed to consider carefully the budget presented by each committee, 'not with the object of questioning or objecting to the ordinary operating expenditure, but with the obligation to satisfy itself in regard to extraordinary or additional expenditure.' The procedure has been described as follows: 'The procedure followed by the Stewardship and Budget Committee provides machinery whereby the committees may put forward their claims to finance, but the methods by which conflicting claims can be reconciled are limited by the authority conferred on the Stewardship and Budget Committee . . . If, as has so far been the case, the total of the budgeted requirements for the coming year exceeds the expected available income, the Stewardship and Budget Committee has no power to require any committee to reduce its budget and, if it could not achieve a balance by negotiation, it would have to submit the problem to the next General Assembly to determine priorities. So far, the requisite balance has always been achieved by negotiation, i.e. a balance between the total budgets of the committees and the total annual expected income. The Stewardship and Budget Committee has no power to discriminate between the requirements of the various committees and can only strive to reduce the total in an arbitrary manner.'[17]

It seems very likely that the 'total of the budgeted requirements' for future years will continue to exceed 'expected available income', for at least two reasons. The first is that most, if not all, of the committees within the fund face what is potentially an almost unlimited demand for the services they provide, whether it be homes for the old or missionary aid to less developed countries. The potential demand for funds is thus almost unlimited. Secondly, the competitive bidding situation in which the committees draw up their budgets may encourage each committee, fortified by the acknowledged demand for its services, to bid for rather more funds than it hopes to get, on the basis that it will not get more than it asks for, and on the basis of previous experience it will probably get rather less.

Once budgets are determined, a further regulation helps to ensure that the money is spent. The regulation is that a committee within the Co-ordinated Appeal cannot build up reserves out of ordinary income, since the amount of any surplus arising in a particular year is deducted from that committee's budget in a subsequent year.[18] This measure provides a strong incentive for committees to spend all of their ordinary income, and indeed, has been suggested as the reason for the relatively low level of the reserves of the Mission and Service Fund.

4 National church extension

The function of the National Church Extension Committee is to decide, in consultation with presbyteries, where new church buildings are required to serve the needs of new housing areas, and then to arrange and finance such projects as are agreed. The income and expenditures of National Church Extension for the period 1961-75 are shown in table 30; the corresponding figures in real terms at 1975 prices are given in table 31. As with the other committees, income is derived partly from congregational contributions received through the Mission and Service Fund, and partly from income from other sources received direct by the committee. The income from congregations has followed a fairly steady upward trend in money terms, though variations in other income has tended to lead to fluctuations in total income. Other income formed the larger part of total income in most years between 1961 and 1971, but in the last few years the position has been reversed. In 1975 the total income of the committee was £568,000, or 3.2 per cent of the Church's total income. When expressed in real terms, the total income of National Church Extension has fluctuated considerably from year to year. However, it may be significant that in the three years 1973-5 annual real income averaged £571,000, as compared with £761,000 in the three years 1961-3. The difference between the figures is largely explained by the much lower level of real income from other sources in the later period.

Administration expenditures have amounted to about 5 per cent of total expenditure in recent years, the remaining expenditures being devoted to building work. The significant aspect of expenditures is that they increased very sharply in 1964 and 1965, reaching totals of £534,000 and £580,000 respectively as compared with £333,000 in 1963. As a result, the funds of the committee fell from a surplus of £95,000 at the end of 1963 to deficits of £156,000 in 1964 and £484,000 at the end of 1965. These changes reflect a deliberate change of policy towards accelerating the building programme, which was approved by the General Assembly of 1963. The policy was based on the assumption, later proved to be mistaken, that the completion of the outstanding building programme estimated at £3 millions would see an end to the need for church extension. The expected debt to be incurred by the committee was to be financed by inter-committee borrowing, together with a loan of up to £500,000 from the (then) five Scottish banks. In the event, the facilities arranged with the banks were not required. By 1966, however,

TABLE 30.
The income and expenditure of National Church Extension, 1961-75 (in money terms)

	1961	1962	1963	1964	1965	1966	1967	1968	1969	1970	1971	1972	1973	1974	1975
INCOME															
congregational contributions	108	124	135	130	131	152	159	164	167	193	204	218	232	248	285
income from other sources	183	150	198	153	121	188	159	128	258	143	211	217	153	225	283
TOTAL	291	274	333	283	252	340	318	292	425	336	415	435	385	473	568
EXPENDITURE															
building work	248	293	319	520	561	405	238	301	329	384	448	399	359	303	412
administration	12	13	14	14	19	18	18	17	19	20	21	24	25	27	32
TOTAL	260	306	333	534	580	423	256	318	348	404	469	423	384	330	444
Surplus(+)/deficit(−)	+31	−32	0	−251	−328	−83	+62	−26	+77	−68	−54	+12	+1	+143	+124
add: profit(+)/loss(−) on investment transactions									−88		−5			−7	
funds at beginning of year	96	127	95	95	(156)	(484)	(567)	(505)	(531)	(542)	(610)	(669)	(657)	(656)	(520)
FUNDS AT END OF YEAR	127	95	95	(156)	(484)	(567)	(505)	(531)	(542)	(610)	(669)	(657)	(656)	(520)	(396)

SOURCE: 'Report of the General Finance Committee', *Reports to the General Assembly*, 1969 and 1973, appendix II, schedule C (1969) and schedule B (1973). Information for recent years was supplied by the general treasurer.
Figures to nearest £000. The bracketed numbers indicate deficits.

TABLE 31.

The income and expenditure of National Church Extension, 1961-75 (in real terms at 1975 prices)

	1961	1962	1963	1964	1965	1966	1967	1968	1969	1970	1971	1972	1973	1974	1975
INCOME															
congregational contributions	282	314	336	313	303	336	346	339	327	357	345	344	335	308	285
income from other sources	477	380	493	369	280	415	346	264	505	265	356	342	221	280	283
TOTAL	759	694	829	682	583	751	692	609	832	622	701	686	556	588	568
EXPENDITURE															
building work	647	742	795	1254	1296	894	518	622	644	711	757	629	518	376	412
administration	31	33	35	34	44	40	39	35	37	37	35	38	36	34	32
TOTAL	678	775	830	1288	1340	934	557	657	681	748	792	667	554	410	444
Surplus(+)/deficit(−)	+81	−81	0	−605	−758	−183	+135	−54	+151	−126	−91	+19	+1	+178	+124
add: profit(+)/loss(−) on investment transactions									−172		−8			−9	
funds at beginning of year	250	322	237	229	(360)	(1069)	(1234)	(1043)	(1039)	(1003)	(1031)	(1054)	(948)	(815)	(520)
FUNDS AT END OF YEAR	331	241	237	(376)	(1118)	(1252)	(1099)	(1097)	(1060)	(1129)	(1130)	(1035)	(947)	(646)	(396)

SOURCE: Figures converted to real terms from those in table 30.
Figures to nearest £000. The bracketed numbers indicate deficits.

the General Finance Committee reported 'grave concern . . . that, if the desired and planned building programme continues, the maximum debt of £750,000 permitted by the General Assembly will be exceeded in 1966.'[19] It was feared that further growth in the debt would have to be financed by bank overdraft facilities, which would involve 'heavy interest charges'. It was decided, therefore, that the committee should defer and adjust its building programme 'in order to ensure that the maximum debt of the committee would not exceed £750,000'. As a result, the commencement of new building was 'virtually suspended' in 1967. Not surprisingly, the expenditure of the committee dropped very sharply in that year, leading to a surplus on the year of £62,000, as shown in table 30.

From 1967 onwards the annual expenditure of the committee was held at a lower level, and the question turned on how the accumulated debt could be paid off. In 1968 the General Finance Committee reported that 'the initial (debt) estimates were far short of requirements and, even now, a substantial and costly building programme remains to be carried out. On the limited income of the National Church Extension Fund it is impossible to maintain the building programme and repay debt simultaneously.'[20] The Stewardship and Budget Committee also urged the need to repay the debt in order to reduce the potential liability on the Mission and Service Fund, and in the following year gained the support of the General Assembly for such a policy. The National Church Extension Committee agreed to repay in 1972 and thereafter a sum equivalent to one-third of the amount it actually received from the Mission and Service Fund until the repayment of the debt was completed, and that, if the actual debt was lower than £750,000 in the first year of repayment, the difference between the actual debt and £750,000 would count towards the first repayment instalment.[21] The first repayment date was, in the event, postponed by one year until 1973, and then no repayment was actually made in that year, because the committee's debt had fallen below the maximum permitted level of £750,000 by more than the required payment of one-third of the 1973 income received from the Mission and Service Fund. The first instalment in the repayment of the debt was thus made in 1974. In the following year the committee reported that, on the assumption that the income received from the Mission and Service Fund continued its present momentum, it hoped that the debt would be extinguished by 1980.[22]

5 Total income and expenditure

In this section we attempt to present a general picture of the total income and expenditure of the Church by aggregating the income and expenditure of its constituent spending agencies.

Table 32 presents a summary of the income of the Church of Scotland broken down by major spending agency for the period 1961-75. The same information is given in table 33 where it is expressed in real terms at 1975 prices. The income of each spending agency is divided between 'liberality' and 'other income', all such figures having been drawn from the earlier tables. However, there is a problem in that, whereas the sum of the liberality accruing to all spending agencies equals the published total liberality figure, there is a large deficit in the calculated total of other income as compared with the known total. It transpires that this apparently 'missing' portion of other income comprises items of income from trusts, legacies, and the like, which are tied by the donors to specific purposes in the Church

142   *The Church of Scotland: An Economic Survey*

TABLE 32.

Summary of the income of the Church of Scotland broken down by major areas of expenditure, 1961-75 (in money terms)

		1961	%	1962	%	1963	%	1964	%	1965	%	1966	%
Congregations	CL	2,921	44	3,007	43	2,981	41	3,125	38	3,253	40	3,463	39
Payment of stipend	CL	1,140	17	1,206	17	1,384	19	1,459	18	1,550	19	1,630	19
Church and ministry	CL	269	4	285	4	298	4	329	4	358	4	384	4
	OI	639	10	680	10	685	9	791	10	772	9	750	9
Mission and service	CL	595	9	622	9	647	9	689	8	708	9	729	8
	OI	300	4	339	5	377	5	428	5	456	6	375	4
National church	CL	108	2	124	2	135	2	130	2	131	2	152	2
extension	OI	183	3	150	2	198	3	153	2	121	1	188	2
'Tied' funds	OI	463	7	540	8	549	8	1,081	13	855	10	1,190	13
Total	CL	5,033	76	5,244	75	5,445	75	5,732	70	6,000	73	6,358	72
Total	OI	1,585	24	1,709	25	1,809	25	2,453	30	2,204	27	2,503	28
TOTAL INCOME		6,618	100	6,953	100	7,254	100	8,185	100	8,204	100	8,861	100

SOURCE: tables 22, 25, 28 and 30.
Figures rounded to nearest £000; percentages rounded.
CL = Christian liberality
OI = other income

TABLE 33.

Summary of the income of the Church of Scotland broken down by major areas of expenditure, 1961 – 75 (in real terms at 1975 prices)

		1961	%	1962	%	1963	%	1964	%	1965	%	1966	%
Congregations	CL	7,619	44	7,620	43	7,428	41	7,534	38	7,518	40	7,646	39
Payment of stipend	CL	2,973	17	3,056	17	3,448	19	3,517	18	3,582	19	3,599	19
Church and ministry	CL	702	4	722	4	743	4	793	4	827	4	848	4
	OI	1,667	10	1,723	10	1,707	9	1,907	10	1,784	9	1,656	9
Mission and service	CL	1,552	9	1,577	9	1,612	9	1,662	8	1,636	9	1,610	8
	OI	782	4	859	5	939	5	1,032	5	1,054	6	828	4
National church	CL	281	2	314	2	336	2	313	2	303	2	336	2
extension	OI	477	3	280	2	493	3	369	2	208	1	415	2
'Tied' funds	OI	1,209	7	1,469	8	1,368	8	2,606	13	2,048	10	2,628	13
Total	CL	13,127	76	13,289	75	13,567	75	13,819	70	13,866	74	14,038	72
Total	OI	4,135	24	4,331	25	4,507	25	5,914	30	5,094	26	5,527	28
TOTAL INCOME		17,262	100	17,620	100	18,074	100	19,733	100	18,960	100	19,565	100

SOURCE: Tables 23, 26, 29 and 31.
Figures rounded to nearest £000; percentages rounded.
CL = Christian liberality
OI = other income

Expenditure

TABLE 32. (*continued*)

	1967	%	1968	%	1969	%	1970	%	1971	%	1972	%	1973	%	1974	%	1975	%
	3,579	39	3,565	37	3,919	39	3,632	35	3,789	34	4,195	36	4,819	37	5,877	39	7,115	40
	1,678	18	1,808	19	1,924	19	2,001	19	2,143	19	2,259	19	2,553	20	2,798	19	3,365	19
	399	4	419	4	462	4	492	5	524	5	568	5	593	5	636	4	988	5
	817	8	776	8	769	8	836	8	802	7	883	8	848	7	922	6	1,064	6
	761	8	777	8	816	8	887	8	1,000	9	995	8	1,061	8	1,123	8	1,224	7
	484	5	422	4	439	5	484	5	439	4	557	5	526	4	741	5	812	5
	159	2	164	2	167	2	193	2	204	2	218	2	232	2	248	2	285	2
	159	2	128	1	258	3	143	1	211	2	217	2	153	1	225	1	283	2
	1,271	14	1,580	17	1,360	13	1,699	17	1,914	18	1,727	15	2,133	16	2,365	16	2,508	14
	6,576	71	6,733	70	7,288	72	7,205	69	7,660	69	8,235	70	9,258	72	10,682	72	12,977	73
	2,731	29	2,906	30	2,826	28	3,162	31	3,366	31	3,384	30	3,660	28	4,253	28	4,667	27
	9,307	100	9,639	100	10,114	100	10,367	100	11,026	100	11,619	100	12,918	100	14,935	100	17,644	100

TABLE 33. (*continued*)

	1967	%	1968	%	1969	%	1970	%	1971	%	1972	%	1973	%	1974	%	1975	%
	7,787	39	7,361	37	7,666	39	6,721	35	6,401	34	6,611	36	6,956	37	7,301	39	7,115	40
	3,651	18	3,733	19	3,764	19	3,704	19	3,620	19	3,560	19	3,685	20	3,476	19	3,365	19
	868	4	865	4	904	4	911	5	885	5	895	5	856	4	790	4	988	6
	1,777	8	1,602	8	1,504	8	1,547	8	1,355	7	1,392	8	1,224	7	1,145	6	1,064	6
	1,656	8	1,604	8	1,595	8	1,641	8	1,689	9	1,568	8	1,531	8	1,395	8	1,224	7
	1,053	5	871	4	859	4	896	5	742	4	878	5	759	4	921	5	812	4
	345	2	339	2	327	2	357	2	345	2	344	2	335	2	308	2	285	2
	346	2	264	1	505	3	265	1	356	2	342	2	221	1	280	1	283	2
	2,767	14	3,264	17	2,659	13	3,145	17	3,233	18	2,720	15	3,079	17	2,938	16	2,509	14
	14,307	71	13,902	70	14,256	72	13,334	69	12,941	69	12,978	70	13,363	72	13,270	72	12,977	74
	5,943	29	6,001	30	5,527	28	5,853	31	5,686	31	5,332	30	5,283	29	5,284	28	4,668	26
	20,250	100	19,903	100	19,783	100	19,187	100	18,627	100	18,310	100	18,646	100	18554	100	17,645	100

and Ministry Department and in the committees within the Mission and Service Fund. Because these spending agencies have no freedom to allocate those funds as they wish, they are excluded from the reckoning in the income and expenditure statements published by the General Finance Committee. The volume of these 'tied' funds can be calculated by subtracting the sum of the 'other income' accruing to the spending agencies each year from the known total 'other income' for the year. These figures are shown as a separate item of income in tables 32 and 33.

The proportion of tied funds to total income has increased considerably over recent years, from 7 per cent in 1961 to 14 per cent in 1975. The reason for this increase is not known. Even the General Treasurer was not able to supply us with the breakdown of the tied funds between the benefiting committees, although the breakdown of other income for 1973 shows that they formed 58 per cent of the total, as follows:

	(£m)	(%)
Total 'other income' (approx.)	3.6	100
For general distribution (approx.)	1.5	42
Tied to particular purposes (approx.)	2.1	58

SOURCE: General Treasurer's Department.

Table 34 gives a summary of the expenditures of the Church for the period

TABLE 34.
Summary of the expenditures of the Church, 1961-75 (in money terms)

	1961	%	1962	%	1963	%	1964	%	1965	%	1966	%	1967	%
Congregations +	2,921	45	3,007	44	2,981	41	3,125	38	3,253	39	3,463	38	3,579	39
Payment of stipend	1,140	18	1,206	17	1,384	19	1,459	18	1,550	18	1,630	18	1,678	18
Church and ministry	871	13	865	13	964	13	961	12	992	12	1,087	12	1,170	13
Mission and service	877	13	947	14	1,029	14	1,103	13	1,137	14	1,230	14	1,236	13
National church extension	260	4	306	4	333	5	534	6	580	7	423	5	256	3
Expenditure of 'tied' funds +	463	7	540	8	549	8	1,081	13	855	10	1,190	13	1,271	14
TOTAL EXPENDITURE	6,532	100	6,871	100	7,240	100	8,263	100	8,367	100	9,023	100	9,190	100

SOURCE: Tables 22, 25, 28 and 30.
Figures are rounded to nearest £000; percentages are rounded.
+ Expenditure arbitrarily assumed to equal income.

TABLE 35.
Summary of the expenditures of the Church, 1961-75 (in real terms at 1975 prices)

	1961	%	1962	%	1963	%	1964	%	1965	%	1966	%	1967	%
Congregations +	7,619	45	7,620	44	7,428	41	7,534	38	7,518	39	7,646	38	7,787	39
Payment of stipend	2,973	18	3,056	17	3,448	19	3,517	18	3,582	18	3,599	18	3,651	18
Church and ministry	2,272	13	2,192	13	2,403	13	2,317	12	2,293	12	2,400	12	2,545	13
Mission and service	2,287	13	2,400	14	2,564	14	2,659	13	2,627	14	2,716	14	2,689	13
National Church Extension	678	4	775	4	830	5	1,288	6	1,340	7	934	5	557	3
Expenditure of 'tied' funds +	1,209	7	1,469	8	1,368	8	2,606	13	2,048	10	2,628	13	2,767	14
TOTAL EXPENDITURE	17,038	100	17,512	100	18,041	100	19,921	100	19,408	100	19,923	100	19,996	100

SOURCE: Tables 23, 26, 29 and 31.
Figures are rounded to nearest £000; percentages are rounded.
+ Expenditure arbitrarily assumed to equal income.

Expenditure

1961-75. Table 35 presents the same information expressed in real terms at 1975 prices. Unfortunately, there are no expenditure figures available for congregations or for the tied funds. Consequently, we have had to assume that the income of congregations and the tied funds are entirely spent each year, so that in those two cases expenditure is simply set equal to income. The assumption must lead to a slight exaggeration of total Church expenditure, since savings are undoubtedly made from the income of congregations, and possibly also from tied funds. On the other hand, from the viewpoint of the central authorities, money once allocated to the congregations for local purposes is as good as spent, in which case the assumption is not unreasonable.

The total income and expenditure of the Church for the period 1961-75 is shown in table 36 in both money terms and in real terms at 1975 prices. Column 5 of the table gives the annual surplus (+) or deficit (−) as a percentage of total annual income. The deficit years of 1964-6 are clearly shown. Taking the period as a whole, total expenditure almost exactly balances total income, with a small surplus of 0.8 per cent. In the deficit years the deficits would have been met from reserves, which were themselves bolstered by certain extraordinary items of income, particularly special distributions from the F.G. Salvesen bequest.

The Church total income and expenditure figures given in table 36 are plotted

TABLE 34. (*continued*)

1968	%	1969	%	1970	%	1971	%	1972	%	1973	%	1974	%	1975	%
3,565	37	3,919	39	3,632	35	3,789	34	4,195	37	4,819	37	5,877	40	7,115	42
1,808	18	1,924	19	2,001	19	2,143	20	2,259	20	2,553	20	2,798	19	3,365	20
1,231	13	1,187	12	1,185	12	1,272	12	1,240	11	1,334	10	1,464	10	1,611	9
1,228	13	1,331	13	1,370	13	1,453	13	1,413	13	1,612	13	1,931	13	1,937	11
318	3	348	4	404	4	469	4	423	4	384	3	330	2	444	3
1,580	16	1,360	13	1,699	17	1,914	17	1,727	15	2,133	17	2,365	16	2,508	15
9,730	100	10,069	100	10,291	100	11,040	100	11,257	100	12,835	100	14,765	100	16,980	100

TABLE 35. (*continued*)

1968	%	1969	%	1970	%	1971	%	1972	%	1973	%	1974	%	1975	%
7,361	37	7,666	39	6,721	35	6,401	34	6,611	37	6,956	37	7,301	40	7,115	42
3,733	18	3,764	19	3,704	19	3,620	20	3,560	20	3,685	20	3,476	19	3,365	20
2,541	13	2,322	12	2,193	12	2,149	12	1,954	11	1,925	10	1,818	10	1,611	9
2,535	13	2,604	13	2,536	13	2,455	13	2,227	13	2,326	13	2,399	13	1,937	11
657	3	681	4	748	4	792	4	667	4	554	3	410	2	444	3
3,264	16	2,659	13	3,145	17	3,233	17	2,720	15	3,079	17	2,938	16	2,508	15
20,091	100	19,696	100	19,047	100	18,650	100	17,739	100	18,525	100	18,342	100	16,980	100

146   The Church of Scotland: An Economic Survey

TABLE 36.
The total income and expenditure of the Church in money terms and in real terms at 1975 prices, 1961-75.

	Total income money 1	Total income real 2	Total expenditure money 3	Total expenditure real 4	Annual surplus (+) or deficit (−) as a percentage of total income 5
	(£000s)	(£000s)	(£000s)	(£000s)	%
1961	6,618	17,261	6,532	17,038	+1.3
1962	6,953	17,620	6,871	17,512	+0.6
1963	7,254	18,074	7,240	18,041	+0.2
1964	8,185	19,732	8,263	19,921	−1.0
1965	8,204	18,958	8,367	19,408	−2.4
1966	8,861	19,564	9,023	19,924	−1.8
1967	9,307	20,248	9,190	19,994	+1.3
1968	9,639	19,903	9,730	20,091	−0.9
1969	10,114	19,784	10,069	19,696	+0.4
1970	10,367	19,185	10,291	19,047	+0.7
1971	11,026	18,627	11,040	18,650	−0.1
1972	11,619	18,311	11,257	17,739	+3.1
1973	12,918	18,645	12,835	18,525	+0.6
1974	14,935	18,554	14,765	18,342	+1.1
1975	17,645	17,645	16,981	16,980	+3.8
TOTAL	153,645	282,111	152,454	280,909	+0.8[+]
ANNUAL AVERAGE	10,243	18,807	10,164	18,727	+0.8[+]

SOURCE: Tables 32, 33, 34 and 35.

[+] Because of the change in the weighting of the annual figures in the period total induced by the conversion of the money figures into real terms, the period surplus in real terms is 0.4 per cent.

in figure 11. The plots indicate that both income and expenditure have risen every year over the period 1961-75, with both increasing overall by more than 150 per cent. As expected, income and expenditure do closely correspond, with expenditure tending to be just below income in order to produce a small surplus. This sggests that the spending agencies do budget for a small surplus. The major exception occurs in the period 1964-6 when expenditure rose significantly above income. The deficit is explained by the planned acceleration in the building programme of the National Church Extension Committee which took the committee heavily into debt. This debt was, and continues to be, financed by the reserves of the other committees in the Mission and Services Fund. The surplus of the last four years is largely explained by the surplus generated by the National Church Extension Committee in order to pay off its debt.

The financial position of the Church appears rather different when the total income and expenditure figures are expressed in real terms, as shown in figure 11. Real income reached a high point in 1967, when it stood 17.3 per cent above the level in 1961. Between 1967 and 1975 the trend was reversed, with income falling every year except 1973, so that by 1975 it stood 12.9 per cent below the peak level.

Taking the period 1961-75 as a whole, therefore, the real income of the Church stood 2.2 per cent higher in 1975 than in 1961. Real expenditure shows a similar

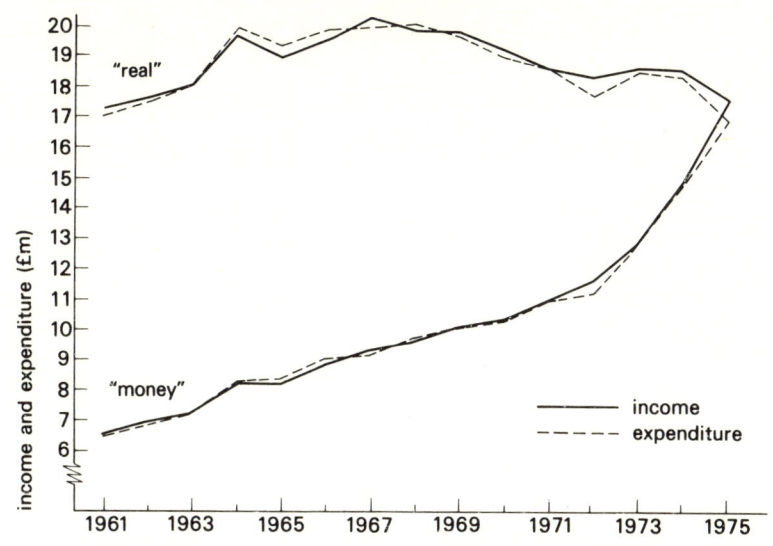

Expenditure

FIGURE 11: The total income and expenditure of the Church in money terms and in real terms at 1975 prices, 1961-75.

trend, reaching a high point one year later than income in 1968, and thereafter declining steadily. As we pointed out above, falling real income and expenditure poses difficult questions of priority and readjustment for the Church. From the evidence examined above, it seems that the greatest problems have been faced by the committees within the Mission and Service Fund.

4 Forecasts of the income of the ministry and mission and service, 1981 and 2001

There are no published figures in accessible form giving a complete breakdown of the total income and expenditure of the Church between the major spending agencies. The difficulty lies in apportioning the tied funds element of the Church's 'other income'. However, in the Report of the Stewardship and Budget Committee for 1963[23] the total income of the committees within the Mission and Service Fund for 1962 is given in full; these figures are shown in column (1) of table 37, where they are compared to total Church income in the same year (column 2). The calculations in column 3 suggest that in 1962 mission and service received 14.2 per cent of congregational liberality and 22.0 per cent of 'other income,' or 16.1 per cent of total Church income.

These figures can be used as the basis for estimating the breakdown of total Church income between mission and service on the one hand and the ministry on the other for 1975. Column 4 of table 37 gives the total income of the Church in 1975 broken down by major component, and column 5 gives the estimated income figures for mission and service for that year on the basis of the percentages in column 3. The figure for liberality of £1,509,000 is the actual figure; at 11.6 per cent of total liberality it falls rather below the 1962 proportion of 14.2 per cent. The proportion of income accruing to mission and service from the other income of the Church is estimated at 27.2 per cent, as compared to the 1962 figure of 22.0 per cent. Overall it is estimated that the committees within the

148

TABLE 37.
The proportion of total Church income received by the committees within the Mission and Service Fund, 1962 and 1975 (£000s)

	Mission and service income in 1962	Total church income in 1962	$\frac{1}{2} \times 100$	Total church income in 1975	Estimated income of mission and service in 1975	$\frac{5}{4} \times 100$	Estimated income of the ministry in 1975 4−5	$\frac{7}{4} \times 100$
	1	2	3	4	5	6	7	8
	£	£	£	£	£		£	
CONGREGATIONAL INCOME	746	5,244	14.2	12,976	1,509*	11.6	11,467	88.4
OTHER INCOME								
donations, grants, etc.	174	435	40.0	1,852	741	40.0	1,111	60.0
bequests	106	393	27.0	854	231	27.0	623	73.0
income from investments	96	464	20.7	1,446	299	20.7	1,147	79.3
standardized stipend	0	417	0.0	516	0*	0.0	516	100.0
Sub-total	376	1,709	22.0	4,668	1,271	27.2	3,397	72.8
TOTAL INCOME	1,122	6,953	16.1	17,644	2,780	15.8	14,864	84.2

* Actual figure.

TABLE 38.
The apportionment of the total income of the Church for 1975, and the forecasts for 1981 and 2001, between the ministry and mission and service. (£000s)

	Figures for 1975			1981				2001			
	Total income	The ministry	Mission and service	Total income	The ministry	Mission and service	Percentage change between 1976 and '81	Total income	The ministry	Mission and service	Percentage change between 1975 and 2001
(1)	17,644	14,864	2,780	18,280	15,392	2,888	+3.6	17,855	15,034	2,821	+1.2
(2)	17,644	14,864	2,780	17,120	14,415	2,705	−3.0	11,629	9,792	1,837	−34.1
(3)	17,644	14,864	2,780	16,002	13,474	2,528	−9.3	6,864	5,779	1,085	−61.1

Mission and Service Fund absorbed 15.8 per cent of the total income of the Church in 1975, or just below the figure of 16.1 per cent for 1962. The remaining 84.2 per cent of total Church income was accounted for by the ministry. This estimate should be fairly reliable, since the apportionment of liberality and the standardized stipend is exact. In 1975 those items constituted 76.5 per cent of the total income of the Church, and 54.3 per cent of the income of mission and service.

In the previous chapter we produced forecasts of the total income of the Church for 1981 and 2001. These income figures can be apportioned between the ministry and mission and service areas of the Church's work by assuming that the ratio of 84.2: 15.8 between the two in 1975 is maintained in the forecast period. On the basis of this rather arbitrary assumption, the breakdown in the forecasts of total income for 1981 and 2001 between the ministry and mission and service are shown in table 38. Because the ratio is assumed constant, the percentage changes in the income accruing to those two sections of the Church in the various forecasts are the same as the precentage changes in the corresponding total income figures in table 38. It can be seen that, depending upon which of the forecasts is used, the income of the ministry and of mission and service may change in a range of $+3.6$ per cent to -9.3 per cent by 1981, and in a range of $+1.2$ per cent to -61.1 per cent by 2001. The implications of these forecasts for the two areas of the Church's work are examined in chapter 9.

5 Conclusions

While the main purpose of this chapter has been to examine the expenditure of the Church, the major theme has been that expenditure is in fact largely determined by income, so that a simultaneous consideration of income and expenditure is desirable. The Church raises income to carry out its various activities, and if income falls, expenditure has to be curbed. This follows because the Church, like other institutions, has to balance its financial accounts. The Church cannot increase expenditure indefinitely to match the potential demand for its services, and choices inevitably have to be made between competing alternatives. One of the main reasons for looking at expenditure is to see how the question of choice is resolved in practice.

In section 2 we saw that the process by which congregational income, or liberality, which constitutes about 70 per cent of the Church's income, is apportioned to the major spending agencies has been formalized in the 'available balance' method. This method involves calculating for every congregation the average of its normal recurring income over a recent three-year period. From this sum is subtracted the congregation's contribution to the maintenance of the ministry, and the remainder is the 'available balance' upon which the Mission and Service Fund levy is raised. The sum remaining after the levy has been deducted, together with the congregation's special or non-recurring income, is retained by the congregation to meet local expenses.

The 'available balance' procedure of apportioning income – and, therefore, expenditure – illustrates the interdependence of the spending agencies; for the winning of a larger share of liberality by one agency necessarily reduces the share accruing to the other two. A number of factors influence the allocation process. One of the most important is the recognition that the ministry receives priority, since without the ministry there can be no mission and service. The scope of the mission and service work thus depends very much upon the ability of the Stewardship and Budget Committee to organize the raising of a 'surplus' income beyond the needs of the ministry to finance the wider work of the Church.

A further consideration is the stance taken by the congregations. We have suggested that the response of congregations to the introduction of the 'available balance' method has been to reclassify their income in order to reduce the proportion of normal recurring income, and thereby to reduce the size of their Mission and Service Fund allocation. This may help to account for the fact that, while the proportion of liberality accruing to congregations declined from 58 per cent to 49 per cent over the period 1961-71, the downward trend was reversed subsequently when the proportion climbed back to 55 per cent in 1975.

The spending agency which had lost most ground is the Mission and Service Fund, whose share of liberality declined from 16 per cent in 1971 to 12 per cent in 1975. Over the same period the Church and Ministry Department's share declined from 35 to 33 per cent. A further reason for the strengthened position of the congregations *vis-à-vis* the central spending agencies may be the difficulty found by those agencies in budgeting ahead in a period of high inflation.

The apportionment of the Church's 'other income' amongst the major spending agencies is rendered difficult by the fact that a large proportion is tied by the donors to specified purposes. Consequently, these sums are excluded from the published summaries of the incomes of those agencies, and to that extent the income (and expenditure) figures are understated.

In section 3 we examined the income and expenditure of the three spending agencies. It was found that, although the money incomes of all three had increased very considerably over the period 1961-75, the conversion of those figures to real terms produced a different picture. The liberality accruing to congregations fell by 6.6 per cent in real terms, from £7,619,000 in 1961 to £7,115,000 in 1975. However, when the decline in the number of congregations over the period was taken into account, it was found that the real income per congregation had actually increased by 5.2 per cent, from £3,444 in 1961 to £3,623 in 1975.

Although the real income of the Church and Ministry Department increased sharply after 1961, reaching a peak of £2,700,000 in 1964, it thereafter declined on a fluctuating trend. Between 1961 and 1975 the real income fell by 13.4 percent from £2,369,000 to £2,080,000. While income from liberality rose by 40.7 per cent in real terms over the period, this was more than offset by the real decline in income from other sources, caused largely by the decline in the real value of the standardized stipend. As a result, the proportion of liberality to total income increased from 29.6 per cent in 1961 to 48.1 per cent in 1975.

The bulk of the expenditure of the Church and Ministry Department – 68.8 per cent in 1975 – comprised contributions by the Maintenance of the Ministry Committee to congregations in aid of stipend, together with contributions to ministerial expenses, such as car grants, driving grants, and removal expenses. The remaining expenditures are taken up by retiring allowances paid by the Aged and Infirm Ministers' Fund, endowments for stipend, and Departmental administration.

Total expenditure fell below total income in every year except 1968 over the period 1961-75, so that the real level of the reserves have more than doubled over the period. At the end of 1975 the reserves stood at £2,567,000, which comfortably exceeded the year's expenditure of £1,611,000. The increase was due to the policy of holding down increases in the minimum stipend below the level which would have been permitted by the reserves, in order not to jeopardize the contributions to the Mission and Service Fund of charges on the margin of support. The fact that the Minimum Stipend still increased by 8.2 per cent in real terms between 1961 and 1975 indicates the significance of the reduction in the number of charges to be supported through the policy of union and readjustment.

The income of the Committees within the Mission and Service Fund (excluding National Church Extension) has been roughly the same as the Church and Ministry Department, hovering around £2.5 millions in real terms. However, the committees receive a much larger proportion of their income (roughly two-thirds) in the form of liberality, so that they are much more dependent upon the annual contributions of congregations. Although total real income increased sharply after the inception of the Co-ordinated Appeal in 1961, reaching a peak of £2,659,000 in 1964, it declined sharply in 1966, and then again over the period 1972-5. The real income of £2,036,000 in 1975 stood 12.8 per cent below the 1961 income.

The expenditure of the committees has closely followed income, with deficits in a number of years. Allowing for special distributions from the F.G. Salvesen bequest, real reserves fell by 40.9 per cent from £1,541,000 in 1961, to £910,000 in 1975. This is an indication of the weakness of the financial position of the mission and service work of the Church.

The National Church Extension Committee was treated separately, although it receives funds from the Mission and Service Fund. In 1975 the total income of the committee was £568,000, or 3.2 per cent of the Church's income. This was composed of liberality and income from other sources in about equal measure, although formerly the 'other income' component tended to form the bulk of the total. The total real income of the committee has fluctuated considerably from year to year over the period 1961-75, although it may be significant that annual real income averaged £571,000 in the last three years of the period, compared to £761,000 in the first three years.

A deliberate acceleration in the building programme approved by the General Assembly in 1963 led to sharp increases in expenditure, and to deficits in 1964 and 1965. The policy was based on the mistaken assumption that the completion of the outstanding building programme estimated at £3 millions would see an end to the need for Church extension. By 1966 the General Finance Committee was expressing concern that the debt, which was financed by the reserves of the other committees in the Mission and Service Fund, would exceed the maximum of £750,000 permitted by the General Assembly. In 1967 new building work was virtually suspended, and thereafter the annual expenditure was held at a lower level. The repayments of the debt was started in 1973, and it is hoped to extinguish the debt by 1980.

In section 3 we presented a general picture of the total income and expenditure of the Church by aggregating the income and expenditures of its constituent spending agencies. In addition, we were able to calculate the volume of the tied funds element of 'other income' by subtracting the sum of the 'other income' received by the spending agencies from the published 'other income' figure. Because there were no expenditure figures for the congregations, we assumed arbitrarily that total expenditure equalled total income. The data showed that expenditure closely matched income, with the exception of the deficit years 1964-66 caused by the acceleration in the expenditure of the National Church Extension Committee. Taking the period 1961-75 as a whole, total income exceeded total expenditure by 0.8 per cent.

The total income and expenditure of the Church increased every year over the period 1961-75. When the figures are expressed in real terms, however, the picture is rather different. Both income and expenditure increased through the first half of the 1960s, income reaching a high point in 1967, when it stood 17.3 per cent above the level in 1961, and expenditure 'peaking' a year later in 1968. Between 1967 and 1975 the trend was reversed, with income and expenditure falling every year except 1973. By 1975 real income stood 12.9 per cent below the 1967 peak, and only 2.2 per cent above the 1961 level.

Finally, in section 4 we attempted to apportion the total income of the Church for 1975 between the two main areas of Church activity – the ministry (i.e. the congregations and the Church and Ministry Department) and mission and service. The difficulty lies in apportioning the 'tied funds' element of the Church's 'other income'. The calculation was based on information showing the total income of the committees within the Mission and Service Fund in 1962, which suggested that they received 16.1 per cent of total Church income in that year. On the basis of that information, it was calculated that mission and service received about 15.8 per cent of the Church's total income in 1975. The remaining 84.2 per cent of total income was accounted for by the ministry.

Notes

1 The financial planning period was formerly a quinquennium, but this was reduced to a triennium in 1973 because of budgeting problems caused by inflation.

2 Church of Scotland, 'Joint Report on Consultations between the Maintenance of the Ministry Committee and the Stewardship and Budget Committee', *Reports to the General Assembly, 1969* p. 299.

3 'Report of the Joint Consultative Committee of the Maintenance of the Ministry Committee and the Stewardship and Budget Committee', *Reports to the General Assembly, 1972,* p. 273.

4 'Supplementary Report of the General Finance Committee', *Reports to the General Assembly, 1967,* p. 97.

5 ibid., p. 101.

6 The operation of the Maintenance of the Ministry Fund is described in chapter 10.

7 'Report of the Joint Consultative Committee of the Maintenance of the Ministry Committee and the Stewardship and Budget Committee', *Reports to the General Assembly, 1972,* p. 273.

8 Church policy towards fund-raising and stewardship is examined in chapter 17.

9 'Report of the Stewardship and Budget Committee', *Reports to the General Assembly, 1971,* pp. 103-4.

10 The policy of union and readjustment is described in chapter 8.

11 'Supplementary Report of the General Finance Committee', *Reports to the General Assembly, 1967,* p. 98.

12 A. Herron (ed.), *The Church of Scotland Yearbook, 1976* (Saint Andrew Press, 1976), p. 31.

13 All of these expenses are described in chapter 10.

14 The various types of endowment grants are described in chapter 10.

15 'Report of the Committee on the Maintenance of the Ministry', *Reports to the General Assembly, 1963*, pp. 124-5.

16 'Report of the Stewardship and Budget Committee', *Reports to the General Assembly, 1965*, p. 59.

17 'Supplementary Report of the General Finance Committee', *Reports to the General Assembly, 1967*, pp. 96-7.

18 ibid., p. 98.

19 'Report of the General Finance Committee', *Reports to the General Assembly, 1966*, p. 81.

20 'Report of the General Finance Committee', *Reports to the General Assembly, 1968*, p. 87.

21 'Report of the Stewardship and Budget Committee', *Reports to the General Assembly, 1969*, p. 116.

22 'Report of the National Church Extension Committee', *Reports to the General Assembly, 1975*, p. 262.

23 'Report of the Stewardship and Budget Committee', *Reports to the General Assembly, 1963*, p. 110.

Chapter 7

Ministers and lay workers

1 Introduction
The so-called 'shortage' of ministers has been a feature of the Church of Scotland for many years. As long ago as 1878 the number of students in training for the ministry was said to have fallen far below the requirements of the Church, and the problem has not eased in recent years. The 1942 report of the wartime Commission for the Interpretation of God's Will in the Present Crisis found 'more than a little cause for anxiety as to the number of young men . . . being attracted to the work of the ministry.'[1] The problem remains today. In 1969 the *Ad Hoc* Committee on Recruitment and Training of the Ministry made the following statement: 'Today the Church finds herself with an annual intake of 55 candidates, to meet a requirement officially estimated as "not less than 80" in the 1964 Report of the Education for the Ministry Committee, and as "60 to 70" in the 1966 Report of the Special Committee Anent Manpower. . . . Moreover, since the present intake includes a higher proportion of older candidates than formerly, a large number of the Church's present ministers will give fewer years of service with a consequent increase in replacement needs.'[2]

A new fear is that the impending retirement of the 'bulge' of men in their early sixties will lead to a further drastic decline in the number of ministers.[3]

However, in the following chapter we show that the steady decline in the number of parish ministers since the war has facilitated the process of rationalization of the parish structure through unions and readjustments. We argue that the policy of reducing the number of charges must continue in the future, and that this requires a continuation of the current declining trend in the numbers of parish ministers.

The main purpose of this chapter, however, is to make a forecast of ministerial manpower in the ministry over the years up to 2001. This is done on the basis of statistical information about how the size of the ministerial work-force has changed in the recent past.

Three major changes affect the population of parish ministers each year, as follows:
(i) the population of ministers ages one year each year;
(ii) a number of new ministers are added to the population each year, but the age distribution of that number is likely to differ from that of the existing population;
(iii) a number of ministers leave each year, and the age distribution of their number is also likely to differ from that of the existing population.

A manpower forecast, therefore, starts with the current stock of ministers stratified by age, and calculates how the stock will change year by year into the future on the basis of assumptions about the size and age distribution of the future annual inflows and outflows of ministers. These assumptions about the flows of ministers are usually based on the extrapolation of the trends discernible in the recent past. The forecast made is thus subject to the limitation, given that all the data required are available so that it is possible to ascertain what the trends have been, that the trends may not continue in the future, and that they may be subject to random influences or to change resulting from changes in the policy of the Church. Consequently, a manpower forecast can, at best, only provide a tentative estimate of the number of ministers in the Church in the future.

In section 2 we start by describing the process of data collection and manipulation, including an assessment of the accuracy of the data collected. Then in section 3 the results of the forecast are produced on the basis of given assumptions about future trends in ministerial manpower. This forecast is compared with an alternative forecast based on calculations made by the Church actuary. Finally, in section 4 we examine trends in the number of lay workers associated with ministers in parish work.

2 Data collection and processing

In this section we present the basic information required for the manpower study, and where necessary indicate how it was obtained.

Table 39 gives the age-distribution of the 1,675 active parish ministers in the Church of Scotland in July 1974, by individual age and by five-year age cohorts. This information is plotted in figure 12. The age-distribution shows a pronounced

FIGURE 12: Age-distribution of active parish ministers in the Church of Scotland as at July, 1974.

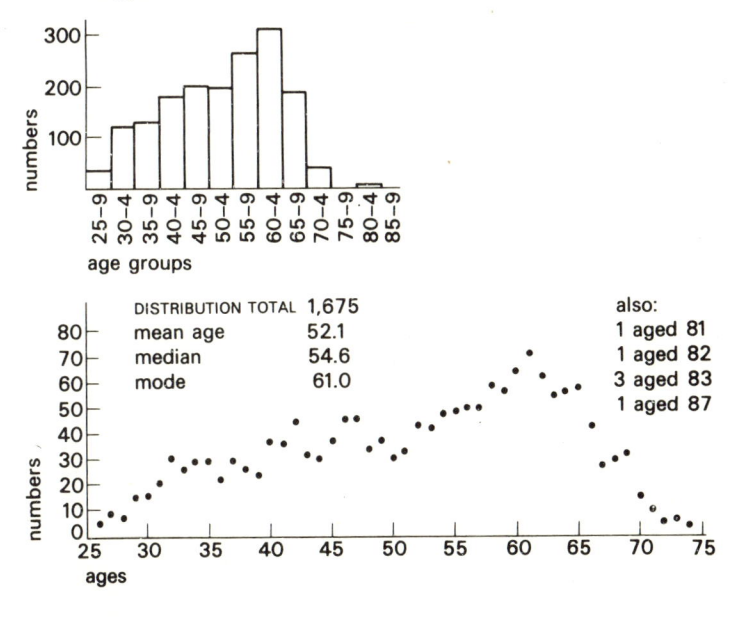

negative skew (i.e. the long 'tail' in figure 12 stretches out to the left). As a result, the modal age is 61 years, and the average (mean) age of parish ministers is 52.1

TABLE 39
Age-distribution of active parish ministers in the Church of Scotland as at July 1974.

Age	Numbers at each age	Numbers in 5-year cohorts
26	5	
27	8	35
28	7	
29	15	
30	16	
31	21	
32	30	122
33	26	
34	29	
35	29	
36	22	
37	29	130
38	26	
39	24	
40	37	
41	36	
42	45	180
43	32	
44	30	
45	37	
46	45	
47	46	199
48	34	
49	37	
50	31	
51	34	
52	43	198
53	42	
54	48	
55	49	
56	50	
57	50	265
58	59	
59	57	
60	65	
61	71	
62	63	311
63	55	
64	57	
65	58	
66	43	
67	27	189
68	29	
69	32	
70	15	
71	10	
72	5	40
73	6	
74	4	
75	0	
76	0	
77	0	0
78	0	
79	0	
80	0	
81	1	
82	1	5
83	3	
84	0	
85	0	
86	0	1
87	1	
TOTAL	1,675	

years. This is an unusual distribution, for nearly one-half of all ministers are at age 55 or over, whereas in a normal work-force distribution the proportion would be nearer one-fifth, according to the actuarial consultant employed by the Aged and Infirm Ministers' Fund.[4]

Although the pension of ministers starts at age 65 there is no fixed age of retirement, except for those ministers entering the ministry, or 'translating' between charges, from 1972 onwards, when the maximum age of service was fixed at 70.[5] Hence there are a number of aged ministers: 40 are in their 70s and 6 in their 80s, with the oldest at age 87. The employment of so many aged people is probably almost unknown outside the Churches.

The information presented in table 39 we take as the existing population of ministers for the purposes of the manpower forecast. We have deliberately excluded ministers not serving in parishes from the forecast, preferring to concentrate our attention on the parish ministry. However, the total number of ministers employed by the Church of Scotland in July 1974 in different areas of work is given in table 40. It can be seen from the table that the bulk of ministers − 96 per cent in fact − are serving in parish charges.

The main flows of ministers into and out from the ministry of the Church of Scotland are shown in a generalized way in the simple flow diagram in figure 13. The central spine of the diagram represents the given population of ministers at any particular time. Inflows of ministers to swell the existing population merge from the left, while the outflows, which serve to reduce the existing number of ministers, leave to the right of the diagram. The inflow comprises mainly newly ordained ministers who have undergone a lengthy period of training.[6] The outflow of ministers from the ministry includes demitting ministers (i.e. those who leave for service in other parts of the Church and outside the Church), ministers dying in active service (as opposed to those who die *after* retiring), early disablements (i.e. ministers retiring for reasons of poor health), and retirements.

Information on the numbers and age-distributions of the inflow of ministers to, and outflow of ministers from, the ministry could only be obtained indirectly by examining the pension fund cards kept for every minister by the Aged and Infirm Ministers' Fund and Pension Fund. By sifting through the cards, it proved possible to assemble the numbers and ages of those ministers who had either

TABLE 40

Number of ministers employed by the Church as at July 1974

		%
Serving in charges	1,675	96.2
Employed overseas	17	1.0
Employed by the Home Board	8	0.5
Employed as hospital chaplains	9	0.5
Working in the Iona Community	3	0.2
Staff of the Church offices	13	0.7
Employed in youth work	3	0.2
Others	13	0.7
TOTAL	1,741	100.0

SOURCE: Church and Ministry Department, Church of Scotland.

FIGURE 13: The main flows of ministers into and out of the ministry.

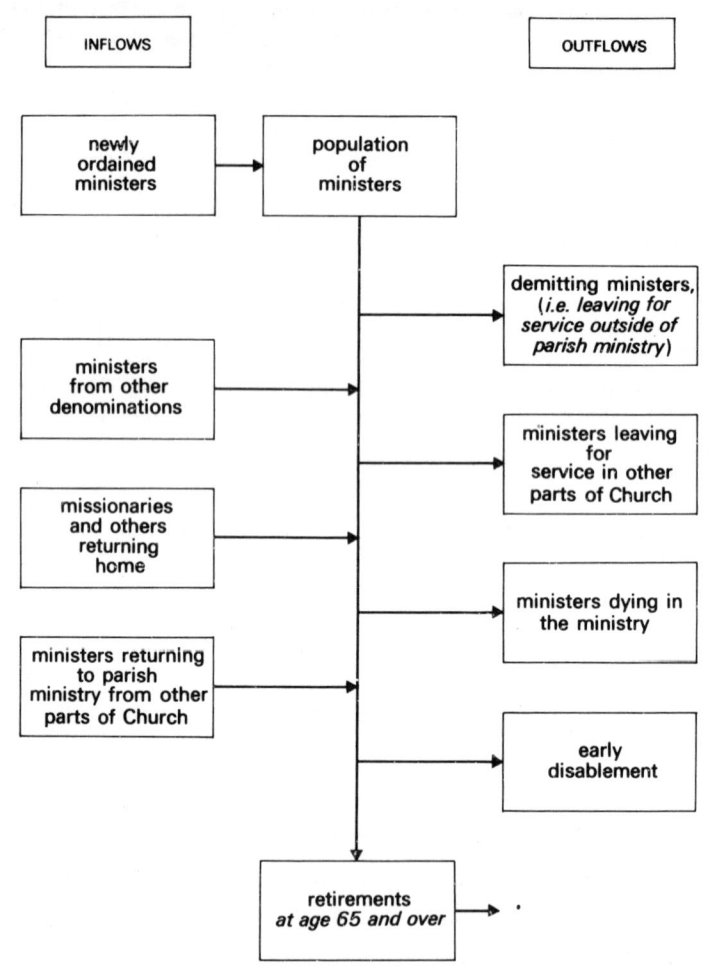

```
         INFLOWS                                    OUTFLOWS

    newly              population
    ordained    →      of
    ministers          ministers
                           │
                           ├──────────→  demitting ministers,
                           │             (i.e. leaving for
    ministers                             service outside of
    from other    ─────────┤              parish ministry)
    denominations          │
                           ├──────────→  ministers leaving
                           │             for
    missionaries           │             service in other
    and others    ─────────┤             parts of Church
    returning              │
    home                   ├──────────→  ministers dying in
                           │             the ministry
    ministers returning    │
    to parish     ─────────┤
    ministry from other    │
    parts of Church        ├──────────→  early
                           │             disablement
                           ↓
                      retirements    ──→
                    at age 65 and over
```

entered or left the ministry in recent years. Such information was collected for the six years 1969 to 1974, but it was decided to ignore the 1974 figures since they were not complete at the time of collection (October 1974).

We also attempted to collect information for 1963 in order to test whether the trends in the numbers and age-distributions of the various flows had changed. Such changes seem a definite possibility, for there has been a tendency for the average age of new entrants to the ministry to increase since the war. Moreover, the actuary called in to make a valuation of the Pension Fund believes that there might in future be a slight trend towards the earlier retirement of ministers because of the reduction in 1968 of the minimum pension age from 70 to 65.[7] Unfortunately, the information available from the pension cards proved to be incomplete for years in the early 1960s, so that the information collected for 1963 was of no value. As a result, it is not easy to discern trends with data for only five consecutive years.

Ministers and lay workers

Table 41 gives the information collected on the inflow of ministers into the ministry of the Church of Scotland for each of the years 1969-73. The numbers entering each year are given from age 24, the age of the youngest entrant, to age 59, the age of the oldest entrant. Thus, for example, the number of ministers entering the Church at age 27 was 3 in 1969, 4 in 1970, 9 in 1971, 1 in 1972, and 7 in 1973. These total 24 for the five-year period, giving an annual average intake of 4.8 at age 27. The last column in table 41 shows that the age cohort 25-9 has an average annual inflow of ministers at each age of 3.20.

TABLE 41
Inflow of ministers into the ministry of the Church of Scotland by age, 1969-73

Age	1969	1970	1971	1972	1973	TOTAL	Annual average	Annual average in 5 – year cohorts
24	0	0	1	0	0	1	0.2	0.20
25	0	1	0	0	0	1	0.2	
26	1	4	1	2	4	12	2.4	
27	3	4	9	1	7	24	4.8	3.20
28	14	1	1	2	4	22	4.4	
29	4	2	6	8	1	21	4.2	
30	3	2	4	4	4	17	3.4	
31	11	3	6	3	1	24	4.8	
32	2	1	3	2	2	10	2.0	3.12
33	3	2	1	5	3	14	2.8	
34	3	4	1	2	3	13	2.6	
35	1	1	3	1	3	9	1.8	
36	2	3	3	1	1	10	2.0	
37	1	0	2	1	3	7	1.4	1.88
38	2	2	1	1	2	8	1.6	
39	2	4	3	3	1	13	2.6	
40	1	3	2	1	3	10	2.0	
41	3	0	0	3	2	8	1.6	
42	1	2	0	4	1	8	1.6	1.32
43	1	0	0	0	1	2	0.4	
44	0	0	1	1	3	5	1.0	
45	2	2	3	2	0	9	1.8	
46	0	3	1	1	2	7	1.4	
47	1	1	2	1	0	5	1.0	1.04
48	0	1	0	1	1	3	0.6	
49	0	0	1	1	0	2	0.4	
50	0	0	1	0	0	1	0.2	
51	0	0	1	1	0	2	0.4	
52	0	0	0	0	0	0	0.0	0.32
53	0	0	0	0	2	2	0.4	
54	1	1	1	0	0	3	0.6	
55	0	1	2	1	1	5	1.0	
56	0	0	0	0	0	0	0.0	
57	0	0	0	0	0	0	0.0	0.24
58	0	0	0	0	0	0	0.0	
59	1	0	0	0	0	1	0.2	
TOTAL	63	48	60	53	55	279	55.8	

Table 41 indicates that the bulk of the entrants to the ministry are at age 34 or less; 159 out of the 279 entrants, or 57.0 per cent, fall in this category. Perhaps what is more surprising, however, is that a large number of entrants lie within older age groups; 80 people, or 28.7 per cent of the total, became ministers in the period 1969-73 at ages between 35 and 44, and there was a sizeable trickle of entrants in their late 40s and early 50s. Finally, table 41 shows that the total inflow of ministers into the ministry each year varied from 48 in 1970 to 63 in 1969, but that over the five years the average was 55.8 per year.

Table 42 provides similar information on those ministers who left the ministry over the period 1969-73. It shows that the numbers leaving the younger five-year age cohorts was quite small, and that the bulk of the outflow occurred with ministers between the ages of 60 and 74. In fact, 36.2 per cent of the total of ministers left at ages 65-9, 50.1 per cent at ages 60-9, and 64.1 per cent at ages 60-74.

The total outflow of ministers from the ministry each year varied from 59 in 1969 to 85 in 1970, but averaged 74.6 for the five-year period as a whole.

The breakdown of the total outflow of ministers for the period 1969-73 is presented in table 43.[8] This table shows that 171 out of the 373 ministers who left the ministry in the period, or 45.8 per cent, did so to retire. Another quarter (24.7 per cent) demitted, and over a fifth (21.7 per cent) died in active service. The remaining 7.8 per cent were accounted for by early disablements. The numbers of demitting ministers are spread most evenly over the age range, although there are minor concentrations around age 40 and again in the late 50s. In contrast, the numbers of ministers leaving in the other three groups is negligible until about age 55, when the numbers increase to reach a peak about age 65. Large numbers of ministers retired, for example, between ages 65 and 71.

A comparison of the numbers and age-distributions of ministers entering and leaving the ministry is shown in the bar-graph in figure 14, the information plotted being obtained from the last columns of tables 41 and 42 respectively. This shows the numbers in five-year age-cohorts (starting with those under 25), each bar indicating the number of ministers entering or leaving the ministry as an average for each age in the age-cohort. Not unexpectedly, the age-distribution of the inflow exhibits a marked positive skew, having an average (mean) age of 35.2 years, while the age-distribution of the outflow has a marked negative skew, with an average age of 60.2 years. The diagram clearly shows that up to and including the 45-9 age-cohort, the number of ministers entering the ministry exceeds the number leaving. In the age cohorts of 50 and over the reverse happens, with outflows greatly exceeding inflows, particularly in the 60-4 age-cohort and beyond, when the number of entrants has fallen to zero.

A cursory examination of figure 14 suggests that the net effect of the flows is to produce a decline in the number of parish ministers, and this is so. We have already seen that over the period 1969-73 the average inflow of ministers was 55.8 per year, compared with an average annual outflow of 74.6, which gives a net drain on the number of parish ministers of 18.8 per year. As a check on the accuracy of the data collected, the net flow figure of −18.8 can be compared with those derived from the number of parish ministers published each year in the *Reports to the General Assembly*.[9] The calculations involved are presented in table 44. Column 1 shows the number of parish ministers each year from 1953,

TABLE 42
Outflow of ministers from the ministry of the Church of Scotland, 1969-73

Age	1969	1970	1971	1972	1973	TOTAL	Annual average	Annual average in 5 – year cohorts
29	1	0	0	0	1	2	0.4	0.40
30	0	0	1	2	0	3	0.6	
31	0	0	0	0	0	0	0.0	
32	0	0	0	0	0	0	0.0	0.36
33	0	1	1	0	1	3	0.6	
34	0	1	0	1	1	3	0.6	
35	1	0	0	3	0	4	0.8	
36	0	0	0	1	0	1	0.2	
37	0	3	1	0	1	5	1.0	0.72
38	1	0	1	0	1	3	0.6	
39	1	1	1	1	1	5	1.0	
40	0	2	2	4	1	9	1.8	
41	0	1	0	2	1	4	0.8	
42	0	2	0	2	1	5	1.0	1.04
43	1	1	0	0	0	2	0.4	
44	0	0	2	2	2	6	1.2	
45	0	0	0	0	0	0	0.0	
46	1	0	1	0	1	3	0.6	
47	0	2	1	0	0	3	0.6	0.48
48	0	1	0	0	1	2	0.4	
49	0	1	1	1	1	4	0.8	
50	1	0	2	0	0	3	0.6	
51	2	2	0	1	0	5	1.0	
52	1	2	0	2	0	5	1.0	0.84
53	1	0	1	0	2	4	0.8	
54	2	1	0	1	0	4	0.8	
55	1	0	2	0	0	3	0.6	
56	1	2	0	1	2	6	1.2	
57	4	9	1	0	0	14	2.8	1.68
58	1	4	2	1	1	9	1.8	
59	1	4	1	1	3	10	2.0	
60	1	2	2	0	2	7	1.4	
61	2	0	1	1	1	5	1.0	
62	3	3	2	2	0	10	2.0	2.08
63	2	4	3	2	2	13	2.6	
64	3	2	4	4	4	17	3.4	
65	3	13	11	13	6	46	9.2	
66	4	1	6	10	8	29	5.8	
67	4	6	3	5	2	20	4.0	5.32
68	8	5	6	2	4	25	5.0	
69	4	3	4	2	0	13	2.6	
70	1	3	8	7	3	22	4.4	
71	2	1	3	5	6	17	3.4	
72	0	1	2	1	3	7	1.4	2.08
73	1	0	1	1	2	5	1.0	
74	0	0	0	0	1	1	0.2	
75	0	0	0	0	1	1	0.2	
76	0	0	0	0	0	0	0.0	
77	0	0	1	0	0	1	0.2	0.12
78	0	0	1	0	0	1	0.2	
79	0	0	0	0	0	0	0.0	
80	0	1	0	0	0	1	0.2	
81	0	0	0	0	0	0	0.0	
82	0	0	0	0	0	0	0.0	0.04
83	0	0	0	0	0	0	0.0	
84	0	0	0	0	0	0	0.0	
85	0	0	1	0	0	1	0.2	
86	0	0	0	0	0	0	0.0	
87	0	0	0	0	0	0	0.0	0.08
88	0	0	0	1	0	1	0.2	
TOTAL	59	85	81	80	68	373	74.6	

TABLE 43
Breakdown of the outflow of ministers from the ministry, 1969-73.

Age	Demitted	Early disablement	Retired	Died	TOTAL
29	2	0	0	0	2
30	3	0	0	0	3
31	0	0	0	0	0
32	0	0	0	0	0
33	3	0	0	0	3
34	3	0	0	0	3
35	4	0	0	0	4
36	1	0	0	0	1
37	5	0	0	0	5
38	3	0	0	0	3
39	4	1	0	0	5
40	7	0	0	2	9
41	4	0	0	0	4
42	5	0	0	0	5
43	1	0	0	1	2
44	5	0	0	1	6
45	0	0	0	0	0
46	3	0	0	0	3
47	2	0	0	1	3
48	2	0	0	0	2
49	2	0	0	2	4
50	1	1	0	1	3
51	4	0	0	1	5
52	3	0	0	2	5
53	2	0	0	2	4
54	0	2	0	2	4
55	0	1	0	2	3
56	2	0	0	4	6
57	6	1	3	4	14
58	1	3	2	3	9
59	1	2	2	5	10
60	3	2	0	2	7
61	0	1	0	4	5
62	1	1	3	5	10
63	4	2	4	3	13
64	0	6	5	6	17
65	0	4	38	4	46
66	0	1	23	5	29
67	2	1	15	2	20
68	1	0	21	3	25
69	1	0	11	1	13
70	1	0	20	1	22
71	0	0	14	3	17
72	0	0	5	2	7
73	0	0	4	1	5
74	0	0	0	1	1
75	0	0	1	0	1
76	0	0	0	0	0
77	0	0	0	1	1
78	0	0	0	1	1
79	0	0	0	0	0
80	0	0	0	1	1
81	0	0	0	0	0
82	0	0	0	0	0
83	0	0	0	0	0
84	0	0	0	0	0
85	0	0	0	1	1
86	0	0	0	0	0
87	0	0	0	0	0
88	0	0	0	1	1
TOTALS	92	29	171	81	373
	24.7%	7.8%	45.8%	21.7%	100%

FIGURE 14. The numbers of ministers entering and leaving the ministry each year over the period 1969-73, averaged by age for each age group.

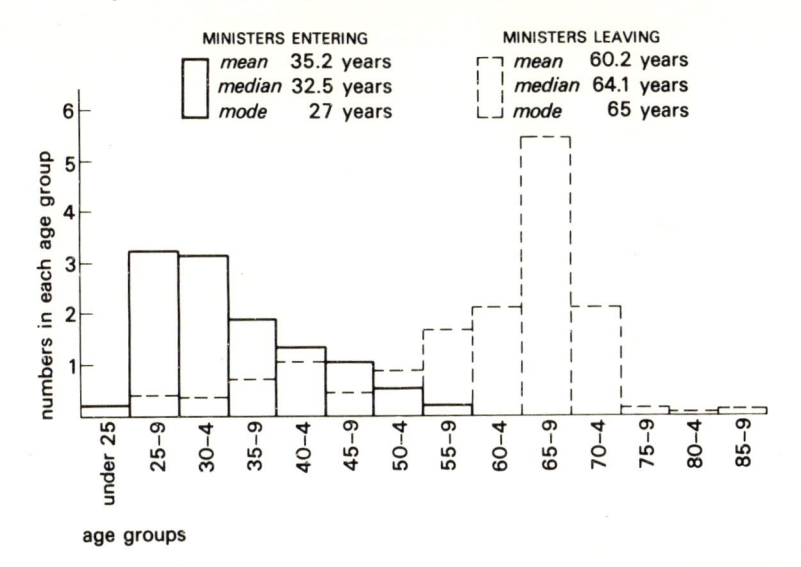

MINISTERS ENTERING
- mean 35.2 years
- median 32.5 years
- mode 27 years

MINISTERS LEAVING
- mean 60.2 years
- median 64.1 years
- mode 65 years

when there were 2,149, to 1973, when the number had fallen to 1,660. Column 2 gives the annual changes in the number of parish ministers each year, mainly negative, which produce a fall of 489 in the total over the whole period. The annual changes vary considerably from year to year, the decline in numbers of ministers being particularly heavy in the late 1950s, and again, to a lesser extent, in the last few years. The average annual net flow over the period 1954-73 is −24.45, which is rather above the figure calculated from our data.

An alternative measure of the annual net flow is shown in columns 3 to 5 of table 44. The Church and Ministry Department of the Church of Scotland provided us with the annual numbers of ordinations and admissions, and the numbers of retirements, resignations and deaths, for the period 1954-73, and these are shown in columns 3 and 4 respectively. The net change in the total number of ministers over the period shown in column 5 is −492, which is almost identical with the change implied by movements in the total number of ministers, although the annual changes differ considerably between the two sets of information. The number of ordinations and admissions total 1,257 for the period, giving an annual average of 62.85, or rather above our inflow figure of 55.8. The number of retirements, resignations and deaths total 1,749, giving an annual average of 87.45, which is well above our outflow figure of 74.6. It seems clear, therefore, that our data for 1969-74 has not completely captured all those entering and leaving the ministry, and suggests that the data has to be modified accordingly. These adjustments are made in tables 45 and 46.

Table 45 shows the annual inflow and outflow figures supplied by the Church and Ministry Department for the five years 1969-73, as given in table 44. This five-year period is taken because it coincides with the time period of our data. The annual average inflow is 58.6, or slightly above our figure of 55.8, whereas the annual average outflow is 87.2, which is well above our figure of 74.6. These

164   *The Church of Scotland: An Economic Survey*

TABLE 44
Changes in the numbers of parish ministers in the Church, 1953-73.

	Numbers of parish ministers* 1	Annual change in 1 2	Ordinations and admissions 3	Retirements, resignations and deaths+ 4	Annual change in manpower (i e 3−4) 5
1953	2,149	−	−	−	−
1954	2,160	+11	62	111	−49
1955	2,113	−47	62	88	−26
1956	2,080	−33	61	77	−16
1957	2,042	−38	72	83	−11
1958	1,982	−60	63	102	−39
1959	1,942	−40	63	96	−33
1960	1,959	+17	66	76	−10
1961	1,928	−31	69	81	−12
1962	1,927	− 1	64	81	−17
1963	1,890	−37	63	79	−16
1964	1,888	− 2	60	78	−18
1965	1,885	− 3	68	90	−22
1966	1,859	−26	57	87	−30
1967	1,814	−45	57	100	−43
1968	1,827	+13	77	84	− 7
1969	1,789	−38	65	78	−13
1970	1,754	−35	53	100	−47
1971	1,745	− 9	64	89	−25
1972	1,687	−58	53	95	−42
1973	1,660	−27	58	74	−16
TOTAL	−	−489	1257	1749	−492
ANNUAL AVERAGE	−	24.45	62.85	87.45	24.60

*SOURCE: 'Report of the Committee on General Administration', *Reports to the General Assembly*, 1946-74, appendix C.
+SOURCE: supplied by the Church and Ministry Department, Church of Scotland.

TABLE 45
Inflows and outflows of parish ministers to the ministry, 1969-73

	Ordinations and admissions 1	Retirements, resignations and deaths 2	Annual change in numbers of ministers (i.e 1−2) 3
1969	65	78	− 13
1970	53	100	− 47
1971	64	89	− 25
1972	53	95	− 42
1973	58	74	− 16
TOTAL	293	436	− 143
ANNUAL AVERAGE	58.6	87.2	− 28.6

SOURCE: Table 44, columns 3, 4 and 5.

Ministers and lay workers 165

higher figures lead to an annual decline in ministerial numbers of 28.6, as compared to 18.8 using our original data.

Table 46 shows how the annual average inflows and outflows of ministers in each five-year age-cohort are scaled up, using the multiplier 58.6/55.8 for the inflows, and the multiplier 87.2/74.6 for the outflow figures. The revised figures for inflows and outflows are given in columns 3 and 4 respectively. The scaling-up process is somewhat arbitrary, in that it assumes that the age-distribution of the ministers apparently missing from the original data is the same as that for the data. This consideration is probably not important in the case of the inflows, where the discrepancy is small, but it could be significant for the outflows, where the discrepancy of about 13 per year raises the possibility that a particular category of ministers with a special age distribution is missing. Unfortunately we have been unable to explain this discrepancy.

TABLE 46
The scaling-up of the inflow and outflow figures of parish ministers (see text).

Age Cohort	Annual average inflow at each age*	Annual average outflow at each age×	$1 \times \dfrac{58.60}{55.80}$	$2 \times \dfrac{87.20}{74.60}$
	1	2	3	4
24	0.20	–	0.21	–
25–9	3.20	0.40+	3.36	0.47+
30–4	3.12	0.36	3.28	0.42
35–9	1.88	0.72	1.97	0.84
40–4	1.32	1.04	1.39	1.22
45–9	1.04	0.48	1.09	0.56
50–4	0.32	0.84	0.34	0.98
55–9	0.24	1.68	0.25	1.96
60–4	–	2.08	–	2.43
65–9	–	5.32	–	6.22
70–4	–	2.08	–	2.43
75–9	–	0.12	–	0.14
80–4	–	0.04	–	0.05
85–9	–	0.08	–	0.09
ANNUAL TOTAL	55.80	74.60	58.61	87.17

*SOURCE: Table 41.
×SOURCE: Table 42.
+Figure refers to age 29 only.

The slight disparity between the scaled-up total inflow and outflow figures produced in table 46 from those anticipated arises because it is impossible to make the two correspond exactly while keeping the numbers down to two decimal places.

3 A ministerial manpower forecast for the parish ministry of the Church of Scotland

In this section we describe the calculations involved in producing the ministerial manpower forecast, and discuss the results produced. Both questions can be examined in relation to table 47.

TABLE 47.
The ministerial manpower forecast for the ministry: basic data and the results for selected years.

Age	Annual rate of inflow* (1)	Annual rate of outflow+ (2)	July 1974 stock of parish ministers × (3)	1975	1976	1977	1978	1979	1980	1981	1986	1991	1996	2001
24	0.21	0	0	0.21	0.21	0.21	0.21	0.21	0.21	0.21	0.21	0.21	0.21	0.21
25	3.36	0	0	3.36	3.57	3.57	3.57	3.57	3.57	3.57	3.57	3.57	3.57	3.57
26	3.36	0	5	3.36	6.72	6.93	6.93	6.93	6.93	6.93	6.93	6.93	6.93	6.93
27	3.36	0	8	8.36	6.72	10.08	10.29	10.29	10.29	10.29	10.29	10.29	10.29	10.29
28	3.36	0	7	11.36	11.72	10.08	13.44	13.65	13.65	13.65	13.65	13.65	13.65	13.65
29	3.36	0.47	15	10.36	14.72	15.08	13.44	16.80	17.01	17.01	17.01	17.01	17.01	17.01
30	3.28	0.42	16	17.81	13.32	13.54	17.89	16.30	19.55	19.76	19.76	19.76	19.76	19.76
31	3.28	0.42	21	18.86	20.62	16.25	16.46	20.70	19.15	22.32	22.52	22.52	22.52	22.52
32	3.28	0.42	30	23.86	21.76	23.49	19.20	19.41	23.57	22.05	25.35	25.35	25.35	25.35
33	3.28	0.42	26	32.86	26.81	26.47	26.44	22.21	22.42	26.52	28.28	28.28	28.28	28.28
34	3.28	0.42	29	28.86	35.61	29.66	29.32	29.29	25.13	25.34	31.10	31.10	31.10	31.10
35	1.97	0.84	29	30.55	30.41	37.06	31.20	30.87	30.84	26.74	32.62	32.62	32.62	32.62
36	1.97	0.84	22	30.13	31.64	31.50	37.96	32.27	31.95	31.92	33.46	33.65	33.65	33.65
37	1.97	0.84	29	23.13	30.95	32.40	32.27	38.48	33.01	32.70	31.39	34.34	34.34	34.34
38	1.97	0.84	26	30.13	24.43	32.02	33.43	33.31	39.34	34.02	33.75	35.32	35.32	35.32
39	1.97	0.84	24	27.13	31.13	25.61	32.96	34.32	34.20	40.04	31.16	36.15	36.15	36.15
40	1.39	1.22	37	24.55	27.57	31.43	26.10	33.20	34.51	34.39	31.28	36.27	36.27	36.27
41	1.39	1.22	36	37.17	25.13	28.05	31.78	26.63	33.50	34.76	34.99	36.30	36.46	36.46
42	1.39	1.22	45	36.17	37.30	25.67	28.49	32.09	27.12	33.75	35.22	34.11	36.61	36.61
43	1.39	1.22	32	45.17	36.58	37.68	26.36	29.11	32.61	27.77	35.91	35.68	37.01	37.01
44	1.39	1.22	30	32.17	44.84	36.58	37.63	28.75	29.39	32.76	40.28	32.79	36.99	36.99
45	1.09	0.56	37	29.87	31.95	44.11	36.18	37.19	26.75	29.28	35.01	32.39	36.58	36.58
46	1.09	0.56	45	37.53	30.51	32.56	44.53	36.72	37.72	27.44	35.66	35.86	36.97	37.12
47	1.09	0.56	46	45.53	38.15	31.22	33.24	45.07	37.35	38.34	35.24	36.53	35.56	37.75
48	1.09	0.56	34	46.53	46.07	38.78	31.93	33.93	45.61	37.99	29.70	37.39	37.19	38.38
49	1.09	0.56	37	34.53	46.85	46.40	39.23	32.49	34.46	45.95	35.00	41.81	35.03	38.84
50	0.34	0.98	31	36.78	34.35	46.48	46.04	38.98	32.34	34.28	31.80	37.12	34.68	38.59
51	0.34	0.98	34	30.36	35.96	33.60	45.35	44.92	38.09	31.66	28.85	36.37	36.56	37.56
52	0.34	0.98	43	33.36	29.82	35.26	32.97	44.38	43.97	37.33	37.49	34.71	35.88	34.99
53	0.34	0.98	42	42.36	32.94	29.48	34.80	32.56	43.71	43.31	36.11	28.74	35.58	35.41
54	0.34	0.98	48	41.36	41.71	32.51	29.13	34.33	32.14	43.04	42.24	32.56	38.58	32.59
55	0.25	1.96	49	47.27	40.77	41.11	32.10	28.79	33.88	31.73	31.68	29.49	34.17	32.02
56	0.25	1.96	50	47.29	45.63	39.39	39.72	31.07	27.89	32.77	29.02	26.57	33.13	33.29

TABLE 47 *(continued)*

167

Age															
57	0.25					50	48.29	45.69	44.09	38.06	38.41	30.10	27.05	33.52	33.67	31.26	32.26
58	0.25					59	48.29	46.65	44.15	42.61	36.82	37.15	29.17	37.96	31.85	25.61	31.41
59	0.25					57	57.29	46.94	45.35	42.93	41.44	35.85	36.61	37.28	36.61	28.49	33.55
60	—	2.43	65	55.04	55.32	45.33	43.79	41.45	40.02	34.62	27.16	27.12	25.31	29.18
61	—	2.43	71	62.57	52.98	53.25	43.64	42.15	39.90	38.52	27.86	24.83	22.72	28.09
62	—	2.43	63	68.57	60.43	51.17	51.43	42.15	40.71	38.53	23.00	28.39	28.52	26.49
63	—	2.43	55	60.57	65.93	58.10	49.20	49.45	40.52	39.14	24.55	31.89	26.79	21.58
64	—	2.43	57	52.57	57.89	63.02	55.53	47.03	47.27	38.73	29.84	30.75	30.20	23.49
65	—	6.22	58	54.57	50.33	55.42	60.33	53.16	45.03	45.25	28.32	22.22	22.19	20.70
66	—	6.22	43	51.78	48.72	44.93	49.48	53.86	47.46	40.20	29.22	21.15	18.84	17.23
67	—	6.22	27	36.78	44.29	41.67	38.43	42.32	46.07	40.59	25.88	15.45	19.07	19.16
68	—	6.22	29	20.78	28.31	34.09	32.07	29.58	32.57	35.46	21.05	13.21	17.15	14.41
69	—	6.22	32	22.78	16.32	22.24	26.78	25.19	23.24	25.58	17.12	13.19	13.59	13.35
70	—	—	—	25.78	18.35	13.15	17.92	21.57	20.29	18.72	16.83	10.53	8.27	8.25
Less CR[a]												0.28	0.65	1.67	2.93
70	—	2.43	15	25.78	18.35	13.15	17.92	21.57	20.29	18.72	16.55	9.88	6.50	5.32
71	—	2.43	10	12.57	21.60	15.38	11.02	15.02	18.08	17.00	13.86	9.67	6.18	3.91
72	—	2.43	5	7.57	9.52	16.35	11.64	8.34	11.37	13.69	12.45	7.68	4.00	4.35
73	—	2.43	6	2.57	3.89	4.89	8.40	5.98	4.29	5.84	7.29	4.20	2.50	2.83
74	—	2.43	4	3.57	1.53	2.31	2.91	5.00	3.56	2.55	4.00	2.61	1.92	1.76
75	—	0.14	0.4	1.57	1.40	0.60	0.91	1.14	1.96	1.40	1.43	1.26	0.75	0.50
76	—	0.14	0.4	0.26	1.02	0.91	0.39	0.59	0.74	1.27	1.01	0.82	0.57	0.33
77	—	0.14	0.4	0.26	0.17	0.66	0.59	0.25	0.38	0.48	0.70	0.63	0.39	0.20
78	—	0.14	0.4	0.26	0.17	0.11	0.43	0.38	0.16	0.25	0.37	0.46	0.27	0.16
79	—	0.14	0.4	0.26	0.17	0.11	0.07	0.28	0.25	0.10	0.18	0.28	0.18	0.14
80	—	0.05	0.4	0.26	0.17	0.11	0.07	0.05	0.18	0.16	0.16	0.16	0.14	0.09
81	—	0.05	0.4	0.35	0.23	0.15	0.10	0.06	0.04	0.16	0.20	0.16	0.12	0.09
82	—	0.05	0.4	0.35	0.31	0.20	0.13	0.09	0.05	0.03	0.10	0.15	0.14	0.08
83	—	0.05	0.4	0.35	0.31	0.17	0.11	0.08	0.08	0.04	0.07	0.10	0.15	0.08
84	—	0.05	0.4	0.35	0.31	0.17	0.15	0.10	0.07	0.07	0.03	0.07	0.10	0.07
85	—	0.09	0.4	0.35	0.31	0.17	0.15	0.13	0.09	0.06	0.08	0.08	0.08	0.07
86	—	0.09	0.4	0.31	0.27	0.24	0.13	0.12	0.10	0.07	0.07	0.09	0.07	0.06
87	—	0.09	0.4	0.31	0.24	0.21	0.19	0.10	0.09	0.08	0.01	0.04	0.06	0.07
88	—	0.09	0.4	0.31	0.24	0.19	0.16	0.15	0.08	0.07	0.01	0.02	0.03	0.07
89	—	0.09	0.4	0.31	0.24	0.19	0.15	0.12	0.12	0.06	0.02	0.01	0.02	0.03
TOTAL	58.61	87.17	1675	1646.13	1616.72	1583.34	1550.49	1519.38	1489.73	1460.73	1347.89	1304.14	1298.01	1298.32

*SOURCE: Table 46, column 3.   +SOURCE: Table 46, column 4.   ×SOURCE: Table 39.   [a]CR = compulsory retirements at age 70 (see text).

The calculations involve two major assumptions. The first is that the annual rate of inflow of ministers will be constant over the period of the forecast, being the scaled-up average for the five years 1969-73 averaged by five-year age-cohorts as calculated in table 46. These figures are shown in column 1 of table 47. Each year the inflow is 58.61, and is assumed to be exogenously determined. It might be possible to relate the inflow of ministers to certain features of the Scottish population such as the birth-rate, and thus to derive a separate forecast for inflow; but it was thought that the extra sophistication of the results which might be produced was not justified in view of the large amount of work involved.

The second major assumption is that the annual outflow of ministers is not a constant figure, but is related to the size and age distribution of the population of ministers in the year concerned. Column 2 of table 47 shows the scaled-up average outflow figures for the five years 1969-73 averaged by five-year age-cohorts (except for age 29, which is the figure for a single age) as calculated in Table 46. Column 3 gives the actual number of ministers at each age as at July 1974. We assume that the pairs of numbers in columns 2 and 3 are directly related, so that the annual outflow at any particular age is determined by multiplying the number of ministers at the age concerned by the ratio of the annual average outflow at that age (column 2) to the number at that age in the original July 1974 stock. For example, at age 29 the outflow ratio is 0.4/15. Consequently, the larger the stock at age 29 in a particular year, the greater will be the absolute outflow figure. Consequently, although the total outflow figure is initially 87.17 per year, this figure will change as the population of ministers changes.

As an example of the way in which the process works, we can see what happens to the fifteen ministers at age 29 in July 1974 when the July 1975 manpower forecast is calculated. During the period from July 1974 to July 1975, 0.47/15 of 15, or 0.47, ministers will drop out, so that by July 1975 the original 15 ministers at age 29 will be 14.53 ministers at age 30. During the same period, however, there will be an inflow of 3.28 ministers at age 30, so that by July 1975 the new number of ministers at age 30 will be 17.81 (i.e. 14.53 + 3.28). This process is repeated for each age from 24 to 89, and results in the forecast numbers and age distribution of parish ministers for 1975. The process is then repeated for each succeeding year up to 2001, and the results for selected years are shown in table 47.

The use of decimals rather than whole numbers may seem rather odd when dealing with persons, but this is inevitable with the averaging techniques used. The decimal parts of the numbers are also important when the figures are being worked through for a period of twenty-seven years. The resulting total manpower figures need to be rounded to produce the forecast figures.

At this point three complications need to be mentioned, all relating to older ministers. Firstly, we noted above that in May 1972 the General Assembly accepted an overture whereby ministers appointed from that date would be subject to the compulsory termination of their ministry on attaining the age of 70.[10] The overture also applies to ministers appointed *ad vitam aut culpam*[11] prior to that date who 'translate' to another charge. The implications of both elements for the manpower forecast are significant.

All ministers entering at age 41 and over in 1972 would be compulsorily retired at age 70 by the year 2001; those entering at age 59 (the oldest inflow age in our data) in 1972 would be compulsorily retired as early as 1983. Similarly, all ministers entering the ministry in 1973 at age 42 and over would be retired by 2001, all ministers entering in 1974 at age 43 and over would be retired by 2001, and so on. With a given number and age distribution of inflow, the number of new ministers potentially affected by the overture by the year 2001 gradually falls in later years, the last group effected being those entering at age 59 in 1990. Of course, it can be assumed that these ministers will be subject to the same rates of outflow as those entering at a younger age, so that a much smaller number will actually reach age 70 than those who originally entered. A separate calculation was done to discover the numbers involved, and this extra outflow of ministers at age 70 is incorporated in table 47. It can be seen, however, that the numbers involved are very small. Even by 2001 the number of ministers compulsorily retired at age 70 is only about three.

However, this calculation ignores the impact of the overture on ministers who translate to another charge after May 1972. We were unable to calculate the impact of this part of the overture because of the lack of readily available data on the age of translating ministers. We should guess that the impact on ministerial numbers of that part of the overture will be somewhat greater than that part concerning new entrants to the ministry, although again it will not be felt until towards the end of the century.

The second complication with the calculations is that we need to fix an age by which all ministers will have left the ministry. In the forecast we have fixed that age at 90. This assumption is needed to round off the calculations neatly, and has practically no impact on the results, since very few ministers reach such an age; in 1974 there were only six ministers aged 75 and over, of which the oldest was 87.

The third complication with the calculations conerns those ministers in the 75 + age-cohorts, and relates to a technical problem. Because in the 1974 stock of ministers there are a number of ages in the upper part of the range where there happen to be no ministers, there is no denominator for the outflow ratio. Consequently, the calculations produce a zero outflow at those ages, which means that a sizeable number of ministers in the forecast were reaching a great age while still in employment. This seems implausible when there were only six ministers in the 75 + age group in 1974. Admittedly, there is a bulge of ministers about to retire over the next ten or fifteen years, so one might expect a slight increase in the number of aged ministers in the longer term; but, on the other hand, the earlier availability of a pension from the Aged and Infirm Ministers' Fund may tend to discourage many from continuing in service to a great age. On balance, it was thought appropriate to strengthen the outflow ratio in the 75 + age-cohorts. This was done by averaging the 1974 population of six ministers in those cohorts over the fifteen years spanned by the group (75 – 89) – i.e. 0.40 per year. As a result, the forecast number of ministers in the 75 + age-group falls from 6 in 1974 to 5.56 in 1976, 4.46 in 1986, and 2.04 in 2001.

Table 48 presents the result of the manpower forecast. Column 1 shows the constant annual inflow figure of 58.61, while column 2 gives the calculated outflow figures. These rise slightly in the first few years from 87.17 in 1974 to 91.99 in 1977, after which they fall gradually, reaching the level of the inflow figures by the end of the century. Consequently, the total number of parish ministers falls at a rate of around 30 a year for the first several years (see column

TABLE 48.
A forecast of the parish ministerial manpower of the Church of Scotland, 1975-2001

	Ministerial manpower forecast I				Ministerial manpower forecast II				Ministerial manpower forecast III
	Inflow 1	Outflow 2	Annual change in numbers (i.e. 1 — 2) 3	Total number of ministers 4	Outflows 5	Annual change in numbers (i.e. 1 — 5) 6	Total number of ministers 7	8
1974	58.61	87.17	—	1631+		—	1631+	1677
1975	58.61	87.48	−29	1602	115	−56	1575	1656
1976	58.61	88.02	−29	1573	115	−56	1519	1635
1977	58.61	91.99	−34	1539	115	−56	1463	1614
1978	58.61	91.46	−33	1506	115	−56	1417	1593
1979	58.61	89.72	−31	1475	105	−46	1371	1572
1980	58.61	88.26	−29	1446	105	−46	1325	1552
1981	58.61	87.61	−29	1417	105	−46	1289	1531
1982	58.61	86.02	−28	1389	95	−36	1253	1510
1983	58.61	83.60	−25	1364	95	−36	1227	1489
1984	58.61	81.69	−23	1341	85	−26	1201	1468
1985	58.61	78.57	−20	1321	85	−26	1185	1448
1986	58.61	76.01	−17	1304	75	−16	1189	1427
1987	58.61	72.84	−14	1290	75	−16	1163	1406
1988	58.61	70.13	−12	1278	65	−6	1157	1385
1989	58.61	67.23	−8	1270	65	−6	1151	1364
1990	58.61	64.46	−6	1264	65	−6	1155	1343
1991	58.61	62.14	−4	1260	55	+4	1159	1323
1992	58.61	61.38	−3	1257	55	+4	1163	1302
1993	58.61	58.86	0	1257	55	+4	1167	1281
1994	58.61	59.84	−1	1256	55	+4	—	1260
1995	58.61	59.97	−1	1255	—	—	—	1239
1996	58.61	59.13	−1	1254	—	—	—	1219
1997	58.61	59.25	−1	1253	—	—	—	1198
1998	58.61	58.06	+1	1254	—	—	—	1177
1999	58.61	59.07	−1	1253	—	—	—	1156
2000	58.61	57.72	+1	1254	—	—	—	1135
2001	58.61	58.74	0	1254	—	—	—	1114

+ Actual figure for 31 December, 1974.

3), after which the rate of decline slowly levels off, so that by the mid-1990s the annual rate of change in numbers is zero. The forecast total number of ministers is shown in column 4. The numbers decline fairly quickly at first, but begin to level off in the late 1980s, reaching a steady state of about 1,255 ministers in 1995. It should be noted that the starting point of the forecast is the 1,631 ministers in the ministry as at 31 December 1974, rather than the 1,675 ministers recorded at July 1974; the former figure is used because it is one of those published annually by the General Administration Committee,[12] which should enable the forecast to be compared with the actual outcome in the forecast period. We have not been able to explain the unexpectedly large difference between that figure and the second, relating to a point six months earlier, supplied by the Church and Ministry Department.

In order to test the sensitivity of the manpower forecast to the inflow and outflow figures used, the forecast was reworked using the original figures of 55.80 and 74.60 respectively. The basic figures are given in table 48. These show that, despite the fact that the initial annual rate of decline in the number of ministers under the alternative assumptions (B in table 49) is 9.76 less than the forecast assumptions (A in table 49), the total number of ministers predicated by 2001 is 1,282, which is only 28 higher than the forecast. Rather surprisingly, therefore, the forecast does not seem to be very sensitive to quite large changes in the initial net flow figure, given that the age-distributions of the two flows are the same.

TABLE 49
The ministerial manpower forecast under alternative assumptions (see text).

		Annual inflow	Initial annual outflow	Initial annual change in numbers of ministers (i.e. 1−2)	Forecast number of ministers in 2001
		1	2	3	4
A	Manpower forecast	58.61	87.17	−28.56	1254
B	Forecast under alternative assumptions	55.80	74.60	−18.80	1282
C	A−B	2.81	12.57	−9.76	−28

A further aspect of the process of movement towards a stable state in the population of ministers is shown in figure 15, which presents for certain selected years the forecast of the age distribution of ministers. The negative skew of the age frequency distribution found for the 1974 population (see figure 15) is still distinct in 1976, but by 1981 this feature is much reduced. In succeeding years the changes in the distribution are less marked, but the statistics of central tendency show that it moves slowly towards a normal distribution and then overshoots, so that by 2001 the median age is slightly higher than the mean age, indicating a small positive skew. At the same time, as one would expect, the mean age of ministers falls, from 51.89 years in 1976 to 49.29 years in 1986 and 47.86 years in 2001.

FIGURE 15: A forecast of the age-distribution of parish ministries for selected years, based on the manpower forecast.

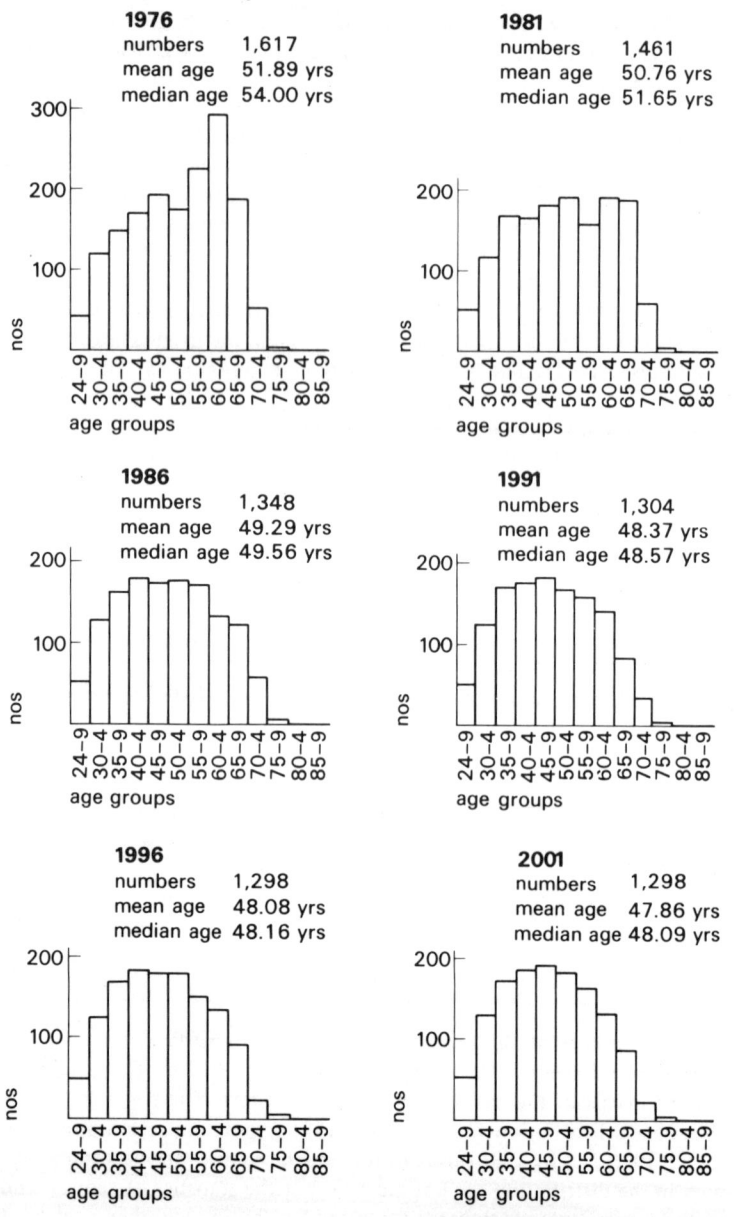

1976
numbers 1,617
mean age 51.89 yrs
median age 54.00 yrs

1981
numbers 1,461
mean age 50.76 yrs
median age 51.65 yrs

1986
numbers 1,348
mean age 49.29 yrs
median age 49.56 yrs

1991
numbers 1,304
mean age 48.37 yrs
median age 48.57 yrs

1996
numbers 1,298
mean age 48.08 yrs
median age 48.16 yrs

2001
numbers 1,298
mean age 47.86 yrs
median age 48.09 yrs

An alternative forecast of ministerial numbers is shown in columns 5 to 7 of table 48. This forecast is based on the estimates of retirements and deaths made by the actuarial consultant to the Aged and Infirm Ministers' Fund. He expects exits from active service by retirements and deaths in service to average 100 per year for the next three years, gradually declining to a level of 40 per year by 1990. Assuming an outflow of demitting ministers of 15 a year (the current annual rate), the total annual outflow figures are given in column 5 of table 48. With the constant inflow of 58.61 per year (column 1), the annual change in the number of parish ministers is shown in column 6, and the manpower forecast is given in column 7. In this second manpower forecast the decline in ministerial numbers is at a much steeper rate over the next decade, so that by 1984 the gap between the two forecasts has widened to a maximum figure of 140. The downward trend flattens out rather earlier, however, with numbers reaching a low of about 1,150 in 1989. At that point the distance between the two forecasts has narrowed to about 120, and this distance is subsequently reduced to less than a hundred by 1993, as the first forecast levels off and the second starts slowly to rise.

A third forecast of ministerial numbers can be made by using an entirely different technique, that of fitting a linear trend to a time series of annual ministerial numbers by means of statistical least squares regression analysis. Trends were fitted for the periods 1945-72 and 1961-72 with the following results, where M denotes the number of ministers and Y the year:

$M = 2319.59 - 21.58Y$ ... (6)
   (10.36) (0.62)
   $N = 28$ (*1945-72*)
   $R^2 = 0.9787$
   Durbin-Watson statistic $= 0.6817$.

$M = 2301.24 - 20.82Y$ ... (7)
   (33.79) (1.48)
   $N = 12$ (*1961-72*)
   $R^2 = 0.9516$
   Durbin-Watson statistic $= 1.6181$.

In both equations the standard errors of the constant and coefficient terms (in brackets) are very small, and the R^2 are high, indicating that the equations 'fit' the data well. The second equation is superior, however, because the Durbin-Watson statistic has probably reached an acceptably high level at which autocorrelation is not significant. This cannot be said of the first equation. The linear regression forecast is therefore based on equation 7. The forecast is given in column 8 of table 48. The figure of 1,677 ministers in 1974 is rather above the actual figure of 1,631, but it is an estimate based on the trends over the preceding twelve years. If these trends were to continue into the future, then the number of ministers would continue to decline steadily year after year, reaching about 1,114 by 2001.

The linear regression forecast is based not so much on an appreciation of the underlying forces at work which determine ministerial numbers, as are the first two forecasts, but rather on a simple extrapolation of recent trends in total numbers; it is not surprising, therefore, that it differs significantly from those forecasts. All three forecasts are plotted in figure 16. Assuming a constant rate of inflow of ministers, the first forecast produces a 'steady state' population of ministers of about 1,250 in 1995, while the second forecast leads to a steady state of about 1,150 ministers in 1989. These forecasts represent declines of about 23

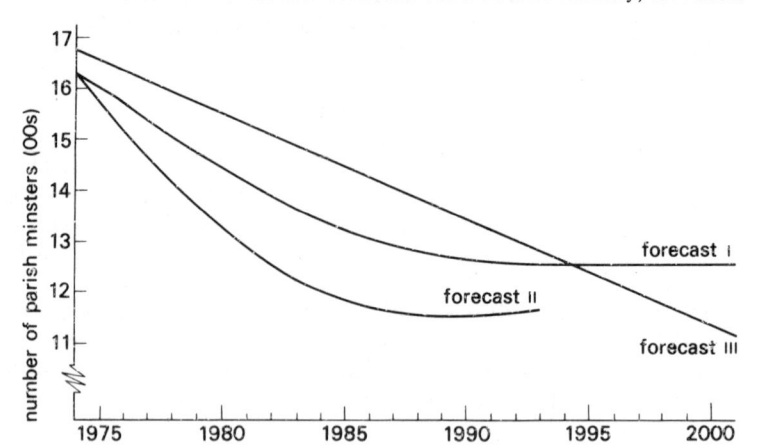

FIGURE 16: Forecasts of the number of ministers in the Parish Ministry, 1974-2001.

and 30 per cent, respectively, in the number of parish ministers over the period 1974-2001. The linear regression trend line suggests that ministerial numbers might fall continuously to 1,114, giving a decline of about 32 per cent on the actual 1974 figure.

The first two manpower forecasts, which are likely to be the more accurate, indicate the possibility that the decline in the number of ministers will cease in the long-run, thereby solving the problem of the shortage of ministers, providing that the number of charges continues to be reduced by the policy of union and readjustment. This is after an initial period during which the problem may become somewhat more severe, as a result of the likely acceleration of the decline in ministerial numbers over the next few years as the 'bulge' in the numbers of older ministers passes through the system. However, the solution of the problem of the shortage of ministers may conflict with the requirements of the policy of union and readjustment. We turn to the examination of that question in the following chapter.

5 Office-bearers and other lay workers

The purpose of this final section is to analyse briefly the trends in the numbers of office-bearers and other lay workers associated with the minister in the work of the parish. These include elders, the members of the financial courts of congregations, and Sunday School teachers. Measures of the work of the parish might include the number of members, and the numbers of Sunday School and Bible Class pupils.

The broad trends in these groups over the period 1949-73 are given in table 50. The table shows that the number of ministers has declined by about a quarter (24.5 per cent), while the number of members, after increasing a little during the early part of the period, has declined overall by 14.1 per cent. As a result of the faster rate of decline in ministerial numbers, the average number of members for each minister has increased from 577 in 1949 to 644 in 1957 and 656 in 1973. This suggests that on average the pastoral care work of ministers has become rather heavier since the war.

The number of elders has increased steadily from 38,486 in 1949 to 50,963 in 1973, a rise of almost one-third (32.4 per cent). When matched with the decline in membership, the number of members per elder is found to have fallen from 33 in 1949 to 21 in 1973. This parallels the trend evident in many western Churches towards greater lay participation. In the Church of Scotland, however, it seems that the main reason for the growing number of elders is that, while elders are ordained for life, many have become 'inactive' for reasons of age and infirmity. The increase in numbers, therefore, largely reflects the Church's desire to maintain the numbers of active elders. It is also possible that the number of elders may have been increased as a means of off-setting the falling minister/member ratio, thereby helping to preserve standards of pastoral care. Moreover, during the period since the war the increased mobility of the population may have made pastoral care more difficult, especially in urban areas where many members travel outside their parish to attend church.

Table 50 shows that the number of office-bearers other than elders has also risen, but at a slower rate. Over the period 1949-73 the increase was from 19,805 to 22,317, or 12.7 per cent. 'Other office-bearers' comprise mainly the members of the financial courts of charges other than *quoad omnia* charges. Unlike elders, these officials are usually (but not always) appointed for a fixed term of a few years (often three years).

TABLE 50
Comparisons of the numbers of members, ministers and layworkers for 1949, 1957 and 1973

	1949	1957	Percentage change between 1947 and 1957	1973	Percentage change between 1957 and 1973	Percentage change between 1949 and 1973
Ministers	2,198	2,042	−7.1	1,660	−18.7	−24.5
Members	1,268,315	1,315,630	+3.7	1,088,873	−17.2	−14.1
Number of members per minister	577	644	−11.6	656	−1.9	−13.7
Elders	38,486	43,677	+13.5	50,963	+16.7	+32.4
Number of members per elder	33	30	+9.1	21	+30.0	+36.4
Other office-bearers	19,805	21,936	+10.8	22,317	+1.7	+12.7
Total office-bearers	58,291	65,613	+12.6	73,280	+11.7	+25.7
Charges	2,357	2,272	−3.6	1,791	−21.2	−24.0
Number of office-bearers per charge	25	29	+8.0	41	+41.4	+64.0
Sunday School teachers and other workers	36,731	41,193	+12.1	30,512	−25.9	−16.9
Sunday School pupils	273,592	307,218	+12.3	167,733	−45.4	−38.7
Teacher/pupil ratio	1:7	1:7	0.0	1:5	+28.6	+28.6
Bible Class pupils	49,897	71,856*	+44.0	51,418	−28.4	+3.0

*Figure for 1960, the highest reached.

The number of elders and other office-bearers taken together has increased over the period by about a quarter (25.7 per cent), while the number of charges has declined by about a quarter (24.0 per cent). The number of office-bearers per charge has thus increased from 25 to 41. In 1973 the ratio of elders to other office-bearers was 2.3:1.

Sunday School teachers and other workers increased in numbers by 12.1 per cent from 36,731 in 1949 to 41,193 in 1957, and thereafter declined, reaching 30,516 by 1973 for an overall fall of 16.9 per cent. The number of Sunday School pupils follows a broadly similar pattern, increasing by 12.3 per cent from 273,592 in 1949 to 307,218 in 1957, but falling steeply in subsequent years to reach 167,733 by 1973, giving an overall decline of 38.7 per cent. Consequently, the teacher/pupil ratio, which was 1:7 in 1947 and in 1957, increased to 1:5 by 1973. These trends in Sunday School teachers and pupils are similar to those of membership, which reached a post-war 'peak' one year earlier in 1956.

The numbers of Bible Class pupils also reached a 'peak' in the post-war period in 1960, when a figure of 71,856 was recorded. Between 1960 and 1973 the number fell by 28.4 per cent to 51,418.

In order to examine more closely the trends in the numbers of lay-workers and pupils, straight lines were fitted by means of least squares regression analysis to the numbers in recent years, stretching as far back as a continuous trend is discernible. The following equations were estimated, where Y is the dependent variable and X denotes the year:

elders $Y = 38,550 + 525.5X$ ... (8)
$N = 24, 1949\text{-}73$
$R^2 = 0.96$
Durbin-Watson statistic $= 0.478$

other office-bearers $Y = 20,430 + 121.65X$ ... (9)
$N = 24, 1949\text{-}73$
$R^2 = 0.68$
Durbin-Watson statistic $= 0.039$

Sunday School teachers and other workers $Y = 42,550 - 608X$ ... (10)
$N = 17, 1957\text{-}73$
$R^2 = 0.82$
Durbin-Watson statistic $= 0.208$

Sunday School pupils $Y = 314,500 - 6564X$ ... (11)
$N = 17, 1957\text{-}73$
$R^2 = 0.977$
Durbin-Watson statistic $= 1.90$

Bible Class pupils $Y = 74,320 - 2533X$ ... (12)
$N = 14, 1960\text{-}73$
$R^2 = 0.988$
Durbin-Watson statistic $= 5.311$

In all but one case (that of 'other office-bearers') the R^2 is high, indicating that the equations provide good fits for the data. In three cases the Durbin-Watson statistic is rather low, suggesting the existence of auto-correlation.

Rough forecasts for future years can be made by extrapolating the trend lines into the future. Forecasts for 1981 and 2001 are given in table 51. These suggest that on the basis of recent trends, the number of elders might be expected to increase by 29.3 per cent to 65,876 by 2001, and the number of other office-bearers might rise by 20.0 per cent to 26,756. Sunday School teachers and other workers fall by almost a half over the period from 30,512 in 1973 to 15,798 in 2001, while Sunday School pupils decline by 84.7 per cent from 167,733 in 1973 to 25,684 in 2001. Consequently, the teacher/pupil ratio increases from 1:5 to 1:2. The number of Bible Class pupils falls at such a steep downward trend that they reach zero by 1990. The forecast steep declines in the numbers of Sunday School pupils and Bible Class pupils are unlikely to be vindicated, but they indicate the seriousness of the present trends if they are allowed to continue.

TABLE 51.
Forecasts of members and layworkers for 1981 and 2001

	Actual figure for 1973	1981	Percentage change between 1973 and 1981	2001	Percentage change between 1981 and 2001	Percentage change between 1973 and 2001
Elders	50,963	55,366	+8.6	65,876	+19.0	+29.3
Other office-bearers	22,317	24,323	+9.0	26,876	+10.0	+20.0
Total office-bearers	73,280	79,689	+8.7	92,632	+16.2	+26.4
Sunday School teachers and other workers	30,512	27,958	−8.4	15,798	−43.5	−48.2
Sunday School pupils	167,733	156,964	−6.4	25,684	−83.6	−84.7
Teacher/pupil ratio	1:5	1:6	−20.0	1:2	+66.7	+60.0
Bible Class pupils	51,418	21,127	−58.9	0*	—	—

*The downward trend in numbers of Bible Class pupils reaches zero in 1990.

6 Conclusions

The main purpose of this chapter has been to make a forecast of the ministerial manpower available for the ministry over the period from the present up to the turn of the century. We saw that any such forecast is based on the existing population of ministers, and on the projected trends in the annual inflows to, and outflows from, the ministry.

Our starting population was that at July 1974, when there were 1,675 active parish ministers. The age distribution of these ministers exhibited a marked negative skew, with an average age of 52.1 years and a modal age of 61.0 years. The annual inflow and outflow figures by age cohort were an average for the five year period 1969-73 calculated from information obtained from the Aged and Infirm Ministers' Fund, but scaled up to accord with the flows recorded by the Church and Ministry Department, namely 58.61 and 87.17 respectively. Over the period, 57.0 per cent of the ministers entering the ministry did so at age 34 or less, while 64.1 per cent of the outflows took place in the age range 60-74. Of the ministers leaving the ministry, 45.8 per cent did so to retire, 24.7 per cent demitted, and 21.7 per cent died in active service.

The manpower forecast calculations are based on two major assumptions. The first is that the size and age distribution of the annual inflow of ministers is constant throughout. The second assumption is that the annual outflow in any year depends upon the size and age distribution of the ministerial population in the previous year. The annual outflow will therefore vary from year to year, being greater the larger and older the population. Special allowance was made for those ministers appointed since May 1972 who will be retired compulsorily at age 70, but the numbers affected seem likely to be very small in the years up to 2001. It was not possible to take account of the same ruling on those ministers who translate after 1972, where the impact is likely to be greater.

The main results of the forecast are as follows:

(a) The total number of parish ministers would decline a little more quickly over the next few years, at the rate of about 30 a year, but the rate of decline would then gradually level off. The population of ministers would reach a stationary state of around 1,250 by 1995. This represents a decline of about 23 per cent from the 1974 figure.

(b) As the ministerial population shrinks, the age distribution would move from having a marked negative skew to one which by 2001 has a slight positive skew. During this period the average age of parish ministers would fall from 52.10 in 1974 to 47.86 in 2001. Thus the current bulge of ministers in their late 50s and early 60s disappears from the distribution.

An alternative forecast based on the calculation of the outflows by the Church actuary suggests that, while the trend in ministerial numbers will follow a similar pattern to the first forecast, the overall decline will be greater. The forecast suggests that a low point of 1,150 ministers will be reached in 1989, giving a fall on the 1974 figure of about 29 per cent.

A third forecast was made by the fitting of a linear time-trend by means of least squares regression analysis to the annual number of parish ministers for the period 1961-72. The resulting equation suggested that ministerial numbers might fall continuously to 1,114, giving a decline of about 32 per cent on the 1974 figure.

It must be emphasized, however, that the forecasts are only as good as the assumptions on which they are based. The first two forecasts are likely to have the greater predictive ability, because they attempt to take into account the underlying forces at play. If the assumptions about these forces are justified by future events, then the forecasts suggest that the problem of the 'shortage' of ministers may solve itself in the long run, providing that the policy of the union and readjustment of charges is continued. The connection between the number of parish ministers and the number of charges is the subject to which we turn our attention in the following chapter.

Finally, in section 5 we analysed briefly the trends in the numbers of office-bearers and other lay workers associated with the minister in the work of the parish. We saw that, since the war, there has been an increase of about a quarter in the number of office-bearers, caused largely by a rise in the number of elders appointed to take over the work of those elders who have become 'inactive' for reasons of age or ill-health. The numbers of Sunday School teachers and pupils, and of Bible Class pupils, increased after the war up to 1957 (1960 in the case of Bible Class pupils) but thereafter declined very sharply. If these trends persist in the future their numbers should become very small by the end of the century, and even sooner in the case of Bible Class pupils.

Notes

1 Reported in Church of Scotland 'Report of the *Ad Hoc* Committee on Recruitment and Training of the Ministry', *Reports to the General Assembly, 1969*, p. 813.

2 ibid., p. 813.

3 'Report of the Special Commission on Priorities of Mission in Scotland in the 1970s', *Reports to the General Assembly, 1971*, p. 694.

4 'Supplementary Report of the Committee on Aged and Infirm Ministers' Fund and Pension Fund, 1974', *Reports to the General Assembly, 1974,* appendix, p. 644.

5 'Report of Standing Committee for Classifying Returns to Overtures, 1972', *Reports to the General Assembly, 1972*, pp. 792-3.

6 The education and training of ministers is described in chapter 14.

7 'Report of the Committee of the Aged and Infirm Ministers' Fund and Pension Fund, 1969', *Reports to the General Assembly, 1969*, p. 313.

8 A similar breakdown for the inflow of ministers is not available, but it is known that the great bulk of the inflow comprises newly ordained ministers.

9 'Report of the Committee on General Administration', *Reports to the General Assembly*, appendix C.

10 'Report of Standing Committee for Classifying Returns to Overtures, 1972', pp. 792-3.

11 The phrase *ad vitam aut culpam* (i.e. for life or until fault) is used to describe the parish minister's tenure of office.

12 'Report of the Committee on General Administration', op. cit.

Chapter 8

Charges and congregations

1 Introduction
Since before the Second World War the numbers of charges and congregations in the Church of Scotland have declined steadily. This is a result of the policy of union and readjustment, which is aimed at rationalizing the parish structure of the Church. The rationalization process has been made necessary by the high cost of maintaining excessive numbers of congregations, which has been caused by a number of factors, including the following: the widespread duplication of charges inherited from the 1929 Union; the shifts in the distribution of the Scottish population, especially from inner-city areas to the suburbs, and the depopulation of rural areas, rendering certain charges unnecessary; the decline in membership since 1956; the continuing financial pressures on the Church; and the decline in the number of parish ministers. Until the potency of these factors abates, the need for the policy of union and readjustment will remain pressing.

An analysis of the costs and economies of the policy is made in chapter 13. The purpose of this chapter is to examine the trends in the numbers of charges and congregations since the war, to explain the underlying forces at play, and to make future projections of numbers. In section 2 the procedures used by the Committee on Unions and Readjustments in effecting readjustments are described. Then in sections 3 and 4 we examine the factors which determine the rate at which unions and readjustments are carried out, and show the downward trend in the numbers of charges and congregations which has resulted from previous readjustment activity. Finally, in section 5 forecasts of the number of charges are made for the years up to 2001.

2 Procedures of union and readjustment
In 1966 the Committee on Unions and Readjustments produced a 'memorandum on procedure'[1] which outlined those lines of procedure which experience had shown were helpful in the negotiations between the Committee, Presbyteries and congregations over matters of union and readjustment. The purpose of this section is to outline these procedures and to describe the various types of readjustment which take place.

It is the duty of the Presbytery to report each vacancy in a parish charge to the Committee on Unions and Readjustments (henceforth 'the committee'), together with the Presbytery's position as to whether or not the question of union or readjustment should be raised. In forming its opinion, the Presbytery is required to take account of the following factors:

(i) The membership and general condition of the vacant congregation.
(ii) The population and extent of the parish and any changes taking place or in prospect, either in it or its neighbourhood, e.g. erection of new housing.
(iii) The number of congregations and ministers sufficient to serve the spiritual needs of the community.
(iv) The number of other congregations and Church agencies in the vicinity, their circumstances and resources.
(v) The number of ministers available to serve the whole Church.

On receiving the report of the Presbytery, the Committee makes its own decision as to whether the question of union or readjustment should be raised. If either the Committee or the Presbytery decides that the question should be raised, the case must be enquired into.

When the question of union or readjustment is raised, the practice of the Committee is to remit the case to its sub-committee for the area of the Synod. Generally, each sub-committee has two joint convenors, one or both of whom act for the central Committee in cases remitted to the sub-committee. The duty of the convenors is to keep in close touch with the Presbytery, to take part in negotiations with local parties, to give counsel and guidance, and to make independent reports direct to the Committee 'as occasion demands', and when the Presbytery's decision is submitted. The sub-committee is a panel of ministers and elders on whose services the convenors may call.

It is the duty of the Presbytery when the question of readjustment is made to appoint a committee to confer with parties and conduct negotiations. The convenor of the Presbytery's Committee should preside at all meetings of office-bearers and congregations held in connection with the case. For the efficient conduct of the case, it is essential that close co-operation between the Presbytery's Committee and the Synodical convenors be maintained throughout.

In many cases there is an obvious union or readjustment which the Presbytery's committee in conjunction with the Synodical convenors should endeavour to accomplish; in other cases it may be necessary to keep several possibilities in view. Generally, the first step is to confer with the office-bearers of the vacant congregation, followed by a conference with the office-bearers of the other congregation or congregations concerned. It is seldom desirable to hold meetings of congregations until negotiations are sufficiently advanced to enable concrete proposals to be put forward. The vote is taken by the congregation. Wherever the interests of a minister are involved, an interview should be arranged with him at an early stage in the negotiations, and he must be kept informed of all matters that affect him.

When a substantial measure of agreement has been reached with office-bearers, the Presbytery's Committee in conjunction with the Synodical convenors should prepare a 'draft basis' embodying the terms agreed upon. The draft basis should then be submitted to the secretary of the department for revision, and then submitted to the office-bearers and congregations for their approval. To become effective, a Basis of Union or Linking requires the approval of the congregations concerned, the Presbytery, and the Committee.

In the course of negotiations for union or readjustment, the Presbytery's Committee and Synodical convenors may encounter exceptional difficulties. It is required that these difficulties should be reported to the Committee, which may appoint special deputies to confer with the parties.

When agreement has been reached with all the parties concerned, the Presbytery will unite the congregations. The moderator, or interim moderator, should then without delay constitute the Kirk Session of the United Charge and prepare the new communion roll, and also the electoral roll if required. The method of administration of the temporal affairs of the united congregation should also be put into operation, and arrangements made to collect from all members for the Maintenance of the Ministry and the Mission and Service Funds.

Before going on to examine the different types of readjustment available, two important definitions need to be stated. Firstly, a 'charge' means 'a sphere of pastoral duty to which a minister or ministers are appointed *ad vitam aut culpam*'. In the ministry, the term 'charge' is synonymous with 'parish', but there are charges of a different kind outside the ministry – e.g. as chaplains to H.M. Forces. On the other hand, a 'congregation' is defined as 'a company of persons associated together in a particular locality for Christian worship, instruction, fellowship, and work . . .' Normally, each parish charge has only one congregation, but there are a large number of 'linked' charges which comprise two or even three congregations, under the care of one minister.

We now go on to describe the various types of readjustment used in the Church of Scotland.

1 Union of congregations

'Union' means 'the joining of two or more congregations . . . so that they are made into one'. The congregations concerned are merged under one minister and one Kirk Session; this leads to a saving in the stipend and expenses of one minister, and the cost of upkeep of the buildings of one congregation. The redundant buildings may be sold, and the proceeds used as a fabric fund for the united charge.

On the occurrence of a vacancy in a case where union is desirable, the two congregations may unite under the pastoral charge of the remaining minister. It is considered that 'this form of union is specially to be welcomed'. A vote taken by the vacant congregation agreeing to unite or link with the other congregation under its minister constitutes the election of that minister to the united or linked charge.

When a vacancy occurs and a union of congregations is proposed, the minister of the other congregation may see it as his duty to retire so as to facilitate union. In such a case, financial arrangements will fall to be made according to the individual case. A joint sub-committee of the three committees in the Church and Ministry Department, known as the 'Sub-Committee on Retirement for the Sake of Union', considers the cases as they arise and makes the appropriate recommendations to the committee concerned.

The most usual arrangements are:

(i) A minister approaching the age of retirement may retire earlier than he would otherwise have done, and receive from the date of union a retiring allowance calculated on the basis of the rate applicable if he were retiring because of age or infirmity.

(ii) A minister may be guaranteed the minimum stipend for eighteen months while he seeks a new charge.

(iii) A minister may be accepted 'at the service of the Church', where the minister is available for pulpit supply (*locum tenens*) and terminable appointments, etc., and is prepared to reside where the work is to be done. He receives the minimum stipend.

With the consent of local parties, the retiring minister may receive life occupancy of the manse not required by the united congregation on the same terms as his existing manse.

In every case in which readjustment is considered advisable, a union of congregations is given priority in the thinking of the Committee because of the large potential economies involved, but in many cases linking has been considered more desirable because of the distance between the two congregations concerned.

2 Linking of congregations

'Linking' means 'the joining of two or more congregations as one charge under one minister, with each congregation retaining its own identity, courts, services, and organizations'. The two Kirk Sessions meet once a year to appoint a representative elder to Presbytery and Synod, and to discuss stipend arrangements. The savings in this form of readjustment amount to the stipend of one minister, together possibly with a manse.

The Committee considers that there are two types of cases where linking is 'the correct form of readjustment'. The first case is where union or some other form of adjustment is desirable, but only a linking arrangement is practicable at the time; such an arrangement is regarded as temporary, and merely a step towards union or some other readjustment. The second case is where two or more congregations are at such a distance from each other as to make united worship impracticable, and to make difficult the effective working of united congregational courts and organization, but where one minister can serve the congregations, conduct their services, and supervise their Sunday Schools. Here the congregations may be linked permanently, and share the minister and representative elder. Experience has shown that linking is more effective than union where the two places of worship are not less than two, and not more than ten, miles apart.

The Committee avoids the linking of urban with rural congregations.

3 Transportation

'Transportation' means 'the moving of a congregation from one place of worship to another with or without a change of parish'. The redistribution of population necessitates the redistribution of charges, so that a charge or congregation can be 'transported' to another district in which a new community is being, or has been, formed by the building of new houses; it carries with it its identity, status, and congregational funds. If the buildings left are sold, the proceeds usually are used to defray the share of the cost of the erection of the church buildings that normally is borne by the congregation of a church extension charge.

It is not necessary to wait for a vacancy to occur before taking steps for the transportation of a charge to a new district. The charge can be transported with the consent of the minister, office-bearers and congregation.

4 Restricted choice of ministers

A 'restricted charge' means 'the ministry of a congregation that is permitted to call the minister *ad vitam aut culpam* but who is not under a stated age, or a minister or probationer whose name is on the special list kept by the Committee on Probationers and Transference of Ministers'. A restricted ministry 'may be imposed on a vacant charge by the Presbytery of the bounds, with the concurrence of the Committee on Unions and Readjustments . . .'

A *Restricted choice of ministers (age)*

Some charges are small and unlikely to grow; they are placed so that they cannot be united or linked with neighbouring charges, and the pastoral work required is comparatively light. Such charges are suitable for ministers getting on in years, and when one becomes vacant the Presbytery can restrict the congregation's choice of minister to one of not less than a given age, usually 55 years.

In other cases a union is desirable but not immediately practical, and the minister of the other charge is due to reach the normal age of retirement in ten or fifteen years. Here the vacant congregation may have the choice of a new minister restricted by the Presbytery to a given age, with a view to ultimate union.

This enables the Church to make good use of those ministers having a claim to relief from heavy responsibilities, while conserving the younger ministers for the charges where they are most needed.

B *Restricted choice of ministers (special list)*

In certain cases in which efforts to unite congregations have failed, the Presbytery and the Committee may agree to permit vacant congregations to make an appointment *ad vitam aut culpam*, but restricting the choice of congregations to ministers on the special list, i.e. the list of ministers willing to be translated and whose translations would open the way for the union of their present congregation with another. The list may also include probationers.

5 Continued vacancy

A 'continued vacancy' means 'an interim arrangement to cover a period during which it is considered undesirable to suppress or reduce a charge, and negotiations towards union or readjustment are suspended.' The Presbytery and the Committee may agree to a continued vacancy in cases of 'extreme difficulty'. The vacancy continues under an interim moderator, and it is very desirable that he be the minister of a neighbouring charge who is able to conduct services and undertake pastoral duties.

6 Deferred union or linking

A 'deferred union' or 'deferred linking' means 'the agreement to a basis of union or linking between the congregation of a vacant charge and another congregation, which basis shall not be put into effect until a vacancy occurs in the other charge, and then under a minister who has been elected by both congregations to the first-mentioned vacant charge.'

This occurs where the Presbytery and the Committee may be convinced that there is a clear case for the union or linking of two congregations, one of which is vacant, and where local parties may agree that such a move ought to take place, but where 'for cogent reasons' the minister of the charge is unable to undertake the work of the united or linked congregations, or retire for the sake of union. Here a deferred union or linking may be effected, where a provisional basis is prepared, and both congregations participate in the election and call of a minister to the vacant charge. The condition of his induction is that as soon as the other incumbency ends, he will become minister of the united or linked charge.

7 Terminable appointments (suppressed charges)
The 'suppression' of a charge means 'the withdrawal from a congregation of the right to have its minister or ministers appointed *ad vitam aut culpam*. The work of the congregation may be carried on under a terminable appointment by a minister without a charge, or licentiate.'

A minister without charge may be appointed for a term of years, if thought desirable by the Presbytery in conference with the Committee, but all such engagements may be terminated sooner by the Presbytery in the event of the question of union or readjustment again arising. The congregations involved retain all the rights and privileges of congregations, except that of life appointment to the ministry.

A necessary condition for a terminable appointment is that the Presbytery and the Committee take the view that union or readjustment is desirable in the case. There are two types of cases where a terminable appointment may be an advantage: the first is where one congregation is vacant and another adjacent congregation may be expected to become vacant in the not too distant future, i.e. a minister is approaching retirement or is likely to be translated to another charge; the second situation is where the movement of population from the territorial area which the vacant congregation serves is such as to make its future uncertain.

8 Reduction
'Reduction' means 'the alteration of the status of a congregation to that of a mission station.' Such cases arise when a Presbytery finds that from the depopulation of a parish or other causes, it is not advisable to maintain a congregation. 'Mission stations' are found in small communities in the Highlands and Islands which are within a parish but are remote from the parish church, and are served by a lay missionary; he is financed largely by the Home Board, and is responsible to the minister. The Presbytery consults with the committees on Union and Readjustments and Maintenance of the Ministry and the Home Board as to whether the congregation should be reduced to a mission station, and makes a report. The Presbytery's report, together with the representation of the congregation concerned, is heard in the Synod.

9 Dissolution
'Dissolution' means 'the termination of the existence of a congregation.' This may occur where a charge, through depopulation or other causes, has become unnecessary, and no readjustment can be made. Dissolutions tend to occur in inter-city areas. The procedure is the same as that for reductions: the Synod makes the decision, and, if it is for the reduction, then it must ensure that adequate provision is made for the pastoral oversight of the former parish.

10 Transference
'Transference' means 'the change of a congregation and its parish from the bounds of one Presbytery or Synod to the bounds of another without any change

of site.' Transference arises from the desire of the Kirk Session that the charge should be transferred, and a petition is presented to that effect to the Synod via the Presbytery.

11 Basis of association
'In some of our cities and burghs where the time is not ripe, nor the circumstances suitable, for an effective union, a basis of association has been negotiated between two or more neighbouring congregations, whereby the congregations, while maintaining their separate identity and status of ministers . . . get to know each other a great deal better than perhaps has hitherto been possible.'[2] The Committee is strongly in favour of such associations if a closer tie cannot be arranged immediately, in the hope that such congregations may eventually move towards union.

12 Special areas of readjustment
When the Committee and a Presbytery are agreed on a plan of readjustment in rural areas which the Presbytery is prepared to put into effect without delay, it is possible for the Committee, together with the Maintenance of the Ministry Committee, to the declare the area a 'special area of readjustment'. The plan involves the establishment of team ministries consisting of ministers, and/or assistants, probationers, missionaries and deaconesses.[3]

The variety of readjustment measures available probably reflects the differing circumstances of charges and congregations and the problems of carrying out readjustment, particularly that posed by the 'life interest' of ministers at a time when adjustment is a pressing problem for the Church.

3 The scope for union and readjustment
Since ministers are usually inducted to a parish charge *ad vitam aut culpam* (i.e. they have a life interest), the question of union and readjustment can normally only be raised when a charge falls vacant. The rate at which readjustments can proceed, therefore, depends partly upon the rate at which vacancies occur, and partly upon the criteria used in deciding in what proportion of vacancies the question should be raised. In this section we examine the vacancy rate, and in the following section the criteria apparently used by the Committee and the Presbyteries in selecting in which vacancies the question is raised.

The number of vacancies each year depends upon two factors; the shortfall in the number of ministers below the number of charges (i.e. 'net vacancies'), and the annual rate of translations of ministers between charges (i.e. 'turnover'). These two factors together constitute 'gross vacancies'. It is important to note that the existence of translations, or turnover, is not sufficient in itself to facilitate the policy of union and readjustment. If the number of parish ministers equals the number of charges (i.e. there are no net vacancies), then any policy of union and readjustment would result in ministerial unemployment. A vacancy caused by a translation often provides the occasion on which the question of union and readjustment is raised, but there must be net vacancies if the policy is to be carried through without causing ministerial unemployment. A continuing policy of union and readjustment thus requires a continuing decline in ministerial numbers in order that a number of net vacancies can be preserved. This is exactly the situation that has prevailed since the war, as shown in table 52 and plotted in figure 17.

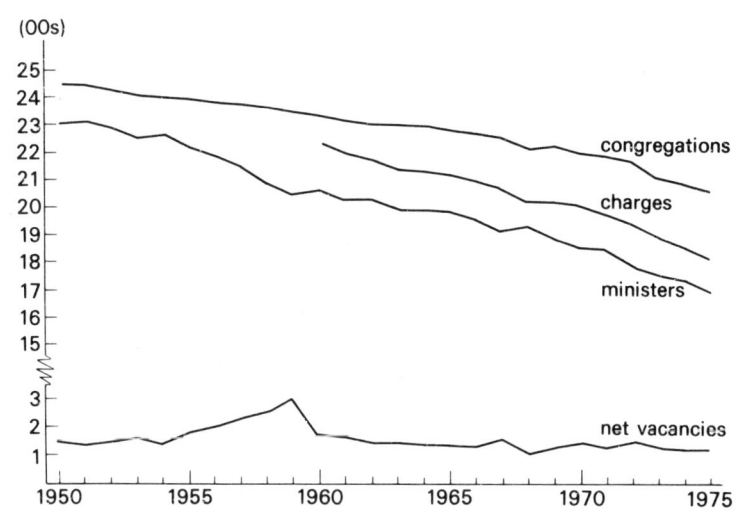

FIGURE 17: The number of congregations, charges, ministers and net vacancies in the Church, 1950-75.

The data show that the number of congregations has declined steadily over the period 1950-75 from 2,426 to 1,964, a fall of 19.0 per cent. This has been caused by unions (i.e. making two or more congregations into one); reductions (i.e. reducing the status of a congregation to that of a mission station); and dissolutions (i.e. terminating the existence of a congregation). The decline in the number of congregations thus arises directly from the work of the Committee.

The number of charges has also declined over the period 1960-75 for which information is available, but from a lower level and at a faster rate than the number of congregations, i.e. the vertical distance between the two in figure 17 has widened. The number of charges fell by 19.5 per cent from 2,130 in 1960 to 1,714 in 1975; the vertical distance between charges and congregations widened from 119 in 1961 to 250 in 1975. This distance is accounted for by the growing number of those congregations which, as the result of linking arrangements, are no longer designated as charges, but retain their separate identity as congregations. For example, the linking of two charges makes them one charge, but the two congregations involved remain intact. Thus the number of charges is reduced by one, but the number of congregations remains unchanged.

The number of parish ministers also exhibits a fairly steady decline over the period 1950-75, and as expected always stays below the corresponding yearly figures for charges. Between 1960 and 1975 the number of ministers declined from 1,959 to 1,588, the fall of 18.9 per cent closely paralleling the 19.5 per cent fall in the number of charges over the period. This is a further pointer to the process of union and readjustment described above. In figure 17 the vertical distance between the numbers of charges and ministers measures the numbers of

TABLE 52.
The numbers of congregations, charges, ministers and vacancies as at 31 December, 1945-75

	1945	1946	1947	1948	1949	1950	1951	1952	1953	1954	1955	1956	1957	1958
1 Congregations	2,426	2,410	2,387	2,377	2,357	2,348	2,340	2,322	2,303	2,296	2,289	2,280	2,272	2,257
2 Charges	–	–	–	–	–	–	–	–	–	–	–	–	–	–
3 Ministers serving parishes	2,265	2,246	2,242	2,218	2,198	2,206	2,210	2,182	2,149	2,160	2,113	2,080	2,042	1,982
4 Net vacancies (i.e. 2 – 3)×	–	–	–	–	–	–	–	–	–	–	–	–	–	–
5 Translations (turnover)	84	108	110	132	113	118	88	90	82	110	109	110	103	106
6 Gross vacancies (i.e. 4 + 5)+	–	–	–	–	–	–	–	–	–	–	–	–	–	–

	1959	1960	1961	1962	1963	1964	1965	1966	1967	1968	1969	1970	1971	1972	1973	1974	1975
1	2,242	–	2,212	2,200	2,199	2,192	2,179	2,166	2,150	2,115	2,124	2,097	2,088	2,067	2,009	1,993	1,964
2	–	2,130	2,093	2,069	2,031	2,027	2,016	1,994	1,969	1,927	1,919	1,902	1,874	1,838	1,791	1,756	1,714
3	1,942	1,959	1,928	1,927	1,890	1,888	1,885	1,859	1,814	1,827	1,789	1,754	1,745	1,687	1,660	1,631	1,588
4	–	171	165	142	141	139	131	135	155	100	130	148	129	151	131	125	126
5	109	104	94	86	63	71	60	93	103	89	79	63	83	73	71	58	54
6	–	275	259	228	204	210	191	228	258	189	209	211	212	224	202	183	180

SOURCE: 'Report of the Committee on General Administration', *Reports to the General Assembly*, 1946-76, appendices B and C.
× Calculated on the basis that 'net vacancies' equals the number of charges less the number of ministers; these figures differ from those in the source.
+ Arising during year.

Charges and congregations 189

net vacancies which have fluctuated from year to year around 139 on a declining trend. Table 52 shows that the number of translations (or turnover) has also tended to follow a declining trend. In most years between 1945 and 1960 the number of translations exceeded a hundred, but in the later period the number has fallen to reach about sixty in recent years. The numbers of net vacancies and translations together form gross vacancies. The gross vacancies measure the number of opportunities for the union and readjustment of charges arising during each year. Over the period 1960-75 gross vacancies have averaged 216, being rather higher than this in the earlier part of the period and rather below it at the end.

4 The policy of the Committee
In the previous section it was argued that the number of unions and readjustments depends partly upon the annual number of gross vacancies, and partly upon the criteria used by the authorities in deciding in which cases to raise the question of union and readjustment. In this section we examine the second aspect of the question.

Table 53 presents a summary of the progress of the policy of union and readjustment since the war. Row 1 gives the number of cases per year where the opportunity for readjustment arose because of a vacancy in a charge, but where it was decided that no change should be made. Row 2 shows the number of cases per year where the opportunity for readjustment arose, and where the question of readjustment was raised either by the Presbytery or by the Committee. Finally, the number of cases undecided at the end of the previous year, and brought forward for consideration and decision in the current year, is shown in row 3. The total of all the cases considered in each year, therefore, comprises the sum of rows 1, 2 and 3, and this is shown in row 4. The total number of cases per year where the question was raised, however, is rather less since it comprises the sum of rows 2 and 3, as given in row 5. Row 6 gives the number of cases out of the total shown in row 5 in which decisions were reached during the year. These remaining cases where decisions were not taken during the year are presented in row 7, and these are carried forward for further consideration in the following year (see row 3).

The remaining five rows deal with the number of unions and linkings which constitute the major forms of readjustment. Row 8 shows the number of unions carried through during each year, while row 9 gives the running total of unions arranged since the union of 1929 as at the end of the year (i.e. including the unions arranged during the current year). Similarly, row 10 presents the number of linkings (including temporary linkings) arranged during each year, and row 11 indicates the cumulative total of linkings made since 1929. Finally, row 12 gives the number of unions and linkings combined (i.e. row 8 + row 10) for each year, which provides some measure of the union and readjustment activity during the year.

At this point two warnings concerning deficiencies in the figures shown in table 53 should be made. Firstly, the annual time-periods used change in the middle of the series. From 1945 to 1955 the year runs from 1st April to 31st March, while from 1957 to 1975 the year used corresponds to the chronological year. Since the change-over is made in 1956, the figures relating to that year cover only the nine months from 1 April to 31 December.

TABLE 53.

A summary of the work of the Committee on Unions and Readjustments for the period 1945-75

Classification of cases	1945	1946	1947	1948	1949	1950	1951	1952	1953	1954	1955
1 Number of cases where question not raised (i.e. no change)	47	22	33	38	26	39	28	26	28	25	36
2 Number of cases where question raised during year	77	71	75	83	85	89	84	98	84	106	99
3 Number of cases brought forward from previous year	38	19	29	23‡	34‡	26‡	19	34‡	41‡	31	43
4 TOTAL OF ALL CASES CONSIDERED DURING YEAR (i.e. 1 + 2 + 3)	162	112	137	144	145	154	131	158	153	162	178
5 TOTAL NUMBER OF CASES WHERE QUESTION RAISED DURING YEAR (i.e. 2 + 3)	115	90	104	106	119	115	103	132	125	137	142
6 Number of cases in which decisions taken during year	96	61	83	75	87	95	71	96	94	93	92
7 Number of cases carried forward to next year (i.e. 5 − 6)	19	29	21	31	24‡	19‡	32	36	31	43	50
8 Number of unions arranged during year	23	18	22	7	25	18	13	27	22‡	15	15
9 TOTAL NUMBER OF UNIONS SINCE 1929 AS AT END OF YEAR	527	545	567	574	599	617	630	657	680	695	710
10 Number of linkings arranged during year	1	0	5	2	2	4	2	4	4	5	13
11 TOTAL NUMBER OF LINKINGS SINCE 1929 AS AT END OF YEAR	‡	‡	‡	2	4	8	10	14	18	23	36
12 Number of unions and linkings arranged during year (i.e. 8 + 10)	24‡	18‡	27‡	9	27	22	15	31	26	20	28

TABLE 53 *(continued)*

	1956+	1957	1958	1959	1960	1961	1962	1963	1964	1965	1966	1967	1968	1969	1970	1971	1972	1973	1974	1975
	25	21	29	40	37	29	30	31	28	17	127	131	124	105	104	92	111	71	65	73
	60	105	114	128	101	100	94	88	47	49	55+	52	54	63	73	59	70	57	72	71
	50	42	45	45	36	41	38‡	34	34	18	22	24‡	31	39	43	42	46	46	42	43
	135	168	188	213	174	170	162	153	109	84	204+	207	209	207	220	193	227	174	179	187
	110	147	159	173	137	141	132	122	81	67	77+	76	85	102	116	101	116	103	114	114
	68	102	101	137	94	111	98	88	63	45	51+	45	46	59	74	55	70	61	71	73
	42	45	45‡	36	41‡	30	34	34	18	22	26	31	39	43	42	46	46	42	43	41
	18	15	16	25	11	17	16	19	12	11	11	17	17	9	13	14	23	23	27	29
	728	743	759	783	794	811	827	846	858	869	880	897	914	923	936	950	973	996	1,023	1,052
	10	17	22	19	16	15	16	18	15	13	3	13	10	9	15	8	17	17	15	18
	46	63	85	105‡	121	136	152	170	185	198	201	214	224	233	248	256	273	290	305	323
	28	32	38	44	27	32	32	37	27	24	14	30	27	18	28	22	40	40	42	47

SOURCE: 'Reports of the Committee on Unions and Readjustments', *Reports to the General Assembly*, 1946-74.
+Covers only nine months from 1st April to 31st December, 1956.
‡Discrepancy in figures.
§Estimated from incomplete information.

Secondly, there are discrepancies in some of the figures from year to year. These are of two kinds. Firstly, the annual numbers of linkings arranged and the cumulative total were traced 'backwards' — that is to say, starting with the figures for 1975 and working back year by year to 1945. Unfortunately, by 1947 the cumulative total of linkings had reached zero, whereas linkings were apparently carried out in 1945 and 1947. The probable explanation of this discrepancy is that some linkings arranged were only of a temporary nature, and on their subsequent dissolution were deducted from the count.

Secondly, there are several examples where the number of cases undecided in one year and carried forward to the next (row 7), differ from the number of cases in the next year reported as having been brought forward from the previous year (row 3). In some of these cases at least the discrepancy can be explained by the fact that the number of cases carried forward included some cases where linkings or unions were pending, in that the decision had been taken but the readjustment had not been completed. Such cases subsequently disappear from the figure showing the number of cases brought forward in the following year.

The points of interest in table 53 are brought out in figure 18, where five of the classifications of cases are plotted for the year 1950 to 1975. Firstly, the TU line plots the cumulative total number of unions since 1929 (row 9, table 53); the line slopes upwards to the right, and is more or less linear. By the end of 1945, 527 unions had been completed, and by the end of 1975, 1,052 unions, making a total of 525 for the period since the war. The line would not remain linear if projected back to 1929, for the period immediately following the reunion saw a large number of unions; 93 unions took place in the year up to 31 March 1930, with 48 and 52 unions respectively in the following two years, as compared with an average of 17 unions per year over the period 1945 to 1975.

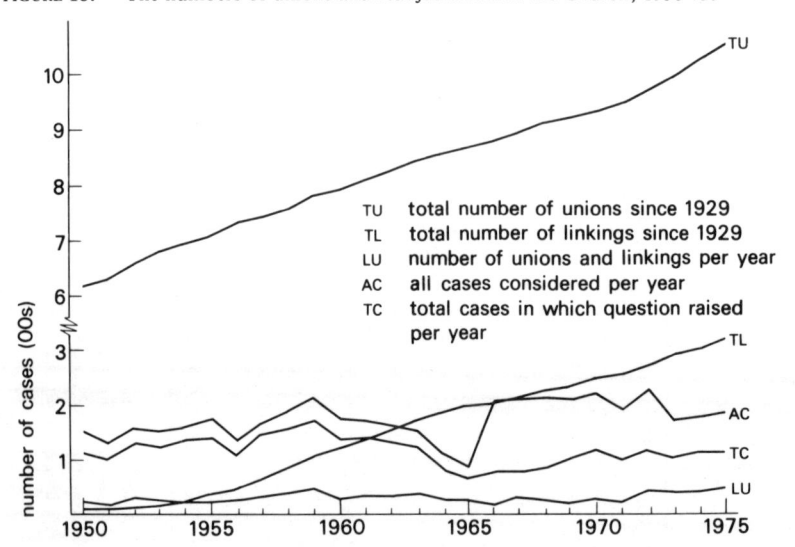

FIGURE 18: The numbers of unions and readjustments in the Church, 1950-75.

TU total number of unions since 1929
TL total number of linkings since 1929
LU number of unions and linkings per year
AC all cases considered per year
TC total cases in which question raised per year

Secondly, the TL line plots the cumulative total number of linkings in the Church of Scotland since 1929 (row 11, table 53). Like the TU line, the TL line slopes upwards to the right, but rather less evenly. Linkings seem to have started in the second half of the 1940s, although this is a little uncertain because of the discrepancies in the figures mentioned above. In the early 1950s the line rises only slowly, but then more quickly from about 1955. There appears to be a slight pause in the mid-1960s, but by the early 1970s the line is again rising comparatively steeply.

Thirdly, the LU line plots the combined number of unions and linkings which were arranged in each year over the period 1945-75 (row 12, table 53). The line fluctuates from year to year around an average of 27. It may be that the number of unions and linkings are related to the number of cases considered each year (TC), although the relationship does not appear to be a very close one. In the last four years (1972-5) the number of unions and linkings combined reached 40 and more per year, which is much above the average, and is exceeded only in one previous year (1959), when the number reached 44. This may indicate a desire on the part of the Committee to increase the rate at which readjustment is carried out.

The AC line plots the total number of all cases considered during the year (row 4, table 53), while the TC line plots the total number of cases per year in which the question of readjustment is raised (row 5, table 53). The gap between the TC and AC lines in figure 18 is accounted for by the group of cases where the question of readjustment was not raised. The relationship between these two lines over the period 1950-73 is an interesting one, and may be broken down into two parts. In the first period between 1950 and 1965 the lines first rise and then fall. Between 1950 and 1959 there is a slow upward trend leading to peaks in both curves in 1959. There are dips in the general trend in 1951 and 1956, but the latter can be explained by the fact that 1956 covered only a nine month period, as mentioned above. Over the period 1959-65 there is a sharp downward trend in both curves, leading to troughs in 1965. The interesting point is that during these movements the two curves correspond very closely. With one minor exception in 1961, the curves rise and fall together, and the distance between them varies remarkably little. TC averages 80.1 per cent of AC over the period 1950-65, but varies from year to year over the comparatively small range of 71.0 − 87.5 per cent. This suggests that, whatever criteria are used for selecting charges for readjustment (TC) out of the total possible number of charges to be adjusted (AC), those criteria were used fairly consistently over the period. The variations which do occur in the proportion of charges to be readjusted might be explained by random variations in the characteristics of each year's group of vacant charges.

However, the period between 1966 and 1975 presents a very different picture, largely brought about by the very large increase in AC from 84 in 1965 to 204 in 1966. We have not been able to account for such a large increase in the number of vacancies, and no explanation is given in the 1966 report of the committee, where the figure is disguised. The new high level of AC is roughly maintained over the rest of the period, declining in the last two years. The TC line, instead of rising sharply to maintain the previously established gap, increases only very slowly over the period to 1975, so that the gap starts very large and is only slowly reduced. Thus, full advantage does not seem to have been taken of the opportunity to increase the rate of readjustment, although the number of unions and linkings has been rather higher in the last four years. If the proportion of TC to AC of 80.1 per cent had been maintained over the period 1966-75, the number of cases of readjustment would have totalled 1,648 instead of 776. As it happened, the ratio of TC to AC averaged 50.1 per cent over the period 1966-75. However, the gap between AC and TC, although narrowing, is still wide, thus offering the opportunity for increasing the rate of readjustment in the future.

In deciding in which cases to raise the question of union and readjustment, the Committee considers that the 'spiritual welfare of the community' is of prime importance in its work, but that financial considerations should also be taken into account. It is beyond our competence to examine the 'spiritual welfare' criterion, since this must be determined by the subjective judgement of the Committee. We can, however, investigate the financial aspects using information published by the Church.

The names of charges involved in unions and readjustments each year, together with those charges which fall vacant but where the question of readjustment is not raised, are published in the *Reports to the General Assembly* in the following year.[4] We have used the information for 1972 since that is the last year for which the financial information is published. The 'no change' charges form an ideal control group with which to compare the charges undergoing adjustment. The number of charges in the 'no change' group, together with the numbers under the different categories of adjustment, are given in table 54, column 1. Note that column 1 gives the number of charges involved; but, since some types of adjustment involves more than one charge, a separate figure is given after the name of the form of adjustment where the two differ. For example, in 1972, there were 23 unions involving 50 charges.

The financial and other information for each of the 239 parishes involved, which forms the basis of the figures presented in columns 2 to 12 of table 54, was obtained for the year 1971, that is to say, the year immediately preceding the year in which the adjustments were carried out.[5] In this way we can examine the financial state of the charges immediately prior to their adjustment, using the same information as that presumably available to the Committee at the time.

In table 54, column 1 gives the number of charges involved in 1972; 111 in the 'no change' group, and 128 in the 'readjusted, charges group. Of the 128 charges in the 'readjusted' groups, the largest single group was 'unions', which involved 50 charges. The membership figures of the charges are given in columns 2 and 3. Column 2 shows the total membership of each group of charges, while column 3 provides the average membership per charge of each group. It can be readily seen that the 'no change' charges' average membership of 689.6 is higher than any of the 'adjusted' groups of parishes, which overall have an average membership of 332.8.

Column 4 in table 54 presents the total congregational support of each group of charges in pounds sterling, while column 5 gives the congregational support per member of each group. Examination of these figures reveals that the congregational support per member is £2.2 per year in the 'control' group of charges, but this figure is equalled or exceeded by six out of the ten 'adjusted' groups of charges, which together average £2.5 per member per year. Column 6 provides the figures for the congregational support per charge in each of the groups; these figures show that the average support is much higher in the 'no change' charges

TABLE 54.
Analysis of the financial position in 1971 of those charges considered for union or readjustment in 1972

Unions and readjustments to charges	Number of charges involved	Total membership of charges	Average membership of charge	Total congregational support	Congregational support per member	Congregational support per charge	Total endowment of charge	Stipend Average endowment per charge	Stipend from all sources	Average stipend per charge	Total aid given to (+) or drawn from (−) the fund	Average aid given (+) or drawn (−) per charge
	1	2	3 £	4 £	5 £	6 £	7 £	8 £	9 £	10 £	11 £	12 £
A No change	111	76,550	689.6	172,120	2.2	1,550.6	25,690	231.4	151,263	1,362.7	+17,874	+161.0
B Age restrictions	11	3,161	287.4	9,385	3.0	853.3	3,969	360.1	12,900	1,172.7	− 2,810	− 255.5
C Terminable appointments	4	1,767	441.8	4,234	2.4	1,058.5	600	125.0	4,059	1,014.8	− 101	− 25.3
D Continued vacancy	6	2,598	433.0	6,446	2.5	1,074.3	552	92.0	5,920	986.7	− 18	− 3.0
E Unions (23)	50	21,418	428.4	53,250	2.5	1,065.0	5,539	110.8	45,540	910.8	+ 5,828	+116.5
F Deferred unions (4)	8	3,619	452.4	7,162	2.0	895.3	1,847	230.9	7,443	930.4	+ 372	+ 46.5
G Linkings (14)	28	7,053	251.9	14,945	2.1	533.8	8,617	307.8	23,280	831.4	− 4,836	−172.7
H Temporary linkings (3)	6	3,061	510.2	6,604	2.2	1,100.7	891	148.5	5,545	924.2	+ 753	+125.5
I Linkings terminated (5)	11	2,707	246.1	6,087	2.2	553.4	2,444	222.2	8,848	804.4	− 1,109	−100.8
J Reduction to mission station	2	56	23.0	101	1.8	50.5	—	—	—	—	− 1,503	−751.5
K Dissolution of congregations	2	411	205.5	140	0.3	70.0	—	—	—	—	+ 140	+ 70.0
L AGGREGATE, B to K	128	42,593	332.8	108,354	2.5	846.5	24,459	191.1	113,535	887.0	− 3,289	− 25.7
M $\frac{L}{A} \times 100$	—	—	48.3%	—	113.6%	54.6%	—	82.6%	—	65.1%	—	—

than in the 'readjusted' charges, averaging £1,550.6 per year compared to £846.5. Thus, although the congregational support per member is a little higher in the 'readjusted' groups of charges, this is more than offset by the much higher average membership figures in the 'no change' charges.

Columns 7 to 10 of table 54 deal with stipend. Column 7 gives the total endowments for stipend in each group, while column 8 presents the average endowment per charge in each group. Although the 'control' group of charges have a higher average endowment than the rest (£231.4 per year as compared to £191.1), the difference is not great, and two of the 'readjusted' groups have much higher average endowments than the 'control' group. Endowments are probably not a good indicator of the financial viability of charges, partly because they form a relatively small proportion of total stipend (18.9 per cent. in the charges in table 54), and partly because they do not appear to be related to the current level of congregational support. The total figures for stipend from all sources in each group is shown in column 9, with the respective average figures in column 10. The average stipend in the 111 'no change' charges was £1,362.7, as compared to only £887.0 in the readjusted group. Even the higher of the two figures is below the 1971 minimum stipend of £1,392, but this is no doubt explained by the fact that most of the charges concerned underwent a period of vacancy, when no stipend was paid.[6]

The figures for 'stipend' are thus somewhat misleading, since in most cases they amount to only a proportion of the total stipend of the charges that would have been paid had they not fallen vacant. The lower 'average stipend' paid in the adjusted charges may at least partly reflect the fact that such charges probably underwent a longer period of vacancy; the difficulty of attracting a new minister may in some cases have been a factor leading to their readjustment. Allowance for the vacancy factor can be made as follows. In 1971 there was only 1 vacancy in the 'control' group of charges, but 16 vacancies in the 'readjusted' group. Taking this factor into account raises the stipend figures for the two groups from £1,362.7 and £887.0 to £1,375.1 and £1,013.7 respectively. In addition, a number of charges are designated as 'vacant for part of the year', and again these 'part-time' vacancies occur much more frequently in the 'readjusted' charges (in 46, or 36 per cent. of the total) than in the 'no change' charges (in 11, or 13 per cent of the total). Assuming in such cases that only half the total stipend is paid, the two adjusted average stipend figures are raised further to £1,468.6 and £1,275.7 respectively. On the basis of these rather arbitrary assumptions, the average stipend in the 'no change' charges exceeded the stipend in the 'readjusted' charges by nearly £200. Although the stipend of the 'adjusted' group still falls below the minimum, this is probably explained by the roughness of the calculations.

No figures for stipend are given for the two congregations reduced to mission stations (row J) or the two charges which were dissolved in 1972 (row K).

The amount of aid given or drawn from the Fund for the Maintenance of the Ministry are shown in the last two columns of table 54. Column 11 gives the net aid given to (+) or drawn from (−) the fund by each group of charges, while column 12 supplies the corresponding figures per charge. The 'no change' charges appeared to be comfortably in surplus, contributing on average £161 in aid to the fund in 1971. Amongst the 'readjusted' charges, four of the ten groups were aid givers, but overall the average such charge drew £25.7 in aid in 1971.

In general, therefore, it seems that those charges which underwent some form of union or readjustment in 1972 were much less strong financially in the previous year than those charges which fell vacant but where the question of union or readjustment were not raised in 1972. The average membership in the readjusted charges was much lower, averaging only 48.3 per cent. of the membership of the no change charges. On the other hand the congregational support per member was a little higher, but the congregational support per charge, which is a function of the average membership and the *per capita* contribution, was much lower at 54.6 per cent. The average endowment for stipend is a little lower in the readjusted parishes at 82.6 per cent, but this is a relatively small proportion of total stipend (less than 20 per cent), and therefore probably not a good indicator of financial viability. The adjusted figures for stipend show that the average stipend in the 'readjusted' group exceeded that of the 'no change' group by nearly £200. Finally, the no change charges contributed on average £161.0 in aid to the central fund in 1971, whereas the readjusted charges on average drew £25.7 of aid from the fund in 1971.

However, it should be remembered that the figures in table 54 are averages for groups of charges which individually show considerable variations about the mean. For example, some of the no change charges drew considerable sums from the fund in 1971, while a number of the readjusted charges, particularly those which subsequently underwent union, contributed large sums to the fund. Nonetheless, the evidence provided here suggests that financial considerations do sway the judgement of the Committee, and that the tendency is to readjustment of those charges which are of below average financial strength.

5 Forecasts of the number of charges, 1974 – 2001

So far we have been concerned to explain the mechanics of the close link between the number of parish ministers and the number of charges in the Church. Table 55 indicates that in the post-war period the decline in ministerial numbers (29.9 per cent) has been almost exactly matched by the fall in the number of charges (29.3 per cent). Over the next decade the forecasts of an acceleration in the decline of the number of ministers should lead to an increase in the annual number of 'net vacancies'. This presents the Church with an opportunity to accelerate the rate of union and readjustment, even if the proportion of cases in which the question is raised remains constant.

TABLE 55.
The numbers of charges, congregations, parish ministers and net vacancies, 1945-75

	1945	1961	Percentage change 1945-61	1975	Percentage change 1961-75	Percentage change 1945-75
No. of charges	2,426*	2,093	13.7	1,714	18.1	29.3
No. of congregations	2,426	2,212	8.8	1,964	11.2	19.0
No. of ministers	2,265	1,928	14.9	1,588	17.6	29.9
No. of net vacancies	161	165	—	126	—	—

* Approximate figure only

It is not easy, however, to determine what is the optimum number of charges towards which the Church should work. One possible guide might be provided by the situation obtaining in 1928 just prior to the Union. At that time the Church of Scotland had 1,457 charges and the United Free Church had 1,441 charges. Since those two Churches were in competition with each other, the appropriate number of charges for the two Churches when united in 1929 might be taken as half the joint number of charges (i.e. about 1,450). However, even by 1975, after many years of unions and readjustments, the number of charges at 1,714 still exceeded the 1929 figure by over 250. Moreover, since 1929 the membership of the Church has declined by 18.1 per cent, so it is arguable that the 1929 'appropriate' number of charges should be reduced by the same proportion. On this basis, the 1975 'appropriate' number of charges would be 1,188, which the present number exceeds by 526. It is possible that with only about 1,200 charges the Church would not be able to fulfil 'its distinctive call and duty to bring the ordinances of religion to the people in every parish of Scotland through a territorial ministry'. However, the widespread use of the motor car, together with the increasing urbanisation of the Scottish population, may make 1,200 charges an appropriate target at which to aim by the end of the century.

If the policy of union and readjustment continues to maintain the close relationship between the numbers of charges and ministers, then a forecast of the number of charges can be related to the forecast of the number of ministers. This forecast can be calculated by adding the forecast for the number of ministers to the forecast number of net vacancies (i.e. the number by which ministers are expected to fall below charges). Regression analysis suggests that the number of net vacancies will continue to fall slowly from an average level of 130 in 1974 to 98 in 2001, this rate of decline maintaining the proportion of net vacancies to ministers at between 7 and 8 per cent as the number of ministers declines.

The three forecasts for the number of charges over the period 1974-2001, based on the three manpower forecasts made in the previous chapter, are shown in table 56. All three forecasts give rise to patterns of decline similar to the ministerial forecasts from which they are derived. Under the first forecast the number of charges falls to about 1,350 by the end of the century, giving an overall decline of 23.2 per cent from the 1974 level. In the second forecast the number falls more quickly to about 1,270 by the late 1980s, giving a fall of about 28 per cent. In the third forecast, based on the linear membership trend, the number of charges falls by 32.9 per cent to 1,212 by the end of the century.

While the falls in the first two forecasts are substantial, the number of charges even in the lower of the two will still exceed by a sizeable margin the suggested target number of 1,200 for 2001. Only the less realistic linear projection is on target, with 1,212 charges by 2001. On the other hand, if the number of ministers reaches a stable state towards the end of the century, and a halt is called on the policy of reducing the number of charges, then the number of net vacancies could be considerably reduced. This would reduce the forecast number of charges to between 1,150 and 1,250 under the first two forecasts, or about the number required. Alternatively, if it was intended to reduced further the number of charges around the turn of the century and after, then measures would have to be taken in the 1980s to ensure that the downward trend in ministerial numbers does not level off.

TABLE 56.
A forecast of the number of charges in the Church of Scotland, 1974-2001

| | Manpower forecast ||| Number of net vacancies | Forecast number of charges |||
	I	Ii	III		I (i.e. 1 + 4)	II (i.e. 2 + 4)	III (i.e. 3 + 4)
	1	2	3	4	5	6	7
1974	1631	1631	1677	130	1761	1761	1807
1975	1602	1575	1656	128	1730	1703	1784
1976	1573	1519	1635	127	1700	1646	1762
1977	1539	1463	1614	126	1665	1589	1740
1978	1506	1417	1593	125	1631	1542	1718
1979	1475	1371	1572	124	1599	1495	1696
1980	1446	1325	1552	122	1568	1447	1674
1981	1417	1289	1531	121	1538	1410	1652
1982	1389	1253	1510	120	1509	1373	1630
1983	1364	1227	1489	119	1483	1346	1608
1984	1341	1201	1468	118	1459	1319	1586
1985	1321	1185	1448	116	1437	1301	1564
1986	1304	1169	1427	115	1419	1284	1542
1987	1290	1163	1406	114	1404	1277	1520
1988	1278	1157	1385	113	1391	1270	1498
1989	1270	1151	1364	112	1382	1263	1476
1990	1264	1155	1343	111	1375	1266	1454
1991	1260	1159	1323	109	1369	1268	1432
1992	1257	1163	1302	108	1365	1271	1410
1993	1257	1167	1281	107	1364	1274	1388
1994	1256	—	1260	106	1362	—	1366
1995	1255	—	1239	105	1360	—	1344
1996	1254	—	1219	103	1357	—	1322
1997	1253	—	1198	102	1355	—	1300
1998	1254	—	1177	101	1355	—	1278
1999	1253	—	1156	100	1353	—	1256
2000	1254	—	1135	99	1353	—	1234
2001	1254	—	1114	98	1352	—	1212

6 Conclusions

In this chapter we have attempted to account for the decline which has taken place in the number of charges since the Second World War and before, and to forecast the number of charges over the years up to 2001. It has been shown that the decline has been brought about by the deliberate policy of the Church authorities.

In section 2 we saw that on the occurrence of a vacancy in a parish charge, the question of union and readjustment may be raised by the Presbytery or the Committee. If either decides that the question should be raised, the case must be enquired into. In the subsequent negotiations the Committee gives priority in its thinking to a union, i.e. the joining of two or more charges under one minister and Kirk Session. However, linkings (i.e. the joining of two or more charges under one minister), with the congregations concerned retaining their separate status and organization, are considered best when the congregations are more than two miles apart. In addition to unions and linkings, other forms of readjustments include restricted choice of ministers, terminable appointments and dissolutions.

In sections 3 and 4 we saw that the rate at which unions and readjustments are effected depends upon the annual number of vacancies, and the criteria used by the authorities in deciding in which cases the question of union and readjustment should be raised. The number of vacancies depends partly upon the 'net vacancies', (i.e. the figure by which the number of parish ministers falls below the number of charges), and partly upon 'translations' (or 'turnover', i.e. the number of ministers who change charges every year). We saw that as the number of ministers falls the number of net vacancies increases, which lays those charges open to union and readjustment, thereby enabling the number of charges to be reduced. The number of 'translations' widens the range of charges which can be considered for readjustment. Over the period 1945-75 the number of parish ministers has fallen by 29.9 per cent and the number of charges by 29.3 per cent, which indicates the closeness of the relationship between the two.

The criteria used by the authorities in deciding in which vacancies the question of union and readjustment should be raised has changed in the period since the war. In the first part of the period between 1946 and 1965, the question of union and readjustment was raised in an average of 80.1 per cent of all cases, the percentage varying from year to year over the comparatively small range of 71.0 per cent to 87.5 per cent. This suggests that whatever criteria were used for selecting vacant charges for readjustment were applied fairly consistently. In the later part of the period up to 1975, a large increase in the number of vacancies resulted in a fall in the proportion, though not the number, of cases in which the question was raised. The proportion averaged 50.1 per cent over the period. It was suggested that an opportunity had been missed for an acceleration in the rate of union and readjustment.

We then went on to consider how far financial criteria played a part in deciding which vacant charges should undergo readjustment. The financial characteristics in 1971 of those charges which underwent some form of readjustment in 1972 were compared to the characteristics of those charges which fell vacant in 1972 but where no readjustment took place. It was found that although there were considerable variations between charges in each group, the 'readjusted' charges in 1972 were much less strong financially in the previous year than the 'no change' charges. Both the membership and congregational support of the readjusted charges were on average about half that of the control group of charges.

Finally, in section 5 we turned to the question of forecasting the number of charges over the years to 2001. Because the number of charges and parish ministers are closely related through the policy of union and readjustment, it was possible to make a forecast by adding estimated net vacancies to the forecasts of ministerial numbers given in the previous chapter. On this basis, charges are expected to decline by about a quarter from a little over 1,700 in 1975 to between 1,270 and 1,350 by 2001 using the two manpower forecasts. While this fall is substantial, the end-of-century forecast still exceeds by a sizeable margin the suggested target of 1,200 charges. However, it was suggested that if the number of net vacancies was to be reduced as the number of ministers levels off towards the end of the century, the number of charges might be brought down to the 1,200 target. Such a policy would have the disadvantage of limiting the scope for further unions and readjustments at the turn of the century.

Notes

1 Church of Scotland, 'Report of the Committee on Unions and Readjustments, 1966', *Reports to the General Assembly, 1966,* appendix II, pp. 288-311.
2 'Report of the Committee on Unions and Readjustments, 1974, *Reports to the General Assembly, 1974,* p 216.
3 The question of team and group ministries is discussed in chapter 15.
4 'Report of the Committee on Unions and Readjustments, 1973', *Reports to the General Assembly, 1973,* appendix, tables I-XII, pp. 268-72.
5 *Reports to the General Assembly, 1972,* table A, pp. 817-64.
6 'Stipend' is described in chapter 10.

Chapter 9

Forecasts of the financial position in 1981 and 2001

1 Introduction
In the previous five chapters forecasts have been made of membership, real total Church income, ministerial manpower, numbers of charges, and numbers of lay workers. All of these forecasts have been based on an extrapolation of trends over recent years. In the case of membership, a range of three forecasts was made, because of the importance of the membership variable and the difficulty of making a precise forecast so far ahead; these suggest that membership might fall from 1,041,772 in 1975 by between a third and a half to reach between 680,000 and 450,000 in 2001. Because membership was found to have an important influence on real total income, a range of three income forecasts was also made. These indicate that on the most optimistic membership forecast, real total income might improve slightly on the 1975 figure of £17.644 millions, but that on less optimistic membership forecasts real income might fall by up to sixty per cent to reach £6.864 millions by 2001. Our preferred forecast 2 suggests that membership might fall by about 45 per cent to 570,000 by 2001, and real income by about 34 per cent, to £11.655 millions. The two forecasts for ministerial manpower and the number of parish charges suggest that both will fall by about a quarter by 2001. If the steady upward trend in the number of elders since the war continues, the figure should increase by 29 per cent from 50,963 in 1973 to 65,876 in 2001.

The purpose of this chapter is to use the forecasts of these variables to produce some statistics to indicate the likely financial position of the Church in 1981 and 2001. We have a greater confidence in the forecasts for 1981 than those for 2001 because of the much nearer time-horizon involved.

2 Financial forecasts of the Church, 1981 and 2001
In making forecasts of the financial position of the Church in 1981 and 2001, we deal separately with the ministry and the mission and service work.

1 The ministry
The forecasts for the ministry are based largely on projections of the financial position of the average charge. The term 'average charge' refers, not to any existing charge or group of charges which might be taken in some way as representative of the Church, but to the statistical average produced from aggregate data. It is important to remember that such an average will conceal the wide variations which exist between individual charges.

Tables 57 and 58 indicate the projections of the numbers of members per charge for 1981 and 2001 respectively based on the three membership forecasts and two forecasts for the number of charges. Consequently, there are six alternative projections for each year; in 1981 these range from 589, for the projection based on the lowest membership forecast (906,157) and the higher of the two forecasts of the number of charges (1,538), to 681 for the highest membership forecast (959,993) and the low forecast of charges (1,410). All but two of the projections are thus above the 1975 actual figure of 608 members per charge. This arises because the number of charges will tend to fall by a proportionately greater amount than the membership forecasts. If we take forecast 2 of membership as the most likely outcome, it seems that the number of members per charge should lie between 607 and 662 in 1981, a change on the 1975 figure of 608 of between -0.2 and +8.9 per cent.

TABLE 57.
Projections of members per charge in 1981*

Forecasts of membership in 1981°	Number of charges[×] I 1,538	II 1,410
1. 959,993	624	681
2. 933,075	607	662
3. 906,157	589	643

TABLE 58.
Projections of members per charge in 2001*

Forecasts of membership in 2001°	Number of charges[×] I 1,352	II 1,274[+]
1. 687,395	507	540
2. 570,751	422	448
3. 454,108	336	356

* In 1975 the figure was 608.
[×] SOURCE: Table 56.
° SOURCE: Table 17.
[+] Assumed the same as the 1993 figure.

By 2001 the position is reversed, with all of the projections of members per charge lying below the 1975 figure, as indicated in table 58. This reflects partly the slackening in the rate of decline in the number of charges as the two forecasts approach a stable state around 1990, and partly the continuing decline in the membership implied by the linear forecasts.

The projections range from 336 to 540, but the most likely forecast suggests that the members per charge by 2001 should be between 422 and 448, giving a decline from the 1975 figure of between 26.3 and 30.6 per cent.

An important assumption underlying the projected figures of members per charge is that there is no link between the number of members and the number of charges, so that an increase in the rate of decline of charges does not cause an increase in the rate of decline of the membership. There is some evidence, however, which is presented in chapter 13,[1] that the process of uniting congregations does not produce an immediate fall in their memberships which is significantly greater than that occurring in those charges which fall vacant but do not undergo some form of readjustment. It seems unlikely, however, that this factor would have any great impact on the figures in tables 57 and 58, which suggest that over the next several years at least the pastoral care work for the average minister will become heavier as the number of members per charge rises. In the longer term the position should become easier as the numbers of members per charge declines, which may suggest that the policy of union and readjustment should be continued after 1990 in order to maintain the numbers of members per charge at nearer the 600 level.

Projections of the income per charge in real terms (at 1975 prices) for 1981 and 2001 are given in tables 59 and 60 respectively. Again the three forecasts of the income of the ministry together with the two forecasts of the number of charges produces a range of six projections of income per charge for each year. In examining these income figures it is important to remember that they are gross figures based on the total income of the ministry, which were calculated in chapter 6. This includes not only congregational income, or liberality, but also the standardized stipend and the income accruing separately to the Church and Ministry Department in the form of bequests, donations, grants and investment income. The income per charge figures thus are based on the income to be spent by, and on behalf of, the charges.

Table 59 indicates that in 1981 the projections of income per charge in real terms at 1975 prices range between £8,761 and £10,916, compared to the 1975 actual figure of £8,672. The most likely outcome for 1981 is forecast 2, which gives an income per charge of between £9,373 and £10,223. These figures represent increases over the 1975 actual figure of between 8.1 and 17.9 per cent respectively. This increase reflects the fact that, while the real income of the ministry has fallen, the number of charges to be supported has fallen by a proportionately larger amount. By 2001 the range in the real income per charge has widened considerably to between £4,274 and £11,801. The further reduction in the number of charges continues to have a buoying effect, but this is offset in forecasts 2 and 3 by the sharp decline of the real income of the ministry between 1981 and 2001. The most likely outcome is taken to be forecast 2, which suggests that the income per charge in 2001 might be of the order of £7,243 to £7,686. These figures represent falls over the 1975 actual figure of between 11.4 and 16.5 per cent.

In calculating the income per charge figures in tables 59 and 60, it is assumed that the number of charges does not influence the income of the ministry. However, the continuing decline in the number of charges implies that some members may have to travel a greater distance to church. This in turn may cause reduced rates of attendance and of liberality.

Tables 61 and 62 give projections of liberality per member in real terms (at 1975 prices) for 1981 and 2001 respectively. The forecasts of total liberality, or

Forecasts of the financial position in 1981 and 2001

TABLE 59.
Projections of real income per charge (at 1975 prices) in 1981*

Forecasts of the income of the ministry in 1981⁰	Forecasts of number of charges[×]	
	I 1,538	II 1,410
£	£	£
1. 15,392,000	10,008	10,916
2. 14,415,000	9,373	10,223
3. 13,474,000	8,761	9,556

TABLE 60.
Projections of real income per charge (at 1975 prices) in 2001*

Forecasts of the income of the ministry in 2001⁰	Forecasts of number of charges[×]	
	I 1,352	II 1,274+
£	£	£
1. 15,034,000	11,120	11,801
2. 9,792,000	7,243	7,686
3. 5,779,000	4,274	4,536

* In 1975 the figure was £8,672.
× SOURCE: Table 56.
⁰ SOURCE: Table 19.
+ Assumed the same as the 1993 figure.

congregational income, were made on the assumption that liberality will continue to form 71.1 per cent of total income, as it did with little annual variation for the ten-year period 1966-75. Since the three forecasts of liberality for each year are linked with one of the three forecasts of membership (through the income forecasting equation), there are only three projections of liberality per member for each year. In 1981 these projections range between £12.56 and £13.54, but the 'best estimate' forecast is £13.05. This figure represents an increase in real terms

TABLE 61.
Projections of real liberality per member (at 1975 prices) in 1981*

Forecasts of total income[×]	Forecasts of liberality	Forecasts of membership+	Forecasts of liberality per member
£	£	£	£
1. 18,280,000	12,997,000	959,993	13.54
2. 17,120,000	12,172,000	933,075	13.05
3. 16,002,000	11,377,000	906,157	12.56

*In 1975 the liberality per member was £12.46.
× SOURCE: Table 19.
+ SOURCE: Table 17.

TABLE 62
Projections of real liberality per member (at 1975 prices) in 2001*

Forecasts of total income[×]	Forecasts of liberality	Forecasts of membership⁺	Forecasts of liberality per member
£	£	£	£
1. 17,855,000	12,695,000	687,395	18.47
2. 11,629,000	8,268,000	570,751	14.49
3. 6,864,000	4,880,000	454,108	10.75

*In 1975 the liberality per member was £12.46.
[×]SOURCE: Table 19.
⁺SOURCE: Table 17.

of 4.7 per cent over the 1975 actual figure of £12.46. By 2001 the projections of real liberality per member range between £10.75 and £18.47, but the best forecast is £14.49, which gives an increase over the 1975 figure of 16.3 per cent. The rise in the average member's contribution to liberality reflects the growth in real personal income *per capita* over the period.

TABLE 63.
Estimates of the expenditure of the average charge in real terms (at 1975 prices) for 1975, 1981 and 2001, under different assumptions.

	Assumptions about expenditures	Expenditure per charge		
		1975 (actual)	1981 (forecast)	2001 (forecast)
		£	£	£
A	Held constant in real terms at 1975 level	8,672	8,672	8,672
B	Allowing for increase in real stipend	8,672	9,129	11,399
C	Allowing for increase in real labour costs	8,672	9,348	13,152
D	Allowing for increase in real stipend and labour costs	8,672	9,805	15,879

The income forecasts are not only of interest in themselves, but also in relation to the forecast level of congregational expenditures. We saw in chapter 6 that no information is published centrally on congregational expenditure, but that, apart from making small savings, congregational income is completely expended each year. One assumption, therefore, is that the expenditure of the average charge can be taken to equal income, i.e. £8,672 in 1975. Like the income figure, this expenditure figure is a gross one based on the expenditure of the ministry as a whole. In forecasting real expenditure for the average charge over the period 1976–2001, one might assume that money expenditure will increase in line with prices. Real expenditure would then be maintained at the level of £8,672 obtaining in 1975. This forecast is shown in row A of table 63 for the years 1981 and 2001, and for the period 1976-2001 in column 2 of table 64. However, this assumption has important implications for the income positions both of ministers and of other Church employees. We examine each group in turn.

A Ministers

If the expenditure of the average charge was to be maintained in the future at the 1975 level in real terms, then it is implied that the average level of stipend might also be maintained in real terms over the years to 2001. However, over the same period it is likely that the real earnings of other groups of professional employees will increase more or less in parallel with the growth of the British economy. Consequently, the maintenance of a constant level of real stipend would result in ministers slipping further and further behind the income position of comparable professional groups. Indeed, this process has been in progress for many years, as will be shown in chapter 11.[2] Whereas in 1929 the minister was one of the wealthier members of the community, his income today (including the manse and other goods in kind) is roughly equivalent to that of a graduate school teacher in the mid-range of the profession. If this trend were to continue in the future, with incomes (including those of school teachers) nearly doubling in real terms by 2001 while the real income of the ministers stayed constant, then at the turn of the century the income of the minister would be at approximately one-half of that of the mid-range school teacher. It seems to us desirable that the relative income position of ministers should not be allowed to decline further. To this end, the policy of the Maintenance of the Ministry Committee should be as far as possible to increase the real level of the minimum stipend in line with the growth in real incomes of the community as a whole (i.e. at about 3 per cent a year). However, the success of such a policy depends ultimately upon the fund-raising efforts in each and every congregation.

Such real increases in stipend represent an increase in the real cost of the average charge, and would need to be added to the 1975 expenditure of £8,672. According to the calculations made in chapter 11, the average stipend paid in 1975 was approximately £2,460, as compared to the minimum stipend of £2,258. In addition, each charge paid a further 15 per cent of the previous year's stipend, or about £305, as a contribution to the Aged and Infirm Ministers' Fund. This gives an average stipend and pension contribution of £2,765 in 1975. In chapter 5 we estimated that real personal income *per capita* increased by 0.06 per cent in 1976, and forecast that in subsequent years it will rise by 2.7 per cent a year.[3] Over the period 1975-81, therefore, real personal income *per capita* should increase by 14.3 per cent. If the average stipend is to keep pace it should increase by the same proportion, or from £2,460 to £2,812. In 1981 the congregational contribution to the Aged and Infirm Ministers' Fund would be about £410, giving a stipend and pension payment of £3,222 in 1981 at 1975 prices. The real increase in the stipend and pension payment in 1981 over 1975 is thus £457, which added to the 1975 expenditure for the average charge of £8,672 gives a forecast real expenditure for 1981 of £9,129.

The same procedure is extended to calculate the increase in real costs of the average charge in 2001. The increase in real personal income *per capita* between

1975 and 2001 is forecast to be 94.8 per cent. Applied to the 1975 average stipend, this produces a figure of £4,792 for 2001. Allowing a further 15 per cent for the pension contribution (about £700), the stipend and pension contribution amounts to £5,492. The increase over the 1975 figure is £2,727, which, added to the expenditure of the average charge in 1975 of £8,672, gives a figure of £11,399 for 2001. The forecast expenditures for the average charge which incorporate these increases in real stipend are shown for 1981 and 2001 in table 63, row B, and for every year over the period 1975-2001 in column 4 of table 64.

B Other employees

The maintenance of real expenditure at the 1975 level would also have implications for the income positions of other Church employees. The average wage paid might be maintained in real terms over the years to 2001, but like ministers, the employees would gradually slip behind the earnings of other comparable groups or workers. The Church would find it increasingly difficult to retain the services of these employees, and in the end would probably be forced to raise real wages in order to compete with other employers. The Church, like other service-providing institutions, is necessarily labour-intensive, and would find it difficult to offset increased labour costs with improved productivity.[4] Similarly, other expenditures, such as those on the repair and maintenance of buildings, will tend to have a high labour content, and might be expected to increase in real terms in line with increasing real labour costs.

The impact of the prospective increase in real costs of other labour should therefore be included in the forecast of the expenditure of the average charge. This can be done by assuming arbitrarily that labour costs comprise 80 per cent of the non-stipend expenses of £5,907 of the average charge in 1975, and that they too increase in line with the forecast increase in real personal income *per capita* in the United Kingdom. On this basis, non-stipend expenses of the average congregation would rise from £5,907 in 1975 to £6,583 in 1981 and to £10,387 in 2001. If the average stipend and pension contribution of £2,765 in 1975 is held constant in real terms, then the expenditure of the average charge in 1981 and 2001 would be £9,348 and £13,152 respectively. These forecasts are shown in table 63, row C, while those covering every year over the period 1975-2001 are given in column 6 of table 64. Alternatively, if the calculated increases in the 'real' stipend are also included, the expenditure figures would rise to £9,805 and £15,869 in 1981 and 2001 respectively, as shown in table 63, row D. The forecasts for the period 1975-2001 are presented in column 8 of table 64.

An important assumption underlying these projections of the expenditure of the average charge is that the level of expenditure is not influenced by the size of the membership. The statistical analysis in chapter 12 below indicates that this assumption is incorrect, and, since the membership of the average charge is likely to fall by 2001, the forecast expenditure figures calculated for that year may prove to be overestimates. By the same token, the expenditure figures for 1981 are likely to be understated, since the membership of the average charge in that year is expected to be larger than in 1975.

The various forecasts of real total expenditure of the ministry, together with forecasts of real total income, for every year over the period 1975-2001 are presented in table 64. The four forecasts of total expenditure have been calculated by multiplying together the four forecasts of expenditure of the average charge,

TABLE 64.
Forecasts of the income and expenditure of the ministry in real terms (at 1975 prices), 1975-2001.

		EXPENDITURES									INCOME		
	Number of charges ×	Forecast A		Forecast B		Forecast C		Forecast D					
		Average	Total i.e. 1 × 2	Average	Total i.e. 1 × 4	Average	Total i.e. 1 × 6	average	Total i.e. 1 × 8	Forecast 1	Forecast 2	Forecast 3	
	1	2	3	4	5	6	7	8	9	10	11	12	
		£	£	£	£	£	£	£	£	£	£	£	
1975+	1,714	8,672	14,864,000	8,672	14,864,000	8,672	14,864,000	8,672	14,864,000	14,864,000	14,864,000	14,864,000	
1976	1,672	8,672	14,508,000	8,737	14,617,000	8,675	14,513,000	8,740	14,622,000	14,993,000	14,843,000	14,694,000	
1977	1,627	8,672	14,109,000	8,804	14,324,000	8,803	14,322,000	8,935	14,537,000	15,084,000	14,777,000	14,475,000	
1978	1,587	8,672	13,762,000	8,882	14,096,000	8,934	14,178,000	9,144	14,512,000	15,168,000	14,702,000	14,244,000	
1979	1,547	8,672	13,416,000	8,962	13,864,000	9,068	14,028,000	9,358	14,477,000	15,249,000	14,616,000	14,000,000	
1980	1,508	8,672	13,077,000	9,045	13,640,000	9,207	13,884,000	9,580	14,447,000	15,323,000	14,521,000	13,744,000	
1981	1,474	8,672	12,782,000	9,129	13,456,000	9,348	13,779,000	9,805	14,453,000	15,392,000	14,415,000	13,474,000	
1982	1,441	8,672	12,496,000	9,217	13,282,000	9,495	13,682,000	10,040	14,468,000	15,455,000	14,298,000	13,192,000	
1983	1,415	8,672	12,271,000	9,306	13,168,000	9,644	13,646,000	10,278	14,543,000	15,511,000	14,169,000	12,896,000	
1984	1,389	8,672	12,045,000	9,398	13,054,000	9,798	13,609,000	10,524	14,618,000	15,561,000	14,029,000	12,588,000	
1985	1,369	8,672	11,872,000	9,492	12,995,000	9,956	13,630,000	10,776	14,752,000	15,604,000	13,879,000	12,266,000	
1986	1,352	8,672	11,725,000	9,589	12,964,000	10,118	13,680,000	11,035	14,919,000	15,638,000	13,715,000	11,933,000	
1987	1,341	8,672	11,629,000	9,689	12,993,000	10,285	13,792,000	11,302	15,156,000	15,666,000	13,539,000	11,587,000	
1988	1,331	8,672	11,542,000	9,791	13,032,000	10,456	13,917,000	11,575	15,406,000	15,685,000	13,352,000	11,229,000	
1989	1,323	8,672	11,473,000	9,895	13,091,000	10,632	14,066,000	11,855	15,684,000	15,695,000	13,152,000	10,860,000	
1990	1,321	8,672	11,456,000	10,003	13,214,000	10,813	14,284,000	12,144	16,042,000	15,697,000	12,939,000	10,480,000	
1991	1,319	8,672	11,438,000	10,114	13,340,000	10,998	14,506,000	12,440	16,408,000	15,689,000	12,714,000	10,088,000	
1992	1,318	8,672	11,430,000	10,228	13,481,000	11,188	14,746,000	12,744	16,797,000	15,672,000	12,477,000	9,687,000	
1993	1,319	8,672	11,438,000	10,335	13,632,000	11,384	15,015,000	13,057	17,222,000	15,644,000	12,227,000	9,277,000	
1994	1,318	8,672	11,430,000	10,464	13,792,000	11,585	15,269,000	13,377	17,631,000	15,607,000	11,964,000	8,859,000	
1995	1,317	8,672	11,421,000	10,587	13,943,000	11,791	15,529,000	13,706	18,051,000	15,559,000	11,689,000	8,433,000	
1996	1,316	8,672	11,412,000	10,714	14,100,000	12,003	15,796,000	14,045	18,483,000	15,500,000	11,402,000	8,000,000	
1997	1,315	8,672	11,404,000	10,843	14,259,000	12,220	16,069,000	14,391	18,924,000	15,430,000	11,103,000	7,562,000	
1998	1,315	8,672	11,404,000	10,976	14,433,000	12,444	16,364,000	14,748	19,394,000	15,350,000	10,792,000	7,119,000	
1999	1,314	8,672	11,395,000	11,113	14,602,000	12,673	16,652,000	15,114	19,860,000	15,256,000	10,469,000	6,674,000	
2000	1,314	8,672	11,395,000	11,253	14,786,000	12,909	16,962,000	15,490	20,354,000	15,152,000	10,136,000	6,227,000	
2001	1,313	8,672	11,386,000	11,399	14,967,000	13,152	17,269,000	15,879	20,849,000	15,034,000	9,792,000	5,779,000	

× This forecast is an average of forecasts I and II which are shown in 5 and 6 columns of Table 56.
+ Expenditure of the ministry in 1975 assumed to equal income.

shown in columns 2, 4, 6 and 8, and the average of forecasts I and II of the number of charges. The corresponding figures of total expenditure are shown in columns 3, 5, 7 and 9, and are plotted in figure 19. Each of the forecasts of real total expenditure results from the interplay of two different factors; the first is the gradual rise in the real expenditure of the average charge (with the exception of forecast A) which serves to increase real total expenditure. In the early part of the period 1975-2001, when the number of charges is falling faster than real costs are increasing, real total expenditure falls in all four forecasts. Subsequently, as the rate of decline in the number of charges diminishes, the rise in real costs becomes the dominant factor, and all but forecast A show rising real total expenditure.

Apart from forecast A, which is based on a constant real expenditure of the average charge so that real total expenditure reaches a plateau level of about £11.46 millions in 1990, all the forecasts plotted in figure 19 are convex to the horizontal axis, and therefore reach a minimum point. These minimum points are £12.96 millions in 1986 for forecast B; £13.61 millions in 1984 for forecast C; and £14.45 millions in 1980 for forecast D. By 2001 these forecasts rise to £14.97 millions, £17.27 millions, and £20.85 millions respectively, giving increases over their respective minimum points of 15.5, 26.9 and 44.3 per cent.

FIGURE 19: Forecasts of the income and expenditure of the Ministry in real terms (at 1975 prices), 1975-2001.

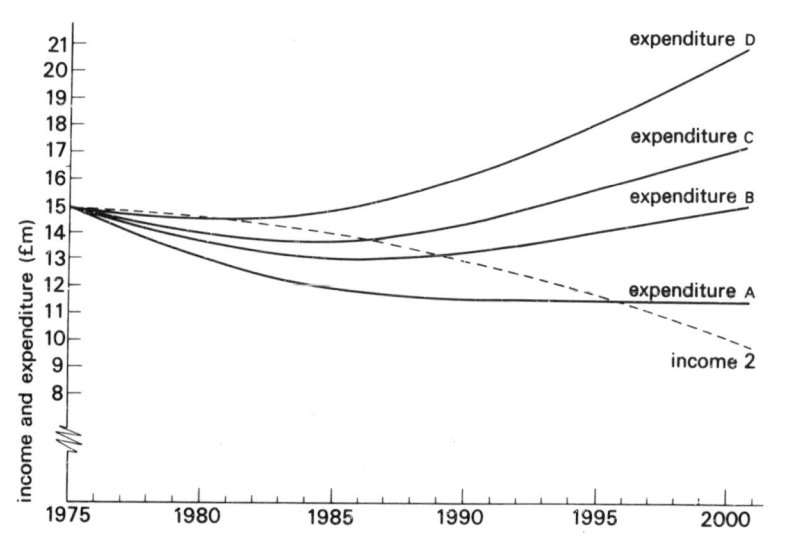

Probably the best of these forecasts is that which incorporates increases both in real stipend and labour costs (forecast D). Under this forecast the real total expenditure of the ministry falls by 2.8 per cent from £14.86 millions in 1975 to £14.45 millions in 1981, and then rises by 44.3 per cent to reach £20.85 millions in 2001.

The three forecasts of the real total income of the ministry are given in columns 10, 11 and 12 of table 64. These are derived from the forecasts of real total Church income made in chapter 5, and have been calculated in the manner described in chapter 6.[5] The best forecast (2) is plotted in figure 19.

The projections of the real total expenditure and income (at 1975 prices) of the ministry for the years 1975-2001 enable us to show the likely changes in the financial position over the period. Where the income line in figure 19 lies above the expenditure line, the vertical distance between the two measures the size of the resulting surplus; where the income line lies below the expenditure line, the gap measures the deficit. The figure indicates that, whichever of the four expenditure forecasts is used, the short-term prospect is one of financial surplus in the ministry. The surplus persists only as far as 1981 with expenditure forecast D, which incorporates increases in real stipend and labour costs. On this forecast, the ministry would move into a deficit position after 1981 which would become very large by 2001. With forecast C, which includes increases in real labour costs only, the break-even point would be reached in 1986, after which the ministry would move into a growing deficit position. Alternatively, on the basis of forecast B, which is based on increasing real stipend costs only, the ministry would pass from a surplus to a deficit financial position in 1989. Finally, using forecast A, under which the real expenditure of the average charge is assumed to remain constant over the period, the ministry does not move into a deficit position until after 1996.

These projections suggest that the financial position of the ministry appears to be not unfavourable in the short-term, but that the position in the long-run, although hazardous to forecast, could be very difficult if present trends persist. The forecasts of the financial position of the ministry for 1981 and 2001 are given in tables 65 and 66. The three income forecasts and four expenditure forecasts

TABLE 65.
Projections of the financial position of the ministry in real terms (at 1975 prices) in 1981*

	Income forecasts[+]	Expenditure forecasts[×]			
		A £12,782,000	B £13,456,000	C £13,779,000	D £14,453,000
		£	£	£	£
1.	£15,392,000	+2,610,000	+1,936,000	+1,613,000	+939,000
2.	£14,415,000	+1,633,000	+ 959,000	+ 636,000	− 38,000
3.	£13,474,000	+ 692,000	+ 18,00	− 305,000	− 979,000

TABLE 66.
Projections of the financial position of the ministry in real terms (at 1975 prices) 2001*

	Income forecasts[+]	Expenditure forecasts[×]			
		A £11,386,000	B £14,967,000	C £17,269,000	D £20,849,000
		£	£	£	£
1.	£15,034,000	+3,648,000	+67,000	− 2,235,000	− 5,815,000
2.	£ 9,792,000	−1,594,000	−5,175,000	− 7,477,000	−11,057,000
3.	£ 5,779,000	−5,607,000	−9,188,000	−11,490,000	−15,070,000

*NOTE: '+' denotes a financial surplus, and '−' a financial deficit.
[×] SOURCE: Table 64.
[+] SOURCE: Table 19.

give rise to twelve alternative forecasts of the financial position in each year. In 1981 the forecasts range from a deficit of £979,000 to a surplus of £2,610,000, with only three of the forecasts showing a deficit position. Perhaps the most likely outcome is forecast 2D, which gives rise to a break-even position in 1981. By 2001 the range of the projections of the financial position of the ministry has widened considerably, with all but two of the forecasts showing a deficit position. The forecasts range from a surplus of £3,648,000 to a deficit of £15,070,000, with forecast 2D giving a deficit of £11,057,000.

One way in which the Church might react to the prospective long-term financial difficulties, as it has in the past, is to limit money increases in the minimum stipend to a level which only maintains its real value. The appropriate projections of the financial position of the ministry given in table 65 and 66 would be 2C, which allow for increases in real labour costs only. This shows an enlarged surplus of £636,000 in 1981 and a reduced, but still very large, deficit of £7,477,000 in 2001. However, although this alternative forecast is an improvement on the first forecast quoted, the position of the long-run finances of the ministry remains a serious one. Moreover, the improvement is achieved at the expense of a serious decline in the relative income position of ministers.

While we have chosen forecast 2D as the most likely outcome, there is no entirely scientific basis on which to choose between the forecasts, and much depends upon the efforts of the Church on its own behalf. The forecasts are based on recent trends and on likely future trends, and do not incorporate the impact of improvements brought about by the Church, or by a possible change in the trends for the better at some future date. If the Church makes great efforts to staunch the loss of members, to raise income, and to carry on with a vigorous policy of union and readjustment, the actual outcome may be better than that indicated by forecast 2D. On the other hand, if the financial situation suffers a setback, with membership and income declining at a steeper rate and real labour costs increasing more rapidly than anticipated, then the actual outcome may be worse than that in forecast 2D; this might not be serious in the short-run, but could result in the ministry moving into a large deficit position in the years after 1981.

2 Mission and service work
The financial position of the mission and service work can also be forecast for the last quarter of the twentieth century. If it can be assumed that in general all income contributed for mission and service work is spent, then in 1975 the total expenditure would have equalled the estimated income of £2,780,000.[6] Assuming further that labour costs comprise 80 per cent of total expenditure, and that these costs increase in line with real personal income *per capita*, then the real expenditure on mission and service (at 1975 prices), on the basis of the present level of activity, should rise to £3,098,000 by 1981, and to £4,888,000 in 2001. The real expenditure figures for every year over the period 1975–2001 are shown in column 1 of table 67. Also given in table 67 are three alternative forecasts of the real income of mission and service, with are derived from the forecasts of real total Church income as described in chapter 6.

The expenditure and income forecasts for mission and service are plotted in figure 20. The expenditure line slopes upwards to the right under the influence of

TABLE 67.
Forecasts of the income and expenditure of mission and service in real terms (at 1975 prices), 1975-2001.

	Expenditure	Income		
		Forecast 1 2	Forecast 2 3	Forecast 3 4
	£	£	£	£
1975[x]	2,780,000	2,780,000	2,780,000	2,780,000
1976	2,781,000	2,814,000	2,785,000	2,757,000
1977	2,841,000	2,830,000	2,773,000	2,716,000
1978	2,903,000	2,846,000	2,759,000	2,673,000
1979	2,966,000	2,861,000	2,743,000	2,627,000
1980	3,032,000	2,875,000	2,725,000	2,579,000
1981	3,098,000	2,888,000	2,705,000	2,528,000
1982	3,167,000	2,900,000	2,683,000	2,475,000
1983	3,238,000	2,911,000	2,659,000	2,420,000
1984	3,310,000	2,920,000	2,633,000	2,362,000
1985	3,384,000	2,928,000	2,604,000	2,302,000
1986	3,461,000	2,935,000	2,574,000	2,239,000
1987	3,539,000	2,940,000	2,541,000	2,174,000
1988	3,620,000	2,943,000	2,505,000	2,107,000
1989	3,702,000	2,945,000	2,468,000	2,038,000
1990	3,787,000	2,945,000	2,428,000	1,966,000
1991	3,875,000	2,944,000	2,386,000	1,893,000
1992	3,964,000	2,941,000	2,341,000	1,818,000
1993	4,056,000	2,936,000	2,294,000	1,741,000
1994	4,151,000	2,929,000	2,245,000	1,662,000
1995	4,248,000	2,920,000	2,194,000	1,582,000
1996	4,347,000	2,909,000	2,139,000	1,501,000
1997	4,450,000	2,896,000	2,083,000	1,419,000
1998	4,555,000	2,880,000	2,025,000	1,336,000
1999	4,663,000	2,863,000	1,965,000	1,252,000
2000	4,774,000	2,843,000	1,902,000	1,168,000
2001	4,888,000	2,821,000	1,837,000	1,085,000

[x] Expenditure of Mission and Service in 1975 is assumed to equal income.

FIGURE 20: Forecasts of the expenditure of mission and service in real terms (at 1975 prices), 1975-2001.

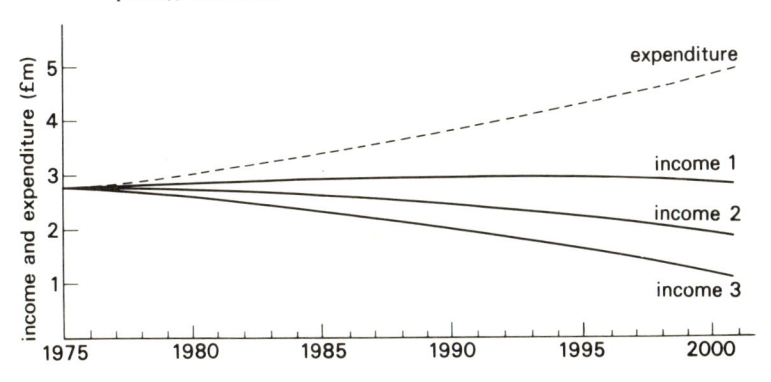

increasing real labour costs. Income forecast 1 shows a slight increase in real income during the early years of the period 1975-2001, but income forecasts 2 and 3 produce a substantial real decline. Consequently, although mission and service is assumed to be in financial balance in 1975, it quickly moves into a substantial and growing deficit position in the following years, no matter which income forecast is used.

The financial position of mission and service in 1981 and 2001 is examined in detail in tables 68 and 69 respectively, which give the various income and expenditure forecasts and the deficits which arise. In 1981 the forecasts produce deficits ranging from £210,000 to £570,000, with the most likely outcome being a deficit of £393,000. By 2001 the position has deteriorated seriously, with forecast deficits ranging from £2,067,000 to £3,803,000. The best forecast produces a deficit of £3,051,000, which is equivalent to 166.1 per cent of income.

TABLE 68.
Projections of the financial position of mission and service in 1981*

Forecasts of the income of mission and service in 1981[x]	Forecasts of financial position (assuming expenditure is £3,098,000)
£	£
1. 2,888,000	−210,000
2. 2,705,000	−393,000
3. 2,528,000	−570,000

TABLE 69.
Projections of the financial position of mission and service in 2001*

Forecasts of the income of mission and service in 2001[x]	Forecasts of financial position (assuming expenditure is £4,888,000)
£	£
1. 2,821,000	−2,067,000
2. 1,837,000	−3,051,000
3. 1,085,000	−3,803,000

*Note: '+' indicates a financial surplus, '−' a financial deficit.
The figures are expressed in real terms at 1975 prices.
[x] SOURCE: Table 67.

The reason for the poorer financial prospect of mission and service compared to that of the ministry lies, not in its income, but rather in its expenditure. In forecast 2 the real income of both the ministry and mission and service is forecast to fall by about 3 per cent between 1975 and 1981, and then to fall by about a further 32 per cent between 1981 and 2001. But while the ministry can offset the rise in its real labour costs by reducing the number of charges to be supported and still maintain its overall effectiveness, mission and service can only cut its costs by cutting back on the range of activities in which it is engaged. Mission and service thus faces increasing real costs of labour on the whole of its present activities, and in the future these extra costs are likely to outweigh any improvement in real income. This forecast implies that a severe curtailment in mission and service work will be necessary in the long-term in order to protect the real average stipend, unless the Church is successful in raising its income much faster than the current trends suggest is likely.

4 Conclusions

The purpose of this chapter has been to forecast the financial position of the Church for 1981 and 2001 using the forecasts that were developed in previous chapters for certain key Church variables viz. the membership, real total income, ministerial manpower, the number of charges, and the number of lay workers. The financial positions of the ministry (including the average charge) and of mission and service were dealt with separately.

A range of forecasts was produced because of the difficulties of forecasting membership and income, but the 'best guess' forecast is as follows:

(i) Membership might decline from 1,041,772 in 1975 to 933,075 in 1981 and 570,751 in 2001, giving falls over the 1975 figure of 10.4 and 45.2 per cent respectively.

(ii) Income in real terms at 1975 prices should fall by 3.0 per cent from £17,644,424 in 1975 to £17,120,000 in 1981, and then decline by 32.1 per cent between 1981 and 2001 to reach £11,629,000.

(iii) The number of ministers is expected to fall steeply over the next decade as the bulge of men in their early sixties reach retirement. The rate of decline should then slacken, so that a stable population is achieved by about 1990. Numbers should fall from 1,631 in 1974 to about 1,353 in 1981, and to about 1,211 by 2001. The overall fall by 2001 is about 25.8 per cent of the 1974 figure.

(iv) The number of charges should follow a similar trend to that of ministers if an active policy of unions and readjustments is pursued. Numbers are expected to fall from 1,714 in 1975 to about 1,474 in 1981, and to about 1,313 by 2001. The overall decline for the period 1975-2001 is about 23.4 per cent.

(v) On the present trends, the number of elders should rise steadily from 50,963 in 1973 to 65,876 by 2001, an increase of 29.3 per cent.

(vi) The number of members per charge is expected to rise from 608 in 1975 to about 635 in 1981, depending upon the relative rates of decline of membership and charges, and then to fall to about 435 by 2001.

(vii) The real income per charge should rise by 13.0 per cent from £8,672 in 1975 to about £9,798 in 1981, and then fall by 23.8 per cent to reach about £7,465 by 2001.

(viii) The real liberality per member at 1975 prices should rise from £12.46 in 1975 to about £13.05 in 1981 and £14.49 in 2001, these representing increases of 4.7 and 16.3 per cent respectively over the 1975 figure.

(ix) Assuming that the estimated income of the average charge in 1975 equals its expenditure, and that the average stipend and other wage costs rise in line with the forecast rise in real personal income *per capita* in the United Kingdom, then the expenditure of the average charge should increase from £8,672 in 1975 to £9,805 in 1981 and to £15,879 in 2001. These forecasts represent increases of 13.1 and 83.1 per cent respectively over the 1975 figure.

(x) Given the forecast of the number of charges and the real expenditure of the average charge over the period 1976-2001, it is possible to calculate the total expenditure of the ministry for those years. According to the best forecast, total expenditure should fall from £14,864,000 in 1975 to about £14,453,000 in 1981, and then rise sharply to about £20,849,000 by 2001. These forecasts are the outcome of two conflicting forces: the increasing real costs of labour, and the decline in the number of charges which serves to reduce costs.

(xi) On the basis of these projections of real income and expenditure, the ministry is likely to have a small surplus over the next few years before reaching a break-even point in 1981. In later years, however, the position is reversed, with the ministry moving into a large deficit (expressed in real terms at 1975 prices) of several millions by 2001.

(xii) Forecasts of the real income and expenditure of the committees within the Mission and Service Fund suggest that in maintaining the present level of activities, the fund should move into a growing deficit position. By 1981 the deficit may reach £393,000, and by 2001 it may be over £3 millions, which is considerably in excess of income in that year. The main cause of this financial setback is the prospective near doubling of real labour costs by the end of the century compared to a fall in real income.

It should be emphasised that all forecasts are subject to error, and that the long-term forecasts for 2001 can at best be only very tentative. Much will depend upon the efforts of the Church to improve its financial position. If great efforts are made to that end, then the forecasts may be bettered; this would be particularly likely if the present rate of decline of the membership could be reduced, or if economies could be made in the use of labour. On the other hand, if fund-raising and the policy of union and readjustment are not pursued vigorously, then the actual outcome may fall below the forecast.

What seems to emerge clearly from our forecasting work is that over the next few years the Church should have a respite in which to put its financial affairs in order. If this opportunity is not grasped, then the long-term future appears bleak.

Notes

1 See chapter 13, pp. 309-10.
2 See chapter 11, pp. 250-3.
3 See chapter 5, p. 108.
4 This theme has been developed in relation to the performing arts by W.J. Baumol and W.G. Bowen, 'On the performing arts: the anatomy of their economic problems', *American Economic Review (Papers and Proceedings)*, (1965), vol. 55, no 2, pp. 495-502.
5 See above, pp. 147-9.
6 SOURCE: Table 37, p. 148.

PART III

The Ministry

Chapter 10

Funding the Ministry

1 Introduction
The purpose of this chapter is to describe the sources of stipend in the Church of Scotland and the administration of the stipend funds by the Committee on the Maintenance of the Ministry. By setting out the present arrangements for stipend, the chapter should provide a background against which proposals for stipend can be made. These proposals are presented in the following chapter. The present account is based on certain sources, especially Cox and Gibson,[1] and on information supplied by the Church and Ministry Department.

In section 2 a brief outline is given of the historical development of stipend in the Church of Scotland. Then in section 3 the Maintenance of the Ministry Committee is introduced and its role briefly outlined. This is followed in section 4 by a detailed description of the funds for stipend, dealing first with the endowment funds and then with the annual funds. The sub-section *1* on the endowment funds deals with the standardized stipend (*1.A*) and other endowments for stipend (*1.B*), and then describes the operation of the central endowment funds through which the endowment monies pass (*1.C*). The second sub-section deals with the annual funds, derived from the contributions of congregations towards stipend, which form the bulk of the total stipend payments. These monies pass through two central funds — the General Fund (*2.A*) and the Minimum Stipend Fund (*2.B*). We also describe the small Supplementary Fund (*2.C*). In this sub-section we consider the factors which help determine the level at which the committee sets the minimum stipend each year. Finally, in section 5 the regional and local organization and procedure for maintenance of the ministry business is described (*1*), along with the non-stipend expenses of the fund (*2*) and the listed expenses (*3*).

2 Stipend: a brief historical background
Ministers in the Church of Scotland receive a stipend. The term 'stipend' means either the total income of a minister in a year, which is the stipend of the minister's parish or charge, or any of the various payments from any source which make up ministerial income.[2] The meaning of stipend has widened over the centuries, in that the various elements of stipend have increased in number. At first stipend meant only teind stipend, the teinds being the tithe or tenth part of the annual produce of the parish; these were the 'spiritualities' of the parish. Before the Reformation, stipend came also to include the 'temporalities', such as glebe or glebe rent, glebe monies, and any other official income of the minister from kirklands and local bequests, if any. At the Reformation the amount of

stipend was much reduced. Ministers received only one-third of what the parish priest had received as spirituality; this was meant only as a temporary measure while the life interests of priests existed, but the situation was never redressed. At the same time, practically the whole of the temporalities, except some glebes, were alienated from the Church.

The meaning of the term stipend changed little until the mid-eighteenth century, when it was expanded to include the offerings of the supporters of the ministers of the Secession Church, who had no other source of maintainance for themselves. This source of stipend was to increase very greatly so that it now forms the bulk of stipend payments in the Church. Later new sources of stipend arose, including burgh church stipends, exchequer grants and the statutory endowments of parliamentary and *quoad sacra* parishes. These were followed by further endowments and by the many new glebe monies arising from feus, minerals, etc.

From its very beginning in 1843, the Free Church had to supplement the stipend paid by many local congregations with a grant from a central fund, and this also happened later in the United Presbyterian Church and the Established Church. These grants were made to ensure that all ministers received at least a certain minimum level of stipend. The grants were in all cases not regarded as part of the stipend of the parish or charge, but as an addition to it. The term 'minimum stipend', although used widely, is therefore a misnomer, since it often includes payment from a central fund that is not properly stipend at all.

Recently there has been another change. Stipend used to differ from salary in that it was subject to the deduction of the necessary expenses incurred by the minister in the course of his duties, and only the remainder could be used for the maintenance of himself and his dependants. Salaries are not normally liable to such deductions. There were three exceptions: the provision of a manse, a glebe, and a communion elements allowance. The modern development of such exceptions are the 'Listed Expenses', which are six kinds of ministerial expense which must be paid by every congregation to, or on behalf of, the minister; these expenses are not regarded as stipend. As the Listed Expenses cover the majority of the necessary expenses of a minister, the old distinction between stipend and salary has more or less disappeared. They are described in section 5 below.

Stipend vests in a minister on a *de die in diem* basis. It is subject to deductions of income tax, Widows' and Orphans' Fund dues, Pension Fund contributions and Furnishing Loan refunds. Under the 1961 Finance Act, an important provision effecting the Church concerns the heating, lighting and cleaning of the manse and the maintenance of the manse garden. If the Church or the congregation meets this expenditure, or if it reimburses the minister in respect of such expenditure, the amount so paid does not form part of the minister's taxable income. For example, if a minister's stipend is £2,500, and the above expenses amount to £350, then the minister would show in his return for income tax purposes a sum of £2,150 as his stipend — i.e. saving the income tax on the £350 (at 35 per cent), or £122.50.

3 The committee on the maintenance of the ministry

In the Church of Scotland Act, 1921, that came into effect in 1926, were laid out the *Articles Declaratory of the Constitution of the Church of Scotland in Matters*

Spiritual. The third of these Articles ends as follows: 'As a national Church representative of the Christian Faith of the Scottish people, it acknowledges its distinctive call and duty to bring the ordinances of religion to the people in every parish of Scotland through a territorial ministry.'

Provision for the ministry was set out in the *Basis and Plan of Union,* 1929, under which the General Assembly established a standing committee, called the 'Committee on the Maintenance of the Ministry', 'responsible for ingathering from the General Trustees and all other available sources, and for their distribution, all funds destined for stipend.' The committee is composed of 72 members, of whom 48 are Presbytery representatives and 24 are appointed by the Nominations Committee of Assembly. The committee administers a fund, called the Maintenance of the Ministry Fund, the purpose of which is 'to secure the maintenance of religious ordinances throughout the land, so that the strong may be enabled to help the weak in a systematic as well as a brotherly manner.' All stipend payments are now made through the fund, and it is through the fund that the minimum stipend is maintained in all congregations. The minimum stipend is declared each autumn for the following year, and is the level of income below which no minister's income is allowed to fall. The minimum stipend for 1976 is £2,460.

Every congregation, in the management of its finance, is required to aim primarily at providing the minimum stipend for its minister, inclusive of any sum payable to the minister from endowments and other stipend sources. Every congregation that achieves this is self-supporting; the others are aid-receiving. A self-supporting congregation which gives aid to the fund is 'aid-giving'. Broadly speaking, the committee 'maintains the ministry' by making grants in aid of stipend to aid-receiving congregations, which are unable to raise enough income to meet the minimum stipend, from the contributions to the fund of aid-giving congregations sufficiently affluent to be able to support themselves. In this way the minimum stipend is maintained even in poor congregations. The more affluent congregations usually pay their minister rather more than the minimum, but the great majority of ministers are on or very close to the minimum.

4 The funds for stipend

The funds for stipend which are administered by the Maintenance of the Ministry Committee are made up of two complementary sets of funds: *1,* endowment funds, and *2,* annual funds. We shall examine each in turn.

1 Endowment funds

Endowment funds comprise *A,* standardized stipend, and *B,* other endowments. We discuss each of these in turn, and then in a third sub-section examine the actual funds for endowment appearing in the books of the General Treasurer.

A Standardized stipend

The principal part of the endowments for stipend of the Church of Scotland consists of the standardized stipend, which is the modern form of the teinds of Scotland. The teinds (tithes) originated at about the end of the eleventh century, and were the result of the consecration by landowners of a tenth of the produce of their lands to sustain a Christian ministry for the people on their estates. The custom spread rapidly, and soon covered practically the whole country. In 1567 an Act of Council described the tenths or teinds as the 'proper patrimonie' of the Church. They continued thereafter with little change for nearly 300 years as the main source of income of the ministry.

In 1617 an Act of Parliament reformed the law of teinds to the effect that they were no longer paid into a common pool, but were kept by each parish for its own uses. This Act established in Scotland the principle *decimae debentur parocho* (i.e. the teinds are owed to the parish), which is still a guiding principle in the administration of these endowments. From 1617 each minister of a *quoad omnia* parish collected himself, or through an agent, the stipend due to him from the heritors of the parish, who were the persons responsible for the payments. He also collected the rent of the glebe, if let, and any other fruits of the benefice.

In 1808 an Act decreed that all victual stipends payable hitherto in kind were thenceforward to be paid in money at fiars prices. The fiars prices depended upon the prices fetched by grain and oatmeal of the recent harvest, and were fixed annually for each county by local Fiars Courts. These courts met annually about the end of the winter or beginning of spring, and the prices fixed by them ruled the amount of stipend paid in respect of the previous 'crop and year'. Stipend thus rose or fell with the prices of grain and the cultivation or rental of the glebe, so that the minister shared in the prosperity or adversity of his parishioners.

The next important change occurred with the passing of the Church of Scotland (Property and Endowments) Act, 1925. The purpose of the Act was 'to amend the law relating to Teinds and to the Stipends of Ministers of the Church of Scotland and the tenure of the Property and Endowments of that Church, and for purposes connected therewith.' Under this Act, all standardized stipend became a 'standard charge' on land 'preferable to all other securities or burdens, not incidents of tenure.' The standard charge was calculated on an average of the fiars prices for each county for the fifty year period 1873-1922 inclusive. Standardization took place automatically on a vacancy occurring in a parish. A minister could also elect at any time during his incumbancy that his stipend be standardized (i.e. standardization by election). It was also possible for the General Trustees to require that a teind stipend be standardized (i.e. standardization by notification). The last teind was standardized in 1974.

From standardization the stipend was payable by the heritors, no longer to the minister of the parish, but to the General Trustees of the Church. After a deduction of a flat-rate commission to meet the expenses of administration, the standardized stipend is made over to the Maintenance of the Ministry Committee for payment to the stipend of ministers entitled.

A trust was established over these moneys in the following declaration of the 1925 Act: 'All moneys received by the General Trustees with respect to any parish . . . shall be appropriated in the first place to meeting the proper requirements of that parish or its neighbourhood (as such requirements may be determined by the General Assembly or by any body to which the General Assembly may delegate the necessary power), and any remainder after these requirements have been fully met shall form part of a general fund at the disposal of the General Assembly.' The declaration needs to be examined in some detail. The first point concerns the delegated body. Under a 1931 Act of the General Assembly the responsibility for the standardized stipend was delegated to the Maintenance of the Ministry

Committee. This Act was superseded by an Act of 1953, which renewed the delegation, but laid down the procedure to be followed by any interested parties who disagreed with the decision reached by the delegated body.

Secondly, there is the meaning of the term 'proper requirements'. This is undefined in the Act, and is left to the General Assembly or the delegated body to determine; so far the General Assembly has not found it necessary to compile an official list of what may be regarded as proper requirements. The determination of the monetary value of the proper requirements of a parish or its neighbourhood is made, invariably, for one incumbency only. The value may be increased during an incumbency, but not decreased unless the full amount is no longer being received by the fund. On the occurrence of a vacancy in a parish a change in the determination may be called for. The question then is the proper distribution amongst the necessary congregations within the area of preference of the parochial endowments that have become available.

Thirdly, there is the question of the interpretation of the phrase 'parish or its neighbourhood'. The phrase was subject to various interpretations in the early years of the operation of the Act. In 1933 it was submitted for opinion to two leading counsel of the day, who made the following assessment: 'The area in question may be the civil parish, or the parish *quoad omnia,* or an area approximating to these units, for the significant qualification "or its neighbourhood" absolves the General Assembly from the necessity of the paying exact regard to precise boundaries so long as the area which receives the preference substantially corresponds to the area contributing the funds or endowments to which the preference implies.'

This interpretation was accepted by the General Assembly. Gibson argues that it has the consequence that a contiguous parish is not to be regarded as being automatically within the area of preference, but only if it fulfils certain conditions. These conditions cannot be rigidly defined, but it can safely be said that any *quoad sacra* parish, part of whose area was taken from the *quoad omnia* parish in question, is in the area of preference under this definition. This applies also to any other congregation to which the Presbytery has delimited an area that includes part of the parish in question. In cases where no situation of that kind obtains, an adjacent parish is outwith the area of preference, and if it is self-supporting, has no valid claim on the endowments of its neighbour.

Finally, there is the question of the 'remainders' in section 36 of the 1925 Act. The probable intention of the last clause was to secure possession of these remainders by the Church. The committee's practice has been to allocate any remainder to an aid-receiving congregation outwith the area of preference, thereby relieving the Minimum Stipend Fund.

Since 1931 the Maintenance of the Ministry Committee has been responsible for the standardized stipend. This responsibility is exercised through a stipend sub-committee, which deals with all cases in which the question of the redistribution of standardized stipend is involved. The procedure is as follows. Every vacancy in which stipend endowments are involved (other than private endowments) is reported to the sub-committee, which considers whether the Maintenance of the Ministry Committee should raise with the Presbytery the question of whether some new use of part of the endowments should or should not be made. If it decides not, it can be asked to do so by any other interested party. If the question of union and readjustment is raised, the normal practice is to delay consideration of the question of endowments until the first question is settled.[3]

The question of endowments is not likely to be raised in cases in which there is only one congregation in the area of preference, and which, although enjoying the whole of the parochial endowments, is still aid-receiving. If, however, endowments are more than adequate in view of the general circumstances of the vacant parish, it is the duty of the Presbytery (or its committee) to advise the Maintenance of the Committee regarding the figure at which the proper requirements should be fixed for a new incumbency. The Presbytery meets the office-bearers of the vacant congregation in order to seek their support for the recommendation likely to be made to the Maintenance of the Ministry Committee. Agreement is only final when approved by the Presbytery and confirmed by the Committee. The Presbytery's recommendation is submitted to the stipend sub-committee for approval. One of the principle duties of the sub-committee is to keep Presbyteries roughly in line with each other, so that similar cases are dealt with broadly in the same way by each Presbytery.

It is important to note that a balance does not become available for distribution until after an induction to the vacant charge has taken place. Up to then the stipend is vacant stipend, and it accrues to the central Vacant Stipend Fund (see below).

The policy towards redistribution of endowments is governed broadly by the following points:

(i) First consideration is given to any necessary aid-receiving congregation in the area of preference, and then to those struggling to remain self-supporting. The word 'necessary' is generally used to mean either that there is no likelihood in the forseeable future of the congregation being united with another, or that a life interest makes the congregation necessary so long as that life interest exists. Gibson states that 'No better use can be found for the standardized stipend of a parish than that of making the parish self-supporting.'

(ii) The broad, and most important, distinction is between congregations within the area of preference and those without. An allocation may be made to a congregation within the area no matter what the stipend from other sources is, but can only be made to a congregation outside that area if it reduces aid from the fund. This distinction is rigidly adhered to.

(iii) The Presbytery (or its committee) makes a broad survey of the congregations in the area of preference, particularly any that are aid-receiving, or only self-supporting after a struggle, with a view to estimating the share that might reasonably be distributed amongst them. This is usually done easily and quickly, but there are urban parishes in which six or more other congregations have a valid claim. In such cases the task is simplified by consideration that it is rarely helpful to divide whatever sum is likely to be available, so that only small token sums are allocated to several congregations in recognition of the validity of their claim; it is thought best to select a few congregations, so that the allocated sum will make an appreciable difference. At the same time it has to be borne in mind how much can be taken from the endowments of the formerly benefiting congregation.

The operation of the procedure for the reallocation of endowments for stipend of vacant charges has changed over the period since 1925. Standardization of stipend meant in many cases that the payment derivable from the teinds was reduced, sometimes by a large margin. This reflects the fact that, while standardization took place in the period after 1925, the standard charge is based on the average of the fiars prices for an earlier period (1873-1922). In many such cases it was found that the whole amount of the standardized stipend of a vacant charge was required to meet the proper requirements of the formerly benefiting parish church. Here the committee made no allocations to other charges in the parish, unless these had been certified by the Presbytery as necessary for the adequate provision of religious ordinances in the parish or its neighbourhood.

Some distributions were made in these early years. The allocations varied in amount, but it was not unusual to find that allocations of 10, 15 and 20 per cent of the total standardized stipend was being allocated to charges other than the formerly benefiting parish church. In some cases of higher stipends the allocation was as much as 45 per cent. The pre-Second World War experience is summarized in table 70. This table shows that in the period 1930-9 (but excluding 1934) the total standardized stipend in cases in which the question of reallocation was raised was £42,867, of which £10,503, or 24.5 per cent, was allocated to charges other than the formerly benefiting charge.

TABLE 70
The reallocation of standardized stipend in the period 1930-9.

	Total standardized stipend in cases in which question raised	Allocated to formerly benefiting parish churches	Allocated to other charges	Proportion re-allocated (i.e. 3/1 × 100)
	1	2	3	4
	£	£	£	%
1930-33	12,429	8,661	3,768	30.3
1935-38	17,336	13,514	3,822	22.0
1939	13,102	10,189	2,913	22.2
TOTAL	42,867	32,364	10,503	24.5

In the post-war period it became clear that much higher stipends were required. But at the same time, the general rise in prices was reducing year by year the real value of endowments. In 1925, when the minimum stipend was £300, a charge that had endowments of £450 was regarded as affluent. Today the minimum stipend is £2,460, while the endowments that were £450 in 1925 are still at about that figure. The 'proper requirements' of the parish today are thus very different from those at the time of the Act in 1925. A further consideration is that since 1929, owing to the large number of unions and readjustments, there has been a large increase in the number of parishes in which there is no other congregation than the formerly benefiting parish church in the area of preference.

The consequences of these two factors are as follows. In parishes where, as a result of union, there is only one charge, the proper requirements of the parish church must be set at a higher amount than regarded as 'proper' in earlier years. In most cases the proper requirements are so high in comparison with the amount of standardized stipend usually available, that the committee's procedure is simply to raise no question regarding the use of the endowments for a new incumbency. In all other cases of vacancy involving the use of parochial endowment where there is more than one necessary charge in the parish, the sum available could in only a few cases be regarded as sufficient to meet fully all the proper requirements of the parish church, let alone the requirements of the other charges. So the question of determining the proper requirements of such parishes resolves itself into determining the fairest and best distribution of the sum available amongst all the necessary charges. The proper requirements of the parish are now recognized as including the provision of transport for ministers in rural parishes.

Recent developments with regard to the standardized stipend are summarised in the 1972 Report of the Committee on the Maintenance of the Ministry, as follows: 'A very large number of *quoad sacra* parishes have suffered, or will suffer, a considerable loss of endowment income because of the compulsory redemption of many feu-duties or ground annuals on derelict property. There are also the redemption implications of the recent government legislation to end the Scottish feuing system of land tenure . . . The present situation is so extensive that it will involve many aid-receiving congregations. The committee, in an endeavour to mitigate this situation in some measure, has been setting up by transfer a new Capital Fund presently amounting to £99,998, of which one-half is invested in units of the Church of Scotland Trust and one-half comprised of fixed interest loan stocks in the industrial and commercial sector. The purpose of this fund will be to give a partial replacement of endowment income lost in this way to certain aid-receiving *quoad sacra* parishes.'[4]

In its report of the following year, the committee stated that it had invested a further sum of £49,572 in debenture stock. The Capital Fund then amounted to £149,570, of which one-third was in units of the Church of Scotland Trust and the remainder in fixed-interest loan debenture stocks.

B *Other endowments*

The Church possesses other endowments for stipend besides the standardized stipend. These include burgh church stipends, Exchequer monies for Exchequer grants and the stipends of Parliamentary parishes, statutory stipends or initial endowments, further endowments of various kinds, and basal endowments. Manses, manse grants, glebes, and glebe monies are also forms of parochial endowment for the maintenance of the ministry. We will deal with each in turn.

(*i*) *Burgh church stipends.* Soon after the Reformation, church extension became necessary, especially in the growing cities and towns of Scotland. In all of them the city or burgh was obliged to shoulder the responsibilities discharged by the heritors in the *quoad omnia* parishes. They built and maintained churches, and provided a stipend for the minister as well as salaries for other functionaries. The common practice was to charge seat rents, which were paid to the corporation or council to offset the costs. Stipend was generally paid from the fund for the common good, but in some cases certain taxes were levied. The principal of these in Edinburgh was a tax on every citizen according to the rent of his house.

The situation regarding burgh church stipends was changed under the 1925 Act. The Act set up a new body called the Ecclesiastical Commissioners for Scotland, one of whose duties was to consider each burgh church in turn, and to issue for each an appropriate order and scheme which required the city or burgh to redeem the stipend and pay the redemption money to the General Trustees. These monies are still called burgh church stipends. In 1925 there were 45 burgh churches still in existence, of which 14 were in Edinburgh, 8 in Glasgow, 6 in Aberdeen, 4 in Dundee, 3 each in Paisley and Perth, 2 each in Greenock and Stirling, and 1 each in Queensferry, Dumfries amd Kilmarnock.

(*ii*) *Exchequer monies.* Under the Teinds Act, 1810, a sum of £10,000 per annum, increased by the Teinds Act, 1824, to £12,000 per annum, was payable out of the Consolidated Fund of the United Kingdom for the purpose of raising the stipends of parishes of the Church of Scotland to £150 per annum with manse and glebe, or £180 per annum with manse or glebe, or £200 with neither, in all parishes where stipend was below these levels. This was the first minimum stipend fund of the Church. The subsidy was paid by the government to help ministers whose real income had shrunk as the result of the inflation of the Napoleonic War years. Such inflation would not have mattered if all teind stipends had continued to be paid in kind or in accordance with fiars prices. But a provision had been included in an Act on the teinds whereby a heritor could substitute a fixed money payment in place of the sum which varied from year to year. Many heritors had taken advantage of this provision.

Also, under an Act of 1824 the government set aside a sum of £5,040 per annum for the payment of stipends of £120 per annum in the 42 parliamentary parishes. These had been established in the remote, rural areas of Scotland with the aid of government funds.

Both of these sums – £12,000 per annum for Exchequer grants, and £5,040 per annum for Exchequer livings – were redeemed by Parliament under the Scottish Ecclesiastical Commissioners Order and Scheme no. 1, 1926. On redemption the money was transferred to the General Trustees, since when they have been administered by the Church. On a vacancy occurring in one of the parishes endowed with an Exchequer grant (but not an Exchequer living), such monies are subject to reallocation in the same way as the standardized stipend described above. Reallocations are made infrequently, however, since most Exchequer grants are held by congregations in the more remote areas which are aid-receiving.

(*iii*) *Statutory stipends.* The statutory stipends of *quoad sacra* parishes are regarded as the equivalent of the endowment stipends of Parliamentary parishes. From 1844 until the 1925 Act, virtually all new parishes in Scotland were erected under the provisions of the New Parishes Act, 1844, after application to the Teind Court. Over 500 *quoad sacra* parishes were erected in this way. It was necessary to satisfy the Teind Court that a stipend of at least £120 per annum was provided in perpetuity by an endowment, although at first it might be only £100 per annum if a manse was also provided. The normal arrangement was that the congregation raised half the endowment, and the Endowment Committee of the Church raised the other half. From 1873 most congregations received substantial help from the Baird Trust, which was established in that year. Such endowments are known as 'statutory endowments'.

The Teind Court was reluctant to accept as security for stipend anything other than Consols or feu-duties, and, as the former were considerably more expensive, the Church was restricted in practice to investing the capital raised for endowment of stipend in feu-duties. According to Gibson, the court in some cases accepted feu-duties submitted by local office-bearers that were not well secured, and since the Second World War the Church has suffered considerable loss through such feu-duties losing almost all their value.

After the 1925 Act it was no longer necessary for a church extension charge to apply to the Teind Court for erection into a *quoad sacra* parish. It therefore became possible to simplify the procedure and ease the heavy financial burdens on the new congregation. Since 1930 the arrangement has been that, instead of a statutory endowment, a new congregation, on fulfilling certain conditions, receives an initial or original endowment. One important condition is that the congregation is able to make an annual contribution to stipend of not less than the minimum stipend less £150. An initial endowment of £150 per annum is then made, of which £100 is provided by the Maintenance of the Ministry Committee and £50 by the Baird Trust.

(iv) *Further endowment.* Further endowment is another form of endowment of stipend. It is open to every congregation that fulfils two conditions. The first condition is that the congregation is recognized both by the Presbytery and the Maintenance of the Ministry Committee to be a 'necessary' congregation.[5] The second is that the stipend from all sources does not exceed the limits set out in the regulations. From 1 January 1975 these were that the average level of the stipend in the three years preceding the application is less than £2,100 (excluding aid received),[6] and that the stipend from endowment is less than £900.

A congregation qualifies for further endowment by raising new capital for the purpose. The local capital attracts a grant on a sliding scale, and the total endowment is held by the Church of Scotland Investment Trust for the Maintenance of the Ministry Committee on behalf of the charge. The grant is made in relation to the maximum qualifying level of endowments of £900. Where endowments are less than £700, the grant is paid at the rate of two units in the trust for each unit purchased by the congregation; where endowments lie between £701 and £900, the grant is made unit for unit. When funds are available, the committee will make a grant towards endowment for travelling expenses at the rate of three units for every two units purchased by a congregation.

Over the period 1969-75 the committee made grants for further endowment amounting to 22,743 units to 183 congregations. About two-thirds of the units were granted for stipend, and almost all of the remainder for travelling expenses.

In January 1972 the committee considered the earning power and structure of the Capital Fund, the income from which is used for further capitalization prior to the allocation of capital for endowment grants. Although the committee recognized that the current demand for grants could be funded by the current level of income from the F.G. Salvesen Trust, it was felt that the Capital Fund itself should produce greater income, and that in future, investment should be made in fixed interest government stocks. During 1972 the committee invested £24,000 in 8 per cent Treasury stock 2002 – 6 and £20,963.83 in 6¾ per cent Treasury stock 1995-8. In 1973 a further £20,000 was invested in 8 per cent Treasury loan 2002-6.

(v) *Basal endowment.* A third form of direct endowment of congregations is through basal endowment, which is restricted to necessary congregations in full status which have little or no endowment for stipend. To be eligible, congregations must have a stipend of less than the minimum plus £100.

When the funds available for endowment grants appear to be more than sufficient to meet the likely call for initial and further endowment and manse grants, the committee may choose a charge that seems to be eligible for this particular form of endowment. With the concurrence of the Presbytery concerned, a grant, usually of £150 per annum, is then made in units of the Church of Scotland Trust. In recent years it has been the policy of the committee to make such grants to four congregations every year.

No regulations have been framed to cover basal endowments, because the initiative must lie with the committee.

(*vi*) *Manse and manse grants.* The possession of a manse for the minister is a form of parochial endowment. In 1973 the Church was in possession of 1,865 manses; with an average value of at least £15,000, these are worth in excess of £30 millions.

A congregation which is aid-receiving or just self-supporting, where the stipend does not exceed the minimum, and that has no manse, may apply to the committee for a grant to help it either build or buy a house as a manse. The grant is £1,000. In 1974 it was estimated that only 19 congregations in the Church had no manse. Most grants are now made to the National Church Extension Committee, and thereby serve to reduce that committee's expenditure on manses.

(*vii*) *Glebe* The glebes are a survival of the social life of Scotland in the seventeenth century when the parish minister had to be a small farmer as well as a country gentleman. In those days the glebe was cultivated to supply the manse with food, and used as grazing for the pony which the minister used to convey him about the parish. Nowadays, the glebe is often leased by a local farmer (under an Act of 1866), and the rent forms part of the stipend. When the minister does not let the glebe, he is regarded as having received the assessed rent. In either case the minister is responsible for the upkeep of fences, drainage, etc.

Today, more than 600 parishes have glebes, and many of those have more than one glebe. Most glebes are less than twenty acres, but some in the Highlands are as large as 500 acres of poor land. The average size is estimated at 20 – 30 acres.

In many cases there are also glebe monies derived from minerals, feu-duties, etc. It does not necessarily follow that the minister who receives the income from the agricultural glebe also receives the income from the glebe monies.

All the endowments for stipend described above – the standardized stipend, burgh church stipends, Exchequer monies statutory, stipends, further endowment and basal endowment – are held either by the Church of Scotland Trust or the Church of Scotland General Trustees. The income from the endowments is paid by these bodies into the Endowment General Fund (see below), and thence by the committee to the ministers entitled.

Of all the endowments described above, only the standardized stipend and Exchequer grants are subject to reallocation on a vacancy occurring in a congregation. During the vacancy, all the endowments for stipend are treated like the standardized stipend as vacant stipend, and are paid into the Vacant Stipend Fund (see below).

C The endowment funds

The actual funds for endowment appearing in the books of the General Treasurer are: (i) the Endowment General Fund, (ii) the Uninvested Fund available for endowment grants, (iii) the Endowment Vacant Stipend Fund, and (iv) the Capital Fund. In addition, there is the F.G. Salvesen Trust: General Fund and

Invested Fund. We deal with each in turn.

(*i*) *Endowment General Fund.* This is the account into which is paid the annual income from all the endowments enumerated above, and from which that income is paid out to the ministers entitled. The income derives partly from the General Trustees and partly from the Church of Scotland Investment Trust. The bulk of the income is made up of the standardized stipend, but a substantial portion also accrues in the form of interest on capital. In 1975 the income to the Fund totalled over £650,000; details of the fund as at 31 December 1975 are given in table A of the appendix.

(*ii*) *Univested Fund.* The Uninvested Fund receives all congregational contributions for endowment, together with donations and grants for this purpose. It also receives all legacies destined by the testator for endowment, together with a share (currently £2,500) as a first charge on all legacies to the fund not specially destined by the testators. The income to the fund in 1975 was £67,410.

Manse grants are paid in cash from this fund. The rest of the free income is transferred as required to the General Investment Fund of the Church of Scotland Investment Trust. All other endowments are effected by appropriating the amount of capital needed from the sum at the credit of the committee in that Investment Fund.

The position of the fund as at 31 December 1975 is shown in table B of the appendix.

(*iii*) *Endowment Vacant Stipend Fund.* The income of this fund consists almost entirely of the endowment income of vacant charges paid from the Endowment General Fund, although income is received occasionally from other sources. In 1975 this income totalled £30,344. The right to receive Vacant Endowment Stipend was transferred to the Maintenance of the Ministry Committee from the Trustees of the Widows' Fund of the pre-Union Church of Scotland, this arrangement being ratified by the Churches and Universities (Scotland) Widows' and Orphans' Fund Order Confirmation Act, 1930. The right was transferred to the committee on payment of £140,000, made in forty annual instalments of £3,500 over the period 1931–70 inclusive. The committee bought the right in order to meet vacancy expenses, and these, together with widows and next-of-kin grants, make up the bulk of the expenditure from the fund. The balance of the fund is used flexibly by the committee, subject to approval by the General Assembly. In the past it has been used for the provision of car grants (to help ministers buy cars in parishes where the work cannot be done effectively without a car), and in support of the Uninvested Fund for Endowment Grants.

Details of the fund as at 31 December 1975 are given in table C of the appendix.

(*iv*) *Capital Fund.* The Capital Fund shows the book and market values of the funds of the Endowment Section invested in the Church of Scotland Trust by the committee.

At 31 December 1975 the funds invested were as follows:

	Book value	Market value
	£	£
Endowment General Fund	1,612,487	1,458,753
Fund available for endowment grants	84,838	66,717
Special funds	325,486	269,265
	2,022,811	1,794,735

These figures ignore the capital representing the standardized stipend.

(v) *Special funds.* There are seven special funds for endowment, of which the largest by far is the F.G. Salvesen Trust: General Endowment. The income from this trust of £53,733 in 1975 (£49,754 in 1974) was transferred to the Uninvested Fund for endowment grants, where it made up the bulk of the income.

2 Annual Funds

The annual funds for the maintenance of the ministry pass through the General Fund, the Minimum Stipend Fund and the Supplementary Fund. The first two of these funds together make up what is generally (and loosely) known as the Maintenance of the Ministry Fund. We shall deal with each in turn.

A General Fund

At the beginning of the year a stipend statement is sent from the Church and Ministry Department to the minister and congregational treasurer of each charge showing the amount of stipend for the year and its composition (e.g. endowments, glebe rent, congregational contribution, etc.), together with a note of the appropriate aid to be contributed to the fund by aid-giving congregations, and aid to be received from the fund in the case of aid-receiving congregations. It is to the General Fund that all congregations remit their share of their minister's stipend and, if aid-giving, their appropriate contribution to the fund, by monthly banker's order. In the case of aid-receiving congregations, quarterly remittances are usually made. From this fund all ministers' stipends are paid on the last weekday of each month.

Congregational contributions amount to over 90 per cent of the income of the General Fund, and these are derived largely from the giving of members. In 1974 and 1975 congregational contributions to the fund amounted to about £1.4 million and over £3 millions respectively. The large increase between the two years resulted from the centralization of stipend payments from 1 April 1975. Prior to that date many affluent congregations made over their payment of stipend direct to their minister, without it passing through any central fund. From that date, the total stipend payments from all congregations have been made through the central funds. Apart from congregational contributions, other sources of income to the General Fund include income from donations, grants and trusts, legacies, income on capital and miscellaneous items. Two large items included are interest of over £5,000 on capital handed over by the Smaller Livings Association, and an annual sum of about £18,000 from a legacy to the Church for its small livings from the late Mr F.G. Salvesen. These items are given in table D of the appendix, which shows the position of the general fund as at 31 December 1975.

The practice of the committee with regard to legacies destined simply to maintenance of the ministry is that all received in the calendar year are lodged in a Legacy Suspense Account, and the total treated at the year end as one legacy. From the total is transferred £2,500 to the Uninvested Fund for Endowment grants. The remainder is divided into five equal parts and transferred to a Legacy Distribution Account. From that account, one of the fifth parts, together with a similar one-fifth of the legacies of each of the four preceding years, is transferred to the ordinary income of the General Fund account before its account for the year is closed. The purpose of this procedure is to even out the annual variations in the income received from legacies.

Apart from the payments of stipends, other charges on the General Fund include office expenses; vacancy expenses and widows' and next-of-kin grants other than payable from the Vacant Stipend Fund; car grants, purchases and expenses; driving grants and removal expenses; expenses in connection with retirements in the interest of union; and miscellaneous expenses (see section 5, 2 below).

The balance on the General Fund at the year end, after all charges have been met, is transferred to the Minimum Stipend Fund. The General Fund is thus peculiar in that it starts each year with a clean sheet. The larger the balance transferred the more there is to distribute as minimum stipend, and other things being equal, the higher the minimum stipend the committee can declare for the year ahead.

B Minimum Stipend Fund

The position of the Minimum Stipend Fund as at 31 December 1975 is given in the appendix, Table E. About three-quarters of the income of the Minimum Stipend Fund is made up of the credit balance transferred from the General Fund at the end of each calendar year. Since this income is received at the end of the financial (i.e. calendar) year, while payments in aid of stipend to ministers in aid-receiving charges are made month by month throughout the year, the balance in the fund gradually runs down through the year. But the fund carries forward from year to year a credit balance known as the 'cushion'. Gibson reports that in 1960 the cushion was £15,000, but in more recent years it has been increased gradually to over £800,000. Originally the cushion was intended as a protection against the possibility of a particular minimum stipend costing the fund more than expected. While the cushion still fulfils this purpose, it has now become so large as to prevent the Minimum Stipend Fund from running into deficit.

The object of the committee in deciding, in the previous autumn, the level of the minimum stipend for the year in question, is to set it at a figure that will use up the whole of that year's prospective income. This requires a fine degree of judgement. Much depends upon the size of the credit balance transferred from the General Fund to the Minimum Stipend Fund at 31 December of the previous year. The size of this transfer is not known at the time the decision on the minimum stipend is taken, although estimates can be made. The estimates are made difficult, however, by the fact that many congregations fail to reach their appropriate stipend and aid to the fund contributions, and some also their contributions to the Aged and Infirm Ministers' Fund. In addition, there are the non-stipend expenses of the fund which are not always easy to predict. All these involve an additional drain on the General Fund, and thus reduce the size of the credit balance to be transferred to the Minimum Stipend Fund for the following year.[7]

Perhaps the chief danger is that the minimum stipend may be set too high. This may happen because the income of congregations will tend to rise from year to year, and there is a certain pressure to raise stipends in line with increases in the incomes of comparable professional groups. Also, it is sometimes felt that congregations are likely to respond better financially if they are given a target that is not easily attainable at which to aim. If the minimum stipend is set too high, then many aid-receiving congregations may require even larger amounts of aid in order to pay their minister the minimum, and some self-supporting congregations may become aid-receiving for the first time. The expenditure of the Minimum Stipend Fund will thus be greater than expected, and the size of the cushion will fall in consequence. At the same time, some of the aid-giving congregations whose stipend is linked to the minimum, may not be able to meet their appropriate contributions of aid to the fund.[8] This will reduce the income received by the General Fund during the year, and therefore the size of the credit balance to be transferred to the Minimum Stipend Fund at the end of the year. As a result, the minimum stipend declared for the following year is likely to show a smaller increase than for the year in question, partly because of the smaller size of the transfer, and partly because of the reduced size of the cushion in the Minimum Stipend Fund, which will need to be topped up.

On the other hand, if the minimum stipend is set too low, the converse of the above situation will tend to occur. Some of the aid-giving congregations whose stipend is linked to the minimum may meet their appropriate stipend and contribution to the fund with ease. These congregations will use any surplus income either to increase the stipend of the minister above the appropriate stipend or on congregational expenses. In the former case, the committee is required to ensure that the congregation gives 'further contributions to the Minimum Stipend Fund, and to the Mission and Service Fund, deemed by the Presbytery to be appropriate.'[9] The income of the General Fund will thus show a tendency to rise beyond what would otherwise be expected, so producing a larger credit balance to be transferred to the Minimum Stipend Fund at the end of the year. At the same time, many aid-receiving congregations will be able to meet their appropriate stipends fairly easily with a margin to spare. However, aid-receiving congregations may not supplement their minister's stipend either directly or indirectly (i.e. through the gift of goods in kind) without reporting the payment to the secretary of the committee. Such a report is likely to result in the amount of aid received by the congregation being reduced accordingly, which may discourage the initiative. In a further ruling, aid-receiving congregations are required, after meeting the usual congregational expenses and making a contribution to stipend and to the Mission and Service Fund, to use towards reaching self-support any credit balance at the end of the year on their general fund, apart from a normal working balance. This ruling may help to ensure that any surplus income beyond that required to produce a 'normal working balance' may, in fact, be spent.

The upshot of these rulings is thus somewhat uncertain, but the general tendency may be that, when the minimum stipend for any year is set too low, the amount of aid paid to aid-receiving congregations may tend to fall (and congregational expenses to increase.) This will in turn lead to an increase in the size of the cushion in the Minimum Stipend Fund. This, together with the larger than expected transfer from the General Fund, will allow a larger increase to be made in the minimum stipend for the following year, other things being equal.

It can be seen that the under-setting of the minimum stipend probably has a lesser impact in building up the level of the fund than the over-setting of the minimum has on lowering the level of the fund. When the minimum stipend is set too low, surplus income accumulates in the congregations, rather than in the fund, where, despite various rulings, it is not easy to tap. On the other hand, when the minimum is set too high, extra payments have to be made from the fund to congregations in difficulties, so that the impact on the fund is felt immediately.

Prior to the introduction of the Appropriate Stipend Scheme in 1952, the method of fixing stipends differed somewhat from that used today. Except for minimum stipend charges for which a minimum stipend was declared each year, the stipends of other charges could remain at the same level for some years, unless a Revision Schedule was called for by the Presbytery or the committee, or the charge fell vacant, or the congregation decided to pay an increase. Under the Appropriate Stipend Scheme the committee, in consultation with the Presbytery of the bounds, fixes an 'appropriate stipend' and (in the case of aid-giving congregations) an 'appropriate contribution' in aid to the fund for every charge in the Church. In fixing these two figures, account is taken of the financial history of the congregation and the expected increase in its income on past trends, and in that sense the figures are 'appropriate' to the resources of the congregation. The 'appropriate' figures are forward projections to be attained over a period of years; each congregation is bound to take all necessary steps to secure and pay these sums, including the adoption of the most suitable and effective organization for fund-raising.

In the case of aid-giving charges, the appropriate stipend is thus the stipend which will actually be paid to the ministers concerned. In aid-receiving charges, where the appropriate stipend is less than the prospective minimum stipend, the stipend actually paid will depend upon the level at which the minimum stipend is set from year to year. The difference is made up by aid received from the Minimum Stipend Fund. It can be seen that, providing appropriate stipends are accurately assessed, the Appropriate Stipend Structure determines within broad limits the level of the minimum stipend for each year over the period in which it operates.

However, in recent years the high rate of inflation has made such forward planning difficult. For example, in some aid-giving charges whose income has increased faster than anticipated, the stipend of the minister has been raised above the appropriate stipend. As noted above, such congregations are expected to give further contributions to the Minimum Stipend Fund, and to the Mission and Service Fund, deemed by the Presbytery to be appropriate.

Inflation has also affected the length of the financial planning period. The Appropriate Stipend Structure used to be calculated in advance on a five-year basis to allow congregational boards and other financial bodies to budget for five years ahead. The 'appropriate' figures were to be attained in annual instalments each of not less than one-fifth of the increase. While this method worked well when inflation was proceeding at a rate of only a few per cent a year, so that income forecasts for congregations could be made with some certainty, the high rates of inflation in recent years have made such projection very difficult. Also, the large money increases required in the 'appropriate' figures tends to create a certain amount of doubt in the minds of office-bearers as to the ability of the congregation to reach the figure in the given period. Consequently, in 1972 the quinquennial period was reduced to a triennium, and it has recently been suggested in the *Memorandum on Stipend*[10] that the planning period be further reduced to a yearly basis.

The whole of the income of the Minimum Stipend Fund is devoted to maintaining the minimum stipend. Grants are made to bring stipends below the

minimum up to that level. In certain special cases approved by the General Assembly, the fund is also used by the Committee to guarantee supplementary payments made by congregations to their ministers, as follows:
(i) to ministers in city charges who were inducted to their present charge prior to 30th June, 1960 — £50.
(ii) to a minister in a Church Extension charge, payable by the Home Mission Sectional Committee — £200.
(iii) to minister in a charge on an island which is itself his parish, and where he is the sole ordained minister of the Church of Scotland residing on and ministering to the people of that island — £150.
(iv) to a minister of a congregation which is united or linked with another congregation during his incumbency, and who conducts services each Sunday in both churches — £150.
(v) to a minister inducted to a charge already united or linked, and in which he has to conduct public worship each Sunday in churches not less than two miles apart — £100.
(vi) to a minister in a charge in certain remote districts designated as 'Special areas of readjustment' — £50.
(vii) ministers serving as hospital, prison and officiating chaplains to H.M. Forces receive payments which can also be regarded as supplementary payments.

The committee cannot in any one year make to any minister any payment which would have the effect of increasing his supplementary payments beyond £250. The committee may ask the authority of the General Assembly to declare a particular charge one of strategic importance in which a special additional supplementary payment may be made from the fund, if necessary for the duration of an incumbency. A minister who is on the minimum stipend who receives one or more supplementary payments is still regarded as being on the minimum.

C Supplementary Fund
The Supplementary Fund was raised by the United Free Church, not for stipend, but for purposes ancillary to stipend, such as driving grants and removal expenses. The fund is a capital fund, the income of which was used to help ministers whose stipend was on or just above the minimum who were hard pressed to meet the travelling expenses incurred in their work. However, after the 1929 Union the income of the fund was never great enough to meet the greatly increased costs that were laid on it, despite efforts to increase the size of its capital. Apart from the interest on the capital of the fund, the responsibilities of this fund are now met from the General Fund.

5 Organization and procedure
In this section we deal in turn with the regional organization of the administration of stipend, the grants and other non-stipend expenses of the fund, and the Listed Expenses paid to ministers by their congregations.

1 Regional organization
In every Synod and Presbytery there is a standing committee whose business it is to deal with all matters in its area concerning the maintenance of the ministry. This committee has the very important duty of watching over the contributions

made by congregations, and of satisfying itself that every congregation has contributed to the stipend of its minister and to the fund up to the limit of its resources. The General Assembly has instructed financial courts to give authority to congregational treasurers to remit all contributions to stipend and in aid to the fund to the General Treasurer monthly, except in the case of aid-receiving congregations, when remittances may be made quarterly.

When a vacancy occurs, or is about to occur, the central Maintenance of the Ministry Committee considers the question of union and readjustment. When this question has been settled the committee goes on to consider, in cases in which endowments are involved, whether it will raise the question of other possible use for the stipend of the vacant charge for a new incumbency. If this question is raised, it is referred with a suggested figure to the Presbytery, which makes its views known to the committee as soon as possible.

When these questions are disposed of, a Vacancy Schedule is issued by the Maintenance of the Ministry Committee. This is completed by the appropriate court of the congregation in the presence of a representative of the Presbytery. The schedule requires the congregation to state what it proposes to contribute to the fund, and that it will pay the Listed Expenses. The schedule is then judged by the Presbytery, and if passed, sent to the committee for approval. Both the Presbytery and the committee must be satisfied with the proposals in the Vacancy Schedule, both as to stipend and as to the annual contribution, before the Presbytery is free to sustain a call for a new minister from the vacant charge.

Every Presbytery is required to prepare a rota for the issue of Revision Schedules to congregations within their bounds. Every congregation should complete a schedule at least once every five years, except where the appropriate stipend and contribution to the fund are being met. A Revision Schedule is also issued to a charge when any change occurs which is likely to affect the appropriate stipend or contribution. A Presbytery at its discretion may call for, or a committee may issue, a Revision Schedule to any charge.

When a congregation is united or linked with another congregation which is vacant, both the stipend and the contribution to the fund is affected. These changes are regularised under a Revision or Vacancy Schedule, as the case may be.

In addition to Vacancy and Revision Schedules, there is also the special schedule used by church extension charges on petitioning to be made into a *quoad sacra* parish. All three schedules are issued by the committee, and not by the Presbytery, although in the case of Revision Schedules, usually at its request

2 Grants and other expenses of the fund.
As already noted, the committee makes a number of grants and loans to ministers and to congregations. These include car and driving grants, car loans, removal expenses, widow's and next-of-kin grants and furnishing loans. We shall deal with each of these in turn.

A Car grants
Grants towards the purchase of a car are provided to enable ministers in certain linked, united or very remote charges to conduct services and to undertake pastoral visitation. Grants may only be made where the Presbytery and the committee agree that without a car the work of the parish cannot be undertaken.

Careful consideration is given to every application for a car grant, since a shortage of funds makes it impossible to provide a grant in every case. The grant will not exceed £400, and will not exceed two-thirds of the cost if less than £600.

The number of ministers receiving grants each year, and the total annual outlays on grants, for the period 1968-74 is shown in row 1 of table 71. Over the seven-year period an average of 44 ministers per year received £13,727 in grants, giving an average per minister of £312.

As the grant is made in respect of the parish, the minister, if translated to another parish or retiring, is not entitled to take away the car without the sanction of the committee. Apart from this proviso, the car is the property of the minister, and he is responsible for insurance, the licence, and all running, repair and maintenance costs. He may receive a driving grant towards these costs.

B Provision of cars in the special areas
Comprehensive plans were adopted some years ago for the special areas of readjustment. The special areas are normally coincident with Presbytery areas, and involve the widespread union and readjustment of charges. Ministers, associate ministers and lay missionaries in the linked and united charges in such areas are provided with transport. The number of cars owned and maintained by the committee, together with the annual cost of purchase, replacement and maintenance, for the period 1968-74 are shown in row 2 of table 71. The number of vehicles owned has increased fairly steadily from 59 in 1968 to 84 in 1974. The total annual cost of the scheme over the period has risen from £13,510 to £35,316.

C Driving grants
Driving grants up to an agreed mileage are made by the committee to the ministers of certain linked congregations and in very remote areas (see section 5, *3* below, under *Listed Expenses*). Such grants are also usually made to a minister under whose ministry another congregation has been united or linked with his own. In normal cases the grant is up to three-quarters of an agreed mileage, the congregation being required to meet the remaining one-quarter of the grant. From 1 January, 1973 driving grants have been paid at the following rates: 5p per mile for the first 3,000 miles, and thereafter at 3p per mile for the next 3,000 miles, up to a maximum of £240.

The same rates apply to travelling expenses, i.e. to those transport costs of ministers in congregations where no driving grant is payable from central funds, but where the committee and the Presbytery agree that the work of the parish involves the minister in travelling expenses. Congregations which are self-supporting and which have met their commitments to stipend and aid to the fund (but which are not in receipt of a driving grant) are permitted to pay up to £100 per annum for car depreciation without such payments being taken into account for the purpose of calculating assessments for the Aged and Infirm Ministers' Fund.

D Car Loan Fund
The purpose of the fund is the granting of loans to ministers of charges which are considered as 'car essential charges' by Presbytery and committee. Preference is given to ministers in remote areas who do not qualify for a car grant.

The regulations of this fund provide for interest-free loans of up to £400, repayable in equal monthly instalments over three years, to ministers in minimum

TABLE 71.
Details of some of the grants and other expenses met by the Maintenance of the Ministry Fund, 1968-74 (see text)

Grant	Details	1968	1969	1970	1971	1972	1973	1974
1 Car grants	number of ministers	44	34	28	47	38	62	55
	total cost	£11,873	£9,667	£8,325	£14,671	£13,269	£21,118	£17,168
2 Special areas	number of vehicles	59	57	64	70	81	89	84
	total cost	£13,510	£16,656	£20,696	£16,461	£25,713	£28,323	£35,316
3 Car Loan Fund	number of ministers	30	18	16	22	23	*	49
	total loans	£8,242	£5,186	£3,978	£6,353	£6,898	*	*
	repayments	£7,396	£6,931	£6,099	£6,015	£5,703	*	*
4 Young Ministers' Furnishing and Loan Fund	number of ministers	*	18	*	13	27	13	12
	total loans	*	£5,186	*	£4,464	£5,350	£5,200	£4,450
	repayments	*	£6,931	*	*	£1,193	£1,580	£2,197
5 Widows' or next-of-kin grants	total grants	£16,850	£18,148	£27,762	£17,649	*	£32,500	£42,925

SOURCE: 'Report of the Committee on the Maintenance of the Ministry', *Reports to the General Assembly, 1969-75.*
* Not available.

stipend charges for the purchase of new cars or of second-hand cars not more than eighteen months old or with a mileage of 12,000 or less. Loans may also be made to ministers in receipt of stipends above the minimum, but not exceeding the minimum plus £150 in the year prior to the application; in these cases, interest at six per cent per annum is charged. As the loan is made in respect of the charge, the minister, if translated or retiring, is not entitled to take away the car without the sanction of the committee, except in cases where the loan is repaid in full. Subject to this proviso, the car is the property of the minister, and he is responsible for comprehensive insurance, licence and all running costs, repairs and replacements.

Row 3 of table 71 shows for each year of the period 1968-74 (where available) the number of ministers receiving loans, the total cost of the loans, and the amount or repayments. The number of ministers receiving loans in 1974 was 49.

E Removal expenses

The General Assembly have instructed Presbyteries that when a congregation within the bounds is given leave to elect a minister, its attention be drawn to the heavy costs of removal that a new minister may have to face, and that wherever possible the congregation should meet part, at least, of these expenses.

In 1976 the General Assembly approved regulations which authorized the Maintenance of the Ministry Committee to make grants towards the removal expenses of ministers in certain cases, mainly involving ministers moving to and from minimum stipend charges in the Islands.

F Young Ministers' Furnishing Loan Fund

The object of this fund is to make loans to young ministers in their first charge where the stipend is the minimum to assist them in furnishing the manse. During 1970 the fund, which hitherto had been administered by the General Finance Committee, was transferred to the Maintenance of the Ministry Committee. Row 4 of table 71 provides incomplete information for the period 1968-74 on the number of ministers receiving loans, the total loans made, and the annual repayments. In the five years for which information is complete, 83 ministers received total loans of £24,650 giving an average of £297 per minister.

G Widow's or Next-of-Kin Grant

On the death of a minister in a parish, or the death of a retired minister who is in receipt of an annuity from the Aged and Infirm Ministers' Fund, a grant is paid to his widow or next-of-kin keeping house for him at the time of his death; where there is no widow, the grant may be paid to a sister or daughter who has lived with him and kept house for him for a period of not less than ten years, or to a sister, daughter or his mother who has lived in the same house with him and looked after him for a period of at least two years immediately prior to death.

Prior to April 1973 this *ex gratia* payment was £500, but from 18 April 1973 the committee agreed to increase the amount to £1,000. The grant was further increased to £1,250 as from 1st March, 1976. Row 5 of table 71 indicates the total annual sums paid in grants over the period 1968-74. In 1974 the total payment was £42,925.

H Pulpit supply expenses in a vacancy

During a vacancy, congregations are expected to collect and remit their contributions to the fund regularly and in full. But the fund helps congregations to meet the cost of supplying the pulpit in a vacancy. The cost is borne by the congregation and by the fund jointly in the same proportions as they were liable for stipend during the last full year of the previous incumbency.

The permitted expenses are as follows:
(i) Where the stipend for the last full year did not exceed the minimum plus £200, the fee is £8.00. Where the stipend exceeded that level, the fee is £10.00.
(ii) A neighbouring minister who supplies a vacant pulpit without providing supply for his own pulpit may receive an honorarium of £2.10 each Sunday, plus a refund of travelling expenses, but no fee.
(iii) Weekend board and lodging may be claimed at a maximum of £8.00 for the weekend. Travelling expenses shall be paid.
(iv) Instead of weekly supply a *locum tenens* may be employed by the congregation.

The normal procedure is that the congregational tresurer pays the supply out of congregational funds and periodically claims refund from the committee of its share. The proportion paid by the committee is shared by the Endowment Vacant Stipend Fund and the General Fund in accordance with their respective liabilities for stipend prior to the vacancy.

I Retirement for the sake of union or readjustment.
The question of union and readjustment sometimes involves a minister who holds the life interest in a neighbouring parish. He may be unwilling for health or other reasons to undertake the additional work and responsibility resulting from a union or linking, but would otherwise be happy to continue working in his own parish. In such cases, special financial arrangements may be made by the Presbytery and the Committee on Unions and Readjustments to secure his retirement sooner than would otherwise have been the case. If the minister concerned is not eligible for the normal retiring allowance of a minister retiring through age or infirmity, a substitute payment for this allowance has to be found. This payment falls on the Maintenance of the Ministry Fund.

Each such case is considered separately, but the normal arrangements are as follows:
(i) The retiring minister receives from the Maintenance of the Ministry Fund the equivalent of the normal retiring allowance until he qualifies to receive it from the Aged and Infirm Ministers' Fund.
(ii) As a manse is usually freed by the union or readjustment, he may be given life occupancy of that manse, or an allowance in lieu of the manse which is derived from its sale or let.

Payment under (i) usually lasts only a few years, and may be regarded as a temporary reduction in the savings arising from the union or readjustment.

3 The Listed Expenses.
Every congregation, whether aid-giving or aid-receiving, is expected to repay their minister, or pay on his behalf, certain 'Listed Expenses'. These are not stipend payments, but congregational expenses. From 1963 there have been six Listed Expenses, as follows:
(a) (i) The Communion expenses incurred.
    (ii) Any fee or expenses due to a visiting minister at Communion seasons if such payment be authorized by Kirk Session.
(b) (i) The rates on the manse.

(ii) The rates on any house owned or rented by the minister, and occupied by him in lieu of a manse, the rates in such cases to be calculated on a rateable value limited to £60 in ordinary cases and £100 in the four large cities.
(c) One month's holiday supply, and supply during the minister's attendance at the General Assembly as a commissioner.
(d) Telephone rental and calls incurred in performance of ministerial duties, where the Presbytery deems a telephone necessary.
(e) Notepaper and postage stamps for his official use.
(f) (i) In parishes which receive a driving grant, the remaining proportion of the cost of transport (if any) as may be approved by the committee . . . shall be a charge on the congregation.
(ii) In congregations where no driving grant is payable from central funds, and where the committee and the Presbytery agree that the work of the parish involves the minister in travelling expenses, the congregation shall pay on the same basis as the committee's grants the cost of such travelling either by car or public transport, as may be approved by the committee.

6 Conclusions

In this chapter we have presented an account of the present arrangements for stipend in the Church of Scotland. We have seen that the stipend of a minister may be derived from a number of sources, including congregational support (the most important source), aid drawn from the Minimum Stipend Fund (by aid-receiving charges), standardized stipend (i.e. the former teinds), burgh church stipends, Exchequer monies, statutory endowments (in the case of *quoad sacra* charges), further and basal endowments, and glebe rents, feu duties and monies (the last being the interest on the capital realized from the sale of a glebe). Although not discussed in the chapter, there are in addition a number of trusts for stipend relating to particular charges, or to charges in particular districts of Scotland (e.g. the Pringle Trust benefits charges in Moray).

All these monies for stipend pass through the funds administered by the Maintenance of the Ministry Committee. The endowment monies, received either from the General Trustees or General Treasurer, are paid into the Endowment General Fund, from which they are disbursed to the ministers eligible. When a charge is vacant the endowment income is paid into the Endowment Vacant Stipend Fund. New endowments are made through the Uninvested Fund, the income from which is derived from donations, grants and income from trusts.

The congregational support for stipend, which forms the bulk of stipend payments, is paid into the General Fund, from which it is disbursed to the ministers concerned. The fund also receives the aid given by aid-giving charges, and this, together with a relatively small income from other sources, is used to meet various non-stipend expenses, such as removal and vacancy expenses, car and driving grants, and widows' and next-of-kin grants. The credit balance on the General Fund at the end of the year is made over to the Minimum Stipend Fund, and is its main source of income. The income of the Minimum Stipend Fund is devoted exclusively to making grants to aid-receiving charges to bring the stipend of the minister up to the minimum stipend. The larger the credit balance transferred from the General Fund, therefore, the more there is to distribute in support of the minimum stipend in the coming year, and other things being equal, the higher the minimum stipend the committee can declare for the year ahead. The mainstay of the Minimum Stipend Fund is thus the General Fund, and the mainstay of the General Fund is the contributions of congregations.

The contributions of congregations to stipend are projected for three year periods in advance in the Appropriate Stipend Scheme. The committee, in consultation with the Presbytery of the bounds, fixes an 'appropriate stipend', and an 'appropriate' sum to be given or received in aid, for every charge in the Church, the contributions being 'appropriate' to the resources of the congregation. In the case of aid-giving charges, the 'appropriate stipend' is the stipend that will actually be paid. For aid-receiving charges, the stipend will normally be the minimum. The amount by which the 'appropriate stipend' falls below the minimum is made up by a grant from the Minimum Stipend Fund. The level at which the committee sets the minimum stipend each year thus basically depends upon the success of congregations in meeting their 'appropriate stipends', and in particular the success of aid-giving congregations in meeting their 'appropriate' contributions in aid to the fund. This most important point should be borne in mind by those commissioners to the General Assembly who every year press for the minimum stipend to be increased by larger amounts. The annual rate of increase of the minimum stipend depends not so much upon the policy of the committee, but more upon the contributions to stipend of every congregation.

Notes

1 Cox, *Practice and Procedure*. 6th ed. (1976); A.J.H. Gibson, *Stipend in the Church of Scotland* (Blackwood, 1960); H.C.M. Eggo, *Memorandum on Stipend,* private memorandum, (Church of Scotland, 1976); Church of Scotland, 'Report of the Committee on the Maintenance of the Ministry', *Reports to the General Assembly, 1961-75*; A. Herron (ed.), *The Church of Scotland Yearbook 1976,* (St Andrew Press, 1976).
2 'Stipend' does not include a minister's non-Church sources of income, such as fees for published articles or for radio and television appearances.
3 The policy of union and readjustment of congregations is described in chapter 13.
4 'Report of the Committee on the Maintenance of the Ministry', *Reports to the General Assembly, 1972,* p. 269.
5 The meaning of the term 'necessary' in regard to a congregation is defined above on p. 224.
6 The minimum stipend for the three years prior to 1 January 1975 averaged £1,682.
7 The centralization of all stipend payments from 1 April 1975 has probably helped in the setting of the minimum stipend by requiring that all remittances to the fund be made at monthly intervals (and quarterly by aid-receiving congregations) by banker's order. This should overcome the problem in the former Basic Stipend Fund, that remittances from congregations on the basic stipend, which were to be made quarterly, were often delayed. As a result, the fund was usually in deficit until the end of the year. This not only led to interest charges being incurred, but also made it more difficult to assess the state of the funds at the time when the minimum stipend for the following year had to be decided.
8 It is for this reason that charges, when completing a Revision or Vacancy Schedule for stipend, are being discouraged from fixing their stipends on a 'minimum plus' basis.
9 Deliverance of the General Assembly on the *1972* Report of the Maintenance of the Ministry Committee. See: *Reports to the General Assembly, 1972,* p. 21.
10 Eggo, op. cit., p. 9.

Chapter 11

Stipend

1 Introduction

In the previous chapter we described the financial organization of the ministry, with particular emphasis on the various elements of stipend and the funds through which they pass. The purpose of this chapter is to carry out a statistical analysis of the stipends actually received by ministers, and then to put forward proposals for changes to the present system by which stipends are fixed.

We start in section 2 by assessing the total income of a parish minister in 1976, which comprises not only his stipend (or money income), but also goods in kind, such as the manse, non-contributory pension, and the like. His income is then compared to that of a member of a comparable professional group of salary earners. Then in section 3 we examine how the minimum stipend, which is frequently used as an indicator of the financial position of ministers, has increased in money and real terms over recent years, and how far these increases have reached targets set at various times in the past. The statistical section of the chapter is completed in section 4 with a cross-section analysis, based on a representative sample of charges, of the relationship between stipend on the one hand and the financial characteristics of the charge and the experience of the minister on the other.

The principles which may be used to determine the fixing of stipends between different charges and ministers, and in relation to the minimum stipend, are examined in section 5; the importance of the voluntary principle is strongly emphasized. Then in section 6 we examine two sets of proposals for modifying the present stipend system in such a way as to enhance the voluntary principle. The first proposal concerns the reallocation of the standardized stipend, and possibly all endowment stipend, to aid-receiving congregations. The second concerns modifications to the way in which stipends are fixed.

2 Stipend and the total income of ministers in 1976

In this section an attempt is made to estimate the total income of a parish minister in 1976. The total income includes not only the stipend, but also the non-contributory pension, and certain goods in kind (such as the manse), which accrue to the incumbent of a parish charge. We examine each of these items in turn.

1 Stipend

All ministers in the parish ministry receive a stipend. In 1976 the minimum stipend (the stipend below which no minister is allowed to fall) was £2,460, plus £100 car maintenance allowance.

In order to examine the degree of variation in the stipends paid to ministers in 1976, a weighted sample of 34 charges broadly representative of the Church as a whole was taken; the sample is given in table 72. By comparing the percentage figures in table 72 it can be seen that the proportions of recently united, linked, rural, small town and urban charges in the sample correspond closely to the proportions in the Church total. This sample of charges is based on the sample of congregations used in the statistical analysis of congregational finance,[1] the sole difference being that the ten linked *congregations* (representing 460 linked congregations) have been replaced by four linked *charges* (representing 206 linked charges). This was done in order to preserve the representative nature of the sample in the change from congregations to charges. The charge is the more appropriate unit to use in the analysis of stipend, since it is the unit for which a minister is responsible, and which pays the minister his stipend.

TABLE 72
A representative sample of 34 charges drawn from the Church total in 1974.

	Church total		Weighted sample	
	no. of charges	%	no. of charges	%
United	76	4.6	1	2.9
Linked	206	12.5	4	11.8
Rural	666	40.4	14	41.2
Small town	276	16.8	6	17.6
Urban	423	25.7	9	26.5
	1,647	100.0	34	100.0
Vacant charges	121	—	—	—
GRAND TOTAL	1,768	—	—	—

Information on the stipends paid to the ministers in the 34 charges in 1976 was collected from the Church and Ministry Department files. The distribution of these stipends is shown in table 73. The £100 car maintenance allowance has been omitted from the figures, and is dealt with below.

TABLE 73
The distribution of the stipends of the sample of 34 charges in 1976

	no.	%
£2,460 (the minimum)	9	26.5
Over £2,460 – £2,560	6	17.6
Over £2,560 – £2,660	5	14.7
Over £2,660 – £2,760	5	14.7
Over £2,760 – £2,860	4	11.8
£2,895	1	
£2,977	1	
£3,186	1	14.7
£3,285	1	
£3,880	1	
	34	100.0

The table indicates that in nine charges, or 26.5 per cent of the total, the stipend is on the minimum. In addition, all four linked charges in the sample received supplementary payments to stipend (two at £100 and two at £150), which had the effect of raising the stipend above the minimum stipend figure, although all four remained, technically, minimum stipend charges. The number of minimum stipend charges was thus 13, or 38.2 per cent of the total. This proportion is rather smaller than expected, although it is thought that the sample is biased slightly in favour of the more affluent charges.

Table 73 also shows that 58.8 per cent of the ministers received a stipend of no more than £200 above the minimum in 1976, and 91.2 per cent received a stipend of less than £3,000, or £540 above the minimum. On the other hand, three ministers in the sample, or 8.8 per cent of the total, received stipends of over £3,000, the largest of those being £3,880.

The highest stipend that was paid in the Church in 1976 was £4,428, which was 80.0 per cent above the minimum. This differential between the highest and lowest stipends is rather smaller than expected, but it seems that the differential has narrowed somewhat in recent years. In 1973, for example, when the minimum stipend was £1,674 and the highest stipend was £3,175, the differential was 89.7 per cent.

The average stipend in the sample is £2,688, or £228 above the minimum, as compared to the median stipend of £2,606, which is £146 above the minimum. The distribution of stipends in the sample thus exhibits a positive skew, i.e. the majority of stipends are less than the sample average, although the skewedness is less marked than is often supposed. A smaller proportion of ministers are on the minimum stipend than expected, and some of those receive supplementary payments which have the effect of raising the stipend above the minimum figure. At the other end of the scale, the highest stipends are well under double the minimum.

Finally, it should be noted that the old distinction between 'stipend' and 'salary' has more or less disappeared. Formerly a stipend, unlike a salary, was subject to the deduction of the necessary expenses incurred by the minister during the course of his duties, and only the remainder could be used to support himself and his dependants. Nowadays there are six kinds of ministerial expense which must be paid by every congregation to, or on behalf of, the minister. These 'Listed Expenses' cover the majority of the necessary expenses of a minister. They are not regarded as stipend.

2 Manse

The position at present is that a parish minister is entitled to a manse, or an allowance in lieu of a manse, the allowance being £500 a year in the four large cities and £350 elsewhere (including rates). According to the Church and Ministry Department only 19 ministers received manse allowance in 1975. In 1973 there were 1,865 manses, of which 604 (32.4 per cent) were in the cities and large burghs, and 1,261 (67.6 per cent) were in rural and other communities. It is not easy to estimate an average value for the manses, because they vary so much in size and location. However, in chapter 19 we suggest that the average value of a manse in cities and towns in 1975 might have been about £25,000, and in other areas about £15,000. On the basis of these estimates, table 74 indicates that the total value of the manses in 1975 was about £34 millions, or £18,239 per manse.

TABLE 74
The number and estimated value of manses in 1975

Location	Number	Average values £	Total value £
Cities and large burghs	604	25,000	15,100,000
Rural and other communities	1,261	15,000	18,915,000
TOTAL	1,865	18,239	34,015,000

The value to the average minister of living in an £18,000 house might be measured in terms of the opportunity cost rental (i.e. the rental which he would have to pay for such a house on the private market). Assuming that the annual rental would be set at 6 per cent of the capital value of the house, the rental would be £1,080 (i.e. a little under £21 per week).

The regulations of the Church require that every manse should be 'free', in the sense that the minister is not responsible for any of the normal financial burdens in connection with it, such as rates, insurance, maintenance and feuduty (if any). Also, where manses are vested in or leased to the Church, a 50 per cent remission of rates is mandatory on the local authority. Taking these into account, it was estimated in 1973 that the average cost to a congregation of maintaining an urban manse was £300.[2] This sum was made up as follows:

Rates(50% of total rates)	(say)	£ 80
Insurance	(say)	£ 10
Repairs and maintenance	(say)	£210
TOTAL		£300

However, the figure of £300 has to be amended in two ways. Firstly, the true cost of the manse as a private house would include rates of 100 per cent, which would raise the annual maintenance cost from £300 to £380. Secondly, allowance has to be made for the rise in maintenance costs (including rates) over the period 1973-6 as a result of inflation. Between mid-1973 and April 1976 the Retail Price Index rose by 64.2 per cent, from 179.4 to 294.6. Assuming that manse maintenance costs rose at the same rate, then the £380 in 1973 prices becomes £624 in April 1975 prices. The figure of £624 for maintenance costs has to be added to the rental value of the manse.

In addition, following from the 1961 Finance Act there are certain income tax concessions in respect of heating, lighting and cleaning of the manse, plus the maintenance of the manse garden, which are personal to the minister occupying a manse which is vested in or leased to the Church. If the minister meets these expenses, or the congregation does so on his behalf, the minister can claim them as allowances against tax. In the sample of 34 congregations these expenses averaged £348 in 1975. Assuming that the average figure remains the same in 1976, and that the average minister has income subject to tax of at least that amount, then the minister will save tax on £348 at 35 per cent, or £122.

The income in kind provided to the average minister by the manse in 1976, measured in terms of the expenses he would have to meet in living in a house of similar size and location to the manse but outside the Church, is calculated as follows:

Rent	£1,080
Rates, insurance and maintenance	£ 624
Loss of tax allowance	£ 122
TOTAL	£1,826

The income in kind provided by the average manse to the minister in 1976 is thus estimated at £1,826. On the other hand, it has to be remembered that the present manse arrangements leave the parish minister without a house to which to retire.[3]

3 Non-contributory pension
Parish ministers benefit from a non-contributory pension paid through the Aged and Infirm Ministers' Fund. Congregations contribute 15 per cent of the previous year's stipend of their minister to the fund (prior to 1 January 1975 the contribution was set at 5 per cent). The average contribution to be paid to the fund by the 34 charges in the sample for 1976 was £373. The range of contributions was from £339 for a minimum stipend charge to £552 for the charge with the highest stipend of £3,880. The present normal payment to annuitants is at the rate of £780 per annum, and this is normally available from age 65.

4 Cars
There are a number of benefits received by many ministers in respect of the purchase and running of cars. These are as follows:
(i) The minimum stipend declared for 1976 includes for the first time a car maintenance allowance of £100. The allowance is tax-free. In cases where a minister does not own a car, the £100 will form a part of stipend and be subject to tax.
(ii) Aid-giving congregations which have met all their 'appropriate' payments to stipend and their Mission and Service Fund contribution are permitted to make a car depreciation allowance to their minister of up to £100. This now appears to be a fairly widespread practice amongst such congregations.
(iii) Some affluent congregations provide their minister with a car and meet all the expenses connected therewith. The minister thus has the use of the car for private purposes. This situation was found to exist in one of the 34 charges in the sample.
(iv) In 1974 the Maintenance of the Ministry Committee owned 84 cars. The total cost of purchase, maintenance and running costs amounted to £35,316. These cars are used by the ministers, associate ministers and lay missionaries in the linked and united charges in the special areas of readjustment. Since there were 1,631 parish ministers at 31 December 1974, the figures suggest that as many as one in twenty ministers had the benefit of such cars for private use.
(v) Car grants (and loans at a low rate of interest) are available from the Maintenance of the Ministry Committee to a limited number of ministers in charges which the Presbytery and committee agree are 'car essential' charges. The grant or loan covers a part of the cost of purchasing a car, and again the minister concerned benefits in that the car may be used for private purposes.

The car situation is thus not easy to assess with respect to the average minister. In 1976 all car-owning ministers will receive a car maintenance allowance of £100, and a sizeable proportion also a car depreciation allowance of £100. A small proportion of ministers will have the use of a car provided by the Maintenance of the Ministry Committee or by their congregation. A few ministers in 1976 will receive a car grant or loan towards the purchase of a car.

5 Other sources of income

Ministers also benefit from having certain expenses and grants met by the Maintenance of the Ministry Committee. Removal expenses are met in some cases of ministers removing to and from the Islands. Young ministers in their first charge where the stipend is the minimum are eligible for loans to assit them in furnishing the manse. Also, *ex gratia* payments of £1,000 are made to the widow, or in some cases next-of-kin, of a minister at his death.

Ministers are also in a position to make private earnings from the writing of articles and books, through television and radio appearances, from summer lecture tours in the United States, and the like. It could be argued that similar outlets are available to other professional people, such as university lecturers, although the nature of the minister's job puts him very much in the public eye.

Ministers are also said to receive gifts in money or in kind from parishioners, particularly in rural areas. However, it is not known how widespread is this practice.

6 The total income of ministers in 1976

It is not easy to estimate the total income of the average minister in 1976. One or two items in total income can be measured fairly precisely (e.g. stipend), but a lack of information makes certain items much less easy to measure (e.g. private earnings, gifts from parishioners), while some items accrue to only a proportion of ministers (e.g. car depreciation allowances, 'free' cars in the special areas). However, if we concentrate on those items which can be measured fairly readily, then the total income of the average minister in 1976 would be made up as follows:

Stipend	£2,688
Car maintenance allowance	£ 100
Car depreciation allowance	£ 100
Manse	£1,826
TOTAL	£4,714

The total income figure is £4,714. This excludes any income from private earnings or in the form of gifts from parishioners. With a stipend of £228 above the minimum, the charge is unlikely to be in one of the special areas where a car is provided by the Maintenance of the Ministry Committee, nor is it likely to be rich enough to be able to provide the minister with a car from its own resources. We assume that it is an aid-giving charge which has met all its financial obligations to the centre, and is able to pay a car-depreciation allowance of £100 to the minister. The non-contributory pension contribution of £373 has been excluded from the total income figure in order to retain comparability with other professional workers.

The estimated total income figure of £4,714 for the average minister in 1976 can be compared with similar estimates for the minister on the minimum stipend and the minister in an affluent charge, as follows:

	Minimum stipend charge £	Affluent charge £
Stipend	2,460	3,880
Car maintenance allowance	100	100
Car depreciation allowance	–	100
Manse	1,646	2,246
TOTAL	4,206	6,326

The minister is a minimum stipend charge is estimated to have a total income of £4,206. It is assumed that, since the charge is likely to be in a rural community, the value of the manse is put at £15,000, or rather below the average value. Assuming further that the maintenance costs of such a manse, together with the loss of the tax allowance, are the same as the average, its worth to the minister in 1976 will be £1,646. The minister in a minimum stipend charge will not receive a car depreciation allowance.

The minister is an affluent city-centre charge with a stipend of £3,880 is estimated to have a total income of £6,326 in 1976. This includes income in kind from an urban manse valued at £25,000.

The calculations suggest that stipend will make up about 60 per cent of the total income of ministers in 1976. The actual figures are 58.4, 57.0 and 61.3 per cent respectively for minimum stipend, average, and affluent charges respectively. The bulk of the remainder is made up by the income in kind provided by the manse.

The difference in total incomes between the minister in a rural minimum stipend charge and the minister in a wealthy urban charge was £2,120 in 1976. The proportion of this differential to the income of the minimum stipend charge is 50.4 per cent, which is similar to the figure of 57.7 per cent calculated when only the stipends are compared. These differentials are likely to be widened, however, when variations in the cost of living between the regions of Scotland are brought into consideration. It has been suggested that ministers living in the more remote areas of the north and west, and particularly those on the Islands, tend to face a cost of living which may be 10 per cent or more above the level in the central lowland belt.

7 The relative income position of ministers

The relative income position of ministers can be assessed by comparing the total income figures calculated above for 1976 with the incomes of comparable groups of professional workers. One such comparison can be made with university academic staff, who are paid on incremental salary scales. The results are shown in table 75. University academic staff benefit from a pension contribution amounting to 15 per cent of the salary, but a third of the contribution is paid by the staff member. The salaries of academic staff have therefore been reduced by 5 per cent in making the comparisons with the incomes of ministers in table 75, since the pension scheme of ministers is entirely non-contributory. The private earnings of both groups have also been excluded from consideration.

TABLE 75
*A comparison of the incomes of ministers with
the salary scales of university academic staff, 1976*

Ministerial total incomes	University academic staff equivalent*
Minimum stipend charge (£4,206)	a little below the middle of the lecturers' scale — about 7th point out of 17 (age 32?)
Average charge (£4,714)	a little above the middle of the lecturers' scale — just below the 10th point (age 35?)
Affluent charge (£6,326)	below the middle of the senior lecturer reader scale — about the 3rd point out of 8 (age 40?); alternatively about £1,200 below the minimum salary of professors

* Salary scale operative from 1 October 1975 to 30 September, 1976

Table 75 suggests that in 1976 the minister in the minimum stipend charge (£4,206) and the minister in the average charge (£4,714) had respective incomes a little below and a little above the middle of the university lecturers' scale. The minister in a wealthy charge (£6,326) should have a total income a little below the middle of the senior lecturer scale, or about £1,200 below the professorial minimum salary. The range of incomes is thus relatively small compared to that of other professional groups; this probably reflects the principle that all ministers are regarded as being equals in the Presbyterian system of Church government.

3 Changes in the real value of the minimum stipend since 1929

The calculations in the previous section suggest that stipend will make up about 60 per cent of the total income of ministers in 1976. While the value of the manse and the car allowances, which make up the remaining 40 per cent or so of ministerial income, can be expected to increase roughly in line with the rate of inflation, the money value of stipend has to be increased from year to year in order that its real value is at least maintained. Hence the level of the minimum stipend, and the extent to which it changes from year to year, are usually taken as an index of the living standards of ministers, the success of the Maintenance of the Ministry Committee, and even the general financial well-being of the Church.

While many people in the Church of Scotland, including members of the Maintenance of the Ministry Committee, have expressed their unhappiness with the present level of stipend, the minimum stipend paid does compare very favourably with those paid to clergy in other British Churches. The minimum stipends for 1975 and 1976 (where known) for a number denominations are presented in table 76. The table shows that the minimum stipend in the Church of Scotland is higher, and in some cases considerably higher, than those in other denominations. In the case of the Church of England the recommended minimum in 1975 of £1,846 was over £400 below the minimum in the Church of Scotland. In fact, about one-third of the parish clergy received less than the recommended minimum, while the average stipend paid to parish clergy was about £2,000, or about £250 below the Church of Scotland minimum.

TABLE 76
A comparison of the minimum stipends paid in several United Kingdom churches, 1975 and 1976

	Church of Scotland	Church of England	Scottish Episcopal Church	Baptist Church	Free Church
	£	£	£	£	£
1975	2,258	1,846*	1,812	1,650	1,750
1976	2,560	–	2,226	–	1,750

*Recommended minimum

The minimum stipend of the Church of Scotland is approached most closely by that of the Scottish Episcopal Church. In 1976 the minimum stipend in that Church was £2,226, or £334 below the minimum in the Church of Scotland. On the other hand, the Free Churches appear to have much lower stipends. The minimum stipend of the Baptist Union in 1975 was £1,650, while that of the Free Church was £1,750 in both 1975 and 1976.

Since stipend payments form a large proportion of total expenditure in most Churches, the level at which the minimum stipend is set is often taken as an indicator of the financial health of the Church. By this measure the Church of Scotland, where stipend payments account for about a quater of total income, is in a comparatively favourable position.

However, viewed from a different standpoint the position is less good. In the *Basis and Plan of Union* of 1929 the Church gave the Maintenance of the Ministry Committee the target of raising the minimum stipend from the existing level of £300 (with a manse) to £400 (with a manse) at 1929 prices. However, according to information published by the Maintenance of the Ministry Committee,[4] over the forty years or more since 1929 the money value of the minimum stipend has been increased at such a rate as to keep it roughly in line with the equivalent of £300 in 1929 prices, but at no time has it approached the £400 equivalent. Indeed, during the late 1940s, 1950s and early 1960s the minimum stipend fell below the £300 equivalent, and only rose above it in the second half of the 1960s. Over the same period the incomes of most professional groups have increased substantially in real terms (i.e. faster than the rise in prices), so that the income position of ministers has declined seriously relative to those professional groups. Whereas in 1929 the minister was one of the more affluent members of the community, his total income now (including the non-stipend elements) is broadly equivalent to that of a middle-range professional man.

Evidence on the progress made in the minimum stipend in recent years is given in table 77. Column 1 shows that over the period 1961 to 1976 the minimum stipend increased by more than three times from £800 in 1961 to £2,560 (including the £100 car maintenance allowance) in 1976. Column 2 shows the value of the Retail Prices Index for each year over the same period, while Column 3 gives the minimum stipend inflated to 1976 prices by means of the Index. These figures indicate that the real value of the minimum stipend has fluctuated within a comparatively narrow range over the period 1961-76. From a value of £2,580 in 1961 it followed a cyclical pattern, reaching a peak of £2,811 in 1973, and then dropping back to £2,560 in 1976, a figure which is just below the 1961 real value.

TABLE 77
Changes in the minimum stipend in money and real terms, and compared to average earnings, 1961-76.

	Minimum stipend	Retail Prices Index* (Jan. 1962 = 100)	Minimum stipend at 1976 prices	Index of minimum stipend (1966 = 100)	Retail Prices Index (1966 = 100)	Index of average earnings[Ø] (Jan. 1966 = 100)
	1	2	3	4	5	6
	£		£			
1961	800	–	–	80	–	–
1962	870	101.6	2,580	87	87	–
1963	900	103.6	2,617	90	89	84.3
1964	925	107.0	2,605	93	92	90.3
1965	950	112.1	2,553	95	96	97.0
1966	1,000	116.5	2,586	100	100	103.3
1967	1,100[+]	119.4	2,776	110	102	106.7
1968	1,150	125.0	2,772	115	107	115.3
1969	1,200	131.8	2,743	120	113	124.3
1970	1,250	140.2	2,686	125	120	139.3
1971	1,392	153.4	2,734	139	132	155.1
1972	1,500	164.3	2,751	150	141	175.1
1973	1,674	179.4	2,811	167	154	198.2
1974	1,872	208.2	2,709	187	179	233.3
1975	2,258	258.7	2,630	226	222	295.7
1976	2,560[x]	301.3	2,560	246	259	341.8

*SOURCE: *Department of Employment Gazette,* vol. 85, no. 3 (1977), p. 324, table 132.
[Ø] ibid., p. 319, table 127.
[+] Increase deferred for six months until 1st July 1967 because of prices and incomes standstill
[x] Includes the car maintenance allowance of £100.

In charting the changes in stipend over time, it is important to remember that the travelling expenses incurred by a minister in carrying out his pastoral duties (up to a maximum mileage) were added in 1963 to the Listed Expenses which congregations are expected to pay for, or on behalf of, their ministers. This addition to the Listed Expenses more or less ended the old distinction between stipend and salary which was discussed above. Consequently, the income of ministers on the minimum stipend was effectively increased by more than the £30 rise in the minimum stipend in 1963, since a portion of the stipend of the previous year would in many cases have been spent by the minister on travelling expenses.[5] However, the making compulsory of travelling expenses on congregations could only be effective for minimum stipend charges if guaranteed by the Maintenance of the Ministry Committee. Since in many aid-receiving congregations the extra expense could only be met from income which otherwise would have been allocated to stipend, the amount of aid received had to be increased. This consideration probably explains why the minimum stipend was increased by relatively small sums in 1964 and 1965.

A further consideration in examining the changes in the Minimum Stipend in recent years is that seniority payments, or payments for years of service, were made to ministers over the period 1966-70. By increasing the stipend of some ministers, they had the effect of reducing the minimum stipend below what it might otherwise have been during the period of operation.

In its 1965 Report to the General Assembly, the Maintenance of the Ministry Committee presented some draft regulations governing the minimum stipend.[6] Note (c) to these regulations was as follows: 'In every revision of the appropriate stipend, etc., figures the aim shall always be to provide a standard minimum stipend which has the same purchasing power as will have the minimum stipend of £1,000 in 1966. This shall also apply to any revisal of appropriate stipends in the upper brackets.'

In table 77 we examine whether the target of maintaining the minimum stipend in real terms at 1966 prices has actually been attained. Columns 4 and 5 give an index of the minimum stipend and the Retail Price Index respectively, both indices being based on 1966 = 100. A comparison of these two indices indicates that in 1967 the Minimum Stipend Index increased sharply by ten points, as compared to only two points for the Retail Price Index. In subsequent years the Minimum Stipend Index stayed ahead of the Retail Price Index, but was finally overhauled in 1976. Thus apart from the very end of the period, the committee has exceeded its target, in that the living standard of ministers in absolute terms has been better than in 1966.

However, the living standard of ministers has declined seriously relative to other groups over the same period. This is shown by a comparison of the Minimum Stipend Index with the index of average earnings given in Column 6 of table 77. Over the period 1963-76 the Minimum Stipend Index increased by 173.3 per cent, as compared to an increase of 305.5 per cent in the average earnings index. These represent annual compound rates of increase of approximately 8 per cent and 11¼ per cent respectively.

It can be argued that the relative income position of ministers should not be allowed to decline further (but see the proposals for changes in the minimum stipend system in section 6, *2* below). If this end was agreed, then the policy of the Maintenance of the Ministry Committee would be as far as possible to increase the level of the minimum stipend in line with the growth of average earnings in the community as a whole, i.e. at about 11 per cent a year. However, the success of such a policy depends upon the progress made in improving the financial position of the Church. This responsibility rests as much with the congregations as with the central authorities of the Church. The Church's financial position can be improved by a variety of means, including more effective fund-raising in the congregations, which should increase Church income at a faster rate, and by the policy of union and readjustment which holds down expenditure by reducing the number of ministers and charges to be supported. Much can be done to encourage fund-raising in the congregations by the publicizing of suitable methods by the Stewardship and Budget Committee.[7] We suspect, however, that the present arrangements for stipend in the Church, while admirable in certain respects, may tend to discourage active fund-raising in many congregations. This problem is discussed in sections 5 and 6 below, when proposals for changing the present stipend arrangements are suggested.

4 A cross-section analysis of stipend, 1973
The purpose of this section is to present a cross-section analysis of the stipends of

a sample of charges. The aim of the analysis is to examine how closely stipend is related to the financial position of the charge and to the experience of the minister. This is done through the fitting of linear regression lines by means of least squares regression analysis. The sample used is the 34 charges employed in section 2 above (shown in table 72), but reduced to 28 charges by the exclusion of six that paid no stipend in 1973 because they were vacant. Data for each of the 28 charges in the sample was compiled for the following variables, all the data relating to 1973:

S = the stipend of the charge, as given in the 1975 *Yearbook* 'List of Synods, Presbyteries and Parishes'.

I = the total income of the charge from parish sources as given in the *Schedule of Financial Statistics*, returned annually to the General Treasurer's Department. This includes endowment income for stipend, but excludes aid received (if any) from the Fund for the Maintenance of the Ministry.

E = the expenditure on the upkeep of the congregation, as shown on the expenditure side of the balance sheet in the charge's annual statement of accounts. This includes aid received (if any) and endowment income for stipend, but excludes aid given and all payments for extra-parochial work carried out by the Mission and Service Fund and by outside charities.[8]

M = the number of members and adherents of the congregation, as given in the *Schedule of Financial Statistics*.

MM = the appropriate aid to be given to (+) or received from (−) the maintenance of the Ministry Fund, as given in the *Reports to the General Assembly*, 1974, table A.

ORD = The number of years the minister has been ordained, as given in the *1975 Yearbook*.

IND = the number of years since the minister was inducted into the charge, as given in the *1975 Yearbook*.

The first four equations relate stipend to various financial indicators of the charge. All prove to be significant, with low standard errors (in brackets) for both intercept (a) and b terms and high R^2. The equation relating stipend to the income of the charge is as follows:

$$S = 1530.0 + 0.04986 I \qquad \ldots \qquad (13)$$
$$\quad\;\;(40.66)\;\;\;(0.00461)$$
$$R^2 = 0.818$$
$$F = 116.7$$

Equation (13) is plotted in Figure 21 (i). It shows that a good estimate of the stipend of a charge in 1973 can be calculated by adding about five pence (0.04986p) for every £ of income of the charge to the base sum of £1,530. The 5p in the £ might be looked upon as a kind of commission to the stipend of the minister who is successful at fund-raising. The actual minimum stipend in 1973 was £1,674, or rather above the value of the intercept term in the equation, as shown in figure 21(i). This is probably explained by the fact that at low levels of income all the ministers concerned will be on the minimum stipend, whereas at higher

FIGURE 21. Linear regressions of stipend against congregational income, expenditure, membership, and aid for a sample of charges, 1973.

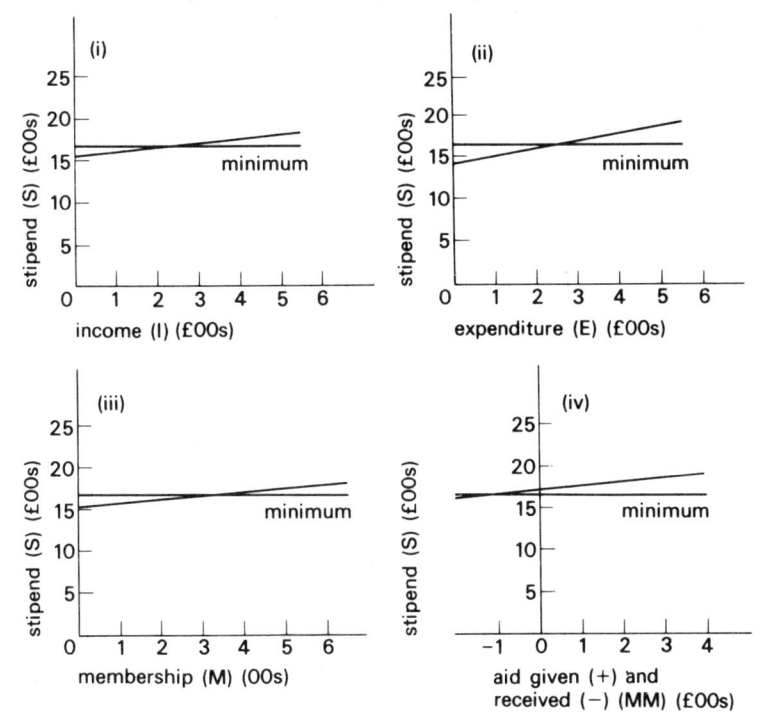

levels of income the stipend may tend to rise well above the Minimum. The slightly lower than expected intercept term may thus be the result of fitting a straight line to a scatter of points which is slightly curved. Nonetheless, the fit of the line is very good.

The equation relating stipend to expenditure is as follows:

$$S = 1437.0 + 0.9138E \qquad \ldots \qquad (14)$$
$$(44.78) \quad (0.00788)$$
$$R^2 = 0.838$$
$$F = 134.2$$

The relationship between stipend and congregational expenditure is also very close; but this was not unexpected, as stipend forms a substantial proportion of expenditure. The equation is plotted in figure 21(ii). It suggests that a good estimate of the stipend in a particular charge in 1973 can be made by adding about nine pence (0.09138p) for every £ of expenditure to a base figure of £1,437.

The equation giving stipend as a function of the number of members is as follows:

$$S = 1531.0 + 0.4117M \qquad \ldots \qquad (15)$$
$$(48.43) \quad (0.04604)$$
$$R^2 = 0.754$$
$$F = 79.87$$

Since we know from our work on congregational finance that congregational income is closely related to the number of members,[9] and from equation (13) above that stipend and income are closely correlated, it is not surprising that there is a similarly close relationship between stipend and membership. The equation suggests that a good estimate of the stipend of a charge in 1973 can be made by adding about 41 pence (0.4117p) for every member and adherent to a base figure of £1,531. As with the income equation (13) the base figure is below the 1973 minimum stipend, and the explanation is probably the same as that given in the analysis of that equation. The membership equation is plotted in figure 21 (iii).

The fourth equation relates stipend to the appropriate aid to be given or received in 1973 as follows:

$$S = 1730.0 + 0.5120 MM \quad \ldots \quad (16)$$
$$\quad\quad (34.48) \quad (0.06064)$$
$$R^2 = 0.733$$
$$F = 71.27$$

The equation indicates that the stipend of a charge in 1973 can be estimated by adding about 51 pence (0.512p) for every £1 of aid given (or subtracting 0.512p for every £1 of aid received) to a base figure of £1,730. The equation is plotted in figure 21(iv). Again, the fit of the equation is good.

Equations (13) to (16) thus show that the stipend which a charge pays its ministers is closely related to the level of its income. Moreover, since congregational expenditure and the number of members are closely correlated to income, and the appropriate aid given or received to the difference between income and expenditure, it is not surprising that stipend is also closely related to these three factors.

The last two equations examine the extent to which the stipend a minister receives is related to his experience in the parish ministry. Experience can be measured by the number of years since the minister was ordained, and the number of years since he was inducted to his present charge. For the ministers in the sample of 28 charges in 1973, it was found that the average period of ordination was 19.46 years, with a range from 2 to 38 years. The average period since the last induction was 9.35 years, with a range from 2 to 23 years. The equations estimated were as follows:

$$S = 1687.1 + 10.165 ORD \quad \ldots \quad (17)$$
$$\quad\quad (97.68) \quad (4.267)$$
$$R^2 = 0.179$$

$$S = 1785.1 + 10.452 IND \quad \ldots \quad (18)$$
$$\quad\quad (89.27) \quad (7.534)$$
$$R^2 = 0.069$$

In both cases the R^2 is very low and the value of the b term is insignificant. The stipend a minister receives thus appears not to be related at all to his experience in the ministry. This result is somewhat surprising, for, although it is recognized that the stipend system in the Church is based largely on the ability of the charge to pay, rather than on the requirements and seniority of the minister, it was thought that senior and experienced ministers would tend to gravitate to the more affluent charges which pay higher stipends. The results of the two equations suggest that this is not the case.

5 Principles of stipend

The guiding principles of stipend in the Church of Scotland are that it shall be fixed in accordance with the financial resources of the charge, and that this is done by the Presbytery in conjunction with the Maintenance of the Ministry Committee.[10] The implication is that the voluntary principle (i.e. that the charge pays the minister a stipend that it can afford) is dominant. This is confirmed by the closeness of the statistical relationship between the stipend and the income and expenditure of charges shown in the previous section. The main exception to the full exercise of the voluntary principle arises from the fact that a minimum stipend is declared each year. Since as many as one-third of the charges in the Church are unable to pay their minister the minimum from their own resources, a significant amount of subsidization of stipend does occur. The amount of the subsidy is increased by the supplementary payments which are paid to certain ministers, many of them on the minimum stipend in aid-receiving charges. The subsidization principle may be taken as the reverse of the voluntary principle.

The extent of the subsidization of stipend is revealed by the following breakdown of total stipend payments of the Church in 1975:[11]

	£	%
Congregational contributions	3,117,272	77.5
Endowments for stipend	543,079	13.5
Aid from Minimum Stipend Fund	362,128	9.0
TOTAL	4,022,479	100.0

The figures indicate that the payment of aid from the Minimum Stipend Fund amounted to £362,128, or to 9.0 per cent of the total stipend payments of £4,022,479. Endowments for stipend accounted for a further 13.5 per cent of total stipend payments, while the bulk of such payments — 77.5 per cent — derived from direct congregational contributions. In addition, aid-giving charges contributed £456,000 in aid to the Fund in 1975.

In our view the present system of payment of stipend, admirable as it is in many respects, may of its nature tend to act as a disincentive to fund-raising efforts by congregations. The reasons for this belief are as follows:

(i) A certain 'subsidy mindedness' appears to exist in some long-standing aid-receiving congregations; this situation is partly induced by the 'poverty trap' in which such congregations find themselves. Even if they manage to raise their income, the amount of the subsidy they receive from the Minimum Stipend Fund is reduced accordingly, so that they are no better off unless they can wipe out the subsidy altogether. Also, the minister's stipend cannot normally be increased above the minimum while the charge remains aid-receiving, so that there is no incentive to the minister to engage in fund-raising activities. These factors may discourage fund-raising efforts by such charges; indeed, there is some evidence to suggest that elements of congregational income may be concealed by some aid-receiving charges in order to avoid a reduction in the amount of aid received.

(ii) The aid-receiving congregations are subsidised through the aid given by aid-giving congregations. These aid-giving congregations may at present pay a relatively high marginal rate of levy of aid (especially if the Mission and

Service fund contribution is included), i.e. a large proportion of each extra pound of income raised is taken in the levy. This being the case, aid-giving congregations may also face some disincentive to fund-raising.

(iii) Although a young minister is relatively well off compared to his peers, in most cases his relative income position steadily worsens with age. This is partly because most stipends are on or very close to the minimum, and partly because there is almost no link between the stipend a minister receives and his experience in the job. At the same time the lack of an explicit link between increases in the income of the charge and increases in his stipend may discourage fund-raising efforts, in so far as they are instigated and encouraged by the minister. It is often said that the interests of the minister is an important factor in determining the success of a charge in stewardship and fund-raising.

It is extremely difficult, owing to the nature of these arguments, to offer convincing scientific evidence that they are valid. However, there is a body of opinion which holds that individuals and institutions do respond to economic incentives. We tend to the opinion that the financial position of the ministry would be strengthened, and the level of stipend raised more quickly, if the voluntarist principle was to be further emphasized, and the amount of subsidization was in consequence to be reduced as far as possible. It is often said that the financial strength of the congregations in the pre-1929 United Free Church arose from the voluntarist principle, enforced by the fact that those congregations had no endowment income on which to rely. We recommend, therefore, that the various proposals for stipend currently under consideration should be judged in the light of the extent to which they enhance the voluntarist principle.

Local circumstances

The proposals for stipend broadly fall into two categories: those which seek to relate the stipend to the circumstances of the minister, and those which seek to relate the stipend to the circumstances of the charge.

An example of the first type of proposal is given by the overture on stipends presented to the 1975 General Assembly by the Presbytery of Glasgow. The overture suggested, amongst other things, that a system of seniority payments, children's allowances and responsibility payments should be added to the stipend structure. The difficulties of introducing such payments and allowances have been clearly laid out by Rev. H.C.M. Eggo in his memorandum on stipend.[12] Seniority payments were made in the period 1966-70. They were discontinued on the grounds that the benefits were small, because the payments for years of service to some ministers had the effect of depressing the minimum stipend, and thus the income of many young ministers. On the question of children's allowances, it is argued that to superimpose such allowances for ministers upon the present state allowances would place ministers in a privileged position *vis-à-vis* the members of their congregation, and that this would harm the social witness of the Church. For the same reason the committee could not agree to the introduction of family allowances in its *Report to the General Assembly* of 1965. Finally, the introduction of responsibility payments is rejected on the grounds that there is no common denominator by which responsibility can be assessed.

According to our criteria, however, the greatest drawback of a proposal to relate stipend more closely to the circumstances of the minister is that it is likely to result in a greater amount of subsidization of stipend, and thus a withdrawal from the voluntary principle. This would arise because many of the ministers who would benefit under such a proposal would be in minimum stipend charges, many of which would be aid-receiving. The aid paid to these charges would have to be increased, and this would require greater amounts of aid to be given by aid-giving charges. In our view, proposals which lead to an increase in the amounts of aid given and received are likely to have an adverse effect on congregational fund-raising, and for that reason should be avoided. Such proposals are also likely to be resisted by the aid-giving charges who would have to supply the additional aid to the fund.

The proposals for stipend which we favour are those which seek to relate the stipend to the financial position of the charge, a feature which already exists to a considerable extent in the stipend structure. We believe that by putting the emphasis even more strongly on self-support, congregations would be encouraged to seek ways of improving their financial position. Two such proposals are put forward in the following section.

6 Proposals for stipend

In this section we examine two proposals for stipend which are designed to enhance the voluntary principle outlined above. These proposals could be implemented separately or together. The first proposal concerns the reallocation of the standardized stipend, and possibly the other endowment stipend, to aid-receiving charges. The second discusses modifications to the present policy on the minimum stipend which are designed to link stipends more closely to the financial position of charges. Each proposal is examined in turn.

1 Reallocation of endowment stipend

The present procedure with regard to the standardized stipend was described in the previous chapter. When a charge falls vacant its standardized stipend is subject to reallocation to other charges. The reallocation normally only occurs within 'the area of preference', which is 'the parish or its neighbourhood'. In recent years the amount of reallocation has been small. A similar procedure applies to Exchequer grants, but not to the other types of endowment stipend, e.g. Exchequer livings, burgh stipends, further and basal endowment, etc.

The proposals examined here involve a large change in present practice. The standardized stipend, and possibly all endowment stipend, would be transferred to a central pool, from whence it would be reallocated, preference being give to aid-receiving charges. The effect of the reallocation would be to reduce, and possibly eliminate, all payments of aid-receiving congregations: such congregations would become just self-supporting. The amount of aid given by aid-giving congregations would also be reduced. The total amount of subsidization of stipend would thus be greatly reduced, and with it the associated disincentives to fund-raising. The process by which many aid-giving congregations would lose a part, or all, of their endowment stipend can be compared to a lump-sum tax, which would have no disincentive effect. It is not certain whether this change in policy towards the reallocation of the standardized stipend could be accomplished within the terms of the Church of Scotland (Property and Endowments) Act, 1925, or whether amending legislation would be required.[13]

The proposal would effect charges in different ways, depending upon their financial position at the time the reorganization is carried out. A variety of cases would arise, as follows:

A *Self-supporting charges* (i.e. neither giving to, nor receiving aid from, the fund)
(i) those which have no standardized stipend would not be affected by the reorganization;
(ii) those having standardized stipend would retain it, so that their positions would remain unchanged.

B *Aid-giving charges*
(i) those which have no standardized stipend would not be effected by the reorganization;
(ii) those with standardized stipend *less* than the aid given would lose *all* of the standardized stipend, and the amount of aid given would be reduced accordingly. For example, a charge with standardized stipend of £200 and appropriate aid of £300 would, as a result of the reorganization, lose all of its standardized stipend and have its appropriate aid reduced to £100. The disposable (or 'after tax') income of the charge would not be changed, but the marginal rate of 'tax' on aid would be reduced;
(iii) those with standardized stipend *greater* than the aid given would give up an amount of standardized stipend equivalent to the aid given. For example, a charge with standardized stipend of £350 and appropriate aid of £250 would lose standardized stipend worth £250, and would become just self-supporting. As in the last case, the disposable income of the charge would not be changed, but the marginal rate of 'tax' on aid would be reduced.

C *Aid-receiving charges*
(i) those having no standardized stipend would receive an allocation equal to the amount of aid received;
(ii) those having standardized stipend would retain it, and receive an additional allocation equivalent to the amount of appropriate aid received.

All aid-receiving charges (*c*) would thus become just self-supporting, providing that sufficient standardized stipend was available for reallocation. This would depend upon the amount of standardized stipend given up by the aid-giving charges (*b* (ii), (iii)). This question was put to the test with a sample of 157 congregations, divided into five classes and representative of the Church as a whole. Data was collected for each of the congregations for 1973 with respect to the amount of aid given to or drawn from the fund, and the amount of endowment stipend.[14] The effect of the proposal on each of the congregations, and for each of the five classes of congregations, was then calculated, from which it was possible to estimate the position for all 1,647 congregations in the Church. The results are summarized in table 78. Column 1 shows for each of the five classes and for the Church as a whole the numbers of congregations in the sample and the total number. Column 2 shows in respect of each class the aid drawn by the sample of congregations, the aid drawn per congregation, and the estimated total aid drawn by all the congregations in the class. Similarly, column 3 indicates for each class the stipend endowments which could be relinquished by the aid-giving congregations under the proposal, firstly for the sample, then the average figure, and finally the estimated total for the class.

TABLE 78

Estimating the impact of the proposal to reallocate endowment stipend, based on a sample of 157 congregations, 1973.

Classification of congregations	Number of congregations 1	Aid drawn by aid-receiving congregations 2	Endowments yielded by aid-giving congregations 3
		£	£
UNITED			
sample	32	419.0	7,263.0
average	1	13.1	227.0
total	76	995.6	17,252.0
LINKED			
sample	29	7,400.0	2,807.0
average	1	255.2	96.8
total	206	52,571.2	19,940.8
RURAL			
sample	31	6,717.0	3,349.0
average	1	216.7	108.0
total	666	144,322.2	71,928.0
SMALL TOWN			
sample	33	775.0	5,716.0
average	1	23.5	173.2
total	276	6,486.0	47,803.2
URBAN			
sample	32	1,587.0	5,517.0
average	1	49.6	172.4
total	423	20,980.8	72,925.2
AGGREGATE			
sample	157	—	—
average	1	—	—
total	1,647	225,355.8	229,849.2

The aggregate estimates suggest that in 1973 the endowment stipend that would have been relinquished by aid-giving congregations under the proposal would have amounted to £229,849, a figure slightly in excess of the aid drawn by aid-receiving congregations of £225,356. It appears, therefore, that the scheme might have produced the desired effect in 1973 providing that all endowment stipend, and not just the standardized stipend, had been included.

However, the high rates of inflation experienced since 1973 may have changed the situation significantly. The amount of aid drawn by aid-receiving congregations has increased sharply. At the same time, the volume of aid given by aid-giving congregations will also have risen, and this will mean an increase in the transfer of endowments in those congregations where in 1973 endowments were greater than the appropriate aid figure. But the money value of such endowments will have changed little. On balance, therefore, it seems likely that the situation has deteriorated somewhat since 1973, and that it may not still be possible to eliminate all of the aid drawn. However, this could only be confirmed by a further detailed examination using up-to-date information.

Even if the ideal position of eliminating all of the aid drawn could still be achieved, the position might be difficult to maintain, for in an inflationary world the real value of standardized stipend endowments would continue to decline.[15] Against this, however, would have to be placed a number of off-setting factors:

(i) The continuing decline in the number of congregations through the policy of union and readjustment will result in the endowment stipend becoming more concentrated.

(ii) The criteria used in the reallocation of standardized stipend on a vacancy occurring would be changed under the proposal. Aid-giving charges would be required to relinquish a part or all of their standardized stipend. They would lose an amount equivalent either to the total standardized stipend held or to the aid given, whichever is the smaller (as in b (ii) and (iii) above). Standardized stipend would no longer be reallocated to the 'parish or its neighbourhood', but only to aid-receiving congregations.

(iii) If the proposal has the desired effect of improving fund-raising in the congregations, then the chances of many self-supporting congregations slipping back into an aid-receiving position should be much reduced.

(iv) The funds currently used by the Committee for Further and Basal Endowments could be used entirely for increasing the endowments of aid-receiving congregations, provided certain conditions were met.

(v) The previous two points could be reinforced by imposing stringent conditions on a congregation which requested aid. The fund-raising methods, organization and account balances of the charge could be subject to searching scrutiny by the Committee on the Maintenance of the Ministry and by the Presbytery of the bounds. The charge could be compelled to undertake a fund-raising campaign organized with the help of the Stewardship and Budget Committee.

(vi) In order to reduce the financial strain on charges which are barely self-supporting, and which are on the minimum stipend, a policy of restraining increases in the minimum stipend might be introduced. Such charges would also be helped if the supplementary payments, many of which are made to ministers in linked minimum stipend charges which are aid-receiving, were to be discontinued. These and other questions are discussed in the context of the second proposal.

2 Proposals for change in the minimum stipend system
These proposals for change in the minimum stipend system are presented here partly as an alternative to the previous proposal on endowment stipend, in that they assume, for example, the continued existence of a large number of aid-receiving congregations. However, they would fit in very well with the previous one. The prime purpose of the proposals is to reduce the amount of subsidization of stipend by reducing the amounts of aid given by aid-giving congregations, and drawn by aid-receiving congregations. A further aim is to make explicit the link which already exists between the stipend and the total income of a charge.

The proposals are as follows:
(i) All supplementary payments would be discontinued. These payments are made largely to minimum stipend charges, many of which are aid-receiving.

The effect of this proposal would be to reduce the amount of aid drawn from the fund, and to shift a number of the congregations concerned to a self-supporting position.

(ii) All aid-receiving and self-supporting charges would automatically be minimum stipend charges. The effect of this proposal would be more or less to regularize present practice.

(iii) The minimum stipend would be increased in money terms from year to year, as at present. The rate of increase in the minimum would be less than the rate of increase in total Church income. Thus if the income of the Church should in the future rise significantly in real terms from year to year, the minimum stipend might be increased at such a rate as to maintain its real value. If total Church income should only be maintained in real terms, then the real value of the minimum stipend would be allowed to fall.

The effect of proposals (i), (ii) and (iii) would be to reduce the strain on the minimum stipend fund and aid-giving congregations of supporting the minimum stipend in aid-receiving congregations. Over a period of time many marginal aid-receiving congregations would become self-supporting and even small givers of aid, thereby rising out of the 'poverty trap'. The marginal rate of levy of aid from aid-giving congregations would be reduced, so encouraging their fund-raising activities.

Also, aid-receiving congregations would be pressured into improving their financial position since they might find it more difficult to attract and keep a minister on the less attractive minimum stipend, while a continuing vacancy would render them liable to some form of readjustment.

(iv) Aid-giving congregations would be able, and should be encouraged, to increase the margin by which the stipends of their ministers exceeds the minimum. This would reverse the trend towards a narrowing of the differential between the minimum stipend and the maximum stipends paid, which we consider to be desirable. The proposal should also encourage a larger number of stipends in the middle range.

(v) Proposal (iv) could be reinforced by a ruling to the effect that, while aid-giving charges would be free to determine the stipend of their minister in consultation with the Presbytery of the bounds and the Committee on the Maintenance of the Ministry, they could not pay a stipend *less* than that determined by the following formula: the minimum plus 5p for every £1 by which the income of the charge exceeds, say, £4,500. The figure of £4,500 is not exact, but it is roughly equivalent to the income of the average self-supporting charge in the previous year. The figure would be linked to the Retail Price Index and changed each year.

It is likely that the suggested formula underestimates the likely stipend payments of aid-giving charges in most cases, which is probably desirable. The main advantage of the proposal, however, is that it makes explicit the link between the stipend of a charge and the income of that charge. Thus a successful minister who managed to raise the income of his charge above £4,500, always assuming that the charge is aid-giving, would receive a proportion of the increase (5 per cent) above £4,500.

(vi) The emphasis placed upon the level of the minimum stipend declared each year should be reduced. The anticipated level of the average stipend to be paid in the Church should be given equal, if not greater, publicity. Under these proposals, the average level of stipend should increase more quickly than the minimum stipend.

It is important to note that these proposals for changes in the minimum stipend system do not alter the basic structure of the system. Neither the operation of the appropriate stipend scheme nor the Minimum Stipend Fund would be changed if the proposals were to be implemented. Some may find the proposals rather strong, but we feel that they are necessary to ensure that all congregations contribute to stipend up to the limit of their capacity in the straitened financial circumstances in which the Church finds itself.

7 Conclusions

In this chapter we have carried out a statistical analysis of stipend, leading in the later sections to two sets of proposals for modifications to the present stipend system.

We started in section 2 by assessing the total income of ministers, which comprises not only the stipend, but also income in kind derived from the manse and from certain other benefits. A difficulty lies in the fact that some items are difficult to value (e.g. non-contributory pension), and other benefits are received by only a proportion of ministers (e.g. free cars in the special areas, car grants etc.). The minimum stipend declared for 1976 was £2,460, plus £100 car maintenance allowance. From a representative sample of 34 charges it was found that 13 (38.2 per cent) had stipends on the minimum, although in 4 cases supplementary payments were made; 53 per cent of the charges had stipends between the minimum and £3,000; and the remaining 8.8 per cent had stipends over £3,000, the highest being £3,880. The differential of 80.0 per cent between the highest stipend paid (£4,428) and the minimum was less than expected. The average stipend in the sample was £2,688, or £228 above the minimum.

We suggested that the average minister would have a manse of average value, which was put at £18,000. It was estimated that the annual opportunity cost of such a house (i.e. rent, rates, insurance, maintenance and running costs, and loss of tax allowance) would be £1,826. Such a minister would probably also receive a car depreciation allowance of £100. These items together give a total measurable income for the average minister of £4,714 in 1976. A pension contribution amounting to 15 per cent of the previous year's stipend, or £373, was also paid by the congregation on his behalf.

Similar estimates were made for the total income of a minister on the minimum stipend in a rural charge, and for a minister in an affluent city-centre charge. The figures produced were £4,206 and £6,326 respectively. Nearly all the variation is accounted for by differences in the stipend and opportunity cost of the manses. In all three cases stipend forms about 60 per cent of total income.

Comparisons were made between the estimated total income figures of ministers and the current salary scales of university academic staff, after making allowance for the different pension contributions. It was found that the total income of ministers coincided with the middle range of academic staff salaries, i.e. from about the mid-lecturer scale to the mid-senior lecturer scale. The range of ministerial income is thus a good deal smaller than that of university staff.

Stipend is the major element in the total income of ministers. The minimum stipend is usually taken as an indicator of the financial position both of ministers, and of the Church through its ability to pay its servants a reasonable money income. In section 3 we found that, although the minimum stipend is higher today than in any of the other major British churches, the relative income position of ministers has deteriorated seriously over the years since 1929. While the real value of the minimum stipend has roughly maintained its level of £300 in 1929, the incomes of other professional people have increased substantially in real terms; thus, whereas in 1929 the stipend of the minister alone made him one of the more affluent members of the community, his total income today (including the manse and allowances) is the equivalent of that of a middle-range professional man. The deteriorating relative income position of ministers has continued in recent years, despite the fact that the value of the minimum stipend has increased faster since the mid-1960s than at any time since 1929. Over the period from 1963 to 1976 the minimum stipend increased by 220.0 per cent, as compared to an increase in average earnings of 305.5 per cent.

In section 4 the statistical part of the chapter was completed with a cross-section analysis of stipend, using the sample of 34 charges for 1973. The analysis found very close positive linear relationships between stipend and the four independent variables representing the financial position of charges — income, expenditure, members and 'appropriate' aid. In all four equations the standard errors of the intercept (a) and b terms were significant, and the R^2 varied between 0.73 and 0.84. These results indicate that the stipend system in the Church of Scotland is based largely on the ability of the charge to pay.

We also examined whether stipend is related to the experience of the minister, as measured by the number of years since ordination, and the number of years since the last induction. It was thought that although stipend is charge-related, the more experienced ministers would tend to gravitate to the wealthier charges. This hypothesis was disproved as there appeared to be virtually no link between stipend and ministerial experience.

The principles used in fixing stipend were discussed in section 5. It was found that all but 9.0 per cent of the total stipend payment in the Church in 1975 was paid by congregations from their own resources (including endowments). This further confirms that voluntarism is the guiding principle used in the fixing of stipends. However, we argued that the subsidization of stipend which does occur may discourage fund-raising in many charges. This results from the 'poverty trap' situation of aid-receiving charges, and the possibly high marginal rate of levy faced by aid-giving congregations. It was also suggested that the lack of an explicit link between changes in the income of a charge and changes in the stipend paid might put fund-raising low on the priority of ministers.

It was argued that these disincentives might be removed by modifying the present stipend system in such a way as to reduce or eliminate subsidization of stipend, thereby further emphasizing the voluntary principle. Proposals for relating stipend more closely to the minister were rejected, in that they would have the reverse effect.

In section 6 we examined two sets of proposals designed to enhance the voluntary principle. The first concerned the re-allocation of endowment stipend from aid-giving to aid-receiving charges, the amount of aid given and received in each case being reduced accordingly. It was estimated that in 1973 there would have been a sufficiently large transfer of endowment stipend to eliminate completely the aid received by deficit congregations, thus making such charges just self-supporting. This should have had a beneficial effect on the fund-raising efforts of such charges, as well as on the more affluent charges whose marginal rate of levy would be reduced. However, it is uncertain whether this position was still achievable after the rapid inflation since 1973, or could be maintained with the continued decline of the real value of endowments through inflation in future years.

Under the second set of proposals all supplementary payments would be discontinued, and all aid-receiving and self-supporting charges would automatically be minimum stipend charges. The money figure of the minimum stipend would in future years be increased at a slower rate than total Church income, so that it might not maintain its real value if Church income did not increase sufficiently quickly. These proposals should have the effect of substantially reducing the rate of increase in the total aid received by aid-drawing congregations. The amount of aid required from aid-giving charges would therefore increase more slowly, allowing such charges to increase the stipends paid to their own ministers more quickly, and thus restoring differentials. The proportion of subsidised stipend in total stipend payments should be reduced, with beneficial effects on fund-raising. It was also suggested that the link between changes in the income of a charge and changes in stipend should be made explicit. This could be done by means of a formula by which the stipend of a charge could be calculated from its income.

Notes

1 See chapter 12, table 92, p. 282.

2 Church of Scotland, *Housing for the Ministry Memorandum no 3*, (Church and Ministry department, 1973), p. 1.

3 At present, retiring ministers generally take one of three options. About a half of them apply for a loan from the Housing and Loan Fund for Retired Ministers and Widows of Ministers. The loan is charged at 2½ per cent interest (1% for widows), and the original capital sum is repaid from the estate of the minister at his death (or his widow when she dies). A further quarter of retiring ministers apply for local authority housing. A final quarter make their own arrangements; for example, some young ministers have their own cottages which they are in the process of renovating.

4 Church of Scotland, 'Report of the Committee on the Maintenance of the Ministry,' *Reports to the General Assembly, 1973*, p. 242.

5 Some congregation deferred starting the payment of travelling expenses to their ministers until after 1963, in a number of cases by a matter of years.

6 'Report of the Committee on the Maintenance of the Ministry', *Reports to the General Assembly, 1965*, appendix iii, pp. 90-2.

7 Measures to improve Church stewardship and fund-raising are examined in chapter 17.

8 An analysis of congregational finance is presented in the following chapter, where these terms are explained more fully.

9 See Chapter 12, pp. 283-6.

10 Eggo, *Memorandum on Stipend*, op. cit., p. 2.

11 SOURCE: Minutes of the Committee on the Maintenance of the Ministry, 18.2.76, in the *Church and Ministry Departmental Files*, pp. 711-14. The figure for the congregational contributions is an estimated figure.

12 Eggo, pp. 4-9.

13 This proposal raises certain legal problems which we do not enter into here.

14 SOURCE: *Reports to the General Assembly, 1974*, table A, pp. 593-639.

15 Losses have also been suffered from the redemption of feuduties arising out of the compulsory acquisition of derelict property, and from redemption under the recent legislation to end the present Scottish system of land tenure, when feuduties have been redeemed at less than their book value. See: 'Report of the Committee on the Maintenance of the Ministry', *Reports to the General Assembly, 1975*, p. 163.

Chapter 12

Congregational finance

1 Introduction

So far we have seen that the congregations raise the bulk of the income of the Church in the form of congregational income or liberality, and that they are required to make certain contributions from this income to the central authorities. The major contributions are made to the Maintenance of the Ministry Fund in respect of stipend, and to the Mission and Service Fund in support of the wider work of the Church; congregations also make contributions to the General Purposes Fund to meet the expenses of the General Assembly, the committees without funds and other objects; and they pay Synod and Presbytery dues to meet the costs of those courts within whose bounds they are situated. The residual income is used to meet the various expenses of the congregation. Superimposed upon this general pattern is the wide variations between congregations in urban and rural districts, and between the different regions of Scotland.

The purpose of this chapter is to undertake a statistical analysis of congregational finance. In section 2 we examine the geographical distribution of members and congregations by Presbytery and Synod. The resulting variations in the size and financial viability of congregations in different districts and regions of Scotland leads us to formulate a theory of congregational finance; this is developed and tested in section 3. The importance of such a theory is that it enables predictions to be made of the effects of alternative policies, particularly with regard to union and readjustment.

In section 4 an effort is made to calculate the income of congregations derived from various subsidiary funds which does not normally appear in the congregational returns of income to the central authorities. Finally, in section 5 a list of recommendations on the presentation and auditing of congregational accounts is made.

2 Regional variations in membership and finance

The purpose of this section is to investigate the membership and finance of congregations as aggregated and averaged by Presbytery and Synod.[1] Since individual Presbyteries and Synods often cover districts and regions of Scotland which exhibit roughly similar characteristics, it is possible to examine the resulting variations in the financial viability of congregations in different parts of the country. For example, in 1973 there were presbyteries covering city and urban districts like those of Edinburgh, Glasgow, Hamilton, Aberdeen and Dundee; then there are Presbyteries in the remote rural areas of the Highlands and Islands, such as those of Sutherland, Orkney, Shetland, Mull, Skye, Uist, and Argyll. A further broad category of Presbytery may be discerned in those covering small towns and villages in a rural setting, and would include those of Peebles, Annandale, St Andrews and Turriff. In this way, indications of regional variations in the financial position of the ministry should come to light.

In 1973 there were 12 Synods, 58 Presbyteries and 2,018 congregations in the Church of Scotland in Scotland; the 59th Presbytery, that of England, had eleven congregations. In Scotland the average number of congregations per Presbytery was 35. The Presbyteries of Orkney, Shetland, and England are not part of any Synod, although each has synodical powers. In the following tables these three small Presbyteries have been included in the Synod of Ross, Sutherland and Caithness (XII). The ten Synods composed of more than one Presbytery had an average of between five and six Presbyteries (or about 200 congregations) each.

Table 79 shows the frequency distribution of the number of congregations per Presbytery. The distribution exhibits a marked positive skew, with 41 of the 59 Presbyteries having less than the average number of congregations of 34. Consequently, the range of the distribution is very large, with the Presbytery of Islay having only seven congregations, and the three largest Presbyteries of Glasgow, Edinburgh and Hamilton having 212, 115 and 102 congregations respectively.

TABLE 79
The frequency distribution of the number of congregations per Presbytery, 1973

Congregations per Presbytery	Numbers
0 – 10	6
11 – 20	15
21 – 30	16
31 – 40	6
41 – 50	6
51 – 60	3
61 – 70	3
71 – 80	0
81 – 90	1
over 90	3
TOTAL	59

The large Presbyteries tend to cover urban areas having a high density of population, and therefore of congregations. The Presbyteries of Glasgow (212 congregations), Edinburgh (115), Aberdeen (81) and Dundee (70), which cover the four cities of Scotland account for 478 congregations, or 23.6 per cent of the total of 2,029. The four Synods in which the four 'city' Presbyteries are found – those of Lothian and Tweeddale (I), Clydesdale (V), Angus and Mearns (IX), and Aberdeen (X) – account for 1,111 or 54.8 per cent of the total number of congregations. The territorial boundaries of these Synods are shown on the map in figure 22.

270   *The Church of Scotland: An Economic Survey*

FIGURE 22:   A map of Scotland showing the four 'city' Synods

```
I   Edinburgh
V   Clydesdale
IX  Angus and Mearns
X   Aberdeen
(The boundaries of the Synods
are approximate)
```

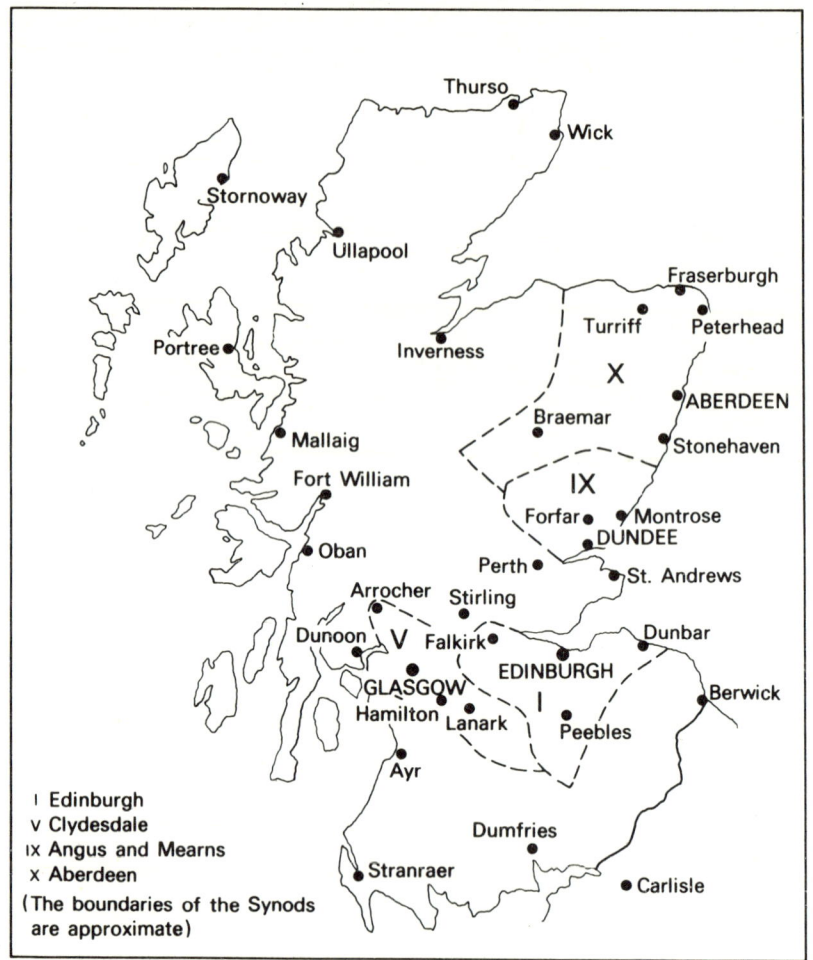

The frequency distribution of membership by Presbytery is given in table 80. The distribution exhibits a marked positive skew, with 40 of the 59 Presbyteries having less than the average membership of 18,533. This again seems to reflect the concentration of membership in a few large urban Presbyteries. Thus the four 'city' Presbyteries account for 353,701 members, or 32.2 per cent of the total membership in 1973 of 1,093,459. Moreover, the four Synods in which those Presbyteries are found take up 730,964 members, or 66.8 per cent of the total. The largest Presbytery in terms of membership is that of Glasgow, with 140,543 members; the smallest is that of Lochcarron, with 309.

The frequency distribution of the average membership per congregation by Presbytery is given in table 81. The average congregational membership by Presbytery in 1973 was 539, but 42 of the 59 Presbyteries fell below the average,

TABLE 80.
The frequency distribution of Presbytery memberships, 1973

Membership by Presbytery (000s)	Numbers
under 5	16
over 5 – 15	20
over 15 – 25	10
over 25 – 35	4
over 35 – 45	4
over 45 – 55	1
over 55	4
TOTAL	59

again indicating a marked positive skew in the distribution. There seems to be a tendency for the large congregations to be found in urban areas, since the four 'city' Presbyteries all have average congregational memberships well above the mean, including the two largest of Edinburgh (841) and Aberdeen (820). Similarly, the four 'city' Synods have an average congregational membership of 658, or more than a fifth (22.1 per cent) above the average. This contrasts with an average congregational membership of only 149 in the Synod of Ross, Sutherland and Caithness (XII, Figure 23) (excluding the Presbytery of England), which covers a large part of the really remote areas of Scotland.

It would be interesting to compare the membership figures with the actual population figures by Presbytery, but these are not easily available. However, the Committee of Forty has produced figures which suggest that the four 'city' presbyteries account for 35.0 per cent of the Scottish population.[2] This compares roughly with the 32.3 per cent of the membership of the Church in those Presbyteries, which seems to indicate the broad comparability of membership rates in urban and rural areas.

The Committee of Forty has also estimated that as a rough guide: 'the Church may expect to have one full-time ordained minister to every 7,500 people in urban

TABLE 81.
The frequency distribution of the average membership per congregation by Presbytery, 1973

Average congregational membership by Presbytery (00s)	Numbers
under 1	6
over 1 – 2	8
over 2 – 3	3
over 3 – 4	10
over 4 – 5	11
over 5 – 6	4
over 6 – 7	10
over 7 – 8	5
over 8 – 9	2
TOTAL	59

272   *The Church of Scotland: An Economic Survey*

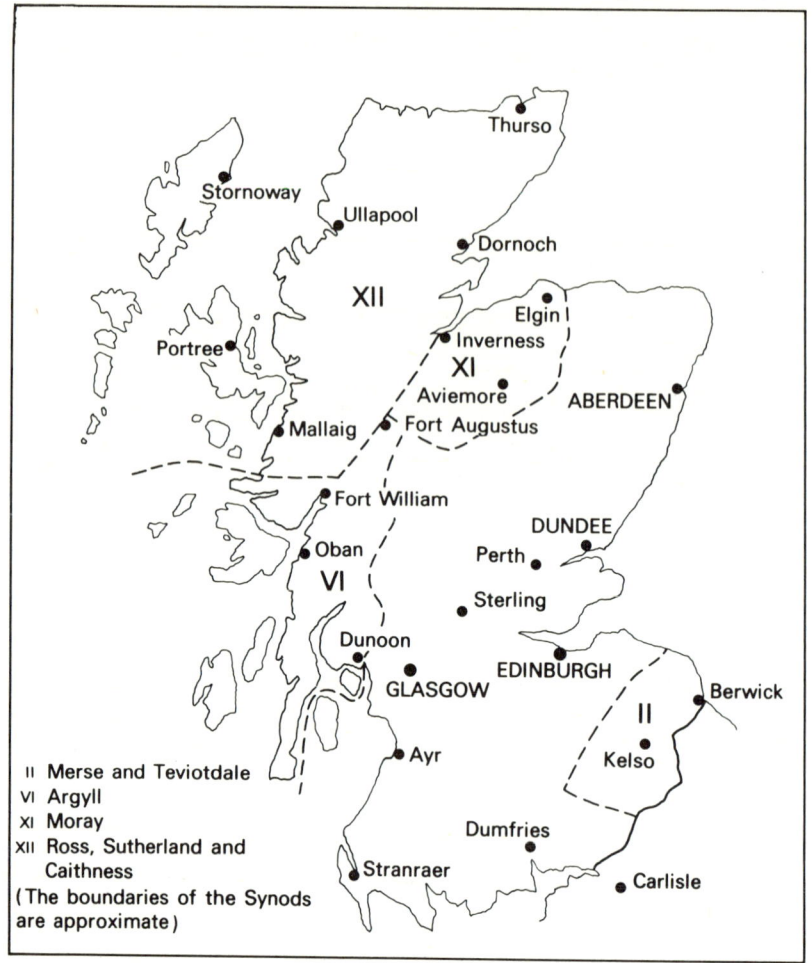

FIGURE 23:   A map of Scotland showing the four net aid-receiving Synods in 1973

```
II   Merse and Teviotdale
VI   Argyll
XI   Moray
XII  Ross, Sutherland and
     Caithness
(The boundaries of the Synods
are approximate)
```

areas, and one to every 2,500 in rural areas. This ratio excludes ministers of other denominations, and ignores the fact that in some areas many Christians do not belong to the Church of Scotland.'[3]

This imbalance in the distribution of ministers in favour of rural areas results largely from the very uneven geographical distribution of the Scottish population, and reflects the difficulty of the Church in ministering to such a population. We return to a discussion of this topic in chapter 15.

We now consider the income of congregations. Table 82 gives the frequency distribution of the average 'normal liberality' per congregation by Presbytery. The frequency distribution again conforms to the now familiar pattern of a distinct positive skew: while the average congregational 'normal liberality' in 1973 was £3,831, 44 out of the 59 Presbyteries had a lower figure. Broadly speaking, the

Presbyteries covering urban districts tend to have a higher average level of 'normal liberality' per congregation than those in rural districts. Thus the Presbyteries of Edinburgh (£7,015), Glasgow (£5,919), Dundee (£4,590) and Aberdeen (£4,544) all have levels of liberality well above the average, whereas such Presbyteries as those of Duns (£1,327), Annandale (£1,476), Dumfries (£2,004), Lorne and Mull (£1,426), Dunkeld (£1,907), Deeside and Alford (£1,791), Sutherland (£1,300) and Shetland (£1,183) all fall well below the average.

TABLE 82.
The frequency distribution of the 'normal liberality' per congregation by Presbytery, 1973

Normal liberality per congregation by Presbytery (£000s)	Numbers
up to 1	1
over 1 − 2	18
over 2 − 3	17
over 3 − 4	7
over 4 − 5	9
over 5 − 6	5
over 6 − 7	1
over 7 − 8	1
TOTAL	59

The four 'city' Presbyteries contributed £2,750,938, or 35.4 per cent of the total 'normal liberality' of £7,773,214 in 1973. Similarly, the four 'city' Synods accounted for £5,181,066, or 66.7 per cent, of the total liberality. These two percentage figures are very close to the corresponding proportions of total membership in the four Presbyteries and four Synods of 32.3 and 66.8 per cent respectively.

The frequency distribution of the 'normal liberality' per member by Presbytery is shown in table 83. The average contribution per member of 'normal liberality' in 1973 was £7.11. Thirty-one of the 59 Presbyteries had a lower figure than that,

TABLE 83
Frequency distribution of the 'normal liberality' per member by Presbytery, 1973

Normal liberality per member by Presbytery (£)	Numbers
up to 5	4
over 5 − 6	13
over 6 − 7	13
over 7 − 8	9
over 8 − 9	4
over 9 − 10	2
over 10 − 11	1
over 11 − 12	3
over 12 − 13	2
over 13 − 14	0
over 14 − 15	1
over 15	7
TOTAL	59

but the normal positively skewed distribution is disturbed by the presence of seven Presbyteries where the average contribution was greater than £15.00 per member. All seven Presbyteries are found in the Synod of Ross, Sutherland and Caithness (XII), which covers the north-west Highlands (i.e. north of the Great Glen from Fort William to Inverness, but excluding Caithness), Skye and the Outer Hebrides. If the Presbytery of Caithness is included (which had a *per capita* liberality of less than £15), then this region had a normal liberality per member of £20.51 in 1973, which was nearly three times the average for the Church as a whole.

There are a number of possible explanations for this phenomenon. Firstly, it could be argued that, since the liberality per congregation is low in the north-west Highlands because of the small memberships, one or two large gifts by wealthy local patrons in each congregation might bias upwards the contribution per member figure. However, this does not seem to apply in apparently similar remote areas like Orkney and Shetland.

A similar doubt is cast on Barber's 'behaviour setting' theory, which states that the smaller the unit of a voluntary organization, the greater the degree of participation by individual members.[4] Since the average membership per congregation is low both in the north-west Highlands and in Orkney and Shetland, one would expect the high level of personal contributions, which might reflect a high degree of participation in the Church, to be found in both areas. The theory is brought into further doubt by the following statement from the Report of the Committee of Forty: 'It has been suggested that in communities with a population of over 1,000, where the parish church has a membership of some hundreds, the Church is still viable and in many cases very active; but, in the words of the Presbytery of Annandale's Report to the Special Committee on Rural Areas, "at less than 150-200 members, it becomes impossible to find leaders, helpers, beadles, cleaners, organists, Sunday School teachers, Women's Guild members and elders. The problem . . . will have to be solved by means other than the methods we have tried hitherto." The report goes on to suggest a team ministry centred on a burgh and serving a wide rural area.'[5]

A third possible explanation for the high level of giving by members in the north-west Highlands lies in the fact that the area was strongly Free Church. At the time of the Disruption in 1843, nearly all the ministers and their congregations in that area 'went out' from the Church of Scotland to join the Free Church,[6] and that Church has a history of high levels of giving by members since, unlike the Established Church, it had no endowment income (the teinds) on which to rely. This high level of giving is said to have persisted to the present time, although the statistical analysis in section 3 below suggests that this is not the case.

A fourth explanation for the high levels of contributions of church members in the north-west Highlands may be that the phenomenon is more apparent than real. This is because there are proportionately large numbers of adherents, as opposed to communicant members, in the congregations in the Highlands. No returns are made by congregations of the numbers of adherents, but they are said to outnumber members by as much as 2:1 in that area. Assuming that that ratio applies throughout the synod of Ross, Sutherland and Caithness, then the average contribution of communicant members together with the estimated number of adherents was £6.84 in 1973, or a little below the Church average. The presence of adherents in the north-west Highlands and Islands is the most likely explanation of the apparently high levels of giving of communicant members in congregations in that region.

Table 84 shows the breakdown in the numbers of congregations between those which gave aid to the Maintenance of the Ministry Fund, and those which received aid from the fund, in 1973. Out of a total of 2,029 congregations, 1,297, or nearly two-thirds, were aid-givers. The total amount of aid given to the fund was £443,845, or £342.20 per congregation. Aid-receiving congregations numbered 571, or more than a quarter of the total number of congregations. They received a total of £267,718 in Aid, or an average of almost £469 per congregation. The remaining 161 congregations were 'break-even' congregations, forming 8 per cent of the total.

TABLE 84
The numbers of congregations giving aid to, or receiving aid from, the Fund for the Maintenance of the Ministry in 1973

	Congregations numbers	%	Total aid given (+) and received (−)	Average per Congregation
			£	£
Aid-giving	1,297	63.9	+443,845	+342.2
Aid-receiving	571	28.1	−267,718	−468.9
'Break-evens'	161	8.0	—	—
TOTALS	2,029	100.0	+176,127	+86.8

The amounts of aid given or received by the congregations in each Presbytery in 1973 were summed, and the total net figure was divided by the number of congregations to produce the average net aid per congregation given or received by Presbytery. The frequency distribution of these figures are given in table 85. The

TABLE 85.
The average net aid per congregation given to (+) or received from (−) the fund by Presbytery in 1973

Average net aid per congregation given to (+) and drawn from (−) the Fund by Presbytery (£00s)	Numbers
−7 or more	1
less than −7 to −6	2
less than −6 to −5	2
less than −5 to −4	5
less than −4 to −3	1
less than −3 to −2	3
less than −2 to −1	7
less than −1 to 0	9
over 0 to +1	13
over +1 to +2	5
over +2 to +3	7
over +3 to +4	4
TOTAL	59

distribution indicates that 29 Presbyteries were net givers of aid to the fund, and that 30 Presbyteries were net receivers of aid from the fund. In over half of the Presbyteries (34, or 57.6 per cent of the total) the average congregation fell in the range −£200 to +£200. An examination of individual Presbyteries suggested that, broadly speaking, the aid-giving Presbyteries tend to cover urban districts and small towns, while the aid-receiving Presbyteries generally cover rural districts. Thus in the Presbytery of Edinburgh the average congregation contributed £394 of aid to the fund in 1973, which was the highest by any Presbytery, while the congregations in the Presbytery of Shetland received the greatest average amount of aid from the fund, with a figure of £841. In the Church as a whole in 1973, the average congregation contributed £86.80 of aid to the fund.

Although 30 of the 59 Presbyteries drew more aid than they gave, only 22 Presbyteries had more aid-receiving congregations than aid-giving congregations. This seems to reflect the fact that the average aid-receiving congregation receives a good deal more aid than the average aid-giving congregation gives in aid, so that it is possible for a Presbytery (or Synod) to be a net aid-receiver and yet have a preponderance of aid-giving congregations. Thirteen of these 22 Presbyteries are found in just two Synods: Argyll (VI), where 5 of the 6 Presbyteries have a preponderance of aid-receiving congregations, and the Synod of Ross, Sutherland and Caithness (XII), where all ten Presbyteries (including Orkney and Shetland) fall in this category. Table 86 gives details of the numbers of congregations involved. It shows in these two Synods that the ratio of aid-receiving to aid-giving congregations in 1973 was 164:60, or nearly 3 to 1, whereas in the Church as a whole the ratio is reversed, with more than twice as many aid-giving (1,297) as aid-receiving (571) congregations. Thus, while Synods VI and XII jointly account for 11.7 per cent of all the congregations in the Church, they have within their bounds 28.7 per cent of all aid-receiving congregations.

TABLE 86
The synods where the numbers of aid-receiving congregations exceeded aid-giving congregations in 1973

		\multicolumn{4}{c}{Numbers of congregations}
		Total	Aid giving	Aid receiving	'Break-even'
VI	Argyll	88	28	55	5
XII	Ross, Sutherland and Caithness (including Orkney and Shetland)	149	32	109	8
	TOTAL (VI + XII)	237	60	164	13
	GRAND TOTAL	2,029	1,297	571	161
	($\frac{\text{Total}}{\text{Grand Total}} \times 100$)%	11.7	4.6	28.7	8.1

The significance of this analysis is that it indicates a geographical concentration of aid-receiving congregations in the more remote rural areas of the north and west. The Synod of Ross, Sutherland and Caithness covers the mainland and islands lying to the north of the Great Glen (but excluding Mull), as shown in figure 23. The Synod of Argyll covers an adjoining area on the west coast roughly corresponding to the former county of Argyll (including Mull). We have seen already that the congregations in the Synod of Ross, Sutherland and Caithness have the lowest average level of membership of any Synod, and that the Synod of Agryll has the next lowest. This suggests that, because of their low populations, the remote areas of Scotland tend to give rise to congregations with small memberships which are unable to raise sufficient income to maintain their parish church without financial support.

Table 87 gives details of the four Synods which are net aid-receivers, as opposed to the two Synods just discussed which also have a preponderance of aid-receiving charges. Here the Synods of Moray and of Merse and Teviotdale are added to the discussion; the geographical extent of each is shown in figure 23. Moray covers the area on the north-east coast between Inverness and Elgin, and extends as far south as the Spey valley, and almost as far west as Fort Augustus; this area adjoins the north-west Highland region. The Synod of Merse and Teviotdale extends over much of the Borders, including the Teviot valley and the broad lowlands of the Tweed below Selkirk (i.e. the Merse). The Table shows that, despite the large area of Scotland covered by the four Synods, they contain a disproportionately small number of congregations, with only about a fifth (19.7 per cent) of the total. Nonetheless, these congregations accounted for almost a half (46.2 per cent) of the total aid paid by the fund to congregations, and contributed only about a fifteenth (6.4 per cent) of the total aid given by congregations. By far the largest aid receiver is the Synod of Ross, Sutherland and Caithness, which alone accounts for 17.3 per cent of the total aid from the fund. The next largest aid-receiver is Argyll, followed by Moray, and finally by Merse and Teviotdale, the last-named only just being a net aid-receiver in 1973.

TABLE 87.
The Synods which were net receivers of aid from the fund in 1973

		Total aid given (£)	Total aid received (£)	Number of congregations
II	Merse and Teviotdale	8,642	9,039	96
VI	Argyll	6,455	31,131	88
XI	Moray	8,978	12,889	67
XII	Ross, Sutherland and Caithness (including Orkney and Shetland)	4,270	70,582	149
	TOTAL	28,345	123,641	400
	GRAND TOTAL	443,845	267,718	2,029
	$\left(\dfrac{\text{Total}}{\text{Grand Total}} \times 100\right)\%$	6.4	46.2	19.7

Further details are presented in table 88, which shows that the 145 aid-giving congregations in those four Synods gave on average £195.5 of aid each, which was well below the Church average of £342.2 for aid-giving congregations. On the other hand, the 220 aid-receiving congregations each received on average £562.0 of aid, which was well above the Church average of £468.9 for such congregations. This further emphasizes the relative financial weakness of the average congregation in the regions covered by the four Synods.

TABLE 88.
Aid-giving and aid-receiving congregations in the four Synods in 1973*

	Aid-giving congregations	Aid-receiving congregations
Number of congregations in the four Synods	145	220
Average aid per congregation given (+) or drawn (−)	+£195.5	−£562.0
Overall average aid per congregation	+£342.2	−£468.9

*The table excludes the 36 'break-even' congregations.

Finally, we deal with congregational contributions to the Mission and Service Fund, through which the wider work of the Church is financed. Every year a budget for this work is drawn up by the Stewardship and Budget Committee, and the sum is allocated to Presbyteries based on an assessment of the position of groups of congregations of differing financial strengths within their bounds.[7] The budget allocated to congregations in 1973 amounted to £1,450,342, while the sum actually raised by congregations was £1,297,335. This represents a deficit of 10.6 per cent, or an average shortfall of £75.40 per congregation.

Further analysis revealed that 28 of the 59 Presbyteries, or just under half (47.5 per cent), actually reached of exceeded their allocations; 15 of these 28 Presbyteries are found in the four net aid-receiving Synods, and 14 of the 15 are themselves net receivers of aid. The fact that these Presbyteries rely on the Maintenance of the Ministry Fund for financial support, yet give more than their allocation to the Mission and Service Fund, suggests that the former fund is to some extent subsidizing the latter.

TABLE 89.
The Mission and Service Fund allocations and contributions of the four 'city' Presbyteries, 1973

	Amount allocated to Presbyteries 1	Amount contributed by Presbyteries 2	Surplus (+) or shortfall (−) (i.e. $\frac{2-1}{1} \times 100\%$) 3
	£	£	
1 Edinburgh	213,266	203,221	− 4.7
19 Glasgow	281,792	201,821	− 28.4
37 Dundee	58,623	54,127	− 7.7
40 Aberdeen	72,654	71,339	− 1.8
TOTAL	626,335	530,508	− 18.1
GRAND TOTAL	1,450,342	1,297,335	− 10.6
($\frac{\text{Total}}{\text{Grand Total}} \times 100$)%	43.2	40.9	—

Also of interest is the fact that the four 'city' Presbyteries all fell short of their allocations, as shown in table 89. In 1973 they were allocated 43.2 per cent of the Mission and Service Fund budget, but only achieved 40.9 per cent of the total contribution, which was itself more than 10 per cent below the total allocation. The four 'city' Presbyteries in aggregate thus fell 18.1 per cent below their allocation, although the Presbytery of Glasgow was the chief offender, with a shortfall of 28.4 per cent.

Table 90 indicates that the four 'city' Synods received 72.5 per cent of the Mission and Service Fund allocation in 1973. This figure is rather more than their share of the total 'normal liberality' of the Church in 1973, which was 66.7 per cent, and reflects the higher average congregational incomes of urban charges and the broadly progressive nature of the 'levy'.[8] The four Synods together fell 13.1 per cent below their allocation, although the Synod of Aberdeen slightly exceeded its allocation by 0.3 per cent. The Synod of Clydesdale, in which the Presbytery of Glasgow is found, made the largest shortfall of 18.7 per cent. It seems clear that the total contribution to the Mission and Service Fund will always fall below the allocation when the four 'city' Synods, which receive about three-quarters of the allocation, themselves fall well below the allocation. Their aggregate shortfall of 13.1 per cent exceeds that of the Church as a whole at 10.6 per cent. In fact, if these four Synods had reached their allocation in full in 1973, the total contribution to the Mission and Service Fund would have fallen short of the total allocation by only £14,895, or 1.0 per cent. This illustrates the disproportionate effect which the four 'city' Synods have on the finances of the Mission and Service Fund.

TABLE 90.
The Mission and Service Fund allocations and contributions of the four 'city' Synods, 1973

		Amount allocated to Synods 1	Amount contributed by Synods 2	Surplus (+) or shortfall (−) (i.e. $\frac{2-1}{1} \times 100\%$) 3
		£	£	
I	Lothian and Tweeddale	304,363	276,067	− 9.3
V	Clydesdale	554,420	450,950	− 18.7
IX	Angus and Mearns	87,387	80,707	− 7.6
X	Aberdeen	105,130	105,464	+ 0.3
	TOTAL	1,051,300	913,188	− 13.1
	GRAND TOTAL	1,450,342	1,297,335	− 10.6
$(\frac{\text{Total}}{\text{Grand Total}} \times 100)\%$		72.5	70.4	—

The picture which emerges from this examination of the membership and financial position of congregations in the Church as aggregated by Presbytery and Synod is the relative dominance of the four 'city' Presbyteries and Synods, and the relative financial weakness of the congregations in the thinly populated rural areas. Table 91 provides the basic statistics for a comparison of the four 'city' Presbyteries and Synods with the four rural Synods which are net receivers of aid from the fund. The table shows that in 1973 the four 'city' Presbyteries accounted for nearly a quarter of all congregations, almost one-third of the total Church membership, over one-third of 'normal liberality', about two-fifths of the aid given to the fund, and just over two-fifths of the Mission and Service Fund contribution. The districts covered by the four Presbyteries also contained approximately 35 per cent of the population of Scotland.

TABLE 91.
The significance in Church finance of certain urban and rural Presbyteries and Synods in 1973

	Church totals	Four 'city' Presbyteries* numbers	% of total	Four 'city' Synods+ numbers	% of total	Four rural Synods× numbers	% of total
Congregations	2,029	478	23.6	1,111	54.8	411	20.3
Members	1,093,459	353,701	32.3	730,964	66.8	96,023	8.8
'Normal liberality'	£7,773,214	2,750,938	35.4	5,181,066	66.7	847,396	10.9
Aid given	£ 443,845	175,516	39.5	311,036	70.1	31,416	7.1
Aid received	£ 267,718	39,058	14.6	98,711	36.9	126,261	47.2
Mission and Service fund contribution	£1,297,335	530,508	40.9	913,188	70.4	109,114	8.4

* Edinburgh, Glasgow, Dundee and Aberdeen.
+ Edinburgh, Clydesdale, Angus and Mearns, and Aberdeen.
× Merse and Teviotdale; Argyll; Moray; and Ross, Sutherland and Caithness.

The position of the four 'city' Synods is even more dominant. In 1973 they accounted for well over half of the total number of congregations, two-thirds of the membership and 'normal liberality', and 70 per cent of the aid given to the fund and the Mission and Service Fund contribution. By contrast, the four rural Synods contain a fifth of the congregations – a little less than the four 'city' Presbyteries – but only one-twelfth of the membership. They accounted for only 10.9 per cent of normal liberality, contributed only 8.4 per cent of the Mission and Service Fund contribution, and received nearly half (47.2 per cent) of the total aid paid from the Maintenance of the Ministry Fund.

The evidence examined thus far seems to suggest the theory that the financial position of the congregation is to an important extent determined by the size of the membership, and that the membership of a congregation is probably some function of the population in the parish. In rural areas, therefore, the small populations lead to low congregational memberships, which in turn give rise to small incomes per congregation and a preponderance of aid-receiving congregations. In urban areas, on the other hand, the large populations produce relatively large memberships, which lead to high incomes per congregation and a preponderance of aid-giving congregations. In the following section we attempt to test this theory statistically.

3 A statistical analysis of congregational finance

In this section is presented a cross-sectional statistical analysis of congregational finance, the aim being to test the theory that the financial position of a congregation depends to a large extent on the size of the membership. We deal in turn with the following topics: the samples of congregations and data collected, congregational income, congregational expenditure, and the financial break-even position. The implications of the theory for the organization of the ministry are then discussed. Finally, the limitations of this model are made clear, and we examine the possibilities of an alternative simultaneous equation model.

1 The samples and data collection
A list of congregations in the Church of Scotland is available in the Presbytery lists published annually in the *Church of Scotland Yearbook*. We were able to obtain an updated version of the lists from the Church and Ministry Department which was correct at the time of collection in December 1974. This updated list constitutes the sampling frame; vacant congregations have been excluded, so that it includes only those congregations with an incumbent minister. Of the 2,042 congregations on the Presbytery list there were 141 vacant, leaving a total from which the sample was extracted of 1,901.

In order to ensure that different types of charge were represented, the congregations were stratified into five categories according to three stratification factors:
(i) *Recently united congregations.* These are defined as those unions which had taken place over the previous five-year period between 1 January 1970 and 12 December 1974. Only recent unions were taken because it was thought that any special features which united congregations might exhibit would be lost after several years of union. There are 76 congregations (or charges) in this category.
(ii) *Linked congregations,* of which there are 460 (in 206 charges).
(iii) *Urban, small-town, and rural congregations.* These remaining congregations were stratified according to their geographical situation. The stratification is based on the number of charges found under the place-name of each local town, village or settlement, as given in the Presbytery lists. Rural charges are defined as all those charges found under local place-names where there are one or two charges only; small-town charges are defined as including those charges found under the place-names of larger settlements with between three and ten charges inclusive; and, finally, urban charges are defined as those remaining charges found in large towns and cities where there are eleven or more charges covered by the same place-name. The numbers of congregations in the rural, small-town and urban groups were 666, 276 and 423 respectively.

However, the definitions are rather arbitrary, since the size of a settlement is not necessarily accurately measured by the number of charges found in it, nor is the size of a settlement necessarily a good proxy measure for social, economic and other factors which may have a bearing on the membership and finance of the local congregations. Nonetheless, it was thought that the classification would be sufficient to indicate any broad differences between the three groups of congregations.

Three different random samples of congregations were taken from the sampling frame. The purpose to which each was put will emerge during the analysis below:
Sample 1: a weighted sample of 40 congregations taken from the full sampling

frame, as shown in table 92. The correspondence of the percentage representation of the five groups of congregations in the weighted sample to that in the Church as a whole is close, apart from a slight under-representation of united congregations. This is caused by the small number of congregations in the united group relative to the other groups.

TABLE 92.
A weighted sample of 40 congregations (sample 1) +

Congregations	Church			Weighted sample	
	nos		%	nos	%
United	76	(76*)	4.0	1	2.5
Linked	460	(206*)	24.2	10	25.0
Rural	666	(666*)	35.0	14	35.0
Small-town	276	(276*)	14.5	6	15.0
Urban	423	(423*)	22.3	9	22.5
	1,901	(1,647*)	100.0	40	100.0
Vacant	141	(121*)			
GRAND TOTAL	2,042	(1,768*)			

+ Information on one rural congregation was unobtainable, reducing the sample to 39 congregations.
* Number of charges

Sample 2: the 29 non-linked congregations in sample 1.

Sample 3: a sample of 31 linked congregations (in 15 charges). Unfortunately incomplete information for a number of congregations reduced the size of the sample to 23. Ten of these congregations are the linked congregations in sample 1.

For each of the fifty-two congregations involved in the three samples, data was compiled for the following variables, all relating to 1973:

I: The total income of the congregation from parish sources as provided by the Schedule of Financial Statistics returned annually to the General Treasurer's Department. Separate income received by the subsidiary accounts (see below, section 4) of the congregation is excluded, as is aid received (if any) from the Fund for the Maintenance of the Ministry. Endowment income for stipend is included.

E: The expenditure on the upkeep of the congregation, as shown on the expenditure side of the balance sheet in the congregation's annual statement of accounts. This includes aid received (if any) and endowment income for stipend, but excludes aid given and all payments for extra-parochial work done by the Mission and Service Fund and by outside charities.

M: The number of members and adherents of the congregation, as given in the Schedule of Financial Statistics.

MM: The amount of aid given to (+) or received from (−) the Maintenance of the Ministry Fund, as given in the *Reports*.[9]

MSC: The contribution to the Mission and Service Fund of the congregations in 1973, as given in the *Church of Scotland Yearbook* for 1975.

2 Congregational income

In the linear equations which follow, the independent (or 'explanatory') variable is membership (M), and the various dependent variables, such as income (I) and expenditure (E), are distinguished by the subscripts 1, 2 or 3 according to the sample of congregations represented. For example, an equation expressing income (I) as a function of membership (M) for sample 1 would take the following form:

$$I_1 = a + bM$$

where a and b are constants. Once the values of a and b have been computed, the value of I can be found for any value of M by inserting the appropriate value of M into the equation.

The first three equations show income as a function of membership for each of the three samples of congregations, as follows:

$$I_1 = 848.3 + 7.035\,M \qquad \ldots \qquad (19)$$
$$(714.6) \quad (0.7694)$$
$$N = 39$$
$$R^2 = 0.693$$
Durbin-Watson statistic = 3.429

$$I_2 = 1{,}182.0 + 6.811\,M \qquad \ldots \qquad (20)$$
$$(1{,}115.0) \quad (1.043)$$
$$N = 29$$
$$R^2 \quad 0.612$$
Durbin-Watson statistic = 2.252

$$I_3 = 840.2 + 6.858\,M \qquad \ldots \qquad (21)$$
$$(491.7) \quad (2.018)$$
$$N = 23$$
$$R^2 = 0.355$$
Durbin-Watson statistic = 1.092

All three equations are of a similar form with positive a and b constant terms. With the exception of the sample of linked congregations (21), their R^2 values are quite high, indicating that the equations provide a fairly good fit for the data. The a, or intercept, term might be interpreted as representing that portion of congregational income which does not vary with the number of members, such as endowment and investment income. However, the relatively high values of the standard errors (in brackets) in all three equations indicate that the value of the term is not significant. The fact that the value of the a term is higher for non-linked congregations (£1,182.0) than for linked congregations (£840.2) is therefore not important. The value of the b term varies little between the three equations, indicating that the average level of giving by members is not much influenced by whether charges are organised in single or linked congregations. The figures of around £7 per member correspond closely with the Church ordinary liberality per member of £7.04 in 1973.

The R^2 of the equation for the aggregate sample of congregations (19) indicates that 69 per cent of the variation of income among congregations can be 'explained' by variations in the size of the membership. This is a striking result when one considers the diversity of the congregations in the sample, and of the larger population from which they are drawn. An estimate of the income of a congregation for 1973 can therefore be made by adding £7.04 per member (the value of the b coefficient) to a 'base' sum of £848.30. Some examples of the average income of congregations with different levels of membership are given in table 93. A small congregation with a membership of 250 might have had an income of about £2,600 in 1973, whereas a large congregation of 1,500 members would have had an income in the region of £11,400.

TABLE 93.
Estimates of the income of congregations in 1973 with different levels of membership, based on equation (19).

Membership (M)	'Base' or 'fixed' income £	'Variable' income at £7.04 per member £	Total income (I) (i.e. 'base' plus 'variable') £
100	848.30	704.00	1,552.30
250	848.30	1,760.00	2,608.30
500	848.30	3,520.00	4,368.30
750	848.30	5,280.00	6,128.30
1,000	848.30	7,040.00	7,888.30
1,500	848.30	10,560.00	11,408.30
2,000	848.30	14,080.00	14,928.30

One possibility is that the unreliability of the intercept term might be caused by large variations in the endowment and investment income of congregations. Consequently, equation (19) was recalculated with income excluding endowment and investment income (II). The result was as follows:

$$II_1 = 601.0 + 6.389\,M \qquad \ldots \qquad (22)$$
$$(605.3)\ \ (0.6561)$$
$$N = 39$$
$$R^2 = 0.719$$
Durbin-Watson statistic = 3.225

Since endowment and investment income has been excluded, there is no ready interpretation of the a term, which again is insignificant. Hence we might substitute an equation which is forced through the origin (i.e. with zero intercept), and use that as the means of estimating the proportion of congregational income derived from the giving of members. This produces the following equation:

$$I2_1 = 6.8835\,M \qquad \ldots \qquad (23)$$
$$(0.6592)$$
$$N = 39$$
$$R^2 = 0.712$$
Durbin-Watson statistic = 4.879

When endowment and investment income is considered separately, it is found that the distribution of such income amongst the congregations in the aggregate sample exhibits a marked positive skew, as shown in figure 24. The following statistics of the distribution were calculated:

$$\text{mean} = £642.90$$
$$\text{median} = £513.16$$
$$\text{first quartile} = £359.21$$
$$\text{third quartile} = £759.37$$

Assuming that the sample distribution is the same as the population distribution, these figures indicate that the mean level of endowment and investment income is £642.90. In half the congregations the endowment and investment income is less than £513.16 (the median), and in half it is greater than £513.16. All but 25 per cent of congregations will have endowment and investment income of at least £359.21, while only a quarter of congregations will have such income exceeding £759.37.

FIGURE 24: Frequency polygon of endowment and investment income

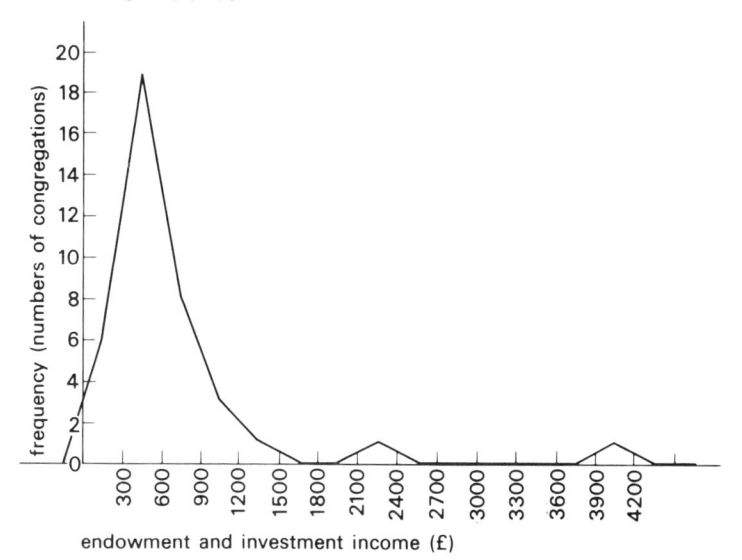

These results for the two components of congregational income can be combined to produce income equations which relate to different groups of congregations according to the size of their endowment and investment incomes. For example, the income equation for a congregation with the mean level of endowment and investment income would be as follows:

$$I3_1 = 642.90 + 6.8835 M \qquad \ldots \qquad (24)$$
$$N = 39$$

Similar composite equations can be constructed for congregations having endowment and investment incomes on the first quartile, the median, and the third quartile.

An alternative approach is to force the total income equation through the origin, which produces the following result:

$$I4_1 = 7.728\,M \qquad \ldots \qquad (25)$$
$$(0.510)$$
$$N = 39$$
$$R^2 = 0.861$$
$$F = 229.60$$

This equation is a distinct improvement on the first equation forced through the origin (equation (23)), the R^2 being 0.861, as against 0.712. It also avoids the problem of the insignificant intercept term, and of calculating the endowment and investment income separately. This equation (25) is selected here as the most appropriate one for forecasting the income of congregations, and is the one used in the subsequent analysis.

While the use of only one 'explanatory' variable — membership — produces results which are highly instructive for the analysis of the financial position of congregations, it is conceivable that the equations might be improved by the addition of other variables. Three such variables were tested, as follows:

(i) It is often claimed in the Church that the historical traditions of congregations affect their income levels, in that congregations which belonged to the former United Free Church tend to have a higher giving per head than those of the pre-1929 Established Church. This was certainly the case in the nineteenth century, when the Free Church congregations, unlike those of the established Church, had no endowment income on which to depend.

(ii) A second factor which might help explain variations in the income of different congregations is whether the congregation is located in an urban or a rural area. It has been suggested that 'religiosity', or church activity, is greater in rural areas, and that this may lead to higher levels of giving per member in rural congregations. For the purposes of the test, a congregation was defined as 'rural' if it was located in a village where it was the only Church of Scotland congregation. 'Urban' congregations made up the rest of the sample.

(iii) The third factor tested for its possible impact on congregational income was deeds of covenant. It was thought that part of the variation in income between congregations might be due to the greater or lesser extent to which members contributed through covenants, since each attracts a tax rebate from the Inland Revenue of about 50 per cent depending upon the base rate of income tax.[10] The variables tested were the amount contributed through Deeds of Covenant, the amount of taxation reclaimed, and the proportion of these taken separately and summed to total income.

All of these variables were subject to the appropriate statistical tests, and all were found to be insignificant, i.e. they had no apparent influence on the level of congregational income.

3 Congregational expenditure

Linear regression equations were also computed for congregational expenditure (E) as a function of membership (M) for each of the samples, with the following results:

$$E_1 = 1262.0 + 4.041\,M \qquad \ldots \qquad (26)$$
$$(372.1) \qquad (0.4007)$$
$$N = 39$$

$$R^2 = 0.734$$
Durbin-Watson statistic = 4.190

$$E_2 = 1469.0 + 3.906\,M \qquad \ldots \qquad (27)$$
$$(578.5) \quad (0.5411)$$
N = 29
$$R^2 = 0.659$$
Durbin-Watson statistic = 2.750

$$E_3 = 829.0 + 4.513\,M \qquad \ldots \qquad (28)$$
$$(152.4) \quad (0.6252)$$
N = 23
$$R^2 = 0.713$$
Durbin-Watson statistic = 4.930

In all three equations the R^2 is reasonably high varying from 0.659 to 0.734, and the standard errors are relatively small, indicating that the equations fit the data well.

The values of the a constant terms may be interpreted as the 'fixed' costs of the congregation, which must be met even when the number of members is reduced to zero. In the case of a non-linked congregation, these costs would include the stipend and expenses of the minister, together with some heating and lighting costs. However, the value of the intercept term in equation (27) of £1,469 is rather lower than anticipated, since the minimum stipend alone in 1973 was larger at £1,674. This may be explained by the fact that, as with the corresponding income equation, the value of the intercept term is not completely reliable, since there are few congregations in the sample with a low membership.

The value of the intercept term of the equation based on the sample of linked congregations (28) is much lower, as was expected. This is because the stipend and expenses of the minister, which are borne by the one congregation in non-linked charges, are shared by the congregations in a linking. Equations (27) and (28) suggest that the fixed cost of a linked congregation is on average little more than half that of a non-linked congregation.

The value of the b term in the expenditure equations is roughly the same in non-linked (£3.906) and linked (£4.513) congregations. This term may be interpreted as representing the 'variable' costs, i.e. those elements of cost which vary with the number of members, which would include part of the upkeep and running costs of buildings (assuming that the size of church buildings is broadly related to the number of members), part of the salary bill of ancillary workers, and expenses such as hymn books, the parish newspaper, and so on.

Equation (27) thus indicates that a fairly good estimate of the expenditure of a non-linked charge in 1973 can be found by adding a 'variable' cost of £3.91 for every member (and adherent) to a 'fixed' cost of £1,469.0. In the case of a linked congregation the annual expenditure can be estimated by adding £4.51 for every member to a fixed cost of £829.0. Examples of the predicted expenditures of non-linked and linked congregations for congregations of different sizes are shown in tables 94 and 95 respectively. It should be remembered that expenditure here is defined as covering only the costs of maintaining the congregation, and excludes aid (if any) given to the Maintenance of the Ministry Fund, Mission and Service

Fund contributions, and other extra-congregational payments. The tables indicate that, with a membership of 500, a non-linked congregation would have had an expenditure of about £3,420 in 1973, whereas a linked congregation's expenditure would have been around £3,085.

TABLE 94.
Estimates of the expenditure of a non-linked congregation in 1973 with increasing levels of membership, based on equation (27)

Membership (M)	'Fixed' cost	'Variable' cost at £3.906 per member	Expenditure (E) (i.e. 'fixed' plus 'variable')
	£	£	£
100	1,469.00	390.60	1,859.60
250	1,469.00	976.50	2,445.50
500	1,469.00	1,953.00	3,422.00
750	1,469.00	2,929.50	4,398.50
1,000	1,469.00	3,906.00	5,375.00
1,500	1,469.00	5,859.00	7,328.00
2,000	1,469.00	7,812.00	9,281.00

TABLE 95.
Estimates of the expenditure of a linked congregation in 1973 with increasing levels of membership based on equation (28)

Membership (M)	'Fixed' cost	'Variable' cost at £4.513 per member	Expenditure (E) (i.e. 'fixed' plus 'variable')
	£	£	£
100	829.00	451.30	1,280.30
250	829.00	1,128.25	1,957.25
500	829.00	2,256.50	3,085.50
750	829.00	3,384.75	4,213.75
1,000	829.00	4,513.00	5,342.00

Equation (26) is the expenditure function for the representative sample, which includes both linked and non-linked congregations. This equation gives rise to an intercept term of £1,262.0 and a b constant term of £4.04, and is plotted in figure 25.

The slope of these regression lines, together with the positive intercepts, reflects economies of scale in the organization of the congregation. Such economies would be indicated by a decline in the expenditure per member as the size of the congregational membership increases. Firstly, a growing congregational membership means that the fixed cost of the congregation, as measured by the value of the intercept term, will be spread over larger and larger numbers of members, so giving rise to economies of scale. Secondly, each new member enrolled causes the annual expenditure of the congregation to rise by the value of the b term. Because b is a constant term, however, there are no economies of scale generated in these variable outlays; economies would be implied by a gradual

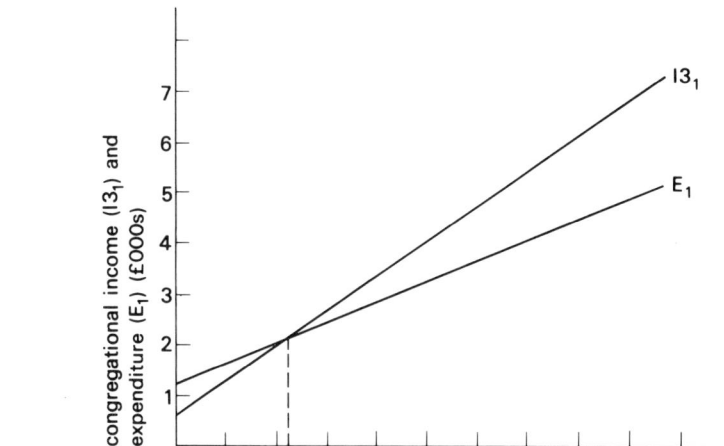

Congregational finance

FIGURE 25: Congregational income and expenditure equations

decline in the value of *b* with increasing membership, and shown graphically by a gradual flattening of the regression line in figure 25. By the same token, there are no diseconomies associated with very large congregations.

Examples of the expenditure per member of congregations of different sizes, based on equation (26), are given in table 96. These indicate that economies of scale are very great in small congregations, but become relatively insignificant for congregations having a membership greater than 500-600. For example, the annual expenditure per member of a congregation with 100 members is estimated to be £16.16, as compared to only £6.56 for a congregation with 500 members. By comparison, the equation suggests that the expenditure per member of a congregation which increased its membership from 1,500 to 2,000 would fall only marginally from £4.88 to £4.67. It seems clear that small congregations are relatively uneconomic in expenditure terms, and that savings would arise if such

TABLE 96.
Estimates of the average expenditure per member of a congregation in 1973 with different levels of membership, based on equation (26)

Membership (M)	Average 'fixed' costs (i.e. $\frac{£1,262.0}{M}$) £	Average 'variable' cost (i.e. £4.04 per member) £	Average expenditure per member (i.e. $\frac{E}{M}$) £
100	12.62	4.04	16.66
250	5.05	4.04	9.09
500	2.52	4.04	6.56
750	1.68	4.04	5.72
1,000	1.26	4.04	5.30
1,500	0.84	4.04	4.88
2,000	0.63	4.04	4.67

congregations could be united or linked with their neighbours to form larger units. We return to this question below.

We also made efforts to find other variables which might have an influence on expenditure, although there were few obvious candidates. Variables linked to the expenses of maintaining and running the buildings of congregations seemed to be the most promising. A short questionnaire was sent to the 39 congregations in the sample, of which 32 duly returned completed questionnaires. Information was elicited on the age of the church building, the seating capacity of the church, and the existence of other buildings. It was hypothesized that expenses on buildings, and therefore total expenditure, would be higher the greater the age of the church building, the greater the size of the building as measured by the seating capacity, and whether there are other buildings to be supported. However, when each of these three variables is related separately to expenditure, only the seating capacity of the church proved to be significant as an explanatory variable. The equation is as follows, where P denotes seating capacity:

$$E_1 = 452.8 + 5.719 P \qquad \ldots \qquad (29)$$
$$(842.10) \quad (1.084)$$
$$N = 32$$
$$R^2 = 0.481$$
$$F = 27.86$$

When seating capacity of the church building is added to membership as 'explanatory' variables of expenditure, the resulting equation is less good than the original expenditure equation.

4 The 'break-even' position

The purpose of this section is to calculate at what number of members (including adherents) a congregation will be, on average, in a financial 'break-even' position, where it neither gives aid to, nor receives aid from, the Fund for the Maintenance of the Ministry. The most obvious way of calculating the 'break-even' point is to regress aid given to (+) or received from (−) the fund (MM) by congregations as a function of their membership (M). The equations estimated for each of the three samples are as follows:

$$MM_1 = -212.6 + 0.6154 M \qquad \ldots \qquad (30)$$
$$(53.75) \quad (0.0579)$$
$$N = 39$$
$$R^2 = 0.753$$
Durbin-Watson statistic = 3.920

$$MM_2 = -239.0 + 0.6336 M \qquad \ldots \qquad (31)$$
$$(78.93) \quad (0.0734)$$
$$N = 29$$
$$R^2 = 0.732$$
Durbin-Watson statistic = 4.232

$$MM_3 = -159.7 + 0.719 M \qquad \ldots \qquad (32)$$
$$(54.85) \quad (0.2251)$$
$$N = 23$$
$$R^2 = 0.327$$
Durbin-Watson statistic = 0.9650

The values of the R² and other statistics are satisfactory in the first two cases, but not in equation (32) for linked congregations. The signs of the coefficients in all three equations are as expected: the negative value of the intercept term indicates that congregations with small memberships on average receive aid from the Fund, while the positive value of the b term shows that the enrolment of extra members serves to reduce the amount of aid received. The 'break-even' point is reached, according to equation (32) for the Church-wide sample, at a membership of 345. In figure 26, this 'break-even' point is found where the MM_1 line cuts the horizontal axis of the graph. Congregations with memberships below 345 tend on average to receive aid from the Maintenance of the Ministry Fund, while congregations with memberships in excess of 345 tend on average to give aid to the fund. The further the membership of a congregation is above or below the figure of 345, the more certain is this forecast likely to apply.

FIGURE 26: The financial 'break-even' membership of congregations

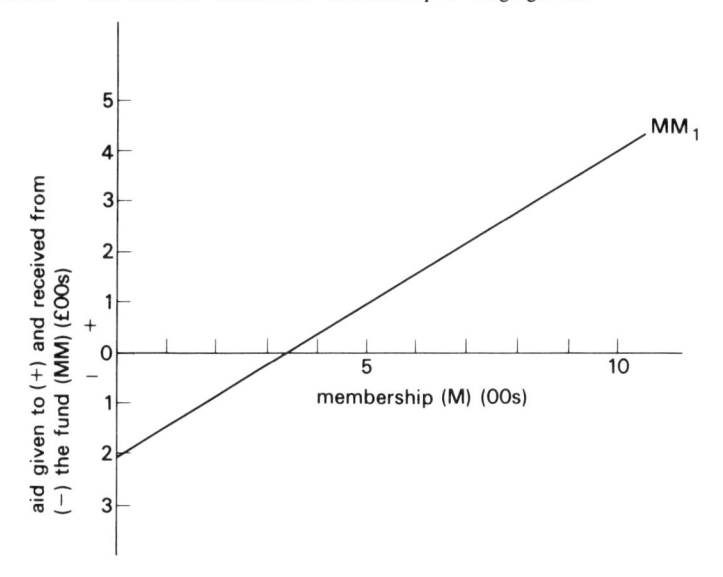

An alternative way of examining the 'break-even' position of congregations, which should produce results similar to equation (30) above, is by relating the income and expenditure equations developed in sections 3.2 and 3 above. Since both sets of equations are correlated significantly with membership, they can be combined in order that the financial position of congregations can be examined.

There are a variety of ways of dealing with the elements of income and expenditure to be included in the equations. In this account we use the expenditure and income equations for the aggregate sample of congregations (1). The various income equations permit a variety of 'break-even' points to be calculated, but for purposes of illustration we start with the equation based on the mean level of endowment and investment income. The income and expenditure equations are therefore as follows:

$$I3_1 = 642.90 + 6.8835M \qquad (24)$$
$$E_1 = 1262.0 + 4.041\,M \qquad (26)$$

Both equations are plotted in figure 25. Since the income line has a lower intercept term and a larger b term than the expenditure line, the two lines intersect. The point of intersection occurs at that level of membership where the income of the congregation exactly balances its expenditure. By justaposing the two equations it is possible to calculate that this financial 'break-even' point occurs at a membership of 218, as shown in figure 25. At lower levels of membership, figure 25 indicates that the expenditure of the congregation exceeds its income, giving rise to a deficit position. This deficit is made up with aid received from the Maintenance of the Ministry Fund. On the other hand, at levels of membership greater than 218, income rises above expenditure, leading to a surplus position; part of this surplus will be given in aid to the Maintenance of the Ministry Fund. The purpose of the fund is thus to transfer aid from the better-off congregations to those which are poorer, in order to ensure that ministers even in the poorest congregations are paid at least the minimum stipend.

The problem to which this analysis gives rise is the discrepancy between the 'break-even' point of 345 members, calculated on the basis of aid given and received, and the mean point of 218 members, based on the intersection of separate income and expenditure equations of congregations. However, on further examination of the data, it was found that both income and expenditure equations were likely to be subject to heteroscedasticity – that is, violation of the assumption underlying the cross-section data that the disturbances in the linear regression model are independently distributed variables with a constant variance (i.e. are homoscedastic). This was confirmed by the application of the Spearman rank correlation coefficient and Goldfeld-Quandt tests. The Glejser test was then applied to identify the mathematical form of the relationship between the disturbance term and the 'explanatory' variable membership. The information gained was then used to make the appropriate transformation to the original model to ensure homoscedasticity. The resulting transformed expenditure equation for sample 1 was as follows:

$$E_1^* = 1{,}185.2 + 4.351\,M \qquad \ldots \qquad (33)$$
$$ (93.64) \quad (0.397)$$
$$N = 39$$
$$R^2 = 0.812$$
$$F = 160.20$$

The appropriate income equation is taken as equation (25), which has been forced through the origin:

$$I4_1 = 7.728\,M \qquad (25)$$

The equation has not been transformed because the degree of heteroscedasticity did not warrant it.

When these two equations are combined, the 'break-even' point at which income equals expenditure is at 351 members. This point is very close to that of 345 calculated by regressing aid given or received against membership.

5 Implications of the theory

The theory of congregational finance outlined and tested above has important

Congregational finance

implications for the structure and organization of the ministry. Because of the high proportion of 'fixed' costs in the annual expenditure of a congregation, those congregations with a small membership of less than about 345 are often unable to raise sufficient income from their own resources to cover their expenses, and so have to rely on aid from the Maintenance of the Ministry Fund to meet the deficit. In contrast, congregations with memberships of medium and large size (i.e. greater than about 345) tend to have a surplus of income over expenditure, and are thus required to give aid to the fund. Table 81 above indicates that 17 presbyteries in 1973 had *average* congregational memberships of 300 or less, and 27 presbyteries had average memberships of 400 or less. It seems clear that, in order to reduce the strain on the fund and on aid-giving congregations of maintaining the minimum stipend in aid-receiving congregations, the small congregations in the Church should as far as possible be merged or linked with their neighbours to form larger and financially more viable units. Considerable progress has already been made in this direction since the Second World War, and the acceleration in the rate of union and readjustment over the next decade forecast in chapter 8 should facilitate continued progress in the future; the economic implications of unions and linkings are examined in chapter 13.

While the evidence suggests that congregations with small memberships should be avoided from the expenditure point of view, it is possible that large congregations may also be undesirable, in that their size hinders the organization of effective fund-raising. To test this hypothesis, an attempt was made to fit a non-linear function to the income-membership relationship. By transforming the original data into logarithms, it is possible to estimate several different forms of curve. By experimentation, it was found that the double log transformation was the most appropriate. The equation produced is as follows:

$$\log I_1 = 1.628 + 0.7485 \log M \qquad \ldots \qquad (34)$$
$$ (0.1620) \quad (0.0597)$$
$$N = 39$$
$$R^2 = 0.810$$
$$F = 157.40$$

The fit of the curve is good, with low standard errors and a high R^2. Since the b term is less than one (0.7485) the slope of the curve increases at a diminishing rate as the number of members increases. This implies that the contribution per member tends to fall as the size of the membership increases. Examples calculated by using the equation are given in table 97. They indicate that the contribution per member in 1973 was likely to fall from £11.2 in small congregations with 250 members, to £8.0 in medium-sized congregations of 750, and to £6.8 in large congregations with a membership of 1,500. These calculations suggest that there are significant diseconomies of scale associated with raising funds in large congregations. However, this should not discourage congregations from attempting to increase their memberships. Over the whole range of membership shown in table 97 from 100 to 2,000 the equations suggest that each additional member adds more to marginal income than he incurs in additional congregational expenditure (marginal cost or average variable cost).[11] These calculations must be distinguished from those involving the enlargement of a congregation as a result of union and readjustment, where the factors involved are rather different.[12]

TABLE 97.
Estimates of the income of congregations in 1973 with different levels of membership, based on equation (34)

Membership (M)	Income of congregation	Income per member
	£	£
100	1,334	13.3
250	2,241	11.2
500	4,448	8.9
750	6,026	8.0
1,000	7,473	7.5
1,500	10,130	6.8
2,000	12,550	6.3

6 An Alternative Model

While the model outlined above has enabled us to go a long way towards understanding congregational finance and explaining variations in the financial positions of different congregations, it may embody assumptions which do not accurately reflect reality. The model assumes, for example, that certain 'necessary' expenditures are required to maintain and run a congregation, and that the size of those expenditures are determined by the number of members. There are certain 'fixed' (or 'overhead') costs which have to be met so long as the congregation continues to function, and the 'variable' (or 'running') costs which increase in proportion to the membership.

In this respect the congregation resembles the business firm; but, whereas the desire to make profits in the business firm ensures that costs are kept down to the minimum 'necessary' level, the same pressure does not necessarily apply in the case of the congregation. In a congregation with a low membership which receives aid from the Maintenance of the Ministry Fund, expenditure is likely to be held down to the 'necessary' level by the scrutiny of the Presbytery and Maintenance of the Ministry Committee; here 'non-necessary' expenses are unlikely to be made, and the congregation will in this respect resemble the business firm. On the other hand, congregations with larger memberships are likely to generate a surplus income, and will not be under the same pressure to curb expenses to the 'necessary' level. A large proportion of the surplus will be contributed as aid to the fund or to the Mission and Service Fund, but the remaining sum will be available for 'non-necessary' expenses. Indeed, the larger and more affluent congregations have in the past been criticized by the Joint Committee of the Maintenance of the Ministry Committee and the Stewardship and Budget Committee for spending on luxuries, and for allocating unduly large sums to Contingency and Fabric Funds. It is possible, therefore, that the expenditure function may show an upward kink at about the 'break-even' level of membership, implying that expenditure may be a function of income rather than membership, i.e. that expenditure is increased to match the available income. This suggests that a simultaneous equation model of congregational income and expenditure may be appropriate. One such model is as follows:

$$I = f(M)$$
$$E = f(I)$$

The equations state that income is a function of membership, and that expenditure is a function of income. Expenditure is thus still related to membership, but now indirectly through the medium of income. There may be a time-lag involved, in that the level of expenditure in a given period may be related to the level of income in a preceding period, the lag arising from the time needed to revise expenditure in line with the actual level of income. A simultaneous equation model embodying a time-lag would become a recursive model. This approach has strong intuitive appeal, in that congregations do tend to budget from year to year with the aim of keeping expenditure within the bounds set by income.

An advantage of recursive models is that ordinary least-squares regression methods for the estimation of parameters (i.e. a and b terms) may be applied. Given the values of the exogenous variables in the first equation, the estimates for the first endogenous variable can be calculated, which can then be used in the second equation to estimate the second endogenous variable, and so on. The equations estimated for the hypothesized model were as follows:

$$I_1^* = 9.694\ M \qquad \ldots \qquad (35)$$
$$(1.163)$$
$$N = 39$$
$$R^2 = 0.768$$
$$F = 69.42$$

$$E_1 = 840.7 + 0.4648\ I \qquad \ldots \qquad (36)$$
$$(148.3) \quad (0.06313)$$
$$N = 39$$
$$R^2 = 0.721$$
$$F = 84.20$$

The income equation is forced through the origin. The R^2 of both equations are quite high, and the constant terms are significant, as indicated by the rela-

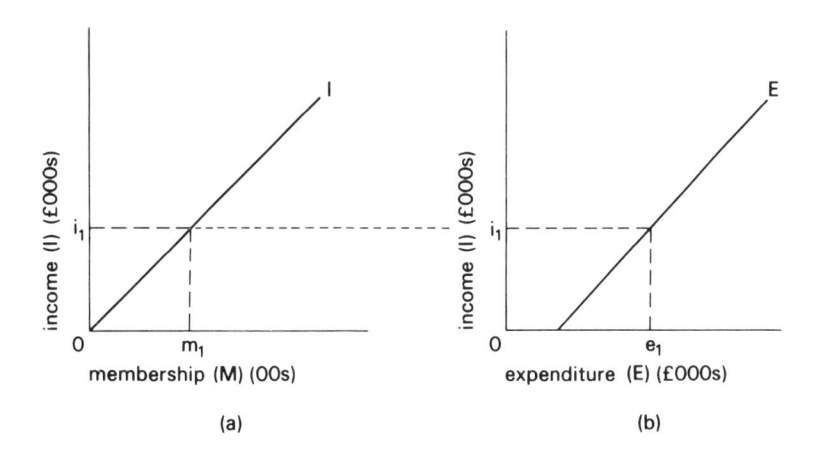

FIGURE 27: The simultaneous equation model of congregational income and expenditure

tively low standard errors. Both equations are plotted in figure 27. Figure 27(a) shows that a membership of m_1 gives rise to an income of i_1, which in figure 27(b) is translated into an expenditure of e_1.

4 An analysis of congregational income

The purpose of this section is to analyse more closely the income of congregations. This is done by comparing the income of a random sample of congregations, as given in their Schedule of Financial Statistic returned to the General Treasurer's Department, with the income as recorded in the congregations' annual accounts which are circulated amongst the membership. All the figures quoted relate to 1973.

The sample of congregations drawn was a stratified random sample reflecting the proportion of recently united, linked, urban, small-town and rural congregations in the Church. Of the thirty-five congregations drawn, two had to be excluded. In the case of one linked congregation, no copy of its accounts for 1973 was available, while for one urban congregation it proved impossible to distinguish between capital balances and income earned.

The Schedule of Financial Statistics requires the itemisation of the income of congregations under receipts for normal purposes, and extraordinary and special receipts. Information on these categories of income is used by the General Finance Committee to calculate the total 'normal' and 'special liberality', or congregational income, of the Church. The receipts for normal purposes are also used by Presbyteries to calculate congregational 'available balances' for the allocation of the Mission and Service Fund budget.[13]

Congregational accounts differ considerably in their presentation. Broadly speaking, however, each account can be divided into two parts – the General Account and Subsidiary Accounts. The General Account is the congregation's balance sheet, which shows the income raised to meet Maintenance of the Ministry expenses, Mission and Service Fund contribution, and much of the expenses of the congregation. The total income figure in the General Account roughly corresponds to that given in the Schedule of Financial Statistics, although it does not usually distinguish between 'normal' and 'special liberality'.

In addition to the General Account, almost all congregational accounts have a number of independent or semi-independent Subsidiary Accounts. These accounts may be divided into two categories. The first category covers those accounts controlled by the body responsible for the management of the financial affairs of the congregation (the Kirk Session, Congregational Board of Management or Deacons' Court), which are sometimes grouped together under the heading of Reserve or Special Accounts; typically such accounts relate to fabric, organ renovation, trust and bequest funds, and benevolent and Kirk Session accounts. The second category of Subsidiary Accounts are those accounts managed independently by affiliated organizations, such as Women's Guilds, Young Wives' and Mothers' clubs, Men's clubs, Sunday School classes, and Boys' Brigades. These accounts may be referred to as Organisation Accounts.

Most of the Subsidiary Accounts have their own sources of income, additional to that income recorded in the General Account or in the Schedule of Financial Statistics. The aim of the study was thus to identify for each congregation in the sample the income accruing to the three categories of accounts: the General

Account, the Reserve or Special Accounts, and the Organization Accounts.

In practice it proved difficult to obtain precise figures for the income accruing to each of the three categories of accounts for all congregations in the sample, because many annual accounts provided incomplete information. For example, some congregations did not include all of the Organization Accounts in the presentation of their annual accounts; this was confirmed by the presence of sums transferred from such accounts and appearing as income in the statements of other accounts. There was similar evidence to suggest that in some congregational accounts only certain Reserve or Special Accounts had been included.

A further difficulty was that some Reserve and Organization Accounts made no distinction between capital balances and the income earned on those balances during the year. This problem appeared most frequently in connection with bequest and trust funds. In other cases, accounts made no mention of the size of capital balances, but recorded only the income earned on the balance. Finally, a few congregational accounts presented income and expenditure statements for only the major Subsidiary Accounts, and only summarized the financial positions of the smaller accounts in terms of the size of the balances at the year end.

Table 98 indicates that a total of 299 Subsidiary Accounts were recorded in the annual accounts of the 33 congregations in the sample. The number of Reserve Accounts was 174, or 58.2 per cent of the total; the number of Organization Accounts 125, or 41.8 per cent of the total. The Reserve Accounts have a higher average income than the Organization Accounts at £185.3 per account, compared to £104.1. The average congregation in the sample had nine Subsidiary Accounts, of which five were Reserve Accounts, and four were Organization Accounts; however, the variation in the numbers of Subsidiary Accounts between congregations was great. In the Reserve category, ten congregations in the sample had fewer than two accounts (including one linked congregation whose annual accounts showed no record of any Subsidiary Account), while nine congregations had eight or more such accounts. The 'Organization' category of Subsidiary Accounts appeared to be absent in fifteen congregations, so that the figure in table 98 of 125 such accounts is provided by just over half the sample of congregations. It seems likely that this figure is a considerable underestimate, and that in many annual accounts the accounts of affiliated organizations are not included. Of the eighteen congregations who did record this type of Subsidiary Account in detail, eight indicated that they had more than eight such accounts.

TABLE 98.

Information on the Subsidiary Accounts which appeared in the annual accounts of the sample of 33 congregations in 1973

	Numbers			Income		
	Total	Average per congregation	%	Total (£)	%	Average income per account (£)
Reserve	174	5.3	58.2	32,246	71.2	185.3
Organization	125	3.8	41.8	13,018	28.8	104.1
TOTAL	299	9.1	100.0	45,264	100.0	151.4

The figures shown in table 98 therefore include only those Subsidiary Accounts for which an itemized income and expenditure statement was given in the annual account. In addition to the 299 Subsidiary Accounts mentioned, another 50 such accounts were traced. Further, it seems clear that other Subsidiary Accounts existed, but were not recorded in the congregational accounts and were not traceable by the method just described. Thus in table 98 the number of Subsidiary Accounts and their income is somewhat understated, although it is probable that most of the large accounts are included in the 229 for which information was available.

In table 99 we attempt to calculate the total income of the sample of congregations in 1973. 'Total income' is defined as that accruing to both the General Account and to the Reserve and Organization Subsidiary Accounts. In order to calculate the income of each of the three categories of accounts, it is necessary to allow for transfers between them. The approach adopted is as follows: where income has been transferred from a Subsidiary Account to the General Account, as for example in the case of a donation by the Women's Guild of the congregation, the transfer is included in the income of the General Account; where transfers occur between two Subsidiary Accounts, the income is attributed to the account which gave it rather than to the account which received it. Finally, the income figures given in table 99 are net of any balances brought forward from previous years.

TABLE 99.
Information on the total income of the sample of 33 congregations, as recorded in their Annual Accounts for 1973

	Total income (£)	Average income per congregation (£)	%
General Account	148,403	4,497	76.7
Subsidiary Accounts			
Reserve	32,246	977	16.6
Organisation	13,018	395	6.8
Sub-total	45,264	1,372	23.4
TOTAL	193,667	5,869	100.0

Table 99 shows that the total income of the 33 congregations in 1973 was £193,667, or £5,869 per congregation. About three-quarters (76.6 per cent) of this income (£148,403, or £4,497 per congregation) appeared in the General Account, and the remaining quarter (23.4 per cent) in the income of Subsidiary Accounts (£45,264, or £1,372 per congregation). Of the £1,372 received by the average congregation through its Subsidiary Accounts, £977 accrued to Reserve Accounts and £395 to Organization Accounts. These figures are only averages, however, and the variation between congregations is large. Moreover, the figures for the average congregation are understated, to the extent that no information was available on the income of a number of Subsidiary Accounts in the sample of congregations.

The income accruing to Subsidiary Accounts (IS) was regressed against membership (M) for the 33 congregations to test the hypothesis that this further category of income is also closely related to membership. The equation produced was as follows:

$$IS = 102.0 + 1.859 M \qquad \ldots \qquad (37)$$
$$(281.0) \quad (0.3244)$$
$$N = 33$$
$$R^2 = 0.515$$
Durbin-Watson statistic = 1.134

The equation indicates that there is a relationship between Subsidiary Account income and membership, but the R^2 of 0.52 is only moderately high. It is possible that the equation might be improved if the data for each congregation were complete. Further, the examination of a scatter diagram of the data suggests that the relationship might be better approximated by a non-linear estimating equation.

From the foregoing analysis it seems clear that the income appearing in a congregation's General Account, which is broadly comparable to the income figure returned in the Schedule of Financial Statistics, forms on average about 75 per cent of its total income. This is not a deliberate understatement of income by congregations, since in the Financial Schedule they are required to return figures of normal and special liberality only. However, the dividing line between what income is included on the Financial Schedule and what is left out appears to be somewhat blurred; for example, in one or two cases the proceeds of exceptional fund-raising efforts have been included in the General Account but not in the Financial Schedule, and, in other cases, the net proceeds of sale of work are given in a Subsidiary Account rather than in the General Account, but the item appears in the Financial Schedule. As a result, in some congregations the Financial Schedule income is greater than the General Account income, and in other cases it is smaller. Since the income returned on the Financial Schedule is used to assess the congregation's Mission and Service Fund allocation, it may be desirable to set out more clearly the items of income which should be included. This would help to ensure that all congregations are treated equally.

In tables 100 and 101 we attempt to calculate the total income of the Church in 1973 to include the income accruing to the Subsidiary Accounts of congregations. This income is normally not included in the congregational income component of total Church income, which is calculated from the 'normal' and 'special liberality' income returned on the Schedule of Financial Statistics. On the other hand, there is a danger of double-counting, in that some of the income of Subsidiary Accounts may be derived from funds invested in the Church of Scotland Trust. Income from the Church of Scotland Trust is included as a separate category of total Church income (see table 13, item 2c, 'Income from Investments'). To the extent that there is an overlap between the estimated Subsidiary Account income and the income from investments, the following calculations will tend to exaggerate the size of the extra income accruing to the Church through Subsidiary Accounts.

In table 100 two different estimates are made of the total income accruing to congregations in 1973. Column 1 shows the total income of the average congregation in 1973, as calculated from the sample of 33 congregations in table 99. In column 2 these figures are multiplied by 2,009, the number of congregations in the Church in 1973, in order to produce a total Church figure. Total congregational income is estimated at £11,790,821, which is composed of £9,034,473 General Account and £2,756,348 Subsidiary Account income. The General Account income should be roughly equivalent to the total liberality figure calculated by the General Finance Committee on the basis of the Financial Schedules. In fact, total liberality in 1973 was £9,258,343, which is only £223,870 (2.5 per cent) greater than the estimate of total General Account income. This result confirms that the sample of 33 congregations is representative of the Church as a whole; it also indicates that the income figures given by congregations in the General Account and Financial Schedule are comparable on average, despite the variations in individual cases.

TABLE 100.
Estimates of Church total congregational income in 1973

Congregational accounts	Estimate I			Estimate II
	Average income per congregation*	1 × 2,009 Congregations in Church	Percentage breakdown in 1	3 × published figure of congregational income in 1973
	1	2	3	4
	£	£	%	£
General account	4,497	9,034,473	76.6	9,258,343
Subsidiary accounts				
Reserve	977	1,962,793	16.6	2,006,377
Organization	395	793,555	6.8	821,889
SUB-TOTAL	1,372	2,756,348	23.4	2,828,266
TOTAL	5,869	11,790,821	100.0	12,086,609

*SOURCE: Table 99, column 2.

An alternative calculation of the total income accruing to congregation in 1973 can be made by assuming that General Account total income is exactly comparable with total liberality. The General Account total income can then be increased to equal the total liberality of £9,258,343. This figure is set equal to 76.6 per cent of the total income of congregation – the proportion of General Account income to total income – and the income of the Subsidiary Accounts is scaled up accordingly, as shown in column 4 of table 100. The resulting estimate of the total income of congregations is £12,086,609.

In table 101 the total income of the Church in 1973 is estimated using the two estimates for total congregational income made in table 100. Column 1 shows that the income recorded by the General Financial Committee for 1973 was £12,918,350, which was composed of £9,258,343 of liberality and £3,660,007 of other income. Column 2 gives the first estimate of total congregational income of £11,790,821, which is 27.4 per cent above the recorded figure. When added to other income, it gives an estimated total Church income of £15,450,828, which is 19.6 per cent above the 1973 recorded figure. The second estimate of total congregational income of £12,086,609, which is 30.5 per cent greater than the

TABLE 101.
Estimates of the actual total income of the Church in 1973

Income categories	Income recorded	Estimate of total income			
		I	Percentage of 1	II	Percentage of 1
	1	2	3	4	5
Congregational income	9,258,343*	11,790,821[+]	127.4	12,086,609[+]	130.5
Other income	3,660,007	3,660,007	100.0	3,660,007	100.0
TOTAL	12,918,350	15,450,828	119.6	15,746,616	121.9

*Calculated by the General Finance Committee on the basis of the Financial Schedules returned by congregations.
[+] Based on alternative definitions of total congregational income (see Table 100).

recorded liberality, is shown in column 4 of table 101. With other income held constant at £3,660,007, the estimate of total Church income in 1973 is £15,746,616 or 21.9 per cent above the recorded figure.

These calculations indicate that the total income of the Church is rather larger than the published figures suggest. Allowing for a possible double-counting of income in Subsidiary Accounts and income from investments on the one hand, with an underestimate of the income of Subsidiary Accounts on the other, it seems likely that the actual figure of Church total income is about 20 per cent above the published figure.

In addition to the income accruing to the various accounts examined above, the accounts also tend to carry forward capital balances from year to year. These balances are defined to include both cash in hand and bank balances held in current and deposit accounts. They have been excluded from the income figures given above, although it is possible in the case of some bequest and trust funds that capital balances held in other forms may have been included in income. A lack of information in the congregational accounts often made it difficult to determine the nature of the balances.

The size of balances carried forward from the previous year (1972), and of balances to be carried forward into the following year (1974), were calculated for each of the three categories of income accounts. The results are summarized in table 102. For the General Accounts of the 33 congregations in the sample, the total balance brought forward from 1972 to 1973 was £7,401.26, giving an average of £224.28 per congregation. The range was from a deficit of £533.00 to a surplus of £1,395.59, with six congregations having balances in excess of £500. An aggregate General Account balance of £7,331.62 was carried forward from 1973 to 1974, an average of £222.17 per congregation. The range was from −£1,600 to £2,095.21, with seven congregations holding balances of over £500. These figures indicate a slight fall of 0.94 per cent in General Account balances in the 33 congregations during 1973.

In Reserve and Special Accounts a total balance of £75,962.62 was transferred from 1972 into 1973, giving an average of £2,301.89 per congregation. The range was from a deficit of £62.64 to a surplus of £11,017.40. Thirteen congregations held balances in excess of £2,500. A balance of £80,952.07 was carried forward from 1973 to 1974, an average of £2,453.09 per congregation. The range was from zero to £8,781.48, with fifteen congregations holding balances of over £2,500. Hence, the value of balances held in Reserve Accounts increased by 6.57 per cent in 1973. The average size of balances per account are also shown in Table 102.

TABLE 102.
Information on the capital balances held in the accounts of the sample of 33 congregations for 1973

	Carried forward from 1972 to 1973			Carried forward from 1973 to 1974		
	Total	Average per congregation	Average per account	Total	Average per congregation	Average per account
	£	£	£	£	£	£
	1	2	3	4	5	6
General Account	7,401.26	224.28	224.28	7,331.62	222.17	222.17
Subsidiary Accounts						
Reserve	75,962.62	2,301.89	436.57	80,952.07	2,453.09	465.24
Organization	6,404.04	194.06	51.23	7,320.78	221.84	58.57
SUB-TOTAL	82,366.66	2,495.95	275.47	88,272.85	2,674.93	295.23
TOTAL	89,767.92	2,720.23	299.23	95,604.47	2,897.10	318.68

In organization accounts a total of £6,404.04 was carried forward from 1972 to 1973, an average of £194.06 per congregation.[14] The size of the balances ranged from zero to £855.57, with eight congregations having balances in excess of £300. From 1973 to 1974 an aggregate of £7,320.78 was transferred, or an average of £221.84 per congregation. The range was from zero to £1,150.02, with nine congregations holding balances of more than £300. These figures indicate that the size of Organization Account balances increased by 14.31 per cent during 1973.

In Table 103 an estimate is made of the total capital balances held by congregations in 1973. Column 1 shows the average balance held in each of the three categories of accounts for the sample of 33 congregations. In column 2 these figures are multiplied by 2,009, the number of congregations in the Church in

TABLE 103.
Estimate of the total capital balances held by congregations in 1973

	Average balance per congregation*	1 × 2,009 congregations in Church in 1973
	1	2
	£	£
General Account	223.23	448,469.05
Subsidiary Accounts		
Reserve	2,377.49	4,776,377.40
Organization	207.95	417,771.55
SUB-TOTAL	2,585.44	5,194,148.95
TOTAL	2,808.67	5,642,618.00

*This is the average balance held in 1973, found by halving the sum of column 2 and 5 in table 102.

1973. The calculations suggest that the balance held in General Accounts in 1973 was about £448,000, and in Subsidiary Accounts about £5,194,000 giving a total balance held by congregations of around £5,643,000. Because of the lack of information on a proportion of Subsidiary Accounts, the estimate of the total balance held in such accounts is likely to be an underestimate.

A large proportion of these balances are probably held in bank accounts, as are the overdrafts of congregations in debt. The Church could make savings on interest payments on overdrafts if it could negotiate certain facilities with the commercial banks, which the Roman Catholic Church already enjoys, whereby the deposits or overdrafts of congregations are pooled for the purposes of interest receipts and payments. For example, if congregation A has a bank deposit of £500 which earns interest at 7 per cent, and congregation B has an overdraft of £200 on which it pays interest at 10 per cent, then the Church as a whole would benefit if B's debt was to be offset against A's savings. Congregation B would no longer have to pay £20 a year in interest charges, while congregation A would lose £14 a year in interest receipts, giving a saving to the Church of £6. Congregation B might pay congregation A the £14 of interest it had sacrificed. Such a facility would have to be negotiated separately with each of the Scottish banks.

5 Recommendations on congregational accounts

Our work on congregational finance described above is based to a large extent on the published annual accounts of a sample of congregations. An examination of these accounts has revealed some deficiencies which would be remedied by the adoption of the following recommendations:

(i) From an examination of the accounts of a random sample of 124 charges it was found that only 13 per cent were audited professionally by a chartered accountant or a similarly qualified person, 70 per cent were audited 'unofficially' by members of the congregation, and the remaining 17 per cent were not audited in any way. We recommend that, whenever practicable, accounts should be audited professionally every second or third year. This would avoid the risk of financial confusion which might adversely affect the Church as a whole, and congregations might benefit from advice on possible economy measures suggested by the auditors. It is quite possible that the resulting savings would outweigh the cost of the professional audit.

(ii) The purposes of preparing annually and circulating congregational accounts to members is to inform the ordinary member of the congregation about the sources of congregational income and the way it is spent. The accounts should therefore be simple and understandable to ordinary people; yet in fact the presentation differs widely between congregations, and in some cases is probably unintelligible to any but an accountant or banker. Cases have come to our attention where the members of congregations were not aware that the contribution of their congregation to the Mission and Service Fund had been below the allocations for several years. We recommend, therefore, that the annual accounts produced by congregations should always be presented on the recommended form devised by the General Treasurer's Department; from a random sample of 124 charges it was found that only 7 per cent made use of the recommended form in 1973.

(iii) We further recommend that every Presbytery should make available each year comparative statistics of the expenditures of the congregations within their bounds. This would provide a basis for the comparison of the accounts of individual congregations by members. Such a development would be in the interest of open government and good financial management in the congregations.

6 Conclusions

In this chapter we have carried out an analysis of congregational finance. We started in section 2 by investigating the membership and finance of congregations as aggregated and averaged by Presbytery and Synod. Most of the Presbytery distributions exhibited a marked positive skew, i.e. more than half were below the average size. They included the following: number of congregations; total membership; average congregational membership; and 'normal liberality', per congregation and per member. These variations seemed to reflect differences between the larger, wealthier, urban congregations and the more numerous, but smaller and poorer, rural congregations. Although 30 of the 59 Presbyteries drew more aid than they gave, only 22 Presbyteries had more aid-receiving than aid-giving congregations. Of those 22 Presbyteries, 13 were located in only two Synods: those of Argyll (5 out of its 6 Presbyteries) and of Ross, Sutherland and Caithness (all 8 Presbyteries). These two Synods, which cover the north-west Highlands and Western Isles, accounted for 28.7 per cent of all aid-receiving congregations and 38.0 per cent of all aid paid from the fund, and only two other Synods, those of Moray and of Merse and Teviotdale, were net aid-receivers. In contrast, the four 'city' Presbyteries, and to a greater extent the four 'city' Synods, dominate the finances of the Church; the latter account for over half of all congregations, two-thirds of the membership and 'normal liberality', and about 70 per cent of the aid given to the fund and the Mission and Service Fund contribution.

The initial work on congregations suggested the hypothesis that the income, expenditure, and thus the financial position, of a congregation would depend to an important extent on the size of its membership. In section 3 this hypothesis was tested using cross-sectional statistical analysis of three samples of congregations representing the total, non-linked and linked congregations in the Church. The results of the linear regression analysis tended to support this hypothesis, with many of the R^2 being around 0.7 or better.

The intercept terms of the income equations were interpreted as the endowment and investment income of the congregations. The value of the b term was about 7.0, which was the level of the Church 'normal liberality' per member in 1973. A problem with the income equations, however, was that the standard error of the intercept term was so large as to make the term insignificant. One approach adopted was to extract endowment and investment income from the income data, and to force the regression line through the origin. The new income equation was taken to represent that proportion of income derived from the offerings of members. It was added to intercept terms calculated from the mean, median and other levels of endowment and investment income. An alternative approach was to force the total income equation through the origin, which avoided the problem of the intercept and was acceptable statistically. Other possible independent variables were tested, but found to be insignificant.

The expenditure equations had rather high intercept terms, reflecting the high proportion of overhead costs in total expenditure. The fixed cost element gives rise to considerable economies of scale in congregations, particularly those of below average size (i.e. of fewer than about 540 members). The variable cost element appeared to be about £4 per member in 1973. According to the curvilinear income equation, small congregations appear to be significantly better at fund-raising than large congregations, because the giving per member is higher. However, the average contribution made by each additional member remains higher than the extra congregational expenses incurred over the whole range of congregational sizes in the Church. This suggests that large congregations are economically more efficient than small congregations. Other independent variables relating to buildings were tested for their influence on expenditure, but only the seating capacity of the Church was found to have some significance.

The 'break-even' level of membership was calculated by regressing amounts of aid given and received against membership, since it was hypothesized that small congregations tend to receive aid and large congregations to give aid. The negative intercept term and positive b term of the linear regression, together with an R^2 of 0.753, confirmed this hypothesis. The 'break-even' point, or point of self-sufficiency, is found to be 345 members. An alternative calculation of the 'break-even' point was made by juxtaposing the expenditure and (composite) income equations for the aggregate sample of congregations. The result was 218 members, or well below the first calculation. It was thought that the break-even point of 218 members was too low. However, tests showed that the expenditure equation in particular was subject to heteroscedasticity. The equation was transformed to correct for this, and the resulting 'break-even' point was 351 members, or very close to the first calculation.

It is possible that the theory of congregational finance might help to explain variations in the financial viability of the ministry in different regions of Scotland. In remote rural areas where the population is sparse, congregations tend to be small and are often aid-receiving. In urban areas, on the other hand, the high population densities give rise to congregations of large average size which tend to be aid-giving.

The theoretical limitation of the static model was that it assumed expenditure was determined by membership, whereas in non-profit-making bodies like congregations expenditure is more likely to be related to income. A simultaneous equation model was devised and tested, in which income was made a function of membership, and expenditure a function of income. The resulting equations were found to be satisfactory statistically.

In section 4 the income of congregations was analysed in greater detail. It was found that the income of congregations returned on the Schedule of Financial Statistics, on which the General Finance Committee bases its compilation of Church congregational income, corresponds closely on average to the income appearing in the General Account of the congregations' annual accounts. For a sample of 33 congregations, the General Account income averaged £4,497 in 1973. But nearly all congregations have a number of subsidiary accounts which relate to fabric, organ renovation, trust and bequest funds, Women's Guilds, Sunday School classes, Boys' Brigades, etc; these usually have their own sources of income, and this income is largely unrecorded by the central Church authorities. In 1973 this extra income amounted to £1,372 per congregation, or 23.4 per cent of the total income of £5,869.

It was estimated that in 1973 the total Subsidiary Account income of congregations was between about £2,756,000 and £2,828,000. These figures represent an addition of about 20 per cent to the recorded total income of the Church in 1973 of £12,918,350.

In addition, congregational accounts tend to carry balances of cash or bank deposits. In 1973 the average congregation in our sample of 33 had a balance of £223.23 in its General Account and £2,585.44 in its Subsidiary Accounts, giving a total balance of £2,808.67. These figures suggest that, in the Church as a whole, in 1973 the total balances held in General Accounts were about £448,000 and in Subsidiary Accounts about £5,194,000, giving a total balance held of about £5,643,000.

Finally, in section 5 some recommendations were made on the presentation and auditing of congregational accounts. We recommend that congregations' annual Accounts should be audited professionally every second or third year, which would avoid financial confusion and give congregations the benefit of the advice obtained. Accounts should be on the recommended form devised by the General Treasurer's Department (only about 7 per cent of congregations do so at the moment).

Notes

1 Information for this study was taken from the following sources: 'List of Synods, Presbyteries and Parishes', *The Church of Scotland Yearbook,* 1975, pp. 100-273; Church of Scotland, 'Report of the Committee on the Maintenance of the Ministry', *Reports to the General Assembly, 1974,* table A, pp. 593-639

2 'Report of the Committee of Forty', *Reports to the General Assembly, 1975,* table 8, p. 556.

3 ibid., p. 521.

4 See A.W. Wicker, 'Size of Church Membership and Members: Support of Church Behaviour Settings', *Journal of Personality and Social Psychology,* no. 3, 1969, pp. 278-88.

5 'Report of the Committee of Forty', op. cit. pp. 527-8.

6 Burleigh, *Church History of Scotland,* (1960), pp. 372-3.

7 The question of budgeting for the Mission and Service Fund, and the allocation of the budget to Presbyteries and congregations, forms the subject matter of chapter 16.

8 See chapter 16, pp. 359-68.

9 *Reports to the General Assembly, 1974,* table A.

10 The use of Deeds of Covenant is examined in chapter 18.

11 Some of the extra income may be taken by the central levies.

12 The economics of union and readjustment are examined in the following chapter.

13 The calculation and allocation of this budget is discussed in chapter 16.

14 Only 18 congregations in the sample provided detailed information for this category of accounts.

Chapter 13

Union and readjustment of congregations

1 Introduction
In chapter 8 we found that the policy of union and readjustment is aimed at rationalizing the parish structure of the Church, and that this policy has been made necessary by a number of factors, which include the duplication of charges inherited from the 1929 union, the shifts in the geographical distribution of the Scottish population, and the decline in the number of members and ministers.

The purpose of this chapter is to examine the economic implications of union and readjustment. In section 2 we analyse the influence on the membership and income of congregations of union and linking. Then in sections 3 and 4 the savings arising from the 'typical' union and 'typical' linking are calculated with the help of the congregational finance equations developed in the previous chapter. On the basis of this analysis, we calculate in section 5 the implications for the Church as a whole of the future extension of the policy of union and readjustment.

All the money figures are expressed in 'real' terms at 1973 prices.

2 The impact of unions and linkings on congregational membership and income
It has been suggested that the merging of congregations may have an adverse effect on membership. One of our early studies of the Presbytery of Edinburgh, which seemed to confirm this view, compared the decline in membership of charges united during the years 1958 to 1970 and the decline in membership throughout the Church in the same period. It was found that the mean fall in membership for united charges was significantly greater than the national rate of decline. Further, it was shown that if the sample of united charges was divided up according to the pre-1929 Union allegiances of the former congregations of which they are composed, then the greatest decline in membership subsequent to union occurred in cases where former United Free Church congregations were united with pre-1929 Church of Scotland Congregations. In such cases the loss of membership was of the order of 28 per cent more than the fall in membership nationally over the twelve-year period. If it were demonstrated that these results hold for the Church throughout Scotland, then there would be important implications to be drawn for the Church's policy on unions and readjustment. For example, it might be necessary for the Church deliberately to promote certain unions and to discourage others.

Consequently, it was decided to examine the membership and income ('normal liberality') figures for all 61 united charges in the Church which underwent union during the years 1965 to 1969. The study also considered those 43 charges, composed of 86 congregations, which were formed from linkings in the years between 1965 and 1969. The purpose of the study was to compare the trends in membership and income in the years prior to the union or linking of the charge to the trends in the years following the reorganisation. Data on membership and income for the years 1960 to 1975[1] yielded the following figures, expressed as percentages, calculated for all charges in the two samples: the average annual change in membership and income for the five years prior to readjustment, the corresponding figure for the five years subsequent to the date of readjustment, and the percentage change between the year immediately preceding readjustment and the year in which it occurred. These changes can then be considered for the united and linked charges as groups, and compared with the changes in the Church as a whole.

Table 104 summarizes the results for membership for the sample of united charges compared with the Church total membership, and also the results for unions classified according to the pre-1929 Union allegiances of the former congregations of which they are composed. One limitation of the percentage figures

TABLE 104.
Comparisons of annual changes in membership of united charges with the Church as a whole, 1960-74

1. Mean percentage annual change in:	%	Comparison of means
(a) all charges, 1960-1969	−1.10	
(b) united charges for five years prior to union	−2.53	(b) is significantly different from (a)
(c) all charges, 1965-1974	−1.78	
(d) united charges for five years following union	−2.67	(d) is not significantly different from (c)
(e) for old Church of Scotland charges united with old Church of Scotland charges	−1.72	(e) is not significantly different from (c)
(f) for old United Free Church charges united with old United Free Church charges	−2.91	(f) is not significantly different from (c)
(g) for old United Free Church charges united with old Church of Scotland charges	−3.03	(g) is not significantly different from (c)
2. Percentage change in year of union:	%	
(a) for united charges	−8.25	
(b) for old Church of Scotland charges united with old Church of Scotland charges	−5.36	
(c) for old United Free Church charges united with old United Free Church charges	−9.67	
(d) for old United Free Church charges united with old Church of Scotland charges	−8.72	

is that their variances tend to be large, which implies that the degree of variation between individual cases is great. Nonetheless, they do indicate that the sample of congregations which subsequently united tended as a group to lose membership more rapidly in the years preceding union than did the Church as a whole for the corresponding period. In the years following the union, however, the decline in the membership of the newly united charges on average did not differ significantly from rest of the Church; this result held, irrespective of the historical allegiances of the uniting congregations. Table 104 also shows that there is a large once-over loss in membership averaging 8.25 per cent in the year of the union. The significance of this result is discussed below.

Table 105 sets out for the income ('normal liberality') of the sample of united charges a list of comparisons similar to those in table 104. The results are consistent with those for membership, with the mean annual increase in income for the congregations of the united charges for five years prior to the union being significantly less than the average increase for total 'ordinary liberality'. Again, the striking feature of the results is the loss of income in the year of union, which

TABLE 105.

Comparisons of annual changes in income (normal liberality) of united charges with the Church as a whole, 1960-74

1. Mean percentage annual change in:	%	Comparison of means
(a) all charges, 1960-1969	+4.70	
(b) united charges for five years prior to union	+2.77	(b) is significantly different from (a)
(c) all charges, 1965-1974	+6.97	
(d) united charges for five years following union	+7.30	(d) is not significantly different from (c)
(e) for old Church of Scotland charges united with old Church of Scotland charges	+8.21	(e) is not significantly different from (c)
(f) for old United Free Church charges united with old United Free Church charges	+7.96	(f) is not significantly different from (c)
(g) for old United Free Church charges united with old Church of Scotland charges	+6.94	(g) is not significantly different from (c)
2. Percentage change in year of union:	%	
(a) for united charges	−11.84	
(b) for old Church of Scotland charges united with old Church of Scotland charges	−8.56	
(c) for old United Free Church charges united with old United Free Church charges	−12.62	
(d) for old United Free Church charges united with old Church of Scotland charges	−12.80	

averaged 11.84 per cent.

Comparable membership and income figures for the sample of linked charges were also compared to the Church figures. They revealed no significantly greater loss of membership either prior to linking, during the year of the readjustment, or in the years following it. Similarly, the growth in income for linked charges was not significantly different from the Church as a whole throughout the entire period under consideration.

These results indicate that the reorganization of congregations by unions and linkings does not have an adverse effect on membership and income in the years following the readjustment. They do demonstrate, however, that in the case of unions there is a large loss of membership and income during the year in which the readjustment is brought into effect. The size of this once-for-all loss of membership can be exaggerated, however, partly because in the year of union the membership of the uniting congregations would on average have declined in any event, and partly because in all vacancies the revision of the Communion Roll produces a larger than average decline in membership for that year. These two factors must be eliminated from the gross fall in membership of 8.25 per cent in the year of union in order to isolate the adverse impact on membership attributable to the union alone.

The impact of the revision of the Communion Roll on membership was found by taking a random sample of 30 charges which fell vacant during 1967 but were not readjusted, and calculating the average change in membership between 1967 and 1968. This average change was found to be -3.13 per cent, as compared to a decline in membership for the Church as a whole of -1.49 per cent between 1967 and 1968. The net effect of a roll revision thus appears to be a 1.64 per cent decline in membership.

The net impact on membership in the year of union for unions occurring between 1965 and 1969 can now be calculated as follows:

Change in membership in year of union	-8.25%
less expected change in membership	-2.53%*
less expected change from roll revision	-1.64%
Change in membership caused by union	-4.08%

*SOURCE: Table 104, 1(b)

The figures indicate that the average union between 1965 and 1969 resulted in a net loss of membership in the year of union of 4.08 per cent. Against this, however, must be set the fact that, while the membership of congregations in the years prior to union declined at a significantly faster rate than the Church average, in the years following union the rate of membership decline was not significantly different from the Church average. This suggests that a union on average improves the long-term membership prospects of the uniting congregations at the expense of an immediate fall in membership of about 4 per cent.

A further point is that a part of the 4 per cent loss of membership of the united charge may not be lost to the Church as a whole. Such members may join a nearby congregation because the union is seen as the appropriate point at which to sever old ties of loyalty with their former congregation, often because they have moved house and now live some distance from it. Assessing this gain in members by congregations adjacent to the united congregation would be very difficult.

The average loss of income in the year of union is much larger than the average loss of membership. Instead of an increase in income of 2.77 per cent there is a fall of -11.84 giving an overall difference of -14.61 per cent. This fall in income is much larger than predicted by the income equation in the previous chapter used in conjunction with the membership decline. Two possible explanations for this result might be offered. The first is that the uniting of two congregations creates some dissatisfaction amongst a proportion of the membership, so that while they do not in general resign from membership the size of their contributions is reduced. The second possible explanation is that the loss of income is caused by a preoccupation with the upheavals brought by the readjustment to the detriment of normal fund-raising activities. Many readjustments are brought about by vacancies occurring in charges, some of which persist for several months. The absence of an incumbent minister for this period of time may also have an adverse effect on income.

The analysis suggests that the Church should examine ways of facilitating a smooth transition to a united charge so as to minimize the loss of membership and income. One possibility is that the linking of congregations could be used as a first step towards union. This procedure is recommended by the fact that the membership and income of linked congregations do not appear to be affected by the linking.

3 The economic implications of unions

A 'union' means the joining of two or more congregations to form one charge. Unions are normally preferred to linkings, partly because the savings involved are potentially larger, but their practicability is limited to those adjacent congregations which are in close proximity to each other; therefore they usually take place in urban areas and small towns.

An investigation of the 38 unions which took place in the period 1967-9 revealed that 35 involved the union of two congregations, and three the union of three congregations. Ignoring the third congregations involved in the three triple unions, it was found that the average membership of the larger congregations prior to union was 599, although actual cases varied from 121 to 1,834, and the average membership of the smaller congregations was 340, with a range from 24 to 623. In the calculations which follow we take the figures of 599 and 340 as the memberships of the two congregations involved in the average union. These give a pre-union combined membership of 939, which is subject to the loss of membership in the year of union of 4.08 per cent calculated above; the post-union membership will therefore be 901. These membership numbers are taken for illustrative purposes only, but they are not unrepresentative.

The calculations are based on the expenditure and income equations developed in the previous chapter on congregational finance. The equations are as follows, where $I4_1$ is the total income equation forced through the origin, E_2 is expenditure for the sample of non-linked congregations, and M is membership:

$$I4_1 = 7.728M \quad (25)$$
$$N = 39$$

$$E_2 = 1,469.0 + 3.906M \quad (27)$$
$$N = 29$$

The two equations are plotted in figure 28.

Firstly, we deal with the financial positions of the two congregations prior to union, where congregation X is assumed to have a membership of 599 and congregation Y one of 340; the positions of the two charges are shown in figure 28. Their income and expenditure are calculated as follows:

	Congregation X		Congregation Y	
	income	expenditure	income	expenditure
	£	£	£	£
Fixed	0	1,469	0	1,469
Variable	4,629	2,340	2,628	1,328
TOTAL	4,629	3,809	2,628	2,797

Given these income and expenditure figures, the financial positions of the two congregations can be summarized as follows:

Congregation X		Congregation Y	
	£		£
Income	4,629	Income	2,628
Expenditure	3,809	Expenditure	2,797
GROSS SURPLUS	820	GROSS DEFICIT	−169
less 40% for aid given	328	less nominal contribution to Mission and Service Fund	−179
less 50% for Mission and Service Fund contribution	410	aid received	179
NET SURPLUS	82	NET POSITION	0

In congregation X income exceeds congregational expenditure, and a proportion of the resulting gross surplus is contributed to central funds. Rough calculations suggest that on average about 40 per cent of such a surplus would be given as aid to the Maintenance of the Ministry Fund, and about 50 per cent would be contributed to the Mission and Service Fund. We use these rather arbitrary percentage figures throughout for the purpose of illustration. Congregation X thus had a net surplus of £82 in 1973. In congregation Y income is exceeded by 'necessary' congregational expenditure, leading to a gross deficit of £169, and the congregation is assumed to make a nominal contribution of £10 to the Mission and Service Fund, as is the practice for aid-receiving congregations. The gross deficit of £179 is met by aid received from the Maintenance of the Ministry Fund.

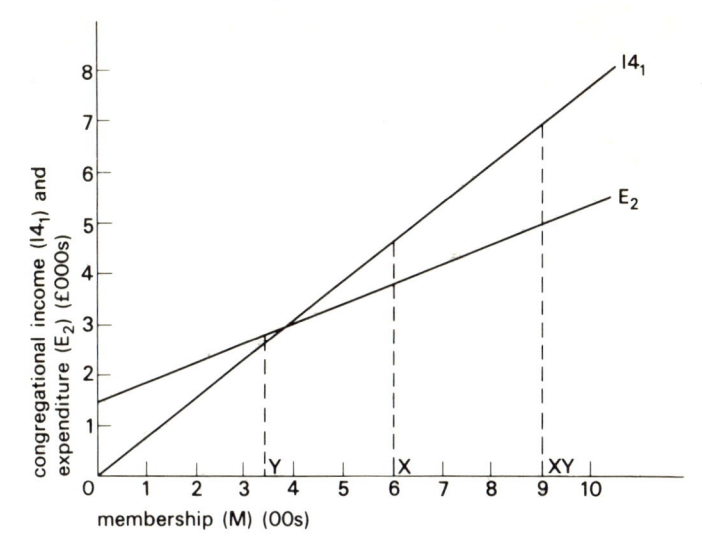

FIGURE 28: Income ($I4_1$) and expenditure (E_2) as functions of membership for a sample of non-linked congregations, 1973

The combined pre-union financial position of the two congregations can now be summarized as follows:

	Income	Expenditure	Aid given (+) or received (−)	Mission and Service Fund contribution	Net surplus/ deficit
	£	£	£	£	£
Congregation X	4,629	3,809	+328	410	82
Congregation Y	2,628	2,797	−179	10	0
TOTAL	7,257	6,606	+149	420	82

In the combined position, income of £7,257 exceeds expenditure of £6,606 to give a gross surplus of £651. A net sum of £149, or 23 per cent of the surplus, is given as aid to the Maintenance of the Ministry Fund, and another 65 per cent, or £420, is contributed to the Mission and Service Fund. Allowing for these deductions, the net surplus amounts to £82.

When the two congregations unite, their joint membership is assumed to fall by 4.08 per cent from 939 to 901, this being the average fall in the year of union calculated in section 2 above.

The position of the new congregation XY is also shown in figure 28 and its income and expenditure is calculated as follows:

	Congregation XY	
	income	expenditure
	£	£
Fixed	0	1,469
Variable	6,963	3,519
TOTAL	6,963	4,988

The financial position of congregation XY can now be given as follows:

	£
Income	6,963
Expenditure	4,988
GROSS SURPLUS	1,975
less 40% for aid given	790
less 50% for Mission and Service Fund contribution	988
NET SURPLUS	197

In order to calculate the savings arising from the union, the financial position of congregation XY can be compared with the combined position of former congregations X and Y, as follows:

	income	expenditure
	£	£
Fixed	0	−1,469
Variable	−294	− 149
TOTAL	−294	−1,618

Income falls by £294, the sum of the annual contributions of the 38 members who were lost at Union. Expenditure falls by £1,618, which comprises the fixed costs of one of the congregations (£1,469), and a decline in variable costs of £149 occasioned by the loss of the 38 members. The net saving to the ministry of the union thus amounts to the reduction in expenditure of £1,618 less the loss of income of £294, or £1,324 for the year at 1973 prices. The saving will continue to accrue to the ministry at £1,324 per year at 1973 prices in perpetuity as a result of the once-for-all readjustment.

Two further factors need to be considered in assessing this annual savings figure for the 'average' union. Firstly, it seems possible that the fixed costs of a non-linked charge in 1973 were rather greater than the figure of £1,469, which is the value of the intercept term in the expenditure equation. The fixed costs would include the ministerial expenses, i.e. the 1973 minimum stipend of £1,674, the contribution of the congregation to the Aged and Infirm Ministers Fund, and the

TABLE 106.

Alternative calculations of the savings arising from the uniting of pairs of congregations with different aggregate levels of membership.

	LOW (memberships 121 and 24 = 145)			LOW MIDPOINT (memberships 360 and 182 = 542)		
	pre-union	post-union	change	pre-union	post-union	change
	£	£	%	£	£	%
Income	1,120	1,074	−4.1	4,188	4,019	−4.0
Expenditure	3,505	2,012	−42.6	5,055	3,500	−69.2
Aid given	0	0	0.0	0	208	+123.4
Aid received	2,405	958	−60.2	887	0	
Mission and Service fund contribution	20	20	0.0	20	260	+1,200.0
NET SURPLUS	0	0	0.0	0	51	—

Listed Expenses, together with some maintenance and running costs of the buildings. These items might tentatively total as much as £2,000. Secondly, calculations in section 2 above based on a sample of fairly recent unions suggest that on average a union leads to a drop in income of 14.61 per cent in the year of union. In our example this would produce a fall in income of £1,060, which is substantially larger than the calculated fall of £294, or 4.1 per cent, based on the decline in membership. It is conceivable that the extra savings on expenditure arising from a higher estimate of fixed costs would be offset by the greater fall in income, leaving the calculated net annual savings figure of about £1,324 unchanged.

A comparison of the financial positions of congregations X and Y before and after the union can be summarized as follows:

	Pre-union	Post-union	Change
	£	£	%
Income	7,257	6,963	− 4.1
Expenditure	6,606	4,988	− 24.5
Aid given (+)	328	790	+430.2
Aid received (−)	179	0	
Mission and Service Fund contribution	420	988	+135.2
NET SURPLUS	82	197	+140.2

A fall in income of 4.1 per cent is submerged by a decline in expenditure of 24.5 per cent. The greatly improved financial position of the united congregation allows the net aid given to the Maintenance of the Ministry Fund to be increased by 430.2 per cent, and the Mission and Service Fund contribution to be increased by 135.2 per cent. The net surplus also increases by 140.2 per cent.

The example of the economic consequences of a 'typical' union is based on congregations which have the median levels of membership for the larger and smaller congregations involved. Examples for a range of congregational memberships are given in table 106. The 'low' and 'high' memberships are those of the

TABLE 106 (continued)

HIGH MIDPOINT (memberships 1,217 and 482 = 1,699)			HIGH (memberships 1,834 and 623 = 2,457)		
pre-union	post-union	change	pre-union	post-union	change
£	£	%	£	£	%
13,130	12,597	− 4.1	18,988	18,215	− 4.1
9,575	7,836	− 18.2	12,535	10,675	− 14.8
1,422	1,904	+33.9	2,581	3,016	+16.9
0	0	0.0	0	0	0.0
1,778	2,381	+33.9	3,227	3,770	+16.8
355	476	+34.1	645	754	+16.9

pairs of larger and smaller uniting congregations at the extremes of their respective size ranges. The 'low' and 'high' midpoints represent the points midway between the 'low' and 'high' figures respectively and the mean used in the above calculations for the larger and smaller congregations. The table indicates that in all cases expenditure falls much more than income, leading to a substantial improvement in the financial position of the united charge over the pre-union joint position. This applies even in the 'low' membership example, where the united charge remains in receipt of aid from the Maintenance of the Ministry Fund. The net annual savings at 1973 prices amount to £1,447, £1,386, £1,206, and £1,087 for the 'low', 'low midpoint', 'high midpoint', and 'high' membership examples respectively.

While it should be emphazised that the impact of union varies enormously between individual cases, not only because of variations in membership sizes but also because of local factors which influence the compatibility of the uniting congregations, these calculations suggest that, on average, a union serves to greatly strengthen the financial position of the united congregations, of the ministry as a whole, and of the Mission and Service Fund.

4 The economic implications of linkings

Two or more neighbouring congregations may be linked together under one minister. Each congregation retains its own church building, Kirk Session, method of congregational management, and separate identity. The Kirk Sessions meet together once a year to appoint a representative elder to the Presbytery and Synod, and to discuss the arrangements for the payment of the minister's stipend and expenses.

Linking is considered to be the appropriate form of readjustment in two types of cases. The first is the case in which union or some other form of readjustment is desirable, but only a linking arrangement is practicable at the time. Such arrangements are regarded as temporary and as a step towards union or some other readjustment. The second is where two or more congregations are at such a distance from each other as to make united worship impracticable, and to make the effective working of united congregational courts and organisations difficult. In such cases, where the minister is able to serve both congregations and conduct their services, they may be linked permanently and share a minister and representative elder. Experience has shown that linking is more effective than union where the two places of worship are not less than two and not more than ten miles apart. Linkings, therefore, are largely restricted to rural areas where congregations are small, and their respective church buildings are often situated some distance from each other.

An investigation of the 41 linkings which took place between 1965 and 1969 showed that all were formed from two congregations. In the larger of the congregations in each linking the membership averaged 304, although the size varied from 40 to 907, while in the smaller the membership averaged 140 with a range of 15 to 362. In section 2 above it was found that linkings, unlike unions, did not suffer a fall in membership in the year of readjustment.

On the basis of these membership figures, and using the income ($I4_1$) and expenditure (E_2) equations given in section 3 above, the savings arising from the 'average' linking can be calculated. The positions of two charges prior to linking is shown in figure 29. Charge S has a membership of 304 and charge T a membership of 140. Their financial positions can be calculated as follows:

	Congregation S		Congregation T	
	income	expenditure	income	expenditure
	£	£	£	£
Fixed	0	1,469	0	1,469
Variable	2,349	1,187	1,082	547
TOTAL	2,349	2,656	1,082	2,016

Given these income and expenditure figures, the financial positions of the two congregations can be summarized as follows:

	Congregation S	Congregation T
	£	£
Income	2,349	1,082
Expenditure	2,656	2,016
Gross deficit	− 307	− 934
less nominal contribution to Mission and Service Fund	− 317	− 944
Aid received	317	944
NET POSITION	0	0

These figures indicate that both congregations have substantial deficits, £307 in the case of congregation S, and £934 in the case of congregation T. Both congregations are again assumed to make nominal contributions of £10 to the Mission and Service Fund, as is the practice in aid-receiving congregations. The total deficit in each case is met by aid received from the Maintenance of the Ministry Fund.

The combined position of the two congregations prior to linking is therefore as follows:

	Income	Expenditure	Aid given (+) or received (−)	Mission and Service Fund contribution	Net surplus/ deficit
	£	£	£	£	£
Congregation S	2,349	2,656	− 317	10	0
Congregation T	1,082	2,016	− 944	10	0
TOTAL	3,431	4,672	− 1261	20	0

When congregation S links with congregation T, their memberships are assumed to remain unchanged at 304 and 140 respectively. The principle impact of the linking appears to be a large drop in the fixed cost of each congregation, arising from the fact that each no longer has to pay the stipend and expenses of its own minister, but instead shares the cost of one minister. The regression of the expenditures of a sample of linked congregations (E_3) against membership (M)

318   The Church of Scotland: An Economic Survey

(see Chapter 12) produced the following equation:

$$E_3 = 829.0 + 4.513M \qquad \ldots \qquad (28)$$
$$(152.4) \quad (0.6252)$$
$$N = 23$$
$$R^2 = 0.713$$

Durbin-Watson statistic = 4.930.

The equation is also drawn in figure 29. The value of the intercept term is rather more than half that for the equation for non-linked congregations (E_2), which probably reflects the fact that the total cost of a minister in a linked charge is rather greater than the cost of the minister in one or other of the pre-linked charges. The extra expense arises because the minister in a linked charge generally receives a special allowance of up to £150 in addition to the minimum stipend, and he may incur higher costs in travelling between the two charges.

The steeper slope of the E_3 line as compared to the E_2 line (see figure 29) may reflect the impact of the allocation of the ministerial expenses between the two charges. Since the costs are probably apportioned roughly in proportion to income, the small charges will receive a smaller proportion of the allocated costs than the large charges. The allocation will thus tend to steepen the slope of the expenditure line so that it approaches more closely the steeper slope of the income line.

The financial positions of the two congregations when linked are as follows:

FIGURE 29: Income ($I4_1$) and expenditure (E_3) as functions of membership for a sample of linked congregations, 1973.

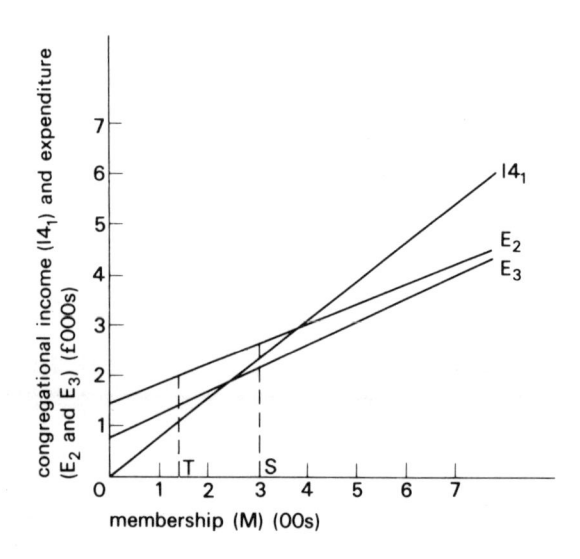

	Congregation S		Congregation T	
	income	expenditure	income	expenditure
	£	£	£	£
Fixed	0	829	0	829
Variable	2,349	1,372	1,082	632
TOTAL	2,349	2,201	1,082	1,461

		£		£
Income		2,349	Income	1,082
Expenditure		2,201	Expenditure	1,461
GROSS SURPLUS		148	GROSS DEFICIT	−379
Less 40% for aid given		59	Less nominal contribution to Mission and Service Fund	−389
Less 50% for Mission and Service Fund contribution		74	Aid received	389
NET SURPLUS		15	NET SURPLUS	0

The financial position of both congregations has improved as a result of the linking. Whereas formerly both were aid-receiving congregations, congregation S is now an aid-giver, and the aid received by congregation T, although still substantial, is much reduced. This improvement is brought about entirely by a reduction in expenditure as follows:

	Expenditure		
	pre-linking	post-linking	Change
	£	£	£
Fixed	2,938	1,658	−1,280
Variable	1,734	2,004	+270
TOTAL	4,672	3,662	−1,010

Fixed costs fall by £1,280 as a result of sharing the minister, but variable costs rise by £270 as a result of the steepening of the expenditure function. The net annual saving on the linking is thus £1,010 per year at 1973 prices. Against this, however, has to be set the fact that, in many cases of linking, a car is provided for the minister at the expense of the Maintenance of the Ministry Committee.

A comparison of the changes in the aggregate financial position of the two congregations before and after the linking can be summarized as follows:

	pre-linking	post-linking	change
	£	£	%
Income	3,431	3,431	0
Expenditure	4,672	3,662	−21.6
Aid received	1,261	389	−73.8
Aid given	0	59	
Mission and Service Fund contribution	20	84	+320.0
NET SURPLUS	0	15	—

The improved financial position of the two congregations brought about by the fall of 21.6 per cent in expenditure has allowed net aid received to be reduced by 73.8 per cent from £1,261 to £330, which includes an increase in aid given from zero to £59. Whereas prior to the linking both congregations were in deficit, following the linking congregation S is a giver of aid, and the deficit of congregation T is much reduced. The Mission and Service Fund contribution has increased from £20 to £84.

Unlike unions, the economic consequences of linkings seem to vary between individual cases only to the extent that the aggregate memberships involved vary. Linkings do not appear to suffer falls in membership and income in the year of linking in the same way as do unions in the year of union. The example given of a 'typical' linking is based on a pair of congregations which have the median levels of membership for the larger and smaller congregations involved. As with unions, we give examples of a range of congregational memberships in table 107. They indicate that in all cases the linking serves to improve the financial position of the congregations concerned compared to their joint pre-linking position, even though the smaller congregations remain in receipt of aid from the Maintenance of the Ministry Fund. The net annual savings at 1973 prices amount to £1,146, £1,129, £759 and £510 for the 'low', 'low midpoint', 'high midpoint' and 'high' membership examples respectively. These savings are less than those for unions, largely because the joint overhead costs of the two congregations concerned are reduced by rather less than half at the linking, whereas in cases of union the overhead costs are assumed to be exactly halved.

5 The savings to the Church of union and readjustment, 1976-85

The purpose of this section is to estimate the savings which might accrue to the Church over the period 1976-85 if the decline in the number of charges forecast in chapter 8 is actually realized.

As in the past, the bulk of the decline in the number of charges will be caused by unions and linkings. Over the ten-year period 1965-74 the number of unions and linkings carried out was 282, or about 28 per year. This figure implies a

TABLE 107.

Alternative calculations of the savings arising from the linking of pairs of congregations with different aggregate levels of membership

	LOW (memberships 40 and 15 = 55)			LOW MIDPOINT (memberships 172 and 78 = 250)		
	pre-linking	post-linking	change	pre-linking	post-linking	change
	£	£	%	£	£	%
Income	425	425	0.0	1,932	1,932	0.0
Expenditure	3,153	2,007	−36.3	3,915	2,786	−28.8
Aid given	0	0	0.0	0	0	0.0
Aid received	2,748	1,602	−41.7	2,003	874	−56.4
Mission and Service fund contribution	20	20	0.0	20	20	0.0
NET SURPLUS	0	0	0.0	0	0	0.0

decline in the number of charges of at least 282 (assuming that each union or linking involved at least two charges), but the actual decline was 260. It is possible that this discrepancy might be explained by the fact that a number of linkings and unions were terminated over the period, so that the figure of 282 overstates the net increase in the number of permanent unions and linkings formed. Also, the decline in the number of charges of 260 has been arrested by the admission of new congregations and the revival of others, although these numbers have been offset to some extent by the dissolution of a number of congregations.

Although it has not proved possible to reconcile these figures, it seems clear that the bulk of the decline in the number of charges has been caused by unions and linkings. We assume for the purposes of this analysis that unions and linkings will in the forecast period be entirely responsible for the decline in the number of charges.

In sections 3 and 4 above it was calculated that the 'typical' union gave rise to an annual saving of £1,324, and the 'typical' linking to an annual saving of £1,010, both figures being expressed in terms of 1973 prices. In order to simplify the calculation of the prospective total savings to the Church of union and readjustment over the next ten years, a weighted annual savings figure per readjustment was calculated. This figure can be produced by taking the average of the two annual savings figures, and weighting it by the proportion of unions and linkings to be carried out. If the ratio of unions and linkings in the future can be assumed to equal the proportion in the period 1965-74, then the ratio will be 165 unions to 117 linkings. On this basis, the weighted annual savings figure per readjustment is £1,194.

In table 108, two estimates are made of the potential savings to the Church of the forecast decline in the number of charges over the next ten years brought about by the policy of union and readjustment. These estimates are based on the two forecasts of the number of charges made in chapter 8. The annual falls in the number of charges for the period 1976-85 for forecasts I and II are shown in columns 1 and 4 respectively. Columns 2 and 5 show the annual savings, at £1,194 per readjustment, which arise from the fall in the number of charges each year. Since the

TABLE 107 (*continued*)

HIGH MIDPOINT (memberships 606 and 251 = 857)			HIGH (memberships 907 and 362 = 1,269)		
pre-linking	post-linking	change	pre-linking	post-linking	change
£	£	%	£	£	%
6,623	6,623	0.0	9,807	9,807	0.0
6,285	5,526	− 12.1	7,895	7,385	− 6.5
339	448	+ 32.2	799	969	+ 21.3
519	32	− 93.8	95	0	0.0
433	569	+ 31.4	1,008	1,211	+ 20.1
85	112	+ 31.8	200	242	+ 21.0

TABLE 108.
Estimates of the savings to the Church (at 1973 prices) of union and readjustment, 1975-86

	Based on forecast I of number of charges			Based on forecast II of number of charges		
	Forecast annual fall in number of charges* 1	Annual savings at £1,194 per charge 2	Cumulative savings over period 3	Forecast annual fall in number of charges* 4	Annual savings at £1,194 per charge 5	Cumulative savings over period 6
		£	£		£	£
1976	35	—	—	57	—	—
1977	34	41,790	41,790	47	68,058	68,058
1978	32	40,596	82,386	47	56,118	124,176
1979	31	38,208	120,594	48	56,118	180,294
1980	30	37,014	157,608	37	57,312	237,606
1981	29	35,820	193,428	37	44,178	281,784
1982	26	34,626	228,054	27	44,178	325,962
1983	24	31,044	259,098	27	32,238	358,200
1984	22	28,656	287,754	18	32,238	390,438
1985	18	26,268	314,022	17	21,492	411,930
Total	281	314,022	1,684,734	362	411,930	2,378,448

*SOURCE: Table 56.

readjustments will be spread evenly throughout the year, the full savings will not be realised until the following year. In order to simplify the calculations, it is assumed that no savings accrue until the year following the year of readjustment.

Once a readjustment has been made, the savings can be considered to accrue, not only in the year of the readjustment, but also for succeeding years in perpetuity. Thus the financial position of the Church is better now than it might otherwise have been, not only because of unions and readjustments carried out last year, but also because of those carried out in the last forty years. In the same way, the Church will benefit cumulatively in the future from future unions and linkings. Columns 3 and 6 of table 108 give the two forecasts of the cumulative savings from the policy of union and readjustment over the next ten years. Under the forecast of the moderate decline in the number of charges (column 3), the cumulative savings at the end of ten years (i.e. by 1985) will be running at £314,000 per year; under the more severe forecast (column 6) the estimate is £412,000 per year. The total savings for the ten-year period are estimated at £1,684,734 and £2,378,448 respectively.

These savings figures are based on the reduction in the expenditures of readjusted charges, less any decline in income caused by the readjustment. We have not taken into account the savings on property arising from union and readjustment, which are likely to be considerable. In a union the buildings (including the manse) of one congregation are usually made redundant, while in a linking the manse of one of the congregations is usually no longer required. Rough calculations suggest that interest earned on the proceeds of sale of redundant property would approximately double the savings calculated in table 108.

The question of Church property is very important and is considered in detail in chapter 19.

6 Conclusions

The purpose of this chapter has been to analyse the economic implications of the union and linking of congregations.

In section 2 we examined the implications for membership and income of union and linking. The study was based on the 61 charges which were united, and the 43 charges which were linked, in the period 1965-69. It was found that the linking of two congregations appeared on average to have no effect on their membership or income. In the case of unions, however, it was found that congregations in the five years prior to union lost members at a significantly faster rate than the Church as a whole, but that in the five years following union the membership loss was not significantly different from the Church average. In the year of union there is a large once-over loss of members of 8.25 per cent. However, when allowance is made for the expected loss of members in the year (2.53 per cent) and for the loss caused by the revision of the Communion Roll which occurs in all vacancies (1.64 per cent), the net loss of members in the year of union which can be attributed to the union is reduced to an average of 4.08 per cent. Not all of these members may be lost to the Church, for certain members take the opportunity to transfer their allegiancies to other congregations at the occurrence of a union. The impact of unions on membership, therefore, may not be on average as adverse as is often supposed.

The impact of unions on income, as measure by 'normal liberality', is broadly consistent with, but more serious than, the changes in membership. In the five years prior to union the income of the sample of congregations increased at a significantly slower rate than the Church average, while in the five years following union the rate was not significantly different. In the year of union, however, there was a large once-over drop in income of 14.61 per cent, which is much larger than anticipated by the fall in membership. It might be explained by a certain dissatisfaction with the union among some members, or by the disruption of normal fund-raising activities caused by the vacancy and subsequent reorganization.

In sections 3 and 4 we went on to analyse separately the economic implications of unions and linkings respectively. This was done by using the income and expenditure equations developed in chapter 12. Taking the typical union as involving congregations with memberships of 599 and 340, it was calculated that the annual savings would amount to £1,324 at 1973 prices; this is composed of a cut in expenditure of £1,618 — mainly the fixed cost of one congregation — less a fall in income of £294, which reflects the 4.08 per cent drop in membership in the year of union. With its enlarged surplus income, the united charge is able to increase the net contribution given to the Maintenance of the Ministry Fund from £149 to £790, and its Mission and Service Fund contribution from £420 to £988. Allowing for these deductions, the net surplus of the charge rises from £82 to £197.

In our examination of the economic implications of linkings, we took the typical linking as involving two congregations with memberships of 304 and 140. According to the income expenditure equations, both congregations would be in deficit, and therefore in receipt of aid from the fund. The main impact of the linking is to reduce the fixed costs of each congregation with the sharing of a minister; we estimate that the resulting annual savings amount to £1,010 at 1973 prices. There is no loss of income, because the membership does not fall as a result of the linking. The improved financial position of the linked charge allows it to reduce a combined aid-receiving position of £1,261 into one of £330, a fall of 73.8 per cent. The mission and service contribution is increased from £20 to £84, and the net surplus rises from zero to £15.

While it should be emphasized that the impact of unions and linkings varies enormously between individual cases, it seems clear that on average both serve to strengthen the financial position of the congregations concerned and of the central funds. Indeed, calculations of the financial impact of unions and linkings of congregations with memberships varying from very small to very large indicated that all showed a considerable improvement in their financial position as a result of the readjustment, although such calculations cannot take account of local factors, such as local opposition to the union, which can sometimes have an adverse effect on membership and income. For this reason it is important that every effort is made by the Presbytery concerned to ensure an easy transition to the united position.

Finally, in section 5 we examined the savings which might accrue to the Church over the period 1976-85 if the decline in the number of charges forecast in chapter 8 is actually realized. Using a weighted annual savings figure per readjustment of £1,194, it was estimated that the cumulative savings at the end of the ten-year period would be running at either £318,907 or £418,225 per year depending upon which forecast of the number of charges was used. These calculations ignore the savings on property brought about by union and readjustment. A rough estimate suggests that the interest earned on the proceeds of sale of property might double the prospective savings figures.

Notes

1 'List of Synods, Presbyteries and Parishes', *The Church of Scotland Yearbook*.

Chapter 14

Education and training for the ministry

1 Introduction
The purpose of this chapter is to examine the education and training of candidates for the ministry. We argue that certain limitations in the present training in practical matters handicaps the newly ordained minister in the efficient conduct of some of his duties. It seems vital to the future security and progress of the Church that its ministers are given an appropriate training for the job. We make recommendations on how the practical training could be improved.

A start is made in section 2 by examining the nature of the education and training received by candidates for the ministry, from the point at which they first apply for a place on a theology course to the time when they are ready to be placed in a charge. The respective roles of university and Church, and the relation between the two, are described.

Then in section 3 we go on to consider how well the courses of education and training for service in the ministry prepare the candidates for the job. Information on the nature and scope of the duties of parish ministers is provided by a Church-conducted questionnaire survey.

2 Education and training for the ministry
The education and training of theological students is conducted in the faculties of Divinity of the four older Scottish universities (those of Aberdeen, Edinburgh, Glasgow, and St Andrews), but candidates for the ministry of the Church of Scotland must also be nominated by their Presbyteries. In this section we examine in turn the nature of the education received by theological students, the recruitment and supervision of candidates for the ministry by the Church, and the relations between Church and university.

1 Education for the ministry
Applications for theological courses need to be made before 31 January for courses starting in the following October. The applicant fills in a schedule obtained from the secretary of the Committee on Education, and at the same time informs the clerk of the Presbytery within whose bounds he normally resides that he desires to be recognized as a student in training for the ministry of the Church of Scotland. The Committee on Education for the ministry arranges for applicants to attend a selection board with a view to determining his fitness for the office of the ministry. If the board is satisfied with the character of the applicant, his (or her) motives for seeking to enter the ministry, and that he has full member-

ship of the Church, it issues its certificate of approval of the candidate to his Presbytery, which, if also satisfied, will nominate him.

There are three different courses for students desiring to enter the ministry:
(i) *the regular course* of not less than six years study, which comprises two main parts: a first degree in Arts, Medicine, Law, Science, etc., or any other suitable professional qualification; and a course of not less than three years theological study leading to a B.D. (Bachelor of Divinity) degree or L.Th. (Licentiate in Theology) qualification of one of the faculties of Divinity of the four universities. This part of the course may be taken outside Scotland in a university or theological college, providing that the course is recognized by the committee as equivalent to at least part of the three years' study for the B.D. or L.Th., in which case a further period of at least three terms at one of the four Scottish Universities is required.

(ii) *the alternative course* under which, with the permission of the Committee on Education for the Ministry, candidates may take a four-year B.D. first degree at one of the four Scottish universities, followed by two years of further study as approved by the committee. A two-year diploma course has been introduced fairly recently to fill this gap. This course has become more popular in recent years.

(iii) *pre-Divinity and Licentiate course*, which is intended for mature students between the ages of 23 and 40 who do not have the necessary qualifications for admission to the universities. Lectures are given on such subjects as English, History, Philosophy and Greek, and the courses are held at Trinity College, Glasgow, and Christ's College, Aberdeen. Candidates are selected by the Central Selection Board, and must have University Prelim. or S.C.E. examination passes in Higher English and at least one other subject, and one 'O'-level pass. The course lasts two years; the first is probationary, and on the basis of a candidate's progress, the committee decides whether he will be permitted to do the second year. On his satisfactory completion of the course, the student is eligible for nomination by his Presbytery, and thereafter he proceeds to the theological course of one of the four universities for his L.Th.

All students must graduate B.D. or L.Th. before proceeding to trials for Licence by the Church. The theological course which leads to the B.D. degree or L.Th. qualification 'is a course conducted by the universities and recognized by the Church.' Students must apply for admission to the Dean of the Faculty of Divinity at the university concerned in the normal way, and pay such fees as the university may require. During the course of theological study, students are under the supervision of the Central Selection Board and the Presbytery, which must confer with students at least once during each recess on the progress of their studies and satisfy itself of their fitness to go forward to the office of the ministry.

Students about to enter their last session of the theological course are required to give the committee the name of the Presbytery to which they intend to apply for licence, and also to apply to the clerk of that Presbytery to be taken on trials for licence (i.e. licence to 'preach the Word'). If no objections are received, the Presbytery will proceed to take the student on trials, although the Central Selection Board must be assured that the student has satisfied its requirements. The trials are undertaken either by the Presbytery, or a committee reporting to the Presbytery, and comprise an oral examination on his knowledge of the principles and practice of the Church of Scotland, and the conduct of public worship at the principal service on a Sunday in the presence of a minister and an elder.

On successful completion of the trials, the candidate becomes a Licentiate of the Church. Before becoming eligible for ordination and induction to a charge, every Licentiate is required to spend a probationary period, normally one year, working under the supervision of one of the Boards of Practical Training (attached to each faculty of Divinity), which directs students to suitable spheres of attachment. Very often probationers act as assistants to the ministers in large urban parishes. During the year all probationers are required to attend a residential school arranged by the Committee on Education for the Ministry.

The Committee on Probationers and Transference of Ministers becomes responsible for Probationers only at the stage when they are ready to be placed in charges. This committee keeps a Roll of Probationers, and congregational Vacancy Committees desiring to consider probationers must, before doing so, apply to the Probationers' Committee for a list of probationers. Thereafter a Vacancy Committee which chooses a probationer as a sole nominee, or as one of the leet, must apply to the committee for his appointment to preach in the vacant charge.

2 Recruitment and supervision of students

The work of recruiting, educating, and supervising candidates for the ministry is the responsibility of the Committee on Education for the Ministry. The committee was reorganized in 1970, and now much of the detailed work is delegated to four sectional committees: (a) Recruitment and Selection of Candidates for the Ministry; (b) Supervision of Students; (c) Supervision of Probationers; (d) 'In-service' Training of Ministers. We will look at the work of each in turn.

A Recuitment and selection of candidates for the ministry

This committee holds selection schools every year for the selection of candidates for the ministry. These are residental, and last two days. Personal interviews form the basis of the selection procedure, but these are supplemented by other tests, both written and oral. The procedure was developed with the help of the Chairman of the Civil Service Selection Board, and are comparable to those used by the Civil Service.

Table 109 gives details of the number of schools held and the number of applicants attending, from the inception of the scheme in 1967 (although one pilot school was held in December 1966). Applicants are accepted subject to the conditions that they attain the appropriate academic qualifications and that they are nominated by Presbyteries. Table 109 shows that on average 79 per cent of applicants are accepted as candidates for the ministry following the selection schools. The rejecting of candidates after the 'extended interview' was felt to be a problem, and this was met in 1969[1] by resolving that rejected applicants should have a right to attend another selection school after one year and to be assessed by different assessors; and that a counsellor should be appointed by the Central Selection Board to be responsible for giving guidance to rejected applicants.

In 1972 a 'deferred' category was introduced, distinguished from the 'not accepted' category in being liable to recall at a later date, whereas in the 'not accepted' group the decision remains with the candidate whether or not to apply again.

From the viewpoint of recruitment, the committee noted in 1971 that the

TABLE 109.
The selection of candidates for the ministry, 1967-75

	Number of schools held	Number of applicants attending	Applicants accepted	Applicants deferred	Applicants not accepted	Percentage of applicants accepted to those applying ($\frac{3}{2} \times 100$) %
	1	2	3	4	5	6
1967[+]	5	81	71	—	10	88
1968	5	83	64	—	19	77
1969	5	80	66	—	14	83
1970	4	69	57	—	12	83
1971	5	69	53	—	16	77
1972	7	109	85	5	19	78
1973	*	90	71	2	17	79
1974	*	90	61	2	27	68
1975	*	72	*	*	*	—
TOTAL	31	743	528	9	134	79[×]

SOURCE 'Report of the Committee on Education for the Ministry', *Reports to the General Assembly,* 1968-76.
[+] Including one 'pilot' school held in December 1966.
[×] Average figure for 1967-74.
* Not available

numbers of applicants accepted as candidates for the ministry has remained fairly constant over the last two decades, with an average of 55 entering the first theological year each session, and that 'very few have failed to finish the course and become Licentiates of the Church.' The committee goes on to remark, however, that 'satisfaction at this consistence has . . . been tempered by the knowledge that this number is barely sufficient to meet the Church's needs.'

Table 110 shows the distribution of students in training for the ministry in each of the four universities for the years 1966/7 to 1975/6. The total student numbers are fairly constant from year to year at a little over 200; about three-quarters of the students are in courses at the universities of Edinburgh and

TABLE 110.
Distribution by university of students in training for the ministry, 1966/7-1975/6

	1966/7	1967/8	1968/9	1969/70	1970/1	1971/2	1972/3	1973/4	1974/5	1975/6
St Andrews	14	13	16	15	15	18	*	*	*	17
Glasgow	88	93	76	81	88	88	*	*	*	93
Aberdeen	35	38	38	35	38	34	*	*	*	27
Edinburgh	69	65	67	75	72	65	*	*	*	73
Cambridge	2	1	3	1	1	1	*	*	*	0
TOTAL	208	210	200	207	214	206	215	226	232	210

SOURCE: 'Report of the Committee on Education for the Ministry', *Reports to the General Assembly,* 1967-76, appendices.
* Not available.

Glasgow. Table 111 gives the distribution of the students in training in the academic year 1975/6 by year of the different courses for each University. The biggest single course is the Regular Course, which accounts for 79 of the 210 students in training, but the variants of the Alternative Course together have a greater number of students.

B Supervision of students

The function of the Committee on the Supervision of Students is 'to examine, supervise and maintain contact with candidates in training for the ministry during the period between nomination by Presbytery and licensing by Presbytery.' Much of the work is done through local liaison committees which are attached to each Divinity Faculty.

Students in training for the ministry are financed in one of the following three ways: Scottish Education Department (S.E.D.) grants; grants from other education authorities; and presentation bursaries. Formerly, small presentation bursaries were given to students in addition to S.E.D. and other grants. However, in recent years inflation has reduced the 'real' worth of the bursary available for distribution, and this, combined with the fact that many students, particularly married men with family responsibilities, are not eligible for S.E.D. grants, has meant that presentation bursaries have increasingly been restricted to 'needy' students.

Many students also used to derive some income from the system of "student assistantships", in which students worked as a part of their training in a limited part-time capacity as assistants to ministers. However, the system of student assistantships attracted a good deal of criticism, not least amongst students, and in 1970 the system was replaced with one of 'student attachments'. The work is of a similar nature, but the time required of the student is less, and he is no longer paid.

C Supervision of probationers

Probationers are employed by the congregations of the parishes in which they serve as assistants to the minister. Up to 1970 there was much dissatisfaction amongst probationers arising from the differences in salaries paid by the different Kirk Sessions, and also from the fact that some congregations provided free or subsidized housing while others did not. As a result, efforts were made in 1969 to standardize the employment situation of probationers by equating their salaries with the minimum stipend less £250. This led to a sharp rise in probationers' salaries from an average of £850 a year in 1968/9 to £1,142 a year in 1971/2.

Students are sometimes exempted from the probationery period on the grounds that older men have no time to lose, that married men cannot fulfil their commitments on a probationer's salary, and that men of experience would like to be out on their own. However, the Report of the *ad hoc* Committee on Recruitment and Training of the Ministry argued in 1969 that none of these reasons is sufficient to justify exemption, and that the probationary period 'ought to be regarded as essential for *all* students.[2] As a result, fewer students were exempted from the probationary period, the number falling from 26 in 1968 to 6 in 1970.

The result of the increase in salary on the one hand and the reduced exemptions on the other has been to cause financial problems for the Home Board, which subsidizes the bulk of those congregations which cannot afford to pay for

TABLE 111

Number of students in training for the ministry by course and university, 1975-6

	Expected completion of course	Regular	1 B.D.+2	1 B.D.+1	1 B.D.	P.D.+1 B.D.	Including L.Th.	Special	Total	
Aberdeen	1976	1	1	—	—	—	—	2	4	
	1977	6	2	1	1	—	—	—	10	
	1978	3	2	—	—	—	3	—	8	
	1979	—	3	—	—	1	—	—	4	27
	1980	—	1	—	—	—	—	—	1	
Edinburgh	1976	15	3	2	1	—	—	3	24	
	1977	11	4	4	—	—	—	1	20	
	1978	11	5	4	1	—	—	—	21	
	1979	—	4	1	2	—	—	—	7	73
	1980	—	1	—	—	—	—	—	1	
Glasgow	1976	9	3	3	6	3	1	7	32	
	1977	11	3	5	2	1	4	1	27	
	1978	5	6	3	2	—	5	—	21	
	1979	—	1	5	—	—	1	—	7	93
	1980	—	4	2	—	—	—	—	6	
St Andrews	1976	—	1	—	—	—	1	1	3	
	1977	6	—	1	—	—	2	—	9	
	1978	1	2	—	—	—	—	—	3	
	1979	—	1	—	—	—	—	—	1	17
	1980	—	1	—	—	—	—	—	1	
TOTAL	1976	25	8	5	7	3	2	13	63	
	1977	34	9	11	3	1	6	2	66	
	1978	20	15	7	3	—	8	—	53	
	1979	—	9	6	2	1	1	—	19	210
	1980	—	7	2	—	—	—	—	9	

SOURCE: 'Report of the Committee on Education for the Ministry', *Reports to the General Assembly, 1976*, appendix, p. 419.

the full probationer's salary. The Home Board itself is helped by funds from the Committee on Education.

D In-service training

Various short courses for ministers are conducted by the Youth Committee, the Education Committee, and different committees of the Home Board. The first course of in-service training was arranged by the Committee on Education for the Ministry in April 1970 at Aberdeen University. Since then in-service training courses for ministers have been held regularly, usually at the rate of two per year.

3 Church and university

The faculties of Divinity in the four older Scottish Universities do not exist to train ministers for the Church of Scotland, although in former days it may have seemed that they did. Nowadays, the faculties include a number of ministers and laymen from other denominations, and amongst the students there are those who are candidates for other Churches, and some who do not contemplate entering the ministry at all; in two of the faculties the candidates for the Church of Scotland ministry form only a minority of students.

Despite recent developments, however, the present system has its origins in history long past. Students preparing for the ministry in the pre-Union Church of Scotland were taught in the faculties of Divinity of the then four Scottish universities.[3] Professorial chairs were 'tested by subscription to the Confession of Faith', and had to be held by ministers of the Church of Scotland. In each university, there were four professors, each teaching one of the traditional disciplines: Old Testament, New Testament, Church history and systematic theology. The fifth discipline of practical theology was introduced around the time of the Union. In negotiations prior to the Union, legislation was introduced which removed the tests, although boards of nomination to the chairs continued to have equal representation from Church and university. As a result, a professor needed no longer to be a minister of the Church of Scotland, and, even if he was a minister, he was responsible to the university court for his teaching and research activities; hence after 1929 the faculties of Divinity had a different relationship to the Church than previously.

In the pre-union United Free Church the situation was different. In three of the four university centres it ran colleges which it had established following the 1843 Disruption, whose teachers were appointed by, and responsible to, the General Assembly of the United Free Church. At the Union these teachers were accepted into the faculties of Divinity on similar appointments to those of the existing staff.

Today the only authoritative statement on what the Church of Scotland requires in the preparation of candidates for the ministry is contained in the *Plan and Basis of Union* of 1929,[4] which outlines the subject-matter of the five disciplines mentioned above. The statement presupposed a uniform degree structure, but at present no two B.D. courses in the four universities are the same in structure and content, and the extent of specialization permitted varies considerably from one faculty to another. This diversity is probably explained by the university control of the B.D. syllabus since 1929, together with the desire of the faculties of Divinity to attract students other than those who are candidates for the Church of Scotland ministry.

3 The duties of parish ministers

So far we have been concerned with the process by which candidates for the ministry are recruited, educated and trained. We now go on to consider how well this process prepares the candidate for the job.

Dissatisfaction seems to be felt in some quarters of the Church over the nature of the training in practical theology, or pastoral care, given to students. The feeling seems to be that the training is not sufficiently practical, and is not designed specifically for Church of Scotland students. Moreover, a survey of the attitudes of students in training suggests that pastoral care does not have, at present, a high rating in their view of the ministry. This suggests that they have not been sufficiently trained in this discipline, or that they have not been given enough practical experience for them to see the importance of this training.

Information on the nature and scope of the duties of parish ministers is provided by the results of a questionnaire survey conducted by the Special Committee Anent Manpower in 1966-7.[5] The questionnaire was sent to the ministers in 15 of the (then) 60 home Presbyteries; this represented 15.3 per cent of the total number of parish ministers in charges, of whom 143, or 8.0 per cent of the total, replied to the questions. As surveys were being carried out by others in Aberdeen and Edinburgh, those Presbyteries were omitted from the survey. The committee considered the sample of Presbyteries to reflect the diverse regions of Scotland.

Table 112 shows the hours spent on his various duties by the average parish minister in an average week. These duties fall into the following five main categories: official, parish visiting, private study, administration, and public duties. The average time spent weekly on official duties amounted to 6.2 hours, of which 4.7 hours were taken up with the actual conduct of Sunday services. A further 1.5 hours per week was taken up with weddings and funerals, although the time spent in individual cases is said to be closely linked to the population of the parish and the number of members.

TABLE 112
Breakdown of the average working week of a parish minister from a survey in 1966-7

	Activity	Hours	%
1	Official:		
	conduct of Sunday services	4.7	
	weddings and funerals	1.5	
TOTAL		6.2	12.2
2	Visiting	16.2	31.8
3	Reading, study, sermon preparation, and private devotions	20.0	39.2
4	Administration		
	administration	2.7	
	secretarial	2.9	
	Presbytery, Synod, etc.	1.5	
TOTAL		7.1	13.9
5	Public	1.5	2.9
TOTAL		51.0	100.0

An average of 16.2 hours per week was given to visiting; this was felt to be adequate in 65 cases, but inadequate in 68. Visits to the sick and aged, in home or hospital, took up most time, and appeared to be covered adequately. Congregational visitation was undertaken fairly consistently, but stated to be inadequate in most cases owing to the pressure of other duties.

Twenty hours per week were spent on private study and sermon preparation.

Administration and committee work involved 7.1 hours, of which 2.7 hours was spent on congregational administration, and 2.9 hours on secretarial work; the preparation of the parish magazine was frequently mentioned in the latter connection. A further 1.5 hours was spent on Presbytery, Synod, and central committee work, but this falls mainly in one week in the month, and more heavily on the convenors of committees; 51 of the 143 ministers were members of Assembly committees.

Outside duties in the community fall more heavily on ministers in rural parishes, but personal interest has an important influence on the time given and the kind of community work engaged in; 126 of the 143 ministers in the sample were chaplains to schools, hospitals, and industry, accounting for an average of 1.5 hours per week.

Overall, the average minister usually worked 51 hours in the week. About half of that time was spent on what were essentially 'religious' activities – the official duties and private study – and half on 'practical' activities – visiting and administration work. This contrasts with the balance in the education of ministers, which is heavily weighted towards liturgical and theological training. In the B.D. course, only one of the five disciplines is concerned with the practical side of the ministry. While the quality of the theological training is considered to be excellent, concern has been expressed at the inadequate level of training in practical theology. For example, the *ad hoc* Committee on Recruitment and Training, while welcoming the recognition of practical theology as the fifth discipline within the faculties of Divinity, also stated their belief that a greater emphasis could be placed on training in 'the every-day aspects and responsibilities of the 'ministry'[6] This is a view that we heartily endorse.

Although the courses in practical theology differ widely between the faculties of Divinity in the four universities, the practical training given is largely confined to the conduct of the official duties, such as services, weddings and funerals, and to parish visiting and dealing with the social problems that arise. In our view, the most important omission is in training in administration and committee management; the parish minister is not only *ex officio* the Moderator of the Kirk Session, but also a member of the financial court (in most *quoad sacra* parishes) and of the various committees of the Kirk Session, such as the membership, liberality, fabric, and visitation committees. The role of the minister in dealing with these committees is well recognized in the theory of small-group management; effectively, it involves encouraging the members of the committees in their various tasks by helping to point out the dimensions of the tasks, by monitoring their work, by helping to recruit suitable members for the committees, and helping to suggest the names of parishioners who might serve on sub-committees or act as agents for the committees. In our view, therefore, the minister in effect delegates the bulk of the practical work to lay members. His work consists of influencing the deliberations of the committees, which he can do by reason of his greater experience and better training for the work involved, his long tenure of office in the committees involved, and by virtue of his good personal relations with the individual members of each of the committees. It should not be necessary for the minister to solicit contributions himself, or even to canvass for members himself.

It seems clear, therefore, that the minister must have knowledge and training, not only in dealing with individual parishioners, but also in dealing with groups of interested elders and other laymen in committee. He must have considerable training in the various alternative procedures which can be made to work in such committees, and knowledge to pass on to the relevant committee of the ways in which membership, stewardship, and fund-raising drives can best be organized. He should also be able to train his elders in methods of routine parish visiting, so leaving himself time to visit the sick, the elderly, and the bereaved. The kind of training we have in mind might be described by the term 'catalytic management'.

These considerations suggest that changes may need to be made in the education and training of ministers. We make the following proposals:

(i) Applicants for the ministry should be selected on the basis of their assessed suitability for the tasks at hand, although the limited number of applicants forthcoming at the present time will unfortunately restrict the degree of selectivity which can be exercised.
(ii) The education and training of candidates for the ministry should be improved by increasing the size and scope of the course on practical theology.
(iii) Students should not proceed to trials for Licence until their general competence at the academic level in practical theology is established by examination.
(iv) It is important that the one-year probationary period should not be spent in one parish, but on a tour of duty covering several parishes, so that the probationer is not influenced unduly by one relatively successful or unsuccessful minister. Ministers with a special capacity in one or another of the various tasks which ministers need to perform should be encouraged to take probationers.
(v) A one-year postgraduate course in pastoral care might be introduced for students who have completed the regular or alternative courses. This course might be sandwiched in the probationary year, so that probationers might spend alternating periods in college and as an assistant to a minister in a parish. It is not certain that the University Grants Committee, through which public funds are supplied to the universities, would be prepared to finance such training; the church itself might have to bear the costs, which could be quite high.
(vi) Because the job of the minister is very complex and varied, he must be subject to regular refresher and retraining courses. These should not be confined to, or even consist mainly of, theology, but should include training in business methods, finance, administration, and pastoral problems.

4 Conclusions

The purpose of this chapter has been to examine broadly how candidates for the ministry are educated and trained, and to make recommendations on the element of practical training where that is found wanting.

In section 2 we saw that candidates for the ministry are taught in the faculties of Divinity of the four older Scottish universities, but that candidates must first be nominated by their Presbyteries after having met the requirements of a selection board. There is a regular course, comprising a first degree followed by a B.D.; an alternative course, comprising a B.D. and two further years of study; and a pre-Divinity and Licentiate course for mature students who do not have the necessary qualifications for admission to the universities. The B.D. and L.Th. qualifications have courses conducted by the universities and recognized by the Church. On graduation, the candidate undertakes a trial for Licence, on the successful completion of which he becomes a Licentiate. The Licentiate normally undergoes a one-year probationary period, usually as an assistant to a parish minister, before becoming eligible for ordination to the ministry and induction to a charge.

The Committee on Education for the Ministry is responsible for recruiting, educating, and supervising candidates for the ministry. Applicants are assessed at two-day residential selection schools. In recent years an average of 79 per cent have been accepted as candidates, and students in training have numbered a little over 200 in each of the past several years, about three-quarters of whom are at the universities of Edinburgh and Glasgow. The regular course remains the largest single course, although the Alternative Course has increased in popularity.

In section 3 we went on to examine how far the training candidates received prepared them for the job of parish minister. In a Church questionnaire survey of the ministers in a sample of Presbyteries in 1966-7, it was found that the average minister worked an average 51 hour week. This time was divided roughly equally between 'religious' activities (official duties and private study) on the one hand, and 'practical' activities (visiting, administration, and public duties) on the other. In contrast, only one of the five courses in the theology degree is concerned with the practical side of the ministry, and contains nothing on administration, business methods, and committee management. We argued that committee management in particular – the recruiting, guiding and vitalizing of congregational committees concerned with membership, income, fabric and the like – was among the most important tasks of the minister. We recommend that all candidates for the ministry should receive adequate training in committee management and group leadership, and that they should not proceed to trials for Licence until their general competence at the academic level in practical theology is established by examination.

We also recommend that because of the variety and complexity of the minister's job, he should be subject to regular in-service training courses.

Notes

1 Church of Scotland, 'Report of the Committee on Education for the Ministry', *Reports to the General Assembly, 1969,* p. 745.
2 'Report of the *ad hoc* Committee on Recruitment and Training of the Ministry', *Reports to the General Assembly, 1969,* p. 809.
3 ibid., pp. 801-4.
4 Reproduced by J.T. Cox in *Practice and Procedure*, 6th ed. (1976), pp. 405-6.
5 *Reports to the General Assembly, 1967,* pp. 777-82.
6 *Reports to the General Assembly, 1969,* p. 806.

Chapter 15

New forms of ministry

1 Introduction
In chapter 12 on congregational finance it was found that the financial position of a congregation can to a significant extent be explained by the size of its membership. Owing to the large fixed-cost element in the expenditure of a congregation, those congregations where the membership is relatively low tend to be in deficit, since the annual expenditure tends to exceed the annual income from congregational sources (i.e. excluding aid received), while in large congregations income tends to exceed expenditure, giving rise to a surplus position. It was further suggested that congregations in rural areas where the population is sparse tend to have small memberships, and often tend to be in receipt of aid from the Maintenance of the Ministry Fund. On the other hand, in urban areas the tendency is for congregations to have relatively large memberships and income, and to be givers of aid to the fund, although the impact of the congregation on the parish as measured by the proportion of members to the population may be small.

The financial weakness of the parish ministry in many rural areas, and the decline of the membership in urban areas, have in recent years encouraged experiments in, and proposals for, new forms of parish ministry in the Church of Scotland. Some salient points in these new experiments and proposals are examined briefly below in section 2. Then in section 3 we discuss the economic implications of a proposal for a radical reorganization of urban parishes into team ministries. Finally, in section 4 the proposal for the introduction of part-time non-stipendiary ministers is examined.

2 New forms of parish ministry
The Report of the Special Committee Anent Manpower in 1966 gives a summary of 'the types of ministry in existence or envisaged by the General Assembly in reports over the past two decades.' Four types of ministry are distinguished.[1]
(i) *The normal parish ministry*. This is defined as follows: 'The first form will continue to be of the familiar pattern of one parish-one minister, where the work of the minister covers the whole field of administering the sacraments, preaching, teaching, administration, organizing, counselling and pastoral duties. In this he may be assisted by part-time, mostly voluntary, workers.'
(ii) *The larger parish ministry*. 'This is found usually where a parish has a numerically large, or potentially large (as in Church Extension charges), Communion Roll. In such, the minister has an assistant, student, Licentiate, or ordained probationer and/or a deaconess, all of whom are paid workers, but who are

under the direction of the minister, and have no direct connection with the courts of the Church in virtue of their appointments.'

The position of these various types of parish assistant is briefly as follows. Firstly, lay missionaries are agents of the Home Board appointed to preach and exercise pastoral care under the direction of the minister and Kirk Session; in 1974 the committee had 57 lay missionaries in its employ. They serve mainly either in 'mission stations' found in the isolated communities in the north-west Highlands and Islands, or now increasingly in the heavily populated urban areas of the central lowlands. They receive a salary amounting to 75 per cent of the minimum stipend, together with supplements after seven and fourteen years of service. A house, or sum in lieu of a house, is provided.

Secondly, the function of deaconesses is 'to exercise a ministry of an evangelistic, pastoral, educational or social nature' in a variety of spheres; of the 46 deaconesses employed by the Home Board in 1974, 37 were parochial assistants. They are to be found mainly in large new housing areas, where the number of ministers is low in relation to the size of the population; here their main work is in parish visitation, congregational youth work, and chaplaincy work in schools. Deaconesses are paid on the same basis as lay missionaries.

The third category of parish assistant is the Licentiate or probationer. These are men or women who have gained their Licence following university training, and who are serving in a parish for a probationary year prior to ordination, at which time they become eligible for induction to a charge. They are employed by, and are responsible to, the Kirk Session, which pays them a salary equivalent to the minimum stipend less £250. A number of congregations receive grants from the Home Board towards the salary of their Licentiate. The great majority of Licentiates serve in urban parishes.

Finally, there are ordained assistants. Some Licentiates stay on in probationary employment for a second year, usually either because they feel the need to serve another year's 'apprenticeship', or because they wish to continue work which they started as probationers. Most seek, and are granted, ordination by Presbytery (i.e. they become ministers), but retain their assistant status. They are paid a salary equivalent to the minimum stipend less £150.

The request for the employment of an assistant comes from the minister and the Kirk Session, who put in an application through the Presbytery. The Home Board deals with requests for lay missionaries and deaconesses, and the Committee on Education for the Ministry with requests for Licentiates.

(iii) *The team ministry*. This is defined as follows: 'By the term "team ministry" is meant a minimum of two ordained ministers, one of whom is inducted to the charge in the usual way, the other having the status of an ordained probationer. . . . Such a team ministry may be enlarged by the addition of other ordained assistants and/or full-time lay workers for special duties . . .'

The report envisages that team ministries would be called into being in three main situations. The first situation is in remote, rural areas where 'a readjustment calls for the continued use of churches in different parishes or districts and for a resident minister in more than one of them . . .' These areas are called 'special areas of readjustment', and are normally co-terminous with a Presbytery area; the Presbytery is required to enter into a planned programme of readjustment. There are special areas of readjustment in the Presbyteries of Inveraray, Kintyre,

Islay, Abernethy, Sutherland, Caithness, Lochcarron, Orkney and Shetland. In every instance the team ministries were formed by associate ministers joining with ministers who had been inducted in the normal way.

The second situation in which the special committee considered that team ministries would be called into being is in 'specialized ministries, such as chaplaincies in industry, etc., [which] would greatly benefit by being more closely associated with the work of the Church at parish and Presbytery level.'

The third situation is in 'large new housing areas where greater impact is needed than can be made by one minister, even with an assistant.'

(iv) *The group ministry.* This is '... a grouping of two or more ministers, preferably more, each in full charge of their own parishes and congregations, along with their Kirk Sessions, working together in the mission of the Church to the area.

'Such a group ministry must of necessity be voluntary and experimental, but should be initiated by the Presbytery of the bounds. Its ministers would continue to be separate and in charge of their own parishes as at present . . . but a basis of group ministry would involve an undertaking, under the Presbytery, to take part in such a group ministry; to meet with such numbers of the Kirk Sessions involved as would seem proper in the particular town or area of a city; to prepare and plan for action by the whole Church, as represented by the particular group, and the gradual building up of the image of the Church in the area as the one Church of Jesus Christ'.

In July 1975 there appeared to be no ministers operating under a basis of group ministry in the Church of Scotland. However, there is a similar form of arrangement called a 'basis of association', which has the effect of setting up a group ministry, although the ultimate aim is to unite the congregations concerned.

The Report of the Special Committee Anent Manpower represents the 'moderate' approach to team and group ministries, where the normal parish ministry remains the basic form of organization, and where any reorganization is limited and based on the present parish structure. Team ministries are suggested for large and difficult parishes, for example, in sparsely populated rural areas ('special areas of readjustment'), where the reorganization takes the form of extended linkings with an assistant minister or lay missionary helping the minister by being stationed in one or more of the linked congregations. Staff costs are reduced in comparison with the normal parish organization, but it is difficult to assess whether the effectiveness of the ministry is maintained. Team ministries also occur in large new housing estates in cities, where it is thought that the minister would benefit from the help of assistants (e.g. ordained assistants, deaconesses or lay missionaries). This form of organization serves to increase personnel costs, but it is an open question as to whether the effectiveness of the ministry is improved commensurately. Group ministries can be formed by ministers and their congregations in adjacent parishes, who otherwise retain their separate status, joining for common services and activities. This form of reorganization is attractive, partly because it may improve the effectiveness of the congregations concerned, so perhaps increasing church membership, attendance and income, and partly because it may form the prelude to the union of the congregations at some later date.

A limited number of experiments in team and group ministries along the lines defined in the report of the special committee are now in progress. In July 1975 five team ministries (apart from the special areas of readjustment) set up by the Church and Ministry Department and the Presbyteries concerned were in operation; two were in Glasgow, and one each in Edinburgh, Dundee and Paisley. At the same time there were four bases of association in operation, two of which have just resulted in the unions of the congregations concerned.

An alternative 'radical' approach to new forms of parish organization was advocated in the 1975 report of the Committee of Forty.[2] The approach taken is based on the proposition that parish boundaries, especially in many urban districts, no longer correspond to the area of the local community, which results in a fall in the effectiveness of pastoral care, and is conditioned by the forecasts of a sharp fall in the number of ministers over the coming decade. The report argues, therefore, the need for a large reorganization of the parish system in urban areas. Existing parishes would be merged into large units which correspond to geographical communities, and the enlarged parishes would be managed by teams composed of a minister and a number of full-time and voluntary assistants. 'A city centre, for instance, such as Aberdeen, might be one such parish; a town like Bathgate might be another; an identifiable rural area such as the islands of Mull and Iona might be treated as a separate parish; present rural parishes with radial links with a country town might become part of a radial parish; a new housing area such as Castlemilk or Craigmillar might be another. A Presbytery in consultation with groups of Kirk Sessions would be best placed to work out its new parishes in detail. But the aim would be to delineate the identifiable area of mission for the Church within the Presbytery's bounds, and to group existing parishes accordingly.'

The report suggests that the precise methods of working such teams will vary from place to place, but that every team 'must have a leader with ability to co-ordinate plans and common efforts.'

This brief survey of new forms of parish ministry has indicated that the main policy issue concerns the organization of team ministries, and the extent to which they should be introduced. The 'moderate' approach to team ministries is reflected in the current official policy of running a limited number of experiments in existing parishes where the circumstances seem especially favourable. The 'radical' alternative rests on the argument that the effective operation of the parish ministry, particularly in urban areas, requires a large-scale reorganization of the parish structure. In the next section we examine the economic implications of the 'radical' form of team ministry as advocated by the Committee of Forty.

3 The economic implications of the radical proposal for team ministries

Although the proposals of the Committee of Forty have not been spelt out in detail, broadly speaking what appears to be proposed is the merger of existing parishes in urban areas to form larger parish units. The new enlarged parishes might be based on 'identifiable' geographical communities, and the ministers in the former parishes covered by the new community parish would be replaced by a single minister in charge of a team of assistants, composed variously of assistant ministers, lay missionaries and deaconesses, together with lay-workers. This arrangement avoids the problems of leadership and the allocation of duties associated with teams composed of two or more ministers. Individual assistants might be required to specialize in different aspects of the work of the parish unit, such as youth work or the visitation of parishioners. The number of church buildings within the enlarged parish might also be reduced, with surplus manses being sold, and the various other buildings being developed for special purposes; for example, one or two churches might be used for the holding of services, while another might be developed as a youth centre.

The implementation of such reorganization on a wide scale in urban areas would have a profound effect on the employment of manpower in the parish ministry. The number of parish ministers would be reduced substantially, while the number of assistants would undergo a large increase. For example, if 600 urban parishes were to be converted into 150 community parishes, there would be a loss of 450 ministerial posts; this amounts to a fall of more than a quarter on the 1,588 ministers serving in parishes in 1975. At the same time the number of parish assistants might be expected to increase by at least 450. The total manpower in the parish ministry – ministers and assistants of various kinds – would probably stay constant, and might rise.

If the difficulties of organizing these new arrangements of manpower could be overcome, it is possible that the new scheme might be more cost-effective. This might arise because assistants are paid a salary below the minimum stipend, so that with a given annual expenditure it is possible to employ a larger number of assistants than ministers. The differential between the cost to the Church of ministers and assistants is further widened when it is remembered that a minister is provided with a manse maintained by the congregation, whereas a house only is provided for ordained assistants, lay missionaries and deaconesses. The actual differentials at 1975 prices, based on salaries and the cost of any housing provided, are given in table 113; these figures indicate that, broadly speaking, the cost of an urban minister to the Church is roughly twice as high as that of a lay missionary, deaconess, or probationer, and about one-and-a-half times that of an ordained assistant.

In reorganizing urban parishes into team ministries, the Church would face a range of policy options from which we will select two for consideration. The first would be a constant manpower option, in which the *number* of personnel employed in the parish ministry would be held constant; for example, a team ministry formed from the merger of four parishes might be staffed by a minister and three assistants in place of the four ministers. The total salary bill for the parish ministry would fall significantly, and an income would accrue from the renting-out of surplus manses. Rough calculations based on the figures in table 113 suggest that, if 600 urban parishes were to be converted into 150 team ministry parishes in this manner, the outcome would be an improvement in the financial position of the Church by nearly £1 million a year at 1975 prices. However, it is an open question as to whether this new arrangement would maintain the effectiveness of the ministry, even though the number of personnel employed remained the same: assistants might not have as great an impact on the parish as the former ministers.

An alternative which the Church would face in reorganizing urban parishes into team ministry parishes would be a 'constant salary bill' option; the number of personnel employed in the parish ministry would be increased (assuming sufficient manpower was available) to the point where the salary bill equalled that

TABLE 113.
Relative costs of ministers and assistants in the Church of Scotland, 1975

	£
MINISTER	
minimum stipend	2,352
opportunity cost of urban manse*	1,750
annual cost to congregation of maintaining manse[x]	375
TOTAL	4,477
LAY MISSIONARY AND DEACONESS	
basic salary set at 75% of the minimum stipend	1,764
(lay missionaries also receive increments for years of service)	
rental of house+	700
TOTAL	2,464
PROBATIONER	
Salary (minimum stipend less £250)	2,102
ORDAINED ASSISTANT	
salary (minimum stipend less £150)	2,202
Rental of house+	700
TOTAL	2,902

*The 'opportunity cost' of the manse is taken to be the potential annual rental, which is set at 7 per cent of the capital value. An urban manse is assumed to be worth on average £25,000.

[x]SOURCE: Church of Scotland, *Housing for the ministry. Memorandum no. 3* (1973), p.1. The figure has been increased by 25% to £375 to allow for price increases since 1973.

+The annual rental of the house is set at 7% of the capital value, which is assumed to be £10,000.

obtaining prior to the reorganization; for example, in a team ministry formed from the merger of four urban parishes, the four ministers could be replaced by a team comprising one minister, one ordained assistant, one probationer, and three or four lay missionaries and deaconesses. In the example quoted above of 600 urban parishes converted into 150 team ministry parishes, the former 600 ministers could be replaced by a combination of 150 ministers, 150 ordained assistants, 150 probationers, and 500 lay missionaries and deaconesses. Again, the question as to how the reorganization would alter the effectiveness of the urban parish ministry is an open one, but it is conceivable that such a large increase in manpower, properly managed in teams, might result in an improvement in effectiveness.

A reorganization of manpower in the parish ministry on such a scale would give rise to obvious, and considerable, difficulties. The conversion of 600 urban parishes into 150 team ministry parishes would result in a loss of 450 ministers, which would reduce the 1974 number from 1,631 to 1,181. According to even the most pessimistic ministerial manpower forecast, a level of 1,181 ministers is unlikely to be reached by the end of the century through natural wastage (see chapter 7). Attempts to speed up the decline in the number of ministers by early retirements, direction of ministers to particular charges, restrictions on tenure, and other measures might prove highly unpopular.

This view is supported by a special report in 1970 on team and group ministries by the Committee on the Maintenance of the Ministry in response to an instruction of the General Assembly in 1968. On the question of the manning of such ministries, it made the following comment: '. . . there is a shortage of ministers already. If we were to talk in terms of team ministries in church extension charges, the Church does not have the ministerial manpower resources to cope. There may be many ministers who are prepared to be the senior minister in the team, ordained and inducted. The committee does not believe that there is a significant number of ministers in the Church who are prepared to undertake for any reasonable time the duties of an associate minister under instruction of the senior minister of the team.'

The committee stated that it had considerable experience of team ministries, and that, while 'one or two have been completely successful', in 'a number of cases the ministers concerned have found it impossible to work together in harmony.'

A second question which emerges over the reorganization of urban parishes into team ministry parishes concerns the effectiveness of the new form of ministry in comparison with conventional forms. The efficiency test is very important, because there is little point in making changes in the parish ministry unless improvements result. In theory at least, the effectiveness of an operation can be measured by the benefit:cost ratio, where an increase in the numerical value of the ratio indicates an improvement in effectiveness, and a decline the reverse. A new form of ministry might show an increase in cost-effectiveness by producing larger benefits, such as higher membership, attendance and liberality, with a given volume of resources; or by maintaining the output of benefits at a given level with a smaller volume of resources, or by some combination of the two. A weakness of the proposals of the Committee of Forty is that there is little evidence, and that generally adverse, to support their claim that the reorganization of parishes into team ministries would improve the effectiveness of the parish ministry.

In order to assess the comparative effectiveness of team ministries, a series of careful experiments would be required. Several experimental team ministries would have to be set up, since an analysis of one or two experiments would be subject to the influence of many chance factors, such as the personality of the minister, the compatibility of the merged congregations, and so on. A suitable control group of parishes would be required to act as a standard against which the impact of the experimental ministries could be judged. But the setting up of several experimental team ministries might prove impractical. A condition for the setting up of each experiment would be that the parishes concerned would have to fall vacant at about the same time, and that the congregations would all have to agree to participate in the Presbytery-sponsored reorganization; this would be somewhat difficult where three or more parishes are involved. The establishment of several experimental team ministries might thus take many years to accomplish. The alternative would be that parish ministers would have to suffer a weakening of their rights of tenure, a possibility recognized by the Committee of Forty. A further difficulty is that the reorganization would probably be irreversible, since they imply the merger of congregations and the rationalization of the buildings in use. It might be dangerous to risk such experiments in several parishes, in case the team ministries proved ineffective.

As an alternative to the introduction of team ministries, the policy of union and readjustment is commended by the fact that it is a well-tested and largely successful policy which has been conducted for a period of more than 40 years; the economic implications of union and readjustment are dicussed above in chapter 13.

4 Part-time non-stipendiary ministers

The introduction of part-time non-stipendiary ministers in rural areas was suggested in the 1975 Report of the Committee of Forty[3] and the whole question is now being given serious consideration by the Church. It is envisaged that such ministers might be recruited from among church-going professional people, such as schoolteachers and doctors, who would undergo an appropriate period of training leading to ordination, or from those who are already fully ordained ministers, in employment outside the Church. Non-stipendiary ministers would remain employed full-time in secular employment, but would be qualified like parish ministers to perform the duties of the ministry of the Word and sacraments. They would be under the direction and control of the minister of the parish to which they were attached. In the longer term it is envisaged that part-time non-stipendiary ministers would come to replace the minister in many small rural congregations in the Highlands. These small congregations would be grouped together in much enlarged linked charges for which one parish minister would be responsible. Non-stipendiary ministers who took over the day-to-day responsibility for a congregation would be eligible to occupy the appropriate manse.

Although the proposal for introducing non-stipendiary ministers is attractive as a means of economizing in the provision of ministerial manpower to the small congregations in the Highlands and Islands, many of which are in receipt of aid from the Maintenance of the Ministry Fund, it does pose difficult problems. Since the non-stipendiary minister would be equal in status to the parish minister, but under his direction and control, there are likely to be disagreements arising over the work assigned to the non-stipendiary minister; experiments in group ministries indicate that this is likely to be so. Where agreement could not be reached, the case would have to be taken to the Presbytery for judgement. Unless the parish minister was found to have acted unreasonably, the non-stipendiary minister would be in the wrong. Difficulties would arise if the non-stipendiary minister were to be assigned to another parish, for he could not be expected to move his home and job accordingly. It seems clear that the predominant position of the parish minister would have to be stressed at the outset.

A further problem is that it is not certain how many would be prepared to come forward as candidates for the non-stipendiary ministry. People are taking a greater interest in leisure and recreational activities, and many would be unwilling to forgo such pursuits for unpaid service. The proposition may be made even less attractive for those who would require a period of training, possibly full-time for one year, prior to ordination.

5 Conclusions

There has been much discussion in recent years about the possibility of new forms of parish ministry in the Church of Scotland. This discussion has been prompted by an awareness of certain weaknesses in the traditional 'one man, one parish' ministry, especially the financial weakness of the ministry in rural areas, and the apparent lack of effectiveness of the ministry in urban areas. The purpose of the chapter has been to examine the merits of proposed alternative forms of ministry.

We found that experiments in new forms of ministry have followed a moderate approach, being based on small adjustments to the present system, and carried out in a limited number of parishes where the conditions are deemed to be favourable. Team ministries have been formed by providing assistants to help ministers in difficult parishes, such as in large new housing areas, and in Presbyteries covering the more remote rural districts where extended linkings have taken place (the 'special areas of readjustment'). In the first case salary costs are increased, and in the second they may be reduced; but in neither is it easy to assess whether the effectiveness of the ministry has changed. Group ministries have also been formed from the joining of adjacent congregations and their ministers in common services and activities. Although the congregations concerned retain their separate identities, these do promote unions at some later date.

Radical proposals for team ministries were put forward in 1975 by the Committee of Forty that involve a considerable reorganization of the parish structure in urban areas. They involve merging groups of four or five parishes which cover 'identifiable' geographical communities, such as small towns or parts of cities, and replacing their ministers with a team comprising a minister and several assistants. This reorganization might produce a number of benefits: parish boundaries might coincide more closely with the boundaries of the local communities; assistants could specialize in different aspects of parish work; and the building facilities could be adapted for special purposes, with surplus elements being sold or rented out. Since assistants are paid at a lower salary than ministers but are generally provided with housing, a given sum will finance the employment of perhaps two assistants for every minister. Consequently the Church could choose to follow a policy whereby the total manpower in the urban parish ministry – ministers and assistants – would be held constant, so leading to considerable savings in salaries, and to extra income from the rental on surplus manses; if 600 urban charges were involved in the reorganization, the annual improvement in the financial position of the Church might be nearly £1 million. An alternative option would be a constant salary option, under which the savings could be used to increase the manpower in the ministry by employing more assistants. In the 600 urban parishes quoted above, the savings would permit an increase in manpower of 350, although it seems highly improbable that sufficient numbers of applicants would be forthcoming.

However, there are a number of serious disadvantages of this radical proposal for team ministries. Firstly, the reorganization would be very difficult to effect, since it would require each group of parishes to fall vacant at about the same time, and for all the congregations in each group to agree to the union. In present circumstances, the progress towards reorganization would at best be slow. Secondly, there would be a problem of organizing simultaneously a reduction in the number of ministers and an increase in the number of assistants; theological students might be discouraged from entering the ministry if they had to become assistants for several years. Thirdly, although the reorganization of urban parishes into team ministry parishes might yield substantial savings in salaries and manses, it seems likely that greater savings are already being realized through the process of union and readjustment. Finally, an important test for new forms of ministry lies in comparisons of their efficiency with that of conventional forms of ministry. Changes in efficiency might be measured by changes in the levels of membership, attendance and liberality. A weakness of the proposals of the Committee of Forty is that there is little evidence – and that generally adverse – to support their claim that the reorganization of parishes into team ministries would improve their effectiveness. Radical new forms of ministry should therefore be subjected to searching scrutiny and experimentation before they are introduced.

In section 4 we examined the proposal for the introduction of part-time non-stipendiary ministers, especially in rural areas. These ministers would enjoy a status equivalent to that of parish ministers, but would be subject to their direction and control. It is envisaged that in the longer term the non-stipendiary ministers might assume responsibility for small congregations in new large-scale linked charges. This would provide a means of economizing in the provision of ministerial manpower in the North-West Highlands and Islands, providing that sufficient numbers would be prepared to serve. To avoid potential conflicts between the parish minister and his part-time non-stipendiary assistant, the predominance of the former would have to be made clear from the outset.

Notes

1 Church of Scotland, *Reports to the General Assembly, 1966*, pp. 792-4.
2 *Reports to the General Assembly, 1975*, pp. 517-21.
3 ibid., pp. 519-20.

IV
Mission and Stewardship

Chapter 16

Mission and service

1 Introduction

In chapter 6 we conducted a general overview of the income and expenditure of the Church, which included the committees within the Mission and Service Fund as one of the three main spending agencies. We saw that roughly two-thirds of the income of those committees consists of congregational contributions, or liberality, and that these sums are raised through the Mission and Service Fund. The purpose of this chapter, along with the next, is to investigate the work of the Stewardship and Budget Committee, which is responsible for promoting the Mission and Service work of the Church.

The Stewardship and Budget Committee was appointed by Act of Assembly in 1959. The committee brought into one fund all contributions made by congregations to the Home Board (including National Church Extension), the Overseas Council, the Social and Moral Welfare Department, and the Department of Education. These committees, by the terms of the Act, have waived their right to appeal directly to congregations for financial support. Originally the fund so created was called 'The Co-ordinated Appeal', but since 1 January 1970 it has been known officially as the Church of Scotland Mission and Service Fund. The Mission and Service work of the Church 'means broadly all those activities of Christian mission and service which stretch beyond the pastoral task in the parishes.'[1] The Stewardship and Budget Committee is therefore complementary to the Maintenance of the Ministry Committee, and together they take in the whole task of evangelism, service and education for which the Church exists in the world.

As its name implies, the work of the Stewardship and Budget Committee is of a twofold nature. Firstly, each year this committee determines, in negotiations with the committees concerned, the size of the total Budget for the Mission and Service Fund for the following year. The committee is also responsible for grouping the congregations, acting on information supplied by the Presbyteries, and for determining the proportion of the total budget required from each group. Secondly, the committee is charged with 'the education of the membership of the Church in the spiritual basis of Christian giving, and in the adoption of the best methods of ingathering and systematic giving.'[2]

In this chapter we concentrate on the budgetary aspects of the committee's work, which concerns the annual preparation, submission and allocation of the Budget. The question of fund-raising and stewardship is left until the next chapter. We start in section 2 by outlining the regulations governing the work of the committee. Then in the following section some of the economic and political factors influencing the determination of the Budget are examined. Finally, in section 4 we assess the 'available balance' formula, which is used to allocate the budget between Presbyteries and congregations.

2 The work of the stewardship and budget committee

The purpose of this section is to examine in some detail the work of the Stewardship and Budget Committee as specified in the amended Act of Assembly of 1959.[3] This Act opens with an introductory passage on the co-ordination of appeals:

> As from 1 January 1961 . . . all committees, associations or other bodies whose funds have hitherto derived support from congregations in Scotland or England shall, with the exception of the Committee on the Maintenance of the Ministry and the Committee on the Aged and Infirm Ministers' Fund, cease to have right to appeal directly to such congregations for contributions to their funds. As from the operative date a co-ordinated appeal, to be known as the Church of Scotland Mission and Service Fund, made through the medium of the Stewardship and Budget Committee shall be the sole method of appealing to such congregations by any committees, associations or other bodies, with the above exceptions.
>
> The appeal to be made through the medium of the Stewardship and Budget Committee shall be confined to the branch of income known as congregational contributions. While, after the operative date, committees, associations and other bodies within the scheme shall cease to have right to appeal direct to congregations in Scotland or England for contributions, nothing in this scheme shall prevent them from making appeals for funds from other sources. In the event of any emergency arising which necessitates a committee, association or body making a special appeal to congregations of the Church for contributions, the Stewardship and Budget Committee may grant permission for such an appeal to be made, and state conditions on which it is to be made.

The Stewardship and Budget Committee is a standing committee of the General Assembly within the Administration and Special Interests Department. The administration expenses of the committee are met by the committees and other bodies within the Mission and Service Scheme *pro rata,* according to the contributions they have received from the congregations during the year.

The Stewardship and Budget Committee assumed the functions of the former Budget Committee and of the General Finance Committee's Sub-Committee on Systematic Giving and Ingathering of Funds. Its duties include the following:

(i) The education of the membership of the Church in the spiritual basis of Christian giving and in the adoption of the best methods of ingathering and systematic giving.

(ii) The preparation of such co-ordinated publicity as may be required.

(iii) The preparation of a draft Act each year for submission to the General Assembly showing the details of the sums required by committees, associations and other bodies from congregational contributions in the ensuing year, and the allocation amongst groups of congregations of the total as approved by the General Assembly.

(iv) The comparison of the response by congregations with the allocations by Presbyteries and the direction of special attention to areas where the response is regarded as inadequate.

(v) To devise such methods as it may see fit for the allocation of the total require-

ments, provided that, before such methods are put into operation, the authority of the General Assembly shall be obtained.
(vi) Guidance to Presbyteries on any special problems that may be raised by them in connection with the scheme.

These items form the work of the Stewardship and Budget Committee. We now go on to examine items (iii)-(v), concerning the preparation, submission and allocation of the budget.

1 Preparation of the budget
Every year in February each committee within the scheme submits to the Stewardship and Budget Committee a budget of its estimated income and expenditure for the ensuing calendar year. It is required that such budgets shall be prepared on a realistic basis, having due regard to the essential needs of the work of the committee.

The budget submitted by each committee is carefully considered by the Stewardship and Budget Committee, 'not with the object of questioning or objecting to the ordinary operating expenditure, but with the obligation to satisfy itself in regard to extraordinary or additional expenditure.' This is important, for the committee cannot criticise a budget, and can only seek to reduce it when required by negotiation with the committee concerned. In the event of a disagreement between the committees, the case has to be taken to the General Assembly for judgement.

If, at the time of submission of any budget under the scheme, a committee has a debt, the debt may be spread over a future period determined by the Stewardship and Budget Committee, having due regard to the additional burden which such sums place upon congregations. If any committee within the scheme has a deficit at the end of the year, the amount of the deficit as agreed with the Stewardship and Budget Committee shall be added to the next estimated amount required by the committee.

The Stewardship and Budget Committee is required to include in the total amount of its annual budget a figure to set against contingencies.

2 Submission of budget to General Assembly
The Stewardship and Budget Committee submits its report direct to each General Assembly. This report includes a statement of approved requirements from congregations of each committee within the scheme for the ensuing calendar year, and the proposed allocation of the total amount of such requirements. These particulars are then incorporated in a draft Act of Assembly to be submitted with the report for approval by the General Assembly.

The method of allocating the budget has changed recently. Prior to 1974 the budget was allocated to Presbyteries, the Stewardship and Budget Committee having regard to such factors as Presbytery membership, Christian liberality and endowments. Subject to General Assembly approval of the total requirements and the allocation among Presbyteries, the Stewardship and Budget Committee then intimated to each Presbytery the amount allocated to it, and stated how it was apportioned among the several funds of the Church. On learning of the share of the budget allocated to the Presbytery, the Presbytery's Stewardship and Budget Committee then proceeded to allocate the amount to each congregation within the bounds of the Presbytery, having regard to local circumstances including membership, liberality, endowments and obligations. The proposed allocation was then confirmed or amended at the next meeting of Presbytery. Individual congregations were informed not later than 15 November in each year of their allocation, these sums representing the minimum contributions they were expected to make. Presbyteries also sent copies of their allocations to congregations to the secretary of the Stewardship and Budget Committee.

However, in 1971, the committee reported that there had been mounting pressure to consider a new approach to the allocation of the Mission and Service Fund budget. The committee therefore appointed a special study group 'to consider a proposal by which allocations be made, not to Presbyteries, but to congregations grouped by Presbyteries, according to a uniform system applied throughout the Church.' This method of allocation, called the 'available balance' method, came into operation in 1974. The Stewardship and Budget Committee allocates the total amount of the budget among groups of congregations on the basis of the available balance figures for each congregation supplied by the Presbyteries. This allocation involves determining the proportion of the total budget required from each group, and then informing each Presbytery of the amount allocated to and required from each group within it.

3 Presbyteries' responsibilities within the scheme
The first main duty of each Presbytery is the preparation of available balance figures for each congregation, in the manner indicated by a Financial Schedule formulated by the General Finance Committee. These schedules have to be completed from time to time in respect of each congregation within the bounds, and provide the following information: (a) normal recurring income for the general purposes of the congregation; (b) net cost of maintenance of the ministry; (c) the available balance for the Mission and Service Fund, local expenses and remaining ministerial expenses, which is the difference between (a) and (b).

In the case of aid-receiving congregations and congregations making repayments for buildings to the National Church Extension Committee, special arrangements apply. These arrangements are agreed between the Stewardship and Budget Committee, the Committee on the Maintenance of the Ministry, and the Home Board respectively.

Each Presbytery is to make a return to the Stewardship and Budget Committee prior to 30 June in each year, giving available balance figures for each congregation.

The second main duty of each Presbytery is to allocate its share of the budget to the congregations within its bounds. On receipt of intimation of the share of the total budget allocated to each group within the Presbytery, the Presbytery's Stewardship and Budget Committee makes a proposed allocation to each congregation within a group, so that the sum of such allocations will equal the proportion of the total budget required from that group; Presbyteries may ask for guidance from the Stewardship and Budget Committee. The proposed allocation is approved or amended at the next meeting of Presbytery, this decision being final in respect of the immediately ensuing calendar year. Then, as previously, the clerk of the Presbytery notifies, not later than 15 November in each year, each congregation of its allocation, and provides information concerning its division amongst the several funds of the Church. The sums thus notified 'represent the minimum contributions they are expected to make.' Presbyteries are also required to transmit copies of their allocations to congregations to the secretary of the Stewardship and Budget Committee.

The third main job of the Presbytery, through its Stewardship and Budget Committee, is to ensure that congregations meet their allocation. Congregations are urged 'to improve their methods of giving, and generally to be responsible for the education of the membership to a fuller understanding of the real meaning of Christian stewardship.'

When Vacancy and Revision Schedules are being completed, Presbyteries arrange that representatives of their Stewardship and Budget Committees have the opportunity to be present, along with representatives of the Presbytery's Maintenance of the Ministry Committee, in order that office-bearers may have in mind at the same time a congregation's allocation to the Mission and Service fund. Moreover, in all cases where congregations fail to meet the requirements of the Mission and Service Fund, the Presbytery's Stewardship and Budget Committee are required to consult with the office-bearers concerned.

4 Responsibility of congregations
The responsibility of congregations towards the Mission and Service fund allocation is described as follows: 'It will be the responsibility of each Kirk Session, Congregational Board, Deacons' Court or Board of Management, on receiving intimation of the allocation, to take steps to inform the congregation of the allocation, to raise at least the sum allocated along with promised minimum contributions to the Maintenance of the Ministry Fund and Aged and Infirm Ministers' Fund, and to give members of the congregation full information with regard to the Mission and Service Fund . . .'

Consultations are also usually held with representatives of the Woman's Guild and other organizations within a congregation concerning their responsibilities towards the wider work of the Church. Each congregation is required to remit its minimum contribution each quarter to the General Treasurer of the Church. Where a congregation raises more than the minimum required, it is free to allocate the excess amongst the funds of the Church as it thinks fit.

5 Conclusion
This completes our overview of the work of the Stewardship and Budget Committee. In the following sections we go on to look more closely at the drawing up of the Mission and Service Fund Budget, and at its allocation to Presbyteries and groups of congregations.

3 The Mission and Service Fund budget
The purpose of this section is to examine briefly how the budget is assessed, and to make recommendations as to the future division of expenditures between the committees concerned.

We have seen that each committee within the Mission and Service Fund submits each year to the Stewardship and Budget Committee a budget of its estimated income and expenditure for the following calendar year. It has invariably

TABLE 114.
Liberality received by committees within the Mission and Service fund, 1961-75*

		1961 Actual	1961 Real	1961 Percentage of total	1965 Actual	1965 Real
		£	£		£	£
A	**WORK AT HOME**					
	Home Board:					
	Home Mission	94,156	245,576	13.39	105,844	244,593
	National Church Extension	108,171	282,130	15.39	130,728	302,097
	Property	6,800	17,736	0.97	12,424	28,710
	Department of Education					
	Parish Education	22,394	58,408	3.19	34,426	79,554
	Education for the Ministry	8,475	22,104	1.20	5,688	13,144
	St Colm's College	—	—	—	—	—
	Committee on Social Responsibility	51,448	134,186	7.32	75,419	174,284
	Other Committees:					
	Deaconess Board					
	Public Worship and Aids to Devotion	12,862	33,547	1.83	19,970	46,148
	Chaplains to H.M. Forces					
	SUB-TOTAL	304,306	793,687	43.29	384,499	888,530
B	**WORK OVERSEAS**					
	Overseas Council:					
	Foreign missions	322,483	841,096	45.87	360,408	832,860
	Jewish missions	22,294	58,147	3.17	15,182	35,084
	Scots' Memorial Church					
	Christian Aid	50,568	131,891	7.19	56,041	129,504
	SUB-TOTAL	395,345	1,031,134	56.23	431,631	997,448
C	CONTINGENCIES (less surpluses carried forward) [+]	3,344	8,722	0.48	22,783	52,649
	TOTALS	702,995	1,833,543	100.00	838,913	1,938,627

*SOURCE: "Report of the Stewardship and Budget Committee", *Reports to the General Assembly*, 1962, 1966, 1971 and 1976, appendix II, schedule I. The aggregate figures in the earlier years are only broadly accurate.
[+] Including special contributions and schemes.

been the case that the sum of the income requirements of the committees has exceeded, often by a substantial margin, the total income which the Stewardship and Budget Committee expects to raise through the fund. The committee, therefore, has had to prune the budgets of individual committees to a level which could be afforded within the total expected income figure. For example, the original budget estimates of committees for 1967 totalled over £980,000; this sum was pruned by 7.0 per cent to £911,000, to which a sum of £19,000 for contingencies was added, making a total requirement of £930,000 from congregations: 'The committee is painfully conscious that the rough and rude method of arbitrarily reducing the budgets to reach down to a figure likely to be contributed is a poor way of doing the Church's business. . . . The committee is also aware that the total budget figure presented to the Assembly year by year presents, not the picture of what the work requires, but what the committees can prudently be authorized to spend in view of the response of the congregations.'[4]

TABLE 114 (*continued*)

	1970			1975		
Percentage of total	Actual	Real	Percentage of total	Actual	Real	Percentage of total
	£	£		£	£	
12.62	116,524	215,642	10.40	181,198	181,198	11.83
15.58	192,704	356,622	17.21	284,873	284,873	18.60
1.48	17,251	31,925	1.54	23,621	23,621	1.54
4.10	45,445	84,102	4.06	77,563	77,563	5.07
0.68	14,557	26,940	1.30	34,767	34,767	2.27
—	5,620	10,400	0.50	9,224	9,224	0.60
8.99	98,610	182,490	8.81	149,216	149,216	9.74
				4,500	4,500	0.29
2.38	13,846	25,624	1.24	1,358	1,358	0.09
				280	280	0.02
45.83	504,557	933,745	45.06	766,600	766,600	50.06
42.96	428,837	793,615	38.30	593,941	593,941	38.79
1.81	12,023	22,250	1.07	16,583	16,583	1.08
6.68	4,221	7,811	0.38	6,269	6,269	0.41
	44,275	81,936	3.95	58,637	58,637	3.83
51.45	489,356	905,612	43.70	675,430	675,430	44.11
2.72	125,836	232,875	11.24	89,312	89,312	5.83
100.00	1,119,749	2,072,232	100.00	1,531,342	1,531,342	100.00

A further factor accounting for the excess of the original budget estimates over the final budgets is that there is an almost limitless scope for further mission and service work. As the funds available are limited, committees may realize that they will not get any more funds than they ask for, and will very likely get rather less, and so tend to overbid, in the hope that their desired budget will not be cut.

The budgetary system tends to be an incremental one. In planning the financial requirements for the following year provision is first made to continue the existing work and to fund the expected increases in cost of that work, and only then is the question raised as to whether money can be found to finance 'extensions of present work' or 'new work'. In this way the base of existing activity becomes sacrosanct, and discussion centres on what expansion can be afforded. The problem has been that in the early years of the scheme the increase in real income was too slow to permit much new work, while in the last few years the decline in real income has required careful budgeting even to maintain existing services. The forecasts of income made in chapter 9 suggest that the prospects for the Mission and Service Fund are not good, and that further cutbacks may be required.

Despite the incremental nature of the budgeting, there has been a gradual shift in the share of liberality accruing to the different committees within the Mission and Service Fund, as shown in table 114. While the share of liberality accruing to the committees engaged in 'work at home' has increased from 43.29 per cent in 1961 to 50.06 per cent in 1975, the share to 'work overseas' has declined from 56.23 per cent to 44.11 per cent over the same period. The income for 'work overseas' has increased substantially over the period from £395,345 to £675,430, but the rise in prices has been greater, so that real income has declined by roughly a third. This illustrates that a substantial reallocation of the budget can be achieved over a period of time without actually cutting any committee's budget, simply through the action of inflation.

In 1966 the Stewardship and Budget Committee appointed a Special Sub-Committee on Priorities within the Co-ordinated Appeal to fulfil the General Assembly's instruction to 'estimate the amount of money likely to be required by 1972 to maintain and advance the effective witness of the Church at home and abroad, and to recommend to the next General Assembly how that sum should be allocated among the committees of the Co-ordinated Appeal.'[5] The sub-committee proved to be influential. It recommended that 'during the next five years' the priorities of the Church lay with religious education, church extension, and foreign mission. On the basis that those urgent matters should be proceeded with, and that the expected rise in prices between 1967 and 1972 would be about 25 per cent, the sub-committee estimated that a minimum sum of £1.5 millions would be required for the Co-ordinated Appeal by 1972. It was aware that on the current trends it was unlikely that such a figure would be reached by 1972, and so it made proposals for a 'dramatic increase in Christian giving'. At the centre of these proposals was the congregational stewardship promoter scheme, whereby a 'salesman' would be appointed in every congregation to promote the interests of the wider work of the Church. However, the financial targets proved to be overambitious, as shown by the committee's report in 1970: '. . . contributions to the Fund in 1969 totalled . . . £995,644 – an increase of only 2 per cent compared with the 1969 figure, whereas the 1969 allocation or requirement was 9½ per cent above the 1968 figure at £1,050,000. The 1969 shortfall of £55,000 was the biggest in the history of the fund, and if this pattern is projected forward to 1972 the gap becomes . . . financially disastrous. In that year contributions to the fund are likely to be some £300,000 short of the target of £1,500,000 set by the General Assembly.'[6]

While the committee decided not to advise the General Assembly to lower the target figure of £1,350,000 set for 1971, although it involved an increase in the requirement over the previous year of £150,000, it did adopt a new measure which effectively moved it half-way towards that end: '. . . the Committee thought it prudent to limit the increase in the allocation to committees to £80,000 as compared with 1970. While therefore it asks congregations for the sum of £1,350,000, it has written £170,000 of that figure against Contingencies.'[7]

Significantly, the figures for contingencies for 1969 and 1970 were £39,368 and £99,434 respectively, indicating a sharply increasing trend. The Contingencies

Fund was thus used to reduce the budget below the allocation, both to minimize the size of deficits and to create a small surplus income to meet any deficits of individual committees which might arise. This method might also have had the advantage, by keeping the allocation higher than it would otherwise be, of encouraging Presbyteries and congregations to strive to produce higher contributions, even if the chance of actually reaching the target set was remote. The Contingencies Fund figure, although still high, has been reduced somewhat in recent years; in 1975 it stood at £89,312.

The reports of the committee in the past few years have laid stress on the adverse impact of inflation on the real income of the Mission and Service Fund. While this situation prevails, the policy of the fund must be one of retrenchment; difficult decisions of priority will have to be made between the different areas of the mission and service work of the Church. In our view, the present trend towards increasing the proportion of the income of the fund spent at home and decreasing that devoted to work overseas should not only be continued, but be accelerated. The present financial position of the Church requires that resources are concentrated in support of it at home rather than abroad. Within the work at home, we feel that resources should be concentrated on the social service work, especially the provision of homes for old people, and on parish education. The former is justified by the increasing proportion of old people in the Scottish population, and by the fact that the homes are self-financing. We feel that the homes should be run so as to make a surplus which can then be used to expand the facilities provided so as to cater for more people. Work on parish education and stewardship needs to be expanded in order to promote stewardship and increase membership in the congregations.

4 Allocating the budget

The purpose of this section is to examine the allocation of the annual Mission and Service Fund budget to congregations by means of the 'available balance' formula. In section 2 we saw that each Presbytery is responsible for establishing, from a Financial Schedule designed by the General Finance Committee, certain information in respect of each congregation within its bounds. The detailed information required is as follows:[8]

1 Normal recurring income

Normal recurring income, which is income for the general purposes of the congregation, was formerly calculated as an average over a period of three years. The allocations for 1974, 1975 and 1976 were based on the average annual normal recurring incomes for the periods 1969-71, 1970-2, and 1971-3 respectively. In 1977 the procedure was changed in that the allocation for that year was worked out on the basis of the income of one year only: 1975. Initially, existing Financial Schedules were used, but from 1972 a revised Financial Schedule has been available, providing information to include: ordinary collections; weekly freewill offering collections; payments under Bonds of Annuity and tax recovered thereon, provided these have not been specifically granted for a particular purpose; donations, including those from congregational organizations for general purposes; interest on endowments, whether invested in stocks and shares or property, and not held for specific purposes; miscellaneous income comprising seat rents, net proceeds of sales of work (if held annually), and any income which could reasonably be regarded as being available annually for general purposes.

2 Net cost of maintenance of the ministry
Items under this head include:
(i) Congregational contributions to appropriate stipend.
(ii) Congregational contributions to salary of assistant minister, if approved by Presbytery.
(iii) Congregational contributions to salary of deaconess or lay missionary.
(iv) Aid given to Maintenance of the Ministry Fund.

As a result of the experience gained in allocating the 1974 budget, the General Assembly approved the Stewardship and Budget Committee's proposal to add the following items to the net cost of maintenance of the ministry:
(v) Contributions to the Aged and Infirm Ministers' Fund.
(vi) Ministerial travelling expenses (the payment of which is obligatory on all congregations) comprising the amount actually paid in the year, or the sum approved by the Maintenance of the Ministry Committee (at present £240), whichever is the less; and any sum paid towards car depreciation up to the amount approved by the Maintenance of the Ministry Committee (in 1975, £100).

3 The Available Balance
The Available Balance for the Mission and Service Fund and local expenses for each congregation is calculated by subtracting the net cost of the maintenance of the ministry (2 above) from normal recurring income (1 above). To this sum is added the annual donations to the Mission and Service Fund from congregational organizations, and from it is deducted any allowances that may be made in special circumstances in particular congregations. For example, an allowance may be given to a congregation with an excessive fabric burden. In such cases, a deduction may be made from the available balance at the discretion of the Presbytery, although these deductions are made only rarely.

In the case of National Church Extension and aid-receiving charges special arrangements are made for these items, as follows:
(i) Charges to new housing areas making repayments for buildings to the National Church Extension Committee form a special group. It is recommended that these charges should make repayments each year at the rate of 20 per cent of annual normal recurring income. This amount is therefore to be deducted from the normal recurring income, after deduction has been made of the net cost of the ministry, and the remainder constitutes the available balance.
(ii) Aid-receiving charges (other than Church Extension charges which are aid-receiving) also form a special group. It has been agreed with the Maintenance of the Ministry Committee that the allocation to aid-receiving charges will in no case be increased above the present figure without prior agreement of the Maintenance of the Ministry Committee; and allocations to all aid-receiving charges will be re-negotiated before the end of the 1973-7 quinquennium, by agreement between the Maintenance of the Ministry Committee, the Stewardship and Budget Committee and the Presbyteries and congregations involved.

It is clear that the 'available balance' formula has an important part to play in the apportioning of congregational income (or liberality) between the three major spending agencies in the Church: the committees within the Mission and Service Fund, the Church and Ministry Department, and the Congregations. The broad forces at play were examined in chapter 6 in the analysis of Church expenditure. We now analyse how the available balance formula is used to raise income for the committees within the Mission and Service Fund. This is done with the aid of table 115.

Column 1 shows the 16 groups into which congregations are divided on the basis of the size of their available balances, which are given in column 2. Column 3 shows the number of congregations in each group in 1974, and column 4 gives their total available balances as the annual average for the years 1969-71. The total available balance for the Church averaged just over £4.4 million per year for the period 1969-71. Column 5 provides the average balance per congregation in each group: these vary between £336 for group B and £18,496 for group Q, but average £2,141 for the Church as a whole.

Columns 6 to 9 then deal with the allocation for 1973 using figures *calculated by the previous formula*: column 6 breaks down the allocation actually made to Presbyteries into an allocation by congregational groups; column 7 presents the allocation to each group as a proportion of the total budget. Column 8 calculates the average congregational allocation by group; unfortunately this had to be done using the numbers of congregations in 1974, since the numbers of congregations by group were not available for 1973. Finally, column 9 gives the average allocation as a percentage of the average available balance per congregation in each group. The figures in this column are thus the effective rate of levy (or 'tax'), imposed by the Stewardship and Budget Committee on each group. In 1973 the levy ranged from 20 per cent for congregations with the lowest available balance to 47 per cent for those with the highest balance. The average levy was 33 per cent.

The calculations in table 115 are then repeated for 1974 in columns 10 to 13 using the allocation determined by the *new formula* for the first time, the effects being limited in the first year of operation to an increase or decrease on the previous allocation of about one-third. The average annual available balances for 1969-71 were again used.

The calculations are repeated once again for 1975, but this time using numbers of congregations for 1975 and figures for annual available balance averaged for the years 1970-2. The allocation was again modified for the second year of operation of the new scheme so as to limit the increase or decrease resulting from the scheme to approximately two-thirds. The large increases in the numbers of congregations in group B, C and D in 1975 (column 14) over 1974 (column 3) is probably explained by the fact that, with the consent of the Maintenance of the Ministry Committee, the group A aid-receiving congregations were distributed amongst the other groups according to the size of their available balances for 1975.

The calculations are repeated one further time in table 115 for 1976, that year marking the end of the transitional period when the available balance scheme came into operation fully for the first time. The calculations use the number of congregations in 1976 and figures for available balances averaged for the years 1971-3.

TABLE 115.
Allocation of Mission and Service Fund budget to groups of congregations, 1973-76

Groups 1	Available balance range 2	Number of congregations in group in 1974 3	Average annual available balances 1969-71 4	Average balance per congregation (i.e. 4/3) 5	Total allocation 6
	£		£	£	£
A	Aid-receiving	543	443,224	816	91,542
B	0-500	113	37,996	336	12,907
C	501-1,000	166	125,123	753	38,019
D	1,001-1,500	213	269,149	1,263	81,970
E	1,501-2,000	224	390,416	1,742	116,171
F	2,001-2,500	209	468,188	2,240	144,947
G	2,501-3,000	150	409,403	2,729	132,252
H	3,001-4,000	175	605,081	3,457	198,079
J	4,001-5,000	107	477,734	4,464	165,525
K	5,001-6,000	54	294,899	5,461	109,870
L	6,001-7,000	42	270,931	6,450	104,963
M	7,001-8,000	13	95,661	7,358	36,363
N	8,001-9,000	22	187,219	8,509	72,156
O	9,001-10,000	8	77,159	9,644	31,916
P	10,001-15,000	10	120,682	12,068	59,457
Q	Over 15,000	7	129,476	18,496	60,970
TOTALS		2,056	4,402,341	2,141	1,457,137

TABLE 115 (continued)

1975

Number of congregations in group in 1975 14	Average annual available balances, 1970-2 15	Average balance per congregation (i.e. 15/14) 16	Modified 1975 allocation 17	Percentage of 17 18	Average annual allocation (i.e. 17/14) 19	Percentage levy (i.e. 19/16) 20
	£	£	£	%	£	%
—	—	—	—	—	—	—
253	84,666	334	14,422	0.9	57	17
388	289,452	746	53,275	3.4	137	18
311	390,757	1,256	83,792	5.3	269	21
251	438,242	1,745	109,042	7.0	434	24
203	460,667	2,269	133,964	8.6	659	29
156	427,230	2,738	136,748	8.7	876	31
187	645,507	3,451	233,257	14.9	1,247	36
113	503,938	4,459	195,624	12.5	1,731	38
54	293,995	5,444	122,330	7.8	2,265	41
41	261,764	6,384	117,508	7.5	2,866	44
29	217,443	7,498	99,566	6.3	3,433	45
13	112,472	8,651	53,705	3.4	4,131	47
10	94,739	9,474	46,505	2.9	4,651	49
14	170,286	12.163	91,622	5.8	6,544	53
6	116,853	19,475	65,640	4.2	10,940	56
2,029	4,508,011	2,221	1,557,000	100.00	767	34

(Edinburgh: Blackwood), 1973 (p.127), 1974 (p.80), and 1975 (p.88).

TABLE 115. (continued)

	1973				1974		
Percentage of 6	Average annual allocation (i.e. 6/3)	Percentage levy (i.e. 8/5)	Modified 1974 allocation	Percentage of 10	Average annual allocation (i.e. 10/3)	Percentage levy (i.e. 12/15)	
7	8	9	10	11	12	13	
	£		£		£		
6.3	168	20	91,542	5.9	168	20	
0.9	114	33	11,092	0.7	98	29	
2.6	229	30	34,391	2.2	207	27	
5.6	384	30	78,551	5.1	368	29	
8.0	518	29	115,251	7.4	514	29	
9.9	693	30	150,023	9.7	717	32	
9.1	881	32	141,929	9.2	946	34	
13.6	1,137	32	216,669	14.0	1,238	35	
11.4	1,546	34	181,554	11.7	1,696	37	
7.5	2,034	37	120,007	7.7	2,222	40	
7.2	2,499	38	115,375	7.4	2,747	42	
2.5	2,797	38	41,039	2.6	3,156	42	
5.0	3,279	38	82,580	5.3	3,753	44	
2.1	3,989	41	36,229	2.4	4,528	46	
4.1	5,946	49	64,460	4.2	6,446	53	
4.2	8,710	47	69,308	4.5	9,901	53	
100.0	708	33	1,550,000	100.0	753	35	

TABLE 115 (continued)

			1976			
Number of congregations in group in 1976	Average annual available balances, 1971–3	Average balance (i.e. 22/21)	Total allocation	Percentage of 24	Average annual allocation (i.e. 24/21)	levy (i.e. 26/23)
21	22	23	24	25	26	27
	£	£	£	%	£	%
—	—	—	—	—	—	—
252	85,060	338	10,207	0.6	41	12
387	286,684	741	48,736	2.8	126	17
294	364,760	1,241	80,247	4.6	273	22
225	388,704	1,728	104,950	6.0	466	27
189	425,567	2,252	129,798	7.4	687	31
186	509,383	2,739	173,190	9.9	931	34
180	622,811	3,460	242,896	13.9	1,349	39
104	464,408	4,465	204,340	11.7	1,965	44
69	374,139	5,422	177,716	10.1	2,576	48
41	266,064	6,489	134,364	7.7	3,277	51
28	210,772	7,528	111,709	6.4	3,990	53
17	143,122	8,419	78,717	4.5	4,630	55
12	113,991	9,499	64,405	3.7	5,367	57
15	178,724	11,915	103,660	5.9	6,911	58
8	143,458	17,932	85,067	4.8	10,633	59
2,007	4,577,647	2,281	1,750,000	100.0	872	38

SOURCE: Church of Scotland, 'Report of the Stewardship and Budget Committee', *Reports to the General Assembly*, (Edinburgh: Blackwood), 1973 (p.127), 1974 (p.80), and 1975 (p.88).

The important calculation in table 115 is the percentage rate at which the levy is imposed on the groups of congregations with increasing size of available balance. The percentage rates of levy for 1973 — the year immediately preceding the introduction of the new method — are shown in column 9, and for the three years 1974-6 covering the transitional period of the scheme up to full operation, in columns 13, 20 and 27 respectively; these results are summarized in table 116. They reveal that the levy is markedly progressive, i.e. that the *proportion* of the available balance required by the allocation increases with the size of the balance. For example, in 1976 group B congregations having an available balance range of £0 – 500 were expected to contribute 12 per cent to the Mission and Service Fund, whereas group Q congregations, having an available balance range of over £15,000, were expected to contribute 59 per cent. The average rate for all contributions was 38 per cent. It is important to remember, however, that these calculations are based on the allocations to the groups of congregations within each Presbytery, and that each Presbytery is free to decide the allocations to congregations within each group total. The degree of progressivity of the levy system may thus be reduced in respect of individual congregations to the extent that Presbyteries exercise this power.

TABLE 116
Minimum (group B) and maximum (group Q) rates of Mission and Service Fund levy on groups of congregations, 1973-6

	1973	1974	1975	1976
Group B	20*	20	17	12
Group Q	47	53	56	59
Average	33	35	34	38

*Figure for Group A

Table 116 also indicates that, while the system of levies was progressive prior to the introduction of the available balance formula in 1973, the effect of the new formula has been to increase the degree of progressivity. Between 1973 and 1976 the lowest rate of levy fell from 20 per cent to 12 per cent, while the highest rate increased from 47 per cent to 59 per cent; the average rate has increased from 33 per cent to 38 per cent.

Perhaps a more important question concerns the *marginal* rate of levy. If a congregation manages to increase its normal recurrent income, and hence its available balance, sufficiently in order to place it in a higher group, then how much extra levy does it have to pay? If the formula works like income tax, the congregation would have to pay the higher levy of its new group only on that last part of its available balance by which its income exceeds the group minimum income. However, it appears that the original intention of the scheme was that the congregation would be required to pay the new higher levy on *all* of its available balance, so that the marginal tax rate was considerably higher. The principle can be illustrated if we take a middle-range congregation in group H having the maximum available balance for the Group of £4,000. Such a congregation would have been required to make, on average, a contribution of 39 per cent of the balance, (or £1,560) to the Mission and Service Fund in 1976. If the available balance of that congregation had been just a pound greater, which would have taken it into Group J, its contribution in 1976 would have been 44 per cent of the balance (or £1,760).

This example shows that an increase in the available balance of the congregation of £1 led to an increase in its required Mission and Service Fund contribution of £200. Such a high marginal rate of levy might cause the congregation to take steps to keep its available balance within the £4,000 ceiling, either by restricting its fund-raising and stewardship activities, or by increasing its maintenance of the ministry costs, e.g. by increasing stipend or ministerial expenses. This problem was recognized in the 1975 Report of the Stewardship and Budget Committee, which stated that a graduated scale was to be used for the first time in the calculation of the 1976 allocations.[9] The scale would have the effect of lessening the abrupt increase in allocation which occurs when a small rise in a congregation's available balance takes it into a higher group. This development is particularly important in view of the recent high rates of inflation, which helped to cause a significant movement of congregations between groups, especially in an upward direction.

The new method has been generally well received, although it has been criticized on the grounds that it bases allocations on the resources of congregations in past years, and so does nothing to stir congregations which are making little effort to improve giving; on the other hand, those congregations which succeed in increasing their income are expected to make a larger contribution. In 1975 the General Assembly approved an overture from the Presbytery of Edinburgh which proposed that the Mission and Service Fund allocation should be calculated from only the latest returns available instead of an average of returns from an earlier three-year period. Allocations for 1977 were thus worked out in 1976 on the basis of figures for 1975,[10] instead of the average for the period 1972-4. This had the unfortunate effect of producing a number of exceptionally high increases in allocations for those congregations with fast rising incomes, thereby further penalizing the successful fund-raisers.

However, the crucial point is that the allocation of the Mission and Service Fund budget cannot be made in such a way as to encourage giving. The allocation takes the form of a semi-voluntary levy, or 'tax', which congregations tend to view as no more than a target at which to aim. This is illustrated by the large proportion of congregations which just reach their allocation, as shown in table 117. In the years 1971-3 about a half of all congregations just met their allocations, and more than a third failed to meet their allocations. The reason lies in the fact that such a levy (or tax) is painful to the taxed person or body, in that it reduces the income at its disposal, and for that reason it tends to be avoided. This probably applies even to those congregations who contribute readily to the wider work of the Church through the fund, for the allocation may well be greater than the completely voluntary contribution which they would be prepared to make. All that can be done is to ensure that the allocation system produces the minimum of disincentive effects to congregational fund-raising and contributions to the fund. Both sources can be helped through the equal treatment of congregations, a point well recognized by the Stewardship and Budget Committee; it should be recognized by all congregations that they are being asked to give on the same basis as all others. Special allowance should be made to individual congregations in special circumstances.

TABLE 117.
A breakdown of the numbers of congregations which met, exceeded, and failed to meet, their Mission and Service Fund allocations in the years 1971-3.

	1971	%	1972	%	1973	%
Allocation:						
met	1,093	52	1,118	54	977	48
exceeded	176	9	205	10	307	15
not met	822	39	740	36	757	37
TOTALS	2,091	100	2,063	100	2,041	100

SOURCE: 'Report of the Stewardship and Budget Committee', *Reports to the General Assembly*, 1972-4.

A progressive levy system on the grounds of ability to pay is desirable, so that congregations with larger available balances are able to contribute a large proportion, because all congregations have to meet certain overhead expenses in respect of fabric costs and the like, regardless of the size of their income. Efforts can be made to minimize the disincentive effects to fund-raising of such a system by avoiding too high a top rate of tax, and by avoiding high marginal rates of tax in moving from one group to the next higher group, as discussed above. These factors could be tested each year by classifying those congregations who fail to meet their allocations into their groups, and comparing the distribution to the degree of progressivity of the levy system. A relative bunching of the congregations concerned towards the low end of the available balance range might suggest that the lower-income congregations were being over-taxed and those with higher incomes were being undertaxed; this would suggest a revision of the tax system so as to increase its progressivity, accompanied by a reduction in the tax rates at the bottom of the scale. A relative bunching of the congregations who failed to meet their allocations towards the top end of the available balance range might suggest that the more affluent congregations were being over-taxed, and that the tax system should be made less progressive. A retrospective analysis of this kind might help the Stewardship and Budget Committee to refine the allocation system in such a way as to ensure that all congregations receive an allocation which they can just meet with effort.

Another possibility we have considered is that the Mission and Service Fund allocations to congregations could be made compulsory. The impact of such a measure on the finances of the fund, if successful, is shown in table 118. The calculations are based on the allocation for 1973, when the total contributions to the fund of £1,297,335 fell below the allocation of £1,450,342 by £153,007, or 10.5 per cent. Part A of the table shows how much extra income would have accrued to the fund if all those Presbyteries which fell below their allocations had actually achieved them. The extra contribution would have amounted to

£168,242, or 11.6 per cent of the allocation; this would have been sufficient to take the total contribution from 10.5 per cent below the allocation to 1.1 per cent above, leading to a surplus of £15,235. The improvement is not greater because, when the Presbyteries which fell short are brought up to their allocations, those congregations within each Presbytery which exceeded their allocation will offset those which fell below, so that the assumption used does not entirely eliminate 'deficit' congregations. The same applies to those Presbyteries which were in overall surplus.

TABLE 118.

A calculation of the increase in income to the Mission and Service Fund in 1973 assuming that (A) all Presbyteries and (B) all congregations had at least achieved their allocations

	Allocations 1	Contributions 2	Percentage of contributions to allocation 3
	£	£	%
A Presbyteries			
actual outcome	1,450,342	1,297,335	89.5
extra contribution	—	168,242	11.6
TOTAL	1,450,342	1,465,577	101.1
B Congregations			
actual outcome	1,450,342	1,297,335	89.5
extra contribution	—	245,469	16.9
TOTAL	1,450,342	1,542,804	106.4

A second, more stringent, assumption is that all congregations in 1973 managed at least to achieve their Mission and Service Fund allocation. Part B of table 118 shows that the increase in contributions to the fund would have been £245,469, or 16.9 per cent of the original allocation. This sum would have raised the total contribution from 10.5 per cent below the allocation to 6.4 per cent above, giving rise to a 'surplus' of £92,462.

Making the Mission and Service Fund allocations to congregations compulsory would thus help to put the extra-parochial work of the Church on a sounder financial footing. It might also encourage congregations to improve their fund-raising methods, since the making compulsory of the allocations both to the Mission and Service Fund and to the maintenance of the ministry would lead to a squeezing of the proportion of liberality accruing to congregations if annual income fell below expectations. On the other hand, such a measure would raise a number of problems. Firstly, a compulsory levy would be difficult to enforce, because there are no sanctions available to the Stewardship and Budget Committee to deal with offending congregations. Moreover, the fact that a substantial proportion of congregations fall below their allocations each year suggests that, unless the measure is matched by more successful fund-raising, the result may be a squeezing of liberality accruing to congregations, or a decline in the aid given to, or an increase in the aid received from, the Maintenance of the Ministry Fund. Secondly, the measure would be strongly resisted by congregations, partly because it would be seen as an infringement of their independence, and partly because it would confer upon the committee the power (in theory at least) to greatly increase the size of the allocations made to them. Thirdly, the method of making the allocations to Presbyteries and congregations would become a sensitive issue, and thus might delay what at present seems to be a smoothly running process of allocation each year.

On balance, therefore, we feel that it would be undesirable to make the Mission and Service Fund allocations to congregations compulsory. A better policy would be to strengthen the superintendance powers of Presbyteries over congregations. Measures to that end are discussed in chapter 20.[11]

In chapter 6 it was suggested that congregations had attempted to reduce the size of their Mission and Service Fund allocations by reclassifying their income, so as to reduce the proportion of normal recurring income and increase the proportion of special, or non-recurring, income. Because the available balances of congregations are calculated on the basis of the normal income only, a reduction in the size of normal income reduces the available balance, and therefore the amount of the allocation made; congregations may have been encouraged to do this by the high marginal rates of levy prior to 1975. Whatever the cause, there is no doubt that this factor has had a considerable adverse effect on the income of the Mission and Service Fund. We strongly recommend that the available balance formula is modified so that allocations are no longer based on the normal recurring income of congregations, but on their total income. This may require a return to the three-year averaging process for the calculation of available balances, at least in the case of the special income component of the total income of congregations, in order to avoid any fluctuations in the sizes of available balances caused by year to year variations in the size of special income.

5 Conclusions

This chapter is the first of two to examine the work of the Stewardship and Budget Committee in promoting the wider work of the Church. The committee was appointed by Act of Assembly in 1959, and brought into one fund – the Mission and Service Fund, established in 1961 under the title of 'the Co-ordinated Appeal' – all contributions made by the congregations to the committees working in mission and service. The Stewardship and Budget Committee is responsible, both for determining the size of the annual budget for the fund in consultation with the committees and allocating the budget to groups of congregations, and for promoting the fund-raising and stewardship work of congregations.

In section 3 we saw that the sum of the annual budgets of the committees within the fund have invariably been greater than the sum which the Stewardship and Budget Committee expected to raise in income. Hence in every year the budget has been pruned by the committee to a size which the Church could afford. This situation probably arises from the fact that each committee, fortified by the knowledge that many areas of work within their remit remain to be done, overstates its requirement in the knowledge that it will not get any more than it asks for, and will very likely get rather less. In this way each committee may get the funds to meet its reasonable budget.

The budgeting process tends to be an incremental one, in that provision is first made to finance the existing base of activities, and only then is consideration given to the financing of new work. Because the real income of the Mission and Service Fund increased only slowly over the first part of the period 1961-75, and then declined, there has been little scope for new work; indeed, in recent years economy has become the watchword. Our income forecasts suggest that the situation will not improve in the foreseeable future.

Nonetheless, there has been a gradual shift in the disposition of the Mission and Service Fund between the constituent committees, particularly from 'work overseas' to 'work at home'. Although the income for work overseas has increased substantially over the period 1961-75, its real income has declined by about a third because of inflation. We recommend that this trend should be accelerated, on the grounds that in the present economic climate the resources for the wider work of the Church would be better concentrated in support of the Church at home rather than the Church abroad.

In section 4 we saw that the method of allocating the total budget to congregations now used is the 'available balance' formula, which was first employed in 1974. The 'available balance' of each congregation, formerly the average for a previous three-year period, and now for a recent single year, is calculated by subtracting the net cost of the maintenance of the ministry from its normal recurring income. The budget is then allocated to congregations, which are grouped according to the size of their 'available balances'. Our analysis showed that the rate of levy (or tax) is progressive, i.e. the proportion of the allocation to the balance increases with the size of the balance, and that the degree of progressivity has increased over the three year period 1974-6 during which the scheme was phased in. Between 1973 and 1976 the rate of levy for the congregations with the smallest balances fell from 20 per cent to 12 per cent, while the rate for the congregations with the highest balances rose from 47 per cent to 59 per cent.

The 'available balance' method has been criticized, like other such methods, for taxing most heavily the successful congregations, while doing nothing to stimulate the inactive congregations into increasing their fund-raising efforts. But no such levy can encourage extra giving; all that can be done is to ensure that the levy method employed minimizes the disincentive effects to fund-raising. This requires the equal treatment of like congregations, special allowance to be made in special cases, and a progressive levy system on the grounds of ability to pay, and in recognition of the fact that all congregations have to meet certain overhead expenses. All three are features of the available balance formula. With regard to the last point, care should be taken to avoid too high a top rate of levy, and to avoid high marginal rates of levy when congregations move from one group to the next higher group.

We considered the proposal to make the Mission and Service fund allocation on congregations compulsory, but rejected it on the grounds that it would be difficult to enforce, that it would be resisted by congregations, and that it might make the annual allocation process more difficult. We did recommend the alternative policy that the available balance calculations should be based on the total liberality of congregations, and not on the normal recurring income, as at present. This measure would prevent congregations from reducing their allocation by reclassifying a greater proportion of their liberality as special income, a phenomenon which occurred in the years after the available balance was first proposed.

Notes

1 *The Church of Scotland Yearbook*, 1976, p. 24.

2 ibid., p. 25.

3 Church of Scotland, 'Report of the Stewardship and Budget Committee', *Reports to the General Assembly, 1973,* Appendix I, pp. 118-23.

4 'Report of the Stewardship and Budget Committee', *Reports to the General Assembly, 1966,* p. 90.

5 'Report of the Stewardship and Budget Committee', *Reports to the General Assembly, 1967,* p. 113.

6 *Reports to the General Assembly*, 1970, p. 89.

7 loc. cit.

8 'Report of the Stewardship and Budget Committee', *Reports to the General Assembly, 1972,* pp. 108-10.

9 'Report of the Stewardship and Budget Committee', *Reports to the General Assembly, 1975,* pp. 79-80.

10 'Report of the Stewardship and Budget Committee', *Reports to the General Assembly, 1976,* pp. 56-7.

11 A proposal to make the Mission and Service Fund allocations on congregations compulsory was rejected by the General Assembly of 1977 as this chapter was being written.

Chapter 17

Fund-raising and stewardship

1 Introduction
In the previous chapter we examined that part of the work of the Stewardship and Budget Committee which was concerned with drawing up and allocating the Mission and Service Fund. The second major aspect of the committee's work, which we investigate here, concerns what the Church calls 'education in Christian stewardship', and is defined as 'the education of the membership of the Church in the spiritual basis of Christian giving and in the adoption of the best method of ingathering and systematic giving.' This work is carried out by the Church in the following ways:[1]
(i) through stewardship campaigns in congregations – by which all members are called upon to make a response in worship, service and giving;
(ii) by publicity about the work of the committees within the Mission and Service Fund;
(iii) by guiding financial authorities in congregations concerning the effective working of the weekly freewill offering, Deed of Covenant and presentation of annual congregational budget;
(iv) by the appointment in each congregation of a stewardship promoter (chosen by the congregation and trained by the committee), to be personally responsible for increased interest in, and giving to, the whole work of the Church at home and abroad.

The purpose of this chapter is to examine the methods which have been, and are being, promoted by the Stewardship and Budget Committee in the congregations to raise funds for the Church, and to suggest ways in which this might be made more effective. The importance of such an investigation will be realized when it is remembered that about 70 per cent of the income of the Church of Scotland comes from liberality, which derives from various sort of contributions at the level of the congregation. Moreover, we have seen that the wider work of the Church carried out by the committees within the Mission and Service Fund depends upon the success of fund-raising by the Stewardship and Budget Committee, and that the slow real increase in these funds over recent years has severely constrained the activities of the committees. An investigation of ways of improving the effectiveness of fund-raising in the congregations in order to increase income, rather than concentrating on ways of cutting costs in order to keep expenditure within the bounds set by income, is a more positive approach towards strengthening the financial position of the Church.

In section 2 we survey the stewardship methods used by the Stewardship and

Budget Committee over the period 1960-75. This is followed in the next section by an examination of the methods adopted by professional fund-raising firms, which have been employed by a number of congregations in the Church. Then in section 4 we conduct a comparative statistical analysis of the efficiency of various forms of congregational fund-raising campaign, measuring efficiency in terms of increases in membership and income. Finally, in section 5 a number of recommendations are made to improve the fund-raising and stewardship performance of the Church.

2 Fund-raising and stewardship, 1960-75

In this section we survey the various methods promoted by the Stewardship and Budget Committee to aid congregations in the raising of funds over the period 1960-75. These methods fall easily into the four categories given above, namely stewardship campaigns, publicity, education and financial guidance, and stewardship promoters. We shall deal with each in turn.

1 Stewardship campaigns

The committee has defined a stewardship campaign as 'an effort to convey to all connected with the congregation the call to Christian stewardship.'[2]

In the early part of the period the stewardship campaigns were of the type involving a family meal. The members of the congregation were invited to attend a family function at which the message of stewardship was conveyed. Thereafter, a visit to every home was made by trained visitors, giving an opportunity to all to pledge financial support and service. These Stewardship Campaigns with Family Meal were first held in 1960. By early 1962 about 50 campaigns had been held, and by early 1964 about 240 campaigns.

In all about 300 campaigns were carried out, most prior to 1967. According to the committee, the campaigns varied greatly in success, depending upon the methods used and the amount of effort put into them. The committee has urged all congregations to seek the advice and experience of the Presbytery's Stewardship Committee and of itself before embarking upon a campaign, and the services of a field assistant are now available (see below).

In 1966 the committee reported that rural congregations 'have consistently maintained that the method of approach to members recommended by the committee in their normal stewardship campaign is unsuitable for their case.'[3] These congregations found difficulty in meeting the initial expense of the campaign, and also in the organization required. Following a conference with ministers of rural charges, the committee produced an inexpensive form of campaign for these congregations, which became the Parish Development Programme. The campaign is based on a programme of visiting members in their homes to convey the message of Stewardship. The committee reported that the Parish Development Programme was welcomed by the rural Presbyteries: 'Some such Presbyteries have taken the decision to recommend to all their congregations that they should carry through the programme simultaneously. In Wigtown and Stranraer, 16 out of 29 congregations accepted the lead given by the Presbytery, and this became the first Presbytery area to hold a combined stewardship campaign. First reports show a position response, in terms of the witness, service and liberality of the members.'[4]

Also in 1966, the committee reported that it had been under pressure to offer more guidance in conducting campaigns than that given by its existing staff: 'Propaganda by fund-raising firms has resulted in many congregations specifically asking for full-time directors supplied, not by outside agencies, but by the Church itself, as is done in many other communions. The committee has now decided to meet that demand by appointing a full-time agent of the committee who will be available to congregations who desire such a service in the conducting of campaigns.'[5]

The services of the field assistant are fully self-supporting, his salary and expenses being paid by the committee out of the fees charged to congregations using his services.

As a result of these two new departures in 1966, congregations embarking upon a systematic campaign of stewardship teaching had a choice of three methods of approach, namely: (i) the Stewardship Campaign with Family Meal, conducted by the congregation; (ii) the Stewardship Campaign with Family Meal, under the direction of a full-time organizer or adviser; and (iii) the Parish Development Programme, in which congregations combined in Presbytery or area groups.

From 1967, however, the Parish Development Programme overtook the stewardship campaign as the principal campaign method. Indeed, the pressure of demand in 1967 and 1968 was so great that the field assistant, who was appointed originally to direct stewardship campaigns, was seconded to the Parish Development Programme. The procedure involved the field assistant in spending six to eight weeks in each Presbytery area, speaking to a meeting of the Presbytery, and then visiting and advising individual congregations. The Parish Development Programme undertaken in Presbytery areas came to an end at the end of 1969, but a large number of individual charges have since used the programme on a congregational basis.

2 Publicity
The committee quickly became aware of 'a demand and need for a steady flow of well-produced literature concerning the principles of Christian stewardship.' In 1962 it reported the 'first modest beginning of co-ordinated publicity' in the production of an illustrated booklet entitled *Co-ordinated Action*, 710,000 copies of which were asked for and distributed. The committee argued that there was 'an urgent demand for well-produced and well-illustrated literature, photographs, sets of slides, film-strips, and even films, to publicize the work of the Church in its wholeness and balance.'

By 1964 the Stewardship and Budget Committee was able to report: 'The committee is convinced that a great effort must be made to win the interest of our members in the work supported by the Co-ordinated Appeal. It has tried to get the best professional advice on effective methods of information. At the same time it is convinced that no technique can dispense with personal contact and sharing of conviction. In its publicity, therefore, the committee must rely on the faithful co-operation of ministers, elders and members in the congregations. The literature and the other helps supplied by the committee are only aids to promote interest and support.'[6]

In 1962 the committee argued the need for 'a department of publicity which will make co-ordinated publicity easier to produce and more efficient.' In 1964 the General Assembly discharged the Publications Committee, which had been a standing commitee of Assembly for over one hundred years, and set up in its place a new Department of Publicity and Publication. The purpose of the new department is 'to carry on the work of the production of periodicals, the publishing of Christian literature, the provision of specialized bookshops, and, in the important field of public relations, providing a service for the Church's internal and external publicity.'[7]

In the following year the Stewardship and Budget Committee reported that representatives of the committee, along with representatives of the Church and Ministry Department and the Department of Publicity and Publication, had met with the General Finance Committee to discuss arrangements for financing the work of the new Department of Publicity and Publication. It was agreed that the Mission and Service Fund should bear 50 per cent of the cost, and the Church and Ministry Department and General Purposes Fund 25 per cent each.

From 1962 an annual leaflet on the Co-ordinated Appeal (now Mission and Service Fund) was published for distribution to all members. This leaflet showed the division of the money contributed among the different committees, and also described in broad outline the nature of the work so supported. In 1971 the committee decided to vary the method by replacing the annual leaflet by three separate efforts:

> (1) Minute for Mission – each month there will be sent to congregations through P.P.I.O. a brief item of news about Mission and Service to be used at Sunday Services in whatever way appears to be suitable;
> (2) *Life and Work* will carry a series of full-page advertisements about the work of the different committees;
> (3) through the good offices of P.P.I.O. news items and articles will be offered to national and provincial newspapers.[8]

It was hoped that the new system would be more economical than producing an annual leaflet, but with an equally wide coverage. However, the committee has emphasized that, although it can produce publicity material, it cannot ensure that such material is used or displayed to the best advantage: 'For this the committee depends upon, and is grateful for, the co-operation of Presbytery covenors, ministers, stewardship promoters and office-bearers. Moreover, no material, however skilfully written or designed, can communicate so effectively as sincere, well-informed and enthusiastic commendation from person to person.'

3 Education and financial guidance
The Stewardship and Budget Committee started its activities in education for stewardship by asking all Presbyteries, at the beginning of 1960, to arrange for area conferences on Christian Stewardship. By 1963 the committee was able to report that 54 Presbyteries had so far arranged such conferences. No attempt was made at those conferences to explain in detail the organization of congregational campaigns; the aim was rather 'to stimulate thought and discussion about stewardship at the right level.'

This was followed up by the Three-Year Plan, approved by the General Assembly in 1964, by which it was hoped that 'the meaning and application of stewardship will be brought more effectively to the notice of Kirk Sessions and office-bearers' by a 'systematic programme of visitation'. The programme was carried through by deputies from Presbyteries' Stewardship and Budget Committees of congregations within their bounds, beginning with those congregations which were finding difficulty in meeting their co-ordinated appeal allocations. The aim was to ensure that sessions and office-bearers had all the help they needed in acquainting their members with the purpose of the co-ordinated appeal and with the meaning and practice of stewardship.

The chief method of raising income is, and has been, through the Weekly Freewill Offering Scheme. This method, when used properly, involves each member in pledging to contribute a given minimum sum per week to the congregation for the year ahead. He receives fifty-two envelopes, one for each week of the year, which he returns sealed with the contribution inside. The pledge is then renewed annually to take account of the person's changing financial circumstances. However, the committee stated in 1965 that there was a great deal of room for improvement in the operation of the scheme: 'According to the statistical returns, 272 congregations do not use the Weekly Freewill Offering System; 1,233 use it without giving members an opportunity to make a financial pledge; 201, which use pledge cards, have not arranged for a review of the pledge within the last five years.'[9]

The Weekly Freewill Offering system was extended in 1971 by the introduction of the scheme known as Give as You Earn (GAYE). The purpose of GAYE is to emphasize that the sum pledged should be related to income, and increased as personal income increases. Efforts are also being made through the system to encourage donors to make their contributions through Deeds of Covenant, which requires that donors undertake to give a stated minimum annual sum to the congregation for a period of seven years; the congregational treasurer can then reclaim the income tax already paid on the contribution from the Inland Revenue.[10]

The value of these methods is that they encourage regular contributions to match the regular outgoings of the Church. The danger is that members may lapse from making regular contributions, or fail to increase their contributions each year to match increasing prices and personal income.

Weekend training courses in stewardship for teams from charges, usually comprising the minister and from three to five laymen, have been organized by the committee since 1962. It was felt that the residential school method was 'a highly effective way of stimulating discussion among office-bearers, and inspiring them to practical action.' By 1970 the committee was able to report that it 'had had close contact with over 3,000 office-bearers in residential schools and courses during the '60s.'

In recent years the weekend training courses have been linked with the membership programme. This programme arose out of a 'Statement on membership', together with educational material, produced by a Joint Committee of the Stewardship and Budget Committee and the Adult Christian Education Committee in 1971. The joint committee argued that the standard of membership in the Church is generally low, and that more than half of the membership give 'only trifling support, in money or in service, to the great enterprises of Christian mission'. The joint committee recommended that greater emphasis should be placed on the training of new members, and that the task of winning new members should be regarded in congregations as a high missionary priority. For present members, teaching in Christian discipleship must be a continuing process after initiation, but for those members who rarely attend church, visiting, especially by elders, is of key importance. These priorities were reflected in the aims of the 1974 training course held at St Ninian's, Crieff, which were defined as follows:

(i) To encourage a deeper understanding of the five points of membership, approved by the General Assembly – worship, prayer, involvement, giving and learning.

(ii) To provide sufficient material and information to enable delegates to set up a visitor training programme in their own congregations.

(iii) To demonstrate the value of role-play and group discussion as training methods.

4 Stewardship promoters

In response to the Report of the Special Sub-Committee in 1967, which recommended that the Mission and Service Fund budget should rise from £930,000 in 1967 to £1,500,000 in 1972, the Stewardship and Budget Committee took up the suggestion, made at the General Assembly in 1966 by the convenor of the General Finance Committee, that a 'salesman' might be appointed in every congregation to promote the interests of the wider work of the Church. After discussions with various other committees, the Committee arrived at the following plan:[11]

> The first stage is the selection of suitable persons . . . Ideally the stewardship promoter should be an office-bearer (a) with organizing ability and energy, (b) clear vision of the missionary nature of the Church's work, and (c) the gift of passing on his enthusiasm to others.
>
> The second stage is the training and equipping of the persons appointed in the congregations. This will be done by Presbytery areas, bringing the stewardship promoters together for briefing and training at least once a year.
>
> Thirdly, it will be necessary to supply the promoters regularly with information to be passed on to other office-bearers and members. At this stage the committee will rely on the Press, Publicity and Information Office for the best ways of maintaining interest among the members.

In the following year the committee was able to report that the scheme for the appointment and training of stewardship promoters had been set in motion. In order to learn by experience, initially the scheme was limited to the three large Presbyteries of Edinburgh, Glasgow and Hamilton. Fourteen area conferences were organised by the Presbytery committees, where 450 congregations were invited to attend. Afterwards 230 congregations made appointments.

The training of the promoters was given at residential schools, and the course covered such subjects as basic Christian stewardship, the work of the Church, organizing Church finance, methods of approach, and literature and other available aids. Each promoter is provided with a working manual as a source of practical information and guidance in his work.

In the autumn of 1968 fifteen further Presbyteries were visited, and those appointed attended training courses in the early months of 1969. In 1970 the committee reported that the promoter plan had been presented in 33 Presbyteries, including all except the Western and Island Presbyteries and those north of Inverness; in the 1,500 congregations concerned over 600 Promoters had been appointed. In some smaller Presbyteries where the scheme was less suitable the aim was to have a team of well-informed people who would be prepared to help congregations in their Presbytery area, instead of having an individual promoter in each congregation.

The work of stewardship promoters has been described as follows: 'It is to promote in their congregations the understanding and practice of Christian stewardship . . . This they do by personal example; by encouraging their fellow office-bearers and members to participate fully in Christian service and giving; by informing themselves about the mission and service of the Church so as to be a source of information to others; and by using opportunities as they arise in the worship and activities of the parish to underline the priorities of mission.'[12]

By the early 1970s two disquieting features appeared in the operation of the stewardship promoter scheme. The first concern was that only about one-third of the congregations in the Church had taken up the idea, and that many of the congregations which had made no appointment were those that, according to the Committee, most needed the stimulus of fresh publicity. The second concern was that although some promoters were active, they were often restricted by the inertia of the Kirk Session; as a result, many fund-raising schemes were watered down to the point of being ineffective – e.g. the Weekly Freewill Offering Scheme being used without pledge cards.

The fact that the Stewardship and Budget Committee seems to rate the stewardship promoters so highly, while as many as two-thirds of the congregations have not appointed a promoter, suggests that this may be a source of friction between the two. Such friction may arise partly because promoters provide a continuing pressure for fund-raising in the congregation, and partly because they have close links with the central committee, thereby giving it a foothold in the congregation. This pressure and interference may be a source of irritation to the minister and office-bearers.

In this section we have traced the development of the various methods promoted by the Stewardship and Budget Committee over the period 1960-75. These methods fall into four categories of work: stewardship campaigns, publicity, education and financial guidance, and stewardship promoters.

3 The employment of fund-raising firms in the church

A large number of congregations in the Church have employed the services of fund-raising firms, the largest of which in Scotland is Wells Organizations Scotland Ltd. This firm offers two types of programmes: the Three-Year and the Seven-Year programmes. The Three-Year programmes are of an elementary type whose object is to introduce congregations to the habit of planned giving; these have now been largely superseded by the Seven-Year programmes, which are of a more advanced nature where families are encouraged to covenant their giving, so that the Church can benefit from the additional tax rebate. Wells claim that the difference between the two programmes is that in the Three-Year programme the churches only just received all the money pledged by members, whereas in the Seven-Year programmes many of them received much more. This is put down to the fact that, by the time the longer programmes were introduced, people were better attuned to good giving, and took their pledges more seriously. Also, Wells give more time to the direction of the Seven-Year programmes (which are more expensive), and are better able to deal with guidance on church management, efficient follow-up and the like.

Wells argue that such covenant campaigns require more care and attention than the earlier planned giving programmes, for in asking families to commit themselves for seven years in advance through covenants, the income of the church is being pegged for that period. This is because most people in practice will make no alteration to their covenant until the seven years have expired. Wells argue from their experience that the only way to encourage people to covenant realistically is as follows:

> 1 Educate them to give generously for the right reason, which is not simply that the church needs more money, but that the giver needs to give to fulfil his Christianity. Such an educational programme takes time, but is invariably time well spent.
> 2 When people have made a decision to give something which is obviously reasonable, then is the time to explain how the church can benefit by more than half again if the amount is covenanted.[13]

The methods used on the Seven-Year programme vary from church to church, but in general there are three stages: the planning study, the report of the planning study, and the campaign. The planning study is a free service offered to any church, and without it Wells never handle a campaign. Wells examine the previous year's accounts of the church, and the distribution of its envelope and covenant giving, and have an interview with the minister about the church's pastoral affairs. A planning meeting is then arranged with the Finance Committee at which the previous year's expenditure is used to work out a forecast of funds needed over the next seven years. Apart from agreeing on future needs, the consultant draws the committee's attention to the current giving of the members, and indicates where an improvement is likely, how lapsed members can be tackled, and how membership might be increased gradually over the years. After the meeting the consultant prepares a typed report for presentation to the Kirk Session or Congregational Board.

The report of the planning study is presented to all office-bearers. It includes Well's suggestions of a suitable plan of action, organization of the campaign, the probable results, and the likely seven-year cash flow. At the end of the meeting it is left to the office-bearers to make what use they will of the report. They can employ Wells, or may try to do the job themselves.

If the congregation decides to employ Wells for the campaign, it is conducted by a consultant who lives in the area for the duration of the campaign. This is governed by the size of the church roll: a covenant campaign in a church of 600 families usually takes about two months. Working initially through a planning committee, the consultant composes a campaign plan, interviews from 15 to 25 people to get their opinion on leadership for the campaign organization, and fairly quickly selects his key leaders. Wells never assume that the Kirk Session will constitute the campaign organization, but goes for the best men, some of whom naturally will be office-bearers. The selected key leaders will then discuss and agree on which other men should be asked to join the organization, until gradually a group of potential visitors – one for each ten families – has been built up. A similar group of women will be recruited to act as hostesses for the promotional meal, but this is done fairly quickly as women are usually less reticent in volunteering for church work. Enlistment is followed by several training meetings, and about two-thirds through the campaign the congregation attends the promotional meal to have the complete programme explained. Family visiting then occupies the next two weeks, during which there will be report meetings to determine the progress of the visitors, the quality of the pledges, and to help any visitor with problems encountered. The last few days are spent training the various continuation groups in the work they will have to do over the next seven years, and the reports Wells expect from them so that they can be given any help and supervision as required.

Although Wells have a good record in increasing the level of financial contributions of congregations, the methods used have been the subject of criticism. In 1965 the special committee appointed by the Stewardship and Budget Committee made a report in fulfilment of the General Assembly's instruction 'to consider anew the issues raised by the work of professional fund-raising consultant organisations for the guidance of the Church.'[14] The special committee sought information from the Churches of various countries where fund-raising firms had been active – in the United States, Canada, Australia, New Zealand, Scotland (the Episcopal Church), and England (the Church of England) – mainly concerning the work of Wells. The official attitude of these Churches to fund-raising firms was found to be largely neutral. The majority of reports said that the operation of such firms had the effect of alerting the Churches to the need for systematic organization of financial support, as a result of which the Churches have created departments which have made the fund-raising firms unnecessary. Criticisms of fund-raising firms were voiced by all the Churches consulted along the following lines:

(i) While they claim not to teach but to organize, it is unavoidable that a certain basic interpretation of the Christian message must underlie an appeal to members for financial support. Such teaching on the part of fund-raising firms tends to be naive, shallow and sometimes misleading. Heavy stress is laid on 'the need of the giver to give'. Such a need, however, is by no means a central Christian motive . . . Fund-raising firms encourage undue optimism concerning the spiritual benefits that derive from financial commitment.

(ii) There is criticism about the methods employed. These tend to be the same as in raising money for secular purposes. Since the firms are in the field for financial profit, their criterion is financial success. It is easier to raise money for local purposes; therefore propaganda is geared to build up interest in and loyalty to the 'needs' of the local congregation. Uniformly the Churches criticize the use of social pressures to induce the people to give. The heavy stress that is laid on financial targets, financial pledges, and financial success obscures the missionary purposes of the Church and the congregation.

The official view of the Church departments consulted is that a proper organization within the Church itself makes it unnecessary to employ fund-raising firms, and that in the long-term even the financial success of operations carried through by the Church itself is more permanent.

The special committee also interviewed certain congregations, as represented by their ministers and selected office-bearers, and sent questionnaires to other congregations, all of whom had employed Wells. All were reported to be 'enthusiastic about the financial success of the Wells campaigns . . . There was little sign of uneasiness about the methods employed. The office-bearers, when asked about methods by which the money had been raised, were in general agreement that the financial results justified them.'

In its conclusions, the special committee asserted that Christian giving grows out of Christian faith, and that teaching about Christian response to the Gospel is the Church's work, and cannot properly be delegated to an outside agency. The Church, therefore, must 'keep careful control of the teaching concerning Christian liberality, and of the methods used to encourage it.' Thus, while not actually condemning the employment by congregations of fund-raising firms, the special committee certainly indicated its disapproval; it asked the General Assembly 'to recommend to all congregations the teaching and methods of the Church's own Stewardship and Budget Committee.'

4 A comparative statistical analysis of fund-raising campaigns

The purpose of this section is to present the results of a study to assess the success of various organized fund-raising campaigns that have been employed in recent years by charges in the Church. These campaigns have been organized by the Stewardship and Budget Committee and by Wells Organizations Scotland Limited. Unfortunately, no information was available on the number of charges which organized their own campaigns without the help of the committee or Wells. Four types of campaign were examined, as follows:

(i) The committee's Stewardship Campaign with Family Meal.
(ii) The committee's Parish Development Programme.
(iii) The Wells Three-Year Plan.
(iv) The Wells Seven-Year Plan.

Information was requested from the committee and from Wells as to the number of charges taking part in each of the campaigns for the years 1967 and 1968; the information provided is given in table 119. For the Wells Three-Year and Seven-Year Plans, the year given is the year in which the campaign was initiated. The table shows that 9 charges undertook the Committee's Stewardship Campaign with Family Meal over the period 1967-70; the number is small because the bulk of those campaigns were conducted prior to 1967. A total of 173 charges took part in the committee's Parish Development Programme in 1967-8, mainly charges in rural areas. In the Wells campaigns, 60 charges conducted a Three-Year Plan in the period 1963-9, and 13 charges undertook the Seven-Year Plan in the years 1964-72.

The geographical distribution by Presbytery of the 254 charges conducting one or other of the campaigns is given in table 120. The table indicates that 32 out of the then total of 58 Scottish Presbyteries had one or more charges participate in a fund-raising campaign. Only three Presbyteries, those of Edinburgh, Glasgow and Dundee, had charges that had been involved in all four types of campaign. The Presbyteries which were most active, as measured by the proportion of the charges conducting campaigns to the total number of charges in the Presbytery, were Greenock (72.7 per cent), Melrose (69.2 per cent), Paisley (49.0 per cent), Ayr (46.8 per cent), Livingston and Bathgate (46.4 per cent), and Dundee (35.7 per cent); all six Presbyteries have been heavily engaged in the Parish Development Programme, which tended to be organized on a Presbytery-wide basis and involved a large number of charges, usually in rural areas. The six Presbyteries account for 113, or 65.3 per cent, of the 172 charges involved in the Parish Development Programme in 1967-8. The Wells campaigns have tended to concentrate in urban areas: one half of the charges utilizing the Three-Year Plan were found

TABLE 119.
The number of charges participating in each of the four types of fund-raising campaign, 1963-72.

| | Stewardship and Budget Committee || Wells Organizations Scotland Limited ||
	Stewardship Campaign with Family Meal	Parish Development Programme	Three-Year Plan	Seven-Year Plan
1963	*	*	1	0
1964	*	*	13	1
1965	*	*	25	0
1966	*	*	11	0
1967	2	57	5	2
1968	2	116	4	1
1969	3	*	1	5
1970	2	*	0	3
1971	*	*	0	0
1972	*	*	0	1
TOTAL	9	173	60	13

* Not available.

in the Presbyteries of Glasgow (8), Dundee (7), Edinburgh (5), Dunbarton (5), and Kirkcaldy (5). Similarly, 8 of the 12 Seven-Year Plan campaigns have been undertaken by charges in Glasgow (4), Edinburgh (2) and Dundee (2). The concentration of these campaigns in a relatively small number of Presbyteries may partly reflect the fact that the urban areas tend to have the more affluent charges which can afford to meet the expenses of the Wells campaign, and partly the 'demonstration effect' which accompanies a successful campaign: the success of a fund-raising campaign in a charge encouraging a neighbouring charge to undertake a similar campaign.

Table 120 shows that overall the charges involved in the four types of fund-raising campaigns were concentrated geographically in an area which extends to the south and east of a line connecting Dunbarton, Dundee and Aberdeen. The absence of charges in the central and north-west Highlands and the Western Isles is very striking; this is explained by the fact that the small charges in those remote areas are generally unable to afford the expense associated with the types of campaign under consideration. The field assistant of the Stewardship and Budget Committee has concentrated his efforts in the lowland Presbyteries where the returns to fund-raising campaigns are likely to be greater.

In order to examine the effectiveness of each of the four types of campaign, a control sample of 45 charges (from which seven were removed because of involvement in readjustments) was drawn from the total number of charges in the Church. These were used as a bench-mark against which the income and membership trends for charges engaged in fund-raising campaigns could be compared. The sample was drawn from the list of charges appearing in the 1968 *Yearbook* after the 254 congregations involved in fund-raising campaigns had been eliminated. However, because our information on the numbers of charges involved in the Stewardship Campaign with Family Meal and the Parish Development Programme was limited to 1967-70 and 1967-8 respectively, it was not possible to

TABLE 120.
The geographical distribution by Presbytery of charges participating in fund-raising campaigns, 1963-72.

Presbytery (number in brackets)	Family Meal	Parish Development	Wells 3-Year	Wells 7-Year	TOTAL	Total as percentage of number of charges in Presbytery
Edinburgh (1)	1	2	5	2	10	8.70
Livingston & Bathgate (2)	—	13	—	—	13	46.43
Linlithgow & Falkirk (3)	—	10	3	—	13	24.07
Peebles (4)	1	—	—	—	1	6.25
Dalkeith (5)	—	3	—	—	3	9.68
Haddington & Dunbar (6)	—	2	1	—	3	9.37
Duns (7)	—	4	—	—	4	14.81
Jedburgh (8)	—	3	1	—	4	10.81
Melrose (9)	—	17	1	—	18	69.23
Annandale (10)	—	—	1	—	1	3.57
Dumfries (11)	—	—	3	—	3	7.32
Wigtown & Stranraer (13)	—	—	2	1	3	10.71
Ayr (14)	1	25	3	—	29	46.77
Irvine & Kilmarnock (15)	—	5	1	1	7	19.44
Ardrossan (16)	1	1	—	—	2	5.40
Paisley (17)	1	21	3	—	25	49.02
Greenock (18)	—	22	2	—	24	72.73
Glasgow (19)	2	4	8	4	18	8.49
Hamilton (20)	1	2	—	—	3	2.94
Lanark (21)	—	—	4	—	4	12.12
Dumbarton (22)	—	1	5	1	7	10.77
Stirling & Dunblane (32)	—	1	—	1	2	4.44
Dunfermline & Kinross (33)	1	3	3	—	7	15.55
Kirkcaldy (34)	—	3	5	—	8	19.51
Dundee (37)	1	15	7	2	25	35.71
Angus & Mearns (39)	—	6	—	—	6	10.71
Aberdeen (40)	—	2	—	—	2	2.47
Deer (43)	—	—	1	—	1	4.00
Strathbogie & Fordyce (45)	—	—	1	—	1	3.33
Inverness (48)	—	1	—	—	1	3.70
Chanonry & Dingwall (49)	—	2	—	—	2	11.11
Orkney (50)	—	4	—	—	4	14.28
TOTAL	10	172	60	12	254	—

exclude from the control sample charges which had engaged in those campaigns prior to or after the sample periods; similarly, it was impossible to exclude from the control sample those charges which had undertaken locally organized campaigns during the period. But these biases should not affect the analysis of the comparative effectiveness of the campaigns under review.

The number of charges in the Wells Three-Year Plan and the Parish Development Programme campaigns were reduced for the purposes of the analysis by taking samples of 36 and 30 charges respectively.

Before proceeding to a more detailed analysis of the impact of fund-raising campaigns on the membership and revenue of the charges involved, it is of interest to examine the average characteristics of charges in each of the four campaign categories, and to compare these with the average characteristics of the control group, which represents the Church as a whole. The figures in table 121 show the average membership, liberality contributed, and liberality per member, for each of the five samples of charges for 1964. A rough guide to the performance of the charges since 1964 can be gained by comparing the figures with those for 1972, also shown in Table 121. The table indicates that in 1964 the 'average' charge in the Church had about 600 members, an income from liberality of £2,785, and a contribution per member of £4.9. The charges in each of the four campaigns categories on average all had memberships above the Church average, ranging from 663 for the Parish Development Programme to 1,281 for the Wells Seven-Year Plan, while contributions per member all fell below the Church average, ranging from £3.1 for the Wells Three-Year Plan to £4.4 for the Seven-Year Plan charges. The average liberality per charge was higher than the Church average in three of the four campaign categories, the impact of the higher average membership offsetting the lower average contribution per member. The exception is provided by the charges in the Parish Development Programme, which had a lower average liberality than the Church average charge because of their relatively low average membership. It seems, therefore, that with the exception of the Parish Development Programme, which was designed as an inexpensive form of campaign for small charges in rural areas, the fund-raising campaigns have tended to attract charges which have larger memberships and are more affluent, but are less successful at fund-raising, than the average; this applies particularly to the Stewardship Campaign with Family Meal and to the Wells Seven-Year Plan. The substantial initial outlays involved probably tended to discourage the less affluent charges from undertaking such campaigns. The Wells Three-Year Plan has tended to attract, in the main, medium-sized charges with relatively small amounts of income derived from liberality.

A rough guide to the performance of the five groups of charges since 1964 can be gained by comparing the 1972 figures with those for 1964. The figures for the change in the average membership per change are difficult to interpret: the control group membership fell by 8.9 per cent. over the period 1964-72, while the average memberships of the charges in the Stewardship Campaign with Family Meal and the Wells Three-Year Plan fell roughly twice as much, and the memberships in the Parish Development Programme and Wells Seven-Year Plan fell less than the Church average. With the exception of the Wells Seven-Year Plan, the average liberality per member was still lower in the four campaign categories of charges than the Church average, but the increase over the period since 1964 had been much greater, except in the case of the charges in the Parish Development Programme. While the average liberality per member increased by 61.2 per cent. for the control group of charges, it increased by 97.3 per cent. for the Stewardship Campaign with Family Meal category, 116.1 per cent for the Wells Three-Year Plan, and 134.1 per cent for the Wells Seven-Year Plan. The average liberality per charge increased faster in all four campaign categories than in the control group, including the charges in the Parish Development Programme, where the very small membership fall over the period more than offset the relatively poor performance in average liberality per member.

The preliminary analysis suggests that the Wells Seven and Three-Year Plans, together with the Stewardship Campaign with Family Meals, were all successful in

TABLE 121

A comparison of the 'average' characteristics of charges in each of the four fund-raising campaign categories with those of the control group between 1964 and 1972.

Sample	Average membership per charge 1964	1972	Percentage change	Average liberality per member 1964 £	1972 £	Percentage change	Average liberality per charge 1964 £	1972 £	Percentage change
(a) Control group (n = 38)	600.4	547.2	− 8.9	4.9	7.9	+ 61.2	2,784.5	3,877.6	+ 39.3
(b) Stewardship Campaign with Family Meal (n = 9)	1,032.5	844.6	−18.2	3.7	7.3	+ 97.3	3,821.0	5,897.4	+ 54.3
(c) Parish Development Programme (n = 28)	663.0	646.3	− 2.5	4.0	6.3	+57.5	2,425.1	3,740.2	+ 54.2
(d) Wells Three-Year Plan (n = 36)	734.3	611.6	−16.7	3.1	6.7	+116.1	2,194.9	3,902.1	+ 77.8
(e) Wells Seven-Year Plan (n = 12)	1,281.3	1,196.0	− 6.7	4.4	10.3	+134.1	5,490.8	11,539.8	+110.2

increasing the income of participating charges more quickly than the Church average, whereas the Parish Development Programme appears to have had little impact on the rate of increase of income. In order to make a more detailed assessment of the impact of the various types of fund-raising campaign on the income and membership of participating charges, data for those variables was assembled for all the charges in the samples for the following periods: for the five years prior to the initiation of a fund-raising campaign; for the years during which the campaign was being carried out; and for the five years subsequent to the completion of the campaign (where possible).

Membership and income figures for the charges in the control group were also collected for the period 1960-73. This means that not only can comparisons be made within a sample between the periods prior to, during, and subsequent to campaigns, but also between the performance of charges participating in fund-raising campaigns and those in the Church as a whole, as represented by the control group.

The approach adopted was to calculate the average annual percentage rate of change in membership and income over the three periods for each charge in each sample; the resulting charge averages are then averaged to arrive at a single figure for each period for each sample. Statistical tests can then be applied to ascertain whether there are significant differences in the rate of change of membership and income between the various samples. Tables 122 to 125 provide such figures for the charges in the Wells Three-Year Plan category (122) and in the Parish Development Programme (123), and for the control group of charges for comparison with each of those types of campaign (124, 125).

Care is needed in the interpretation of these tables. This applies particularly to the income section of table 122, which presents the results for the Wells Three-Year Plan. The table shows that income in the charges concerned increased on average at 1.5 per cent a year in the five years prior to the introduction of the campaign. In the first and second years of the campaign, income increased on average by 56.79 and 46.39 per cent respectively, and then fell by 8.43 and 7.23

TABLE 122.
Mean annual percentage changes in the membership and income of charges participating in the Wells Three-Year Plan, 1963-9.

	Membership		Income	
	Mean annual rate of change	Standard deviation	Mean annual rate of change	Standard deviation
	%		%	
The five years prior to commencement of campaign	−1.7300	2.4539	1.5000	6.7666
First year of campaign	−2.7183	5.0934	56.7914	45.9404
Second year of campaign	−2.0233	5.2339	46.3869	70.6409
Third year of campaign	−1.9197	4.1265	−8.4335	13.9067
Fourth year of campaign	−2.8336	4.2348	−7.2255	13.3194
The five years subsequent to completion of campaign	−1.7064	2.5921	2.8933	7.5137

TABLE 123.
Mean annual percentage changes in the membership and income of charges participating in the Parish Development Programme, 1967-8.

	Membership		Income	
	Mean annual rate of change	Standard deviation	Mean annual rate of change	Standard deviation
	%		%	
The five years prior to commencement of campaign	0.1789	2.2975	5.4293	5.4470
The first year of campaign	0.0121	4.2348	5.7734	9.7736
The second year of campaign	−0.8134	3.4121	6.8631	13.4320
The five years subsequent to completion of campaign	−1.3272	1.6882	9.2858	7.1715

TABLE 124.
Mean annual percentage changes in membership and income of charges in control sample I for comparison with the charges participating in the Wells Three-Year Plan.

	Membership		Income	
	Mean annual rate of change	Standard deviation	Mean annual rate of change	Standard deviation
	%		%	
The equivalent five years to commencement of Wells' campaign	−0.5428	4.9970	4.6110	5.0772
The year of the first year of the Wells' campaign	−1.2416	7.9278	4.4355	13.6423
The year of the second year of the Wells' campaign	−0.4415	4.5289	6.5397	13.3963
The year of the third year of the Wells' campaign	−0.5603	3.5908	2.9007	11.7713
The year of the fourth year of the Wells' campaign	−1.0347	2.6318	7.6869	17.6831
The five years subsequent to completion of the Wells' campaign	—	—	6.7047	4.7646

per cent respectively in the third and fourth years.[15] In the five years following the campaign, income rose on average by 2.89 per cent a year. However, the substantial increase in income for the first two years of the campaign should not be interpreted as meaning that most charges in the sample greatly increased their level of giving in each of the two years. Without exception, all congregations in the sample recorded an increase in income in the first year of the campaign; typically, the new higher level of giving was sustained for the remainder of the campaign, and then drifted downwards slightly from the peak in later years. But in some cases there was a delay before the impact of the campaign was reflected in higher income. Thus the average figure for the increase in income in the first year of the

TABLE 125.
Mean annual percentage changes in membership and income of charges in control sample II for comparison with the charges participating in the Parish Development Programme

	Membership		Income	
	Mean annual rate of change	Standard deviation	Mean annual rate of change	Standard deviation
	%		%	
The equivalent five years prior to commencement of Parish Development Campaign	−1.0968	3.3185	5.0997	4.3216
The year of the first year of the campaign	−0.5603	3.5623	7.6889	17.6822
The year of the second year of the campaign	−1.2739	4.4838	6.5000	16.1311
The five years subsequent to completion of Parish Development Campaign	−0.9753	2.3116	6.9763	5.2512

campaign given in table 122 reflects gains in income by 25 of the charges in the sample, with the second year average increase representing gains by the remaining 11 charges. These two annual figures taken separately understate the increase in income enjoyed by a charge participating in the Wells Three-Year Plan, as the average figure for each year is composed of charges whose income figures incorporate the impact of the fund-raising campaign and those which do not. Taking the two years together, the smallest gain in income by a congregation in the sample was 18.5 per cent, and the largest increase was 272.4 per cent. Of the 36 charges in the sample, 29 recorded increases in income of more than 50 per cent, and 15 increases of more than 100 per cent.

The income of charges in the Parish Development Programme show no marked increase as a result of the campaign. Among the 30 charges in the sample, the largest increase in income recorded in either of the two years in which the campaign could be expected to affect income was 41.7 per cent. Only 7 of the charges in the sample recorded increases of more than 20 per cent in either of those two years.

It is possible to examine the impact of those two types of fund-raising campaign by testing whether the average rates of change of membership and income in each case differ significantly from those of the control sample for comparable time-periods. The null hypothesis is that there is no significant difference between the mean rate of change of membership or income of the control sample and the mean rate of change of membership or income of either the Wells Three-Year Plan charges or the Parish Development Programme charges.

The results of these tests indicate that there was no significant different at the 0.05 per cent level in the mean rate of changes of membership and income between the Parish Development Programme sample and the control group sample. This result suggests that the Parish Development Programme had no significant impact on the changes in membership and income of the charges involved; the membership and income of the charges would have changed over the period of the campaign in much the same way if no campaigns had been carried out.

Comparisons between the results for the Wells Three-Year Plan and those for the control group sample reveal a more complex picture. With regard to membership, it was found that there was no significant difference between the two samples, with the exception of the fourth year of the campaign, when the fall in numbers was significantly greater in the Wells Three-Year Plan charges than in the control group charges. It is possible, therefore, that the Wells Three-Year Plan campaigns may have had some adverse affect on membership numbers in the charges concerned.

In the income comparisons, it was found that the rate of increase in income amongst charges involved in the Wells' campaign differed significantly from the rate of charges in the control group sample in the following ways:

(i) the rate of increase in income was significantly lower for the five years prior to the commencement of the campaign;
(ii) for the first two years of the campaign income increased very much faster on average than for the control group;
(iii) in the final two years of the campaign and for the five years subsequent to its completion, the rate of change of income was significantly less than for charges in the control sample.

These figures provide some justification for the contention that, while fund-raising campaigns of the Wells type do lead to large increases in income during the period of the campaign, the initial raised levels of giving are not sustained in subsequent years. On the other hand, the charges involved in the Wells' Three-Year Plan appear to be those whose pre-campaign income performance is not good, as measured by the annual contribution per member or the rate of increase in total liberality. Moreover, the figures indicate that the initial gain in income greatly outweighs the subsequent falls.

The rise in income of charges which can be attributed to the impact of the Wells Three-Year Plan campaign can be roughly estimated by calculating, for each year of a time-period which covers both the campaign and a number of years following its completion, the difference in income between the charges involved in the campaign and the income of those same charges if they had not had the campaign. These calculations are shown in table 126. The year from which the calculations start, or the 'base' year, is taken as the year preceeding the commencement of the campaign. The income of the 'average' charge in that year is taken as £2,000. Column 1 of table 126 shows the annual 'average' percentage increases in income for charges participating in the Wells' Three-Year Plan, years 1 to 4 being the years in which the campaigns took place, and years 5-9 being the following five-year period. These percentages are taken from table 122. Column 2 gives the corresponding annual income figures, which increase by 124.85 per cent from £2,000 in the 'base' year to £4,497 in year 9. The annual increases in the income of the 'average' control group charge are shown in column 3; these are the figures given in table 126. The corresponding annual income figures are shown in column 4, which indicate that the annual income of a charge not engaged in a fund-raising campaign over the period would have increased on average by 70.55 per cent. The annual differences in income between the campaign charges and control group charges are given in column 5; these figures measure the impact of the campaign over the nine-year period. The total difference attributable to the campaign is £12,083, which is nearly half as much again as the total income of the charge which had the same income nine years previously but did not undertake a Wells Three-Year Plan campaign. Finally, the figures in column 5 are multiplied by 30 in order to show the gross impact on the charges in the Wells sample, and these are given in column 6. The calculated increases in income accruing to the campaign charges may be understated, in that the 30 charges involved appeared on average to be increasing their income more slowly than the Church average, as revealed in the control group sample. If the control group sample reflected this slower rate of growth of income, the impact of the Wells Three-Year Plan in increasing income would be greater.

TABLE 126.
Estimate of the effectiveness of the Wells Three-Year Plan in raising the income of charges.

	INCOME OF 'AVERAGE' CHARGE				Difference in income between Wells and control group i.e. 2 − 4	Increase in income of 30 charges in Wells sample i.e. 5 × 30
	Wells Three-Year Plan		Control group			
Year	Annual change	Income	Annual change	Income		
	1	2	3	4	5	6
	%	£	%	£	£	£
'Base'	–	2,000	–	2,000	0	0
1	56.79	3,136	4.44	2,089	1,047	31,410
2	46.39	4,590	6.54	2,225	2,365	70,950
3	− 8.43	4,204	2.90	2,290	1,914	57,420
4	− 7.23	3,900	7.69	2,466	1,434	43,020
5	2.89	4,012	6.70	2,631	1,381	41,430
6	2.89	4,128	6.70	2,808	1,320	39,600
7	2.89	4,248	6.70	2,996	1,252	37,560
8	2.89	4,370	6.70	3,196	1,174	35,220
9	2.89	4,497	6.70	3,411	1,086	32,580
TOTAL (less 'Base')	224.83	37,085	170.53	24,112	12,973	389,190

So far we have not considered the cost of a Wells Three-Year Plan campaign. According to Wells, the cost is scaled according to the size of the congregation, as measured in the number of families. The costs for the period 1965-7, when the bulk of the campaigns under investigation were initiated, are given in table 127. The cost is composed of the fee charged by Wells, which varied from £1,200 to £1,600, together with the expenses of the congregation on printing, catering, typing, etc., which at about £1.50 per family varied between £300 and £900. Overall, the cost ranged from £1,500 for a medium-sized congregation of 200 families to £2,500 for a large congregation of 600 families. One of the fears of congregations is that they will be unable to raise sufficient income to meet the expenses of the campaign, but the figures in Tables 126 and 127 indicate that on average the expenses are easily met from the extra income raised. This may not apply to the small or very small congregation.

TABLE 127.
The cost of a Wells Three-Year Plan campaign, 1965-7

Size of congregation	Wells services Length of job	Fee	Expenses of congregation	TOTAL COST
	weeks			
200 – 300 families	4	£1,200	£300 – 450	£1,500 – 1,650
350 – 450 families	5	£1,400	£425 – 675	£1,825 – 2,075
450 – 600 families	6	£1,600	£675 – 900	£2,275 – 2,500

SOURCE: Wells Organization Scotland Limited.

So far in our detailed statistical analysis of the impact of fund-raising campaigns, we have concentrated on the Parish Development Programme and the Wells' Three-Year Plan. It is more difficult to assess the impact of either the Stewardship Campaign with Family Meal or the Wells Seven-Year Plan because of the statistical problems which arise when dealing with small samples. There were only nine charges in the Stewardship Campaign with Family Meal sample, with membership and income figures being available in eight cases. Among the charges, the average annual percentage increase in income was 6.4814 per cent for the five years prior to the commencement of the campaign; 13.0905 per cent and 11.8097 per cent respectively for the two years in which the campaign would have had maximum impact; and 3.6645 per cent for the five years following the completion of the campaign. This type of campaign thus on average probably produced a significant improvement in income, and the cost of mounting it was much less than for the Wells Three-Year Plan. Over the period 1967-70 the cost varied from £0.75 to £1.00 per member, together with a fee of £420 for the services of the Stewardship and Budget Committee's field assistant if he was employed on the campaign. The total cost for a medium-sized congregation of 600 members would have been about £600 or £1,000, depending upon the engagement of the field assistant.

We had information on twelve charges which were participating in the Wells Seven-Year Plan. However, only two of these had completed the full programme by 1973, and so it was not possible to derive averages for this sample in the manner employed above. Substantial increases in income, averaging 60.8298 per cent, were recorded in the first year of the campaign. In contrast to the Wells Three-Year Plan, it appears that the higher level of giving was sustained in all twelve charges, at least for the period for which information was available.

In conclusion, it seems clear that the Wells Three-Year and Seven-Year Plans, and probably to a lesser extent the Stewardship Campaign with Family Meal, have all had a significant impact in increasing the income of the charges in our samples when compared to the control group sample. The Parish Development Programme, however, does not appear to have been effective in raising the level of income of the congregations which have participated.

5 Measures to improve fund-raising and stewardship

It could be argued that fund-raising in the Church has been a remarkable success when one considers that the Church is not organizing a campaign of relatively short duration for the achievement of a specific objective, where it may be comparatively easy to harness people's interest and enthusiasm, but is raising income to support work which is on-going from year to year. However, the reports of the Stewardship and Budget Committee have frequently emphasized the low returns of its fund-raising efforts.

The following statement, made in 1956 by the Committee Anent Ingathering of Funds, probably reflects the committee's view of the situation as accurately today as it did twenty years ago: 'The Church of Scotland does not receive from its members sufficient money to support its manifold operations . . . The measure of the Church of Scotland's failure to command the willing and adequate response which it does indicates faithfully the degree of unreality with which many of its people regard their commitment to its duties and privileges.'[16]

The efforts made by the Stewardship and Budget Committee to promote fund-raising and stewardship in congregations have shown that some congregations are very active in fund-raising and are ready to adopt new methods, while others do little active fund-raising and resist the adoption of new methods.

A number of factors have been suggested to account both for the difference between 'active' and 'inactive' congregations, and for the generally inadequate performance of the Church in raising its income. These include the following:

(i) In many congregations the membership listed on the Communion Roll bears little relationship to the contributing membership. Often a third, or even a quarter, of the nominal membership provides the financial support. There is some evidence to suggest that the main contributors are those members who attend church regularly.

(ii) Many congregations are not sufficiently business-like in teaching and organizing their Christian giving. The congregational treasurer is traditionally responsible for fund-raising, but many treasurers see their role as one of accounting for the income and expenditures of the congregation, and of producing the annual accounts. There is a reluctance to use effective methods of raising income, such as the Weekly Freewill Offering Scheme with pledge cards and Deeds of Covenant.

(iii) The view is often expressed that it is the minister who sets the tone for fund-raising and stewardship in his charge.[17] 'It is our experience that when a minister is convinced of the value and importance of Christian stewardship . . . the congregation's enthusiasm, manpower and finance to tackle the work of Christ increase. He will educate his Kirk Session, office-bearers and members in Christian stewardship; he and his Kirk Session will find ways of telling the congregation of the work undertaken by the Church of Scotland in Christ's name.'

Significantly, a proportion of ministers consider that fund-raising and stewardship in their charge is not a matter that concerns them. This applies particularly to ministers of the conservative evangelical persuasion who see their role in terms of spiritual leadership.

Fund-raising campaigns also impose a great deal of extra work on the minister. Older ministers are often reluctant to tackle this work, especially those nearing retirement who may not see the benefits of the work.

(iv) Many Kirk Sessions are resistant to the use of modern fund-raising methods. It has been suggested that in many cases this is because they are composed of elders who are mostly middle-aged and old, and therefore tend to be unwilling or unable to undertake the extra work involved. Many elders report a difficulty in raising the question of money in their discussions with individual Church members. Central allocations on congregations are sometimes declared to be 'unrealistic' or 'unattainable' when only a small contribution per member is involved.

(v) Efforts by the Stewardship and Budget Committee to persuade congregations to undertake stewardship campaigns usually encounter two main problems. The first difficulty lies in persuading the congregation of the need for a campaign to raise the low level of giving per member, in order to benefit both the congregation and the wider Church. The second problem concerns the difficulty of convincing the congregation of its ability to raise funds sufficiently to meet the cost of the campaign.

(vi) Members are not always adequately informed about the financial position of the congregation, or of its budgeted income requirements. Congregational accounts are often too complicated for the average member to understand.

The recognition that these factors operate to hinder active and successful fund-raising in congregations provides an indication of the measures which need to be adopted in order to improve the situation. Some of the measures required are mentioned at various points through this book; we do no more than repeat them without elaboration here. Other measures to improve fund-raising and stewardship are discussed in more detail.

The recommended measures are as follows:

(i) The decline in the number of members needs to be halted or even reversed. This change alone would have a considerable beneficial affect on the rate of increase of Church income. An increase in average attendance rates at services would have a similar affect. Measures to increase Church membership and attendance rates are discussed in chapter 4.

(ii) The approved and successful methods of raising income should be used more widely and more effectively. The Weekly Freewill Offering Scheme should be used with pledge cards in every congregation, and the pledge should be reviewed annually. People using the Weekly Freewill Offering Scheme should be encouraged to contribute through Deeds of Covenant, and the covenants should be reviewed annually. The potential benefits to be derived from a greater use of covenants are examined in chapter 18.

(iii) In chapter 20 we recommend various modifications to Church government and administration which might have the affect of improving congregational fund-raising. These include the ordination of more elders, both younger and with a background in business or commerce, and a strengthening of the Presbyterial superintendance of congregations, including an increase in the rate of parish visitation from quinquennial to triennial visits.

(iv) The proposals for stipend made in chapter 11, which are designed to reduce the amounts of aid given to, and received from, the Maintenance of the

Ministry Fund by congregations, should have a salutary impact on fund-raising.

(v) The proposal for an increase in the emphasis to be placed on training in pastoral care in the education and training of students for the ministry and in the content of in-service refresher courses for practising ministers may encourage ministers to become more aware of the need for congregational fund-raising and stewardship. This proposal is made in chapter 14.

(vi) In chapter 12 we recommend that the annual accounts of congregations should be presented in as simple a format as possible, so that they can be understood by the ordinary Church member. This should encourage a better understanding of the financial position of the congregation and the need to raise extra income.

(vii) The success of the fund-raising campaigns conducted by the Wells organization in a number of congregations is too striking to be ignored. We recommend that the Church should consider anew the methods employed by such professional fund-raising firms, with a view to incorporating such methods in the programmes promoted by the Stewardship and Budget Committee.

6 Conclusions

The purpose of this chapter has been to examine and assess the fund-raising and stewardship methods used by the congregations, and promoted by the Church's Stewardship and Budget Committee and other agencies.

In section 2 we traced the development of the various methods promoted by the Stewardship and Budget Committee over the period 1960-75. These methods can be classified into stewardship campaigns, publicity, education and financial guidance, and stewardship promoters. The early years (1960-3), which followed the inception of the committee in 1959 and of the Co-ordinated Appeal in 1961 saw the establishment of several important promotional activities, including the stewardship campaigns in individual congregations, publicity, and the introduction of courses in stewardship training for ministers and office-bearers.

However, an early optimism over the ability of the committee to increase the income accruing to the Co-ordinated Appeal (renamed the Mission and Service Fund in 1970) was shown to be unfounded, despite the efforts of the committee. This shortcoming was perhaps highlighted by a report in 1965 on the success in raising funds of professional fund-raising agencies employed by certain congregations in the Church, and by the appointment in 1966 of a field assistant to promote stewardship campaigns in congregations. Then in 1967 a special sub-committee produced a report which advocated a sharp acceleration of the expenditure of the committees within the Mission and Service Fund.

It was proposed that the extra income required might be raised by the appointment of stewardship 'salesmen' in each congregation. In the following years stewardship promoters were appointed in about a third of all congregations, although later reports have indicated that many are hampered by a lack of support and encouragement in their congregations. Finally, we saw that in recent years the emphasis in the committee's thinking on stewardship has shifted to developing the Weekly Freewill Offering Scheme through Give As You Earn and Deeds of Covenant.

In section 3 we examined the employment of fund-raising firms in the Church, the largest of which is Wells Organizations Scotland Ltd. The firm used to run three-year planned giving programmes, but these have largely been superseded by the seven-year covenant programmes. In the latter programmes the aim is first to raise individual giving to a reasonable level, and then to encourage the contribution to be covenanted. This avoids the contributions being pegged by the covenant at too low a level.

Wells stresses the need of the giver to give in order to fulfil his Christianity, in contrast to the official Church teaching which treats contributions as a by-product of the education of members in the meaning of stewardship. Although the methods used by Wells have been much criticised, the firm has a good fund-raising record, and has influenced fund-raising methods and organization employed by the Churches.

In section 4 we conducted a comparative statistical analysis of the effectiveness of various forms of fund-raising which have been employed by charges in the Church. These campaigns have been promoted by the Stewardship and Budget Committee and by Wells Organizations Scotland Limited, and are of four types: the Committee's Stewardship Campaign with Family Meal, the Committee's Parish Development Programme, the Wells Three-Year Plan, and the Wells Seven-Year Plan. A sample of charges participatng in each of these campaigns was drawn from a period centring on 1967-8. The 254 charges sampled were drawn from 32 of the (then) 58 Scottish Presbyteries. The absence of charges in the central and north-west Highlands and Islands is explained by their inability to afford the fees charged by Wells, and by the fact that the Presbyteries in those areas were not visited by the committee's field assistant.

Only three Presbyteries, those of Edinburgh, Glasgow and Dundee, had charges involved in all four types of campaign. The most active Presbyteries, as measured by the proportion of charges conducting campaigns to the total number in the Presbytery, were those of Greenock, Melrose, Ayr, and Livingston and Bathgate. All of these were heavily involved in the Parish Development Programme, which tended to be organized on a Presbytery-wide basis. The Wells charges were concentrated in urban areas, with over a half found in only five Presbyteries.

In order to examine the effectiveness of the campaigns, a control sample of 45 charges was selected to represent the Church as a whole. The average annual rates of change of membership and income for each of the campaign samples could then be compared with those of the control group. It was found that in 1964 the campaign samples all had an average membership higher than the Church average of 600, and average contributions of liberality per member of less than the control group figure of £4.90. In three of the four campaign samples the average liberality per charge was higher than the Church average. With the exception of the Parish Development Programme, therefore, the fund-raising campaigns have tended to attract charges of above-average size and income, but below average in contributions per member.

By 1972 the average liberality per member had increased much more in the campaign sample of charges (except the Parish Development Programme) than the Church average of 61.2 per cent, although the average contribution per member still fell below the average in all samples except the Wells' Seven-Year Plan.

The detailed analysis was based on comparisons of the annual rate of change of membership numbers and income; these were aggregated for all the charges in each group for the five years prior to the commencement of the campaign, each year of the campaign, and the five year period following the campaign. There was no significant difference at the 0.05 per cent level between the rates of change of membership and income of the charges in the Parish Development Programme and the rates of change in the control sample. This suggests that the Parish Development Programme had no significant impact on membership or income in the charges concerned.

In the Wells' Three-Year Plan sample, no significant difference was found in the rate of decline of membership with that of the control group, except in the fourth year of the campaign, when the fall in the Wells group was significantly greater. In the income comparisons it was found that the Wells sample differed significantly for all three time periods, in that the rate of increase in income was less in the preceding five-year period, very much greater in the first two years of the campaign, and less in the final two years of the campaign and in the subsequent five-year period; this evidence provides some support for the contention that the large increases in income brought about by fund-raising firms during the campaign is not sustained in subsequent years. However, the net increase to the average charge is considerable. For a charge with an income of £2,000 in 1964, the affect of a Wells Three-Year Plan campaign was to increase the income nine years later by 125 per cent to £4,497, as compared to an increase of 71 per cent to £3,411 for a control group charge. Over the nine-year period the Well's charge would have raised £12,973 more in income, which easily covers the campaign costs of between £1,500 and £2,500.

The small size of the samples made it difficult to produce reliable results for the Stewardship Campaign with Family Meal and Wells Seven-Year Plan samples. The evidence suggests that the former campaign did on average increase income, though by less than the Wells Three-Year Plan. However, the cost of such campaigns were much less — at between £600 and £1,000 for a charge of average size.

By 1973 only two charges had completed the full Wells Seven-Year Plan, but the evidence suggests that a large increase in income, averaging 60 per cent, was recorded in the first year of the campaign for all congregations.

In section 5 we examined the factors which have served to restrict increases in congregational income. Amongst these were included the decline in membership and low rates of attendance; the insufficiently business-like attitude of many congregations, and the unwillingness to use the best fund-raising methods; the lack of interest in fund-raising of some ministers because of theological position or age; the reluctance of many Kirk Sessions to adopt modern fund-raising methods; the unwillingness to risk the initial expenses in a fund-raising campaign; and the lack of simple financial information for members in many congregations. The measures to improve the income position and fund-raising of charges suggested by these considerations included the need to reverse the downward trend in membership and increase attendance; to use approved fund-raising methods, such as the Weekly Freewill Offering System with pledge cards and Deeds of Covenant, more widely; to increase the number of younger elders, and those with a business background; to increase the pastoral care training in the education for the ministry; and to reconsider incorporating the methods used by professional fund-raising firms in the promotional activities of the Stewardship and Budget Committee.

Notes

1 *The Church of Scotland Yearbook*, 1975, p. 25.

2 Church of Scotland, 'Report of the Stewardship and Budget Committee' *Reports to the General Assembly, 1962,* p. 104.

3 'Report of the Stewardship and Budget Committee,' *Reports to the General Assembly, 1966,* p. 93.

4 loc. cit.

5 loc. cit.

6 *Reports to the General Assembly, 1964,* p. 117.

7 *The Church of Scotland Yearbook*, 1974, p. 77.

8 'Report of the Stewardship and Budget Committee', *Reports to the General Assembly, 1971,* p. 105. The P.P.I.O. is the Press, Publicity and Information Office (Department of Publicity and Publication).

9 *Reports to the General Assembly, 1965,* p. 62.

10 The value of Deeds of Covenant to the fund-raising efforts of the Church is examined in chapter 18.

11 'Report of the Stewardship and Budget Committee', *Report to the General Assembly, 1967,* p. 120.

12 'Report of the Stewardship and Budget Committee', *Reports to the General Assembly, 1973,* p. 115.

13 *Scottish Newsletter, 1975-6,* (Wells Organizations Scotland Ltd.).

14 'Report of the Stewardship and Budget Committee', *Reports to the General Assembly, 1965,* pp. 54-6.

15 The fourth year represents the final year figures for those charges where the impact of the fund-raising campaign is not first reflected in higher income until the year following the start of the campaign. The apparent delay is probably caused in such cases by the commencement of the campaign late in the year.

16 Quoted in: Church of Scotland, 'Report of the Stewardship and Budget Committee', *Reports to the General Assembly, 1964,* p. 109.

17 'Report of the Stewardship and Budget Committee', *Reports to the General Assembly, 1974,* pp. 73-4.

V
Further proposals to improve finances

Chapter 18

Deeds of covenant

1 Introduction
The purpose of this chapter is to examine the significance of Deeds of Covenant as a method of raising funds for the Church. In section 2 we describe the additional income, in the form of income tax reclaimed from the Inland Revenue, accruing to the Church from contributions made by covenant, and briefly examine the present position of such covenants in Church finance. Then in sections 3 and 4 we go on to examine to what extent the income of congregations could be augmented if a greater proportion of their ordinary collections were to be raised through covenants. Finally, in section 5 methods to encourage the greater use of covenants in fund-raising are discussed.

2 Deeds of covenant
A Deed of Covenant (or a Bond of Annuity, as it is sometimes known) is an obligation to pay a specified sum to a specified person or body over a period of more than six years; most covenants are therefore granted for a period of seven years. To avoid any additional cost to himself the contributor must have income taxed at the basic rate at least equivalent to the gross amount of the annual contribution.

The significance to charitable institutions such as the Church of contributions made by covenant is that the institution can recover the income tax at the basic rate already paid by the contributor on the sum given. For example, given the current (1977) basic rate of income tax of 35 per cent, then from every portion of £15.38 of an individual's taxable income, £5.38 will be taken in tax, leaving £10 for the person concerned. If that person then contributes £10 to the Church by covenant, the Church can recover the £5.38 tax paid from the Inland Revenue. Thus, with income tax at the basic rate of 35 per cent, an additional 53p is recovered by the Church for every £1 paid in cash by the contributor.

A further advantage of covenants to the funds of the Church is that they tend to consolidate income because of the seven-year commitment to contribute. However, the degree of consolidation is weakened during periods of high inflation, such as we are currently experiencing, when the real value of covenants will fall rapidly. Contributors need to be reminded of this, particularly as their money incomes have probably risen quickly, and they should be encouraged to increase the value of their covenants accordingly.

Contributions by covenant need not necessarily be paid in one annual instalment; they may be made under the Weekly Freewill Offering system or otherwise, by arrangement. In the case of the weekly offering, the Church can reclaim tax provided the total amount given in a year is at least the amount promised. Whatever the arrangement made, tax is recoverable only on contributions made after the date on which the covenant is signed. Stamp duty on covenants was abolished in 1971.

Covenants may be granted in favour of the Church of Scotland or the local congregation, depending on the wishes of the contributor, but the total number of covenants granted within the Church is known, because all have to be registered with the General Treasurer's Department. Table 128 shows that 59,000 Covenants were held by the Church in 1973, compared with 49,000 only two years previously, an increase of 20.7 per cent. Of these about a quarter were granted in favour of the Church of Scotland, and the remainder in favour of the local congregations. In 1973 the value of the covenants held in favour of the Church of Scotland only amounted to £380,000, on which £188,000 tax was reclaimed, making £568,000 in all. The 15,000 donors contributed an average sum of nearly £38, including tax. Separate information on the covenants held in favour of the congregations is not available.

TABLE 128
Details of Deeds of Covenant held by the Church of Scotland

		1971	1972	1973
1	Total number of Deeds of Covenant held by Church of Scotland	49,059	54,529	59,210
2	Number of covenants (approx.) on which General Treasurer recovers tax	*	14,500	15,000
3	Tax recovered on 2	*	£220,000	£188,000
4	Total value of 2 + 3	*	£565,000	£568,000
5	Sum per donor (including tax)	*	£ 38.84	£ 37.87
6	Number of donors (approx. $\frac{4}{5}$)	*	14,547	14,999

SOURCE: 'Reports of the General Finance Committee', *Reports to the General Assembly*, 1973, p. 100, and 1974, p. 64. The total number of covenants held increased to 66,624 in 1974 and 81,567 in 1975.

Figures are for the year ending 31 December.
*Not available.

The level at which the basic rate of income tax is set directly determines the amount of tax which can be recovered on a given sum of convenants. In table 128, for example, the sharp drop (by 14.5 per cent) in the sum of tax recovered in 1973 as compared with 1972 suggests a change in the tax rate, particularly when the total value of the convenants held increased quite sharply (by 10.1 per cent) between the two years. Since the analysis which follows in sections 3 and 4 is based on 1973 data, the following quotation will be significant. 'Under the new Unified Tax System due to come into effect on 6 April 1973, it is proposed that the rate of income tax will be reduced from 38.75% to 30%. Accordingly, from that date tax recoverable on fixed "net" Bonds of Annuity will be less, and it is estimated that the annual income of the Church of Scotland will be reduced by £240,000 through the lower rate of tax recovery.'[1]

However, in his budget speech of 6th March 1973, the Chancellor instituted a scheme of 'transitional relief' to be available over the four years 1973/4 to 1976/7 to help alleviate such a loss. The 'base' on which the transitional reliefs were calculated is the tax recovered by a body or institution in the financial year 1971/2, plus the claims for tax repayments for the year 1972/3 received prior to 6 March 1973. In the first year the institution obtains 100 per cent of the base, but this is reduced by 25 per cent a year to zero in four years. These arrangements were not affected by the April 1974 increase in the basic rate of income tax from 30 per cent to 33 per cent. Fortunately from the point of view of this study, the effective tax recovery rate on covenants thus did not change in 1973 because of the operation of the transitional relief scheme.

3 Collection of data

The purpose of this section and the following one is to examine to what extent the income of congregations could be increased, through the recovery of income tax payments from the Inland Revenue, if contributors could be persuaded to pay a greater proportion of their contributions through Deeds of Covenant. This would seem to be a relatively painless way of increasing congregational income, since contributing by covenant imposes no extra financial burden on people who contribute regularly to the Church.

The source of the information for this study was the 1973 income and expenditure statements for a representative sample of charges in the Church divided into five groups: recently united, linked, rural, small-town and urban. The purpose of this stratification is to examine whether significant differences are discernible in the finances of the different groups of charges. Although the original sample contains 30 charges in each group, or 150 in all, we had accounts from 105 charges at the time of the study. It was thought that this shortfall was not likely to unduly bias the results when extrapolated forward to represent the parish ministry as a whole, particularly as all five groups were fairly evenly represented, as shown in table 129. However, this statement needs to be qualified with respect to the group of linked charges, where at the time of the study only 37 of the 62 congregational accounts in the sample of 30 linked charges were available; of these, 15

TABLE 129
Details of the stratified sample of parishes in the Church

Types of charges	Number of each type at 12/12/74[+] 1	Size of original sample 2	Number available for survey 3	Number actually used in survey 4
Recently united	76	30	22	21
Linked	205(460*)	30(62*)	21(37*)	21(37*)
Rural	667	30	20	20
Small-town	276	30	22	22
Urban	423	30	20	19
TOTAL	1,647	150	105	103

[+] The 121 charges vacant at 12/12/74 were excluded from the sample.
*References to congregations rather than charges.

linked charges were fully represented (with 31 congregations), leaving six other linked charges to be represented by the accounts of only one of their congregations. The sample of linked charges is thus rather small and incomplete, and this may tend to bias the results for this group of charges. Also, two charges, one united and one urban, had to be excluded because their accounts provided too little information to be useful in this study.

The relevant financial information for each of the five groups of charges obtained from the sample of congregational accounts is presented in table 130 under the following headings: total income of the congregations, income from ordinary collections, collections through Deeds of Covenant, and income tax recovered on covenants. All this information was obtained from the income and expenditure balance-sheets of the accounts, called variously the Congregational Account, the General Fund, or the Ordinary Account. The definition of these terms, and their significance is explained as follows:

(i) *Total income of the congregations.* The total income of the congregation is that sum appearing at the foot of the income side of the income and expenditure balance sheet. It includes all sources of both ordinary and special liberality and any income brought forward from the previous year (usually a very small sum), but excludes any income accruing separately to the various (and often numerous) subsidiary accounts, such as fabric funds, reserve accounts, contingency funds, Women's Guild accounts, Bible Class accounts, and so on.[2] The elements of congregational income listed under the following headings all fall within this total income category.

(ii) *Income from ordinary collections.* Income from ordinary collections covers that proportion of total congregational income which is collected on a regular recurring basis, and for that reason is open to the possibility of being redirected (if not already done so) through Deeds of Covenant. Included here is income from Freewill Offering Schemes, ordinary collections and offerings, and Deeds of Covenant (but not the income tax recovered); excluded from this category are donations, investment income, income donated to the congregation from Women's Guilds and other schemes of the congregations, endowments, sales of work, Church collection boxes, and all special collections and appeals.

(iii) *Collections through Deeds of Covenant.* This forms that portion of income from ordinary collections paid through covenants. Occasionally, accounts distinguish between 'direct payments' and payments 'through envelopes', but for our purposes the mode of payment is not relevant. The recovery of income tax on covenants is not included here.

(iv) *Income tax recovered on covenants.* This is self-explanatory. Only a handful of the congregational accounts received were presented on the recommended form drawn up by the General Treasurer's Department so that the financial information required was not always easily available. However, the desired information could usually be obtained at the risk of some imprecision in the figures produced. In a few cases the accounts referred to the year 1972, or to a financial year which did not exactly coincide with the calendar year 1973, but these were included without modification.

Two problems recurred frequently in the accounts. The first concerns the fact that many accounts showed the tax recovered on covenants, but did not distinguish the value of the covenants held from the income from other ordinary collec-

TABLE 130.
A disaggregation of congregational income showing the proportion raised by Deed of Covenant for the five groups of charges in 1973 (see text)

Charges 1		Total congregational income 2	Income from ordinary collections 3	$\frac{3}{2} \times 100$ 4	Collections through Deeds of Covenant 5	$\frac{5}{3} \times 100$ 6	Income tax recovered on covenants 7	$\frac{7}{5} \times 100$ 8
		£	£	%	£	%	£	%
1 Recently united								
a	sample of 21	139,498	98,949	70.9	22,251	22.5	13,715	61.6
b	average of sample	6,643	4,712	70.9	1,060	22.5	653	61.6
c	total of 76	504,868	358,112	70.9	80,560	22.5	49,628	61.6
2 Linked								
a	sample of 21 (37*)	66,263	37,186	56.1	5,188	14.0	3,372	65.0
b	average of sample*	1,791	1,005	56.1	140	14.0	91	65.0
c	total of 205 (460*)	823,810	462,312	56.1	64,499	14.0	41,922	65.0
3 Rural								
a	sample of 20	85,285	53,164	62.3	11,324	21.3	7,382	65.2
b	average of sample	4,264	2,658	62.3	566	21.3	369	65.2
c	total of 667	2,844,255	1,773,019	62.3	377,655	21.3	246,190	65.2
4 Small-town								
a	sample of 22	143,884	93,087	64.7	20,724	22.3	13,487	65.1
b	average of sample	6,540	4,231	64.7	942	22.3	613	65.1
c	total of 276	1,805,040	1,167,756	64.7	259,992	22.3	169,188	65.1
5 Urban								
a	sample of 19	97,718	69,529	71.2	12,665	18.2	7,982	63.0
b	average of sample	5,143	3,659	71.2	667	18.2	420	63.0
c	total of 423	2,175,489	1,547,757	71.2	282,141	18.2	177,660	63.0
All 1,647 charges								
a AVERAGE		4,950	3,223	65.1	647	20.1	416	64.3
b TOTAL		8,153,462	5,308,956	65.1	1,064,847	20.1	684,588	64.3

* Reference to congregations rather than charges (in linked charges).

tions. In the 34 accounts which did provide full information on both items, it was found that on average the total sum of tax recovered was 61.7 per cent of the total value of the covenants held. This percentage was very close to the rate of tax recovery of 63.9 per cent which, together with the transitional arrangements mentioned above, was expected with the pre-March 1973 basic rate of income tax of 38.75 per cent. By using the figure of 63.9 per cent, it was possible to calculate the value of the covenants held from the sum of tax recovered in those congregations where only the latter appeared in the accounts.

A similar problem was that some accounts showed the value of the covenants held and the sum of recovered tax amalgamated in one figure, but it was possible to break down this figure into its two components by assuming the 63.9 per cent rate of tax recovery.

The second major problem was that a number of accounts made no mention either of covenants or of the tax recovered. The numbers involved in each of the five groups in the sample of parishes are shown in table 131. Column 3 indicates that in the samples of small-town, urban, and recently united charges, the proportion of charges which appear not to use covenants is less that 20 per cent, as compared to 30 per cent for rural charges and almost 50 per cent for the congregations of linked charges. The proportion of linked charges in which at least one of the congregations appears not to use covenants is 66.7 per cent.

TABLE 131
Proportions of charges not using Deeds of Covenant

Group	Number of charges in sample+	Number of charges where accounts make no mention of covenants	$\frac{2}{1} \times 100$
	1	2	3
			%
Recently united	21	4	19.0
Linked	21(37*)	14(18*)	66.7(48.6)
Rural	20	6	30.0
Small-town	22	1	4.5
Urban	19	2	10.5

+ SOURCE: Table 129, column 4.
* Reference to congregations rather than charges.

Since only a handful of congregations use the recommended form of accounts drawn up by the General Finance Committee, it is possible that some accounts simply do not bother to distinguish the collecting of income through covenants and the tax recovered from other ordinary collections. However, we can only assume that, where covenants are not mentioned in the accounts, they are not being used.

The financial information necessary for this study is presented in table 130 for each of the five groups of charges, and in aggregate for all 1,647 charges, under the headings given above. Taking recently united charges as an example, row 1(a) shows the aggregate figures for the sample of 21 charges, row 1(b) shows the corresponding figures calculated for the average charge in the sample, and row 1(c) presents the average figures multiplied up to produce estimated aggregate figures for all of the 76 'recently united' charges in the Church. The same calculations have been done for each of the other four groups of charges, except that in the case of linked charges we have used the *congregation* as the basic unit rather than the *charge*. Hence the average figures given in row 2(b) refer to the average congregation; in order to obtain a figure for the average income of a linked charge, the figures in row 2(b) need to be multiplied by 460/205.

Even allowing for these adjustments, the linked charges still had the lowest average total congregational income in 1973, with a figure of £4,019; next came rural charges, with an average income of £4,264; then urban charges at £5,143, small-town charges at £6,540, and finally 'recently united' charges at £6,643. The average income for all 1,647 charges was £4,950, giving a total Christian liberality for 1973 of £8,153,462. This figure falls over £1 million short of the published figure for 1973 of £9,258,343; but a large proportion of the deficit would be made up by the income of the 121 vacant charges which are excluded from the survey. For example, if the average income of the vacant charges was the same as that for the 1,647 occupied charges, then £600,000 of the apparent deficit would be accounted for. We may conclude that the stratified sample of charges used seems to provide a reasonably accurate picture of all charges in the population, and that the small bias is towards an understatement of income.

Columns 3 and 4 of table 130 show the proportion of total congregational income raised by ordinary collections. The proportion varies from 56.1 per cent (for linked charges) to 71.2 per cent (for urban charges), with an average figure for all charges of 65.1 per cent. Columns 5 and 6 deal with the proportion of income from ordinary collections raised through deeds of covenant. Linked charges again have the lowest proportion with a figure of 14.0 per cent, compared to the highest figure of 22.5 per cent for recently united charges, and an average for all charges of 20.1 per cent. Finally, columns 7 and 8 of table 130 give the amount of tax recovered on deeds of covenant. The percentage rate of recovery varies slightly between 61.6 and 65.2, giving an average figure of 64.3. This average corresponds very closely to the expected rate of 63.9 per cent with a basic rate of income tax of 38.75 per cent, although it is not certain why there should be any variations from this rate in the actual figures.

Table 130 shows that in 1973 the average charge raised £647 by covenants, and recovered a further £416 in income tax from the Inland Revenue, out of a total congregational income of £4,950. Thus £1,063, or 21.5 per cent of congregational income, was raised through covenants by the average charge in 1973.

Finally, it may be significant that recently united and small-town charges, which had the highest average levels of congregational income in 1973, also raised the highest proportion of their ordinary income through covenants, whereas linked charges had both the lowest average income and the lowest proportion of ordinary income raised through covenants in 1973. However, it seems unlikely that the level of income of charges can be explained entirely, or even mainly, by the use of covenants. For example, it may be that the members of richer congregations are more likely to channel their contributions through covenants because they tend also to make larger individual contributions. A further consideration is that linked charges raised only 56.1 per cent of their total income through ordinary collections in 1973, compared to figures ranging between 62.3 and 71.2 per cent for the other four groups of charges.

4 Potential increase in income from the greater use of covenants

In this section we attempt to calculate the extra income from income tax recovered on covenants which would have accrued to congregations in 1973 had they managed to raise a greater proportion of their collections of ordinary income through covenants. These calculations are presented in tables 132 and 133. In both tables we treat each of the five groups of charges separately.

If we take recently united charges again as an example, row 1(a) in table 132 shows the breakdown of the income of the average charge in 1973 as given in table 130. The following two rows calculate the potential extra income from recovered tax of the average charge under two different assumptions. Under assumption I the calculation is made on the basis that the charge increases the proportion of its ordinary income raised through covenants from the actual 1973 figure of 22.5 per cent, to the proportion reached by *the 'best' two charges in its group*, in this case 40.2 per cent (see column 6). Thus, although the total income and the income from ordinary collections of the average charge remains unchanged at the 1973 level, the contributions raised through covenants increases from £1,060 to £1,894 (see column 5). Consequently, the income tax recovered on the covenants rises proportionately from £653 to £1,167, a net increase in income to the charge of £514 (see column 9).

Assumption II in row 1(c) is more stringent. It shows the extra tax recovered on covenants if the average recently united charge had reached that proportion of income from ordinary collections raised through covenants achieved by *the 'best' two charges in any of the sample*, in this case 54.3 per cent (see column 6). Here the sum raised through covenants would have been £2,559 rather than £1,060, and the corresponding sum of tax recovered would have been £1,576 rather than £653, a net increase of income to the charge of £923.

This process is repeated for the other four groups of charges in table 132, and the extra tax recovered under assumptions I and II in each case is shown in column 9. The potential increase in tax recoverable per charge in each group varies considerably, depending upon the level of ordinary income per charge, the percentage of covenants to ordinary income obtaining in 1973, and the change in that percentage implied by the proportion achieved by the 'best' two charges in the group. The percentage used in assumption II is, of course, the same for all groups (i.e. 54.3 per cent), as shown in column 6.

Table 133 completes the calculations. Column 2 gives the figures for the extra income per charge from recovered tax for each group of charges under assumptions I and II. Column 3 lists the numbers of charges in each group in the Church as a whole. By multiplying together the two sets of figures, the extra income for each group of parishes under the two assumptions can be calculated. Row 6 gives the figures for the Church as a whole, indicating that for the average (occupied) charge the potential increase in income from recovered tax on covenants in 1973 was £506 under assumption I, and £710 under assumption II. Table 133 shows therefore that, if in 1973 all charges in the Church had reached that proportion of

TABLE 132.

A calculation of the potential increase in income per charge from income tax recovered on covenants in 1973 (see text).

Charges 1	Total congregational income per charge 2 £	Income from ordinary collections per charge 3 £	$\frac{3}{2} \times 100$ 4 %	Contributions through covenants per charge 5 £	$\frac{5}{3} \times 100$ 6 %	Income tax recovered on covenants per charge 7 £	$\frac{7}{5} \times 100$ 8 %	Increase in tax recovered over 1973 situation 9 £
1 Recently united								
(a) 1973 situation[+]	6,643	4,712	70.9	1,060	22.5	653	61.6	—
(b) assumption I	6,643	4,712	70.9	1,894	40.2	1,167	61.6	514
(c) assumption II	6,643	4,712	70.9	2,559	54.3	1,576	61.6	923
2 Linked								
(a) 1973 situation[+]	1,791	1,005	56.1	140	14.0	91	65.0	—
(b) assumption I[*]	1,791	1,005	56.1	460	45.8	299	65.0	208
(c) assumption II[*]	1,791	1,005	56.1	546	54.3	355	65.0	264
3 Rural								
(a) 1973 situation[+]	4,264	2,658	62.3	566	21.3	369	65.2	—
(b) assumption I	4,264	2,658	62.3	1,398	52.6	912	65.2	543
(c) assumption II	4,264	2,658	62.3	1,443	54.3	941	65.2	572
4 Small-town								
(a) 1973 situation[+]	6,540	4,231	64.7	942	22.3	613	65.1	—
(b) assumption I	6,540	4,231	64.7	2,078	49.1	1,353	65.1	740
(c) assumption II	6,540	4,231	64.7	2,298	54.3	1,496	65.1	883
5 Urban								
(a) 1973 situation[+]	5,143	3,659	71.2	667	18.2	420	63.0	—
(b) assumption I	5,143	3,659	71.2	1,160	31.7	731	63.0	311
(c) assumption II	5,143	3,659	71.2	1,987	54.3	1,252	63.0	832

SOURCE: Table, 130.

[+] Figures refer to congregations rather than charges.

income raised by covenants to income raised by ordinary collections achieved by the 'best' two charges in their respective groups, the extra income raised from tax recovered on covenants would have been about £832,000. Alternatively, if all charges had reached that proportion of income from covenants to income from all ordinary collections achieved by the 'best' two charges in the sample, the extra income raised from recovered tax would have been around £1,168,000.

Table 134 indicates that these two figures of extra income correspond to 6.4 per cent and 9.0 per cent of the Church's total income in 1973, and are thus very substantial sums. A big effort by the Church to increase the proportion of ordinary collections raised through covenants would therefore be very worthwhile.

TABLE 133.
A calculation of the potential increase in income of the Church from income tax recovered on covenants in 1973 (see text).

	Charges	Increase in tax recovered per charge +	Number of charges in group in Church	Increase in income from recovered tax in 1973 i.e. 2 × 3
	1	2	3	4
		£		£
1	Recently united			
	assumption I	514	76	39,064
	assumption II	923	76	70,148
2	Linked			
	assumption I	208*	205 (460*)	95,680
	assumption II	264*	205 (460*)	121,440
3	Rural			
	assumption I	543	667	362,181
	assumption II	572	667	381,524
4	Small town			
	assumption I	740	276	204,240
	assumption II	883	276	243,708
5	Urban			
	assumption I	311	423	131,553
	assumption II	832	423	351,936
6	TOTAL			
	assumption I	506	1,647	832,718
	assumption II	710	1,647	1,168,756

+ SOURCE: Table 132, column 9.
* Refers to congregations rather than charges.

TABLE 134.
The potential increase in the income of the Church from income tax recovered on covenants compared to total income in 1973.

	£	%
Assumption I	832,718	6.4
Assumption II	1,168,756	9.0
Total Income of Church	12,918,350	100.0

Perhaps at this point a number of qualifying remarks should be made.

It is possible that many charges which raise little or no income through covenants may have a membership comprising mainly people on low incomes who pay little or no income tax, such as retired and young people. The potential increases in recovered tax from re-channelling a larger proportion of ordinary income through covenants may not be within the reach of such charges. To the extent that this is true, the figures calculated above may be overestimates.

To be set against this, however, is the consideration that the total congregational income for all 1,647 occupied charges calculated from our sample of charges was a little below the published figure for 1973, even allowing for the 121 vacant charges excluded from the analysis. This suggests that our calculations of the potential extra income which could be generated from tax recovered on covenants may also be underestimates.

Of much greater significance, however, is the effect of the exclusion of the 121 vacant charges from the analysis. If these charges on average have the same characteristics as the average of the 1,647 occupied charges, then the potential increase in income that they could have obtained by channelling a greater proportion of their ordinary income through covenants in 1973 would be £506 and £710 under assumptions I and II respectively. If these two figures are multiplied by the 121 charges in the group, the extra income which they as a group might have raised in 1973 was £61,226 and £85,910 respectively; these sums are in addition to those given in table 134. Even though vacant charges may tend to be poorer than the average occupied charge, the fact that they have been excluded from the calculations in table 132 would strongly suggest that the figures given there are underestimates.

5 Methods to encourage a greater use of covenants

The purpose of this section is to suggest measures which might encourage the greater use of covenants as a means of raising funds by congregations.

In the analysis described above it was found that the proportion of ordinary income raised through covenants (excluding recovered tax) by individual congregations varied considerably. In some cases, congregations appeared to make little or no use of covenants, whereas in one or two congregations the proportion of covenants to ordinary income exceeded 50 per cent. The fact that individual charges vary so much in the use made of covenants suggests that at least part of the problem of encouraging a more widespread use of covenants lies in convincing some congregations of their importance in fund-raising. We urge the Stewardship and Budget Committee to redouble its efforts in publicizing the use of covenants in the congregations.

Given that the Kirk Sessions are fully aware of the importance of covenants as a means of raising funds, the second problem lies in encouraging individual members to use them. It is said that members who do not contribute through an envelope system are most unlikely to enter into a covenant, where the commitment to contribute is for a longer period. Evidence from a representative sample of 39 congregations suggests, however, that in 1973 more than two-thirds of members contributed through the Weekly Freewill Offering system, or some other envelope scheme. The next step would be to encourage the members in the envelope systems to covenant their offerings.

6 Conclusions

The purpose of this chapter has been to examine the role of Deeds of Covenant in the fund-raising efforts of the Church of Scotland, and to show how the Church would benefit financially if that role were to be increased.

In section 2 the function of covenants in the Church was described. We found that at the end of 1973 the Church held over 59,000 covenants, of which about one-quarter were in favour of the central authorities of the Church and the rest were in favour of the congregations. In the former group, the average contribution (including tax) was £37.87.

In sections 3 and 4 we set out to calculate the potential increase in income to the congregations from the income tax reclaimed on covenants if they had managed to channel a greater proportion of their ordinary collections through covenants in 1973. The financial information required for the analysis was collected from the accounts of 105 randomly sampled charges, each representing one of five broad classes of charges in the Church: recently united, linked, rural, small-town, and urban. It was found that the average income per charge in each group varied from £4,019 for the linked charges to around £6,600 for the recently united and small-town charges. The proportion of total income raised through ordinary collections varied quite widely between 56.1 per cent and 71.2 per cent, and the proportion of ordinary income raised by covenants varied between 14.0 per cent and 22.5 per cent. However, the average income of all charges was £4,950 in 1973, of which £647 was raised through covenants and £416 was collected in refunded tax. The total covenant income of the average charge was thus £1,063, or 21.5 per cent of income.

In section 4 we went on to calculate for each group of charges how much additional income from tax recovered on covenants could be expected if a greater proportion of ordinary income was raised through covenants. The calculations were based on two different assumptions. Under assumption I we calculated that, if all the charges in each group had reached the proportion of covenants to ordinary income achieved by the 'best' two charges in their group, then the additional income which would have accrued to the Church in 1973 was £832,000. Alternatively, under assumption II, if all charges had reached the proportion of covenants to ordinary income achieved by the 'best' two charges in the sample as a whole, the extra income which would have accrued to the Church in the form of reclaimed tax in 1973 was £1,168,000. Although these two figures are estimates for all the occupied charges in the Church based on a sample of 105, we decided that on balance they probably slightly understate the extra income which could be obtained on the basis of the two assumptions. This was largely because the 121 vacant charges were excluded from the study.

Finally, in section 5 various measures to encourage the greater use of covenants by members were examined. It was suggested that many congregations could do more to encourage the use of covenants amongst their members.

Notes

1 Church of Scotland, 'Report of the General Finance Committee', *Reports to the General Assembly, 1973*, p. 100.

2 The subsidiary accounts of congregations are examined in chapter 12, section 4, on congregational finance.

Chapter 19

Investment and property

1 Introduction
We have seen that over the course of its long history the Church of Scotland has accumulated a great number and variety of investments, endowments and properties. The purpose of this chapter is to examine these investments and properties with a view to recommending an overall investment strategy for the Church. The purpose of such a strategy is to increase as far as possible the income the Church derives from its investments.

In section 2 a brief résumé is given of the break-down of the Church's income in order to distinguish the income deriving from investments. We find that the two major sources of investment income are the standardized stipend and related endowments for stipend, and the income derived from investments in the Church of Scotland Trust; these two items are examined in sections 3 and 4 respectively. Then in section 5 we turn to the question of Church property, which includes the Church buildings, halls, manses, and the like. Finally, in section 6 we put forward an overall investment strategy for the Church.

2 The income of the Church
A breakdown of the income of the Church for the years 1946, 1960 and 1975 is presented in table 135, and the corresponding figures, expressed in 'real' terms at 1975 prices, are shown in table 136.

As we saw in chapter 5, Church income derives from two main sources. The first is congregational income, or liberality, which is the income raised by the congregations, mainly from the contributions of individual members on the plate, by envelope, and by covenant. It forms about 70 per cent of the income of the Church. The second is 'other income', which is that income accruing to the central authorities and collected by the General Treasurer. It comprises the following four major items: donations, grants, income from trusts, and miscellaneous; bequests; income from investments; and the standardized stipend, etc..

Amongst these items of Church income, investment income derives from the following main sources:
(i) Income from investments, which derives from the funds held by the Church of Scotland Trust. In 1975 this item amounted to £1,446,003, or 8.2 per cent of total income. The market value of the funds held amounted to just over £20 millions in 1975. The bulk of the funds are held by the central departments, but substantial sums are also held by, and on behalf of (through the General Trustees), the congregations.

TABLE 135.
A summary of the changes in the income of the Church between 1946, 1960 and 1975 (in money terms)

		1946 £	%	1960 £	%	Percentage change between 1946 and 1960	1976 £	%	Percentage change between 1946 and 1975
1	Congregational income	2,373,878	65.6	4,818,050	76.0	+103.0	12,976,298	73.5	+446.6
2	Other income								
	(a) donations, grants, income from trusts, and miscellaneous	417,209	11.5	401,713	6.3	− 3.7	1,852,470	10.5	+344.0
	(b) bequests	200,400	5.5	267,992	4.2	+ 33.7	853,840	4.8	+326.1
	(c) income from investments	204,718	5.7	433,872	6.8	+111.9	1,446,003	8.2	+606.3
	(d) standardized stipend, etc. collected by and received from the General Trustees	424,013	11.7	421,313	6.7	− 0.6	515,813	2.9	+ 21.7
	(e) SUB-TOTAL	1,246,340	34.4	1,524,890	24.0	+ 22.3	4,668,126	26.5	+274.5
3	TOTAL INCOME OF CHURCH (i.e. 1 + 2)	3,620,218	100.0	6,342,940	100.0	+ 75.2	17,644,424	100.0	+387.4

SOURCE: 'Report of the General Finance Committee', *Reports to the General Assembly*, 1947, 1961, 1976.

(ii) The standardized stipend and other endowments for stipend, which is essentially an investment income composed of the income derived from various endowments for stipend, by far the largest of which is the standardized stipend. Other endowments include the glebe rents and monies, and the income from the invested funds derived from previous *ad hoc* redemptions of the standardized stipend. In 1975 this category of income amounted to £515,813, or 2.9 per cent of the Church total.

(iii) Other categories of investment income include the income of unknown size derived from the investment of congregational income outside the usual central investment channels in bank deposit accounts, stocks and shares, and the like; income from this source is included in congregational income or liberality. There is also a substantial income from trusts, included in the first item of 'other income'. The bulk of this income is derived from the F.G. Salvesen Trust, which has an annual income of approximately £350,000. As far as is known, no other trust has an income in excess of £10,000. Central departments also benefit from the 'overnight' investment of their liquid funds by the General Treasurer.

An examination of Table 136 shows that the Income from Investments (item 2(c)) has had by far the fastest rate of growth of any category of income over the period since the war, increasing in real terms by 58.4 per cent. This compares with a 22.6 per cent increase in real congregational income, which has enjoyed the next fastest rate of growth over the period. On the other hand, the income from the standardized stipend, etc. (item 2(d)) has fallen by 72.7 per cent in real terms since 1946. This 'real' decline is explained by the effect of inflation over the post-war period on a constant money income. Taking these two elements together as the main investment income of the Church, they formed 17.4 per cent of total Church income in 1946 and 11.1 per cent in 1975. In real terms this investment income has declined over the period 1946-75 by 30.0 per cent, from £2,804,140 to £1,961,816.

3 The standardized stipend and other endowments for stipend

The standardized stipend has already been dealt with in some detail in chapters 10 and 11. There it was suggested that these endowments for stipend should be pooled centrally for the benefit of aid-receiving congregations, rather than the present procedure under the 1925 Act of being subject to reallocation to the parish or its neighbourhood when a vacancy occurs. Such a policy might have important indirect economic benefits to the congregations concerned and to the Church as a whole, and would lead to savings on the central administration of these stipends.

A more pertinent question here is the investment of the monies released by the redemption of feus under the Land Tenure Reform (Scotland) Act, 1974. The standardization of the former teinds under the Church of Scotland (Property and Endowments) Act, 1925, proved to be financially very unfavourable to the Church. Whereas prior to standardization the annual income from each teind fluctuated with the price of grain, on standardization these variable sums were transformed into fixed annual figures. With the general rise in the price level over the years since 1925 the real value of these fixed money sums have suffered a

TABLE 136.

A summary of the changes in the income of the Church between 1946, 1960 and 1975 (in real terms at 1975 prices)

	1946* £	%	1960 £	%	Percentage change between 1946 and 1970	1975 £	%	Percentage change between 1960 and 1975
1 Congregational income	10,587,495	65.6	12,944,881	76.0	+22.3	12,976,298	73.5	+22.6
2 Other income								
(a) donations, grants, income from trusts, and miscellaneous	1,860,752	11.5	1,079,301	6.3	−42.0	1,852,470	10.5	−0.4
(b) bequests	893,784	5.5	720,027	4.2	−19.4	853,840	4.8	−4.5
(c) income from investments	913,042	5.7	1,165,704	6.8	+27.7	1,446,003	8.2	+58.4
(d) standardized stipend, etc. collected by and received from the General Trustees	1,891,098	11.7	1,131,961	6.7	−40.1	515,813	2.9	−72.7
(e) SUB-TOTAL	5,558,676	34.4	4,096,993	24.0	−36.3	4,668,126	26.5	−16.0
3 TOTAL INCOME OF CHURCH (*i.e.* 1 + 2)	16,146,172	100.0	17,041,874	100.0	+5.5	17,644,424	100.0	+9.3

SOURCE: figures modified from those in table 135.
* 1946 figure inflated using the Retail Price Index for 1947 (=100)

large decline. Now, with the redemption of the standardized stipend, the Church has the opportunity to thwart any further loss by investing the redemption funds in suitable investments.

Most of the funds have been invested in long-term government stock and local authority bonds. This policy has probably been guided partly by the desire to maximize the income yield for stipend, rather than the capital growth which could not easily be realized, and partly by the need for a constant and predictable annual income figure from each endowment to help simplify the complexities of the administration of stipend. However, the very high rates of inflation over the past few years, which have been greater than the rate of interest of government stock, will have caused the real value of such investments to fall. The Church has thus suffered a substantial and irretrievable capital loss on such investments which might have been avoided had the money been invested elsewhere.

4 Income from investments

By 'income from investments' in the General Treasurer's summarized income statement of the Church is meant that income derived from investments in the Church of Scotland Trust. The Trust, constituted by Act of Parliament in 1932, is empowered to hold heritable properties and investments on behalf of any court, committee or congregation of the Church of Scotland. Under an Amendment Order of 1948 the Trust was given the power to invest in ordinary stocks and shares as distinct from fixed interest-bearing securities. The investment policy of the Trust is determined by the General Assembly through Acts, bye-laws and regulations, but the execution of this policy is the responsibility of the trustees of the Trust. The Trust employs professional investment advisors.

The Trust operates three funds:

(i) *The General Investment Fund* for permanent or long-term investment by committees and congregations. The emphasis in this fund is on long-term capital growth. It is managed on a unit trust basis, and is administered by a committee of thirty-eight members, many of whom are laymen with a particular knowledge of finance and investment. A comparative statement of the investments and income of the Fund for selected years at 31 December over the period 1948-74 is as follows:

	Number of units	Market value £	Value of unit £	Gross income £	Distribution £	Gross income on market value %
1948	–	3,417,018	–	119,389	115,140	3.5
1953	–	3,606,094	–	154,283	147,221	4.3
1958	–	4,283,668	–	214,868	202,186	5.0
1963	967,492	6,048,266	6.25	315,938	315,844	5.2
1968	1,624,817	10,729,776	6.59	570,512	572,764	5.3
1971	–	13,087,400	6.84	697,547	685,059	5.3
1972	–	13,928,244	7.00	740,855	729,976	5.3
1973	2,110,267	10,651,401	5.13	839,319	784,968	7.9
1974	2,193,639	7,439,663	3.49	941,996	896,457	12.7
1975	2,346,418	11,605,487	5.00	901,436	902,344	7.8
1976	2,379,580	11,495,189	4.88	983,980	950,085	8.6

A summary of the investments held in the General Investment Fund as at 31 December 1976 is as follows:

	1976 £	1975 £
Investments at valuation:		
heritable loans	14,652	18,930
feu duties and ground annuals	62,437	67,082
government stocks	2,706,000	2,567,500
corporation and public boards	41,686	41,173
investment trusts	1,569,766	1,709,046
commercial and industrial	6,660,648	6,616,571
short-term dollar deposits	—	5,185
short-term deposits	440,000	580,000
TOTAL	11,495,189	11,605,487

The unit fund is thus composed of a common pool of equity and fixed income investments.

(ii) *Special Investment Account*, the second fund operated by the Church of Scotland Trust, in which the Trust holds specific investments on behalf of committees and congregations. The Special Investment Account is not a unit trust, but a fund in which the investing body specifies the investments to be made; the income is remitted to the investors. A summary of the investments held by the account as at 31 December 1976 is as follows:

	1976 £	1975 £
Investments at valuation:		
heritable loans	4,777	4,777
feu duties and ground annuals	46,403	53,046
government stocks	2,319,375	834,813
corporation and public boards	987,565	407,231
investment trusts	88,853	114,858
commercial and industrial	357,862	482,364
short-term deposits	2,100,000	1,220,000
TOTAL	5,904,835	3,117,089

The interest and dividends received by the Account in 1976 and paid to investors was £392,003 on a capital invested (at market value) of £5,904,835, giving a return of 6.6 per cent.

(iii) *The Deposit Fund,* for short-term investments by committees and congregations. Deposits are made in multiples of £5, with the minimum deposit £100 and the maximum deposit £50,000. No deposits are normally accepted for a period of less than three months, and one week's notice of withdrawal is required. The emphasis in this fund is on high income yield; there is no capital growth. The fund was established in 1967, and by 31 December 1976 its capital stood at £5,950,000. A statement of this capital is as follows:

Held for committees, congregations and General Trustees as at 31st December 1976		£5,920,600
Represented by:		
loans to local authorities	£4,850,000	
loans to finance houses	1,100,000	5,950,000
Over-invested at 31 December 1976		£ 29,400

— analysed thus:

Time to maturity	Average rate (%)	Amount
7 days	14.75	£ 475,000
1 month	11.07	575,000
2 months	14.64	750,000
3 months	9.82	550,000
4 months	10.50	200,000
5 months	10.75	250,000
6 months	11.86	1,050,000
7 months	11.88	200,000
8 months	11.95	400,000
11 months	14.87	500,000
12 months	15.02	1,000,000
	12.88	£5,950,000

Investments earn interest in line with current rates, which is payable gross half-yearly. In 1976 interest received amounted to £669,604, giving a return on capital invested of 11.3 per cent. This fund has proved popular with congregations, whose investments make up the bulk of the total.

A summary of the capital and returns of the Church of Scotland Trust for 1976 is as follows:

	Market value £	Interest and dividends £	Return %
General Investment Fund	11,495,189	983,980	8.6
Special Investment Account	5,904,835	392,003	6.6
Deposit Fund	5,950,000	669,604	11.3
TOTAL	23,350,024	2,045,587	8.7

The income earned by the three separate funds in the trust in 1976 amounted to £2,045,587 on a market value of investments of £23,350,024, giving an overall return on the capital invested of 8.8 per cent.

As the Church is a charity, the interest paid by the trust on investments and deposits is not subjected to the deduction of income tax, and capital gains are not subjected to Capital Gains Tax. Apart from being very favourable to the Church, this provision also influences the areas in which the Church invests its funds. For example, investments in building societies are avoided, as income tax is paid by the societies and cannot be recovered. Also, in the case of certain companies and unit trusts which have interests abroad, only a portion of the income tax deducted from dividends can be recovered.

There is no obligation on departments or committees to use the Church of Scotland Trust for the investment of their funds, but in practice they nearly always do. In some cases the departments or committees do not want to purchase units in the General Investment Fund, but instead indicate to the trustees the equity or fixed stock to be purchased on their behalf through the Special Investment Account.

The investment of funds in no way alters the degree of freedom in the use of the resulting income, or of the capital if later realized; thus, if money with a restricted condition of use is given to a committee, its use is restricted whether it is invested or not, and vice versa.

5 The property of the Church

The property of the Church comprises church buildings, halls, manses, the sites of these buildings, the glebes, and various other buildings like glebe and manse cottages and manse outbuildings. The total value of this property is not known, but rough estimates can be made based on the following considerations. About two-thirds of Church property is vested in the General Trustees. All properties vested in the General Trustees have to be insured with the Church of Scotland Fire Insurance Trust. In 1975 the fire insurances effected by the Trustees over ecclesiastical buildings in their name totalled more than £118 millions. This figure can be used to calculate a rough replacement cost for all Church property, although the figure itself has a number of limitations:

(a) The figure includes certain insurances covering organs, church furnishings and other movable property belonging to Kirk Sessions, protection against damage by storm or flooding, boiler insurance, breakage of glass, burglary, etc..

(b) Recent high rates of inflation, which have included building costs, have probably left many buildings under-insured.

(c) In addition, there is the land on which the buildings stand, together with the glebes. The latter are all vested in the General Trustees, who are responsible for their administration.

An estimate of the total value of Church property might be made up as follows:

	(£ m)
Buildings vested in trustees (3/5)	130.0
Buildings not vested in trustees (2/5)	45.0
Glebes (rents and monies)	1.2
TOTAL	176.2

The replacement cost of the buildings might amount to around £175 millions. The value of the glebes in their present use, assuming a return of 6 per cent., might be valued at about £1.2 millions. These calculations give Church property a total value of just over £175 millions.

So far we have been dealing with the value of buildings in terms of their replacement cost. An alternative measure, which may give a more relevant valuation of buildings from the viewpoint of policy, is 'opportunity cost'; this is the highest price that another party would be prepared to pay for the property in an alternative use. In many cases the opportunity cost of a building is likely to differ from the replacement cost depending upon the type of building, its location, and how easily it could be adapted to other uses. While the majority of manses, and possibly some church halls, may have an opportunity cost in the region of the replacement cost, most churches and halls will have an opportunity cost well below the replacement cost, unless the site is particularly valuable. This is because such buildings are not easily adapted to alternative uses, particularly those situated in the sparsely populated regions. On the other hand, the value of some sites of church buildings in town and city centres may be very high if planning permission can be obtained for their redevelopment. However, planning permission may not be granted in cases where buildings are listed as of architectural or historic importance, or are situated on land which has been zoned for church use. The operation of this factor may artificially limit the opportunity cost of such property.

Rough comparisons can be made between the opportunity cost and replacement cost of different types of church property using information on the prices at which existing property is being sold, and new property purchased. Broadly speaking, buildings normally fall to be sold because they have been made redundant, either through the union and readjustment of parishes or as the result of the acquisition of an alternative building. The sale of a building requires the approval of the body in which the building is vested. The bulk of the property of the Church – about three-fifths – is vested in the Church of Scotland General Trustees, and the sales of this property are recorded in the minutes of the meetings of the trustees and sub-committees. Of the remaining two-fifths of Church property not vested in the trustees, the bulk – as much as 80 per cent, or over 30 per cent of the total property – comprises those properties whose sale is subject to the consent of the General Assembly or Commission of Assembly. The Custodier of Titles is the official who submits proposals for the sale of property in this category to the Assembly for approval, and a record of these sales is given each year in his report to the Assembly. The second category of property not vested in the General Trustees – forming about 20 per cent of the group, or less than 10 per cent of the total – comprises those properties which are vested in local bodies. Since no central body is involved in the sale of such property, no central record is kept of sales.

The main source of information on sales of property is thus the minutes of the meetings of the General Trustees. The volumes run to General Assembly years, that is from 1 June to 31 May; those for the five years 1972/3 to 1976/7 were examined, the last of these years being compiled only to 12th January 1977 at the time of the study. The information on property has been divided into two groups – manses, and all other property (excluding the glebes).

A summary of the information relating to manses is shown in table 137. Over the four-and-a-half year period 114 manses were sold, 10 were rented out, 25 were purchased, and 20 were built. The number of manses disposed of (114) greatly exceeds the number newly acquired (45), thus indicating a steady decline in the

TABLE 137.

Sales and purchases of manses, as reported in the minutes of the General Trustees, 1972/3-1976/7

	1972/3	1973/4	1974/5	1975/6	1976/7	TOTAL
Numbers of manses						
sold	21	21	20	28	24	114
rented out	1	2	4	3	0	10
purchased	4	3+	7	6	5	25
built	1	5	6	4	4	20
net change	−16	−13	−7	−18	−15	−69
Sales of manses						
total annual proceeds (£)x	£314,277	£375,308	£311,358	£532,234	£414,162	£1,947,339
average sale price (£)	£ 14,966	£ 17,872	£ 15,568	£ 19,008	£ 17,257	£ 17,082
range of prices (£)	£ 6,000 –	£ 3,500 –	£ 3,000 –	£ 7,250 –	£ 800 –	£ 800 –
	£ 36,025	£ 35,750	£ 30,033	£ 37,300	£ 31,000	£ 37,300
distribution (£000s)						
0 — 10	7	3	7	4	4	25
over 10 — 20	10	9	6	15	13	53
over 20 — 30	3	7	5	5	5	25
over 30	1	2	2	4	2	11
average price of city manses (number for which information available in parentheses) (£)	£ – (0)	£ 11,036(3)	£ 18,192(5)	£ 19,733(6)	£ 20,350(3)	£ 17,854(17)
New manses						
number for which information available	4	5	8	6	4	28
total cost (£)	47,600	100,175	174,500	128,200	87,056	537,531
average cost (£)	11,900	16,696	21,813	21,367	21,764	19,198
average cost of city manses (number for which information available in parentheses) (£)	£ – (0)	£ 17,500(1)	£ 22,500(2)	£ 19,000(1)	£ 21,352(3)	£ 20,794(17)

SOURCE: Minutes of the General Trustees, 1972/3 – 1976/7, from the files of the secretary's office.
+ One house also being rented.
x In a few cases glebes were included in the sale price of a manse.

number of manses held by the Trustees at the rate of about 10 per year. The range of sale prices has varied considerably over the period from under £1,000 to over £37,000; just under half the manses (53 out of 114) were sold for prices in the £10-20,000 bracket; just under a quarter (25) were sold for £10,000 or less, while another 25 were sold for prices in the £20-30,000 bracket; 11 were sold for more than £30,000. The average annual sale price of manses has varied substantially over each of the five years, and not obviously on an upward trend, which is perhaps surprising in view of the rapid rise in house prices over the period. The lowest average price was £14,966 in 1972/3, the highest – £19,008 – in 1975/6. The total proceeds of sales of manses by the General Trustees over the last four-and-a-half years amount to nearly £2 millions.

In order to test the hypothesis that city manses tend to be more valuable than manses situated outside of the cities, the sale prices of manses sold in the four city Presbyteries were compared to the average. Unfortunately, only 17 city manses were sold in four of the five years, the highest number in any one year being 6. In three of those years the average price of city manses was somewhat greater than the overall average, being £2,624, £2,725, and £3,093 respectively, but these differences were not as large as was expected. The 'city' classification used was rather arbitrary, however.

Finally, the cost of purchasing or building new manses was compared to the sale price of existing manses. Information on costs was available in the case of 28 manses over the five years, the highest number for any year being 8. It was found that in the first two years of the period the average cost of a new manse fell below the average sale price of existing manses (£3,066 and £1,176 respectively), while in the last three years the position was reversed, with the cost of new manses being higher (the differential being £6,245, £2,359 and £4,507 respectively). The figures suggest that there may have been a change of policy towards the purchase or building of more expensive new manses in 1974/5.

Table 138 presents information on the buildings other than manses vested in the General Trustees and sold or purchased by them over the 4½-year period. Purchases of buildings include only complete buildings, as far as it is possible to determine; building extensions, as well as renovations, maintenance and repairs of various kinds, have been excluded. A difficulty with new buildings is that the minutes do not always mention the cost, which is usually an estimate, or, in the case of new constructions, the date of completion. We have arbitrarily chosen to list new buildings in the year in which the decision to start building was made.

In the first part of table 138 the 'number of properties' refers to the number of separate property transactions. Over the period in question 39 properties were purchased or built, an average of about 9 a year; at the same time, 144 properties were sold, rented out, or otherwise disposed of, giving an average of about 30 a year. This is further evidence that the Church is shedding property at a considerable rate, largely as a result of the policy of union and readjustment of parishes. Redundant churches are used mainly for community purposes, storage, and by other denominations. Country churches are occasionally purchased for conversion into private houses. The biggest single category of buyer of redundant churches consists of local councils who normally use them for community purposes.

In the second part of table 138 the sale prices of existing buildings and the cost

TABLE 138.
Sales and purchases of Church properties other than manses, as reported in the minutes of the General Trustees, 1972/3-1976/7

	1972/3	1973/4	1974/5	1975/6	1976/7	TOTAL
No. of properties:						
sold	10	24	15	24	16	89
purchased	6	9	14	8	27	39
demolished	3	1	–	–	–	4
rented out	–	2	3	4	–	9
gifted away	–	–	1	1	–	2
other	–	1	–	–	–	1
net change	−7	−17	−2	−17	−14	−57
Building prices and costs:						
Churches: sold	3,600	1,000	400	2,900	12,500	
	14,500	4,100	22,000	4,500	1,500	
	1,300	**125,000**×	21,000	100	**23,000**	
		600	500	1,050	400	
		32,000	10,000	500	200	
		45,000		**6,500**	6,033	
		8,000		6,750	9,000	
		255,000		650	4,500	
		4,000		**15,000**		
				9,500		
				10,200		
				12,500		
				13,000		
purchased	54,000	–	–	–	–	
Halls: sold	**5,000**	575	7,000	4,820	–	
			3,000ø	2,250		
			4,500	3,000		
			4,000	5,585		
				5,100		
purchased	7,690	**39,000**	11,232	18,870	–	
	7,108	**55,000**+	91,532	12,374		
		900	**6,000**			
		16,300	7,000			
Church and hall: sold	32,500	2,000	22,500	37,000	3,500	
		10,250‡	18,000	5,000	**25,000**	
		30,300	12,000‡	**4,000**	24,000	
		25,000	4,000			
purchased	–	–	–	200,000†	–	
				125,000†		
Manse out-buildings:						
sold	3,150	4,005	–	–	–	
	7,006	4,206‖				
		1,230				
		1,500				
		5,800				
Manse/glebe	1,755	2,600	3,765	2,500	**5,250**	
cottage, etc.: sold	2,911	2,000	1,000	7,000	2,000	

SOURCE: Minutes of the General Trustees, 1972/3 – 1976/7 from the files of the secretary's office.
Key: × three churches   ø price includes cottages
      + halls complex   † church complex
      ‡ price includes a manse   ‖ price includes a glebe
The prices in bold lettering are those of properties situated in one of the four city Presbyteries.

of new buildings have been listed for various broad categories of buildings and for each of the five years. The buildings categories are very general, and some of the entries may have been classified wrongly because of a lack of information. Footnotes provide further information in particular cases. Buildings have been excluded where information for classification purposes is completely inadequate. The prices of buildings sited in the four city presbyteries are in bold lettering. An examination of the figures reveals a number of interesting points. Firstly, most of the properties purchased have been halls, while most of the properties sold have been churches. Secondly, the range of prices is considerable, but most of the higher prices seem to occur on properties found in the four 'city' Presbyteries. Thirdly, it is not easy to compare the cost of new buildings with prices derived from the sale of existing ones, since, apart from halls, there have been relatively few property purchases. However, the limited evidence confirms our original hypothesis that the cost of new buildings tends to be much higher than the sale price of existing buildings. This reflects the difference between replacement cost and opportunity cost of buildings. The three cases of churches being sold for sums in excess of £40,000 almost certainly reflect the value of the sites for development purposes; for example, the sum of £255,000 was paid by a national supermarket chain for a church site in central Glasgow.

We now turn to discussion of three policy issues concerned with church buildings.

1 Fabric funds

One of the financial problems of the Church is that it is burdened with a large stock of old buildings which are very expensive to maintain and run, especially for the small congregation or for the congregation with a very old building. To finance such repair and maintenance work it has been recommended by the General Assembly that the maintenance of an adequate local fabric fund should be a first charge on the income of the congregation. A large number of fabric funds have also been formed from the proceeds of sales of buildings. Many such fabric funds of individual congregations are held centrally by three different departments – the General Trustees, General Treasurer, and the Maintenance of the Ministry Committee. Frequently, a number of funds are held for the benefit of one congregation. It has been suggested that if all such funds held centrally could be transferred to the General Trustees (the largest holding body), arrangements could then be made to amalgamate the funds held for particular congregations. This would simplify the central administration of such funds, and would avoid the present confusion in the congregations with the different bodies administering the funds in different ways. Moves are being made in this direction, but there are difficulties in the way of amalgamating monies in that each fund would normally be held subject to an Act or Deliverance of Assembly and/ or the terms of a Basis of Union or Linking.

The trustees are known to be very unhappy with the overall standard of maintenance of Church property. Although some people in the Church believe that too much money is spent on buildings at the expense of other areas, it can be argued that inadequate maintenance expenditure on a building over the years eventually leads to a large-scale repair job. The congregation is often able to make a special effort to raise the large sum required, whereas it has previously found difficulty in finding money for routine maintenance. Readjustment of congregations is sometimes hastened where large expenditures are required to stave off the decline of buildings. A further difficulty is that the trustees have no funds to undertake maintenance work, yet they are said to incur adverse comment because they insist on knowing what is being done to their buildings although they are unable to assist financially.

Consequently, it has been suggested at various times since the early 1930s that the trustees should take a more active part in ensuring adequate maintenance, and that they could do this if they were in a position to make loans or grants to assist congregations. Various sources of funds have been suggested to form the basis of a Central Fabric Fund, including the funds of the Property Committee, some of the monies from the fabric funds of certain over-endowed congregations, and the possibility of initial and annual funds from the Baird and Pilgrim Trusts; such a fund might also attract bequests. The aim is to channel monies already available for fabric to where they can be best used. No target figure for the fund has been set or even discussed, although a capital sum of £2 millions was once mentioned. The chief danger of such a fund, it is argued, is that it may undermine local congregational involvement and responsibility in property maintenance matters. This problem might be alleviated by limiting the size of central grants for property repairs to a certain maximum proportion of the total cost, which would leave the congregation to raise the remaining proportion. Although it might not be popular, some sort of means test would probably have to be employed in order to avoid giving grants to congregations who could afford to finance the work themselves.

2 Sharing of buildings

Apart from measures to economize on the cost of maintaining and running individual buildings, the chief way of reducing the total burden of such costs would be to reduce the number of buildings. This is happening already in one direction through the policy of uniting congregations, which makes one set of church buildings redundant. The process could be carried further in another direction through a policy of sharing church buildings between congregations. Two possibilities arise. In urban areas the sharing of one church building by two or more congregations in the Church of Scotland might be possible, the church services being staggered; this might be arranged in the case of two adjacent congregations which are too large to be united effectively. Secondly, in rural areas the congregations of two different denominations might arrange to share the use of the same building. The fabric costs, which are often a burden for small congregations, would also be shared. There may be physical, as well as political, difficulties for such arrangements. We recommend, however, that Presbyteries should be encouraged to explore these possibilities in their own localities.

3 New church buildings

New buildings can be looked upon as the capital investment of the Church, although this investment differs from normal commercial investment in at least two important respects. Firstly, Church investment is not intended to be financially productive in the commercial sense, as the following quotation makes clear:

> A sub-division between capital and revenue in Church finances does not have the same significance as in a commercial company. In the latter case, capital sums are normally raised for productive purposes with the intention of writing off the cost

over a period of years out of profits, the inference being that the capital investment will itself provide sufficient profits for this purpose. In general, the Church is not concerned with capital investment of a productive nature in the commercial sense. Its capital expenditure relates primarily to the provision of churches, largely paid for out of the allocation to the National Church Extension Committee from the Co-ordinated Appeal or by borrowings in anticipation of future allocations, and Eventide and other Homes under the control of the Social and Moral Welfare Board, largely paid for out of legacies.

These items of expenditure do not therefore appear in the accounts as capital expenditure in the same way that the acquisition of industrial buildings would appear in the balance sheet of a commercial company. A more realistic sub-division would be between ordinary and extraordinary expenditure although the distinction could not be a clear-cut one.[1]

The point is, however, that the investment in a new church building *could* in principle be subjected to the commercial test, in that the income raised by the congregation accommodated in the building could be seen as the financial return on the original investment; a part of this income could be used to amortize the building. But since the cost of a new building is so high, it is very unlikely that there are any examples in recent years of church extension congregations being able to do more than make the required token repayment of a small part of the cost.

Secondly, investment by the Church in new buildings differs from normal commercial investment in that the completed buildings (churches and halls) usually have an opportunity cost which is less than the replacement cost. Thus, as soon as a new church building is completed, and before it is used, the building is already worth a good deal less than it cost to build. A new church, for example, might cost £50,000 to build, but in alternative use as a warehouse the building might be worth only £5,000. In the strict commercial sense, therefore, the value of investment by the Church in new buildings is open to doubt. In view of the straitened financial circumstances of the Church, we recommend that the following considerations should form the basis of policy:

(i) The erection of new buildings should be kept to a minimum, with the possible exception of new manses.
(ii) Where new buildings have to be built, every effort should be made to design for flexible use, so that a good price can be obtained if and when the building is eventually sold. The most obvious use for redundant churches is as warehouses, so that suitability for this form of use should be designed into the building. This might usefully involve the initial strengthening of floors, the installation (or provision for installation) of lifts, and the provision of access for loading arrangements. While these provisions might cost something initially, they would almost certainly be cheaper to install at once than later. New manses should not be built in remote areas where the sale price is likely to be low.

6 An investment strategy

There appears to be no overall investment strategy in the Church, but rather separate policies in the different spheres of investment and property. From the analysis so far it seems that the main policies are as follows:
(i) To build up income from investments through the three funds in the Church of Scotland Trust. The bulk of the funds are held in shares and in government

and local authority stocks.
(ii) To invest the redeemed feus of the standardized stipend in government and local authority stocks.
(iii) To sell property made redundant by union and readjustment and through the construction of new buildings. The usual practice is for the proceeds of sale to be invested to form a fabric fund for the congregation concerned. It is probably true to say that the great bulk of these funds are invested in the Church of Scotland Trust, mainly the Deposit Fund.
(iv) To improve upon the inadequate standard of property maintenance, possibly by setting up a Central Fabric Fund.

It may be argued that the investment strategy of the Church should be expanded in a variety of directions. In our view, the investment performance of the Church would be improved over a period of years if two new elements were to be introduced into investment policy. Firstly, we recommend that there should be a shift in assets from stocks and shares to property. Secondly, we recommend that liabilities should be considered as much an element of the investment portfolio as assets.

The general portfolio discussion usually centres round which of a variety of assets to hold. However, this is too narrow an interpretation. Any individual of means should hold both assets and liabilities. Thus a prudent person has the liability of a mortgage on his house, as well as assets such as a bank account, government stock, and equities. There are several reasons why he holds a mortgage when he has assets which might enable him to pay off the mortgage. Firstly, there is the cost of paying off the mortgage ahead of time; his assets may be depleted in doing so, and he would lose the services which those assets provide. These services can be divided into the transactionary, precautionary, and speculative services, in the Keynesian fashion; for example, a bank account may be used to purchase goods, to guard against a loss of earning ability as a result of an accident or ill-health, and to speculate in the stock market. Secondly, the composition of an individual's portfolio, like a bank's, is determined by the desire on the one hand to obtain a good return, and on the other to have reserves available to meet unforeseen contingencies. It is proper, therefore, that the individual should hold a certain amount of highly liquid but low-yield assets; a certain amount of higher yield but less liquid assets; and a certain amount of assets which hold the possibility of capital gain. He may find that some illiquid assets like a house may prove over the long-run to yield the highest returns.

It follows from this statement of principles that the Church would do well to accumulate debts as well as to accumulate assets. The Church should borrow money from the banks or insurance companies or the market generally so as to finance long-term investments in real estate holding. This might include equity participation in farmland ownership and management, equity participation in small businesses, and the ownership or part-ownership of commercial buildings, industrial buildings and rental property. When real assets are held with reasonable prospects of appreciation, such as houses, a substantial body of debt owed by the Church would seem to make good sense. This is because the relative cost to the Church of debt, and of tax payments on profits or interest income, may be biased in favour of the Church as compared to the position of the private individual or public company by virtue of its charitable status. The ability of the

Church to provide tied housing offers a golden opportunity for capital appreciation under mortgage finance. Moreover, the availability of government grants on certain types of housing used by older people make this area one which is admirable for development by the Church.

A recognition of the role of liabilities and loans in the portfolio of the Church might greatly improve its financial prospects. This is true even after allowing for the bad record of equities in recent years. In a world of inflation the accumulation of cash assets or even assets in the form of government stock alone would seem to be rather dubious in spite of high money interest rates. The real rates of interest on government stocks are probably negative. One does feel inclined, therefore, to suggest that the holding of equities and government stock should be diminished in favour of real-estate holding, particularly in suburban areas.

We now discuss three specific policies through which the Church could benefit from increased investment in real-estate. The policies are the establishment of a Church building society, the question of the manses, and policy towards the central city churches.

1 A Church of Scotland building society?

There are many building societies, and it might seem pointless to establish a new one. But there are certain advantages possible for the Church in such a foundation, and certain ways in which the Church might make a building society competitive with its rivals. Further, there are a number of ways in which such an institution might act as part of the social outreach of the Church, and do good by stealth.

First of all, there is the confidence and loyalty which a Church-affiliated body could count upon; it might therefore more easily attract depositors, and even some would-be mortgagees. Second, there is the fact that, if the building society were successful, it could make charitable contributions to the Church, either on pure grounds of charity, or on the grounds that its Church connections provided part of its reasons for success, and contributions were therefore legitimate business expenses. The normal way of working of the Church of Scotland Building Society would be entirely on business lines, with the usual caution in the provision of mortgage support. If, however, an applicant wanted more than the normal amount of finance, or to take a mortgage on a property that was more risky than usual, the applicant could, if he wished, apply as a special Church-related person offering the names of ministers and elders as referees. It seems possible that in certain cases, the society might properly feel that they could take a greater risk in such cases than could or would another building society.

Finally, there is the question of social purpose. The policy of the building societies of 'red lining' in some cities, whereby certain areas are designated as 'no mortgage' areas, has been much criticized. It is true that this policy is intended to help the building society and its depositors, but once an area is 'red lined' it may run down rapidly, since neither sales nor repairs or purchases are likely to be easy; property values will fall as property decays. If it were bright enough, a Church society could reverse this trend, especially in collaboration with local authorities. If the society announces it will lend in an area which has been 'red lined', perhaps at slightly higher interest rates (if this were possible in terms of the building societies' cartel), people in the area will flock to it as soon as it is known that funds are available, and the formerly declining area may have a renaissance. Of course, this benevolent aspect would have to be restricted to limited numbers of carefully selected areas at any one time, but an astute investor might cash in on the resulting rise in property values as a proper reward for good work. This aspect could operate in a variety of ways, including singling out areas with substantial Church properties or Church membership.

2 A policy for the manses.
The present position regarding the manses is that a parish minister is entitled to a manse, or an allowance in lieu of one of £500 a year in the four large cities and £350 elsewhere (including rates). In 1973 there were 1,865 manses in the Church, about a third of which (604) were to be found in the cities and large burghs. A survey of a sample of manses in 1967[2] revealed that the average manse had 9.1 rooms, which is substantially bigger than the average family-sized house. The manses ranged in size from 5 to 16 rooms, the larger being mainly in rural areas. Given an estimated average value in 1975 of £25,000 for urban and £15,000 for rural manses, the houses were worth about £34 million.

The regulations require that every manse should be 'free', in the sense that the minister is not responsible for any of the normal financial burdens in connection with it, such as rates, insurance, maintenance, and feu-duty (if any).[3] Also, where manses are vested in or leased to the Church, a 50 per cent remission of rates is mandatory on the local authority. Taking this into account, it was estimated that the average cost to a congregation of maintaining an urban manse was £375 in 1975.[4]

In addition, under the 1961 Finance Act certain income tax concessions in respect of heating, lighting, and cleaning of manses are personal to the minister occupying a manse which is vested in or leased to the Church. Thus if these heating and other expenses amount to £150 a year, the minister can claim the £150 as a personal allowance, in which case he makes a tax saving of roughly £50; in 1975 it was estimated that the tax saving was worth £63 on average to a minister living in an urban manse.

A house can be looked upon as providing a service to the owner-occupier. This service can be measured in money terms by the 'opportunity cost' rent, i.e. the rent which the house could earn if it was to be rented out on the market. When such a house is larger than the occupier really needs, as is the case with most manses, the unused excess capacity constitutes facilities not required. If the capital represented by the excess capacity could be realized, it would yield extra income in the form of rent or interest. In the case of the manses, with their estimated capital value of £34 millions, that extra income could be quite considerable.

A further problem of housing for the Ministry is that ministers have no house in which to retire, and many have no option but to apply for local authority housing.[5] The question lies, therefore, in deciding upon a suitable scheme to reorganize housing for the ministry in such a way as to yield the extra income and be acceptable to the ministers concerned.

One scheme was put forward in 1974 by a Church working party,[6] which was established in response to strongly expressed views in recent General Assemblies and in the correspondence columns of *Life and Work*, that steps should be taken to help ministers to buy their own homes in urban areas.[7] The scheme involved congregations selling their manses, and the proceeds of sales being paid into a central loan fund, which would in turn give loans to ministers towards the purchase of a house. The scheme has two main limitations. Firstly, it involves the sale of an asset which is appreciating in value — the manses — the proceeds of which would form a fund which, by making loans at only 2½ per cent at today's high rates of inflation, would become a depreciating asset. Secondly, ministers would be compensated for the loss of the manse by a manse allowance of £500 per year, which would be subject to tax; such a sum would not be at all adequate to repay a loan even on a small house. In addition, ministers opting to buy a house would forgo the tax concession on the heating and lighting of the manse estimated at £63 a year.

An alternative policy is that the manses should be converted into flats and leased out on the market. The income accruing from rents would be paid into a central fund, which would then pay a housing allowance to the ministers concerned. The housing allowance would be sufficient (net of income tax) to cover the extra cost to the minister of buying a house of normal family size if he decided to buy, or the cost of renting such a house if he decided instead to rent; he would also be compensated for the loss of the heating and lighting tax concession. The minister would benefit by getting a house in which to retire and, if he chooses the purchase option, the capital gains also. Special facilities might be arranged with a building society to help ministers buy their own homes, or, better still, the loans might be provided by the Church of Scotland Building Society proposed above. The costs of maintaining the minister's house are assumed to be met by the congregation, which would no longer have to maintain the manse.

The central fund would also make substantial savings. Rough calculations suggest that, if 90 per cent of all urban manses entered the scheme, total savings would be about £415,000 per year if all ministers decided to buy their house, and about £669,000 if all ministers decided to rent. If 90 per cent of rural manses were to enter the scheme, although that raises further problems, then additional annual savings of between about £380,000 and £624,000 would arise. In addition, the loans used to finance the conversion of the manses into flats would be paid off over a ten-year period, so that when all the loans had been repaid an extra saving of around £285,000 per year would accrue to the fund.

Against these savings a number of factors must be measured. As the result of opposition to the scheme in individual cases from ministers and congregations, a smaller proportion of the manses than 90 per cent might be entered into the scheme, with a consequent fall in the potential savings. Also, a proportion of the savings might be made over to the already existing Housing and Loan Fund to cater for the housing needs of retired ministers and ministers' widows who might fall outside the scheme. A further cost to the Central Housing Fund would be the need to continue to pay the housing allowance to retired ministers who decided to rent a house.

Any scheme to house the ministry raises many problems, not least the resistance of some ministers and many congregations to a minister living in his own house rather than in the manse provided by the congregation. It is possible that the office-space provided in the former manse could be replaced by partitioning off a portion of the church hall for the purpose.

3 A policy towards the central city churches.
Many of the central city churches are amongst the most affluent in the Church, since they are able to attract wealthy members from a wide area; the populations of their own parishes are often very small. The true financial position of such churches may be blurred, however, by the fact that they do not pay rent on the valuable sites occupied. In recent years, for example, sums of £¾ million and just over £¼ million have been realised from the sale of two churches in central Glasgow. While those sums are exceptional, there are probably a number of churches in central city areas whose sites would be worth £50,000 for redevelopment purposes. If the notional rents on such sites were to be included in the balance sheets of the churches concerned, the churches might even be thrown into financial deficit. The argument that such churches sustain the financial strength of the national Church may thus not be altogether accurate.

One policy to be considered is the closing down of selected central city churches in order to take advantage of the valuable sites which they occupy. These sites could be sold, and the proceeds used to form a fund for Church purposes; it is not inconceivable that a sum of £1 million might be raised. The fund might be used to form the nucleus of the Central Fabric Fund discussed above, which would fall within the Church's policy of using the proceeds of sale of property for fabric purposes. Alternatively, the sites could be developed by the Church itself using borrowed funds in the manner described above.

A policy of closing down even a few of the central city churches would undoubtedly raise considerable difficulties. The policy would probably proceed through the merger of the congregation concerned with the congregation of an adjacent parish, on the understanding that the building of the first congregation would be the building disposed of. But some of the buildings might be excluded by virtue of being listed as of special architectural or historic interest, or by being situated on land zoned for Church use. Many of the central city churches are burgh churches, the sale of which often raises problems. Also, the members of the congregations concerned might be strongly opposed to the union of their congregation with another and to the subsequent closing down of the church. It is even conceivable that the congregation might seek to secede from the Church of Scotland under its minister to avoid such a reorganization. The danger is that if the reorganization was carried through the Church might loose a large proportion of the congregation concerned, many of whom might be expected to be affluent members who make substantial financial contributions. The loss of these affluent members would reduce the financial attractiveness of the proposal, and careful efforts would have to be made to avoid such a loss. On the other hand, since the members of the central city churches tend to come from a wide range of suburban parishes, it would be financially advantageous to those parishes if they were able to attract such members to their home parish church.[8] A rationalization process of this kind would also make more sense of the parish system, since it would simplify the parish visitation programmes of ministers and elders.

7 Conclusions
The purpose of this chapter has been to assess the investments, endowments and properties of the Church with the aim of formulating a general strategy for future Church investment and building policy.

In section 2 we saw that the main investment income of the Church is derived from the investments in the Church of Scotland Trust and from the standardized stipend and other endowments for stipend. In 1975 these amounted to £1,961,816, or 11.1 per cent of total income, having declined from 17.4 per cent of total income in 1946. There is also a substantial income from trusts, by far the largest of which is the F.G. Salvesen Trust, worth about £350,000 a year, and an unknown income accruing to congregations from funds invested outside of central channels. This income may have exceeded £½ million in 1975.

In section 3 we saw that the standardized stipend is in the process of being redeemed under the Land Tenure Reform (Scotland) Act, 1974, and that the proceeds are being invested largely in government and local authority stock. It was suggested that this might be a dubious investment in the present economic circumstances, when the real rate of interest is probably negative.

The following section was concerned with the Church of Scotland Trust, which runs three separate investment funds: a General Investment Fund, which is a unit trust for long-term investment and capital growth; a Special Investment Account, in which the specific investments of the central committees are held; and a Deposit Fund, which gives a high income but no capital growth. In 1976 the funds invested in the trust amounted to £23,350,024, the bulk of which were invested in stocks and shares. The income of £2,045,587 gave an overall return of 8.8 per cent.

In section 5 we turned to the property owned by the Church, which comprises church buildings, halls, manses, glebes, and other diverse properties. It was estimated that the replacement cost of these properties was in excess of £175 millions in 1975, although the opportunity cost was substantially less because of the lack of alternative uses to which churches and halls can be put. About two-thirds of all these buildings (and all the glebes) are vested in the General Trustees. An examination of the minutes of the General Trustees for the four-and-a-half year period 1972-3 to mid-January 1977 showed that the Church is shedding property at a steady rate. Manses were being disposed of at the rate of about ten a year, and other properties at more than twenty a year. Such property has been made redundant either through the union and readjustment of congregations or as the result of the acquisition of an alternative building. The sale values of property varied enormously depending upon the type of building and its location. Manses averaged £17,000, but ranged from £1,000 to £37,000. Churches generally had a low sale value unless they occupied a city site valuable for redevelopment.

The Church has a heavy fabric maintenance burden, particularly for small congregations or those with old buildings, and buildings are generally not well maintained. We welcomed the establishment of a Central Fabric Fund to help such congregations, providing that it does not inhibit local responsibilities towards fabric maintenance. We also suggested that congregations ought to share buildings in order to share the maintenance costs.

With regard to new buildings, we argued that from the narrow economic viewpoint they were a poor investment, yielding a relatively low income in terms of liberality and tending to depreciate in value. We recommend that the erection of new buildings should be kept to a minimum, and those that were built should be designed for flexible use.

Finally, in section 6 it was suggested that the Church appeared to have no overall investment strategy, but rather policies for different areas of investment. The policies appear to be to build up the Church of Scotland Trust as the main vehicle for investment in the Church; to invest the standardized stipend redemption monies in government and local authority stocks; to sell off redundant property, and use the proceeds for fabric funds in the congregations concerned; and to improve upon the inadequate standard of property maintenance. It was argued that periods of high inflation tend to favour investment in goods rather than in paper assets, and to favour the debtor rather than the lender. The Church's present portfolio would seem to put it at a disadvantage in both of these respects.

We recommend, therefore, that the Church should borrow from the money market to finance long-term investments in real estate holding, including equity participation in farmland, housing, small businesses, and the like. Proposals were made for a Church of Scotland Building Society, a policy for the manses, and a policy toward central city churches – all designed to benefit the Church from investment in real estate.

Notes

1 Church of Scotland, 'Report of the General Finance Committee', *Reports to the General Assembly, 1967,* p. 92.

2 'Report of the Special Committee Anent Manpower', *Reports to the General Assembly, 1967,* pp. 777-8.

3 A.J.H. Gibson, *Stipend in the Church of Scotland,* p. 113.

4 Figure adapted from that in 'Housing for the Ministry: Memorandum no. 3', Church and Ministry Department files (1973), p. 1.

5 See footnote 3, chapter 11,

6 'Report of the Church and Ministry Department', *Reports to the General Assembly, 1974,* pp. 187-93.

7 But not in rural areas, where there would be a lack of alternative accommodation.

8 The extent to which some central city churches draw their membership from outside their own parishes is shown in the following two examples. In 1973 St Cuthbert's, Edinburgh, had 2,612 members on the Communion Roll, but only about 1,700 people were resident in the parish. In 1974 only 13 of the 867 members of Greyfriars, Edinburgh, lived in the parish; the congregation drew members from all but 11 of the 106 parishes in Edinburgh. (See D.A. Stewart, 'The Geography of the Church of Scotland in Edinburgh', (M.A. dissertation, University of Edinburgh, 1975)).

Chapter 20

Church government and administration

1 Introduction
In Chapter 2 we saw that the Church is governed by a system of courts, inferior and superior, in ascending scale, namely Kirk Session, Presbytery, Synod and General Assembly. Each of these courts has committees made up of its members to deal with specific areas of its business. The most important committees are the standing committees of the General Assembly, which are responsible to the Assembly for the ongoing work of administering the various activities of the Church; included amongst these are the important Maintenance of the Ministry and Stewardship and Budget Committees. These central committees are grouped into seven departments, each staffed by permanent officials or secretaries, supported by professional, clerical and other staff. These departments constitute the central administration of the Church.

Certain measures are already planned to streamline the government of the Church in order to improve its efficiency and reduce its costs. A close watch is also kept on administration expenditures by the General Treasurer and the General Finance Committee. These economy measures are necessary in view of the financial problems which confront the Church.

The purpose of this chapter is to make proposals which would hasten the trend towards efficiency and economy in Church government and administration. In section 2 we briefly outline the various elements which make up the costs of the government and administration of the Church. Then in section 3 we put forward a series of recommendations in respect of Kirk Sessions, Presbyteries, Synods, the General Assembly and its standing committees, and the central secretariat.

2 The costs of Church government and administration
The Church is relatively expensive to govern and administer because of the democratic nature of its organization.[1] However, the estimation of the total cost of Church government and administration is rendered very difficult by the fact that many of the true (i.e. opportunity) costs are concealed.

The elders make up the majority of the membership of the Kirk Session, and many are involved in pastoral visitation. One elder from each charge is a member of the Presbytery and Synod, and the Presbytery elders attend the General Assembly as commissioners by rotation. Some of the elders sitting on the higher courts are members of the committees of those courts. All of these services of elders are voluntary and unpaid, although elders acting as commissioners to the General Assembly or who sit on its standing committees do receive travel and subsistence expenses.

The clerk and treasurer to each of the Church courts provide their services free, or at best receive a small honorarium, with the exception of four of the larger Presbyteries which employ paid full-time clerks,[2] and the clerk and treasurer to the General Assembly.

Parish ministers spend a good deal of time on Church government and administration. They are the moderators of their respective Kirk Sessions, and do much administrative work in respect of their congregations. They are members of the Presbytery and Synod, and attend the General Assembly as commissioners by rotation. They may also sit on one or more of the committees of the higher courts. An indication of how much time parish ministers devote to government and administration work is provided by a survey of a sample of ministers conducted by the Special Committee Anent Manpower in 1966,[3] which we examined in detail in chapter 14. The survey found that ministers in an average week spent 2.7 hours on administration, 2.9 hours on secretarial work, and 1.5 hours on Presbytery and synod work; these together amount to 7.1 hours, or about 13 per cent of the estimated average working week of 51 hours. This information suggests that 13 per cent of ministers' stipends can be apportioned to government and administration work. A calculation of the cost of the ministerial input to Church government and administration is given in Table 139 for 1966 and 1975. The table shows in respect of each year the minimum stipend, the estimated average stipend, and the number of parish ministers; this enables the total stipend, and total minimum stipend, bills to be calculated. Taking 13 per cent of those bills as the stipend attributable to the government and administration work of ministers, we arrive at figures of around £¼ million for 1966 and nearly £½ million for 1975. These figures reveal the considerable concealed costs of Church government and administration. It is possible that the opportunity cost of the contributions of elders and other office-bearers may be as large in total as that of ministers.

TABLE 139.
Estimates of the cost of the ministerial contribution to Church government and administration, 1966 and 1975

Year and stipend	Stipend 1	Number of parish Ministers 2	Total stipend (i.e. 1 × 2) 3	Total stipend attributable to government and administration work (13%) 4
	£		£	£
1966 minimum	1,000	1,859	1,859,000	241,670
average	1,100*	1,859	2,044,900	265,837
1975 minimum	2,258	1,588	3,585,704	466,142
average	2,450*	1,588	3,890,600	505,778

* Estimated figure

The total cost of Church government and administration is also difficult to estimate, because information on the office expenses of Kirk Sessions, Presbyteries and Synods is not collected centrally.[4]

The government and administration costs of the Church which can be ascertained are shown for 1975 in table 140.[5] The first item is the cost of the General Assembly and Commissions of Assembly, which amounted to £50,818. The second item is made up of the administration and organization costs of the central departments. These comprise in general the emoluments to committee secretaries and office staff; printing and stationery; postages and telephones; the expenses of committee meetings, including the travel and subsistence of members; and general office expenses. Also included are the apportioned costs of the accommodation occupied by each of the departments at 121 George Street, amounting in total to £43,391, and of the following service departments: General Treasurer's Office (£70,349); the Stewardship and Budget Committee (£21,233 distributed amongst the Mission and Service Fund Committees); and the Department of Publicity (£44,000, allocated to the Mission and Service Fund Committees, Church and Ministry Department, and General Purposes Fund).

TABLE 140.
The cost of the General Assembly and the central departments in 1975

	Cost £	%
General Assembly (including the Commissions of Assembly)	50,818	7.3
Central Departments		
Administration and Special Interests Department	112,721	16.2
Church and Ministry Department	111,281	16.0
Home Department	80,831	11.7
Department of Social Responsibility	141,282	20.4
Overseas Council	144,586	20.8
Education Department	52,844	7.6
SUB-TOTAL	643,545	92.7
TOTAL	694,363	100.0

In Table 140 the administration and organization costs of the Administration and Special Interests Department includes the cost of the Church of Scotland Trust (£25,509) and of the General-Trustees (£76,054), but excludes the cost of the General Assembly and of grants to ecumenical bodies (£31,517). The administration and organization expenditures of the Department of Social Responsibility includes the cost of the Social Services Committee (£119,897), which was charged against the homes and hostels which it runs.

Table 140 indicates that the total cost of the central departments in 1975 was £643,545. This is equivalent to 3.6 per cent of total income, though the proportion in relation to the total expenditure of each department is, in most cases, much higher. The departments with the highest costs are the Overseas Council and Department of Social Responsibility, each accounting for over a fifth of total departmental cost, followed by the Administration and Special Interests Department and the Church and Ministry Departments, each with rather less than a fifth of the total.

3 Proposals on Church government and administration

1 Kirk Sessions

Our recommendations on Kirk Sessions largely concern the elders. Most are aged between 55 and 75; a survey reported in chapter 4 showed that only about six per cent of elders were aged under 35. Although many have given long and distinguished service to the Church, we feel that their age brings some disadvantages: a resistance to the acceptance of new ideas, and a lack of energy to carry them out; a lack of appeal to young people because they help create the impression that the Church is for the middle-aged and old; and an unwillingness to face the real financial problems confronting the Church, perhaps because they are of a generation which grew up when the financial position of the Church was relatively sound.

In order to overcome these difficulties we recommend that Kirk Sessions should appoint more younger elders in the 30-45 age group.

We also recommend that, in view of the increasing emphasis which needs to be placed on the finances of congregations and on fund-raising, Kirk Sessions should appoint more elders with a background in business, commerce or industry.

Our proposals on the training and re-training of ministers have already been giving in chapter 14. We need only empasize here the need for a definite shift in that training towards the practical side of the ministry, i.e. in congregational administration, meetings, and pastoral care.

2 Presbyteries

In the Church of Scotland it is the Presbytery, rather than the congregation, which traditionally is the linch pin of the organization. A feature of the Presbyterian form of Church government is that the Presbytery exercises a superintendent power over the congregations within its bounds, in roughly the same way as, in the Anglican tradition, the bishop superintends the congregations within his diocese. The Presbytery exercises this power in the following ways: by reviewing the decisions of Kirk Sessions; by attesting congregational books; through the quinquennial visitation of congregations; and by reviewing, through the appropriate committees, the success of congregations in meeting their appropriate stipends and contributions to the Mission and Service Fund.

Our view is that the effectiveness of the work of Kirk Sessions in pastoral care, in stewardship and fund-raising, and in the meeting of central financial allocations, would be improved if the superintending powers of Presbyteries were to be exercised more vigorously. We propose that the following measures be adopted to this end:

(i) At present every congregation is visited once in every quinquennium by the Presbyterial Superintendence Committee of the Presbytery. It so happens that appropriate stipends were formerly fixed for periods of five years; this had later to be reduce to a period of three years, because it proved impossible to forecast stipends so far in advance. It may be that it is advisable to increase the frequency of Presbyterial superintendence visitation of congregations under the same inflationary pressures as have compelled the reduction of the period for forecasting of stipends.

(ii) One of the significant features of Church organisation is the number of Presbyteries. The present pattern of Presbyteries has probably developed out of geographical circumstances and historical accident. Given modern methods of communication and transport, however, the argument for having such a large number of small Presbyteries are diminished. Two benefits would follow from a reduction in their number. Firstly, it is widely believed that there are differences in attitudes between Presbyteries, and that these differences are conditioned by variations in their size. It has been argued that in large Presbyteries the problems posed by those congregations which fall short of their appropriate stipend and Mission and Service Fund contributions can be approached in a dispassionate way without regard to the personalities involved. On the other hand, small Presbyteries are sometimes said to be rather 'cosy' places where such problems are dealt with in less forceful ways, to the detriment of the financial health of the Church. It is possible, therefore, that the unification of smaller Presbyteries may by itself strengthen their role of superintendence. A second benefit of amalgamation is that each Presbytery has certain overhead costs in terms of office and other expenses which would be reduced if Presbyteries were to be enlarged through mergers.

The Church is already moving gradually in the direction of the unification of Presbyteries. Prior to 1st January, 1976, there were 57 Presbyteries in Scotland, with great variations in the number of congregations and number of members from Presbytery to Presbytery. In 21 Presbyteries there are fewer than 20 congregations (compared to over 200 congregations in the Presbytery of Glasgow); 36 Presbyteries had less than 15,000 members (compared to about 140,000 members in the Presbytery of Glasgow). From 1st January 1976, the Presbytery structure of the Church was readjusted, so that their number in Scotland was reduced from 58 to 47. While this is obviously a great improvement, we recommend that further steps in the same direction should be taken.

(iii) One problem facing the Church is posed by those congregations who fail to meet their appropriate stipends and Mission and Service Fund allocations. In such cases the appropriate committee of the Presbytery concerned – the Maintenance of the Ministry Committee or Stewardship and Budget Committee respectively – is required to investigate the reasons for the shortfall. However, the vigour with which such enquiries are conducted, or even whether they are conducted at all, depends very much upon the convenors of the committees concerned. We recommend that all cases of congregations failing to meet their central assessments should be fully investigated by the appropriate Presbytery Committee. To ensure that such enquiries are properly carried out, we recommend that Presbyteries appoint convenors to those two committees who are energetic and forceful in personality, and whose congregations are exemplary in meeting their allocations.

(iv) A more controversial possibility would be the appointment of a full-time Presbytery superintendent who would act as Moderator. Apart from presiding at meetings, his chief functions would be to visit ministers in their parishes, and to discuss with them the problems they face. Such appointments might require extra finance, and it might be difficult to justify the expense unless the role of the Superintendent were extended into pastoral-care training and into the organization of stewardship and fund-raising.

3 Synods

After the Reformation in Scotland the newly established Church was governed by congregational, provincial and national assemblies. No provision was made for Presbyteries; these are said to have arisen later, partly out of the weekly meetings of ministers and church members within districts to discuss the Scriptures, and partly from the need of Synods to delegate some of their duties. The General Assembly of 1581 set out a regular pattern of Presbyteries which formed the prototype of the existing organization. Since then, they have gradually expanded the range of their duties and business at the expense of Synods, so that it is now possible to raise the question as to whether Synods might be abolished.

In recent years, efforts have been made to reorganize Presbyteries into larger units. The greatest advance took place at 1 January 1976, when the number of Presbyteries in Scotland was reduced from 58 to 47. We welcomed this development in sub-section 2, and recommended that the process of unification should be taken further, on the grounds that it would strengthen the superintendent role of Presbyteries. Their increasing size may be a further reason for considering the abolition of Synods.

In 1977 there were twelve Synods in the Church of Scotland. In addition, there are three Presbyteries — those of Orkney, Shetland and England — which are not part of any Synod, but are individually vested with synodical powers. The functions of Synods are rather limited: they exercise a general superintendence of Presbyteries within their separate areas of jurisdiction, and act as courts of appeal between those Presbyteries and the General Assembly. Synods adjudicate finally in all cases of appeal, with the exception of cases involving doctrine, worship, censure of a Minister or other office-bearer, the licensing of students, and cases of union and readjustments; in these cases the General Assembly remains the Court of Appeal. For those Presbyteries with synodical powers, the General Assembly is the court of final appeal.

If Synods were to be abolished, it seems clear that their present duties would be passed over to the General Assembly. The Assembly would become the court of final appeal in all matters, as is presently the case in the three Presbyteries with synodical powers. The Synods' duty of the superintendence of Prebysteries would also be passed to the General Assembly. The successful operation of the three Presbyteries with synodical powers suggests that these changes would pose few problems.

(A) Arguments for abolishing Synods

(i) The duties and responsibilities of Synods are, in fact, rather limited. They act mainly as a staging-post between Presbyteries and General Assembly, and for that reason much of their work is a duplication of that of Presbyteries and General Assembly.

(ii) Attendances at meetings of Synods are said to be poor, sometimes as low as 5 or 10 per cent. Synods are thus unrepresentative bodies in practice.

(iii) The cost of posting material to all Synod members, only a small proportion of whom attend meetings, would be saved, as would the time and travel costs of those who do attend. Against these savings, however, might have to be set the extra costs imposed on the General Assembly arising from the duties transferred from Synods.

(B) Procedure for abolition
A proposal to abolish Synods would be put forward to the General Assembly in the form of an overture. Since such a proposal would probably require a change in the Declaratory Articles of the Church, the procedure for changing those Articles would have to be followed. This requires a vote in favour of the overture by the General Assembly, a two-thirds majority of Presbyteries in favour in two successive years, and finally a resolution by the General Assembly to pass the overture as an Act, at which time the overture would become part of the constitution of the Church.

(C) Conclusion
We recommend that the Church should seriously consider the abolition of Synods.

4 General Assembly and Commission of Assembly
In 1978 the General Assembly is to be reduced in length from nine to seven days, by starting each day half-an-hour earlier at 9.30 a.m. and by leaving each day open-ended in order to finish the day's business. The advantages of compressing the Assembly within one week are partly that it would yield a saving in the cost of commissioners' expenses, and partly that younger elders would be able to attend if given one week's leave.

The savings in commissioners' expenses can be calculated roughly as follows. In 1975 the General Assembly (including the two commissions of assembly held during the year) cost £50,818. Included in this sum are the travelling expenses and subsistence of commissioners, which amounted to £32,468. According to the General Treasurer, about £5,000 of these expenses were attributable to commissioners attending the Commissions of Assembly, leaving over £27,000 of expenses attributable to the General Assembly. On the rather optimistic assumption that the expenses attributable to the General Assembly would be reduced in proportion to the compression in the length of the Assembly, the savings would have amounted to about £6,000 in 1975.

We welcome this plan to curtail the length, and therefore the cost, of the General Assembly, but suggest that the plan could be taken further. This could be done by reducing the proportion of Presbytery members eligible to attend as Commissioners from the present one-quarter to one-sixth or one-eighth. Further savings would be made on the expenses of commissioners, and the Assembly would become a smaller and more manageable body. A reduction in Presbytery representation from one-quarter to one-sixth would, in 1975, have produced further savings of over £7,000, and a reduction in the number of commissioners by a third, from 1,328 to about 885. A reduction in representation from one-quarter to one-half would have led to savings of over £10,500, and a reduction in the number of commissioners by a half to about 664. These savings are not enormous, but they represent a step in the right direction. We recommend that the Church gives serious consideration to reducing the size of the General Assembly as suggested above.

Should the experiments in reducing the length of the General Assembly in 1978 be successful, it is also planned to consider dispensing with the Commission of Assembly. We would support such a move; the Commission is poorly attended, and meets only for a short period, and the membership is virtually identical to that of the General Assembly, although attendance is much lower – usually only around 100-200. The reason is that the long distances which many commissioners would have to travel is hardly justified by the short period for which the Commission meets: in 1976 the meeting lasted less than two hours.

It is believed that the Commission could be abolished if two conditions were to be met: firstly, a small group should be appointed to meet between Assemblies as required to carry out the formal tasks which make up the bulk of the commission's work. Secondly, new methods should be devised to deal with unions and readjustments which would take them off the Commission agenda. The abolition of the Commission of Assembly would have produced savings of about £5,500 in 1975, the bulk of which is composed of the expenses of commissioners. The chief difficulty is that measures requiring early action, which would currently be dealt with at the next meeting of the Commission, would have to wait until the following General Assembly, which might be several months away.

5 Standing committees of the General Assembly

Many of the standing committees of the General Assembly have very large memberships, in part at least because of the constitutional requirement that a representative from each Presbytery should sit on each. We believe that efforts should be made to reduce the size of committees, both to increase their effectiveness and to reduce the cost of members' expenses. The reduction in the number of Presbyteries in 1976, and the further reduction which we propose above, should facilitate this process by allowing a reduction in the number of Presbytery representatives. Two examples are provided by the Church and Ministry Department:

> The Maintenance of the Ministry Committee has recommended to the Advisory Board that its present constitution of 59 members from Presbyteries, plus 41 members appointed by the General Assembly should be reduced to 48 members representing Presbyteries plus 24 members appointed by the General Assembly, thus reducing the membership from 100 to 72.
>
> The Unions and Readjustments Committee has recommended to the Advisory Board that its present membership of 96 should be reduced to 60.[6]

We recommend that all of the standing committees of the General Assembly should examine their memberships with a view to reducing their sizes.

6 The Central Secretariat

In section 2 above it was calculated that the central departments, i.e. the secretariat and standing committees of the General Assembly, cost £643,545 in 1975. This figures is equivalent to 3.6 per cent of total income in 1975.

The cost of the central departments have been strongly criticized in recent years. While we believe these criticisms to be largely unjustified, we would propose that as a general rule great caution should be exercised on administration. This is because administrations exhibit an inborn propensity to grow, even when the organization as a whole is not expanding. There are several reasons for this growth: firstly, the status and salary of senior staff is related to the size of their departments; secondly, a growing department offers greater prospects of promotion. A further reason is that administrators often desire to increase the perfection of the administrative system by undertaking new tasks or by performing existing duties in a more intensive fashion. Finally, there is a tendency for an increase in government-imposed work. Any expansion of the administration, and in particular any increase in the number of staff employed, has to be justified in terms of the gains from the extra work accomplished.

Apart from that guiding principle, there are certain areas of administrative expenditure where potential economies exist:

(i) As we saw in chapter 3, a large number of congregational fabric funds are held centrally by the General Trustees, the General Treasurer, and the Church and Ministry Department; many congregations have more than one fabric fund held centrally. Significant administrative savings would arise if all these centrally held fabric funds were to be vested in one body, and the separate funds of individual congregations were to be amalgamated to form one fund. The General Trustees would be the obvious body to hold these funds, since they already hold the bulk. However, there are legal problems in the way of amalgamating monies, in that each fund is normally held subject to an Act or Deliverance of Assembly and/or the terms of a Basis of Union or Linking. An Act or Deliverance of Assembly would thus be required to effect many amalgamations of fabric monies of individual congregations.

(ii) Substantial administrative expenses result from the necessity to account separately for the various sums received from various sources by way of stipend endowment. In chapter 11 we suggested that these sums should be pooled in a central fund as part of our policy towards stipend. This measure would also have the effect of reducing administration expenses.

(iii) Although we have not explored the matter in detail, it is possible that the administration of stipend payments by the Church and Ministry Department might be more cheaply carried out by a commercial bank. The feasibility of the transfer of this work to an external agency has been increased by the centralisation of stipend payments from April 1974.

(iv) Economies in administration expenditures would follow from cuts in the expenditures of certain committees receiving income from the Mission and Service Fund, as suggested in chapter 16.

4 Conclusions

The purpose of this chapter has been to make proposals for streamlining the government and administration of the Church in order to increase its efficiency and reduce its costs. We saw that the Church is governed by the system of courts − Kirk Session, Presbytery, Synod and General Assembly − and administered by the various court committees, especially the standing committees of the General Assembly, and by the central secretariat. These last two make up the central departments.

For Kirk Sessions we recommended that more younger elders should be appointed to give the Church a more youthful image, and more progressive policies. We also recommmended that more elders with a business background should be appointed to help meet the financial problems facing congregations.

In the case of Presbyteries, our proposals are aimed at making their superintending powers over congregations more rigorous and effective, in order to improve their stewardship and fund-raising. We recommended that the rate of congregational visitation should be increased from quinquennial to triennial visits. We also recommend that there should be a further reduction in the number of Presbyteries through amalgamations to form larger units, since these are thought to exercise their superintending powers in a more vigorous and dispassionate way. A further recommendation was that strong personalities should be appointed to the convenorships of two key Presbytery Committees – the Maintenance of the Ministry Committee and the Stewardship and Budget Committee – to help ensure that congregations meet their central allocations.

We recommend the abolition of Synods on the grounds that they do little work which is not a duplication of work done by Presbytery or General Assembly, the meetings are held only once or twice a year and are poorly attended, and that some savings would arise in postage and other expenses.

We saw that it was already proposed to compress the meeting of the General Assembly into one week; this would reduce the commissioners' travel and subsistence expenses to the Church (potential savings estimated at £6,000 in 1975), and would encourage more younger elders to attend. We further recommended that the proportion of Presbytery members attending as commissioners should be reduced from the present one-quarter to one-sixth or one-eighth. Such a measure would have produced further savings of £7,000 and £10,500 respectively in 1975. We also supported the proposal to dispense with the Commission of Assembly.

We recommended that all standing committees of the General Assembly should examine their memberships with a view to reducing the numbers. The reduction in the number of Presbyteries form 1st January 1976 should allow a reduction in the number of Presbytery representatives, and it may also be possible to reduce the number of members appointed by the Assembly.

The total cost of the central secretariat in 1975 was £643,545, equivalent to 3.6 per cent of total Church income. We recommended that great caution should be exercised in expanding the administration, because of the inborn tendencies of administrations to grow, even when the organization itself is not expanding. We suggested that economies might be found through the vesting in one body of the fabric funds held centrally on behalf of congregations, through the pooling of stipend endowments in one central fund, and by making over the work of stipend payments to a commercial bank.

Notes

1 The degree to which the Church is organized along democratic lines can be questioned. It can be urged that the elders, who along with ministers make up the membership of the Church courts and committees, are a self-perpetuating oligarchy. This is because new elders are selected and ordained by the Kirk Session, which is composed of the minister and elders of the congregation.

2 The four Presbyteries which employ a full-time Presbytery clerk are those of Glasgow (which has two), Edinburgh, Aberdeen, and Paisley; the last is a temporary arrangement only. All of the other Presbytery clerks are employed on a part-time basis, and are usually retired or practising parish ministers.

3 Church of Scotland, 'Report of the Special Committee Anent Manpower', *Reports to the General Assembly, 1967,* pp. 777-82.

4 The expenses of Presbyteries and Synods are met by levies on congregations within the bounds. These levies are amalgamated with the levy for the central General Purposes Fund, which is used to finance the General Assembly, grants to ecumenical bodies, the central committees which do not receive income from the Mission and Service Fund, and certain other items.

5 SOURCE: *Annual Abstracts of Accounts* 1975 (General Finance Committee, 1976).

6 *Reports to the General Assembly,* 1976 p. 157.

Conclusions

The purpose of this book has been to assess the financial position and prospects of a national Church, the Church of Scotland. The analysis has been developed from an examination of the government, practice, and traditions of the Church (chapters 1-3), followed by an analysis of the features, trends, and forecasts of the main Church economic variables: membership, income, expenditure, numbers of ministers and parish charges, and numbers of lay workers (chapters 4-9). We then turned to a more detailed analysis of the ministry, including stipend, congregational finance, the union and readjustment of congregations, the education and training of ministers, and new forms of Ministry (chapters 10-15). Proposals were made to improve the economic efficiency of the Church in all of those areas.

The other main area of the work of the Church – mission and service – was then examined (chapters 16 and 17). This involved an analysis of the financing of the committees within the Mission and Service Fund by the Stewardship and Budget Committee, and of the committee's efforts to promote stewardship and fund-raising in the congregations. Recommendations on finance and fund-raising were made. Finally, we put forward further proposals to strengthen the financial position of the Church. These involved a greater use of Deeds of Covenant in fund-raising, a new investment strategy, and proposals for streamlining the government of the Church (chapters 18-20).

Our studies suggest that the main economic problems which face the Church today are membership, fund-raising, stipend, investment and property, the parish structure, mission and service, the education and training of ministers, and Church government. All of these questions have important spiritual, religious or theological dimensions of concern to the Church, but our interest here lies solely in their economic aspects. In what follows we examine the prospective improvements in the financial position of the Church over the ten year period 1976-1985 which the solution of these problems could bring. These savings are shown in Table 141, where they are expressed in real terms at 1975 prices.

There can be little doubt that the key issue which faces the Church today is membership. The steady decline in the number of members since 1956, which has accelerated from 1967, has been the main factor in restraining the growth of real Church income. If the rate of membership decline could at least be reduced, the improvement in the income prospects of the Church would be dramatic. Columns 1 to 3 of table 141 indicate the beneficial impact on real income on the assumption that the rate of membership decline is reduced from that predicted by forecast 3

TABLE 141.
The estimated real total savings (at 1975 prices) of the main quantifiable proposals, 1976-85

	Membership						Proceeds of sale of property		
	Forecast of total income based on forecast 3* 1	Forecast of total income based on forecast 2* 2	Increase in income from slower membership decline (i.e. 2 − 1) 3	Extra income from tax rebates on covenants 4	Extra income from improved fund-raising 5	Cumulative savings on union and readjustment 6	Manses 7	Churches and halls 8	ANNUAL TOTAL SAVINGS 9
1976	17,450,800	17,628,200	177,400	140,200	102,400		839,000	162,000	420,000
1977	17,191,300	17,550,400	359,100	280,400	204,800	74,100	747,000	144,000	1,919,400
1978	16,917,000	17,460,900	543,900	420,600	307,200	139,300	729,600	138,000	2,302,800
1979	16,627,300	17,359,400	732,100	560,800	409,600	202,900	729,600	138,000	2,773,000
1980	16,322,600	17,246,200	923,600	701,000	512,000	266,600	729,600	138,000	3,270,800
1981	16,002,300	17,119,800	1,117,500	841,200	614,400	320,500	620,100	120,000	3,633,700
1982	15,666,900	16,980,900	1,314,000	981,400	716,800	373,700	601,900	114,000	4,101,800
1983	15,315,900	16,828,200	1,512,300	1,121,600	819,200	416,400	492,500	96,000	4,458,000
1984	14,949,700	16,662,300	1,712,600	1,261,800	921,600	457,400	474,200	90,000	4,917,600
1985	14,568,200	16,482,600	1,914,400	1,402,000	1,024,000	489,700	364,800	72,000	5,266,900
TOTAL	161,012,000	171,318,900	10,306,900	7,711,000	5,632,000	2,740,600	5,599,500	1,074,000	33,064,000

*SOURCE: Table 18.

to that based on forecast 2. These forecasts are given in columns 1 and 2 of table 141 respectively, and the difference between them is shown in column 3. By increasing the membership forecast for 1985 from 815,747 to 860,610, the forecast for real total Church income rises by £1,914,400 from £14,568,200 to £16,482,600. The total improvement in real income for the ten-year period totals £10,306,900.

A second important issue is stewardship and fund-raising. In chapter 18 we showed that a considerable increase in income would ensue if members could be encouraged to channel a greater proportion of their contributions through Deeds of Covenant. It was estimated that the potential increase in income from the tax recovered on covenants in 1973 was between about £832,000 and £1,168,000 per year. The average of these two figures is £1,000,000, and that figure can be adjusted to 1975 levels by adding the 40.2 per cent by which total liberality increased between 1973 and 1975. The 1975 figure is thus estimated at £1,402,000. Since it will take time to build up the use of covenants in the fund-raising efforts of congregations, the figure of £1,402,000 is assumed to be reached in 1985 at the end of the ten year period, as shown in column 4 of table 141. The figures for the intervening years are scaled accordingly. The improvement in the income position of the Church for the ten-year period 1976-1985 through the greater use of covenants is thus estimated at £7,711,000.

So far we have ignored the extra contributions from members which would arise from the implementation of improved fund-raising methods. A rough indication of the sort of improvement which might result is as follows.

In 1973 the 'ordinary liberality' per member was £7.11. It is possible to calculate for each Presbytery whose 'ordinary liberality' per member fell below that figure the additional income which would have been raised had they managed to achieve the Church average figure. This is a modest assumption, since it ignores both the potential for improvement in the fund-raising of congregations in those Presbyteries which exceeded the average, and the possibility of success on the scale which the Wells campaigns have realized. The extra income raised on the basis of the assumption is about £759,000, or 9.76 per cent of the 'ordinary liberality' figure of £7,773,214 in 1973. The same proportion of the 'ordinary liberality' in 1975 of £10,484,603 produces a figure of £1,024,000. In column 5 of Table 141 we assume that the last figure is reached in 1985 by series of equal steps over the years 1976-85. Over the ten-year period the extra income realized is about £5,632,000 in real terms at 1975 prices.

The fourth way in which the Church could substantially improve its financial position over the next ten years is through the policy of union and readjustment. In chapter 13 two estimates were made of the cumulative annual savings arising from union and readjustment, based on alternative forecasts of the decline in the number of charges. The savings shown in column 6 of table 141 are the average of those two estimates, but scaled up from 1973 to 1975 prices by the 34.9 per cent increase in the minimum stipend over the period; the stipend increase was used because the bulk of the savings derive from savings in ministerial manpower. The cumulative annual savings rise from about £74,100 in 1977 to £489,700 in 1985; the savings are cumulative because, once a readjustment has been made, the savings can be considered to accrue not only in the year following readjustment, but also for subsequent years in perpetuity. The total savings for the ten-year period amount to £2,740,600.

Fifthly, there is the savings in property made redundant by union and readjustment. Manses and other buildings are dealt with separately in columns 7 and 8 respectively of table 141. Any estimate of the average value of buildings is rather arbitrary, since much depends upon their size, condition, and location. However, for manses we use the average figure for 1975 of £18,239 calculated in chapter 11 (See table 74). To produce the annual savings arising from the sale of redundant manses, the figures of £18,239 is multiplied by the average of the two forecasts of the decline in the number of charges in each year of the ten-year period. The savings are £839,000 in 1977, gradually declining to £364,800 in 1985. The total proceeds of sale for the ten-year period amount to £5,599,500. These calculations ignore the possibility that the sale of some manses may be delayed as a result of their occupancy by ministers who have retired prematurely for the sake of union, or occupied in the future by part-time non-stipendiary ministers in the rural areas.

The average value of a church together with a church hall is more difficult to estimate because the variation between buildings situated in central city and in remote rural areas is very great. A further consideration is that some congregations, particularly in rural areas, do not have a hall. On the other hand, church buildings and halls are made redundant through the union of congregations, but not through linkings, where the congregations concerned retain their separate identities and buildings. The fact that unions usually take place in cities and towns, and only infrequently in the remote rural areas, will bias upwards the average value of the buildings made redundant. Table 138 (p. 420) suggests that a conservative estimate of the buildings of a congregation other than the manse might be £6,000. The annual proceeds of sale of redundant churches and halls is calculated by mutiplying that figure by the decline in the number of charges brought about by unions in each year of the ten-year period. The savings are £162,000 in 1977, declining to £72,000 in 1985; the total proceeds of sale for the period amount to £1,074,000. As with manses, the savings are greater in the early years of the period because of the steeper rate of decline in the number of charges; like the savings arising from union and readjustment, the proceeds of sale of manses and other buildings are assumed to accrue in the year following the year of readjustment.

Table 141 indicates that the above six measures alone over the period might improve the financial position of the Church by about £33 millions in real terms at 1975 prices. Nearly a third (31.2 per cent) of this improvement is accounted for by the slowing of the rate of membership decline, which might yield extra income of about £10.3 millions. Almost a quarter (23.3 per cent), or roughly £7.7 millions, derives from the greater use of covenants, and a further sixth (17.0 per cent), or approximately £5.6 millions, from improved fund-raising and stewardship; the remaining £9.4 millions, or rather over a quarter of the total savings (28.5 per cent), arises from the policy of union and readjustment. The net savings in congregational expenditure amounts to about £2.7 millions (8.3 per cent), and £5.6 millions (16.9 per cent) and £1.07 millions (3.3 per cent) arise from the proceeds of sales of manses and of other buildings respectively. These savings in aggregate average roughly £3.3 millions per year (in real terms at 1975 prices) over the period 1976-85, which is equivalent to nearly a fifth (18.7 per cent) of the Church's total income in 1975.

In addition to those already described, there are further measures which should improve the financial position of the Church. However, it is difficult to make even rough estimates of their impact. In some cases, as with investment policy, this is because much depends upon the extent to which the policy is implemented. Other measures are difficult to evaluate from the financial viewpoint, because they exert only an indirect influence on Church finances: amongst such measures are included those on stipend, expenditure on mission and service, the education and training of ministers, and Church government. These measures are likely to operate by improving the effectiveness of the Church through an improvement of organizational efficiency, a quickening of interest and involvement in the Church, and a growing vitality in Church life, witness, and social activity. These in turn should lead to increased membership, contributions, and donations.

Our work has shown that there is a considerable scope for improving the financial position of the Church, providing that the necessary policies are implemented successfully. The chief difficulty in implementing new policies lies in the conservatism of the Church courts, which in turn reflect the conservatism of the congregations. While there are congregations which are forward-looking and ready to embrace new ideas, there are many which are very slow in responding to fresh stimuli. Thus even if a new policy is approved by the General Assembly, it is difficult to get the full support of the congregations.

Perhaps the best chance of new policies being introduced lies in their forceful advocacy by the central departments and committees concerned, both in their dealings with individual Presbyteries and congregations, and especially through the deliberations of the General Assembly.

Summary of main recommendations

In this section are outlined the main recommendations and proposals made during the course of this book. The entries are grouped according to subject matter, and while they are listed by page number for ease of reference in the text, all references are not always included for each entry.

1 Young members
Initially the Church should encourage young people to join organizations affiliated to congregations, in the hope that Church membership may come at a later date (p. 91); special efforts should be made to encourage parents to attend Services, since this apparently has an important bearing on the frequency of attendance of their children (p. 91). The Church should press for a return to more formal religious education in the schools (p. 91).

2 Adult members
Efforts should be made to halt the decline in the number of members, in order to increase Church income. An increase in average attendance rates would have the same effect (pp. 90-1). Efforts to recruit older members are likely to be more successful if concentrated on 'fringe' people (i.e. on people who already have some connection with the Church (p. 92). Every Kirk Session should establish a Membership Committee, one of whose functions would be to keep a list of potential members, and to tackle each person on the list annually (p. 92). In all cases where Certificates of Transference are issued to members who are moving house, the minister of the parish to which the members are moving should be given names and addresses; these names should be placed high on the list of people to be visited (p. 92). A loss of members through removals without certificate indicates the need for a strengthening of the pastoral care work of congregations; this would be a responsibility of the proposed Membership Committee (pp. 92-3). Members should be encouraged to attend the church of the parish in which they reside (pp. 93-4).

3 Church income
The 'real' total income of the Church appears to depend largely on real personal income *per capita* in the United Kingdom and on the number of members (pp. 106-7). On current trends, our forecasts suggest that the Church should anticipate a gradual fall in its real income (pp. 112-3); this may be partly offset by the decline in the number of ministers and charges to be supported (p. 204), but

the Mission and Service Fund is likely to come under increasing financial pressure (pp. 212-5). Future trends in membership are crucial to the income position of the Church, and a sure way of consolidating and increasing income is through a policy of membership recruitment and conservation (p. 113).

4 Parish structure

The most effective operation of the parish system requires that the parish boundaries are drawn up in logical fashion, with due regard to geographical and social boundaries (pp. 93-4). Congregations should give consideration to the introduction of house groups within the parish (p. 94).

5 Manpower and congregations

The Church should plan on the assumption that the number of parish ministers will fall by about a quarter between 1974 and 2001 (pp. 173-4). We support the policy of union and readjustment, and recommend that the number of parish charges should continue to be reduced in line with the fall in the number of parish ministers. The Church should plan on the basis that the number of charges might fall by a quarter between 1975 and 2001 (pp. 198-9). While the impact of unions and linkings varies in individual cases, on average both serve to strengthen the financial position of the congregations concerned and of the central funds (p. 324). In order to minimize the adverse effects on income and membership of local frictions when congregations unite, it is important that the Presbytery concerned takes adequate steps to ensure an easy transition (p. 324); a policy of large-scale reorganization of the parish structure into team ministries should not be embarked upon without convincing evidence that it would improve the effectiveness of the ministry. We recommend that the present policy towards team ministries of running a limited number of experiments where the circumstances seem especially favourable should continue (pp. 345-6). If part-time non-stipendary ministers are to be appointed to work with parish ministers in rural parishes, it should be made clear from the outset that the non-stipendiary minister is subordinate to, and responsible to, the parish minister (p. 344).

6 Stipend

The stipend policy of the Maintenance of the Ministry Committee should be as far as possible to increase the real level of the minimum stipend in line with the growth of the incomes of the community as a whole, i.e. at about 3 per cent a year; this would halt the decline in the relative income position of ministers (p. 253). Stipend should be related to the financial position of the charge, and not to the financial requirements of the minister (pp. 257-9). We recommend the reallocation of the standardized stipend, and possibly all endowments for stipend, from aid-giving to aid-receiving congregations; the aim would be to reduce or eliminate the aid given and received, with consequential encouragement for congregational fund-raising and stewardship (pp. 259-262). We recommend alternatively that all supplementary payments for stipend be discontinued, and all aid-receiving and financially marginal charges become minimum stipend charges. The minimum stipend would be increased at a slower rate than Church income in order to reduce the amount of aid given and received (pp. 262-4).

7 Economics of the congregation

We have shown that small congregations are relatively uneconomic in expenditure terms, and that savings would arise if such congregations could be united or linked with their neighbours to form larger units (p. 293). With respect to the central financial assessments on congregations, it should be made clearer in the Schedule of Financial Statistics which items of income are to be included, and which excluded (p. 122). We recommend that the Church should consider negotiating facilities with the Scottish banks whereby congregational bank accounts are pooled for the purposes of calculating interest payments and receipts (p. 303). The annual accounts of congregations should always be presented on the recommended form devised by the General Treasurer's Department (p. 303). Wherever practicable, congregational accounts should be audited professionally every second or third year (p. 303). Every Presbytery should make available each year comparative statistics of the expenditures of the congregations within their bounds (pp. 303-4).

8 Education for the ministry

A greater emphasis should be placed in the education of candidates for the ministry on practical training, in particular, in committee management and group leadership, which might be called 'catalytic management' (pp. 334-5). Applicants for the ministry should be selected on the basis of their assessed suitability for the tasks at hand (p. 335). Students should not proceed to trials for licence until their general competence at the academic level in practical theology is established by examination (p. 335). It would be helpful if the one-year probationary period were not spent in one parish, but on a tour of duty covering several parishes (p. 335). A postgraduate course in pastoral care might be introduced for students who have completed the regular or alternative courses; this might be sandwiched with the probationary year, so that probationers might spend alternating periods in college and as an assistant to a minister in a parish (p. 335). Because the job of a minister is complex and varied, he must be encouraged to take regular refresher and retraining courses; these courses should not be confined to theology, but should emphasize pastoral problems, small group organizations, administration, and finance (p. 335).

9 Mission and service

In the present financial climate the policy towards mission and service by the Stewardship and Budget Committee must be one of retrenchment. The trend towards increasing the proportion of income spent at home at the expense of expenditure overseas might have to be accelerated. Resources for work at home should be concentrated on social service work, residential accommodation for the elderly, and the education and training of members (p. 357). We recommend changes in the 'available balance' method of assessments on congregations to reduce disincentive effects on congregational fund-raising and on contributions to the Mission and Service Fund. Measures include the equal treatment of like congregations, the making of special allowance to individual congregations in special circumstances, and the arrangement of the progressive levy system, so as to avoid too high a top rate of tax and high marginal rates of tax in moving from one group to the next higher group (p. 367). The Mission and Service Fund allocations to congregations should not be made compulsory (pp. 364-6); and the 'available balances' of congregations should be calculated on the basis of total income (i.e. normal and special income), and not only on normal income (p. 366).

10 Covenants and fund-raising

The Weekly Freewill Offering Scheme should be used with pledge cards in every congregation, and pledges should be reviewed annually. People using the Weekly Freewill Offering Scheme should be encouraged to covenant their offerings (p. 390). Efforts should be made to increase the proportion of collections raised through covenants, since this would lead to a substantial increase in total income (p. 406). Greater efforts should be made to publicize the benefits of covenants to congregations, especially in those congregations which make little use of them (p. 407); in attempting to widen the use of covenants, congregations should first approach those members who contribute through envelopes (p. 407). We recommend that the Church should consider the methods employed by professional fund-raising firms, with a view to incorporating such methods in the official programmes for fund-raising (p. 391).

11 Buildings and fabric

We recommend the establishment of a Central Fabric Fund, while ensuring that the fund does not inhibit local responsibilities for fabric maintenance (p. 422). Presbyteries should press for the sharing of church buildings by different congregations. In urban areas two congregations might share the same building; in rural areas the congregations of two different denominations might arrange to share the use of a building (p. 422). The erection of new buildings should be kept to a minimum, with the possible exception of manses; where new church buildings have to be built, efforts should be made to design for flexible use (pp. 422-3).

12 Investments

In order to increase investment income, two new principles of investment policy should be recognized and pursued; firstly, there should be a shift in the distribution of assets from stocks and shares into property; secondly, liabilities should be considered as much an element of the investment portfolio as assets. The Church should borrow money to finance investment in real estate (pp. 423-5). We propose that the Church should consider the establishment of a Church of Scotland building society (pp. 425-7). We recommend a more positive attitude to the use of manses in urban areas; vacant manses could be rented out on the market, and the proceeds put in a fund, which could be used to help ministers buy a house for themselves with building society support (pp. 426-7). The Church should accelerate the redevelopment of selected church sites in city centre areas (p. 428).

13 The Church courts

An increased number of younger elders in the 30-45 age group, and especially those with a background in commerce and industry, should be ordained (p. 434). We recommend that the frequency of Presbyterial superintendance visitation of congregations should be increased from once every five years to once every three years (p. 434). Further steps should be taken to reduce the number of Presbyteries through unification (p. 435). The reasons for congregations failing to meet their appropriate stipend and Mission and Service Fund allocation should be investigated in all cases. Presbyteries should appoint convenors to their Maintenance of the Ministry and Stewardship and Budget Committees who have energetic and forceful personalities (p. 435). We recommend that Synods should be abolished (pp. 436-7), and we welcome the plan to compress the length of the General Assembly into one week; we recommend that the plan be taken a step further by reducing the proportion of Presbytery members eligible to attend as commissioners from the present one-quarter to one-sixth or one-eighth (p. 437). We support the plan to dispense with the Commission of Assembly (p. 437), and we recommend a reduction in the size of the standing committees of the General Assembly (p. 438).

14 Administration

We oppose any expansion of the central secretariat; expansion must be justified in terms of the gains from the extra work accomplished (pp. 438-9). The cost of administering fabric funds held centrally on behalf of congregations would be reduced if these were vested in one body, and the separate funds of individual congregations were amalgamated to form one fund (p. 439); the pooling in a central fund of the sums received from various sources by way of stipend endowment would reduce administration expenditure (p. 439). It is possible that the administration of stipend payments by the Church and Ministry Department might be more economically carried out by a commercial bank (p. 439). Economies in administration would follow from cuts in the expenditures of committees receiving income from the Mission and Service Fund (p. 439).

Appendix

Table A
Endowment General Fund*
Revenue

	1975	1974
Income		
Standardized stipend, endowments etc. collected by the Church of Scotland General Trustees	£485,469	£515,561
Exchequer moneys	20,632	21,137
Interest on capital	149,023	121,238
Miscellaneous	2,308	218
	£657,432	£658,154

less:			
Expenditure			
Standardized stipend, endowments, etc			
Paid	£526,296		£507,791
Transferred to Vacant Stipend Fund	29,560		31,398
	£555,856		£539,189
Exchequer money			
Paid	£16,783		15,728
Transferred to vacant Stipend Fund	784		1,306
		£ 17,567	£ 17,034
Administration and organization	26,735		20,383
General Trustees collection charges	35,479		22,306
Special Grant	2,000		—
		£637,637	£598,912
SURPLUS FOR YEAR		£ 19,795	£ 59,242
Add/deduct credit (debit) balance at 1 January		53,589	(5,653)
		£ 73,384	£ 53,589
less:			
Transfer to Capital		40,000	—
CREDIT BALANCE at 31 December		£ 33,382	£ 53,589

*NOTE: SOURCE of this and subsequent tables: Minutes of the meeting held on 18 February 1976 of the Committee on the Maintenance of the Ministry.

Table B
Uninvested Fund
Revenue

	1975	1974
Income		
Donations, grants and income from trusts	£ 53,749	£ 49,781
Legacies	2,500	2,500
Interest on capital	10,316	8,965
Miscellaneous (repayment of grants)	845	445
	£ 67,410	£ 61,691
less:		
Expenditure		
Manse grants	1,000	—
Surplus for year	£ 66,410	£ 61,691
add:		
Credit balance at 1 January	65,036	33,666
	£131,446	£ 95,357
less:		
Transfer to capital	60,006	30,321
CREDIT BALANCE at 31 December	£ 71,440	£ 65,036

Table C
Vacant Stipend Fund

		1975	1974
Income			
Amount transferred from endowment general fund — standardized stipends, glebe rents, endowment, etc		£ 29,560	£ 33,246
Exchequer moneys		784	1,306
		£ 30,344	£ 34,552
Expenditure			
Widows and Next-of-Kin grants	£19,000		21,463
Vacancy expenses	9,489		15,100
Survey on ministry (Edinburgh University)	10,000		10,000
Grant to Housing and Loan Fund	3,500		3,500
Linlithgow survey	—		1,634
Grant to Calton Club	—		3,744
Widows' and Orphans' Fund: vacant rates	903		954
Grant to Iona Community	—		300
Grant to Young Ministers' Loan Fund	2,500		—
		£ 45,392	£ 56,695
(Deficit) for year		(£ 15,048)	(£ 22,143)
deduct:			
Credit Balance at 1 January		19,093	41,236
CREDIT BALANCE at 31 December		£ 4,045	£ 19,093

Table D
General Fund
Revenue

	1975	1974
Income		
Congregational contributions	£3,083,060	£1,414,294
Donations, grants and income from trusts	17,935	12,441
Legacies	23,370	15,576
Interest on capital	18,354	18,668
Miscellaneous (interest on revenue balance)	56,775	46,897
	£3,199,494	£1,508,506
less:		
Expenditure		
Stipends	£2,626,926	963,240
Cars: grants, purchase and expenses	42,772	44,477
Driving grants, removal expenses, etc.	49,370	46,520
Vacancy expenses	16,120	17,137
Retirements in the Interest of Union	16,897	20,825
Next-of-kin grants	19,000	21,462
Payments in lieu of endowment assurance	11,110	15,620
	£2,782,195	£1,129,281
Administration and organization	70,842	61,399
Miscellaneous:		
Purchase of house for Assistant Secretary £20,000		
Union and Readjustment Committee 4,208		3,355
Probationers and Transference of Ministers Committee 1,365		753
Admission of Ministers Committee 440		102
	£ 26,013	£ 4,210
	£2,879,050	£1,194,890
BALANCE	320,444	313,616
Transfer: Minimum Stipend Fund — revenue	£ 320,444	£ 313,616

Table E
Minimum Stipend Fund
Revenue

	1975	1974
Income		
Balance transferred from general fund — revenue	£320,444	£313,616
Donations, grants and income from trusts	83,458	65,486
Interest on capital	37,075	41,717
	£440,977	£420,819
less:		
Expenditure		
Stipends	£362,128	£268,412
Miscellaneous —		
arrears of contributions to Aged and Infirm Ministers' Fund	1,350	1,217
Sundries	921	893
	£346,399	£270,522
SURPLUS FOR YEAR	£ 76,578	£150,297
add:		
Credit balance at 1 January	£811,923	£603,306
less:		
Payments of stipend therefrom	—	1,409
	£811,923	£601,627
	£888,501	£751,924
add:		
Transfer from capital	—	£100,000
less:		
Amount invested	—	40,001
	—	£ 59,999
CREDIT BALANCE at 31 December	£888,501	£811,923

Selected bibliography

ARGYLE, M. *Religious Behaviour.* London: Routledge and Kegan Paul, 1958.

AZZI, C. and EHRENBERG, R. 'Household allocation of time and church attendance' *Journal of Political Economy* vol. 83, no. 1 (1975), pp. 27-56.

BAUMOL, W.J. and BOWEN, W.G. 'On the performing arts: the anatomy of their economic problems' *American Economic Review* (papers and proceedings) vol. 55, no. 2 (1965), pp. 495-502.

———. *Performing Arts: The Economic Dilemma.* New York: The Twentieth Century Fund, 1966.

BURLEIGH, J.H.S. *A Church History of Scotland.* London: Oxford University Press, 1960.

CHURCH OF ENGLAND. *Church and State: Report of the Archbishop's Commission.* London: Church Information Office, 1970.

CHURCH OF SCOTLAND. *Reports to the General Assembly.* Edinburgh: Blackwood.

COX, J.T. *Practice and Procedure in the Church of Scotland.* 6th ed. edited by Rev D.F.M. Macdonald. Edinburgh: Blackwood, 1976.

GIBSON, A.J.H. *Stipend in the Church of Scotland.* Edinburgh: Blackwood, 1961.

HERRON, A. (ed.) *Church of Scotland Yearbook.* Edinburgh: Saint Andrew Press.

HIGHET, J. *The Churches of Scotland Today.* Glasgow: Jackson, 1950.

———. *The Scottish Churches* London: Skeffington, 1960.

LAZARWITZ, B. 'Some factors associated with variations in Church attendance' *Social Forces* no. 39 (1961), pp. 301-9.

LENSKI, G. 'Social Correlates of Religious Interest' *American Sociological Review* vol. 18 (1953), pp. 533-44.

MACKIE, J.D. *A History of Scotland.* Harmondsworth: Penguin Books, 1973.

MARTIN, D. *A Sociology of English Religion.* London: Heinemann, 1974.

MITTON, C.L. *The Social Sciences and the Churches.* Edinburgh: T. & T. Clark, 1972.

PAUL, L. *The Deployment and Payment of the Clergy.* Church Information Office, 1964.

────── *A Church by Daylight.* G. Chapman, 1973.

OPPENHEIM, A.N. *Questionnaire Design and Attitude Measurement.* Heinemann, 1966.

PHILLIPS, E.H. *Fund-Raising Techniques — and Case Histories.* Business Books, 1969.

RUDGE, P.F. *Ministry and Management.* Tavistock Publications, 1968.

SISSONS, P.L. *The Social Significance of Church Membership in the Burgh of Falkirk.* Church of Scotland, 1973.

WILSON, B. *Religion in Secular Society.* C.A. Watts, 1966.